BOSCH

Automotive Terminology

English · German · French

1st EDITION

SAE INTERNATIONAL ®

Impressum/Imprint/Editeur
Herausgeber/Published by/Publié par:
© Robert Bosch GmbH, 1998
Postfach 30 02 20
D-70442 Stuttgart
Unternehmensbereich Kraftfahrzeugausrüstung,
Abteilung Technische Information (KH/VDT).
Leitung/Management/Direction:
Dipl.-Ing. (FH) Ulrich Adler.

Chefredaktion/Editor-in-chief/ Rédacteur en chef:
Dipl.-Ing. (FH) Horst Bauer.

Redaktion/Editors/Rédacteurs:
Folkhart Dinkler,
Peter Girling,
Paul Lambert,
Dipl.-Ing. (FH) Anton Beer.

Satz/Layout/Composition:
Dipl.-Ing. (FH) Ulrich Adler,
Joachim Kaiser, Thomas Straß,
Jürgen Techert.

Printed in Germany. Imprimé en Allemagne.
1st Edition: November 1998

Exclusive English Language Distribution:
Society of Automotive Engineers, Inc.
400 Commonwealth Dr.
Warrendale, PA 15096-0001 USA
ISBN 0-7680-0338-5

(1,0)

Vorwort

Um die Kommunikation innerhalb der Bosch-Gruppe durch einheitliche Übersetzungen zu erleichtern, haben wir über 4000 Fachwörter der Kraftfahrzeugausrüstung in den Sprachen Deutsch, Englisch und Französisch zusammengestellt.
Grundlage der Fachwortauswahl sind unsere Fachbücher und Begriffssammlungen von Fachabteilungen der Bosch-Gruppe.
Für Hinweise und Ergänzungen sind wir dankbar.
Eine Telefax-Vorlage befindet sich am Schluß dieses Buches.

Hinweise für den Gebrauch

Anordnung der Sprachen
Quell- und Zielsprachen sind tabellarisch dargestellt.
Die Quellsprache ist jeweils alphabetisch geordnet und steht am linken Seitenrand, die Zielsprachen daneben.

Abkürzungen

a	Abkürzung bzw. Akronym
adj	Adjektiv
f	Femininum
loc	Französisch: Redewendung
m	Maskulinum
n	Deutsch: Neutrum Englisch: Substantiv
pl	Plural
pp	Partizip Perfekt
ppr	Partizip Präsens
v	Verb
+	Veraltetete Benennung
x	Fachjargon

Foreword

In order to support communication within the Bosch Group by means of uniform translations, we have assembled more than 4,000 technical terms from automotive technology in German, English, and French.
Our reference books, together with the technical glossaries drawn up by specialized departments of the Bosch Group, served as the basis for the selection of these technical terms.
Suggestions on additions and improvements will be gratefully accepted.
A Fax form can be found inside the rear cover.

Notes on use

Layout of the languages
The terms in the source and target languages are presented in tabular form.
The source-language term is listed alphabetically on the left side of each page and the target languages to the right of it.

Abbreviations

a	Abbreviation or acronym
adj	Adjective
f	Feminine
loc	French: Compound
m	Masculine
n	German: Neuter English: Noun
pl	Plural
pp	Past participle
ppr	Present participle
v	Verb
+	Deprecated term
x	Jargon

Avant-propos

Afin de faciliter la communication entre les différentes entreprises du Groupe Bosch et d'uniformiser les traductions, ce glossaire rassemble plus de 4000 termes techniques du domaine de l'automobile en allemand, anglais et français. Nos manuels et publications ainsi que les vocabulaires techniques des différents départements spécialisés du Groupe Bosch constituent la base de cette sélection de termes techniques.
Nous vous remercions à l'avance pour toutes les remarques et suggestions concernant le présent ouvrage.
Un modèle de télécopie se trouve à la fin de ce manuel.

Conseils d'utilisation

Disposition des langues
Les langues source et cible sont représentées sous forme de table.
La langue source est classée alphabétiquement et positionnée sur le côté gauche de chaque page. Les langues cibles sont juxtaposées à la langue source.

Abréviations

a	abbréviation ou acronyme
adj	adjectif
f	féminin
loc	locution
m	masculin
n	en allemand: neutre en anglais: substantif
pl	pluriel
pp	participe parfait
ppr	participe présent
v	verbe
+	terme plus usité
x	jargon professionnel

Deutsch

Deutsch		Englisch		Französisch	
A					
abblasen (Druckregler)	x v	blow-off (pressure regulator)	v	échappement d'air (régulateur de pression)	m
Abblasestutzen (Druckregler)	m	blow-off fitting (pressure regulator)	n	tubulure d'échappement (régulateur de pression)	f
Abblasgeräusch (Druckregler)	n	blow-off noise (pressure regulator)	n	bruit d'échappement (régulateur de pression)	m
Abblendlicht	n	low beam	n	feu de croisement	m
Abblendscheinwerfer	m	low-beam headlamp	n	projecteur code	m
abbremsen	v	brake	v	freiner	v
Abbremsung	f	braking factor	n	taux de freinage	m
Abdeckrahmen (Scheinwerfer)	m	outer rim (headlamp)	n	collerette (projecteur)	f
Abdeckring	m	cover ring	n	anneau de recouvrement	m
abdichten	v	seal	v	étancher	v
Abdichtstulpe (Radzylinder)	f	sealing cap (wheel-brake cylinder)	n	manchon d'étanchéité (cylindre de roue)	m
Abfallschwellwert (Fahrpedalsensor)	m	decrease threshold value (accelerator-pedal sensor)	n	seuil décroissant (capteur d'accélérateur)	m
Abfallzeit (Einspritzventil)	f	release time (fuel injector)	n	temps de fermeture (injecteur)	m
Abflußbohrung (Elektrokraftstoffpumpe)	f	outlet bore (electric fuel pump)	n	canal de sortie (pompe électrique à carburant)	m
Abgas	n	exhaust gas	n	gaz d'échappement	mpl
Abgasanalysator	m	exhaust-gas analyzer	n	appareil de mesure des gaz d'échappement	m
Abgasanlage	f	exhaust-gas system	n	système d'échappement	m
Abgasausstoß	m	exhaust-gas emission	n	émission de gaz d'échappement	f
Abgasbestandteil	m	exhaust-gas component	n	composant des gaz d'échappement	m
Abgasbestimmungen	fpl	emission-control legislation	n	législation antipollution	f
Abgasemission	f	exhaust-gas emission	n	émission de gaz d'échappement	f
Abgasgegendruck	m	exhaust-gas back pressure	n	contre-pression des gaz d'échappement	f
Abgasgesetzgebung	f	emission-control legislation	n	législation antipollution	f
Abgasgrenzwert	m	emission limits	n	valeur limite d'émission	f
Abgaskomponente	f	exhaust-gas component	n	composant des gaz d'échappement	m
Abgaskonverter	m	catalytic exhaust converter	n	convertisseur catalytique des gaz d'échappement	m
Abgaskrümmer	m	exhaust manifold	n	collecteur d'échappement	m
Abgasleitung	f	exhaust passage	n	conduite d'échappement	f
Abgasmeßgerät	n	exhaust-gas analyzer	n	appareil de mesure des gaz d'échappement	m
Abgasmeßtechnik	f	exhaust-gas measuring techniques	npl	technique de mesure des gaz d'échappement	f
Abgasnachbehandlung	f	exhaust-gas treatment	n	traitement secondaire des gaz d'échappement	m
Abgasprüftechnik	f	exhaust-gas analysis techniques	npl	technique d'analyse des gaz d'échappement	f
Abgasprüfung	f	exhaust-gas test	n	test des gaz d'échappement	m

Deutsch		Englisch		Französisch	
Abgasprüfzelle	*f*	emissions test cell	*n*	cabine de simulation des gaz d'échappement	*f*
Abgasreinigung	*f*	exhaust treatment	*n*	dépollution des gaz d'échappement	*f*
Abgasrohr	*n*	exhaust pipe	*n*	tuyau d'échappement	*m*
Abgasrückführrate	*f*	exhaust-gas recirculation (EGR) rate	*n*	taux de recyclage des gaz d'échappement	*m*
Abgasrückführregelung	*f*	exhaust-gas recirculation (EGR) control	*n*	régulation du recyclage des gaz d'échappement	*f*
Abgasrückführsteller	*m*	exhaust-gas recirculation (EGR) positioner	*n*	actionneur de recyclage des gaz d'échappement	*m*
Abgasrückführung, AGR	*f*	exhaust-gas recirculation, EGR	*n*	recyclage des gaz d'échappement	*m*
Abgasrückführungsventil	*n*	exhaust-gas recirculation (EGR) valve	*n*	électrovalve de recyclage des gaz d'échappement	*f*
Abgasrückführventil	*n*	exhaust-gas recirculation (EGR) valve	*n*	électrovalve de recyclage des gaz d'échappement	*f*
Abgastechnik	*f*	emissions-control technology	*n*	technique des gaz d'échappement	*f*
Abgasteilstrom	*m*	exhaust-gas partial flow	*n*	flux partiel de gaz d'échappement	*m*
Abgastemperaturfühler	*m*	exhaust-gas temperature sensor	*n*	capteur de température des gaz d'échappement	*m*
Abgastest	*m*	exhaust-gas test	*n*	test des gaz d'échappement	*m*
Abgasturbine	*f*	exhaust-gas turbine	*n*	turbine à gaz d'échappement	*f*
Abgasturboaufladung	*f*	exhaust-gas turbocharging	*n*	suralimentation par turbocompresseur	*f*
Abgasturbolader	*m*	exhaust-gas turbocharger	*n*	turbocompresseur	*m*
Abgasvolumen	*n*	exhaust-gas volume	*n*	volume des gaz d'échappement	*m*
Abgasvorschriften	*fpl*	emission-control legislation	*n*	législation antipollution	*f*
Abgaszusammensetzung	*f*	exhaust-gas composition	*n*	composition des gaz d'échappement	*f*
abgegebene Leistung (elektrische Maschinen)	*f*	power output (electrical machines)	*n*	puissance débitée (machines électriques)	*f*
Abgriffbürste	*f*	pickoff brush (potentiometer)	*n*	balai de captage (potentiomètre	*m*
abisolieren	*v*	strip the insulation	*v*	dénuder	*v*
Ablagerung	*f*	deposit	*n*	dépôt	*m*
Ablaßstutzen (Druckregler)	*m*	blow-off fitting (pressure regulator)	*n*	tubulure d'échappement (régulateur de pression)	*f*
Ablaufdrossel	*f*	output throttle	*n*	étranglement de sortie	*m*
ablaufende Bremsbacke	*f*	trailing shoe	*n*	mâchoire secondaire	*f*
abmagern (Luft-Kraftstoff-Gemisch)	*v*	lean-off (air-fuel mixture)	*v*	appauvrir (mélange air-carburant)	*v*
Abmagerung (Luft-Kraftstoff-Gemisch)	*f*	lean adjustment (air-fuel mixture)	*n*	appauvrissement du mélange	*m*
Abregelbeginn	*m*	start of speed regulation	*n*	début de la coupure de débit	*m*
Abregelbereich	*m*	breakaway range	*n*	plage de coupure de débit	*f*
Abregeldrehzahl	*f*	breakaway speed	*n*	vitesse de coupure	*f*
Abregelende	*n*	end of breakaway	*n*	fin de coupure de débit	*f*
Abregelmenge	*f*	breakaway delivery	*n*	débit au moment de la coupure	*m*

Deutsch		Englisch		Französisch	
abregeln (Dieseleinspritzung)	*v*	regulate (diesel fuel injection)	*v*	fin de régulation (injection diesel)	*f*
Abregelpunkt	*m*	start of speed regulation	*n*	début de la coupure de débit	*m*
Abregelung	*f*	speed regulation breakaway	*n*	coupure de débit	*f*
Abregelverlauf	*m*	breakaway characteristic	*n*	caractéristique de coupure de débit	*f*
Abreißfunke	*m*	contact-breaking spark	*n*	étincelle de rupture	*f*
Abreißkante (Spritzzapfen)	*f*	breakaway edge	*n*	arête de rupture (téton d'injection)	*f*
Abriebfestigkeit	*f*	abrasion resistance	*n*	résistance à l'abrasion	*f*
Abrollbewegung	*f*	rolling movement	*n*	mouvement de rotation	*m*
ABS, Antiblockiersystem	*a*	ABS, antilock braking system	*a*	ABS, système antiblocage	*a*
ABS-Funktionskontrolleuchte	*f*	ABS indicator lamp	*n*	lampe témoin de fonctionnement (ABS)	*f*
ABS/ABD, Automatische Brems-Differentialsperre	*a*	automatic brake-force differential lock, ABS/ABD	*n*	blocage automatique du différentiel	*m*
Abschaltdrehzahl	*f*	cutoff speed	*n*	régime de coupure	*m*
Abschaltdruck	*m*	cutoff pressure	*n*	pression de coupure	*f*
Abschaltung (Regler)	*f*	shutoff (governor)	*n*	coupure (régulateur)	*f*
Abschaltventil	*n*	shutoff valve	*n*	valve de barrage	*f*
Abscheidegüte (Filter)	*f*	filtration efficiency	*n*	qualité de séparation (filtre)	*f*
Abscheider (Filter)	*m*	separator (filter)	*n*	séparateur (filtre)	*m*
Abschirmhaube (Zündverteiler)	*f*	shielding cover (ignition distributor)	*n*	calotte de blindage (allumeur)	*f*
Abschirmhülse	*f*	shielding sleeve	*n*	manchon de blindage	*m*
Abschirmung	*f*	shield	*n*	blindage	*m*
Abschleppschutz (Autoalarm)	*m*	tow-away protection (car alarm)	*n*	protection contre le remorquage (alarme auto)	*f*
Abschlußstellung	*f*	final position	*n*	position d'arrêt	*f*
absolutdruckmessender, ladedruckabhängiger Vollastanschlag	*m*	absolute-boost-pressure-dependent full-load stop	*n*	correcteur pneumatique à mesure de pression absolue	*m*
Absolutdrucksensor	*m*	absolute-pressure sensor	*n*	capteur de pression absolue	*m*
Absorptionsanalysator	*m*	absorption analyzer	*n*	analyseur à absorption	*m*
Absorptionsband	*n*	absorption band	*n*	bande d'absorption	*f*
Absperrglied (Kupplungskopf)	*n*	shutoff element (coupling head)	*n*	obturateur (tête d'accouplement)	*m*
Absperrhahn	*m*	stopcock	*n*	robinet d'arrêt	*m*
Absperrventil	*n*	shutoff valve	*n*	valve de barrage	*f*
Abspringdrehzahl	*f*	no-follow speed	*n*	régime de décrochage	*m*
Abspritzstelle	*f*	point of injection	*n*	point d'injection	*m*
Abstandsregelung (Kfz)	*f*	adaptive cruise control, ACC	*n*	régulation auto-adaptative de vitesse de roulage	*f*
Abstandsring	*m*	spacer ring	*n*	bague-entretoise	*f*
Abstelleinrichtung	*f*	shutoff device	*n*	dispositif d'arrêt	*m*
Abstellhebel	*m*	stop (shutoff) lever	*n*	levier d'arrêt	*m*
Abstellung (Regler)	*f*	shutoff (governor)	*n*	coupure (régulateur)	*f*
Abstellvorrichtung	*f*	shutoff device	*n*	dispositif d'arrêt	*m*
Absteuerbohrung	*f*	spill port	*n*	orifice de distribution	*m*

Deutsch		Englisch		Französisch	
absteuern (Dieseleinspritzung)	*v*	fuel-delivery termination (diesel fuel injection)	*n*	fin de refoulement (injection diesel)	*f*
Absteuerquerschnitt	*m*	cutoff bore	*n*	orifice de décharge	*m*
Absteuerstrahl	*m*	cutoff jet	*n*	jet de décharge	*m*
Absteuerung	*f*	end of delivery	*n*	coupure progressive	*f*
Abstrahlgrad (Lüfter)	*m*	noise-emission level (fan)	*n*	degré de rayonnement sonore (ventilateur)	*m*
Abstrahlung (EMV)	*f*	radiation (EMC)	*n*	rayonnement (CEM)	*m*
abstufbar	*adj*	graduable	*adj*	modérable	*adj*
Abstützpunkt (Bremsbacke)	*m*	fulcrum (brake shoe)	*n*	point d'appui (frein)	*m*
Abtastzeitmaxima	*npl*	maximum sampling time	*n*	temps maximum de détection (régulateur)	*m*
Abtriebswelle	*f*	driven shaft	*n*	arbre de sortie	*m*
Abzugskraft	*f*	pull-off force	*n*	force d'extraction	*f*
ACC, adaptive Fahrgeschwindigkeitsregelung	*a*	adaptive cruise control, ACC	*n*	régulation auto-adaptative de vitesse de roulage	*f*
Achsabstand (Fahrzeug)	*m*	wheelbase (vehicle)	*n*	empattement (véhicule)	*m*
Achsantrieb (Kfz)	*m*	final drive (motor vehicle)	*n*	essieu moteur (véhicule)	*m*
Achsgewicht	*n*	axle weight	*n*	poids de l'essieu	*m*
Achskraftverlagerung	*f*	axle-load transfer	*n*	report de charge dynamique de l'essieu	*m*
Achslast	*f*	axle load	*n*	charge (essieu)	*f*
Achslastgeber	*m*	axle-load sensor	*n*	capteur de charge sur essieu	*m*
Achslastsensor	*m*	axle-load sensor	*n*	capteur de charge sur essieu	*m*
Achslastsignal	*n*	axle-load signal	*n*	signal de charge sur essieu	*m*
Achslastverlagerung	*f*	axle-load transfer	*n*	report de charge dynamique de l'essieu	*m*
Achslastverteilung	*f*	axle-load distribution	*n*	répartition de la charge par essieu	*f*
Achsplatte (Zündversteller)	*f*	support plate (ignition-advance mechanism)	*n*	plateau-support (correcteur d'avance)	*m*
Achsresonanz	*f*	axis resonance	*n*	résonance des essieux	*f*
Adapterbox (Wischer)	*f*	adapter box (wipers)	*n*	boîte d'adaptateurs (essuie-glace)	*f*
Adapterkabel	*n*	adapter lead	*n*	câble adaptateur	*m*
adaptive Fahrgeschwindigkeitsregelung, ACC	*f*	adaptive cruise control, ACC	*n*	régulation auto-adaptative de vitesse de roulage	*f*
Additiv (Kraftstoff)	*m*	additive (fuel)	*n*	additif (carburant)	*m*
AGR, Abgasrückführung	*a*	exhaust-gas recirculation, EGR	*n*	recyclage des gaz d'échappement	*m*
Airbag	*m*	airbag	*n*	coussin gonflable (système de retenue des passager)	*m*
Airbag-Auslösegerät	*n*	airbag triggering unit	*n*	déclencheur de coussin d'air	*m*
aktive Masse (Batterie)	*f*	active materials (battery)	*n*	matière active (batterie)	*f*
aktive Ruckeldämpfung, ARD	*f*	surge damping control	*n*	amortissement actif d'à-coups	*m*
aktiver Ruckeldämpfer	*m*	active-surge damper	*n*	amortisseur actif d'à-coups	*m*
Aktivierungssperre (Autoalarm)	*f*	activation blocking (car alarm)	*n*	sécurité de mise en veille (alarme auto)	*f*
Aktivkohlebehälter (Abgastechnik)	*m*	carbon canister (emissions control technology)	*n*	bac à charbon actif (technique des gaz d'échappement)	*m*

Deutsch

Deutsch		Englisch		Französisch	
Aktor	*m*	actuator	*n*	actuateur	*m*
Alarmhorn	*n*	alarm horn	*n*	avertisseur d'alarme	*m*
Alarmschalter	*m*	alarm switch	*n*	commutateur d'alarme	*m*
Alarmton (Autoalarm)	*m*	alarm tone (car alarm)	*n*	tonalité d'alerte (alarme auto)	*f*
Alldrehzahlregler	*m*	variable-speed governor	*n*	régulateur toutes vitesses	*m*
Allgemeine Betriebserlaubnis, ABE	*f*	General Certification	*n*	homologation générale	*f*
Allradantrieb	*m*	all-wheel drive, AWD	*n*	transmission intégrale	*f*
Allradsystem	*n*	all-wheel-drive system	*n*	système de transmission intégrale	*m*
Alterungsschutz (Kraftstoff)	*m*	anti-aging additive (gasoline)	*n*	protection contre le vieillissement (essence)	*f*
Analog-Digital-Wandler	*m*	analog-digital converter	*n*	convertisseur analogique-numérique	*m*
Analogeingang	*m*	anolog input	*n*	entrée analogique	*f*
Analogwertaufbereitung	*f*	analog-value conditioning	*n*	conditionnement de valeur analogique	*m*
Analogwertauswertung	*f*	analog-value evaluation	*n*	exploitation de valeur analogique	*f*
Analogwerterfassung	*f*	analog-value sampling	*n*	saisie de valeur analogique	*f*
Anbauscheinwerfer	*m*	external-fitting headlamp	*n*	projecteur extérieur	*m*
Anbausteuergerät	*n*	add-on ECU	*n*	calculateur adaptable	*m*
Anbremsvorgang	*m*	initial braking	*n*	évolution du freinage	*f*
anfetten (Luft-Kraftstoff-Gemisch)	*v*	enrich (air-fuel mixture)	*v*	enrichir (mélange air-carburant)	*v*
Angebotszeichnung	*f*	project drawing	*n*	plan d'offre	*m*
Angehdrehzahl (drehende Maschinen)	x *f*	self-excitation speed (rotating machines)	*n*	vitesse d'auto-excitation (machines tournantes)	*f*
Angleichbereich	*m*	torque-control range	*n*	plage de correction de débit	*f*
Angleichbolzen	*m*	torque-control shaft	*n*	axe de correction de débit	*m*
Angleichfeder	*f*	torque-control spring	*n*	ressort correcteur de débit	*m*
Angleichhebel	*m*	torque-control lever	*n*	levier de correction de débit	*m*
Angleichlasche	*f*	torque-control bar	*n*	patte de correction	*f*
Angleichmenge	*f*	torque-control quantity	*n*	débit correcteur	*m*
Angleichrate	*f*	torque-control rate	*n*	taux de correction de débit	*m*
Angleichung	*f*	torque control	*n*	correction de débit	*f*
Angleichventil	*n*	torque-control valve	*n*	soupape de correction de débit	*f*
Angleichverlauf	*m*	torque-control characteristic	*n*	caractéristique de correction de débit	*f*
Angleichvorrichtung	*f*	torque-control mechanism	*n*	correcteur de débit	*m*
Angleichweg	*m*	torque-control travel	*n*	course de correction de débit	*f*
Anhalteweg	*m*	total braking distance	*n*	distance totale de freinage	*f*
Anhaltezeit (Bremsvorgang)	*f*	stopping time (braking)	*n*	temps d'arrêt (freinage)	*m*
Anhängefahrzeug	*n*	trailer	*n*	véhicule tracté	*m*
Anhänger	*m*	trailer	*n*	véhicule tracté	*m*
Anhänger-Bremsanlage	*f*	trailer-brake system	*n*	dispositif de freinage de remorque	*m*
Anhängeransteuerung	*f*	trailer pilot control	*n*	pilotage de la remorque	*m*
Anhängerbetrieb	*m*	trailer operation	*n*	exploitation avec remorque	*f*

Deutsch		Englisch		Französisch	
Anhängerbremsausrüstung	*f*	trailer braking equipment	*n*	équipement de freinage de la remorque	*m*
Anhängerbremse	*f*	trailer brake	*n*	frein de remorque	*m*
Anhängerbremsleitung	*f*	trailer brake line	*n*	conduite de frein de remorque	*f*
Anhängerbremsventil	*n*	trailer-brake valve	*n*	valve de frein de remorque	*f*
Anhängererkennung (ABS)	*f*	trailer recognition (ABS)	*n*	détection de la fonction "remorque" (ABS)	*f*
Anhängerkreis (Druckluftanlage)	*m*	trailer circuit (compressed-air system)	*n*	circuit de commande de la remorque (dispositif à air comprimé)	*m*
Anhängerkupplung	*f*	trailer hitch	*n*	accouplement de remorque	*m*
Anhängerrelaisventil	*n*	trailer relay valve	*n*	valve-relais de remorque	*f*
Anhängersteuermodul, ASM	*m*	trailer control module, TCM	*n*	module de commande remorqu(	*m*
Anhängersteuerung	*f*	trailer control	*n*	commande de remorque	*f*
Anhängersteuerventil	*n*	trailer-control valve	*n*	valve de commande de remorque	*f*
Anhängerversorgung	*f*	trailer power supply	*n*	alimentation de la remorque	*f*
Anheizkerze	*f*	flame glow plug	*n*	bougie de préchauffage à flamme	*f*
Anker (ABS-Hydroaggregat)	*m*	armature (ABS hydraulic modulator)	*n*	noyau (groupe hydraulique ABS)	*m*
Anker (Relais)	*m*	armature (relays)	*n*	armature (relais)	*f*
Anker (umlaufende Maschinen)	*m*	armature (rotating machines)	*n*	induit (machines tournantes)	*m*
Ankerabbremsung	*f*	armature braking	*n*	freinage de l'induit	*m*
Ankerhub	*m*	armature stroke	*n*	course du noyau	*f*
Ankerpaket	*n*	armature stack	*n*	noyau feuilleté d'induit	*m*
Ankerrückwirkung	*f*	armature reaction	*n*	réaction d'induit	*f*
Ankerstrom	*m*	armature current	*n*	courant d'induit	*m*
Ankerwelle	*f*	armature shaft	*n*	arbre d'induit	*m*
Ankerwicklung	*f*	armature winding	*n*	enroulement d'induit	*m*
Anlasser	+ *m*	starter	*n*	démarreur	*m*
Anlaufscheibe (Starter)	*f*	friction washer (starter)	*n*	rondelle de friction (démarreur)	*f*
Anlegedruck (Bremsbeläge)	*m*	application force (brake linings	*n*	force de serrage (garnitures de frein)	*f*
anlegen (Bremse)	*v*	apply (brakes)	*v*	appliquer (frein)	*v*
Anlenkhebel (Hubschieberpumpe)	*m*	control-sleeve lever (control-sleeve fuel-injection pump)	*n*	levier de positionnement (pompe d'injection en ligne à tiroirs)	*m*
Anpaßeinrichtung	*f*	add-on module	*n*	groupe d'adaptation	*m*
Anpreßkraft	*f*	downforce	*n*	force d'application	*f*
Anregungsfrequenz	*f*	stimulation frequency	*n*	fréquence d'excitation	*f*
Anregungskennwert	*m*	stimulation characteristic value	*n*	valeur d'excitation	*f*
Anreicherung (Luft-Kraftstoff-Gemisch)	*f*	mixture enrichment	*n*	enrichissement du mélange	*m*
Anreicherungsfaktor (Luft-Kraftstoff-Gemisch)	*m*	enrichment factor (air-fuel mixture)	*n*	facteur d'enrichissement (mélange air-carburant)	*m*
Anreicherungsrate	*f*	enrichment quantity	*n*	taux d'enrichissement	*m*
ansaugen	*v*	suck in	*v*	aspirer	*v*
Ansaugfilter	*n*	intake filter	*n*	filtre d'aspiration	*m*

Deutsch			Englisch		Französisch	
Ansauggebläse		*n*	intake fan	*n*	ventilateur d'aspiration	*m*
Ansauggeräusch		*n*	intake noise	*n*	bruit d'aspiration	*m*
Ansaughub (Verbrennungsmotor)		*m*	intake stroke (IC engine)	*n*	course d'admission (moteur à combution)	*f*
Ansaugkanal		*m*	intake port	*n*	canal d'admission	*m*
Ansaugkrümmer	+	*m*	intake manifold	*n*	collecteur d'admission	*m*
Ansaugleistung		*f*	suction capacity	*n*	capacité d'aspiration	*f*
Ansaugluft		*f*	intake air	*n*	air d'admission	*m*
Ansaugmengenzumessung		*f*	inlet metering	*n*	dosage à l'admission	*m*
Ansaugrohr		*n*	intake manifold	*n*	collecteur d'admission	*m*
Ansaugsystem (Verbrennungsmotor)		*n*	air-intake system (IC engine)	*n*	système d'admission (moteur à combustion)	*m*
Ansaugtakt		*m*	induction stroke	*n*	admission	*f*
Ansaugventil, ASV (ABS/ABD)		*n*	suction valve (ABS/ABD)	*n*	vanne d'aspiration (ABS/ABD)	*f*
Ansaugweg		*m*	intake port	*n*	canal d'admission	*m*
Anschlagbolzen		*m*	stop pin	*n*	axe de butée	*m*
Anschlagfläche		*f*	stop surface	*n*	surface d'arrêt	*f*
Anschlaghebel (Reiheneinspritzpumpe)		*m*	stop lever (in-line pump)	*n*	levier de butée (pompe d'injection en ligne)	*m*
Anschlaghülse		*f*	stop sleeve	*n*	douille de butée	*f*
Anschlaglasche		*f*	stop strap	*n*	patte de butée	*f*
Anschlagnase		*f*	stop lug	*n*	bossage-butée	*m*
Anschlagscheibe		*f*	stop disc	*n*	disque de butée	*m*
Anschlagschraube		*f*	stop screw	*n*	vis de butée	*f*
Anschlagstellwerk		*m*	stop adjustment mechanism	*n*	commande de butée	*f*
Anschliff (Spritzzapfen)		*m*	specially ground pintle	*n*	chanfrein (téton d'injection)	*m*
Anschlußbolzen		*m*	terminal stud	*n*	tige de connexion	*f*
Anschlußklemme (Batterie)		*f*	battery-cable terminal	*n*	cosse de batterie	*f*
Anschlußleitung		*f*	connecting cable	*n*	câble de connexion	*m*
Anschlußmutter (Zündkerze)		*f*	terminal nut (spark plug)	*n*	écrou de connexion (bougie)	*m*
Anschlußnippel		*m*	connection fitting	*n*	raccord fileté	*m*
Anschlußplan		*m*	terminal diagram	*n*	schéma de connexion	*m*
Anschlußpol (Batterie)		*f*	terminal post (battery)	*n*	borne (batterie)	*f*
Anschlußpunkt (Schaltplan)		*m*	terminal location (circuit diagram)	*n*	borne (schéma)	*f*
Anschlußstutzen		*m*	fitting	*n*	raccord	*m*
Ansprechdauer		*f*	initial response time	*n*	temps de réponse initial	*m*
Ansprechdruck		*m*	response pressure	*n*	pression de réponse	*f*
Ansprechschwelle		*f*	response threshold	*n*	seuil de réponse	*m*
Ansprechspannung		*f*	response voltage	*n*	tension de réponse	*f*
Ansprechverzögerung		*f*	response delay	*n*	délai de réponse	*m*
Ansprechweg		*m*	response travel	*n*	course de réponse	*f*
Ansprechzeit		*f*	response time	*n*	temps de réponse	*m*
anspringen (Verbrennungsmotor)	x	*v*	start (IC engine)	*v*	démarrer (moteur à combustion)	*m*
Ansteuerimpuls		*m*	triggering signal	*n*	signal pilote	*m*
ansteuern		*v*	trigger	*v*	piloter	*v*

Deutsch		Englisch		Französisch	
Ansteuersignal	*n*	triggering signal	*n*	signal pilote	*m*
Ansteuerstrom	*m*	control current	*n*	courant de pilotage	*m*
Ansteuerung (ABS-Regelung)	*f*	triggering (ABS control)	*n*	pilotage (régulation ABS)	*m*
Ansteuerungselektronik	*f*	drive electronics	*npl*	électronique de commande	*f*
Anstiegsschwellwert (Fahrpedalsensor)	*m*	increase threshold value (accelerator-pedal sensor)	*n*	seuil croissant (capteur d'accélérateur)	*m*
Anströmwinkel (Seitenwind)	*m*	angle of impact (crosswind)	*n*	angle d'attaque (vent latéral)	*m*
Antenne	*f*	antenna	*n*	antenne	*f*
Antiblockiersystem, ABS	*n*	antilock braking system, ABS	*n*	système antiblocage, ABS	*m*
Antiklopfmittel	*n*	knock inhibitor	*n*	agent antidétonant	*m*
Antiruckelregelung	*f*	surge damping control	*n*	amortissement actif d'à-coups	*m*
Antrieb (Bremskraftregler)	*m*	drive element (braking force regulator)	*n*	transmission (correcteur de freinage)	*f*
Antriebsachse	*f*	powered axle	*n*	essieu moteur	*m*
Antriebsdrehmoment	*n*	drive torque	*n*	couple de traction	*m*
Antriebseinheit (Rollenbremsprüfstand)	*f*	drive unit (dynamic brake analyzer)	*n*	unité d'entraînement (banc d'essai)	*f*
Antriebsexzenter	*m*	drive eccentric	*n*	excentrique d'entraînement	*m*
Antriebshebel (Niveaugeber)	*m*	transfer rod (level sensor)	*n*	levier de transmission (capteur de niveau)	*m*
Antriebskeilriemen	*m*	drive belt	*n*	courroie d'entraînement	*f*
Antriebskraft	*f*	motive force	*n*	force motrice	*f*
Antriebskupplung	*f*	coupling assembly	*n*	accouplement	*m*
Antriebslager (Generator) +	*n*	drive end shield (alternator)	*n*	flasque côté entraînement (alternateur)	*m*
Antriebslagerschild (Generator)	*m*	drive end shield (alternator)	*n*	flasque côté entraînement (alternateur)	*m*
Antriebsleistung	*f*	drive power	*n*	puissance motrice	*f*
Antriebsmoment	*n*	drive torque	*n*	couple de traction	*m*
Antriebsnockenwelle	*f*	camshaft	*n*	arbre à came d'entraînement	*m*
Antriebsrad (Elektrokraftstoffpumpe)	*n*	driving wheel	*n*	roue menante	*f*
Antriebsrad (Kfz)	*n*	driven wheel (motor vehicle)	*n*	roue motrice (véhicule)	*f*
Antriebsriemen	*m*	drive belt	*n*	courroie d'entraînement	*f*
Antriebsrolle (Rollenbremsprüfstand)	*f*	drive roller (dynamic brake analyzer)	*n*	rouleau d'entraînement (banc d'essai)	*m*
Antriebsschlupf	*m*	drive slip (driven wheel)	*n*	antipatinage à la traction	*m*
Antriebsschlupfregelung, ASR	*f*	traction control system, TCS	*n*	régulation d'antipatinage à la traction, ASR	*f*
Antriebsschlupfregler	*f*	traction control system, TCS	*n*	régulation d'antipatinage à la traction, ASR	*f*
Antriebsstrang	*m*	drivetrain	*n*	chaîne cinématique	*f*
Antriebsvorrichtung	*f*	drive assembly	*n*	transmission	*f*
Antriebswelle	*f*	drive shaft	*n*	arbre d'entraînement	*m*
Anzeigediode	*f*	display diode	*n*	diode d'affichage	*f*
Anzeigeeinheit (Fahrdatenrechner)	*f*	display unit (trip computer)	*n*	unité d'affichage (ordinateur de bord)	*f*
Anzeigegerät (Rollenbremsprüfstand)	*n*	display unit (dynamic brake analyzer)	*n*	afficheur (banc d'essai)	*m*

Deutsch		Englisch		Französisch	
Anzeigelampe	*f*	function lamp	*n*	témoin de fonctionnement	*m*
Anzeigeleuchte	*f*	function lamp	*n*	témoin de fonctionnement	*m*
Anzugsdrehmoment	*n*	tightening torque	*n*	couple initial de démarrage	*m*
Anzugszeit (Einspritzventil)	*f*	pickup time (fuel injector)	*n*	durée d'attraction (injecteur)	*f*
Applikationshinweis	*m*	application instructions	*npl*	notice d'application	*f*
Aquaplaning (Reifen)	*n*	aquaplaning (tire)	*n*	aquaplanage (pneu)	*m*
Arbeitshub	*m*	working stroke	*n*	temps de combustion	*m*
Arbeitskammer (Bremskraftverstärker)	*f*	working chamber (brake booster)	*n*	chambre de travail (servofrein)	*f*
Arbeitskolben	*m*	working piston	*n*	piston de travail	*m*
Arbeitsleuchte	*f*	working lamp	*n*	lampe de travail	*f*
Arbeitsluftspalt (ABS-Magnetventil)	*m*	working air gap (ABS solenoid valve)	*n*	entrefer (électrovalve ABS)	*m*
Arbeitsscheinwerfer	*m*	floodlamp	*n*	projecteur de travail	*m*
Arbeitstakt	*m*	power cycle	*n*	temps moteur	*m*
Arbeitszyklus (Verbrennungsmotor)	*m*	working cycle (IC engine)	*n*	cycle de travail (moteur à combustion)	*m*
Arbeitszylinder	*m*	working cylinder	*n*	vérin	*m*
Armaturenbrett	*n*	dashboard	*n*	tableau de bord	*m*
Arretierbolzen	*m*	blocking pin	*n*	axe de blocage	*m*
ASR, Antriebsschlupfregelung	*a*	traction control system, TCS	*n*	régulation d'antipatinage à la traction, ASR	*f*
ASR-Sperrventil	*n*	TCS lock valve	*n*	valve de barrage ASR	*f*
asymmetrisches Abblendlicht	*n*	asymmetrical lower beam	*n*	feu de croisement asymétrique	*m*
atmosphärendruck- und lastabhängiger Förderbeginn	*m*	barometric-pressure and load-dependent start of delivery	*n*	début de refoulement en fonction de la pression atmosph. et de la charge	*m*
atmosphärendruckabhängiger Förderbeginn	*m*	ambient-pressure-dependent port closing	*n*	début de refoulement en fonction de la pression atmosphérique	*m*
atmosphärendruckabhängiger Vollastanschlag, ADA	*m*	altitude-pressure compensator	*n*	correcteur altimétrique	*m*
Atmosphärendruckfühler	*m*	atmospheric-pressure sensor	*n*	capteur de pression atmosphérique	*m*
Atmosphärendrucksensor	*m*	atmospheric-pressure sensor	*n*	capteur de pression atmosphérique	*m*
Atmungsraum (Membran) x	*m*	breathing space (diaphragm)	*n*	côté secondaire (cylindre à membrane)	*m*
aufgewalzt	*pp*	rolled-on	*pp*	appliqué par laminage	*pp*
Aufheizgeschwindigkeit	*m*	pre-heating rate	*n*	vitesse de chauffe	*f*
Aufheizkurve	*f*	preheating curve	*n*	courbe de chauffe	*f*
Aufklemmgeber	*m*	clamp-on sensor	*n*	capteur à pince	*m*
Aufladegrad	*m*	boost ratio	*n*	degré de suralimentation	*m*
aufladen (Verbrennungsmotor)	*v*	supercharge (IC engine)	*v*	suralimenter (moteur à combustion)	*v*
Aufladeverfahren	*n*	supercharging process	*n*	procédé de suralimentation	*m*
Aufladung (Verbrennungsmotor)	*f*	pressure-charging (IC engine)	*n*	suralimentation (moteur à combustion)	*f*
Auflagekraftsteuerung (Wischeranlage)	*f*	force-distribution control (wiper system)	*n*	commande de la force d'appui (essuie-glace)	*f*

Deutsch			Englisch		Französisch	
Auflauf-Bremsanlage		*f*	inertia braking system	*n*	dispositif de freinage à inertie	*m*
Auflaufbremse		*f*	inertia braking system	*n*	dispositif de freinage à inertie	*m*
auflaufende Bremsbacke		*f*	leading shoe	*n*	mâchoire primaire	*f*
Auflaufrolle (Rollenbremsprüfstand)		*f*	secondary roller (dynamic brake analyzer)	*n*	rouleau suiveur (banc d'essai)	*m*
Aufliegerkupplung		*f*	semi-trailer coupling	*n*	accouplement de semi-remorque	*m*
Aufpralldetektion (Airbag)		*f*	crash sensing (airbag)	*n*	détection de collision (coussin gonflable)	*f*
Aufpralleffekt (Filter)		*m*	impact (filter)	*n*	effet d'impact (filtre)	*m*
Aufprallerkennung (Airbag)		*f*	crash sensing (airbag)	*n*	détection de collision (coussin gonflable)	*f*
Aufsatteldruck (Sattelschlepper)		*m*	kingpin load	*n*	pression d'accouplement	*f*
Aufsattelkupplung		*f*	fifthwheel coupling	*n*	sellette de semi-remorque	*f*
Aufschaltgruppe		*f*	add-on module	*n*	groupe d'adaptation	*m*
aufschaukeln (Kfz)		*v*	pitch (motor vehicle)	*v*	oscillation croissante (véhicule)	*f*
aufschwimmen (Reifen)	x	*v*	aquaplaning (tire)	*n*	aquaplanage (pneu)	*m*
Aufstandsfläche (Reifen)		*f*	tire contact patch	*n*	surface de contact du pneu	*f*
ausbrechen (Kfz)	x	*v*	break away (motor vehicle)	*v*	chasser (véhicule)	*v*
Ausfallmechanismus		*m*	failure mechanism	*n*	mécanisme de la défaillance (de l'incident)	*m*
Ausfallsperre (Autoalarm)		*f*	failure protection (car alarm)	*n*	sécurité en cas de panne (alarme auto)	*f*
Ausflußquerschnitt		*m*	outlet cross-section	*n*	section d'écoulement	*f*
Ausführungskennzahl		*f*	type code	*n*	code d'exécution	*m*
Ausgangsschaltung (Steuergerät)		*f*	output circuit (ECU)	*n*	circuit de sortie (calculateur)	*m*
Ausgangsspannung		*f*	output voltage	*n*	tension de sortie	*f*
Ausgleichexzenter		*m*	compensating eccentric	*n*	excentrique de compensation	*m*
Ausgleichgefäß (Bremse)		*n*	compensating reservoir (brakes	*n*	réservoir de compensation (frein)	*m*
Ausgleichsbehälter (Bremse)		*m*	compensating reservoir (brakes	*n*	réservoir de compensation (frein)	*m*
Ausgleichscheibe		*f*	shim (delivery-valve holder)	*n*	cale de réglage	*f*
Ausgleichsplatte		*f*	shim plate	*n*	plaque de réglage	*f*
Ausgleichsvolumen		*n*	compensation volume	*n*	volume de compensation	*m*
Auslaß		*m*	outlet	*n*	sortie	*f*
Auslaßnockenwelle		*f*	exhaust camshaft	*n*	arbre à cames côté admission	*m*
Auslaßsitz	+	*m*	discharge-valve seat	*n*	siège d'échappement	*m*
Auslaßventil (Einspritzpumpe)		*n*	metering spill (fuel-injection pump)	*n*	soupape de dosage (pompe d'injection)	*f*
Auslaßventil (Verbrennungsmotor)		*n*	exhaust valve (IC engine)	*n*	soupape d'échappement (moteur à combustion)	*f*
Auslaßventilsitz		*m*	discharge-valve seat	*n*	siège d'échappement	*m*
Auslenkung (Schwingung)		*f*	excursion (oscillation)	*n*	amplitude (oscillation)	*f*
Auslenkwinkel (Luftmengenmesser)		*m*	deflection angle (air-flow sensor)	*n*	angle de déplacement (débitmètre d'air)	*m*
auslesen (Fehlercode)	x	*v*	read out (error code)	*v*	visualiser (code de défaut)	*v*

Deutsch

Deutsch		Englisch		Französisch	
Ausleuchtung	*f*	illumination	*n*	éclairement	*m*
Auslösegerät (Gurtstraffer)	*n*	seat-belt-tightener trigger unit	*n*	déclencheur de prétensionneur	*m*
Auslösekriterium	*n*	triggering criterion	*n*	critère de déclenchement	*m*
Auslöseschwelle	*f*	trigger threshold	*n*	seuil de déclenchement	*m*
Auslösessystem	*m*	triggering system	*n*	système de déclenchement	*m*
Ausnutzungsgrad (Wickeltechnik)	*m*	power/space ratio (winding technique)	*n*	rendement (technique d'enroulement)	*m*
Auspuffklappe (Motorbremse)	*f*	butterfly valve (engine brake)	*n*	volet d'échappement (frein moteur)	*m*
Auspuffverlangsamer	*m*	exhaust brake	*n*	ralentisseur sur échappement	*m*
Ausregelzeit	*f*	settling time	*n*	délai de régulation	*m*
Ausrichtspiegel (Lichttechnik)	*m*	alignment mirror (lighting)	*n*	miroir d'orientation (éclairage)	*m*
Ausschaltschwelle	*f*	shut-off threshold	*n*	seuil de coupure	*m*
Außendom (Zündverteiler)	*m*	outer tower (ignition distributor)	*n*	cheminée (allumeur)	*f*
Aussetzbetrieb (elektrische Maschinen)	*m*	intermittent-periodic duty (electrical machines)	*n*	fonctionnement intermittent (machines électriques)	*m*
ausspuren (Starterritzel)	*v*	demesh (starter pinion)	*v*	désengrènement	*m*
Aussteuerdruck (Bremskraftverstärker)	*m*	output pressure (brake booster)	*n*	pression maximale (servofrein)	*f*
aussteuern (Bremskraft)	*v*	output (braking force)	*v*	piloter (force de freinage)	*v*
Aussteuerpunkt (Bremskraftverstärker)	*m*	saturation point (brake booster)	*n*	point de régulation finale (servofrein)	*m*
Ausstoßtakt	*m*	exhaust cycle	*n*	échappement (moteur à combustion)	*m*
Austausch-Erzeugnis	*n*	exchange product	*n*	produit d'échange standard	*m*
Austauschgenerator	*m*	exchange alternator	*n*	alternateur d'échange standard	*m*
Austauschprogramm (Werksaustausch)	*n*	exchange program (factory exchange)	*n*	programme d'échange standard	*m*
Auswerfer	*m*	ejector	*n*	éjecteur	*m*
Auswertelektronik	*f*	evaluation electronics	*npl*	circuit électronique de décodage	*m*
Auswertschaltgerät	*n*	signal-evaluation module	*n*	module électronique d'exploitation	*m*
Auswertschaltung	*f*	evaluation circuit	*n*	circuit d'exploitation	*m*
Auto-Alarmanlage	*n*	car alarm	*n*	alarme auto	*f*
Auto-Alarmsystem	*n*	car alarm	*n*	alarme auto	*f*
Automatikgetriebe	*n*	automatic gearbox	*n*	boîte de vitesses automatique	*f*
automatisch lastabhängige Bremskraftregelung, ALB	*f*	automatic load-sensitive braking-force metering	*n*	correction automatique de la force de freinage en fonction de la charge	*f*
automatisch lastabhängige Bremskraftzumessung	*f*	automatic load-sensitive braking-force metering	*n*	correction automatique de la force de freinage en fonction de la charge	*f*
automatische Brems-Differentialsperre, ABS/ABD	*f*	automatic brake-force differential lock, ABS/ABD	*n*	blocage automatique du différentiel	*m*
automatische Bremsanlage	*f*	automatic braking system	*n*	dispositif de freinage automatique	*m*
automatische Bremse	*f*	automatic brake	*n*	frein automatique	*m*
automatische Startmenge	*f*	automatic starting quantity	*n*	surcharge automatique au démarrage	*f*

Deutsch		Englisch		Französisch	
Axialkolben-Verteiler-einspritzpumpe	*f*	axial-piston pump	*n*	pompe distributrice à piston axial	*f*
Axialkolben-Verteilerpumpe	x *f*	axial-piston pump	*n*	pompe distributrice à piston axial	*f*
Axialkolbenmotor	*m*	axial-piston motor	*n*	moteur à pistons axiaux	*m*
Axialkolbenpumpe	x *f*	axial-piston pump	*n*	pompe distributrice à piston axial	*f*
Axiallüfter	*m*	axial fan	*n*	ventilateur axial	*m*
Axialnocken (Radialkolbenpumpe)	*m*	axial cam (radial-piston pump)	*n*	came axiale (pompe à pistons radiaux)	*f*
B					
Backenbremse	*f*	shoe brake	*n*	frein à mâchoires	*m*
Backenkennwert (Bremse)	*m*	shoe factor (brakes)	*n*	facteur de mâchoire (frein)	*m*
Balgdruck (Luftfeder)	*m*	bellows pressure	*n*	pression soufflet	*f*
Balligkeit	*f*	crowning	*n*	bombage	*m*
Bandpaßfilter	*n*	bandpass filter	*n*	filtre passe-bande	*m*
Batterie	*f*	battery	*n*	batterie d'accumulateurs	*f*
Batterie-Set	*n*	battery set	*n*	kit batterie	*m*
Batterie-Tester	*m*	battery tester	*n*	testeur de batteries	*m*
Batterieentladung	*f*	battery discharge	*n*	décharge de la batterie	*f*
Batteriekabel	*n*	battery cable	*n*	câble de batterie	*m*
Batteriekälteprüfstrom	*m*	low-temperature test current (battery)	*n*	courant d'essai au froid (batterie)	*m*
Batteriekapazität	*f*	nominal capacity (battery)	*n*	capacité nominale (batterie)	*f*
Batterieklemme	*f*	battery-cable terminal	*n*	cosse de batterie	*f*
Batterieladegerät	*n*	battery charger	*n*	chargeur de batterie	*m*
Batterieladestrom	*m*	battery charge current	*n*	courant de charge de la batterie	*m*
Batterieladezustand	*m*	state of charge (battery)	*n*	état de charge de la batterie	*m*
Batterieladung	*f*	charging (battery)	*n*	charge (batterie)	*f*
Batteriesäure	*f*	electrolyte	*n*	électrolyte	*m*
Batterieschalter	*m*	battery master switch	*n*	robinet de batterie	*m*
Batteriespannung	+ *f*	steady-state voltage (battery)	*n*	tension au repos (batterie)	*f*
Batterietrennrelais	*n*	battery-cutoff relay	*n*	relais de découplage de batterie	*m*
Batterieumschaltrelais	*n*	battery changeover relay	*n*	coupleur de batteries	*m*
Batterieumschaltung	*f*	battery changeover	*n*	commutation de batteries	*f*
Batteriezange	*f*	crocodile clip	*n*	pince de batterie	*f*
Baugruppe	*f*	assembly	*n*	sous-ensemble	*m*
Baukasten-System	*n*	modular system	*n*	technique modulaire	*f*
Baureihe	*f*	series	*n*	série	*f*
Bauteil (Gerät)	*n*	component (unit)	*n*	composant (appareil)	*m*
BDE, Benzindirekteinspritzung	*a*	gasoline direct injection	*n*	injection directe essence	*f*
Bedieneinheit (Fahrdatenrechner)	*f*	control unit (trip computer)	*n*	unité de sélection (ordinateur de bord)	*f*
Bedientastatur	*f*	keyboard	*n*	clavier de commande	*m*
Bedienteil	*n*	operator unit	*n*	clavier opérateur	*m*
Bedienungsanleitung	*f*	operating instructions	*npl*	notice d'utilisation	*f*
Befestigungsflansch	*m*	mounting flange	*n*	bride de fixation	*f*
Befestigungslasche	*f*	mounting bracket	*n*	patte de fixation	*f*

Deutsch			Englisch		Französisch	
Befestigungsloch		*n*	fixing hole	*n*	trou de fixation	*m*
Befestigungsschelle (Zündspule)		*f*	clamp (ignition coil)	*n*	collier (bobine d'allumage)	*m*
Begrenzungsleuchte		*f*	side-marker lamp	*n*	feu de position	*m*
Beharrungsdrehzahl		*f*	steady-state speed	*n*	vitesse d'équilibre	*f*
beheizte Lambda-Sonde, LSH		*f*	heated lambda sensor, LSH	*n*	sonde de richesse chauffée	*f*
Beifahrerairbag		*m*	passenger airbag	*n*	coussin gonflable côté passager	*m*
Beladungszustand (Kfz)		*m*	laden state (motor vehicle)	*n*	chargement (véhicule)	*m*
Belagbelastung (Bremsbelag)		*f*	lining load	*n*	pression d'appui (garniture de frein)	*f*
Belagverschleiß		*m*	lining wear	*n*	usure de garniture de frein	*f*
Belagverschleißsensor		*m*	wear sensor (brake lining)	*n*	capteur d'usure (garniture de frein)	*m*
Beleuchtung (Kfz)		*f*	lighting (motor vehicle)	*n*	éclairage (automobile)	*m*
Beleuchtungsstärke		*f*	luminous intensity	*n*	intensité lumineuse	*f*
Benzin		*n*	gasoline	*n*	essence	*f*
Benzin-Diesel-Anschlag		*m*	gasoline/diesel stop	*n*	butée essence/gazole	*f*
Benzindirekteinspritzung, BDE		*f*	gasoline direct injection	*n*	injection directe essence	*f*
Benzineinspritzung		*f*	gasoline injection	*n*	injection d'essence	*f*
Berechnungsdruck (Bremswirkung)		*m*	design pressure (braking action	*n*	pression calculée (effet de freinage)	*f*
Beschleunigungsanreicherung		*f*	acceleration enrichment	*n*	enrichissement à l'accélération	*m*
Beschleunigungsaufnehmer	x	*m*	acceleration sensor	*n*	capteur d'accélération	*m*
Beschleunigungsklopfen		*n*	acceleration knock	*n*	cliquetis à l'accélération	*m*
Beschleunigungsloch	x	*n*	flat spot	*n*	trou à l'accélération	*m*
Beschleunigungssensor		*m*	acceleration sensor	*n*	capteur d'accélération	*m*
Bestellnummer		*f*	part number	*n*	référence	*f*
betätigen (Bremse)		*v*	actuate (brakes)	*v*	actionner (frein)	*v*
Betätigungsdauer		*f*	duration of application	*n*	durée d'actionnement	*f*
Betätigungsdruck		*m*	applied pressure	*n*	pression d'actionnement	*f*
Betätigungseinrichtung (Bremsanlage)		*f*	control (braking system)	*n*	commande (dispositif de freinage)	*f*
Betätigungshebel		*m*	actuating lever	*n*	levier de manoeuvre	*m*
Betätigungskraft		*f*	control force	*n*	force de commande	*f*
Betätigungsventil		*n*	control valve (open loop)	*n*	valve de commande	*f*
Betätigungswelle		*f*	actuating shaft	*n*	arbre de commande	*m*
Betriebs-Bremsanlage		*f*	service-brake system	*n*	dispositif de freinage de service	*m*
Betriebsanleitung		*f*	operating instructions	*npl*	notice d'utilisation	*f*
Betriebsbremskreis		*m*	service-brake circuit	*n*	circuit de freinage de service	*m*
Betriebsbremsung		*f*	service-brake application	*n*	freinage de service	*m*
Betriebsbremsventil		*n*	service-brake valve	*n*	valve de frein de service	*f*
Betriebsdatenerfassung		*f*	data acquisition	*n*	saisie des paramètres opérationnels	*f*
Betriebsdatenverarbeitung		*f*	operating-data processing	*n*	traitement des paramètres de fonctionnement	*m*
Betriebsdauer		*f*	period of use	*n*	durée de fonctionnement	*f*
Betriebsdrehzahl		*f*	operating speed	*n*	vitesse de fonctionnement	*f*
Betriebsdruck		*m*	operating pressure	*n*	pression de service	*f*

Deutsch			Englisch		Französisch	
Betriebsfrequenz		*f*	operating frequency	*n*	fréquence d'utilisation	*f*
Betriebsgrenzwert		*m*	operating limits	*n*	valeurs limites de fonctionnement	*fpl*
Betriebsparameter		*m*	operating parameter	*n*	paramètre de fonctionnement	*m*
Betriebssicherheit		*f*	functional security	*n*	sécurité de fonctionnement	*f*
Betriebsspannung		*f*	operating voltage	*n*	tension de service	*f*
Betriebstemperatur		*f*	operating temperature	*n*	température normale de fonctionnement	*f*
Betriebszustand		*m*	operating state	*n*	conditions de fonctionnement	*fpl*
Bewegungsdetektor (Autoalarm)		*m*	motion detector (car alarm)	*n*	détecteur de mouvement (alarme auto)	*m*
Bewegungsenergie		*f*	kinetic energy	*n*	énergie cinétique	*f*
Bezugsmarke		*f*	reference mark	*n*	repère de référence	*m*
Bezugsmarkengeber (Zündung)		*m*	reference-mark sensor (ignition	*n*	capteur de repère de consigne (allumage)	*m*
Bezugsmarkensensor (Zündung)		*m*	reference-mark sensor (ignition	*n*	capteur de repère de consigne (allumage)	*m*
Bezugsmasse (Bordnetz)		*f*	reference ground (vehicle electrical system)	*n*	masse de référence (circuit de bord)	*f*
Biegebalken (Rollenbremsprüfstand)		*m*	flexural sensor (dynamic brake analyzer)	*n*	balancier (banc d'essai)	*m*
Bifokalreflektor		*m*	bifocal reflector	*n*	réflecteur bifocal	*m*
Bipolartechnik		*f*	bipolar technology	*n*	technique bipolaire	*f*
Blasenspeicher		*m*	bladder accumulator	*n*	accumulateur à vessie	*m*
Blasmagnet (Leistungsrelais)		*m*	blowout magnet (power relay)	*n*	aimant de soufflage (relais de puissance)	*m*
Blattfeder		*f*	leaf spring	*n*	ressort à lames	*m*
Blaurauch	x	*m*	blue smoke	*n*	fumées bleues	*fpl*
Blechlamelle (Anker)		*f*	disc (armature core)	*n*	disque de tôle (induit)	*m*
Blei-Akkumulator	+	*m*	lead storage battery	*n*	accumulateur au plomb	*m*
Blei-Kalzium-Batterie		*f*	lead-calcium battery	*n*	batterie plomb-calcium	*f*
Bleibatterie		*f*	lead storage battery	*n*	accumulateur au plomb	*m*
bleifrei (Benzin)		*adj*	unleaded (gasoline)	*pp*	sans plomb (essence)	*loc*
Bleigitter (Batterie)		*n*	lead grid (battery)	*n*	grille de plomb (batterie)	*f*
Blendung (Scheinwerfer)		*f*	glare (headlamp)	*n*	éblouissement (projecteur)	*m*
Blendwirkung (Scheinwerfer)		*f*	glare effect (headlamp)	*n*	effet d'éblouissement (projecteur)	*m*
Blindkupplung		*f*	coupling holder	*n*	accouplement borgne	*m*
Blink Code (Eigendiagnose)		*m*	blink code (self-diagnosis)	*n*	code clignotant (autodiagnostic	*m*
Blinkadapter (Anhänger-ABS)		*m*	flashing adapter (trailer ABS)	*n*	adaptateur clignotant (ABS pour remorques)	*m*
Blinker	+	*m*	direction-indicator lamp	*n*	feu indicateur de direction	*m*
Blinkerschalter		*m*	turn-signal switch	*n*	inverseur des feux clignotants	*m*
Blinkfrequenz		*f*	flash frequency	*n*	fréquence de clignotement	*f*
Blinkgeber		*m*	turn-signal flasher	*n*	centrale clignotante	*f*
Blinkleuchte		*f*	turn-signal lamp	*n*	clignotant	*m*
Blinklicht		*n*	turn signal	*n*	feu clignotant	*m*
Blinklichteinsatz		*m*	turn-signal unit	*n*	module de feu clignotant	*m*
Blinksignal		*n*	flashing signal	*n*	signal clignotant	*m*

Deutsch

Deutsch		Englisch		Französisch	
Blisterverpackung	f	blister pack	n	emballage blister	m
Blockdeckel (Batterie)	m	cover (battery)	n	couvercle de batterie	m
Blockierbeginn (ABS)	m	start of lock-up (ABS)	n	début du blocage (ABS)	m
Blockierdruck	m	locking pressure (brakes)	n	pression de blocage (frein)	f
blockieren (Rad)	v	wheel lock	n	blocage (roue)	m
Blockiergrenze (Rad)	f	wheel-lock limit	n	limite de blocage (roues)	f
Blockierneigung (Rad)	f	incipient lock (wheel)	n	tendance au blocage (roue)	f
Blockierschutz	+ m	antilock braking system, ABS	n	système antiblocage, ABS	m
Blockiervorgang (Rad)	m	wheel lock	n	blocage (roue)	m
Blockkasten (Batterie)	m	battery case	n	bac monobloc (batterie)	m
Blockwegeventil	n	stack-type directional control valve	n	bloc-distributeurs	m
Bodenfreiheit (Kfz)	f	ground clearance (motor vehicle)	n	garde au sol (véhicule)	f
Bodenhaftung	f	road-surface adhesion	n	adhérence au sol	f
Bodenleiste (Batterie)	f	bottom rail (battery)	n	rebord de fixation (batterie)	m
Bohrung (Motorzylinder)	f	bore (engine cylinder)	n	alésage (cylindre moteur)	m
Bordcomputer	m	on-board computer	n	ordinateur de bord	m
Bordnetz	n	vehicle electrical system	n	circuit de bord	m
Bordnetzspannung	f	vehicle system voltage	n	tension du circuit de bord	f
Bordrechner	m	on-board computer	n	ordinateur de bord	m
Bosch-Schwärzungszahl, BSZ	f	Bosch black-smoke number	n	indice de noircissement Bosch	m
Botschaftsformat (CAN)	n	message format (CAN)	n	format de message (multiplexage)	m
Boxfilter	n	box-type fuel filter	n	filtre-box	m
Breitbandstörung	f	broad-band interference	n	perturbation à large bande	f
Brems-Differentialsperre	f	brake-force differential lock	n	blocage du différentiel	m
Bremsabrieb	m	brake dust	n	traces d'abrasion dues au freinage	fpl
Bremsabstimmung	f	brake calibration	n	équilibrage des freins	m
Bremsaggregateprüfstand	m	braking-equipment test bench	n	banc d'essai pour équipement pneumatique de freinage	m
Bremsanlage	f	braking system	n	dispositif de freinage	m
Bremsanlagenauslegung	f	braking-system design	n	conception d'un dispositif de freinage	f
Bremsanschluß	m	brake connection	n	raccordement de frein	m
Bremsarbeit	f	braking work	n	travail de freinage	m
Bremsausrüstung	f	braking equipment	n	équipement de freinage	m
Bremsbacke	f	brake shoe	n	segment de frein	m
Bremsbackensatz	m	brake-shoe set	n	jeu de mâchoires de frein	m
Bremsbeginn	m	start of braking	n	début du freinage	m
Bremsbelag	m	brake lining	n	garniture de frein	f
Bremsdauer	f	braking time	n	temps de freinage	m
Bremsdruck	m	braking pressure	n	pression de freinage	f
Bremsdruckminderer	m	proportioning valve (brakes)	n	réducteur de pression de freinage	m
Bremsdruckmodulation	f	brake-pressure modulation	n	modulation de la force de freinage	f

Deutsch		Englisch		Französisch	
Bremsdruckregelung	*f*	braking-pressure control	*n*	régulation de pression de freinage	*f*
Bremsdynamik	*f*	dynamic braking response	*n*	dynamique du freinage	*f*
Bremse	*f*	brake	*n*	frein	*m*
bremsen	*v*	brake	*v*	freiner	*v*
Bremsenabstimmung	*f*	brake balance	*n*	adaptation des freins (aux différents véhicules)	*f*
Bremsenansprechdauer	*f*	brake response time	*n*	temps de réponse des freins	*m*
Bremsende	*n*	end of braking	*n*	fin de freinage	*f*
Bremsendienst	*m*	brake repair service	*n*	service freins	*m*
Bremseneingriff (ASR)	*m*	brake application (TCS)	*n*	intervention sur les freins (ASR)	*f*
Bremsenergie	*f*	braking energy	*n*	énergie de freinage	*f*
Bremsenkennwert	*m*	brake coefficient	*n*	coefficient d'autoserrage	*m*
Bremsennachstellung	*f*	brake adjustment	*n*	rattrapage de jeu (frein)	*m*
Bremsenprüfung	*f*	brake testing	*n*	essai de freinage	*m*
Bremsensonderuntersuchung, BSU	*f*	braking-system special inspection	*n*	contrôle spécial des freins	*m*
Bremsentester	*m*	brake tester	*n*	contrôleur de freins	*m*
Bremsfading	x *n*	fading (brakes)	*n*	fading (frein)	x *m*
Bremsflüssigkeit	*f*	brake fluid	*n*	liquide de frein	*m*
Bremsflüssigkeitsbehälter	*m*	brake-fluid reservoir	*n*	réservoir de liquide de frein	*m*
Bremsflüssigkeitsstand	*m*	brake-fluid level	*n*	niveau du liquide de frein	*m*
Bremsgerätegruppe	*f*	brake-component group	*n*	groupe de freinage	*m*
Bremsgestänge	*n*	brake linkage	*n*	timonerie de frein	*f*
Bremshebel	*m*	brake lever	*n*	levier de frein	*m*
Bremshysterese	*f*	braking hysteresis	*n*	hystérésis du freinage	*f*
Bremskenndaten	*npl*	brake specifications	*npl*	caractéristiques du freinage	*fpl*
Bremskontakt	*m*	brake contact	*n*	contacteur de freins	*m*
Bremskraft	*f*	braking force	*n*	force de freinage	*f*
Bremskraftaufteilung	*f*	braking-force distribution	*n*	répartition de la force de freinage	*f*
Bremskraftbegrenzer	*m*	braking-force limiter	*n*	limiteur de pression de freinage	*m*
Bremskraftminderer	*m*	braking-force reducer	*n*	réducteur de freinage	*m*
Bremskraftregelung	*f*	braking-force metering	*n*	régulation de la force de freinage	*f*
Bremskraftregler	*m*	load-sensing valve	*n*	modulateur de freinage	*m*
Bremskraftsteuerer	*m*	braking-force controller	*n*	commande de force de freinage	*f*
Bremskraftsteuerung	*f*	braking-force control	*n*	commande de la force de freinage	*f*
Bremskraftverstärker (Pkw)	*m*	brake booster (passenger car)	*n*	servofrein (voiture)	*m*
Bremskraftverteiler	*m*	braking-force metering device	*n*	répartiteur de force de freinage	*m*
Bremskraftverteilung	*f*	braking-force distribution	*n*	répartition de la force de freinage	*f*
Bremskraftzumessung	*f*	braking-force metering	*n*	régulation de la force de freinage	*f*
Bremskreis	*m*	brake circuit	*n*	circuit de freinage	*m*
Bremskreisaufteilung	*f*	brake-circuit configuration	*n*	répartition des circuits de freinage	*f*

Deutsch		Englisch		Französisch	
Bremskupplungskopf	*m*	coupling head "brakes"	*n*	tête d'accouplement "frein"	*f*
Bremslast (Rollenprüfstand)	*f*	retarding force (chassis dynamometer)	*n*	charge de freinage (banc d'essai)	*f*
Bremsleistung	*f*	instantaneous braking power	*n*	puissance instantanée de freinage	*f*
Bremsleitung (allgemein)	*f*	brake line (general)	*n*	conduite de frein (en général)	*f*
Bremsleitung (Zweileitungs-Bremsanlage)	*f*	brake service line (dual-line braking system)	*n*	conduite de commande (dispositif de freinage à deux conduites)	*f*
Bremsleuchte	*f*	stop lamp	*n*	feu de stop	*m*
Bremslicht +	*n*	stop lamp	*n*	feu de stop	*m*
Bremslichtschalter	*m*	brake-light switch	*n*	contacteur de feux de stop	*m*
Bremsmoment	*n*	braking torque	*n*	couple de freinage	*m*
Bremsnocken	*m*	brake cam	*n*	came de frein	*f*
Bremspedal	*n*	brake pedal	*n*	pédale de frein	*f*
Bremsprüfstand	*m*	dynamic brake analyzer	*n*	banc d'essai à rouleaux pour freins	*m*
Bremsprüfung	*f*	brake test	*n*	essai des freins	*m*
Bremsregelkreis (ASR)	*m*	brake control circuit (TCS)	*n*	circuit de régulation du freinage (ASR)	*m*
Bremsregelung	*f*	brake control system	*n*	régulation de freinage	*f*
Bremsregler (ASR)	*m*	brake controller (TCS)	*n*	régulateur de freinage (ASR)	*m*
Bremsrotor	*m*	braking rotor	*n*	rotor de freinage	*m*
Bremssattel	*m*	disc-brake caliper	*n*	étrier de frein à disque	*m*
Bremssattel-Set	*n*	brake caliper set	*n*	kit d'étrier de frein	*m*
Bremsscheibe	*f*	brake disc	*n*	disque de frein	*m*
Bremsschlauch	*m*	brake hose	*n*	flexible de frein	*m*
Bremsschlupf	*m*	brake slip	*n*	glissement au freinage	*m*
Bremsseil (Feststellbremse)	*n*	brake cable (parking brake)	*n*	câble de frein (frein de stationnement)	*m*
Bremssollmoment	*n*	setpoint braking torque	*n*	couple de freinage de consigne	*m*
Bremsstator	*m*	braking stator	*n*	stator de freinage	*m*
Bremsstellung	*f*	brakes-applied mode	*n*	position de freinage	*f*
Bremssystem	*n*	braking system	*n*	dispositif de freinage	*m*
Bremsträger (Bremse)	*m*	brake anchor plate (brakes)	*n*	support de frein	*m*
Bremstrommel	*f*	brake drum	*n*	tambour de frein	*m*
Bremsung	*f*	braking	*n*	freinage	*m*
Bremsventil	*n*	brake valve	*n*	valve de frein	*f*
Bremsverhalten	*n*	braking response	*n*	comportement au freinage	*m*
Bremsverstärker (Nfz)	*m*	brake servo-unit cylinder (commercial vehicles)	*n*	cylindre de servofrein (véhicules utilitaires)	*m*
Bremsverzögerung	*f*	braking deceleration	*n*	décélération de freinage	*f*
Bremsvorgang	*m*	braking action	*n*	mécanique du freinage	*f*
Bremswärme	*f*	braking heat	*n*	chaleur de freinage	*f*
Bremsweg	*m*	braking distance	*n*	distance de freinage	*f*
Bremswertgeber, BWG	*m*	braking-value sensor	*n*	capteur de freinage	*m*
Bremswertsensor	*m*	braking-value sensor	*n*	capteur de freinage	*m*
Bremswicklung	*f*	brake winding	*n*	enroulement de freinage	*m*

Deutsch		Englisch		Französisch	
Bremswirkung	*f*	braking effect	*n*	effet de freinage	*m*
Bremswirkungsdauer	*f*	effective braking time	*n*	temps de freinage actif	*m*
Bremszustand	*m*	braking condition	*n*	situation de freinage	*f*
Bremszyklus	*m*	brake cycle	*n*	cycle de freinage	*m*
Bremszylinder	*m*	brake cylinder	*n*	cylindre de frein	*m*
Brennbeginn	*m*	combustion start	*n*	début de combustion	*m*
Brenndauer (Kraftstoff-Luft-Gemisch)	*f*	combustion time (air-fuel mixture)	*n*	durée de combustion (mélange air-carburant)	*f*
Brenndauer (Zündfunken)	*f*	spark duration	*n*	durée de l'étincelle	*f*
Brennkammer (Abgastester)	*f*	burner (emissions testing)	*n*	chambre de combustion (émissions)	*f*
Brennpunkt (Scheinwerfer)	*m*	focal point (headlamp)	*n*	foyer (projecteur)	*m*
Brennraum (Verbrennungsmotor)	*m*	combustion chamber	*n*	chambre de combustion	*f*
Brennraumgestaltung	*f*	combustion-chamber design	*n*	forme de la chambre de combustion	*f*
Brennspannung (Zündkerze)	*f*	spark voltage (spark plug)	*n*	tension d'arc (bougie)	*f*
Brennweite (Scheinwerfer)	*f*	focal length (headlamp)	*n*	distance focale (projecteur)	*f*
Brückenschaltung	*f*	bridge circuit	*n*	circuit en pont	*m*
brummen (Funkstörung)	*v*	hum (radio disturbance)	*v*	ronflement (perturbation)	*m*
Bügelkralle (Wischer)	*f*	bracket clamp (wipers)	*n*	griffe de palonnier (essuie-glace)	*f*
Bügelsystem (Wischeranlage)	*n*	bracket system (wiper system)	*n*	palonniers (essuie-glace)	*mpl*
Bürstenhalter	*m*	brush holder	*n*	porte-balais	*m*
Bürstenhalterplatte	*f*	brush-holder plate	*n*	plateau porte-balais	*m*
Bürstenschleifer (Potentiometer)	*m*	pickoff brush (potentiometer)	*n*	balai de captage (potentiomètre	*m*
Bürstenträger	*m*	brush holder	*n*	porte-balais	*m*
Bürstenverschleiß	*m*	brush wear	*n*	usure des balais	*f*
Buskonfiguration (CAN)	*f*	bus configuration (CAN)	*n*	structure du bus	*f*
Busstruktur (CAN)	*f*	bus configuration (CAN)	*n*	structure du bus	*f*
Busvergabe (CAN)	*f*	bus arbitration (CAN)	*n*	affectation du bus	*f*
Bypass	*m*	bypass passage	*n*	canal de dérivation	*m*
Bypassventil	*n*	wastegate	*n*	valve de dérivation	*f*
C					
CAN, Controller Area Network	*a*	CAN, controller area network	*a*	CAN, système de multiplexage	*a*
Cetanzahl, CZ	*f*	cetane number, CN	*n*	indice de cétane	*m*
Cloudpoint (Mineralöl) x	*m*	cloud point (mineral oil)	*n*	point de trouble (huile minérale)	*m*
Cockpit-Instrument	*n*	cockpit instrument	*n*	instrument du poste de pilotage	*m*
Codierstecker	*m*	coding plug	*n*	connecteur à module de codage	*m*
Common Rail Hochdruckpumpe	*f*	common-rail high-pressure pump	*n*	pompe haute pression "Common Rail"	*f*
Common Rail Hochdruckverteilerleiste	*f*	common-rail high-pressure fuel rail	*n*	rampe distributrice haute pression "Common Rail"	*f*
Common Rail Injektor	*m*	common-rail injector	*n*	injecteur "Common Rail"	*m*
Common Rail Leitung	*f*	common-rail pipe	*n*	tube "Common Rail"	*m*
Common Rail Pumpe	*f*	common-rail pump	*n*	pompe "Common Rail"	*f*

Deutsch			Englisch		Französisch	
Common Rail System, CR		n	common-rail system, CR	n	système d'injection à pression modulée (Common Rail)	m
Common Rail, CR	x	n	common-rail system, CR	n	système d'injection à pression modulée (Common Rail)	m
Compact-Generator		m	compact alternator	n	alternateur compact	m
Computer Aided Design, CAD		n	Computer Aided Design, CAD	n	dessin assisté par ordinateur, DAO	m
Computer Aided Lighting, CAL		n	Computer Aided Lighting, CAL	n	éclairage assisté par ordinateur	m
CR, Common Rail		a	common-rail system, CR	n	système d'injection à pression modulée (Common Rail)	m
Crashdiskriminierung (Airbag)	x	f	crash sensing (airbag)	n	détection de collision (coussin gonflable)	f
crimpen		v	crimp	v	sertir	v
CVS-Methode (Verdünnungsverfahren)		n	dilution prodedure (CVS method)	n	essai d'évaporation (méthode CVS)	m
D						
Dachantrieb (Kfz)		m	power-sunroof drive unit	n	entraînement du toit ouvrant	m
Dachelektrode (Zündkerze)		f	front electrode (spark plug)	n	électrode frontale (bougie)	f
Dampfblasenbildung		f	vapor-bubble formation	n	percolation	f
Dampfdruck (Benzin)		m	vapor pressure (gasoline)	n	pression de vapeur (essence)	f
Dämpfer (ABS/ASR)		m	damper (ABS, TCS)	n	amortisseur (ABS/ASR)	m
Dämpferkammer (ABS)		f	damper chamber (ABS)	n	chambre d'amortissement (ABS)	f
Dämpfung (Luftfederung)		f	damping (air suspension)	n	amortissement (suspension pneumatique)	m
Dämpfungsdrossel		f	damping throttle	n	orifice calibré	m
Dämpfungskammer (Luftfederventil)		f	damping chamber (height-control valve)	n	chambre d'amortissement (valve de nivellement)	f
Dämpfungsraum (Luftfederventil)		m	damping chamber (height-control valve)	n	chambre d'amortissement (valve de nivellement)	f
Dämpfungsvolumen		n	damping volume	n	volume d'amortissement	m
Datenbus		m	data bus	n	bus de données	m
Datenmodul		m	operating-data module	n	module de données	m
Datenrahmen (CAN)		m	data frame (CAN)	n	cadre de données (multiplexage)	m
Datenübertragung		f	data transmission	n	transmission de données	f
Dauer-Bremsanlage		f	continuous-operation braking system	n	dispositif de freinage additionnel de ralentissement	m
Dauerbeanspruchung		f	continuous loading	n	contrainte permanente	f
Dauerbetrieb (elektrische Maschinen)		m	continuous-running-duty type (electrical machines)	n	fonctionnement permanent (machines électriques)	m
Dauerbremsanlage	+	f	continuous-operation braking system	n	dispositif de freinage additionnel de ralentissement	m
Dauerbremsdruck		m	sustained braking pressure	n	pression de freinage continue	f
Dauerbremse		f	retarder	n	ralentisseur	m
Dauerbremsrelais, DBR		n	retarder relay	n	relais du ralentisseur	m
Dauerbremsung		f	continuous braking	n	freinage prolongé	m
Dauerdrehmoment		n	continuous torque	n	couple permanent	m
dauerglühen		v	continuous glowing	v	incandescence permanente	f

Deutsch		Englisch		Französisch	
Dauerladung (Batterieladung)	*f*	trickle charging (battery charge)	*n*	charge permanente (charge de batterie)	*f*
Dauerlauf	*m*	continuous running	*n*	fonctionnement continu	*m*
Dauerlauferprobung	*f*	endurance test	*n*	essai d'endurance	*m*
Dauerlauftest	*m*	endurance test	*n*	essai d'endurance	*m*
Dauermagnet	*m*	permanent magnet	*n*	aimant permanent	*m*
Dauermagneterregung	*f*	permanent-magnet excitation	*n*	excitation par aimant permanent	*f*
Dauerprüfung	*f*	endurance test	*n*	essai d'endurance	*m*
Dauerstandfestigkeit	*f*	service life	*n*	durabilité	*f*
Dauerton (Autoalarm)	*m*	continuous tone (car alarm)	*n*	tonalité continue (alarme auto)	*f*
Dauerverbraucher	*m*	permanent load	*n*	récepteur permanent	*m*
Dauerversuch	*m*	endurance test	*n*	essai d'endurance	*m*
Dehnmeßstreifen	*m*	strain gage	*n*	jauge de contrainte	*f*
Dehnstoffelement	*n*	expansion element	*n*	élément thermostatique	*m*
dehnungsarm (Keilriemen)	*adj*	low stretch (V-belt)	*n*	peu extensible (courroie trapézoïdale)	*loc*
Deichsel	*f*	drawbar	*n*	timon (remorque)	*m*
DI, Direkteinspritzung (Dieselmotor)	*a*	direct injection, DI	*n*	injection directe	*f*
Diagnose-Taster	*m*			bouton-poussoir diagnostic	*m*
Diagnoseanschluß	*m*	diagnosis connection	*n*	connexion de diagnostic	*f*
Diagnoseanzeige	*f*	diagnosis display	*n*	affichage diagnostic	*m*
Diagnoseausgabe	*f*	diagnosis output	*n*	sortie de diagnostic	*f*
Diagnoselampe	*f*	diagnosis lamp	*n*	lampe de diagnostic	*f*
Diagnoseleitung	*f*	diagnosis cable	*n*	câble de diagnostic	*m*
Diagnosemodul	*m*	diagnosis module	*n*	module de diagnostic	*m*
Diagnoseschnittstelle (elektronische Systeme)	*f*	diagnosis interface (electronic systems)	*n*	interface de diagnostic (systèmes électroniques)	*f*
Diagnosesteckdose	*f*	diagnosis socket	*n*	prise de diagnostic	*f*
Diagnosesystem	*n*	diagnostics system	*n*	système de diagnostic	*m*
Diagnosetestgerät	*n*	diagnosis tester	*n*	testeur de diagnostic	*m*
Diagnosewerkzeug	*n*	diagnosis tool	*n*	outil de diagnostic	*m*
Diagrammscheibe (Tachograph)	*f*	tachograph chart	*n*	disque d'enregistrement (tachographe)	*m*
Dichtheitsprüfung	*f*	air-tightness test	*n*	essai d'étanchéité	*m*
Dichtkegel	*m*	sealing cone	*n*	cône d'étanchéité	*m*
Dichtkonus	*m*	sealing cone	*n*	cône d'étanchéité	*m*
Dichtmanschette	*f*	cup seal	*n*	garniture	*f*
Dichtrahmen	*m*	sealing gasket	*n*	cadre d'étanchéité	*m*
Dichtsitz	*m*	seal seat	*n*	siège d'étanchéité	*m*
Dichtstück	*n*	seal piece	*n*	pièce d'étanchement	*f*
Dickschicht-Membran	*f*	thick-film diaphragm	*n*	membrane à couches épaisses	*f*
Dickschichttechnik	*f*	thick-film techniques	*npl*	technique à couches épaisses	*f*
Diebstahlschutz	*m*	theft-deterrence feature	*n*	dispositif antivol	*m*
Diebstahlwarnanlage, DWA	*f*	car alarm	*n*	alarme auto	*f*
dieselbeständig	*adj*	diesel-fuel resistant	*ppr*	résistant au gazole	*ppr*
Dieseldiebstahlschutz, DDS	*m*	diesel theft deterrent	*n*	antivol diesel	*m*

Deutsch

Deutsch			Englisch		Französisch	
Dieseldirekteinspritzung		*f*	diesel direct injection	*n*	injection directe diesel	*f*
Dieseleinspritzpumpe		*f*	diesel fuel-injection pump	*n*	pompe d'injection diesel	*f*
Dieseleinspritzung		*f*	diesel fuel injection, DFI	*n*	injection diesel	*f*
Dieselkraftstoff		*m*	diesel fuel	*n*	gazole	*m*
Dieselrauch	x	*m*	diesel smoke	*n*	fumées diesel	*fpl*
Dieselregelung		*f*	governing (diesel engine)	*n*	régulation diesel	*f*
Differentialsperre		*f*	differential lock	*n*	blocage des différentiels	*m*
Differenzdruck		*m*	differential pressure	*n*	pression différentielle	*f*
Differenzdrucksensor		*m*	differential-pressure sensor	*n*	capteur de pression différentielle	*m*
Differenzdruckventil		*n*	differential-pressure valve	*n*	régulateur de pression différentielle	*m*
Differenzsollmoment		*n*	desired/setpoint speed differential	*n*	couple différentiel de consigne	*m*
Diffusionseffekt (Filter)		*m*	diffusion (filter)	*n*	effet de diffusion (filtre)	*m*
Diodenmodul		*m*	diode module	*n*	module de diodes	*m*
Diodenträger (Generator)		*m*	diode plate (alternator)	*n*	porte-diodes (alternateur)	*m*
Direkteinspritzer	x	*m*	direct-injection (DI) engine	*n*	moteur à injection directe	*m*
Direkteinspritzmotor		*m*	direct-injection (DI) engine	*n*	moteur à injection directe	*m*
Direkteinspritzung (Dieselmotor)		*f*	direct injection, DI	*n*	injection directe	*f*
Direkteinspritzverfahren		*n*	direct-injection (DI) process	*n*	procédé d'injection directe	*m*
Distanzring		*m*	spacer ring	*n*	bague-entretoise	*f*
Divisions-Steuer-Multivibrator		*m*	division control multivibrator	*n*	multivibrateur-diviseur de commande	*m*
Doppel-Auspuffanlage		*f*	dual exhaust system	*n*	système à double pot d'échappement	*m*
Doppelachsmodul (Anhänger)		*m*	twin-axle module (trailer)	*n*	module d'essieu double (remorque)	*m*
Doppelbettkatalysator		*m*	dual-bed catalytic converter	*n*	catalyseur à double lit	*m*
Doppeldichtung		*f*	double seal	*n*	double joint	*m*
Doppelkolbenspeicher (ASR)		*m*	twin plunger accumulator (TCS)	*n*	accumulateur à double pression (ASR)	*m*
Doppelkonus (Einspritzdüse)		*m*	dual cone (nozzle)	*n*	cône double (injecteur)	*m*
Doppelmagnetventil		*n*	double solenoid-operated valve	*n*	électrovalve double	*f*
Doppelnadeldüse		*f*	twin-needle nozzle	*n*	injecteur à deux aiguilles	*m*
Doppelschlußmotor		*m*	compound motor	*n*	moteur à excitation compound	*m*
Doppelsitzventil		*n*	double-seat valve	*n*	valve à double siège	*f*
doppeltwirkend (Arbeitszylinder)		*ppr*	double-acting (working cylinder)	*ppr*	à double effet (vérin)	*loc*
Doppelzündung		*f*	dual ignition	*n*	système d'allumage double	*m*
Dosierung		*f*	meter	*v*	dosage	*m*
Drall		*m*	swirl	*v*	tourbillon	*m*
Dralldüse		*f*	swirl nozzle	*n*	buse à effet giratoire	*f*
Drallniveausteuerung		*f*	swirl control	*n*	commande de niveau de giration	*f*
Drallsteller (Radialkolbenpumpe)		*m*	swirl actuator (radial-piston pump)	*n*	actionneur à effet giratoire (pompe à pistons radiaux)	*m*
Dralltopf		*m*	swirl plate	*n*	pot de giration	*m*

Deutsch		Englisch		Französisch	
Dreh-Hub-Bewegung	*f*	rotating-reciprocating movement	*n*	mouvement alternatif et rotatif	*m*
Drehanker	*m*	rotating armature	*n*	induit rotatif	*m*
Drehankerrelais	*n*	rotating armature relay	*n*	relais à armature pivotante	*m*
Drehantrieb (Türbetätigung)	*m*	rotary actuator (door control)	*n*	commande de pivotement des portes	*f*
Drehbacke (Trommelbremse)	*f*	rotating shoe (drum brake)	*n*	mâchoire pivotante (frein à tambour)	*f*
Drehdeckel (Kupplungskopf)	*m*	swivel cover (coupling head)	*n*	couvercle pivotant (tête d'accouplement)	*m*
Dreheisenstellwerk	*n*	moving iron actuator	*n*	commande à noyau de ferrite rotatif	*f*
Drehklappe (Motorbremse)	*f*	butterfly valve (engine brake)	*n*	volet d'échappement (frein moteur)	*m*
Drehknopfventil	*n*	rotary-knob valve	*n*	valve à bouton rotatif	*f*
Drehkolben-Gebläse	*n*	rotary-piston blower	*n*	soufflante à piston rotatif	*f*
Drehmagnetstellwerk	*n*	rotating-solenoid actuator	*n*	commande à aimant rotatif	*f*
Drehmomentbegrenzung	*f*	torque limitation	*n*	limitation de couple	*f*
Drehmomenthebel (Rollenbremsprüfstand)	*m*	torque lever (dynamic brake analyzer)	*n*	levier dynamométrique (banc d'essai)	*m*
Drehmomentsensor	*m*	torque sensor	*n*	capteur de couple	*m*
Drehmomentverlauf	*m*	torque curve	*n*	courbe du couple	*f*
Drehnocken (Bremskraftregler)	*m*	cam disc (braking-force regulator)	*n*	disque à cames (correcteur de freinage)	*m*
Drehpotentiometer	*n*	rotary potentiometer	*n*	potentiomètre rotatif	*m*
Drehpunkt	*m*	pivot	*n*	centre de rotation	*m*
Drehratensensor (ESP)	*m*	yaw sensor (ESP)	*n*	capteur de taux de rotation (ESP)	*m*
Drehrichtung	*f*	direction of rotation	*n*	sens de rotation	*m*
Drehschieber	*m*	rotating slide	*n*	tiroir rotatif	*m*
Drehschwingung	*f*	rotary oscillation	*n*	vibration due à la torsion	*f*
Drehsteller (KE-Jetronic)	*m*	rotary actuator (KE-Jetronic)	*n*	actionneur rotatif (KE-Jetronic)	*m*
Drehstrom	*m*	three-phase current	*n*	courant triphasé	*m*
Drehstromgenerator	*m*	alternator	*n*	alternateur triphasé	*m*
Drehstromwicklung	*f*	three-phase winding	*n*	enroulement triphasé	*m*
Drehwinkel	*m*	rotational angle	*n*	angle de rotation	*m*
Drehwinkelsensor, DWS	*m*	angle of rotation sensor	*n*	capteur d'angle de rotation	*m*
Drehzahl im Abregelpunkt	*f*	breakaway speed	*n*	vitesse de coupure	*f*
Drehzahlbegrenzung	*f*	engine-speed limitation	*n*	limitation de la vitesse de rotation	*f*
Drehzahlbereich	*m*	speed range	*n*	plage de vitesses de rotation	*f*
Drehzahlfühler	+ *m*	speed sensor	*n*	capteur de vitesse de rotation	*m*
Drehzahlgeber	*m*	speed sensor	*n*	capteur de vitesse de rotation	*m*
Drehzahlmesser (allgemein)	*m*	tachometer (general term)	*n*	tachymètre (terme général)	*m*
Drehzahlmesser (Kfz)	*m*	revcounter (motor vehicle)	*n*	compte-tours (véhicule)	*m*
Drehzahlpfad	*m*	speed path	*n*	piste de régime	*f*
Drehzahlregelung	*f*	rotational-speed control	*n*	régulation de la vitesse de rotation	*f*

Deutsch		Englisch		Französisch	
Drehzahlregler (Dieseleinspritzung)	*m*	governor (diesel fuel injection)	*n*	régulateur (injection diesel)	*m*
Drehzahlschwelle	*f*	engine-speed threshold	*n*	seuil de régime	*m*
Drehzahlsensor	*m*	speed sensor	*n*	capteur de vitesse de rotation	*m*
Drehzahlverstellung	*f*	engine-speed advance	*n*	correction en fonction du régime	*f*
Dreieckschaltung	*f*	delta connection	*n*	montage en triangle	*m*
Dreifach-Wegeventilblock	*m*	triple directional-control-valve block	*n*	bloc-distributeur triple	*m*
Dreiflügelventil	*n*	triple-fluted valve	*n*	soupape à trois ailettes	*f*
Dreikammerleuchte	*f*	three-chamber lamp	*n*	lanterne à trois compartiments	*f*
Dreikreis-Schutzventil	*n*	triple-circuit protection valve	*n*	valve de sécurité à trois circuits	*f*
Dreiphasenwicklung	+ *f*	three-phase winding	*n*	enroulement triphasé	*m*
Dreistellungsventil	*n*	three-position valve	*n*	valve à trois positions	*f*
Dreiwegekatalysator	*m*	three-way catalytic converter, TWC	*n*	catalyseur trois voies	*m*
Drosselbohrung	*f*	throttle bore	*n*	orifice d'étranglement	*m*
Drosselbolzen	*m*	throttle pin	*n*	axe d'étranglement	*m*
Drosselhub	*m*	throttling stroke	*n*	plage d'étranglement	*f*
Drosselklappe	*f*	throttle valve (IC engine)	*n*	papillon des gaz (moteur à combustion)	*m*
Drosselklappenansteller, DKA	*m*	throttle-valve actuator	*n*	actionneur de papillon	*m*
Drosselklappeneingriff (ASR)	*m*	throttle-valve intervention (TCS)	*n*	intervention sur le papillon (ASR)	*f*
Drosselklappengeber	*m*	throttle-valve sensor	*n*	capteur de papillon	*m*
Drosselklappenpotentiometer	*n*	throttle-valve potentiometer	*n*	potentiomètre de papillon	*m*
Drosselklappenschalter	*m*	throttle-valve switch	*n*	contacteur de papillon	*m*
Drosselklappensensor	*m*	throttle-valve sensor	*n*	capteur de papillon	*m*
Drosselklappensteller	*m*	throttle-valve actuator	*n*	actionneur de papillon	*m*
Drosselklappenstellung	*f*	throttle-valve position	*n*	position du papillon	*f*
Drosselklappenstutzen	*m*	throttle-valve assembly	*n*	boîtier de papillon	*m*
Drosselklappenwelle	*f*	throttle-valve shaft	*n*	axe de papillon	*m*
Drosselklappenwinkel	*m*	throttle-valve angle	*n*	angle de papillon	*m*
drosseln	*v*	choke	*v*	étrangler	*v*
Drosselrückschlagventil	*n*	throttle-type non-return valve	*n*	clapet de non-retour à étranglement	*m*
Drosselschraube	*f*	throttle screw	*n*	vis-pointeau	*f*
Drosselspalt	*m*	throttling gap	*n*	fente d'étranglement (injecteur)	*f*
Drosselstelle	*f*	throttling point	*n*	point d'étranglement	*m*
Drosselventil (Türbetätigung)	*n*	throttle valve (door control)	*n*	valve d'amortissement (pivotement des portes)	*f*
Drosselvorrichtung	*f*	throttle device	*n*	dispositif d'étranglement	*m*
Drosselwirkung	*f*	throttling effect	*n*	effet d'étranglement	*m*
Drosselzapfen	*m*	throttling pintle	*n*	téton d'étranglement	*m*
Drosselzapfendüse	*f*	throttling pintle nozzle	*n*	injecteur à téton et étranglemen	*m*
Druckabbau	*m*	pressure drop	*n*	chute de pression	*f*
Druckabbaustufe (ABS)	*f*	pressure-reduction step (ABS)	*n*	palier de baisse de pression (ABS)	*m*
Druckabfall	*m*	pressure drop	*n*	chute de pression	*f*

Deutsch		Englisch		Französisch	
druckabhängig	*adj*	pressure-sensitive	*adj*	asservi à la pression	*pp*
Druckablaßventil	*n*	pressure relief valve	*n*	soupape de décharge	*f*
Druckanschluß	*m*	pressure connection	*n*	raccord de pression	*m*
Druckanschluß (Einspritzpumpe)	*m*	pressure connection (fuel-injection pump)	*n*	raccord de refoulement (pompe d'injection)	*m*
Druckanstieg	*m*	pressure rise	*n*	montée en pression	*f*
Druckaufbau	*m*	pressure rise	*n*	montée en pression	*f*
Druckausgleich	*m*	pressure compensation	*n*	compensation de pression	*f*
Druckausgleichscheibe (Einspritzdüse)	*f*	pressure-compensation disc (nozzle)	*n*	cale de réglage de pression (injecteur)	*f*
Druckausgleichselement	*n*	pressure-equalization element	*n*	compensateur de pression	*m*
Druckbegrenzer	*m*	pressure limiter	*n*	limiteur de pression	*m*
Druckbegrenzungsventil	*n*	pressure limiter	*n*	limiteur de pression	*m*
Druckbereich	*m*	pressure area	*n*	plage de pression	*f*
Druckbolzen	*m*	pressure pin	*n*	tige-poussoir	*f*
Druckdämpfer (Jetronic)	*m*	fuel-pressure attenuator (Jetronic)	*n*	amortisseur de pression du carburant (Jetronic)	*m*
Druckdifferenz	*f*	pressure differential	*n*	différence de pression	*f*
Druckdose	*f*	vacuum unit	*n*	capsule manométrique	*f*
Druckentlastung	*f*	pressure relief	*n*	délestage de pression	*m*
Druckfeder	*f*	compression spring	*f*	ressort de pression	*m*
Druckfestigkeit	*f*	resistance to pressure	*n*	résistance à la pression	*f*
Druckförderung (Druckluft)	*f*	pressure delivery (compressed air)	*n*	refoulement (air comprimé)	*m*
Druckfühler	+ *m*	pressure sensor	*n*	capteur de pression	*m*
Druckgeber	*m*	pressure sensor	*n*	capteur de pression	*m*
Druckgefälle (Kraftstoff)	*n*	pressure drop (fuel)	*n*	perte de charge (carburant)	*f*
druckgießen	*v*	pressure diecasting	*v*	mouler sous pression	*v*
Druckhaltephase (ABS)	*f*	pressure-holding phase (ABS)	*n*	stade de maintien de la pression (ABS)	*m*
Druckhalteventil (Dieseleinspritzung)	*n*	pressure-holding valve (diesel fuel injection)	*n*	soupape de maintien de la pression (injection diesel)	*f*
Druckkammer (Einspritzdüse)	*f*	pressure chamber (injection nozzle)	*n*	chambre de pression (injecteur)	*f*
Druckkanal	*m*	pressure passage	*n*	canal de refoulement	*m*
Druckknopfventil	*n*	push-button valve	*n*	distributeur à bouton-poussoir	*m*
Druckkolben (Scheibenbremse)	*m*	piston (disc brake)	*n*	piston (frein à disque)	*m*
Druckkorrekturkennfeld	*n*	pressure-correction map	*n*	cartographie de correction de pression	*f*
Drucklager (Rollenbremsprüfstand)	*n*	thrust block (dynamic brake analyzer)	*n*	butée (banc d'essai)	*f*
Druckleitung	*f*	fuel-injection tubing	*n*	tuyau de refoulement	*m*
Druckluft	*f*	compressed air	*n*	air comprimé	*m*
Druckluft-Bremsanlage	*f*	compressed-air braking system	*n*	dispositif de freinage à air comprimé	*m*
Druckluft-Fremdkraft-Bremsanlage mit hydraul. Übertragungseinrichtung	*f*	air-over-hydraulic braking system	*n*	dispositif de freinage hydraulique à commande par air comprimé	*m*

Deutsch		Englisch		Französisch	
Druckluft-Hilfskraft-Bremsanlage	*f*	air-assisted braking system	*n*	dispositif de freinage hydraulique assisté par air comprimé	*m*
Druckluft-Servobremsanlage	*f*	air-assisted braking system	*n*	dispositif de freinage hydraulique assisté par air comprimé	*m*
Druckluftanlage	*f*	compressed-air system	*n*	dispositif à air comprimé	*m*
Druckluftbehälter (Pneumatik)	*m*	compressed-air reservoir (pneumatics)	*n*	réservoir d'air comprimé (pneumatique)	*m*
Druckluftbremse	*f*	compressed-air brake	*n*	frein à air comprimé	*m*
Druckluftkreis	*m*	compressed-air circuit	*n*	circuit d'air comprimé	*m*
Druckluftverbraucher	*m*	compressed-air load	*n*	récepteur d'air comprimé	*m*
Druckluftversorgung	*f*	compressed-air supply	*n*	alimentation en air comprimé	*f*
Druckluftvorrat	*m*	compressed-air reserve	*n*	réserve d'air comprimé	*f*
Druckluftvorratskreis	*m*	compressed-air supply circuit	*n*	circuit d'alimentation (air comprimé)	*m*
Druckmagnet	*m*	pushing electromagnet	*n*	électro-aimant de poussée	*m*
Druckmesser	*m*	pressure gauge	*n*	manomètre	*m*
Druckmeßgerät	*n*	pressure gauge	*n*	manomètre	*m*
Druckminderer (Bremse)	*m*	proportioning valve (brakes)	*n*	réducteur de pression de freinage	*m*
Druckminderventil (Bremse)	*n*	proportioning valve (brakes)	*n*	réducteur de pression de freinage	*m*
Druckmodulation	*f*	brake-pressure modulation	*n*	modulation de la force de freinage	*f*
Druckmodulator (ABS)	*m*	pressure modulator (ABS)	*n*	modulateur de pression (ABS)	*m*
Druckplatte (Bremse)	*f*	pressure plate (brakes)	*n*	plateau de pression (frein)	*m*
Druckpumpe (Scheibenspüler)	*f*	pressure pump (windshield washer)	*n*	pompe de refoulement (lave-glace)	*f*
Druckpunkt (Feststellbremsventil)	*m*	pressure point (parking-brake valve)	*n*	point de pression (valve de frein de stationnement)	*m*
Druckpunkt (Seitenwind)	*m*	pressure point (crosswind)	*n*	centre de pression (vent latéral)	*m*
Druckraum (Bremse)	*m*	pressure chamber (brakes)	*n*	chambre de compression (frein)	*f*
Druckraum (Einspritzpumpe)	*m*	plunger chamber (fuel-injection pump)	*n*	chambre de refoulement (pompe d'injection)	*f*
Druckregelmodul, DRM	*m*	pressure-control module	*n*	modulateur de pression	*m*
Druckregelung	*f*	pressure control	*n*	régulation de pression	*f*
Druckregelventil	*n*	pressure-control valve	*n*	soupape modulatrice de pression	*f*
Druckregler	*m*	pressure regulator	*n*	régulateur de pression	*m*
Druckregler-Ventilblock	*m*	pressure-regulator valve block	*n*	bloc-valves de régulateur de pression	*m*
Druckrohr	*n*	fuel-injection tubing	*n*	tuyau de refoulement	*m*
Druckrolle (Keilbremse)	*f*	pressure roller (wedge brake)	*n*	galet de pression (frein à coin)	*m*
Druckschalter	*m*	pressure switch	*n*	manocontact	*m*
Druckschlauch	*m*	pressure hose	*n*	flexible de pression	*m*
Druckschulter (Düsennadel)	*f*	exposed annular area (nozzle needle)	*n*	cône d'attaque (aiguille d'injecteur)	*m*
Druckschwankung	*f*	pressure variation	*n*	variation de pression	*f*
Druckschwellfestigkeit	*f*	compression pulsating fatigue strength	*n*	tenue aux ondes de pression	*f*
Druckschwingung	*f*	pressure pulsation	*n*	pulsation de pression	*f*

Deutsch		Englisch		Französisch	
Druckseite (Filter)	*f*	pressure outlet (filter)	*n*	côté refoulement (filtre)	*m*
Drucksenkung	*f*	pressure drop	*n*	chute de pression	*f*
Drucksensor	*m*	pressure sensor	*n*	capteur de pression	*m*
Drucksprungschalter	*m*	pressure-contact switch	*n*	contacteur à bond de pression	*m*
Druckstange (Bremskraftverstärker)	*f*	push rod (brake booster)	*n*	tige de poussoir (servofrein)	*f*
Druckstangenkolben	*m*	push-rod piston	*n*	piston à tige-poussoir	*m*
Drucksteller	*m*	pressure actuator	*n*	actionneur manométrique	*m*
Drucksteuerventil (ABS)	*n*	pressure-control valve (ABS)	*n*	valve modulatrice de pression (ABS)	*f*
Druckstift (Zweifeder-Düsenhalter)	*m*	pressure pin (two-spring nozzle holder)	*n*	poussoir (porte-injecteur à deux ressorts)	*m*
Druckstück (Kupplungskopf)	*n*	thrust member (coupling head)	*n*	pièce de pression (tête d'accouplement)	*f*
Druckstufe (Düsennadel)	*f*	differential ratio (nozzle needle	*n*	différentiel d'aiguille	*m*
Drucktaster	*m*	non-locking switch	*n*	interrupteur à touche	*m*
Drucktaupunkt (Lufttrocknung)	*m*	dew point (air drying)	*n*	point de rosée sous pression (dessiccation de l'air)	*m*
Druckventil (Einspritzpumpe)	*n*	delivery valve (fuel-injection pump)	*n*	clapet de refoulement (pompe d'injection)	*m*
Druckventilhalter (Einspritzpumpe)	*m*	delivery-valve holder (fuel-injection pump)	*n*	ensemble de clapet de refoulement (pompe d'injection	*m*
Druckventilkegel	*m*	delivery-valve cone	*n*	cône de soupape de refoulemen	*m*
Druckventilkolben	*m*	delivery-valve plunger	*n*	piston de soupape de refoulement	*m*
Druckventilschaft	*m*	delivery-valve stem	*n*	tige de soupape de refoulement	*f*
Druckventilsitz	*m*	delivery-valve seat	*n*	siège de soupape de refoulement	*m*
Druckventilträger	*m*	delivery-valve support	*n*	porte-soupape de refoulement	*m*
Druckverhältnisventil	*n*	adapter valve	*n*	régulateur proportionnel de pression	*m*
Druckverlauf	*m*	pressure characteristic	*n*	courbe de pression	*f*
Druckverlust	*m*	pressure loss	*n*	perte de pression	*f*
Druckversorgung (ASR)	*f*	pressure generator (TCS)	*n*	générateur de pression (ASR)	*m*
Druckvoreilung	*f*	pressure lead (braking pressure)	*n*	à avance de pression	*loc*
Druckwandler	*m*	vacuum converter	*n*	convertisseur de pression	*m*
Druckwelle	*f*	pressure wave	*n*	onde de pression	*f*
Druckwellenaufladung	*f*	pressure-wave supercharging	*n*	suralimentation par ondes de pression	*f*
Druckwellenlader	*m*	pressure-wave supercharger	*n*	échangeur de pression	*m*
Druckzapfen (Drosselzapfendüse)	*m*	pressure pin (throttling-pintle nozzle)	*n*	téton de pression (injecteur à téton et étranglement)	*m*
Dünnschichttechnik	*f*	thin-film techniques	*npl*	technique à couches minces	*f*
Duo-Duplexbremse	*f*	duo-duplex brake	*n*	frein duo-duplex	*m*
Duo-Servobremse	*f*	duo-servo brake	*n*	servofrein duo	*m*
Duplexbremse	*f*	duplex brake	*n*	frein duplex	*m*
Durchbruchspannung	*f*	breakdown voltage	*n*	tension de claquage	*f*
durchdrehen (Antriebsrad)	x *v*	wheel spin	*n*	patiner (roue motrice)	*v*

Deutsch			Englisch		Französisch	
durchdrehen (Verbrennungsmotor)	x	*v*	cranking (IC engine)	*n*	lancement (moteur à combustion)	*m*
Durchdrehwiderstand (Verbrennungsmotor)		*m*	resistance to rotation (IC engine)	*n*	résistance de lancement du moteur	*f*
Durchflußbegrenzer		*m*	flow limiter	*n*	limiteur d'écoulement	*m*
Durchflußdrossel		*f*	flow throttle	*n*	étrangleur	*m*
Durchflußsensor (Heißfilm-Luftmassenmesser)		*m*	flow sensor (hot-film air-mass meter)	*n*	capteur de flux d'écoulement (débitmètre massique à film chaud)	*m*
durchgehen (Verbrennungsmotor)	x	*v*	speed up out of control (IC engine)	*v*	emballer <s'emballer> (moteur à combustion)	*v*
durchgehende Bremsanlage		*f*	continuous braking system	*n*	dispositif de freinage continu	*m*
Durchlaßkennlinie (Gleichrichterdiode)		*f*	on-state characteristic (rectifier diode)	*n*	caractéristique tension-courant à l'état passant (diode redresseuse)	*f*
Durchlaßspannung (Gleichrichterdiode)		*f*	forward voltage (rectifier diode	*n*	tension à l'état passant (diode redresseuse)	*f*
Durchschlag (elektrisch)		*m*	arcing	*n*	décharge disruptive	*f*
Durchschlagspannung		*f*	breakdown voltage	*n*	tension de claquage	*f*
Durchspülungsverfahren		*n*	flushing method	*n*	méthode de balayage	*f*
Durchströmprinzip		*n*	throughflow principle	*n*	principe de transfert	*m*
Düse (Dieseleinspritzung)		*f*	nozzle (diesel fuel injection)	*n*	injecteur (injection diesel)	*m*
Düsen-Druckkammer		*f*	pressure chamber (injection nozzle)	*n*	chambre de pression (injecteur)	*f*
Düsenachse		*f*	nozzle axis	*n*	axe d'injecteur	*m*
Düsenfeder		*f*	nozzle spring	*n*	ressort d'injecteur	*m*
Düsenhalter		*m*	nozzle-holder assembly	*n*	porte-injecteur	*m*
Düsenhalter-Zwischenscheibe		*f*	adapter plate (nozzle holder)	*n*	glace de porte-injecteur	*f*
Düsenhalterkombination, DHK		*f*	nozzle-and-holder assembly	*n*	ensemble injecteur/porte-injecteur	*m*
Düsenkörper		*m*	nozzle body	*n*	corps d'injecteur	*m*
Düsenkuppe		*f*	nozzle cone	*n*	buse d'injecteur	*f*
Düsenloch		*n*	injection orifice	*n*	trou d'injection	*m*
Düsennadel		*f*	nozzle needle	*n*	aiguille d'injecteur	*f*
Düsennadelhub		*m*	needle lift	*n*	levée de l'aiguille	*f*
Düsennadelsitz		*m*	nozzle-needle seat	*n*	siège de l'aiguille d'injecteur	*m*
Düsenöffnungsdruck		*m*	nozzle-opening pressure	*n*	pression d'ouverture de l'injecteur	*f*
Düsenraum		*m*	nozzle chamber	*n*	chambre d'injecteur	*f*
Düsenschaft		*m*	nozzle stem	*n*	fût d'injecteur	*m*
Düsensitz		*m*	nozzle seat	*n*	siège d'injecteur	*m*
Düsenspannmutter		*f*	nozzle-retaining nut	*n*	écrou-raccord d'injecteur	*m*
Düsenstrahl (aufgelöst)		*m*	spray	*n*	jet pulvérisé	*m*
Düsenstrahl (vor der Auflösung)		*m*	nozzle jet	*n*	jet	*m*
Düsenstrahlrichtung		*f*	spray direction	*n*	direction du jet d'injecteur	*f*
Düsenüberwurfmutter		*f*	nozzle-retaining nut	*n*	écrou-raccord d'injecteur	*m*
Düsenverkokung		*f*	nozzle coking	*n*	calaminage des injecteurs	*m*
dynamische Achslast		*f*	dynamic axle load	*n*	charge dynamique par essieu	*f*

Deutsch		Englisch		Französisch	
dynamische Aufladung	*f*	dynamic supercharging	*v*	suralimentation dynamique	*f*
dynamische Förderbeginn-Einstellung	*f*	dynamic timing adjustment	*n*	calage dynamique du début de refoulement	*m*
dynamische Gewichtsverlagerung	*f*	dynamic weight transfer	*n*	report de charge dynamique	*m*
dynamische Plausibilität	*f*	dynamic plausibility	*n*	plausibilité dynamique	*f*
dynamische Vorsteuerung	*f*	dynamic pilot control	*n*	pilotage dynamique	*m*
dynamischer Funktionsbereich	*m*	dynamic functional range, DFR	*n*	plage de fonctionnement dynamique	*f*
E					
Edelgaslicht	*n*	inert-gas light	*n*	éclairage par lampe à gaz rare	*m*
Effektivhub	*m*	effective stroke	*n*	course effective	*f*
EGAS, elektronische Motorleistungssteuerung	*a*	ETC, electronic throttle control	*a*	EMS, commande électronique du moteur	*a*
EHB, elektrohydraulische Bremse	*a*	electrohydraulic braking system, EHB	*n*	frein électrohydraulique, EHB	*m*
Eichgas (Abgasprüftechnik)	*n*	calibrating gas	*n*	gaz de calibrage	*m*
Eigendiagnose	*f*	self-diagnosis	*n*	autodiagnostic	*m*
Eigendiagnose-Reizleitung	*f*	self-diagnosis initiate line	*n*	câble d'activation de l'autodiagnostic	*m*
Eigenfertigung	*f*	in-house production	*n*	production propre	*f*
Eigenfrequenz	*f*	natural frequency	*n*	fréquence propre	*f*
Eigenlenkverhalten	*n*	self-steering properties	*npl*	comportement directionnel propre	*m*
Einbauanleitung	*f*	installation instructions	*npl*	notice de montage	*f*
einbaugleich	*adj*	interchangeable	*adj*	de montage identique	*loc*
Einbauhinweis	*m*	installation instructions	*npl*	notice de montage	*f*
Einbaulage	*f*	installation position	*n*	position de montage	*f*
Einbauscheinwerfer	*m*	flush-fitting headlamp	*n*	projecteur encastrable	*m*
Einbettkatalysator	*m*	single-bed catalytic converter	*n*	catalyseur à une voie	*m*
Einfachfilter	*n*	single-stage filter	*n*	filtre à un étage	*m*
Einfeder-Düsenhalter	*m*	single-spring nozzle holder	*n*	porte-injecteur à un ressort	*m*
Einfederung	*f*	spring compression	*n*	compression du ressort	*f*
Einflußgröße	*f*	actuating variable	*n*	paramètre d'influence	*m*
einflutig (Lüfter)	*adj*	single-flow (fan)	*n*	monoflux (ventilateur)	*adj*
Einfunktionsleuchte	*f*	single-function lamp	*n*	feu à fonction unique	*m*
Eingangsbeschaltung (Steuergerät)	*f*	input circuit (ECU)	*n*	circuit d'entrée (calculateur)	*m*
Eingangsfilter	*n*	input filter	*n*	filtre d'entrée	*m*
Eingangsgröße	*f*	input variable	*n*	grandeur d'entrée	*f*
Eingangsverstärker (Steuergerät)	*m*	input amplifier (ECU)	*n*	amplificateur d'entrée (calculateur)	*m*
Einhebelsystem (Scheibenwischer)	*n*	single-arm wiper system	*n*	système monobras (essuie-glace)	*m*
Einklemmsicherung (Kfz)	*f*	push-in fuse (motor vehicle)	*n*	dispositif anti-pincement (véhicule)	*m*
einknicken (Sattelzug)	*v*	jacknife (semitrailer unit)	*v*	phénomène de mise en "portefeuille" (semi-remorque) x	*m*
Einkontaktregler	*m*	single-contact regulator	*n*	régulateur monocontact	*m*

Deutsch

Deutsch			Englisch		Französisch	
Einkopplung (EMV)		*f*	couple (EMC)	*v*	couplage (CEM)	*m*
Einkreis-Bremsanlage		*f*	single-circuit braking system	*n*	dispositif de freinage à transmission à circuit unique	*m*
einkreisig (Bremsanlage)		*adj*	single-circuit (braking system)	*n*	à un circuit (dispositif de freinage)	*loc*
Einlaßdrall (Saugrohr)		*m*	intake swirl (intake manifold)	*n*	tourbillon à l'admission	*m*
Einlaßnockenwelle		*f*	intake camshaft	*n*	arbre à cames côté échappemen	*m*
Einlaßquerschnitt (Verteilereinspritzpumpe)		*m*	inlet passage (distributor pump)	*n*	canal d'arrivée (pompe distributrice)	*m*
Einlaßsitz	+	*m*	intake-valve seat (IC engine)	*n*	siège d'admission (moteur à combustion)	*m*
Einlaßsystem (Verbrennungsmotor)		*n*	air-intake system (IC engine)	*n*	système d'admission (moteur à combustion)	*m*
Einlaßventil		*n*	intake valve	*n*	valve d'admission	*f*
Einlaßventilsitz (Verbrennungsmotor)		*m*	intake-valve seat (IC engine)	*n*	siège d'admission (moteur à combustion)	*m*
einlaufen (Bremstrommel, Bremsscheibe)	x	*v*	scoring (brake drum, brake disc)	*n*	trace d'usure (tambour, frein à disque)	*f*
Einlaufstelle (Bremstrommel, Bremsscheibe)		*f*	scoring (brake drum, brake disc)	*n*	trace d'usure (tambour, frein à disque)	*f*
Einleitungs-Bremsanlage		*f*	single-line braking system	*n*	dispositif de freinage à conduite unique	*m*
Einlochelement		*n*	single-port plunger-and-barrel assembly	*n*	élément à un orifice	*m*
Einlochzumessung (Einspritzventil)		*f*	single-orifice metering	*n*	dosage monotrou (injecteur)	*m*
Einparkhilfssystem		*n*	Park Pilot	*n*	guide de parcage	*m*
Einparksystem		*n*	Park Pilot	*n*	guide de parcage	*m*
Einpaßring		*m*	fitting ring	*n*	bague de centrage	*f*
Einpreßdiode		*f*	press-in diode	*n*	diode emmanchée	*f*
Einrückhebel (Starter)		*m*	engagement lever (starter)	*n*	fourchette d'engrènement (démarreur)	*f*
Einrückmagnet (Starter)		*m*	starting-motor solenoid (starter)	*n*	électro-aimant d'engrènement (démarreur)	*m*
Einrückrelais (Starter)		*n*	solenoid switch (starter)	*n*	contacteur électromagnétique (démarreur)	*m*
Einrückstange (Starter)		*f*	engagement rod (starter)	*n*	tige d'engrènement (démarreur)	*f*
Einrückwiderstand (Starter)		*m*	meshing resistance (starter)	*n*	résistance à l'engrènement (démarreur)	*f*
Einschaltbereich		*m*	cutin area	*n*	plage d'enclenchement	*f*
Einschaltdauer		*f*	operating time	*n*	durée d'enclenchement	*f*
Einschaltdrehzahl (Generator)		*f*	cutting-in speed (alternator)	*n*	vitesse d'amorçage (alternateur)	*f*
Einschaltdruck		*m*	cutin pressure	*n*	pression d'enclenchement	*f*
Einschaltpunkt		*m*	cutin point	*n*	point d'enclenchement	*m*
Einschaltschwelle		*f*	switch-on threshold	*n*	seuil d'enclenchement	*m*
Einschaltstrom		*m*	cutin current	*n*	courant de démarrage	*m*
Einschraubstutzen		*m*	screwed socket	*n*	manchon fileté	*m*
Einspritzaggregat (Mono-Jetronic)		*n*	central injection unit (Mono-Jetronic)	*n*	unité d'injection (Mono-Jetronic)	*f*
Einspritzanlage		*f*	fuel-injection installation	*n*	dispositif d'injection	*m*

Deutsch		Englisch		Französisch	
Einspritzanpassung	*f*	injection adaption	*n*	adaptation de l'injection	*f*
Einspritzausblendungszeit (Jetronic)	*f*	injection blank-out period (Jetronic)	*n*	temps d'interruption de l'injection (Jetronic)	*m*
Einspritzausrüstung	*f*	fuel-injection equipment	*n*	équipement d'injection	*m*
Einspritzbeginn	*m*	start of injection	*n*	début d'injection	*m*
Einspritzdauer	*f*	injection time	*n*	durée d'injection	*f*
Einspritzdruck	*m*	injection pressure	*n*	pression d'injection	*f*
Einspritzdüse	*f*	nozzle (diesel fuel injection)	*n*	injecteur (injection diesel)	*m*
Einspritzdüsenhalter	*m*	nozzle-holder assembly	*n*	porte-injecteur	*m*
Einspritzelement (Einspritzpumpe)	*n*	plunger-and-barrel assembly (fuel-injection pump)	*n*	élément de pompage (pompe d'injection)	*m*
Einspritzfolge	*f*	injection sequence	*n*	ordre d'injection	*m*
Einspritzgrundmenge	+ *f*	basic injection quantity	*n*	débit d'injection de base	*m*
Einspritzimpuls	*m*	injection pulse	*n*	impulsion d'injection	*f*
Einspritzleitung	*f*	fuel-injection tubing	*n*	tuyau de refoulement	*m*
Einspritzmasse	*f*	injection mass	*n*	masse injectée	*f*
Einspritzmenge	*f*	injected fuel quantity	*n*	débit d'injection	*m*
Einspritzmengenindikator	*m*	injected-fuel-quantity indicator	*n*	débitmètre instantané	*m*
Einspritzmengenstreuung	*f*	injected-fuel-quantity scatter	*n*	dispersion de débit	*f*
Einspritzmengenverlauf	*m*	rate-of-discharge curve	*n*	loi d'injection	*f*
Einspritzmotor	*m*	fuel-injection engine	*n*	moteur à injection	*m*
Einspritznocken	*m*	injection cam	*n*	came d'injection	*f*
Einspritzpumpe	*f*	fuel-injection pump	*n*	pompe d'injection	*f*
Einspritzpumpen-Kombination	*f*	injection-pump assembly	*n*	ensemble de pompe d'injection	*m*
Einspritzpumpen-Prüfstand	*m*	injection-pump test bench	*n*	banc d'essai pour pompes d'injection	*m*
Einspritzrichtung	*f*	injection direction	*n*	sens d'injection	*m*
Einspritzstrahl	*m*	injection jet	*n*	jet d'injection	*m*
Einspritzsystem	*n*	fuel-injection installation	*n*	dispositif d'injection	*m*
Einspritztakt	*m*	injection cycle	*n*	cycle d'injection	*m*
Einspritztechnik	*f*	fuel injection	*n*	injection de carburant	*f*
Einspritzung	*f*	fuel injection	*n*	injection de carburant	*f*
Einspritzventil	*n*	fuel injector	*n*	injecteur	*m*
Einspritzventil mit axialer Zuführung ("Top-Feed")	*n*	top-feed injector	*n*	injecteur à flux axial	*m*
Einspritzventil mit radialer Zuführung ("Bottom-Feed")	*n*	bottom-feed injector	*n*	injecteur à flux radial	*m*
Einspritzventilgruppe	*f*	injection-valve group	*n*	groupe d'injecteurs	*m*
Einspritzverlauf	*m*	rate-of-discharge curve	*n*	loi d'injection	*f*
Einspritzvolumen	*n*	injected fuel volume	*n*	volume de carburant injecté	*m*
Einspritzvorgang	*m*	injection process	*n*	injection (opération)	*f*
Einspritzzeit	*f*	injection time	*n*	durée d'injection	*f*
Einspritzzeitpunkt	+ *m*	start of injection	*n*	début d'injection	*m*
einspuren (Starterritzel)	*v*	mesh (starter pinion)	*v*	engrènement (pignon)	*m*
Einspurfeder	*f*	meshing spring	*n*	ressort d'engrènement	*m*
Einspurgetriebe	*n*	pinion-engaging drive	*n*	lanceur	*m*
Einspurhub	*m*	pinion travel	*n*	course d'engrènement	*f*
Einspursystem	*n*	engaging system	*n*	système d'engrènement	*m*

Deutsch

Deutsch		Englisch		Französisch	
Einspurtrieb	*m*	pinion-engaging drive	*n*	lanceur	*m*
Einspurvorrichtung	*f*	pinion-engaging drive	*n*	lanceur	*m*
Einstellgerät	*n*	calibrating unit	*n*	appareil de réglage	*m*
Einstellhebel (Verteilereinspritzpumpe)	*m*	control lever (distributor pump)	*n*	levier de réglage (pompe distributrice)	*m*
Einstellhülse	*f*	setting sleeve	*n*	manchon de réglage	*m*
Einstellpotentiometer	*n*	adjusting potentiometer	*n*	potentiomètre de réglage	*m*
Einstellpunkt	*m*	adjustment point	*n*	point de réglage	*m*
Einstellscheibe	*f*	shim (nozzle-holder assembly)	*n*	rondelle de réglage	*f*
Einstellschraube	*f*	adjusting screw	*n*	vis de réglage	*f*
einsteuern (Bremskraft)	*v*	apply (braking force)	*v*	moduler (force de freinage)	*v*
Einstrahl-Drosselzapfendüse	*f*	single-jet throttling-pintle nozzle	*n*	injecteur monojet à téton et étranglement	*m*
Einstrahldüse	*f*	single-hole nozzle	*n*	injecteur monotrou	*m*
Einstrahlfestigkeit (EMV)	*f*	resistance to incident radiation (EMC)	*n*	tenue au rayonnement incident (CEM)	*f*
Einstrahlung (EMV)	*f*	incident radiation (EMC)	*n*	rayonnement incident (CEM)	*m*
Einweggleichrichter	*m*	half-wave rectifier	*n*	redresseur demi-onde	*m*
Einzeleinspritzpumpe (PF)	*f*	single-plunger fuel-injection pump (PF)	*n*	pompe d'injection monocylindrique (PF)	*f*
Einzeleinspritzung	*f*	multipoint fuel injection, MPI	*n*	injection multipoint	*f*
Einzelfunken-Zündspule	*f*	single-spark ignition coil	*n*	bobine d'allumage à une sortie	*f*
Einzelpolgenerator	*m*	salient-pole generator	*n*	alternateur à pôles saillants	*m*
Einzelpolläufer	*m*	salient-pole rotor	*n*	rotor à pôles saillants	*m*
Einzelradregelung (ABS)	*f*	individual control, IR (ABS)	*n*	régulation individuelle (ABS)	*f*
Einzelschwingrohr	*n*	individual runner	*n*	tubulure d'admission	*f*
Einziehtechnik (Wicklung)	*f*	pull-in technique (winding)	*n*	tréfilage (enroulement)	*m*
Einzugswicklung	*f*	pull-in winding	*n*	enroulement d'appel	*m*
Einzylinder-Einspritzpumpe (PF)	*f*	single-plunger fuel-injection pump (PF)	*n*	pompe d'injection monocylindrique (PF)	*f*
Eisenjoch (Leerlaufsteller)	*n*	iron yoke (idle actuator)	*n*	culasse de fer (actionneur de ralenti)	*f*
Eisenkern	*m*	iron core	*n*	noyau de fer	*m*
Eisenverluste (Generator)	x *mpl*	iron losses (alternator)	x *npl*	pertes fer (alternateur)	x *fpl*
Elastomerquellung (Bremsflüssigkeit)	*f*	elastomer swelling (brake fluid)	*n*	gonflement des élastomères (liquide de frein)	*m*
ELB, elektronisch geregelte Bremsanlage	*a*	electronically controlled braking system, ELB	*n*	dispositif de freinage à régulation électronique	*m*
Elektrisch angetriebenes Fahrzeug (Straßenfahrzeug)	*n*	electric vehicle, EV	*n*	véhicule électrique	*m*
elektrische Abstellvorrichtung, ELAB	*f*	solenoid-operated shutoff	*n*	dispositif d'arrêt électrique	*m*
elektrische Verlustleistung	*f*	electrical power loss	*n*	pertes de puissance	*fpl*
elektro-hydraulische Pumpe	*f*	electro-hydraulic pump	*n*	groupe électropompe	*m*
elektro-pneumatische Bremsanlage	*f*	electropneumatic braking system	*n*	dispositif de freinage électro-pneumatique	*m*
Elektroabscheider	*m*	electrical separator	*n*	séparateur électrique	*m*
Elektroblech	*n*	electrical sheet steel	*n*	tôle magnétique	*f*
Elektrode	*f*	electrode	*n*	électrode	*f*

Deutsch		Englisch		Französisch	
Elektrodenabstand (Zündkerze)	*m*	electrode gap (spark plug)	*n*	écartement des électrodes (bougie)	*m*
Elektrodenform (Zündkerze)	*f*	electrode shape (spark plug)	*n*	forme des électrodes	*f*
Elektrodenverschleiß	*m*	electrode wear	*n*	usure des électrodes	*f*
Elektrodenwerkstoffe	*mpl*	electrode materials	*npl*	matériaux des électrodes	*mpl*
elektrodynamischer Verlangsamer	*m*	electrodynamic retarder	*n*	ralentisseur électromagnétique	*m*
Elektrofahrzeug (Straßenfahrzeug)	*n*	electric vehicle, EV	*n*	véhicule électrique	*m*
Elektroförderpumpe	*f*	electric supply pump	*n*	pompe d'alimentation électrique	*f*
elektrohydraulische Abstellvorrichtung, EHAB	*f*	electrohydraulic shutoff device	*n*	dispositif d'arrêt électrohydraulique	*m*
elektrohydraulische Bremse, EHB	*f*	electrohydraulic braking system, EHB	*n*	frein électrohydraulique, EHB	*m*
elektrohydraulischer Drucksteller	*m*	electro-hydraulic pressure actuator	*n*	actionneur de pression électrohydraulique	*m*
Elektrokompressor	*m*	electric compressor	*n*	compresseur électrique	*m*
Elektrokraftstoffpumpe, EKP	*f*	electric fuel pump	*n*	pompe électrique à carburant	*f*
Elektrolyt	*m*	electrolyte	*n*	électrolyte	*m*
Elektrolytkondensator	*m*	electrolytic capacitor	*n*	condensateur électrolytique	*m*
elektromagnetische Abstellvorrichtung	*f*	solenoid-operated shutoff	*n*	dispositif d'arrêt électrique	*m*
elektromagnetische Verträglichkeit, EMV	*f*	electromagnetic compatibility, EMC	*n*	compatibilité électromagnétique, CEM	*f*
Elektromotor	*m*	electric motor	*n*	moteur électrique	*m*
elektromotorische Abstellvorrichtung, EMAB	*f*	electromotive shutoff device	*n*	dispositif d'arrêt électromotoris	*m*
Elektroniklader (Batterie)	*m*	electronic charger (battery)	*n*	chargeur électronique (batterie)	*m*
elektronisch geregelte Bremsanlage, ELB	*f*	electronically controlled braking system, ELB	*n*	dispositif de freinage à régulation électronique	*m*
elektronisch geregelte Luftfederung, ELF	*f*	electronically controlled pneumatic suspension, ELF	*n*	suspension pneumatique à régulation électronique, ELF	*f*
elektronisch gesteuertes Benzineinspritzsystem, Jetronic	*n*	Jetronic (electronic fuel injection)	*n*	Jetronic (injection électronique d'essence)	*m*
elektronische Benzineinspritzung, Jetronic	*f*	Jetronic (electronic fuel injection)	*n*	Jetronic (injection électronique d'essence)	*m*
elektronische Bremsdruckregelung, EPC	*f*	electronic braking-pressure control, EPC	*n*	régulation électronique de pression de freinage, EPC	*f*
elektronische Dieselregelung, EDC	*f*	electronic diesel control, EDC	*n*	régulation électronique diesel, RED	*f*
elektronische Leerlaufregelung, ELR	*f*	electronic idle-speed control	*n*	régulation électronique du ralenti	*f*
elektronische Motorfüllungs-steuerung, EGAS	*f*	electronic throttle control, ETC	*n*	commande électronique du moteur	*f*
elektronische Motorsteuerung, Motronic	*f*	electronic engine-management system, Motronic	*n*	système électronique de gestion du moteur, Motronic	*m*
elektronisches Gaspedal, EGAS	*f*	electronic throttle control, ETC	*n*	commande électronique du moteur	*f*
elektronisches Steuergerät	*n*	electronic control unit, ECU	*n*	centrale de commande électronique	*f*

Deutsch		**Englisch**		**Französisch**	
elektropneumatischer Wandler	*m*	electropneumatic converter	*n*	convertisseur électropneumatique	*m*
Elektrostraßenfahrzeug	*n*	electric vehicle, EV	*n*	véhicule électrique	*m*
Element-Abschaltventil	*n*	element cutoff valve	*n*	soupape de coupure d'élément	*f*
Elementabschaltventil (Common Rail)	*n*	element switchoff valve (common rail)	*n*	électrovanne de désactivation d'élément	*f*
Elementbuchse	*f*	pumping-element bushing	*n*	douille d'élément de pompage	*f*
Elementdruck	*m*	pump-side pressure	*n*	pression dans l'élément	*f*
Elementkolben	*m*	pumping-element plunger	*n*	piston d'élément de pompage	*m*
Elementkopf (Pumpenelement)	*m*	plunger-and-barrel head	*n*	tête de l'élément de pompage	*f*
Elementraum (Common Rail)	*m*	element chamber (common rail	*n*	chambre d'élément (Common Rail)	*f*
Elementverband	*m*	barrel-and-valve assembly	*n*	ensemble élément-soupape	*m*
Elementzylinder	*m*	pumping-assembly barrel	*n*	cylindre d'élément de pompage	*m*
Emissionswerte	*mpl*	emission values	*npl*	valeurs d'émission	*fpl*
Empfänger-Wandler (Autoalarm)	*m*	receiver transducer (car alarm)	*n*	transducteur-récepteur (alarme auto)	*m*
Empfängerkammer (Abgastester)	*f*	receiving chamber (CO test)	*n*	collecteur (gaz CO)	*m*
EMV, elektromagnetische Verträglichkeit	*a*	electromagnetic compatibility, EMC	*n*	compatibilité électromagnétique, CEM	*f*
Endabregelung (Einspritzpumpe)	*f*	full-load speed regulation (fuel-injection pump)	*n*	coupure de vitesse maximale (pompe d'injection)	*f*
Endabstellung (Wischermotor)	*f*	self-parking (wiper motor)	*n*	arrêt en fin de course (moteur d'essuie-glace)	*m*
Enddrehzahl	*f*	high idle speed	*n*	vitesse maximale à vide	*f*
Enddrehzahlregler	*m*	maximum-speed governor	*n*	régulateur de vitesse maximale	*m*
Enderwärmung	*f*	final operating temperature	*n*	température finale de fonctionnement	*f*
Endkontrolle	*f*	final inspection	*n*	contrôle final	*m*
Endlage	*f*	end position	*n*	position de fin de course	*f*
Endpol (Batterie)	*m*	terminal post (battery)	*n*	borne (batterie)	*f*
Endprüfung	*f*	final inspection	*n*	contrôle final	*m*
Endregelfeder	*f*	maximum-speed spring	*n*	ressort de régulation de vitesse maximale	*m*
Endstellung	*f*	end position	*n*	position de fin de course	*f*
Endstufe (Steuergerät)	*f*	driver stage (ECU)	*n*	étage de sortie (calculateur)	*m*
Endstufenbearbeitung (Steuergerät)	*f*	driver-stage processing (ECU)	*n*	traitement à l'étage de sortie (calculateur)	*m*
Endstufenfehlererkennung (Steuergerät)	*f*	driver-stage defect recognition (ECU)	*n*	détection de défaut à l'étage de sortie (calculateur)	*f*
Energieabfluß	*m*	energy output	*n*	départ d'énergie	*m*
Energiefluß	*m*	flow of energy	*n*	flux d'énergie	*m*
Energiehaushalt (Kfz)	*m*	energy balance (motor vehicle)	*n*	bilan énergétique (automobile)	*m*
Energiequelle	*f*	source of energy	*n*	source d'énergie	*f*
Energiereserve (Airbag)	*f*	energy reserve (airbag triggering system)	*n*	réserve d'énergie (coussin d'air)	*f*
Energiespeicher	*m*	energy accumulator	*n*	accumulateur d'énergie	*m*
Energiespeicherung	*f*	energy storage	*n*	accumulation de l'énergie	*f*

Deutsch		Englisch		Französisch	
Energieumsetzung	*f*	energy conversion	*n*	conversion d'énergie	*f*
Energieversorgung	*f*	energy supply	*n*	génération d'énergie	*f*
Energieversorgungs-einrichtung	*f*	energy-supply system	*n*	dispositif d'alimentation en énergie	*m*
Energiezufluß	*m*	energy input	*n*	arrivée d'énergie	*f*
Energiezufuhr	*f*	energy input	*n*	arrivée d'énergie	*f*
Entflammung (Zündung)	*f*	ignition	*n*	allumage	*m*
Entflammungsaussetzer	*m*	ignition miss	*n*	ratés d'inflammation	*mpl*
Entflammungsdauer	*f*	flame-front propagation time	*n*	durée d'inflammation	*f*
Entflammungszeitpunkt	*m*	mixture ignition point	*n*	point d'inflammation	*m*
Entgasungsöffnung (Batterie)	*f*	ventilation opening (battery)	*n*	orifice de dégazage (batterie)	*m*
Entgasungsventil	+ *n*	bleeder valve	*n*	valve de purge air	*f*
entladen (Batterie)	*v*	discharge (battery) <to discharge>	*v*	décharger (batterie)	*v*
Entladestrom	*m*	discharge current	*n*	courant de décharge	*m*
Entladung (Batterie)	*f*	discharge (battery) <noun>	*n*	décharge (batterie)	*f*
Entladungsraum (Gasentladungslampe)	*m*	discharge chamber (gaseous-discharge lamp)	*n*	cellule de décharge (lampe à décharge)	*f*
Entlastungsbund	*m*	relief collar	*n*	épaulement de détente	*m*
Entlastungshub	*m*	retraction lift	*n*	course de détente	*f*
Entlastungskolben	*m*	retraction piston	*n*	piston de détente	*m*
Entlastungsvolumen	*n*	retraction volume (in-line pump)	*n*	volume de réaspiration	*m*
entlüften	*v*	bleed	*v*	dégazage	*m*
Entlüfterschraube	*f*	vent screw	*n*	vis de purge d'air	*f*
Entlüftungsbohrung	*f*	vent bore	*n*	orifice de purge d'air	*m*
Entlüftungsschraube	*f*	vent screw	*n*	vis de purge d'air	*f*
Entlüftungsstutzen	*m*	vent connection	*n*	tubulure de mise à l'atmosphère	*f*
Entlüftungsventil	*n*	bleeder valve	*n*	valve de purge air	*f*
Entmischungsvorgang	*m*	segregation process	*n*	phénomène de démixtion	*m*
Entnahmesonde	*f*	exhaust-sample probe	*n*	sonde de prélèvement	*f*
Entriegelung (Nothahn)	*f*	release (emergency valve)	*n*	déverrouillage (robinet de secours)	*m*
entschärfen (Autoalarm)	*v*	deprime (car alarm)	*v*	mise hors veille (alarme auto)	*f*
Entstördrossel	*f*	interference-suppression choke	*n*	self d'antiparasitage	*f*
Entstörfilter	*n*	suppression filter	*n*	filtre d'antiparasitage	*m*
Entstörgrad	*n*	interference-suppression level	*n*	degré d'antiparasitage	*m*
Entstörklasse	*m*	interference-suppression category	*n*	classe d'antiparasitage	*f*
Entstörkondensator	*m*	suppression capacitor	*n*	condensateur d'antiparasitage	*m*
Entstörmittel	*n*	interference-suppressor	*n*	dispositifs d'antiparasitage	*mpl*
Entstörstecker	*m*	suppressor	*n*	embout d'antiparasitage	*m*
Entstörung	*f*	interference suppression	*n*	antiparasitage	*m*
Entstörwiderstand	*m*	interference-suppression resisto	*n*	résistance d'antiparasitage	*f*
entwässern (Filter)	*v*	drain (drain)	*v*	drainer (filtre)	*v*
Entwässerungsventil	*n*	drain valve	*n*	purgeur d'eau	*m*
Entwicklungszeichnung	*f*	draft drawing	*n*	plan de développement	*m*

Deutsch		Englisch		Französisch	
Erdmagnetfeldsonde (Navigationssystem)	*f*	geomagnetic sensor (navigation system)	*n*	sonde de champ magnétique terrestre (système de navigation)	*f*
ereignisgesteuert	*pp*	event-driven	*pp*	commandé par évènements	*pp*
Erregerdiode	*f*	excitation diode	*n*	diode d'excitation	*f*
Erregerdiodenplatte	*f*	excitation-diode plate	*n*	plaque à diodes d'excitation	*f*
Erregerfeld	*n*	excitation field	*n*	champ d'excitation	*m*
Erregerspannung	*f*	excitation voltage	*n*	tension d'excitation	*f*
Erregerstrom	*m*	exciting current	*n*	courant d'excitation	*m*
Erregerstromkreis	*m*	excitation circuit	*n*	circuit d'excitation	*m*
Erregersystem	*n*	excitation system	*n*	système d'excitation	*m*
Erregerverluste	*mpl*	excitation losses	*npl*	pertes d'excitation	*fpl*
Erregerwicklung	*f*	excitation winding	*n*	enroulement d'excitation	*m*
Ersatzmengenkennlinie	*f*	substitute quantity curve	*n*	courbe de débit substitutif	*f*
Erststart	*m*	first start	*n*	premier démarrage	*m*
ESP, Fahrdynamikregelung	*a*	electronic stability program, ESP	*n*	régulation du comportement dynamique, ESP	*f*
Europalette	*f*	euro-pallet	*n*	palette Europe	*f*
Expansionsphase (Verbrennungsmotor)	*f*	expansion phase (IC engine)	*n*	phase de détente (moteur à combustion interne)	*f*
Exzenter (Feststellbremsventil)	*m*	eccentric element (parking-brake valve)	*n*	excentrique (valve de frein de stationnement)	*m*
Exzenterhub	*m*	eccentric lift	*n*	levée d'excentrique	*f*
Exzenternocken (Common Rail)	*m*	eccentric cam (common rail)	*n*	came à excentrique (Common Rail)	*f*
Exzenterring	*m*	eccentric ring	*n*	bague excentrique	*f*
F					
Fächerkolben (Bremskraftregler)	*m*	fan-type piston (braking-force regulator)	*n*	piston à palettes (correcteur de freinage)	*m*
Fading (Bremse)	x *n*	fading (brakes)	*n*	fading (frein)	x *m*
Fahrbahnbeschaffenheit	*f*	road condition	*n*	état de la chaussée	*m*
Fahrbahrbahnreibmoment	*n*	road frictional torque	*n*	couple de frottement de la chaussée	*m*
Fahrbetrieb	*m*	vehicle operation	*n*	conduite véhicule	*f*
Fahrdatenrechner	*m*	on-board computer	*n*	ordinateur de bord	*m*
Fahrdynamik	*f*	dynamics of vehicular operatioı	*n*	dynamique des véhicules à moteur	*f*
Fahrdynamikregelung, ESP	*f*	electronic stability program, ESP	*n*	régulation du comportement dynamique, ESP	*f*
Fahrdynamikregler	*m*	vehicle dynamics controller	*n*	régulateur de dynamique de roulage	*m*
Fahrerairbag	*m*	driver airbag	*n*	coussin gonflable côté conducteur	*m*
Fahrerhaus	*n*	cab	*n*	cabine de conduite	*f*
Fahrerinformationssystem	*n*	driver-information system	*n*	système d'information de l'automobiliste	*m*
Fahrervorgabemoment	*n*	driver-selected torque	*n*	couple sélectionné par le conducteur	*m*
Fahrervorgabemotormoment	*n*	driver-input engine torque	*n*	couple moteur sélectionné par le conducteur	*m*

Deutsch		Englisch		Französisch	
Fahrerwunsch	*m*	vehicle-operator command	*n*	demande du conducteur	*f*
Fahrgeschwindigkeit	*f*	driving speed	*n*	vitesse de roulage	*f*
Fahrgeschwindigkeits-begrenzer, FGB	*m*	vehicle-speed limiter	*n*	limiteur de vitesse de roulage	*m*
Fahrgeschwindigkeits-begrenzung	*f*	road-speed limitation	*n*	limitation de vitesse de roulage	*f*
Fahrgeschwindigkeitsgeber	*m*	vehicle-speed sensor	*n*	capteur de vitesse de roulage	*m*
Fahrgeschwindigkeitsmessung	*f*	vehicle-speed measurement	*n*	mesure de la vitesse de roulage	*f*
Fahrgeschwindigkeitsregelung	*f*	cruise control (system)	*n*	régulation de la vitesse de roulage	*f*
Fahrgeschwindigkeitsregler, FGR	*m*	vehicle-speed controller	*n*	régulateur de vitesse de roulage	*m*
Fahrgeschwindigkeitssensor	*m*	vehicle-speed sensor	*n*	capteur de vitesse de roulage	*m*
Fahrgestellnummer	*f*	chassis number	*n*	numéro de châssis	*m*
Fahrkomfort	*m*	driving smoothness	*n*	confort de conduite	*m*
Fahrkurve	*f*	driving curve	*n*	caractéristique de conduite	*f*
Fahrkurve (Abgasprüfung)	*f*	test cycle (exhaust-gas test)	*n*	diagramme de test (émissions)	*m*
Fahrpedalmodul	*m*	accelerator-pedal module	*n*	module d'accélérateur	*m*
Fahrpedalsensor	*m*	pedal-travel sensor	*n*	capteur d'accélérateur	*m*
Fahrprogramm (Abgasprüfung)	*n*	driving schedule (exhaust-gas test)	*n*	cycle de conduite (émissions)	*m*
Fahrreglerschalter	*m*	drive-control switch	*n*	commutateur régulateur de marche	*m*
Fahrspur	*f*	lane	*n*	trajectoire	*f*
Fahrstabilität (Fahrverhalten)	*f*	directional stability (driveability)	*n*	stabilité directionnelle (comportement de roulage)	*f*
Fahrstellung	*f*	driving (non-braked) mode	*n*	position de roulage	*f*
Fahrstufe	*f*	gear selection	*n*	rapport de roulage	*m*
Fahrtrichtungsanzeiger	*m*	direction-indicator lamp	*n*	feu indicateur de direction	*m*
Fahrtrichtungsblinken	*n*	direction-indicator signal	*n*	indication de changement de direction	*f*
Fahrtrichtungsstabilität (Kfz)	*f*	directional stability (driveability)	*n*	stabilité directionnelle (comportement de roulage)	*f*
Fahrtschalter	*m*	driving switch	*n*	commutateur de marche	*m*
Fahrtschreiber	*m*	trip recorder	*n*	tachographe	*m*
Fahrverhalten (Kfz)	*n*	driveability (motor vehicle)	*n*	comportement de roulage (véhicule)	*m*
Fahrwerksystem	*n*	chassis system	*n*	système de suspension	*m*
Fahrwiderstand	*m*	total running resistance	*n*	résistance totale à l'avancement	*f*
Fahrzeug-Sicherungssystem	*n*	vehicle security system	*n*	système de protection des véhicules	*m*
Fahrzeugaufbau	*m*	vehicle body	*n*	carrosserie du véhicule	*f*
Fahrzeugbeschleunigung	*f*	vehicle acceleration	*n*	accélération du véhicule	*f*
Fahrzeugführung	*f*	vehicle handling	*n*	guidage du véhicule	*m*
Fahrzeuggeschwindigkeit	*f*	vehicle speed	*n*	vitesse du véhicule	*f*
Fahrzeuggiersollmoment	*n*	vehicle yaw-moment setpoint	*n*	moment de lacet de consigne du véhicule	*m*
Fahrzeughersteller	*m*	vehicle manufacturer	*n*	constructeur automobile	*m*
Fahrzeughochachse	*f*	vehicle vertical axis	*n*	axe vertical du véhicule	*m*

Deutsch		Englisch		Französisch	
Fahrzeugklasse	*f*	vehicle category	*n*	catégorie de véhicule	*f*
Fahrzeugkombination	*f*	vehicle combination	*n*	ensemble de véhicules	*m*
Fahrzeuglängsbeschleunigung	*f*	vehicle longitudinal acceleration	*n*	accélération longitudinale (véhicule)	*f*
Fahrzeuglängsdynamik	*f*	dynamics of linear motion (motor vehicle)	*n*	dynamique longitudinale d'un véhicule	*f*
Fahrzeuglängsverzögerung	*f*	vehicle longitudinal deceleration	*n*	décélération longitudinale du véhicule	*f*
Fahrzeugnavigation	*f*	vehicle navigation	*n*	navigation automobile	*f*
Fahrzeugpneumatik	*f*	automotive pneumatics	*n*	pneumatique automobile	*f*
Fahrzeugquerbeschleunigung	*f*	vehicle lateral acceleration	*n*	accélération transversale (véhicule)	*f*
Fahrzeugquerdynamik	*f*	dynamics of lateral motion (motor vehicle)	*n*	dynamique transversale d'un véhicule	*f*
Fahrzeugstabilität (beim Bremsen)	*f*	vehicle stability (during braking)	*n*	stabilité du véhicule (au freinage)	*f*
Fahrzeugtyp	*m*	vehicle type	*n*	type de véhicule	*m*
Fahrzeugüberschlag	*m*	vehicle rollover	*n*	capotage du véhicule	*m*
Fahrzeugverzögerung	*f*	vehicle deceleration	*n*	décélération du véhicule	*f*
Fahrzyklus (Abgasprüfung)	*m*	driving schedule (exhaust-gas test)	*n*	cycle de conduite (émissions)	*m*
Fall-Bremsanlage	*f*	gravity braking system	*n*	dispositif de freinage à commande par gravité	*m*
fallbeständig	*adj*	drop-proof	*adj*	résistant aux chutes	*ppr*
Fallstrom-Luftmengenmesser	*m*	downdraft air-flow sensor	*n*	débitmètre d'air à flux inversé	*m*
Falltankbetrieb	*m*	gravity-feed fuel-tank operation	*n*	réservoir en charge	*m*
Faltenbalg	*m*	gaiter seal	*n*	soufflet	*m*
Fanfare	*f*	fanfare horn	*n*	fanfare	*f*
Farbtemperatur (Lichttechnik)	*f*	color temperature (lighting)	*n*	température de couleur (éclairage)	*f*
Faustsattel (Bremse)	*m*	floating caliper (brakes)	*n*	étrier flottant (frein)	*m*
Federbein	*n*	spring strut	*n*	jambe de suspension	*f*
Federbeineinsatz	*m*	spring strut insert	*n*	insert de jambe de suspension	*m*
federbelastet	*pp*	spring-loaded	*pp*	taré par ressort	*pp*
Federelement (Luftfederung)	*n*	suspension element (air suspension)	*n*	élément de suspension (suspension pneumatique)	*m*
Federhülse (Drehzahlsensor)	*f*	spring sleeve (wheel-speed sensor)	*n*	douille élastique (capteur de vitesse)	*f*
Federkammer (Kraftstoffdruckregler)	*f*	pressure chamber (fuel-pressure regulator)	*n*	chambre à ressort (amortisseur de pression du carburant)	*f*
Federkapsel	*f*	spring retainer	*n*	coupelle	*f*
Federkennlinie	*f*	spring characteristic	*n*	courbe caractéristique de ressor	*f*
Federkolben (Luftfederventil)	*m*	spring piston (height-control valve)	*n*	piston (valve de nivellement)	*m*
Federkontakt	*m*	spring contact	*n*	ressort de contact	*m*
Federkraft	*f*	spring force	*n*	force du ressort	*f*
federnder Leerlaufanschlag	*m*	spring-loaded idle-speed stop	*n*	butée élastique de ralenti	*f*
Federpaket	*n*	spring assembly	*n*	jeu de ressorts	*m*
Federrate	*f*	spring rate	*n*	raideur de ressort	*f*

Deutsch		Englisch		Französisch	
Federraum	*m*	spring chamber	*n*	chambre de ressort(s)	*f*
Federschiene	*f*	spring strip	*n*	lame-ressort	*f*
Federspannhebel	*m*	tensioning lever	*n*	levier de tension	*m*
Federspeicher	*m*	spring-type brake actuator	*n*	accumulateur élastique	*m*
Federspeicherzylinder (Bremse)	*m*	spring-type brake cylinder	*n*	cylindre de frein à accumulateur élastique	*m*
Federteller	*m*	spring seat	*n*	cuvette de ressort	*f*
Federvorspannung	*f*	initial spring tension	*n*	tension initiale du ressort	*f*
Federweg	*m*	range of spring	*n*	course du ressort	*f*
Fehlerabspeicherung	*f*	error storage	*n*	mémorisation des défauts	*f*
Fehleranzeige	*f*	fault display	*n*	affichage de défauts	*m*
Fehlerart	*f*	failure mode	*n*	type de défaut	*m*
Fehlercode (Eigendiagnose)	*m*	error-code (self-diagnosis)	*n*	code de défaut (autodiagnostic)	*m*
Fehlerdiagnose	*f*	error diagnosis	*n*	diagnostic de défauts	*m*
Fehlererkennung	*f*	fault detection	*n*	détection des défauts	*f*
Fehlermöglichkeits- und Fehlereinfluß-Analyse, FMEA	*f*	failure mode and effects analysis, FMEA	*n*	analyse des modes de défaillance et de leurs effets	*f*
Fehlersignal	*n*	error signal	*n*	signal de défaut	*m*
Fehlersimulation	*f*	error simulation	*n*	simulation des défauts	*f*
Fehlerspeicher	*m*	fault store	*n*	mémoire de défauts	*f*
Fehlerursache	*f*	failure cause	*n*	cause du défaut	*f*
Fehlzündung	*f*	misfiring	*n*	ratés d'allumage	*mpl*
Feinfilter	*n*	fine filter	*n*	filtre fin	*m*
Feinfiltereinsatz	*m*	fine-filter element	*n*	cartouche filtrante fine	*f*
Feldplattensensor	*m*	magnetoresistive sensor	*n*	capteur magnétorésistif	*m*
Feldverzerrung	*f*	field displacement	*n*	distorsion du champ d'excitation	*f*
Feldwiderstand	*m*	field resistor	*n*	impédance de champ	*f*
Fensterantrieb	*m*	power-window drive	*n*	entraînement de lève-vitre	*m*
Fensterheber	*m*	power-window unit	*n*	lève-vitre	*m*
Fensterhebermotor	*m*	power-window motor	*n*	moteur de lève-vitre	*m*
Fensterhebersteuerung	*f*	power-window control	*n*	commande de lève-vitres	*f*
Fernentstörung	*f*	long-distance interference suppression	*n*	antiparasitage simple	*m*
Fernlicht	*n*	high beam	*n*	feu de route	*m*
Fernscheinwerfer	*m*	driving lamp	*n*	projecteur route	*m*
Fernstartleitung (Batterieladung)	*f*	remote-control line (battery charge)	*n*	câble de télécommande (charge de batterie)	*m*
Fertigungsdatum	*n*	manufacturing date	*n*	date de fabrication	*f*
Fertigungsfehler	*m*	manufacturing defect	*n*	défaut de fabrication	*m*
Fertigungsfreigabe	*f*	manufacturing release	*n*	autorisation de fabrication	*f*
Fertigungshinweis	*m*	manufacturing information	*n*	information de production	*f*
Fertigungsstandort	*m*	production location	*n*	lieu de production	*m*
Fertigungszeichnung	*f*	workshop drawing	*n*	dessin d'exécution	*m*
Festdrossel (Drucksteller)	*f*	fixed restriction (pressure actuator)	*n*	étranglement fixe (actionneur de pression)	*m*
feste Drossel	*f*	fixed throttle	*n*	étranglement fixe	*m*
Festnocken	*m*	fixed cam	*n*	came solidaire	*f*

Deutsch

Deutsch			Englisch		Französisch		
Festsattel (Bremse)		*m*	fixed caliper (brakes)	*n*	étrier fixe (frein)		*m*
Feststell-Bremsanlage		*f*	parking-brake system	*n*	dispositif de freinage de stationnement		*m*
Feststellbremse	x	*f*	parking-brake system	*n*	dispositif de freinage de stationnement		*m*
Feststellbremskreis		*m*	parking-brake circuit	*n*	circuit de freinage de stationnement		*m*
Feststellbremsstellung		*f*	parking-brake-applied position	*n*	position de freinage de stationnement		*f*
Feststellbremsventil		*n*	parking-brake valve	*n*	valve de frein de stationnement		*f*
Feststoff-Testergebnis (Dieselrauch)		*n*	particulates test result (diesel smoke)	*n*	résultat du test de particules (fumées diesel)		*m*
Festwertspeicher, ROM		*f*	read-only memory, ROM	*n*	mémoire de valeurs fixes, ROM		*f*
Festwiderstand		*m*	fixed resistor	*n*	résistance électrique fixe		*f*
fett (Luft-Kraftstoff-Gemisch)		*adj*	rich (air-fuel mixture)	*adj*	riche (mélange air-carburant)		*adj*
Fettzugmagnet		*m*	enrichment solenoid	*n*	électro-aimant d'enrichissement		*m*
Filteraufheizung		*f*	filter heating	*n*	réchauffage du filtre		*m*
Filterdeckel		*m*	filter cover	*n*	couvercle de filtre		*m*
Filtereinsatz		*m*	filter element	*n*	cartouche filtrante		*f*
Filterelement		*n*	filter element	*n*	cartouche filtrante		*f*
Filtergehäuse		*n*	filter case	*n*	carter de filtre		*m*
Filterheizung		*f*	filter heating	*n*	réchauffage du filtre		*m*
Filterkuchen		*m*	filter cake	*n*	gâteau de filtre	x	*m*
Filtersieb		*n*	filter strainer	*n*	crépine		*f*
Filterstandzeit		*f*	filter service life	*n*	durabilité du filtre		*f*
Filterverstopfung		*f*	filter clogging	*n*	bouchage du filtre		*m*
Filterwirkung		*f*	filter effect	*n*	effet de filtration		*m*
Filtrationsabscheider		*m*	filtration separator	*n*	séparateur à filtration		*m*
Fixierstift		*m*	locating pin	*n*	broche de positionnement		*f*
Flachbettbefestigung		*f*	flatbed mounting	*n*	fixation par base plane		*f*
Flachdichtsitz		*m*	flat seat	*n*	siège plat		*m*
Flächendruckventil		*n*	delivery-valve with flat	*n*	soupape de pression à méplat		*f*
Flächenzapfendüse		*f*	flatted pintle nozzle	*n*	injecteur à téton plan		*m*
Flachmotor		*m*	flat motor	*n*	moteur plat		*m*
Flachsitzventil		*n*	flat-seat valve	*n*	soupape à siège plan		*f*
Flachstecker		*m*	blade terminal	*n*	fiche plate		*f*
Flachsteckergehäuse		*n*	blade terminal housing	*n*	boîtier pour fiches plates		*m*
Flammen-Ionisations-Detektor, FID		*m*	flame ionization detection analyzer, FID	*n*	détecteur d'ionisation à flamme, FID		*m*
Flammenfront		*f*	flame front	*n*	front de flamme		*m*
Flammenweg		*m*	flame travel	*n*	course de flamme		*f*
Flammglühdrahtkerze		*f*	wire-type flame glow plug	*n*	bougie d'inflammation à filament		*f*
Flammglühkerze		*f*	flame glow plug	*n*	bougie de préchauffage à flamme		*f*
Flammglühstiftkerze		*f*	flame glow plug	*n*	bougie de préchauffage à flamme		*f*
Flammglühstiftkerze		*f*	sheathed-element flame glow plug	*n*	bougie-crayon de préchauffage à flamme		*f*

Deutsch		Englisch		Französisch	
Flammkern (Zündkerze)	*m*	arc (spark plug)	*n*	coeur de la flamme (bougie)	*m*
Flammkerze	*f*	flame glow plug	*n*	bougie de préchauffage à flamme	*f*
Flammstart	*m*	flame start	*n*	démarrage par flamme	*m*
Flammstartanlage	*f*	flame starting system	*n*	dispositif de démarrage à flamme	*m*
flankenoffen (Keilriemen)	*adj*	open flank (V-belt)	*n*	à flanc ouvert (courroie trapézoïdale)	*loc*
Flankenspiel (Zahnrad)	*n*	backlash (gear)	*n*	jeu entre dents (engrenage)	*m*
Flanschbefestigung	*f*	flange mounting	*n*	fixation par bride	*f*
Flanschbuchse	*f*	flange bushing	*n*	manchon à bride	*m*
Flanschelement	*n*	barrel-and-flange-element	*n*	élément de pompage à bride	*m*
Flanschzylinder	*m*	flange cylinder	*n*	vérin à bride	*m*
flexible Leitung	*f*	flexible line	*n*	tuyau flexible	*m*
Fliehgewicht	*n*	flyweight	*n*	masselotte	*f*
Fliehgewichtsbolzen	*m*	flyweight bolt	*n*	axe de masselottes	*m*
Fliehgewichtsmeßwerk	*n*	flyweight speed-sensing elemer	*n*	mécanisme de détection à masselottes	*m*
Fliehgewichtsteil	*n*	flyweight assembly	*n*	bloc de régulation	*m*
Fliehgewichtsträger	*m*	flyweight mount	*n*	porte-masselottes	*m*
Fliehgewichtsweg	*m*	flyweight travel	*n*	course des masselottes	*f*
Fliehkraftabscheider	*m*	centrifugal separator	*n*	séparateur centrifuge	*m*
fliehkraftgesteuerter Drehzahlregler	*m*	mechanical governor	*n*	régulateur mécanique	*m*
Fliehkraftregler	*m*	mechanical governor	*n*	régulateur mécanique	*m*
Fliehkraftverstellung	*f*	centrifugal advance	*n*	correction centrifuge	*f*
Fliehkraftzündversteller	*m*	centrifugal advance mechanism	*n*	correcteur d'avance centrifuge	*m*
fließgepreßt	*pp*	extruded	*pp*	extrudé	*pp*
Flüchtigkeit (Benzin)	*f*	volatility (gasoline)	*n*	volatibilité (essence)	*f*
Flügelzellen-Förderpumpe	*f*	vane-type supply pump	*n*	pompe d'alimentation à palettes	*f*
Flügelzellenlader	*m*	sliding-vane supercharger	*n*	compresseur à palettes	*m*
Flutlichtstrahler	*m*	floodlight	*n*	projecteur d'ambiance	*m*
Folgefunken	*m*	follow-up spark	*n*	trains d'étincelles	*mpl*
Folgeschadenschutz (Überspannung)	*m*	consequential-damage protection (overvoltage)	*n*	protection contre les incidences (surtension)	*f*
Förderabstand (Pumpenelement)	*m*	phasing (plunger-and-barrel assembly)	*n*	phasage (élément de pompage)	*m*
Förderbeginn (Einspritzpumpe)	*m*	start of delivery (fuel-injection pump)	*n*	début de refoulement (pompe d'injection)	*m*
Förderbeginn-Normal (Einspritzpumpe)	*n*	master pump	*n*	pompe de référence de début de refoulement	*f*
Förderbeginngeber, FBG	*m*	port-closing sensor	*n*	capteur de début de refoulemen	*m*
Förderbeginnregelung	*f*	start-of-delivery control	*n*	régulation du début de refoulement	*f*
Förderbeginnversatz	*m*	start-of-delivery offset	*n*	décalage du début de refoulement	*m*
Förderbeginnversteller	*m*	timing device	*n*	variateur d'avance	*m*
Förderdauer	*f*	delivery period	*n*	durée de refoulement	*f*
Förderdruck	*m*	delivery pressure	*n*	pression de refoulement	*f*

Deutsch		Englisch		Französisch	
Förderende (Einspritzpumpe)	*n*	spill (fuel-injection pump)	*n*	fin de refoulement (pompe d'injection)	*f*
Förderenderegelung	*f*	end-of-delivery control	*n*	régulation de la fin de refoulement	*f*
Förderhub	*m*	delivery stroke	*n*	course de refoulement	*f*
Förderhubphase	*f*	delivery-stroke phase	*n*	course d'admission	*f*
Förderkennlinie +	*f*	fuel-delivery curve	*n*	courbe caractéristique des débits	*f*
Förderkolben	*m*	delivery plunger	*n*	piston de refoulement	*m*
Förderleistung	*f*	fuel-delivery rate	*n*	taux de refoulement	*m*
Fördermedium	*n*	flow medium	*n*	fluide de refoulement	*m*
Fördermenge (Einspritzpumpe)	*f*	delivery quantity (fuel-injection pump)	*n*	débit de refoulement (pompe d'injection)	*m*
Fördermenge (Luftkompressor)	*f*	delivery capacity (air compressor)	*n*	débit du compresseur d'air	*m*
Fördermengen-Kennlinie	*f*	fuel-delivery curve	*n*	courbe caractéristique des débits	*f*
Fördermengenhauptnormal	*n*	audit calibration pump	*f*	pompe de référence étalon	*f*
Fördermengenmeßgerät	*n*	fuel-delivery measurement device	*n*	appareil de mesure du débit	*m*
Fördermengennormal	*n*	calibration pump	*n*	pompe de référence de débit	*f*
Fördermengennormal-Prüfbank	*f*	calibration-pump test bench	*n*	banc de contrôle de pompe de référence	*m*
Fördermengenregelung	*f*	fuel-delivery control	*n*	régulation des débits d'injection	*f*
Fördermengenverlauf	*m*	fuel-delivery characteristics	*npl*	courbe du débit d'injection	*f*
Förderphase	*f*	delivery phase	*n*	phase de refoulement	*f*
Förderpumpe (Kraftstoff)	*f*	fuel-supply pump	*n*	pompe d'alimentation (carburant)	*f*
Förderpumpendruck	*m*	supply-pump pressure	*n*	pression de transfert (pompe d'alimentation)	*f*
Förderrate	*f*	fuel-delivery rate	*n*	taux de refoulement	*m*
Förderrichtung	*f*	delivery direction	*n*	sens de refoulement	*m*
Fördersignal-Sensor	*m*	delivery-signal sensor	*n*	capteur de signal de refoulement	*m*
Förderwinkel am Nocken	*m*	cam angle of fuel-delivery	*n*	angle de refoulement sur la came	*m*
Formänderungsarbeit (Reifen)	*f*	deformation process (tire)	*n*	travail de déformation (pneu)	*m*
Freibrand	*m*	burn-off	*n*	autonettoyage	*m*
Freibrenngrenze	*f*	self-cleaning temperature	*n*	température d'autonettoyage	*f*
Freibrenntemperatur	*f*	self-cleaning temperature	*n*	température d'autonettoyage	*f*
Freigabe (Fertigung)	*f*	release (manufacturing)	*n*	autorisation (fabrication)	*f*
Freilauf (Starter)	*m*	roller-type overrunning clutch (starter)	*n*	dispositif de roue libre (démarreur)	*m*
Freilaufdiode	*f*	free-wheeling diode	*n*	diode de récupération	*f*
Freilaufgetriebe (Starter)	*n*	overrunning clutch (starter)	*n*	lanceur (à roue libre)	*m*
Freilaufring	*m*	clutch shell	*n*	bague de roue libre	*f*
Fremdantrieb	*m*	external drive	*n*	entraînement extérieur	*m*
Fremdbelüftung	*f*	auxiliary ventilation	*n*	ventilation externe	*f*
Fremdbezug	*m*	out-sourcing	*n*	origine étrangère	*f*

Deutsch		Englisch		Französisch	
Fremderregung (drehende Maschinen)	*f*	external exitation (rotating machines)	*n*	excitation extérieure (machines tournantes)	*f*
Fremderzeugnis	*n*	non-Bosch product	*n*	produit d'autre marque	*m*
Fremdkraft (Bremsbetätigung)	*f*	external force (brake control)	*n*	énergie étrangère (commande de frein)	*f*
Fremdkraft-Bremsanlage	*f*	power-brake system	*n*	dispositif de freinage à énergie non musculaire	*m*
Fremdzündung	*f*	externally supplied ignition	*n*	allumage par appareillage externe	*m*
Frequenzmodulation	*f*	frequency modulation, FM	*n*	modulation de fréquence	*f*
Frequenzteiler	*m*	frequency divider	*n*	diviseur de fréquence	*m*
Fresneloptik	*f*	fresnel optics	*npl*	optique de Fresnel	*f*
Frischgas (Verbrennungsmotor)	*n*	fresh A/F mixture (IC engine)	*n*	gaz frais (moteur à combustion)	*mpl*
Front-Wischblatt	*n*	front wiper blade	*n*	raclette de pare-brise	*f*
Frontairbag	*m*	front airbag	*n*	coussin gonflable avant	*m*
Frontantrieb	*m*	front-wheel drive	*n*	traction avant	*f*
Frontblende (Scheinwerfer)	*f*	front screen (headlamp)	*n*	cache avant (projecteur)	*m*
Frontleuchte	*f*	front lamp	*n*	feu avant	*m*
Frontscheibe	*f*	windshield	*n*	pare-brise	*m*
Frostschutzeinrichtung	*f*	antifreeze unit	*n*	dispositif antigel	*m*
Frostschutzmittel	*n*	antifreeze	*n*	antigel	*m*
Frostschutzpumpe	*f*	antifreeze pump	*n*	pompe antigel	*f*
Frostschutzvorrichtung	*f*	antifreeze unit	*n*	dispositif antigel	*m*
Früh-Verstellsystem	*n*	early (advance) adjustment system	*n*	système de correction "avance"	*m*
Frühverstellung (Einspritzbeginn)	*f*	advance (start of injection)	*n*	avance (début d'injection)	*f*
Frühverstellung (Zündwinkel)	*f*	ignition advance	*n*	avance (angle d'allumage)	*f*
Frühzündung	*f*	advanced ignition	*n*	avance à l'allumage	*f*
Führungsbolzen	*m*	guide pin	*n*	axe de guidage	*m*
Führungsbuchse	*f*	guide bushing	*n*	douille de guidage	*f*
Führungshebel	*m*	guide lever	*n*	levier de guidage	*m*
Führungsschlitz	*m*	guide slot	*n*	rainure de guidage	*f*
Führungsstift	*m*	guide pin	*n*	axe de guidage	*m*
Füllfaktor (drehende Maschinen)	*m*	slot fill factor (rotating machines)	*n*	facteur de remplissage des rainures (machines tournantes)	*m*
Füllphase	*f*	filling phase	*n*	phase de remplissage	*f*
Füllpulver (Glühstiftkerze)	*n*	filling powder (sheathed-element glow plug)	*n*	poudre isolante (bougie-crayon de préchauffage)	*f*
Füllstandsanzeige	*f*	fuel-level indicator	*n*	jauge de niveau	*f*
Füllstandsgeber (Elektrokraftstoffpumpe)	*m*	level sensor (in-tank unit)	*n*	capteur de niveau (pompe électrique à carburant)	*m*
Füllstück	*n*	filler piece	*n*	cale	*f*
Füllungseingriff (Luftversorgung)	*m*	charge adjustment (air supply)	*n*	régulation du remplissage des cylindres	*f*
Füllungsgrad (Batterie)	*m*	electrolyte level (battery)	*n*	taux de remplissage (batterie)	*m*
Füllungsregelung (Luftversorgung)	*f*	charge adjustment (air supply)	*n*	régulation du remplissage des cylindres	*f*

Deutsch			Englisch		Französisch	
Füllungssteuerung (EGAS)		*f*	cylinder-charge control (EGAS	*n*	commande de remplissage (EMS)	*f*
Funk-Fernbedienung		*f*	radio remote control	*n*	radiocommande	*f*
Funk-Handsender (Autoalarm)		*m*	radio hand transmitter (car alarm)	*n*	émetteur manuel radio (alarme auto)	*m*
Funkenbahn		*f*	creepage-discharge path	*n*	éclateur	*m*
Funkendauer		*f*	spark duration	*n*	durée de l'étincelle	*f*
Funkendurchbruch (an den Elektroden)		*m*	flashover (at electrodes)	*n*	éclatement de l'étincelle (aux électrodes)	*m*
Funkenerosion		*f*	spark erosion	*n*	érosion ionique	*f*
Funkenkopf		*m*	spark head	*n*	tête de l'étincelle	*f*
Funkenlage		*f*	spark position	*n*	position de l'éclateur	*f*
Funkenlänge		*f*	spark length	*n*	longueur d'étincelle	*f*
Funkenschwanz		*m*	spark tail	*n*	queue de l'étincelle	*f*
Funkenstrecke		*f*	spark gap	*n*	distance d'éclatement	*f*
Funkenstrom		*m*	spark current	*n*	courant d'arc	*m*
Funkentstörung		*f*	interference suppression	*n*	antiparasitage	*m*
Funkenüberschlag (an den Elektroden)		*m*	flashover (at electrodes)	*n*	éclatement de l'étincelle (aux électrodes)	*m*
Funkenzahl		*f*	sparking rate	*n*	nombre d'étincelles	*m*
Funkfernbedienung		*f*	radio remote control	*n*	télécommande radio	*f*
Funkstörspannung (EMV)		*f*	radio interference voltage (EMC)	*n*	tension perturbatrice (CEM)	*f*
Funkstörspannungspegel (EMV)		*m*	interference level (EMC)	*n*	niveau de perturbations (CEM)	*m*
Funkstörung (Ursache)		*f*	radio disturbance	*n*	perturbation radioélectrique	*f*
Funkstörung (Wirkung)		*f*	radio interference	*n*	brouillage radioélectrique	*m*
Funktionsblock (Steuergerät)		*m*	function module (ECU)	*n*	bloc fonctionnel (calculateur)	*m*
Funktionskontrolleuchte		*f*	function lamp	*n*	témoin de fonctionnement	*m*
Fußbremse	x	*f*	service-brake system	*n*	dispositif de freinage de service	*m*
G						
Gabelhebel (Starter)		*m*	fork lever (starter)	*n*	levier à fourche (démarreur)	*m*
Gabelkopf		*m*	fork head	*n*	chape	*f*
Ganganzeigeschalter		*m*	gear-indicator switch	*n*	interrupteur-témoin de rapport de vitesse	*m*
Gangschalter		*m*	gear switch	*n*	commande de changement de vitesse	*f*
Gangvorwahlschalter		*m*	gear-preselector switch	*n*	présélecteur de vitesses	*m*
Garagentor-Antrieb		*m*	garage-door drive	*n*	commande de porte pour garages	*f*
Gasannahme (Verbrennungsmotor)	x	*f*	throttle response (IC engine)	*n*	admission des gaz (moteur à combustion)	*f*
Gasdruck-Stoßdämpfer		*m*	gas-filled shock absorber	*n*	amortisseur à pression de gaz	*m*
Gasentladungslampe		*f*	gaseous-discharge lamp, GDL	*n*	lampe à décharge dans un gaz	*f*
Gasgenerator (Airbag)		*m*	gas inflator (airbag)	*n*	générateur de gaz (coussin gonflable)	*m*
Gasgestänge		*n*	accelerator-lever linkage	*n*	timonerie d'accélérateur	*f*
Gaskolbenspeicher (ASR)		*m*	piston gas accumulator (TCS)	*n*	accumulateur de gaz à piston (ASR)	*m*

Deutsch			Englisch		Französisch	
Gaslaufzeit (Lambda-Regelung)		*f*	gas travel time (lambda closed-loop control)	*n*	temps de transit des gaz (régulation lambda)	*m*
Gasungsspannung		*f*	gassing voltage	*n*	tension de dégagement gazeux	*f*
Gaswechsel		*m*	gas exchange	*n*	renouvellement des gaz	*m*
Gaswechselverlust		*m*	charge-cycle losses	*npl*	pertes au renouvellement des gaz	*fpl*
Geber	+	*m*	sensor	*n*	capteur	*m*
Geberkennlinie		*f*	sensor characteristic	*n*	courbe caractéristique de capteur	*f*
Geberkennwort		*n*	sensor ID	*n*	identificateur de capteur	*m*
Geberrad (Zündung)		*n*	trigger wheel (ignition)	*n*	noyau synchroniseur (allumage)	*m*
Geberspannung		*f*	pulse-generator voltage	*n*	tension du générateur d'impulsions	*f*
Geberzylinder (Bremse)		*m*	master cylinder (brakes)	*n*	cylindre capteur (frein)	*m*
Gebläse		*n*	fan	*n*	ventilateur	*m*
Gebläseregler		*m*	blower control unit	*n*	régulateur de ventilateur	*m*
gefederte Masse		*f*	sprung weight	*n*	masse suspendue	*f*
Gefrierschutzmittel		*n*	antifreeze	*n*	antigel	*m*
Gegendruck		*m*	back-pressure reaction	*n*	réaction de contre-pression	*f*
Gegenlaufsystem (Scheibenwischer)		*n*	opposed-pattern wiper system	*n*	système antagoniste (essuie-glace)	*m*
gegenlenken (Kfz)		*v*	countersteer (motor vehicle)	*v*	contre-braquage (véhicule)	*m*
gegensteuern (Kfz)		*v*	countersteer (motor vehicle)	*v*	contre-braquage (véhicule)	*m*
Gegenüberstellung		*f*	cross-reference	*n*	table de correspondance	*f*
Gehäuse (Leuchtkörper)		*n*	housing (lamps)	*n*	boîtier (lampes)	*m*
Gehäuseanschlag		*m*	housing stop	*n*	butée sur carter	*f*
Gehäusebefestigung		*f*	housing mounting	*n*	fixation sur carter	*f*
gehäusefeste Leerlauffeder, LFG	x	*f*	idle-speed spring attached to governor housing	*n*	ressort de ralenti solidaire du corps de pompe	*m*
Gehäusemasse		*f*	equipment ground	*n*	masse (du boîtier)	*f*
Gelenk-Deichselanhänger		*m*	draw bar trailer	*n*	remorque à timon articulé	*f*
Gelenkfahrzeug		*n*	articulated vehicle	*n*	véhicule articulé	*m*
Gelenkgabel		*f*	link fork	*n*	fourchette d'articulation	*f*
Gemisch (Luft-Kraftstoff)		*n*	air-fuel mixture	*n*	mélange air-carburant	*m*
Gemischabmagerung		*f*	lean adjustment (air-fuel mixture)	*n*	appauvrissement du mélange	*m*
Gemischadaption		*f*	mixture adaptation	*n*	adaptation du mélange	*f*
Gemischanpassung		*f*	mixture adaptation	*n*	adaptation du mélange	*f*
Gemischanreicherung		*f*	mixture enrichment	*n*	enrichissement du mélange	*m*
Gemischaufbereitung		*f*	mixture formation	*n*	préparation du mélange	*f*
Gemischbildung		*f*	mixture formation	*n*	préparation du mélange	*f*
Gemischkorrektur		*f*	mixture adaptation	*n*	adaptation du mélange	*f*
Gemischregler (Jetronic)		*m*	mixture-control unit (Jetronic)	*n*	régulateur de mélange (Jetronic)	*m*
gemischte Übertragungseinrichtung (Bremsanlage)		*f*	combined transmission (braking system)	*n*	transmission combinée (dispositif de freinage)	*f*
Gemischturbulenz		*f*	mixture turbulence	*n*	turbulence du mélange	*f*
Gemischverteilung		*f*	mixture distribution	*n*	répartition du mélange	*f*

Deutsch		Englisch		Französisch	
Gemischzumessung	*f*	air-fuel-mixture metering	*v*	dosage du mélange	*m*
Gemischzusammensetzung	*f*	mixture composition	*n*	composition du mélange	*f*
Generator	*m*	generator	*n*	génératrice	*f*
Generatorkontrolleuchte	*f*	charge-indicator lamp	*n*	lampe témoin d'alternateur	*f*
Generatorleistung	*f*	alternator output power	*n*	puissance de l'alternateur	*f*
Generatorregler	*m*	voltage regulator (alternator)	*n*	régulateur de tension (alternateur)	*m*
Generatorstromkreis	*m*	main circuit (alternator)	*n*	circuit principal (alternateur)	*m*
geometrische Reichweite (Scheinwerfer)	*f*	geometric range (headlamp)	*n*	portée géométrique (projecteur)	*f*
gepulst (Drucksteuerung)	x *pp*	pulse-controlled (pressure)	*pp*	par impulsions (modulation de pression)	*loc*
Geradeauslauf (Fahrverhalten)	*m*	directional stability (driveability)	*n*	stabilité directionnelle (comportement de roulage)	*f*
Geradeauslauf (Kfz)	*m*	straight-ahead running stability (motor vehicle)	*n*	trajectoire rectiligne (véhicule)	*f*
Gerätegruppe (Druckluftanlagen)	*f*	component group (air-brake systems)	*n*	ensemble d'appareils de freinage	*m*
Geräuschdämpfer	*m*	silencer	*n*	amortisseur de bruit	*m*
Geräuschkapselung	*f*	noise encapsulation	*n*	encapsulage antibruit	*m*
Geräuschminderung	*f*	noise suppression	*n*	atténuation du bruit	*f*
Geräuschpegel	*m*	noise level	*n*	niveau de bruit	*m*
Geräuschprüfstand	*m*	noise-level test bench	*n*	banc d'essai acoustique	*m*
Geräuschprüfung	*f*	noise-level test	*n*	essai de niveau sonore	*m*
Gesamtbremsdauer	*f*	total braking time	*n*	temps total de freinage	*m*
Gesamtbremskraft	*f*	total braking force	*n*	force de freinage totale	*f*
Gesamtbremsweg	*m*	total braking distance	*n*	distance totale de freinage	*f*
gesamte Bremskraft	*f*	total braking force	*n*	force de freinage totale	*f*
Gesamtfahrwiderstand	*m*	total running resistance	*n*	résistance totale à l'avancement	*f*
Gesamtgewicht	*n*	permissible total weight	*n*	poids total admissible	*m*
Gesamtgewichtskraft	*f*	permissible total weight	*n*	poids total admissible	*m*
Geschäftsbereich	*m*	division (business)	*n*	division (entreprise)	*f*
Geschäftsfeld	*n*	business area	*n*	domaine de spécialisation	*m*
geschirmt	*pp*	shielded	*pp*	blindé	*pp*
geschlossene Bauweise	*f*	closed-type design	*n*	version fermée	*f*
Geschwindigkeits-Sollgeber	*m*	speed-preselect, SP	*n*	capteur de vitesse de consigne	*m*
Geschwindigkeitsbegrenzung	*f*	speed limiting	*n*	limitation de vitesse	*f*
Geschwindigkeitsdiagramm	*n*	velocity diagram	*n*	diagramme des vitesses	*m*
Geschwindigkeitsrampe	x *f*	vehicle-speed ramp	*n*	rampe de vitesse	*f*
Geschwindigkeitsregelung (Kfz)	*f*	cruise control (system)	*n*	régulation de la vitesse de roulage	*f*
gesetzliche Vorschriften	*fpl*	legal requirements	*npl*	législation	*f*
Gestängeregler (Radbremse)	*m*	slack adjuster (wheel brake)	*n*	dispositif automatique de rattrapage de jeu (freins des roues)	*f*
Gestängesteller (Radbremse)	*m*	slack adjuster (wheel brake)	*n*	dispositif automatique de rattrapage de jeu (freins des roues)	*f*
gesteuerte Muffendämpfung	*f*	controlled sleeve damping	*n*	amortisseur de manchon piloté	*m*

Deutsch		Englisch		Französisch	
gestufte Startmenge, GST	*f*	graded start quantity	*n*	surcharge étagée	*f*
gestufter Absteuerquerschnitt	*m*	stepped spill port	*n*	trou de fin d'injection étagé	*m*
Getriebedifferentialbremse	*f*	differential brake	*n*	frein de différentiel	*m*
Getriebeeingriff	*m*	transmission-shift control	*n*	commande de boîte de vitesses	*f*
Getriebefahrstufe	*f*	gearbox stage	*n*	rapport de vitesse	*m*
Getriebemotor	*m*	motor-and-gear assembly	*n*	motoréducteur	*m*
Getriebesteuerung	*f*	transmission-shift control	*n*	commande de boîte de vitesses	*f*
Getriebeübersetzung	*f*	gearbox step-up ratio	*n*	rapport de transmission de la boîte de vitesses	*m*
Getriebewählhebel	*m*	selector lever	*n*	sélecteur de rapport de vitesse	*m*
Gewaltbremsung +	*f*	panic braking	*n*	freinage en situation de paniqu€	*m*
gewichtete Schadstoffemission	*f*	weighted emissions	*n*	émission quantifiée de polluant:	*f*
Gewichtskraft	*f*	weight (force)	*n*	poids	*m*
Gewichtsverlagerung (Bremse)	*f*	weight transfer (brakes)	*n*	report de charge (frein)	*m*
Gewichtsverteilung (Bremse)	*f*	weight distribution (brakes)	*n*	répartition du poids (frein)	*f*
Gewindeanschluß	*m*	threaded port	*n*	orifice taraudé	*m*
Gewindehalsbefestigung	*f*	threaded-neck mounting	*n*	fixation par bague filetée	*f*
Gewindehülse	*f*	threaded sleeve	*n*	corps fileté	*m*
Gierbewegung	*f*	yaw motion	*n*	mouvement de lacet	*m*
gieren (Kfz) x	*v*	yaw (motor vehicle)	*v*	lacet (véhicule)	*m*
Giergeschwindigkeit (Kfz-Dynamik)	*f*	yaw velocity (vehicle dynamics)	*n*	vitesse de braquage (dynamique d'un véhicule)	*f*
Giermoment	*n*	yaw moment	*n*	moment de lacet	*m*
Giermomentaufbau	*m*	yaw-moment build-up	*n*	formation du moment de lacet	*f*
Giermomentaufbau-verzögerung, GMA	*f*	yaw moment buildup delay	*n*	temporisation de la formation du couple de lacet	*f*
Giermomentbegrenzung	*f*	yaw-moment limitation	*n*	limitation du moment de lacet	*f*
Gierwinkel	*m*	yaw angle	*n*	angle d'embardée	*m*
Gitterbox	*f*	meshed container	*n*	conteneur à claire-voie	*m*
Glasbruchmelder (Autoalarm)	*m*	glass-breakage detector (car alarm)	*n*	détecteur de bris de glaces (alarme auto)	*m*
Glasschmelze (elektrisch leitend)	*f*	conductive glass seal	*n*	ciment à base de verre conducteur	*m*
Gleichdruckventil, GDV	*n*	constant-pressure valve	*n*	clapet de refoulement à pression constante	*m*
Gleichfeld	*n*	constant field	*n*	plage neutre	*f*
Gleichfeldeinstreuung	*f*	constant field pick-up	*n*	perturbation par champ continu	*f*
Gleichförderung	*f*	uniformity of fuel delivery	*n*	égalisation des débits	*f*
gleichförmige Verzögerung	*f*	uniform deceleration	*n*	décélération uniforme	*f*
Gleichlaufsystem (Scheibenwischer)	*n*	tandem-pattern wiper system	*n*	système tandem (essuie-glace)	*m*
Gleichraumventil, GRV	*n*	constant-volume valve	*n*	clapet de refoulement à volume constant	*m*
Gleichrichter (Generator)	*m*	rectifier (alternator)	*n*	redresseur (alternateur)	*m*
Gleichrichterdiode	*f*	rectifier diode	*n*	diode redresseuse	*f*
Gleichrichterverluste	*mpl*	rectifier losses	*npl*	pertes redresseurs	*fpl*
Gleichrichtung (Wechselstrom)	*f*	rectification (alternating current)	*n*	redressement (courant alternatif)	*m*
Gleichstrom	*m*	direct current	*n*	courant continu	*m*

Deutsch		Englisch		Französisch	
Gleichstromgenerator	*m*	direct-current generator	*n*	génératrice de courant continu	*f*
Gleichstrommotor	*m*	DC motor	*n*	moteur à courant continu	*m*
Gleichstromrelais	*n*	DC relay	*n*	relais à courant continu	*m*
Gleichverteilung (Luft-Kraftstoff-Gemisch)	*f*	even mixture distribution (air-fuel mixture)	*n*	répartition uniforme (mélange air-carburant)	*f*
Gleitfunkenkerze	*f*	surface-gap spark plug	*n*	bougie à étincelle glissante	*f*
Gleitfunkenzündkerze	*f*	surface-gap spark plug	*n*	bougie à étincelle glissante	*f*
Gleitpaste	*f*	slip paste	*n*	pâte antigrippage	*f*
Gleitreibung	*f*	sliding friction	*n*	frottement de glissement	*m*
Gleitreibungszahl	*f*	coefficient of sliding friction	*n*	coefficient de frottement de glissement	*m*
Gleitstein	*m*	sliding block	*n*	tête coulissante	*f*
Gleitstößel	*m*	sliding tappet	*n*	poussoir coulissant	*m*
Gleitstück (Bremszylinder)	*n*	slider (brake cylinder)	*n*	coulisseau (cylindre de frein)	*m*
Gleitstück (Unterbrecherhebel)	*n*	cam follower (breaker lever)	*n*	toucheau (rupteur)	*m*
Gleitvorgang	*m*	slip	*n*	glissement	*m*
Gleitwiderstand (Rollenbremsprüfstand)	*m*	slip resistance (dynamic brake analyzer)	*n*	résistance de glissement (banc d'essai)	*f*
Glimmentladung	*f*	glow discharge	*n*	décharge d'arc	*f*
Glüh-Start-Schalter	*m*	glow-plug and starter switch	*n*	commutateur de préchauffage-démarrage	*m*
Glühdauer	*f*	glow duration	*n*	durée d'incandescence	*f*
Glühkerze	*f*	glow plug	*n*	bougie de préchauffage	*f*
Glühkörper	*m*	glow-plug tip	*n*	corps chauffant (crayon)	*m*
Glührohr	*n*	glow tube	*n*	tube incandescent	*m*
Glühstift	*m*	glow element	*n*	crayon de préchauffage	*m*
Glühstiftkerze, GSK	*f*	sheathed-element glow plug	*n*	bougie-crayon de préchauffage	*f*
Glühüberwacher	*m*	glow indicator	*n*	contrôleur d'incandescence	*m*
Glühzeit	+ *f*	preheating time	*n*	durée de préchauffage	*f*
Glühzeitablauf	*m*	preheating sequence	*n*	période de préchauffage	*f*
Glühzeitsteuergerät, GZS	*n*	glow control unit	*n*	module de commande du temps de préchauffage	*m*
Glühzündung	*f*	auto-ignition	*n*	auto-allumage	*m*
Glykol-Bremsflüssigkeit	*f*	glycol-based brake fluid	*n*	liquide de frein à base de glycol	*m*
Grad Kurbelwelle (°Kurbelwelle)	x *n*	crankshaft angle	*n*	angle vilebrequin	*m*
Granulat (Lufttrockner)	*n*	desiccant (air drier)	*n*	déshydratant (dessiccateur)	*m*
Greifring (Bremse)	*m*	grip ring (brakes)	*n*	bague d'attaque (frein)	*f*
Grenzbeanspruchung	*f*	limit stress	*n*	contrainte limite	*f*
Grenzdrehzahl	*f*	limit speed	*n*	régime limite	*m*
Grenzfrequenz (Regler)	*f*	cutoff frequency (governor)	*n*	fréquence limite (régulateur)	*f*
Grenzmenge	*f*	limit quantity	*n*	débit limite	*m*
Grenztemperatur	*f*	limit temperature	*n*	température limite	*f*
Griffigkeit (Reifen)	*f*	tire grip	*n*	adhérence (pneu)	*f*
Grobfilter	*n*	course filter	*n*	filtre grossier	*m*
Großschaltkreis (Steuergerät)	*m*	LSI circuit (large scale integration)	*n*	circuit à haute intégration (calculateur)	*m*
Grundeinspritzmenge	*f*	basic injection quantity	*n*	débit d'injection de base	*m*

Deutsch			Englisch		Französisch		
Grundeinspritzzeit		*f*	basic injection timing	*n*	durée d'injection de base		*f*
Grundplatte (Relais)		*f*	cap (relay)	*n*	embase (relais)		*f*
Grundreflektor		*m*	basic reflector	*n*	réflecteur de base		*m*
Gruppeneinspritzung		*f*	group injection	*n*	injection groupée		*f*
Gummimanschette		*f*	rubber sleeve	*n*	douille en caoutchouc		*f*
Gummirollbalg		*m*	rubber bellows	*n*	soufflet en caoutchouc		*m*
Gummitülle		*f*	rubber grommet	*n*	passe-fil caoutchouc		*m*
Gurtbremse (Sicherheitsgurt)		*f*	seat-belt brake	*n*	frein de ceinture de sécurité		*m*
Gurtbringer		*m*	seat-belt extender	*n*	serveur de ceinture		*m*
Gurtlose (Sicherheitsgurt)	x	*f*	seat-belt slack	*n*	jeu de ceinture de sécurité		*m*
Gurtstraffer (Sicherheitsgurt)		*m*	seat-belt tightener	*n*	prétensionneur de ceinture		*m*
Gurtstraffer-Auslösegerät		*n*	seat-belt-tightener trigger unit	*n*	déclencheur de prétensionneur		*m*
Gurtverriegelung (Sicherheitsgurt)		*f*	seat-belt locking	*n*	verrouillage de ceinture de sécurité		*m*
Gut-Schlechtlehre		*f*	go/no-go gauge	*n*	jauge "bon/mauvais"		*f*
Gütefaktor		*m*	quality factor	*n*	facteur de qualité		*m*
H							
Haftreibung		*f*	static friction	*n*	frottement statique (adhérence)		*m*
Haftreibungs-Schlupfkurve		*f*	adhesion/slip curve	*n*	courbe caractéristique glissement/adhérence		*f*
Haftreibungszahl (Reifen/Straße)		*f*	coefficient of friction (tire/road	*n*	coefficient d'adhérence (pneu/route)		*m*
Hakenbefestigung (Scheibenwischer)		*f*	hook-type fastening (wipers)	*n*	fixation par crochet (essuie-glace)		*f*
Hakeneinhängung (Wischer)		*f*	hook-type fastening (wipers)	*n*	fixation par crochet (essuie-glace)		*f*
Halbleiterplättchen		*n*	semiconductor wafer	*n*	plaquette semi-conductrice		*f*
Hall-Auslösesystem		*n*	Hall triggering system	*n*	système de déclenchement Hall		*m*
Hall-Effekt		*m*	Hall effect	*n*	effet Hall		*m*
Hall-Element		*n*	Hall element	*n*	élément Hall		*m*
Hall-Geber		*m*	Hall generator	*n*	générateur de Hall		*m*
Hall-Schicht		*f*	Hall layer	*n*	couche Hall		*f*
Hall-Schranke		*f*	Hall vane switch	*n*	barrière Hall		*f*
Hall-Sensor		*m*	Hall generator	*n*	générateur de Hall		*m*
Hall-Spannung		*f*	Hall voltage	*n*	tension Hall		*f*
Halogenlampe		*f*	halogen lamp	*n*	lampe à halogène		*f*
Halogenlicht		*n*	halogen-gas light	*n*	éclairage par lampe à halogène		*m*
Halteplatte		*f*	cover plate	*n*	platine		*f*
Haltespannung		*f*	holding voltage	*n*	tension de maintien		*f*
Haltestern (Wirbelstrombremse)		*m*	star-shaped bracket (electromagnetic retarder)	*n*	support en forme d'étoile (frein à courants de Foucault)		*m*
Haltestrom		*m*	holding current	*n*	courant de maintien		*m*
Halteventil (ABS)		*n*	pressure-holding valve (ABS)	*n*	valve de maintien (ABS)		*f*
Haltewicklung		*f*	hold-in winding	*n*	enroulement de maintien		*m*
Handbremsbacke		*f*	hand-brake shoe	*n*	mâchoire de frein à main		*f*
Handbremse		*f*	hand brake	*n*	frein à main	x	*m*
Handbremshebel		*m*	hand-brake lever	*n*	levier du frein à main		*m*
Handbremsventil		*n*	hand-brake valve	*n*	valve de frein à main		*f*

Deutsch			Englisch		Französisch	
Handbuch		*n*	manual	*n*	manuel	*m*
Handelsprogramm		*n*	aftermarket program	*n*	programme Commerce	*m*
Handfahrgeber		*m*	hand throttle	*n*	accélérateur manuel	*m*
Handförderpumpe		*f*	hand primer pump	*n*	pompe à main	*f*
Handpumpe		*f*	hand primer pump	*n*	pompe à main	*f*
Handschalt-Getriebe		*n*	manually shifted transmission	*n*	boîte de vitesses classique	*f*
Handscheinwerfer		*m*	hand-portable searchlight	*n*	projecteur portable	*m*
Handsender (Autoalarm)		*m*	hand transmitter (car alarm)	*n*	émetteur manuel (alarme auto)	*m*
Handsteuergerät		*n*	manual electric control unit, MECU	*n*	boîtier de commande manuel	*m*
Hangabtrieb	x	*m*	downgrade force	*n*	force de déclivité	*f*
Hangabtriebskraft		*f*	downgrade force	*n*	force de déclivité	*f*
Hauptanschluß		*m*	main terminal	*n*	connexion principale	*f*
Hauptbremszylinder	+	*m*	brake master cylinder	*n*	maître-cylindre de frein	*m*
Hauptbrennraum		*m*	main combustion chamber	*n*	chambre de combustion principale	*f*
Haupteinspritzung		*f*	main injection	*n*	injection principale	*f*
Hauptkontakt (Relais)		*m*	main contact (relay)	*n*	contact principal (relais)	*m*
Hauptprogrammlaufzeit		*f*	main-program running time	*n*	temps opérationnel du programme principal	*m*
Hauptrelais		*n*	main relay	*n*	relais principal	*m*
Hauptrelaistest		*m*	main-relay test	*n*	test du relais principal	*m*
Hauptschlußmotor		*m*	series motor	*n*	moteur série	*m*
Hauptstrom (Generator)		*m*	primary current (alternator)	*n*	courant principal (alternateur)	*m*
Hauptstromkreis (Generator)		*m*	main circuit (alternator)	*n*	circuit principal (alternateur)	*m*
Hauptstufe (Peripheralpumpe)		*f*	main stage (peripheral pump)	*n*	étage principal (pompe à accélération périphérique)	*m*
Hauptuntersuchung, HU		*f*	general inspection	*n*	contrôle technique	*m*
Hauptverbrennungsraum		*m*	main combustion chamber	*n*	chambre de combustion principale	*f*
Hauptzylinder		*m*	brake master cylinder	*n*	maître-cylindre de frein	*m*
Hebelverband		*m*	lever assembly	*n*	groupe de leviers	*m*
Heck-Wischblatt		*n*	rear-window wiper blade	*n*	raclette de lunette arrière	*f*
Heckscheibe		*f*	rear window	*n*	vitre arrière	*f*
Heckscheibenwischer		*m*	rear wiper	*n*	essuie-glace arrière	*m*
Heckwischer		*m*	rear wiper	*n*	essuie-glace arrière	*m*
Heißbenzinverhalten	x	*n*	hot-fuel handling characteristic:	*npl*	comportement avec carburant chaud	*m*
Heißbremswirkung		*f*	effectiveness of hot brakes	*n*	effet de freinage à chaud	*m*
heißfahren (Bremse)		*v*	overheat (brakes)	*v*	surchauffer (frein)	*v*
Heißfilm-Luftmassenmesser		*m*	hot-film air-mass sensor	*n*	débitmètre d'air à film chaud	*m*
Heißfilm-Luftmassenmesser, HMM		*m*	hot-film air-mass meter	*n*	débitmètre massique à film chaud	*m*
Heißfilmsensor		*m*	hot-film sensor	*n*	capteur à film chaud	*m*
Heißförderung		*f*	hot-fuel delivery	*n*	refoulement à chaud	*m*
Heißlaufverhalten (Verbrennungsmotor)		*n*	hot-engine driving response	*n*	comportement en surchauffe (moteur à combustion)	*m*
Heißleiter		*m*	NTC resistor	*n*	thermistance CTN	*f*

Deutsch

Deutsch		Englisch		Französisch	
Heißstart	*m*	hot start	*n*	départ à chaud	*m*
Heißstartmenge	*f*	hot-start fuel quantity	*n*	débit de démarrage à chaud	*m*
Heißstartverhalten	*f*	hot-start response	*n*	comportement au démarrage à chaud	*m*
Heißtest (Abgasprüfung)	*m*	hot test (exhaust-gas test)	*n*	cycle départ à chaud (émissions)	*m*
Heizautomatik	*f*	automatic heater	*n*	chauffage automatique	*m*
Heizelement	*n*	heater element	*n*	élément chauffant	*m*
Heizergebläse	*n*	heater blower	*n*	ventilateur de chaufferette	*m*
Heizflansch	*m*	heating flange	*n*	bride de réchauffage	*f*
Heizrohr	*n*	heating tube	*n*	tube chauffant	*m*
Heizstab (Lufttrockner)	*m*	heating element (air drier)	*n*	tige chauffante (dessiccateur)	*f*
Heizungsanlage	*f*	heater system	*n*	chauffage	*m*
Heizungsregelung	*f*	heating regulator	*n*	régulation du chauffage	*f*
Heizwasserventil	*n*	hot-water valve	*n*	vanne d'eau chaude	*f*
Heizwendel	*f*	helical heating wire	*n*	filament chauffant hélicoïdal	*m*
Hell-Dunkel-Grenze, HDG (Scheinwerfer)	*f*	light-dark cutoff (headlamp)	*n*	limite entre la clarté et l'obcurité (projecteur)	*f*
Hell-Dunkel-Kontrast (Scheinwerfer)	*m*	light-dark cutoff contrast (headlamp)	*n*	contraste entre clarté et obscurité (projecteur)	*m*
Helligkeitsregler (Scheinwerfer	*m*	luminosity controller (headlamp)	*n*	régulateur de luminosité (projecteur)	*m*
High-Rad (ABS) x	*n*	high wheel (ABS)	*n*	roue à sélection "haute" (ABS)	*f*
Hilfs-Bremsanlage	*f*	secondary-brake system	*n*	dispositif de freinage de secour:	*m*
Hilfsbremsleitung	*f*	secondary-brake line	*n*	conduite de secours	*f*
Hilfsbremsventil	*n*	secondary-brake valve	*n*	valve de frein de secours	*f*
Hilfsbremswirkung	*f*	secondary braking effect	*n*	effet de freinage auxiliaire	*m*
Hilfsdrehzahlgeber	*m*	auxiliary engine-speed sensor	*n*	capteur auxiliaire de régime	*m*
Hilfsgebläse	*n*	auxiliary ventilator	*n*	ventilateur auxiliaire	*m*
Hilfskraft-Bremsanlage	*f*	power-assisted braking system	*n*	dispositif de freinage assisté par énergie auxiliaire	*m*
Hilfslöseeinrichtung (Bremse)	*f*	auxiliary release device (brakes)	*n*	dispositif auxiliaire de desserrage (frein)	*m*
Hilfssteuergröße	*f*	auxiliary actuating variable	*n*	grandeur convergente	*f*
Hinterachsdifferential	*n*	rear-axle differential	*n*	différentiel de l'essieu arrière	*m*
Hinterachssperre	*f*	rear-axle lock	*n*	blocage de l'essieu arrière	*m*
Hitzdraht (Luftmassenmesser)	*m*	hot wire (air-mass meter)	*n*	fil chaud (débitmètre massique)	*m*
Hitzdraht-Luftmassenmesser, HLM	*m*	hot-wire air-mass meter	*n*	débitmètre massique à fil chaud	*m*
Hitzdrahtanemometer	*m*	hot-wire anemometer	*n*	anémomètre à fil chaud	*m*
Hochachse (Kfz)	*f*	vehicle vertical axis	*n*	axe vertical du véhicule	*m*
Hochdruck-Bremsanlage	*f*	high-pressure braking system	*n*	dispositif de freinage à haute pression	*m*
Hochdruckanlage	*f*	high-pressure braking system	*n*	dispositif de freinage à haute pression	*m*
Hochdruckeinspritzung	*f*	high-pressure fuel injection	*n*	injection haute pression	*f*
Hochdruckförderung	*f*	high-pressure delivery	*n*	refoulement haute pression	*m*
Hochdruckladepumpe (ASR)	*f*	high-pressure charge pump (TCS)	*n*	pompe de suralimentation haute pression (ASR)	*f*

Deutsch			Englisch		Französisch	
Hochdruckleitung		*f*	high-pressure delivery line	*n*	tuyauterie haute pression	*f*
Hochdruckmagnetventil		*n*	high-pressure solenoid valve	*n*	électrovanne haute pression	*f*
Hochdruckprüfung		*f*	high-pressure test	*n*	essai de haute pression	*m*
Hochdruckpumpe		*f*	high-pressure pump	*n*	pompe à haute pression	*f*
Hochdruckraum		*m*	plunger chamber (fuel-injection pump)	*n*	chambre de refoulement (pompe d'injection)	*f*
Hochdruckspeicher (Common Rail)		*m*	high-pressure accumulator (common rail)	*n*	accumulateur haute pression (Common Rail)	*m*
Hochdruckteil		*n*	high-pressure stage	*n*	partie haute pression	*f*
Hochfrequenzinduktivgeber		*m*	high-frequency inductive senso	*n*	capteur inductif haute fréquence	*m*
Hochgeschwindigkeitsklopfen		*n*	high-speed knock	*n*	cliquetis à haut régime	*m*
hochgesetzte Bremsleuchte (zusätzliche Bremsleuchte)		*f*	auxiliary stop lamp	*n*	feu stop supplémentaire	*m*
Hochlaufdauer		*f*	running-up time	*n*	temps de montée en régime	*m*
hochlaufen (Verbrennungsmotor)	x	*v*	run-up to speed (IC engine)	*v*	montée en régime (moteur à combustion)	*f*
Hochleistungs-Zündspule		*f*	high-performance ignition coil	*n*	bobine d'allumage à hautes performances	*f*
Hochniveau (Luftfederung)		*n*	high level (air suspension)	*n*	niveau haut (suspension pneumatique)	*f*
Hochspannungsleitung		*f*	high-voltage cable	*n*	câble haute tension	*m*
Hochspannungsverteiler		*m*	high-voltage distributor	*n*	distributeur haute tension	*m*
Höchstdrehzahl		*f*	high idle speed	*n*	vitesse maximale à vide	*f*
Hochtaktventil (ELB)		*n*	pressure-buildup valve (ELB)	*n*	valve à impulsions progressives (ELB)	*f*
Hochtonhorn		*n*	high-tone horn	*n*	avertisseur à tonalité aiguë	*m*
Höhenanschlag		*m*	altitude control	*n*	correcteur altimétrique	*m*
Höhengeber		*m*	altitude sensor	*n*	capteur altimétrique	*m*
höhengesteuerter Vollastmengenanschlag		*m*	altitude-controlled full-load stop	*n*	butée de pleine charge en fonction de l'altitude	*f*
Höhenkorrektur		*f*	altitude compensation	*n*	correction altimétrique	*f*
Höhensensor		*m*	altitude sensor	*n*	capteur altimétrique	*m*
Hohlachse		*f*	hollow axle	*n*	axe creux	*m*
Hohlrad		*n*	internal gear (ring gear)	*n*	roue à denture intérieure	*f*
Hohlschraube		*f*	hollow screw	*n*	vis creuse	*f*
Hohlwelle		*f*	hollow shaft	*n*	arbre creux	*m*
Homofokal-Reflektor		*m*	homofocal reflector	*n*	réflecteur homofocal	*m*
Homologation		*f*	homologation	*n*	homologation	*f*
Horn		*n*	horn	*n*	avertisseur sonore	*m*
Hub am Förderende		*m*	stroke at end of delivery	*n*	course en fin de refoulement	*f*
Hub-Drehzähler		*m*	stroke-counting mechanism	*n*	compte-tours et compte-coups	*m*
Hubanschlag		*m*	lift-stop	*n*	butée de course	*f*
Hubbegrenzung		*f*	stroke limiter	*n*	limiteur de course	*m*
Hubgetriebe		*n*	lifting gear assembly	*n*	réducteur à course de levée	*m*
Hubkolbeneinspritzpumpe		*f*	piston injection pump	*n*	pompe d'injection à piston	*f*
Hubkolbenmotor		*m*	reciprocating-piston engine	*n*	moteur à pistons alternatifs	*m*
Hubkolbenverdichter		*m*	reciprocating-piston supercharger	*n*	compresseur à piston	*m*

Deutsch		Englisch		Französisch	
Hubkontrolle	*f*	stroke limiter	*n*	limiteur de course	*m*
Hubmagnet	*m*	tractive solenoid	*n*	électro-aimant de commande	*m*
Hubphase	*f*	stroke phase	*n*	série de courses	*f*
Hubraum (Verbrennungsmotor)	*m*	piston displacement (IC engine)	*n*	cylindrée (moteur à combustion)	*f*
Hubscheibe	*f*	cam plate	*n*	disque à cames	*m*
Hubschieber	*m*	control sleeve	*n*	ligne à tiroirs	*f*
Hubschieber-Reiheneinspritzpumpe (PE)	*f*	control-sleeve in-line fuel-injection pump (PE)	*n*	pompe d'injection en ligne à tiroirs (PE)	*f*
Hubschieber-Verstellwelle	*f*	control-sleeve shaft	*n*	arbre de déplacement des tiroirs	*m*
Hubschieberelement	*n*	control-sleeve element	*n*	élément à tiroir	*m*
Hubschieberpumpe (PE) x	*f*	control-sleeve in-line fuel-injection pump (PE)	*n*	pompe d'injection en ligne à tiroirs (PE)	*f*
Hubschieberstellwerk	*n*	control-sleeve actuator	*n*	actionneur de ligne à tiroirs	*m*
Hubvolumen (Verbrennungsmotor)	*n*	piston displacement (IC engine)	*n*	cylindrée (moteur à combustion)	*f*
Hüllkurve	*f*	envelope	*n*	enveloppe	*f*
Hybridregler	*m*	hybrid regulator	*n*	régulateur hybride	*m*
Hybridschaltung	*f*	hybrid circuit	*n*	circuit hybride	*m*
Hybridtechnik	*f*	hybrid technology	*n*	technique hybride	*f*
Hydraulik-Bremskraftverstärker	*m*	hydraulic brake booster	*n*	servofrein hydraulique	*m*
Hydraulik-Hauptzylinder	*m*	brake master cylinder	*n*	maître-cylindre de frein	*m*
Hydraulik-Radzylinder	*m*	wheel-brake cylinder	*n*	cylindre de frein de roue	*m*
Hydraulikbehälter +	*m*	hydraulic fluid reservoir	*n*	réservoir de fluide hydraulique	*m*
Hydraulikbremskreis	*m*	hydraulic brake circuit	*n*	circuit de freinage hydraulique	*m*
Hydraulikflüssigkeit	*f*	hydraulic fluid	*n*	fluide hydraulique	*m*
Hydraulikleitung	*f*	hydraulic line	*n*	conduite hydraulique	*f*
hydraulisch betätigte Angleichung, HBA	*f*	hydraulically controlled torque control	*n*	correcteur hydraulique de débit	*m*
hydraulische Abstellvorrichtung, HYAB	*f*	hydraulic shutoff device	*n*	dispositif d'arrêt hydraulique	*m*
hydraulische Bremse	*f*	hydraulic-actuated brake	*n*	frein à commande hydraulique	*m*
Hydroaggregat (ABS)	*n*	hydraulic modulator (ABS)	*n*	groupe hydraulique (ABS)	*m*
hydrodynamischer Verlangsamer	*m*	hydrodynamic retarder	*n*	ralentisseur hydrodynamique	*m*
Hydropumpe	*f*	hydraulic pump	*n*	pompe hydraulique	*f*
Hydrospeicher	*m*	hydraulic accumulator	*n*	accumulateur hydraulique	*m*
Hysterese-Prüfung	*f*	hysteresis test	*n*	contrôle d'hystéresis	*m*
I					
IDI, indirekte Einspritzung	*a*	indirect injection, IDI	*n*	injection indirecte	*f*
Impulsaufladung	*f*	pulse turbocharging	*v*	suralimentation pulsatoire	*f*
Impulsformer	*m*	pulse shaper	*n*	conformateur d'impulsions	*m*
Impulsgeber	*m*	pulse generator	*n*	générateur d'impulsions	*m*
Impulsgeberrad (Zündung)	*n*	trigger wheel (ignition)	*n*	noyau synchroniseur (allumage)	*m*
Impulsrad (ABS/ASR) +	*n*	sensor ring (ABS/TCS)	*n*	disque d'impulsion (ABS/ASR)	*m*
Impulsring (ABS/ASR)	*m*	sensor ring (ABS/TCS)	*n*	disque d'impulsion (ABS/ASR)	*m*

Deutsch			Englisch		Französisch	
Impulssteuerung		*f*	impulse control	*n*	commande à impulsions	*f*
Impulsteiler		*m*	pulse divider	*n*	diviseur d'impulsions	*m*
indirekte Einspritzung, IDI		*f*	indirect injection, IDI	*n*	injection indirecte	*f*
Indirekteinspritzer, IDI (Verbrennungsmotor)	x	*m*	indirect-injection (IDI) engine	*n*	moteur à injection indirecte	*m*
Indirekteinspritzmotor, IDI		*m*	indirect-injection (IDI) engine	*n*	moteur à injection indirecte	*m*
Individualregelung, IR (ABS)		*f*	individual control, IR (ABS)	*n*	régulation individuelle (ABS)	*f*
indiziertes Motormoment		*n*	indicated torque	*n*	couple indiqué	*m*
Induktionsgeber (Zündung)		*m*	induction-type pulse-generator (ignition)	*n*	générateur à induction (allumage)	*m*
Induktionsspannung		*f*	induction voltage	*n*	tension d'induction	*f*
Induktionswicklung		*f*	induction coil	*n*	enroulement d'induction	*m*
Induktivgeber		*m*	induction-type pulse-generator (ignition)	*n*	générateur à induction (allumage)	*m*
Infolampe	x	*f*	indicator lamp	*n*	lampe de signalisation	*f*
Informationsanzeige, INA (ABS)	+	*f*	info display (ABS)	*n*	visuel d'information (ABS)	*m*
Informationslampe		*f*	indicator lamp	*n*	lampe de signalisation	*f*
Infrarot-Analysator		*m*	infrared analyzer	*n*	enregistreur infrarouge à absorption	*m*
Infrarot-Handsender (Autoalarm)		*m*	infrared hand transmitter (car alarm)	*n*	émetteur manuel infrarouge (alarme auto)	*m*
Initialisierungsfehler		*m*	initialization error	*n*	erreur d'initialisation	*f*
Injektor (Common Rail)		*m*	injector (common rail)	*n*	injecteur (système "Common Rail")	*m*
Inkremental-Winkel-Zeit-System		*n*	increment-angle-time system	*n*	système incrémentiel angle-temps	*m*
Innenbackenbremse		*f*	internal-shoe brake	*n*	frein à segments à expansion interne	*m*
innenbelüftet (Bremsscheibe)		*pp*	internally ventilated (brake disc)	*pp*	ventilation interne (disque de frein)	*f*
innenbelüftete Scheibenbremse		*f*	ventilated disc brake	*n*	frein à disque ventilé	*m*
Innenleuchte		*f*	interior light	*n*	éclairage intérieur	*m*
Innenraumüberwachung (Kfz)			intrusion detection (motor vehicle)	*n*	surveillance de l'habitacle (véhicule)	*f*
Innenzahnradpumpe		*f*	internal-gear pump	*n*	pompe à engrenage intérieur	*f*
Insassen-Rückhaltesystem		*n*	occupant-protection system	*n*	système de protection des passagers	*m*
Insassenschutzsystem		*n*	occupant-protection system	*n*	système de protection des passagers	*m*
Instandsetzung		*f*	repairing	*n*	remise en état	*f*
Instrumentenleuchte		*f*	instrument-panel lamp	*n*	lampe de tableau de bord	*f*
Instrumententafel		*f*	dashboard	*n*	tableau de bord	*m*
Integralbremsanlage		*f*	combination braking system	*n*	dispositif de freinage combiné	*m*
integrierte Diagnose		*f*	integrated diagnostics	*n*	diagnostic intégré	*m*
integrierter Schaltkreis, IC		*m*	integrated circuit, IC	*n*	circuit intégré, C.I.	*m*
intermittierende Kraftstoffeinspritzung		*f*	intermittent fuel injection	*n*	injection intermittente de carburant	*f*
Ionenstrom		*m*	ionic current	*n*	courant ionique	*m*
Isodromregler		*m*	isodromous governor	*n*	régulateur isodromique	*m*

Deutsch			Englisch			Französisch		
Isolator (Zündkerze)		*m*	insulator (spark plug)		*n*	isolant (bougie)		*m*
Isolatorfuß (Zündkerze)		*m*	insulator nose (spark plug)		*n*	bec d'isolant (bougie)		*m*
Isolierdeckel (Zündverteiler)		*m*	insulating cover (ignition distributor)		*n*	couvercle isolant (allumeur)		*m*
Isolierkörper (Zündspule)		*m*	insulator (ignition coil)		*n*	isolateur (bobine d'allumage)		*m*
Isolierpapier		*n*	insulating paper		*n*	papier isolant		*m*
Isolierscheibe		*m*	insulating washer		*n*	rondelle isolante		*f*
Isolierschlauch		*m*	insulating tubing		*n*	gaine isolante		*f*
Isolierung		*f*	insulation		*n*	isolation		*f*
Istdrehzahl		*f*	actual speed		*n*	vitesse de rotation réelle		*f*
J								
jacknifing (Sattelzug)	x	*v*	jacknife (semitrailer unit)		*v*	phénomène de mise en "portefeuille" (semi-remorque)	x	*m*
Jetronic (elektronische Benzineinspritzung)		*f*	Jetronic (electronic fuel injection)		*n*	Jetronic (injection électronique d'essence)		*m*
Justierplatte (Rollenbremsprüfstand)		*f*	adjustment plate (dynamic brake analyzer)		*n*	plateau d'ajustage (banc d'essai)		*m*
K								
Kabelbaum		*m*	wiring harness		*n*	faisceau de câbles		*m*
Kabelbruch		*m*	cable break		*n*	rupture de câble		*f*
Kabeldurchführung		*f*	cable lead-through		*n*	passage de câble		*m*
Kabelquerschnitt		*m*	cable cross-section		*n*	section de câble		*f*
Kabelschuh		*m*	cable lug		*n*	cosse		*f*
Kalibriergas		*n*	calibrating gas		*n*	gaz de calibrage		*m*
Kälteprüfstand		*m*	cold-test test bench		*n*	banc d'essai au froid		*m*
Kälteprüfstrom (Batterie)		*m*	low-temperature test current (battery)		*n*	courant d'essai au froid (batterie)		*m*
Kälteviskosität		*f*	cold viscosity		*n*	viscosité à basse température		*f*
Kaltlaufanreicherung		*f*	cold-running enrichment		*n*	enrichissement au fonctionnement à froid		*m*
Kaltstart		*m*	cold start		*n*	démarrage à froid		*m*
Kaltstartanpassung		*f*	cold-start compensation		*n*	adaptation au démarrage à froid		*f*
Kaltstartanreicherung		*f*	cold-start enrichment		*n*	enrichissement de départ à froid		*m*
Kaltstartbeschleuniger, KSB		*m*	cold-start accelerator		*n*	accélérateur de démarrage à froid		*m*
Kaltstartdüse		*f*	starting nozzle		*n*	gicleur de départ à froid		*m*
Kaltstartgrenze		*f*	cold-start limit		*n*	limite de démarrage à froid		*f*
Kaltstarthilfe		*f*	cold-start aid		*n*	aide au démarrage à froid		*f*
Kaltstartsteuerung		*f*	cold-start control		*n*	pilotage de démarrage à froid		*m*
Kaltstartventil		*n*	cold-start valve		*n*	injecteur de départ à froid		*m*
Kammermotor		*m*	indirect-injection (IDI) engine		*n*	moteur à injection indirecte		*m*
kapazitive Zange (EMV)		*f*	capacitive clamp (EMC)	x	*n*	pince capacitive (CEM)		*f*
Kardanwellenmoment		*n*	propshaft torque		*n*	couple de l'arbre à cardan		*m*
Karosserie-Elektrik		*f*	body electrics		*n*	électrotechnique de carrosserie		*f*
Karosserie-Elektronik		*f*	body electronics		*n*	électronique de carrosserie		*f*
Katalysator		*m*	catalytic converter		*n*	catalyseur		*m*
Katalysatorfenster		*n*	catalytic converter window		*n*	créneau de pot catalytique		*m*

Deutsch

Deutsch		Englisch		Französisch	
Kavitation (Lochfraß)	*f*	cavitation	*n*	cavitation (formation de cavités gazeuses)	*f*
Kavitationsschaden	*m*	cavitation damage	*n*	dommages par cavitation	*mpl*
Kegeldichtsitz	*m*	conical seat	*n*	siège conique	*m*
Kegelsitz	*m*	conical seat	*n*	siège conique	*m*
Kegelstrahl	*m*	tapered spray	*n*	jet conique	*m*
Kegelwinkel	*m*	cone angle	*n*	angle de cône	*m*
Keilbremse	*f*	wedge-actuated brake	*n*	frein à coin	*m*
Keilriemen	*m*	V-belt	*n*	courroie trapézoïdale	*f*
Keilrippenriemen	*m*	ribbed V-belt	*n*	courroie trapezoïdale à nervures	*f*
Kennfeld	*n*	program map	*n*	cartographie	*f*
kennfeldgesteuert (Zündung)	*pp*	map-controlled (ignition)	*pp*	piloté par cartographie (allumage)	*pp*
Kennfeldregelung	*f*	map-based control	*n*	régulation cartographique	*f*
Kennfeldzündung	*f*	map-controlled ignition	*n*	allumage cartographique	*m*
Kennleuchte	*f*	identification lamp	*n*	feu spécial d'avertissement	*m*
Kennlinie	*f*	characteristic	*n*	courbe caractéristique	*f*
Kennzeichenbeleuchtung	*f*	license-plate lamp	*n*	feu d'éclairage de plaque d'immatriculation	*m*
Kennzeichenleuchte	*f*	license-plate lamp	*n*	feu d'éclairage de plaque d'immatriculation	*m*
Keramikschicht (Lambda-Sonde)	*f*	ceramic layer (lambda oxygen sensor)	*n*	couche de céramique (sonde lambda)	*f*
Keramikträger	*m*	ceramic substrate	*n*	support en céramique	*m*
Kerbverzahnung	*f*	grooved toothing	*n*	cannelure	*f*
Kerzengehäuse	*n*	spark-plug shell	*n*	culot de bougie	*m*
Kerzenstecker	*m*	spark-plug connector	*n*	embout de bougie	*m*
Kickdown-Schalter	*m*	kick-down switch	*n*	contacteur de kickdown	*m*
Kippfrequenz (Multivibrator)	*f*	switching frequency (multivibrator)	*n*	fréquence d'oscillation (multivibrateur)	*f*
Kippschaltung	*f*	multivibrator	*n*	multivibrateur	*m*
Klappankerrelais	*n*	hinged-armature relay	*n*	relais à armature battante	*m*
Klappgehäuse	*n*	hinged housing	*n*	boîtier rabattable	*m*
Klappscheinwerfer	*m*	retractable headlight	*n*	projecteur escamotable	*m*
Klaue (Kupplungskopf)	*f*	claw (coupling head)	*n*	griffe (tête d'accouplement)	*f*
Klauenführung (Kupplungskopf)	*f*	claw guide (coupling head)	*n*	glissière (tête d'accouplement)	*f*
Klauenpol	*m*	claw pole	*n*	plateau à griffes	*m*
Klauenpolabhebung	*f*	claw-pole chamfer	*n*	chanfrein des pôles à griffes	*m*
Klauenpolgenerator	*m*	claw-pole alternator	*n*	alternateur à rotor à griffes	*m*
Klauenpolläufer	*m*	claw-pole rotor	*n*	rotor à griffes	*m*
Klebeschild	*n*	adhesive label	*n*	autocollant	*m*
Kleinlader (Batterie)	*m*	small charger (battery)	*n*	chargeur compact (batterie)	*m*
Kleinrelais	*n*	minirelay	*n*	petit relais	*m*
Klemmenbezeichnung	*f*	terminal designation	*n*	identification des bornes	*f*
Klemmenspannung	*f*	terminal voltage	*n*	tension aux bornes	*f*
Klemmhülse (Drehzahlsensor)	*f*	spring sleeve (wheel-speed sensor)	*n*	douille élastique (capteur de vitesse)	*f*

Deutsch			Englisch		Französisch	
Klemmschelle (Zündspule)		*f*	clamp (ignition coil)	*n*	collier (bobine d'allumage)	*m*
Klimaanlage		*f*	air conditioner	*n*	climatiseur	*m*
Klimaeingang (Luftzufuhr Klimakompressor)	x	*m*	air-conditioner input	*n*	entrée climatiseur	*f*
Klimakompressor		*m*	air-conditioner compressor	*n*	compresseur de climatiseur	*m*
Klimaprüfstand		*m*	climate test bench	*n*	banc d'essai climatique	*m*
Klimaregelung		*f*	air-conditioning	*n*	régulateur de climatisseur	*m*
klingeln (Verbrennungsmotor)	x	*v*	knock (IC engine)	*v*	cliquetis (moteur à combustion)	*m*
Klopfbremse	x	*f*	knock inhibitor	*n*	agent antidétonant	*m*
klopfen (Verbrennungsmotor)	x	*v*	knock (IC engine)	*v*	cliquetis (moteur à combustion)	*m*
klopfende Verbrennung		*f*	combustion knock	*n*	combustion détonante	*f*
klopffest (Kraftstoff)		*adj*	knock-resistant (fuel)	*adj*	antidétonant (carburant)	*adj*
Klopffestigkeit		*f*	antiknock quality	*n*	indétonance	*f*
Klopfgrenze		*f*	knock limit	*n*	limite de cliquetis	*f*
Klopfneigung		*f*	tendency to knock	*n*	tendance au cliquetis	*f*
Klopfregelung		*f*	knock control	*n*	régulation du cliquetis	*f*
Klopfsensor		*m*	knock sensor	*n*	capteur de cliquetis	*m*
knacken (Funkstörung)		*v*	click (radio disturbance)	*v*	claquement (perturbation)	*m*
Kneeling-Funktion (Luftfederung)	x	*f*	kneeling-function (air suspension)	*n*	fonction d'inclinaison (suspension pneumatique)	*f*
Kneeling-Niveau (Luftfederung)	x	*n*	kneeling level (air suspension)	*n*	niveau d'inclinaison (suspension pneumatique)	*m*
Knickpunkt (Kennlinie)		*m*	knee point (characteristic curve)	*n*	coude (courbe caractéristique)	*m*
Knickregler (Bremse)	x	*m*	dynamic load-sensing valve (brakes)	*n*	régulateur à caractéristique coudée (frein)	*m*
Kniehebel		*m*	toggle lever	*n*	levier à rotule	*m*
Knopfdiode		*f*	button diode	*n*	diode-bouton	*f*
Köcherbürstenhalter		*m*	cartridge-type brush holder	*n*	porte-balais tubulaire	*m*
Kochschutzmenge		*f*	overheat-protection quantity	*n*	volume de protection anti-ébullition	*m*
Kofferraumsicherung (Autoalarm)		*f*	trunk protection (car alarm)	*n*	protection du coffre (alarme auto)	*f*
Kohlebürste (elektrische Maschinen)		*f*	carbon brush (rotating machines)	*n*	balai de charbon (machines tournantes)	*m*
Kohlebürstenhalter		*m*	brush holder	*n*	porte-balais	*m*
Kohlebürstensatz		*m*	carbon-brush set	*n*	jeu de balais	*m*
Kolben-Einspritzpumpe		*f*	reciprocating fuel-injection pump	*n*	pompe d'injection alternative	*f*
Kolbenbohrung (Pumpenkolben)		*f*	plunger passage	*n*	alésage de piston (piston de pompe)	*m*
Kolbendruckregler		*m*	plunger-type pressure regulator	*n*	régulateur de pression à piston	*m*
Kolbenfahne (Pumpenkolben)		*f*	plunger control arm	*n*	entraîneur (piston de pompe)	*m*
Kolbenfeder (Pumpenkolben)		*f*	plunger return spring	*n*	ressort de rappel du piston (piston de pompe)	*m*
Kolbenfresser		*m*	piston seizure	*n*	grippage de piston	*m*
Kolbenhub		*m*	plunger lift	*n*	course du piston	*f*
Kolbenhub bis Förderbeginn (Vorhub des Pumpenkolbens)		*m*	plunger lift to cutoff port closing	*n*	précourse du piston (jusqu'au début de refoulement)	*f*

Deutsch		Englisch		Französisch	
Kolbenhub bis Förderende (Pumpenkolben)	*m*	plunger lift to spill-port opening	*n*	course du piston en fin de refoulement (piston de pompe)	*f*
Kolbenkraft	*f*	piston force	*n*	force de piston	*f*
Kolbenlenkarm (Pumpenkolben)	*m*	plunger control arm	*n*	entraîneur (piston de pompe)	*m*
Kolbenmulde	*f*	piston recess	*n*	cavité du piston	*f*
Kolbenringnut	*f*	piston-ring groove	*n*	rainure annulaire de piston	*f*
Kolbenrückführfeder	*f*	plunger return spring	*n*	ressort de rappel du piston (piston de pompe)	*m*
Kolbenrücklauf (Pumpenkolben)	*m*	plunger return stroke	*n*	course de retour du piston (piston de pompe)	*f*
Kolbenschaft (Druckventil)	*m*	pressure-valve stem	*n*	tige de piston (clapet de refoulement)	*f*
Kolbenspeicher	*m*	piston accumulator	*n*	accumulateur à piston	*m*
Kolbenstange	*f*	piston rod	*n*	tige de piston	*f*
Kolbenventil (Pumpenkolben)	*n*	plunger-type valve	*n*	soupape à piston (piston de pompe)	*f*
Kolbenweg	*m*	plunger lift	*n*	course du piston	*f*
Kolbenzylinder	*m*	piston cylinder	*n*	cylindre à piston	*m*
Kollektorbahn	*f*	collector-track	*n*	piste à résistance	*f*
Kombi-Bremsanlage	*f*	combination braking system	*n*	dispositif de freinage combiné	*m*
Kombibremszylinder	*m*	combination brake cylinder	*n*	cylindre de frein combiné	*m*
Komfortelektronik	*f*	comfort and convenience electronics	*npl*	électronique de confort	*f*
Komfortsysteme	*npl*	comfort and convenience systems	*npl*	systèmes de confort	*mpl*
Kommutator	*m*	commutator	*n*	collecteur	*m*
Kommutatorlager (Generator)	*n*	commutator end shield (alternator)	*n*	flasque côté collecteur (alternateur)	*m*
Kommutierung	*f*	commutation	*n*	commutation	*f*
Kommutierungsszone (Kohlebürste)	*f*	commutating zone (carbon brush)	*n*	partie commutateur (balai)	*f*
Komparator	*m*	comparator	*n*	comparateur	*m*
Kompensationsklappe	*f*	compensation flap	*n*	volet de compensation	*m*
Kompressibilität	*f*	compressibility	*n*	compressibilité	*f*
Kompressionsdruck	*m*	compression (IC engine)	*n*	compression (moteur à combustion)	*f*
Kompressionshub	*m*	compression stroke	*n*	course de compression	*f*
Kompressionsvolumen	*n*	compression volume	*n*	volume de compression	*m*
Kompressor x	*m*	air compressor	*n*	compresseur d'air	*m*
Kondensator	*m*	capacitor	*n*	condensateur	*m*
konfigurieren (Steuergerät)	*v*	configure (ECU)	*v*	configurer (fonction du calculateur)	*v*
Königszapfen	*m*	fifth wheel	*n*	pivot central	*m*
Konstantdrossel (Motorbremse)	*f*	constant throttle (engine brake)	*n*	étranglement constant (frein moteur)	*m*
Kontaktabbrand	*m*	contact erosion	*n*	érosion des contacts	*f*
Kontaktfeder	*f*	contact spring	*n*	contact à ressort	*m*
kontaktgesteuert	*pp*	breaker-triggered	*pp*	à déclenchement par rupteur	*loc*

Deutsch		Englisch		Französisch	
kontaktlos	*adj*	breakerless	*adj*	sans rupteur mécanique	*loc*
Kontaktprellung	*f*	contact chatter	*n*	rebondissement des contacts	*m*
Kontaktregler	*m*	contact regulator	*n*	régulateur à vibreur	*m*
Kontaktsatz (Zündung)	*m*	contact set (ignition)	*n*	jeu de contacts (allumage)	*m*
Kontaktschalter	*m*	contact switch	*n*	contacteur	*m*
Kontaktschiene (Kraftstoffverteiler)	*f*	contact rail (fuel rail)	*n*	rail de contact (rampe distributrice)	*m*
Kontrollmaß	*n*	control dimension	*n*	cote de contrôle	*f*
Kopfkreis (Zahnrad)	*m*	tip circle (gear)	*n*	cercle de tête (engrenage)	*m*
Kopfspiel (Pumpenelement)	*n*	head clearance (plunger-and-barrel assembly)	*n*	jeu en tête (élément de pompage)	*m*
Koppelfeder	*f*	coupling spring	*n*	ressort de couplage	*m*
Koppelkraft (elektronisch-pneumatisches Bremssystem)	*f*	coupling force (electronic/compressed-air braking system)	*n*	force de couplage (dispositif de freinage électronique-pneumatique)	*f*
Koppelkraftsensor (elektronisch-pneumatisches Bremssystem)	*m*	coupling-force sensor (electronic/compressed-air braking system)	*n*	capteur de force de couplage (dispositif de freinage électro-pneumatique	*m*
Koppelortungssystem (Navigationssystem)	*n*	compound navigation (navigation system)	*n*	système de localisation à l'estime (système de navigation	*m*
Körperschall	*m*	structure-borne noise	*n*	bruits d'impact	*mpl*
Körperschallaufnehmer	*m*	knock sensor	*n*	capteur de cliquetis	*m*
Korrekturmenge	*f*	correction quantity	*n*	volume de correction	*m*
korrigierter Luftdruck	*m*	corrected air pressure	*n*	pression d'air corrigée	*f*
Korrosionsfestigkeit	*f*	corrosion resistance	*n*	résistance à la corrosion	*f*
Korrosionsschutz	*m*	corrosion protection	*n*	protection anticorrosion	*f*
Kostenstelle	*f*	cost center	*n*	code d'imputation	*m*
krachen (Funkstörung)	x *v*	crackle (radio disturbance)	*v*	craquement (perturbation)	*m*
Kraftfahrtechnisches Taschenbuch (Bosch-Schriftenreihe)	*n*	Automotive Handbook (Bosch publication)	*n*	Mémento de technologie automobile (publication Bosch)	*m*
Kraftfahrzeugausrüstung	*f*	automotive equipment	*n*	equipement automobile	*m*
Kraftfahrzeugbremsen	*fpl*	motor-vehicle brakes	*npl*	freins d'un véhicule à moteur	*mpl*
Kraftfahrzeugleuchte	*f*	motor-vehicle lamp	*n*	feu (véhicule automobile)	*m*
Kraftlinienfeld	*n*	field of force	*n*	champ de lignes de force	*m*
Kraftmeßeinrichtung (Rollenbremsprüfstand)	*f*	load sensor (dynamic brake analyzer)	*n*	dynamomètre (banc d'essai)	*m*
Kraftschluß (Reifen/Straße)	*m*	adhesion (tire/road)	*n*	adhérence (pneu/route)	*f*
Kraftschlußbeiwert (Reifen/Straße)	*m*	coefficient of friction (tire/road	*n*	coefficient d'adhérence (pneu/route)	*m*
Kraftstoff-Massenverbrauch	*m*	fuel consumption by mass	*n*	consommation massique de carburant	*f*
Kraftstoff-Mehrmenge	*f*	excess fuel	*n*	surdébit de carburant	*m*
Kraftstoffanzeiger	*m*	fuel gauge	*n*	jauge à carburant	*f*
Kraftstoffbehälter	*m*	fuel tank	*n*	réservoir de carburant	*m*
Kraftstoffdruckdämpfer (Jetronic)	*m*	fuel-pressure attenuator (Jetronic)	*n*	amortisseur de pression du carburant (Jetronic)	*m*
Kraftstoffdruckregler	*m*	fuel-pressure regulator	*n*	régulateur de pression de carburant	*m*

Deutsch		Englisch		Französisch	
Kraftstoffdrucksensor	*m*	fuel-pressure sensor	*n*	capteur de pression du carburant	*m*
Kraftstoffeinlaß	+ *m*	fuel inlet	*n*	arrivée de carburant	*f*
Kraftstoffeinspritzmenge	*f*	injected fuel quantity	*n*	débit d'injection	*m*
Kraftstoffeinspritzpumpe	*f*	fuel-injection pump	*n*	pompe d'injection	*f*
Kraftstoffeinspritzung	*f*	fuel injection	*n*	injection de carburant	*f*
Kraftstoffilter	*n*	fuel filter	*n*	filtre à carburant	*m*
Kraftstoffkammer (Kraftstoffdruckregler)	*f*	fuel chamber (fuel-pressure regulator)	*n*	chambre à carburant (amortisseur de pression du carburant)	*f*
Kraftstoffleitung	*f*	fuel line	*n*	conduite de carburant	*f*
Kraftstoffluftabscheider	*m*	fuel-air separator	*n*	séparateur d'air du carburant	*m*
Kraftstoffmasse-Sensor	*m*	fuel-mass sensor	*n*	capteur de masse de combustible	*m*
Kraftstoffmengenkorrektur	*f*	fuel-quantity correction	*n*	correction de débit de carburant	*f*
Kraftstoffmengenteiler	*m*	fuel distributor	*n*	doseur-distributeur de carburan	*m*
Kraftstoffördermenge (Einspritzpumpe)	*f*	delivery quantity (fuel-injection pump)	*n*	débit de refoulement (pompe d'injection)	*m*
Kraftstofförderpumpe	*f*	fuel-supply pump	*n*	pompe d'alimentation (carburant)	*f*
Kraftstofförderung	*f*	fuel supply and delivery	*n*	refoulement du carburant	*m*
Kraftstoffpumpe	*f*	fuel-supply pump	*n*	pompe d'alimentation (carburant)	*f*
Kraftstoffrückführventil	*n*	fuel-recirculation valve	*n*	vanne de recyclage de carburan	*f*
Kraftstoffrückleitung	*f*	fuel-return line	*n*	conduite de retour du carburant	*f*
Kraftstoffspeicher	*m*	fuel accumulator	*n*	accumulateur de carburant	*m*
Kraftstoffsystem	*n*	fuel system	*n*	système d'alimentation en carburant	*m*
Kraftstofftank	+ *m*	fuel tank	*n*	réservoir de carburant	*m*
Kraftstofftröpfchen	*n*	fuel droplet	*n*	gouttelette de carburant	*f*
Kraftstoffverbrauch	*m*	fuel consumption	*n*	consommation de carburant	*f*
Kraftstoffverdampfung	*f*	fuel vaporization	*n*	vaporisation du carburant	*f*
Kraftstoffverdunstungs-Rückhaltesystem	*n*	evaporative-emissions control system	*n*	système de retenue des vapeurs de carburant	*m*
Kraftstoffversorgung	*f*	fuel supply	*n*	alimentation en carburant	*f*
Kraftstoffverteiler	*m*	fuel rail	*n*	rampe distributrice de carburan	*f*
Kraftstoffverteilerstück (Einzeleinspritzung)	*n*	fuel-distribution pipe (multipoint fuel injection)	*n*	rampe d'injection (injection multipoint)	*f*
Kraftstoffverteilung	*f*	fuel distribution	*n*	répartition du carburant	*f*
Kraftstoffvorreiniger	*m*	fuel prefilter	*n*	préfiltre à carburant	*m*
Kraftstoffwasserabscheider	*m*	fuel-water separator	*n*	séparateur d'eau du carburant	*m*
Kraftstoffzerstäubung	*f*	fuel atomization	*n*	pulvérisation du carburant	*f*
Kraftstoffzufuhr	*f*	fuel supply	*n*	alimentation en carburant	*f*
Kraftstoffzulauf	*m*	fuel inlet	*n*	arrivée de carburant	*f*
Kraftstoffzumessung	*f*	fuel metering	*n*	dosage du carburant	*m*
Kraftstoffzuteiler	*m*	fuel rail	*n*	rampe distributrice de carburan	*f*
Kraftstoffzuteilung	*f*	fuel metering	*n*	dosage du carburant	*m*
Krallenschleifer	*m*	claw-type sliding contact	*n*	curseur à griffes	*m*

Deutsch			Englisch			Französisch		
Kreisabsicherung (Bremssystem)		*f*	circuit safeguard (braking system)		*n*	protection des circuits d'alimentation (système de freinage)		*f*
Kreisdruck (ESP)		*m*	circuit pressure (ESP)		*n*	pression de circuit (ESP)		*f*
Kreisellader		*m*	centrifugal turbo-compressor		*n*	compresseur centrifuge		*m*
Kreuzlenker (Wischeranlage)		*m*	transversely jointed linkage (wiper system)		*n*	articulation en croix (essuie-glace)		*f*
Kreuzscheibe		*f*	yoke		*n*	croisillon		*m*
Kriechneigung (Fahrzeuge mit Automatikgetriebe)		*f*	creep tendency (vehicles with automatic gearbox)		*n*	tendance au rampement (véhicules à boîte automatique)		*f*
Kriechstrom (Zündkerze)		*m*	insulator flashover (spark-plug)		*n*	courant de fuite (bougie)		*m*
Kriechweg		*m*	leakage path		*n*	chemin de fuite		*m*
Kugelbolzen		*m*	ball pin		*n*	rotule		*f*
Kugelkäfig (Türbetätigung)		*m*	bearing cage (door control)		*n*	cage à billes (commande des portes)		*f*
Kugelstift	x	*m*	spherical pin		*n*	axe à profil sphérique		*m*
Kugelumlauf (Türbetätigung, Lenkung)		*m*	recirculating-ball device (door control, steering system)		*n*	rampe à billes (commande des portes, direction)		*f*
Kugelventil		*n*	ball valve		*n*	clapet à bille		*m*
Kugelzapfen		*m*	ball pivot		*n*	tourillon sphérique		*m*
Kühlblech		*n*	heat sink		*n*	refroidisseur		*m*
Kühlergebläse		*n*	radiator blower		*n*	ventilateur de radiateur		*m*
Kühlerventilator		*m*	radiator blower		*n*	ventilateur de radiateur		*m*
Kühlkanal (Bremsscheibe)		*m*	cooling channel (brake disc)		*n*	canal de circulation d'air (frein à disque)		*m*
Kühlkörper		*m*	heat sink		*n*	refroidisseur		*m*
Kühlluft		*f*	cooling air		*n*	air de refroidissement		*m*
Kühlmittel		*n*	coolant		*n*	liquide de refroidissement		*m*
Kühlnoppe		*f*	cooling pip		*n*	plateau en plastique		*m*
Kühlung		*f*	cooling		*n*	refroidissement		*m*
Kühlwasser		*n*	cooling water		*n*	eau de refroidissement		*f*
Kühlwasseranschluß		*m*	water port		*n*	raccord d'eau de refroidissemen		*m*
Kulisse (Dieseleinspritzung)		*f*	sliding-block guide (governor)		*n*	guide-coulisse (injection diesel)		*m*
Kulisse (Feststellbremsventil)		*f*	detent element (parking-brake valve)		*n*	coulisse (valve de frein de stationnement)		*f*
Kulissenführung (Diesel-Regler)		*f*	sliding-block guide (governor)		*n*	guide-coulisse (injection diesel)		*m*
Kulissenplatte		*f*	template		*n*	coulisse		*f*
Kulissenstein		*m*	guide block		*n*	coulisseau		*m*
Kundendienst		*m*	service		*n*	service après-vente		*m*
Kundenspezifikation		*f*	customer specification		*n*	spécification client		*f*
Kupferkern (Zündkerze)		*m*	copper core (spark plug)		*n*	noyau de cuivre (bougie)		*m*
Kupferlackdraht		*m*	varnished copper wire		*n*	fil de cuivre laqué		*m*
Kupferpaste		*f*	copper paste		*n*	pâte de cuivre		*f*
Kupferspray		*m*	copper spray		*n*	spray au cuivre		*m*
Kupferverluste (Generator)	x	*mpl*	copper losses (alternator)	x	*npl*	pertes cuivre (alternateur)	x	*fpl*
Kupplungsanschluß		*m*	coupling port		*n*	raccord d'accouplement		*m*
Kupplungseingang		*m*	clutch input		*n*	entrée embrayage		*f*
Kupplungskopf		*m*	coupling head		*n*	tête d'accouplement		*f*

Deutsch		Englisch		Französisch	
Kupplungskopf "Bremse"	*m*	coupling head "brakes"	*n*	tête d'accouplement "frein"	*f*
Kupplungskopf "Vorrat"	*m*	coupling head "supply"	*n*	tête d'accouplement "alimentation"	*f*
Kupplungsschalter	*m*	clutch switch	*n*	contacteur d'embrayage	*m*
Kurbeltrieb	*m*	crankshaft drive	*n*	mécanisme d'embiellage	*m*
Kurbelwellen-Drehzahlsensor	*m*	crankshaft speed sensor	*n*	capteur de vitesse de rotation du vilebrequin	*m*
Kurbelwellenstörfrequenz	*f*	crankshaft disturbance frequency	*n*	fréquence perturbatrice du vilebrequin	*f*
Kurbelwellenwinkel	*m*	crankshaft angle	*n*	angle vilebrequin	*m*
Kurbelwinkel (Grad Kurbelwelle)	*m*	crankshaft angle	*n*	angle vilebrequin	*m*
Kurbelwinkelgeber	*m*	crank-angle sensor	*n*	capteur d'angle vilebrequin	*m*
Kurbelwinkelsensor	*m*	crank-angle sensor	*n*	capteur d'angle vilebrequin	*m*
Kurvenbremsung	*f*	braking during cornering	*n*	freinage en virage	*m*
Kurvenbremsverhalten	*n*	curve braking behavior	*n*	comportement au freinage en virage	*m*
Kurvenfahrt	*f*	cornering	*ppr*	conduite en virage	*f*
Kurvengrenzgeschwindigkeit	*f*	cornering limit speed	*n*	vitesse limite en virage	*f*
Kurvenplatte	*f*	plate cam	*n*	plaque à came	*f*
Kurvenprofil	*n*	curve profile	*n*	profil de courbe	*m*
Kurvenradius (Fahrbahn)	*m*	radius of bend (road)	*n*	rayon de courbure (virage)	*m*
Kurvenscheibe (Bremskraftregler)	*f*	cam disc (braking-force regulator)	*n*	disque à cames (correcteur de freinage)	*m*
kurzschließen	*v*	short-circuit <to short-circuit>	*v*	court-circuiter	*v*
Kurzschluß	*m*	short-circuit <noun>	*n*	court-circuit	*m*
kurzschlußfest	*adj*	short-circuit resistant	*adj*	résistant aux courts-circuits	*ppr*
Kurzschlußring	*m*	short-circuiting ring	*n*	bague de court-circuitage	*f*
Kurzschlußringgeber	*m*	short-circuit-ring sensor	*n*	capteur à bague de court-circuitage	*m*
Kurzschlußringsensor	*m*	short-circuit-ring sensor	*n*	capteur à bague de court-circuitage	*m*
Kurzschlußscheibe	*f*	short-circuit shim	*n*	rondelle court-circuit	*f*
kurzschlußsicher	*adj*	insensitive to short-circuit	*adj*	insensible au court-circuit	*loc*
Kurzschlußstrom	*m*	short-circuit current	*n*	courant de court-circuit	*m*
Kurzzeitbetrieb (elektrische Maschinen)	*m*	short-time-duty type (electrical machines)	*n*	fonctionnement de courte durée (machines électriques)	*m*
Kurzzeitverbraucher	*m*	short-term load	*n*	récepteur à fonctionnement de courte durée	*m*
Kurzzeitverhalten	*n*	short-term behaviour	*n*	comportement à court terme	*m*
L					
Ladebetrieb (Batterieladung)	*m*	charging mode (battery charge)	*n*	mode "charge" (charge de batterie)	*m*
Ladebilanz (Batterie)	*f*	charge balance (battery)	*n*	bilan de charge (batterie)	*m*
Ladedruck	*m*	charge-air pressure	*n*	pression de suralimentation	*f*
ladedruckabhängiger Vollastanschlag, LDA	*m*	manifold-pressure compensator	*n*	limiteur de richesse	*m*
Ladedruckanschlag	*m*	manifold-pressure compensator	*n*	limiteur de richesse	*m*

Deutsch		Englisch		Französisch	
Ladedruckfühler	*m*	boost-pressure sensor, BPS	*n*	capteur de pression de suralimentation	*m*
Ladedruckregelung	*f*	boost-pressure control	*n*	régulation de la pression de suralimentation	*f*
Ladedruckregler	*m*	pressure-charging regulator	*n*	régulateur de pression de suralimentation	*m*
Ladedrucksensor	*m*	boost-pressure sensor, BPS	*n*	capteur de pression de suralimentation	*m*
Ladedrucksteller (Radialkolbenpumpe)	*m*	charge-pressure actuator	*n*	actionneur de pression de suralimentation (pompe à pistons radiaux)	*m*
Ladegerät (Batterie)	*n*	battery charger	*n*	chargeur de batterie	*m*
Ladekennlinie (Batterie)	*f*	charging characteristic (battery)	*n*	caractéristique de charge (batterie)	*f*
Ladeklips (Batterieladung)	x *m*	crocodile clip	*n*	pince de batterie	*f*
Ladekolbeneinheit (ESP)	*f*	charging-piston unit (ESP)	*n*	unité de piston de charge (ESP)	*f*
Ladekontrollampe	*f*	charge-indicator lamp	*n*	lampe témoin d'alternateur	*f*
Ladeleitung	*f*	charging cable	*n*	câble de charge	*m*
Ladeluft	*f*	charge air	*n*	air de suralimentation	*m*
Ladeluftdruck	*m*	charge-air pressure	*n*	pression de suralimentation	*f*
Ladeluftkühler	*m*	charge-air cooler	*n*	refroidisseur d'air de suralimentation	*m*
Ladeluftkühlung, LLK	*f*	charge-air cooling	*n*	refroidissement de la charge d'air	*m*
Lademenge	*f*	pressure-charge fuel-delivery quantity	*n*	débit de suralimentation	*m*
Ladepumpe (EHB)	*f*	charging pump (EHB)	*n*	pompe de charge	*f*
Lader	*m*	supercharger	*n*	compresseur (suralimentation)	*m*
Ladesessel (Handscheinwerfer)	*m*	charging unit (hand-portable searchlight)	*n*	chargeur (projecteur portable)	*m*
Ladespannung (Batterie)	*f*	charge voltage	*n*	tension de charge	*f*
Ladestrom (Batterie)	*m*	battery charge current	*n*	courant de charge de la batterie	*m*
Ladezeit (Batterie)	*m*	charging time (battery)	*n*	temps de charge (batterie)	*m*
Ladezustand (Batterie)	*m*	state of charge (battery)	*n*	état de charge de la batterie	*m*
Ladezustandsanzeige	*f*	charge indicator	*n*	indicateur de charge	*m*
Ladung (Batterie)	*f*	charging (battery)	*n*	charge (batterie)	*f*
Ladungsschichtung	*f*	charge stratification	*n*	stratification de la charge	*f*
Ladungsträger (Zündkerze)	*m*	charged carrier (spark plug)	*n*	porteur de charge (bougie)	*m*
Ladungswechsel	*m*	charge cycle	*n*	alternance de charge	*f*
Lagerbuchse	*f*	bushing	*n*	coussinet	*m*
Lageregelkreis (Drosselklappe)	*m*	position control loop (throttle)	*n*	circuit de régulation de position (papillon)	*m*
Lageregelung	*f*	closed-loop position control	*n*	régulation de position	*f*
Lagergehäuse	*n*	bearing housing	*n*	carter de palier	*m*
Lagerring	*m*	bearing ring	*n*	bague de guidage	*f*
Lagesensor	*m*	position sensor	*n*	capteur de position	*m*
Lambda s. Luftzahl	*a*	excess-air factor (lambda)	*n*	coefficient d'air (lambda)	*m*
Lambda-Kennfeld	*n*	lambda program map	*n*	cartographie de richesse (lambda)	*f*

Deutsch

Deutsch		Englisch		Französisch	
Lambda-Regelung	*f*	lambda closed-loop control	*n*	régulation de richesse	*f*
Lambda-Sonde	*f*	lambda sensor	*n*	sonde de richesse	*f*
Lamellenkontakt	*m*	lamination contact	*n*	contact à lamelles	*m*
Lamellenkupplung	*f*	multiplate clutch	*n*	embrayage multidisques	*m*
Lamellenpaket (Generator)	*n*	stator lamination (alternator)	*n*	paquet de lamelles de tôle (alternateur)	*m*
Längsbohrung	*f*	longitudinal passage	*n*	canal axial	*m*
Längsgeschwindigkeit (Kfz-Dynamik)	*f*	longitudinal velocity (vehicle dynamics)	*n*	vitesse longitudinale (dynamique d'un véhicule)	*f*
Längsnut (Pumpenkolben)	*f*	vertical groove (pump plunger)	*n*	rainure verticale (piston de pompe)	*f*
Längssperre (Allradantrieb)	*f*	inter-axle lock (all-wheel drive)	*n*	blocage longitudinal (transmission intégrale)	*m*
Längsstrang (Allradantrieb)	*m*	longitudinal train (all-wheel drive)	*n*	train longitudinal (système de transmission intégrale)	*m*
Last-Leer-Ventil	*n*	load-proportioning valve	*n*	valve vide-charge	*f*
lastabhängig	*adj*	load-sensitive	*adj*	asservi à la charge	*pp*
lastabhängiger Förderbeginn, LFB	*m*	load-dependent start of delivery	*n*	initiateur de refoulement	*m*
lastabhängiger Spritzbeginn	*m*	load-dependent start of injection	*n*	début d'injection variable en fonction de la charge	*m*
Lastabschaltung (Bordnetz)	*f*	load dump (vehicle electrical system)	*n*	délestage (circuit de bord)	*m*
Lastabwurf (Bordnetz)	*m*	load dump (vehicle electrical system)	*n*	délestage (circuit de bord)	*m*
Lastgröße (Bremskraftregelung)	*f*	load value (braking-force metering)	*n*	charge (correction automatique de la force de feinage)	*f*
Lastmoment	*n*	load moment	*n*	couple de charge	*m*
Lastschalter	*m*	load switch	*n*	commutateur de charge	*m*
Lastschlag-Dämpfer	*m*	power on/off damper	*n*	amortisseur d'à-coups de charge	*m*
Lastschlagdämpfung	*f*	load-reversal damping	*n*	amortissement des à-coups de charge	*m*
Lastsensor (Fahrwerk)	*m*	axle-load sensor	*n*	capteur de charge sur essieu	*m*
Lastsensor (Motor)	*m*	load sensor (engine management)	*n*	capteur de charge (moteur)	*m*
Lastsignal	*n*	load signal	*n*	signal de charge	*m*
Laststeuerung	*f*	load control	*n*	commande de la charge	*f*
Laststrom	*m*	load current	*n*	courant en charge	*m*
Lastventil (ASR)	*n*	load valve (TCS)	*n*	valve asservie à la charge (ASR)	*f*
Lastverstellung	*f*	load adjustment	*n*	correction à dépression	*f*
Lastwechsel	*m*	load changes	*npl*	variation de la charge	*f*
Lastzustand	*m*	load condition	*n*	état de charge du moteur	*m*
Läufer (Druckwellenlader)	*m*	rotor (pressure-wave supercharger)	*n*	rotor (échangeur de pression)	*m*
Läuferscheibe (Rollenzellenpumpe)	*f*	rotor plate (roller-cell pump)	*n*	rotor à cages (pompe multicellulaire à rouleaux)	*m*
Läuferwelle	*f*	rotor shaft	*n*	arbre de rotor	*m*
Läuferwicklung	*f*	rotor winding	*n*	enroulement rotorique	*m*

Deutsch			Englisch		Französisch	
Lauffläche (Bremstrommel, Bremsscheibe)		*f*	contact surface (brake drum, brake disc)	*n*	surface de friction (tambour, disque de frein)	*f*
Laufgeräusch		*n*	running noise	*n*	bruits de fonctionnement	*mpl*
Laufgrenze		*f*	lean misfire limit, LML	*n*	limite de stabilité du moteur	*f*
Laufkultur (Verbrennungsmotor)		*f*	smooth running (IC engine)	*n*	fonctionnement régulier (moteur à combustion)	*m*
Laufrad (Peripheralpumpe)		*n*	impeller ring (peripheral pump)	*n*	rotor (pompe à accélération périphérique)	*m*
Laufradschaufel (Elektrokraftstoffpumpe)		*f*	impeller blade (electric fuel pump)	*n*	ailette de rotor (pompe électrique à carburant)	*f*
Laufrolle (Rollenbremsprüfstand)		*f*	drive roller (dynamic brake analyzer)	*n*	rouleau d'entraînement (banc d'essai)	*m*
Laufruhe (Verbrennungsmotor)		*f*	smooth running (IC engine)	*n*	fonctionnement régulier (moteur à combustion)	*m*
Laufruheintegrator		*m*	cylinder-balancing integrator	*n*	intégrateur de régulation poste à poste	*m*
Laufruheregelung		*f*	smooth-running control	*n*	régulation de la stabilité de fonctionnement	*f*
Laufruheregler		*m*	smooth-running regulator	*n*	régulateur de la stabilité de fonctionnement	*m*
Laufunruhe		*f*	uneven running	*v*	instabilité de fonctionnement	*f*
Laufzeitelektronik		*f*	elapsed-time electronics	*n*	horamètre électronique	*m*
Lebensdauer		*f*	service life	*n*	durabilité	*f*
Leckage	x	*f*	leakage	*n*	fuite	*f*
Leckgas		*n*	blowby gas	*n*	gaz de fuite	*mpl*
Leckkraftstoff		*m*	leak fuel	*n*	carburant de fuite	*m*
Leckkraftstoff-Rückführung		*f*	leakage-return duct	*n*	canal de retour des fuites	*m*
Leckkraftstoffmenge		*f*	leak-fuel quantity	*n*	débit de carburant de fuite	*m*
Leckkraftstoffsperre (Einspritzpumpe)		*f*	oil block (fuel-injection pump)	*n*	barrage d'huile (pompe d'injection)	*m*
Leckmenge		*f*	leak-fuel quantity	*n*	débit de carburant de fuite	*m*
Lecköl	+	*n*	leak fuel	*n*	carburant de fuite	*m*
Leckölanschluß		*m*	leakage-fuel connection	*n*	raccord d'huile de fuite	*m*
lecköllose Düse		*f*	non-leak-off nozzle	*n*	injecteur sans retour de fuite	*m*
Leckölrücklauf		*m*	leakage-return duct	*n*	canal de retour des fuites	*m*
Leckrückführnut		*f*	leakage-return slot	*n*	rainure de retour des fuites	*f*
Leckrückführung	+	*f*	leakage-return duct	*n*	canal de retour des fuites	*m*
Lecksperre	x	*f*	oil block (fuel-injection pump)	*n*	barrage d'huile (pompe d'injection)	*m*
Leckstrom		*m*	leakage flow	*n*	courant de fuite	*m*
Leckverlust		*m*	leakage losses	*npl*	pertes par fuites	*fpl*
Leergasschalter		*m*	low-idle switch	*n*	contacteur de ralenti	*m*
Leerkupplung		*f*	coupling holder	*n*	accouplement borgne	*m*
Leerlauf		*m*	idle	*n*	ralenti	*m*
Leerlauf- und Enddrehzahlregler		*m*	minimum-maximum-speed governor	*n*	régulateur mini-maxi	*m*
Leerlauf- und Endregler		*m*	minimum-maximum-speed governor	*n*	régulateur mini-maxi	*m*
Leerlauf-Fördermenge		*f*	idle delivery	*n*	débit de ralenti	*m*

Deutsch		Englisch		Französisch	
Leerlauf-Solldrehzahl	*f*	low-idle setpoint speed	*n*	régime consigne de ralenti	*m*
Leerlauf-Zusatzfeder	*f*	auxiliary idle-speed spring	*n*	ressort additionnel de ralenti	*m*
Leerlaufanhebung	*f*	idle-speed increase	*n*	ralenti accéléré	*m*
Leerlaufanschlag	*m*	low-idle stop	*n*	butée de ralenti	*f*
Leerlaufanschlagschraube	*f*	idle-speed stop screw	*n*	vis de butée de ralenti	*f*
Leerlaufbetrieb (Druckregler)	*m*	idle (pressure regulator)	*v*	fonctionnement à vide (régulateur de pression)	*m*
Leerlaufdrehsteller	*m*	rotary idle actuator	*n*	actionneur rotatif de ralenti	*m*
Leerlaufdrehzahl	*f*	idle speed	*n*	vitesse de ralenti	*f*
Leerlaufdrehzahlregelung	*f*	idle-speed control	*n*	régulation de la vitesse de ralenti	*f*
Leerlaufeinstellpunkt	*m*	idle-speed adjustment point	*n*	point de réglage de ralenti	*m*
Leerlauffeder	*f*	idle-speed spring	*n*	ressort de ralenti	*m*
Leerlaufintegrator	*m*	low-idle integrator	*n*	intégrateur de ralenti	*m*
Leerlaufkennlinie	*f*	no-load charcteristic	*n*	caractéristique à vide	*f*
Leerlaufkolben (Lufttrockner)	*m*	idle piston (air drier)	*n*	piston de marche à vide (dessiccateur)	*m*
Leerlaufkontakt	*m*	idle contact	*n*	contact de ralenti	*m*
Leerlaufmenge	+ *f*	idle delivery	*n*	débit de ralenti	*m*
Leerlaufregelung, LLR	*f*	idle-speed control	*n*	régulation de la vitesse de ralenti	*f*
Leerlaufregler	*m*	idle controller	*n*	correcteur de ralenti	*m*
Leerlaufstabilisierung	*f*	idle stabilization	*n*	stabilisation du ralenti	*f*
Leerlaufsteller	*m*	idle actuator	*n*	actionneur de ralenti	*m*
Leerlaufstufe	*f*	idle-speed stage	*n*	étage de ralenti	*m*
Leerlaufventil	*n*	idle valve	*n*	soupape de marche à vide	*f*
Lehnenverstellung	*f*	backrest adjuster	*n*	réglage du dossier de siège	*m*
Leichtmetallgehäuse	*n*	light-metal housing	*n*	carter en alliage léger	*m*
Leiselaufvorrichtung	*f*	smooth-idle device	*n*	dispositif d'injection différée	*m*
Leistungsabgabe (elektrische Maschinen)	*f*	power output (electrical machines)	*n*	puissance débitée (machines électriques)	*f*
Leistungsaufnahme	*f*	power input	*n*	puissance absorbée	*f*
Leistungsbedarf (Stromverbraucher)	*m*	electrical load requirements	*n*	puissance des récepteurs	*f*
Leistungsdiode	*f*	power diode	*n*	diode de puissance	*f*
Leistungsendstufe (Steuergerät)	*f*	driver stage (ECU)	*n*	étage de sortie (calculateur)	*m*
Leistungsmodul	*m*	power module	*n*	module de puissance	*m*
Leistungsrelais	*n*	power relay	*n*	relais de puissance	*m*
Leistungsschalter	*m*	circuit breaker	*n*	interrupteur de circuit	*m*
Leistungsstufe (Steuergerät)	*f*	power stage (ECU)	*n*	étage de puissance (calculateur)	*m*
Leistungsteil (Zündsystem)	*n*	power section (ignition system)	*n*	bloc de puissance (allumage)	*m*
Leistungstransistor	*m*	power transistor	*n*	transistor de puissance	*m*
Leistungsverlust	*m*	performance drop	*n*	perte de puissance	*f*
Leistungszone (Kohlebürste)	*f*	power zone (carbon brush)	*n*	partie puissance (balai)	*f*
Leiterbahn	*f*	conductor	*n*	piste de contact	*f*
Leiterfolie (Drehwinkelsensor)	*f*	conductive foil (angle of rotation sensor)	*n*	feuille conductrice (capteur d'angle de rotation)	*f*
Leiterplatte	*f*	printed-circuit board	*n*	carte à circuit imprimé	*f*

Deutsch		Englisch		Französisch	
Leiterplattenrelais	*n*	PC-board relay	*n*	relais pour cartes imprimées	*m*
Leiterquerschnitt	*m*	conductor cross section	*n*	section du conducteur	*f*
Leiterschleife	*f*	conductor loop	*n*	boucle conductrice	*f*
Leitstück	*n*	conductive element	*n*	pièce conductrice	*f*
Leitstückläufer (Generator)	*m*	windingless rotor (alternator)	*n*	rotor à pièce conductrice (alternateur)	*m*
Leitungsberechnung	*f*	calculation of conductor sizes	*n*	calcul des conducteurs	*m*
Leitungsbruch (Bremssystem)	*m*	line break (braking system)	*n*	rupture de conduite (système de freinage)	*f*
Leitungsdruck	*m*	line pressure	*n*	pression dans conduite	*f*
Leitungseinbaupumpe	*f*	in-line pump (fuel supply)	*n*	pompe sur conduite	*f*
Leitungsfilter	*n*	line filter	*n*	filtre de conduite	*m*
Leitungskreuzung	*f*	conductor crossover	*n*	croisement de conducteurs	*m*
lenkbar (Kfz)	*adj*	steerable (motor vehicle)	*adj*	dirigeable (véhicule)	*adj*
Lenkbarkeit	*f*	steerability	*n*	dirigeabilité	*f*
Lenkdrehachse	*f*	steering axis	*n*	axe de pivotement de la direction	*m*
Lenkhebel	*m*	linkage lever	*n*	levier articulé	*m*
Lenkhilfpumpe	*f*	power-steering pump	*n*	pompe de direction assistée	*f*
Lenkradmoment (Kfz-Dynamik)	*n*	steering-wheel force (vehicle dynamics)	*n*	couple appliqué au volant de direction (dynamique d'un véhicule)	*m*
Lenkradverstellung	*f*	steering-wheel positioner	*n*	positionneur de volant	*m*
Lenkradwinkelsensor (ESP)	*m*	steering-wheel angle sensor (ESP)	*n*	capteur d'angle de braquage (ESP)	*m*
Lenksprung	*m*	sudden steering input (vehicle dynamics)	*n*	réaction transitoire de lacet (dynamique d'un véhicule)	*f*
lenkunfähig (Kfz)	*adj*	unsteerable (motor vehicle)	*adj*	incontrôlable (véhicule)	*adj*
Lenkwinkel (Kfz-Dynamik)	*m*	steering angle (vehicle dynamics)	*n*	angle de braquage (dynamique d'un véhicule)	*m*
Lenkwinkelsprung (Kfz-Dynamik)	*m*	sudden steering input (vehicle dynamics)	*n*	réaction transitoire de lacet (dynamique d'un véhicule)	*f*
Lenkwinkelverlauf	*m*	steering-angle characteristic	*n*	évolution de l'angle de braquage	*f*
Leseleuchte	*f*	reading lamp	*n*	lampe de lecture	*f*
Leuchtdichte (Lichttechnik)	*f*	luminance (lighting)	*n*	luminance (éclairage)	*f*
Leuchte	*f*	lamp	*n*	feu	*m*
Leuchtengehäuse	*n*	lamp housing	*n*	boîtier de feu	*m*
Leuchtkörper	*m*	light source	*n*	lampe	*f*
Leuchtweiteeinstellung	*f*	headlight leveling (manually operated)	*n*	correction de la portée d'éclairement	*f*
Leuchtweitenregelung, LWR	*f*	headlight leveling control	*n*	correcteur de site des projecteurs	*m*
Leuchtweiteregler, LWR	*m*	headlight leveling control	*n*	correcteur de site	*m*
Lichtablenkung	*f*	light deflection	*n*	déviation de la lumière	*f*
Lichtabsorptionsmeßgerät	*n*	opacimeter	*n*	opacimètre	*m*
Lichtaustrittsfläche (Lichttechnik)	*f*	lens aperture area (lighting)	*n*	surface de sortie de la lumière (éclairage)	*f*
Lichtbandeinheit	*f*	lighting-strip unit	*n*	bande d'éclairage	*f*

Deutsch		Englisch		Französisch	
Lichtfilter	*n*	light filter	*n*	filtre (projecteur)	*m*
Lichthupe	*f*	headlamp flasher	*n*	signal optique	*m*
Lichtleitring (Autoalarm)	*m*	wire loop (car alarm)	*n*	câble en boucle (alarme auto)	*m*
Lichtscheibe (Leuchte)	*f*	lens (lamp)	*n*	glace de diffusion (feu)	*f*
Lichtsignal	*n*	visual signal	*n*	signal lumineux	*m*
Lichtstärke	*f*	luminous intensity	*n*	intensité lumineuse	*f*
Lichtstrom	*m*	luminous flux	*n*	flux lumineux	*m*
Lichttechnik	*f*	lighting techniques	*n*	technique d'éclairage	*f*
Lichtverteilung (Lichttechnik)	*f*	light pattern (lighting)	*n*	répartition de la lumière (éclairage)	*f*
Lichtwellenleiter	*m*	optical waveguide	*n*	fibre optique	*f*
Lichtwischer	*m*	headlamp wiper	*n*	lavophare	*m*
Lichtwischeranlage	*f*	beamwash	*n*	lavophare	*m*
Lichtwischerarm	*m*	beamwash wiper-arm	*n*	bras de lavophare	*m*
Lichtwischerblatt	*n*	beamwash wiper-blade	*n*	raclette de lavophare	*f*
Lichtwischerhebel	*m*	beamwash wiper-lever	*n*	levier de lavophare	*m*
Lichtwischermotor	*m*	beamwash motor	*n*	moteur de lavophare	*m*
Liefergrad (Verbrennungsmotor)	*m*	volumetric efficiency (IC engine)	*n*	rendement volumétrique (moteur à combustion)	*m*
Liftachse	*f*	lifting axle	*n*	essieu relevable	*m*
Linearsteller (ASR)	*m*	linear actuator (TCS)	*n*	actionneur linéaire (ASR)	*m*
Linkslauf	*m*	counterclockwise rotation	*n*	rotation à gauche	*f*
Litronic (Scheinwerfer mit Gasentladungslampe)	*f*	Litronic (headlamp system with gaseous-discharge lamp)	*n*	Litronic (projecteur avec lampe à décharge)	*m*
Lochblende (Zusatzluftschieber)	*f*	perforated plate (auxiliary-air device)	*n*	diaphragme (commande d'air additionnel)	*m*
Lochdüse	*f*	hole-type nozzle	*n*	injecteur à trou(s)	*m*
Lochform (Einspritzdüse)	*f*	spray-hole shape (injector)	*n*	forme des trous d'injection	*f*
Lochlänge	*f*	spray-hole length	*n*	longueur des trous d'injection	*f*
Lochplatte	*f*	orifice plate	*n*	pastille perforée	*f*
Lochzapfendüse	*f*	hole pintle nozzle	*n*	injecteur à téton perforé	*m*
Löschdiode	*f*	decay diode	*n*	diode de décharge	*f*
Lösedauer (Bremse)	*f*	release time (brakes)	*n*	temps de desserrage (frein)	*m*
Lösedruck	*m*	release pressure	*n*	pression de desserrage	*f*
Löseeinrichtung (Federspeicherzylinder)	*f*	mechanical release (spring-type brake actuator)	*n*	dispositif de desserrage (cylindre à accumulateur élastique)	*m*
Lösestellung	*f*	release position	*n*	position de desserrage	*f*
Löseventil	*n*	release valve	*n*	valve de desserrage	*f*
Low-Rad (ABS) x	*n*	low wheel (ABS)	*n*	roue à sélection "basse" (ABS)	*f*
Luft-Kraftstoff-Gemisch	*n*	air-fuel mixture	*n*	mélange air-carburant	*m*
Luft-Kraftstoff-Verhältnis	*n*	air-fuel (A/F) ratio	*n*	rapport air-carburant	*m*
Luftansaugdeckel	*m*	intake cover	*n*	capot d'aération	*m*
Luftansaugstutzen	*m*	air-intake fitting	*n*	tubulure d'aspiration d'air	*f*
Luftanschluß	*m*	air connection	*n*	orifice d'air	*m*
Luftbedarf (Verbrennungsmotor)	*m*	air requirement (IC engine)	*n*	débit d'air nécessaire (moteur à combustion)	*m*

Deutsch		Englisch		Französisch	
Luftbehälter (Pneumatik)	*m*	compressed-air reservoir (pneumatics)	*n*	réservoir d'air comprimé (pneumatique)	*m*
Luftdichte	*f*	air density	*n*	densité atmosphérique	*f*
Luftdruck	*m*	air pressure	*n*	pression d'air	*f*
Luftdruck-Kontrollschalter	*m*	air-pressure sensor	*n*	contacteur de contrôle de pression d'air	*m*
Luftdurchsatz	*m*	air throughput	*n*	débit d'air (disponible)	*m*
Lüfter	*m*	fan	*n*	ventilateur	*m*
Lüftermotor	*m*	fan motor	*n*	moteur de soufflante	*m*
Lüfterschaufel	*f*	fan blade	*n*	ailette	*f*
Luftfeder	*f*	air spring	*n*	soufflet de suspension	*m*
Luftfeder-Ventileinheit	*f*	height-control-valve unit	*n*	bloc-valves (suspension pneumatique)	*m*
Luftfederanlage	*f*	pneumatic suspension	*n*	dispositif de suspension pneumatique	*m*
Luftfederbalg	*m*	air-spring bellows	*n*	soufflet à air	*m*
Luftfederung	*f*	pneumatic suspension	*n*	suspension pneumatique	*f*
Luftfederventil	*n*	height-control valve	*n*	valve de nivellement	*f*
Luftfilter	*n*	air filter	*n*	filtre à air	*m*
Luftfiltereinsatz	*m*	air-filter element	*n*	cartouche de filtre à air	*f*
Luftförderungsstellung (Druckregler)	*f*	air-supply position (pressure regulator)	*n*	position de refoulement	*f*
Luftfüllung	*f*	air charge	*n*	charge d'air	*f*
Luftfunken (Zündkerze)	*m*	air gap (spark plug)	*n*	étincelle dans l'air (bougie)	*f*
Luftfunkenstrecke (Zündkerze)	*f*	spark air gap (spark plug)	*n*	éclateur dans l'air (bougie)	*m*
Luftfunkentechnik (Zündkerze)	*f*	air-gap design (spark plug)	*n*	éclateur à étincelle dans l'air (bougie)	*m*
luftgekühlt	*pp*	air-cooled	*pp*	refroidi par air	*pp*
Luftgleitfunken (Zündkerze)	*m*	surface air-gap (spark plug)	*n*	étincelle glissante (bougie)	*f*
Luftgleitfunkenstrecke (Zündkerze)	*f*	semi-surface gap (spark plug)	*n*	distance d'éclatement et de glissement (bougie)	*f*
Luftkammer	*f*	air chamber	*n*	chambre d'air	*f*
Luftkissen (Sicherheitssystem)	*n*	airbag	*n*	coussin gonflable (système de retenue des passager)	*m*
Luftkompressor	*m*	air compressor	*n*	compresseur d'air	*m*
Luftkraft	*f*	air force (pneumatics)	*n*	force de l'air	*f*
Luftkühlung	*f*	air cooling	*n*	refroidissement par air	*m*
Luftmangel (Luft-Kraftstoff-Gemisch)	*m*	air deficiency (air-fuel mixture)	*n*	déficit d'air (mélange air-carburant)	*m*
Luftmasse	*f*	air mass	*n*	masse d'air	*f*
Luftmassendurchsatz	*m*	air-mass flow	*n*	débit massique d'air	*m*
Luftmassenmesser	*m*	air-mass meter	*n*	débitmètre massique d'air	*m*
Luftmengendurchsatz	*m*	air-quantity flow	*n*	débit volumique d'air	*m*
Luftmengenmesser	*m*	air-flow sensor	*n*	débitmètre d'air	*m*
Luftpumpe	*f*	air pump	*n*	pompe à air	*f*
Luftreiniger	*m*	air cleaner	*n*	épurateur d'air	*m*
Luftsack (Sicherheitssystem)	*m*	airbag	*n*	coussin gonflable (système de retenue des passager)	*m*
Luftspalt	*m*	air gap	*n*	entrefer	*m*

Deutsch		Englisch		Französisch	
Lüftspiel (Bremsbacken)	*n*	clearance (brake shoes)	*n*	jeu (segments de frein)	*m*
Luftsteuerung (Ansaugluft)	*f*	intake-air adjustment	*n*	commande de l'air d'admission	*f*
Lufttemperaturfühler	*m*	air-temperature sensor, ATS	*n*	capteur de température d'air	*m*
Lufttrichter (KE-Jetronic)	*m*	air funnel (KE-Jetronic)	*n*	divergent d'air (KE-Jetronic)	*m*
Lufttrockner	*m*	air drier	*n*	dessiccateur d'air	*m*
Luftüberschuß	*m*	excess air	*n*	excès d'air	*m*
Luftumfassung (Einspritzventil)	*f*	air-shrouding (fuel injector)	*n*	enveloppe d'air (injecteur)	*f*
Lüftung	*f*	ventilation	*n*	ventilation	*f*
Luftverhältnis	*n*	excess-air factor (lambda)	*n*	coefficient d'air (lambda)	*m*
Luftversorgung	*f*	air supply	*n*	alimentation en air	*f*
Luftverwirbelung	*f*	air turbulence	*n*	turbulence de l'air	*f*
Luftvorrat	*m*	compressed-air reserve	*n*	réserve d'air comprimé	*f*
Luftwiderstand	*m*	aerodynamic drag	*n*	résistance de l'air	*f*
Luftwiderstandsbeiwert	*m*	drag coefficient	*n*	coefficient de pénétration dans l'air	*m*
Luftzahl (Lambda)	*f*	excess-air factor (lambda)	*n*	coefficient d'air (lambda)	*m*
Luxmeter	*n*	luxmeter	*n*	luxmètre	*m*
M					
mager (Luft-Kraftstoff-Gemisch)	*adj*	lean (air-fuel-mixture)	*adj*	pauvre (mélange air-carburant)	*adj*
Magerkonzept	*n*	lean-burn concept	*n*	concept à mélange pauvre	*m*
Magermotor	*m*	lean-burn engine	*n*	moteur pour mélange pauvre	*m*
Magnetanker	*m*	solenoid armature	*n*	armature d'électro-aimant	*f*
Magnetfeld	*n*	magnetic field	*n*	champ magnétique	*m*
Magnetfeldsensor	*m*	magnetic-field sensor	*n*	capteur de champ magnétique	*m*
Magnetisierungsverlust	*m*	magnetization loss	*n*	pertes d'aimantation	*fpl*
Magnetkreis	*m*	magnetic circuit	*n*	circuit magnétique	*m*
Magnetkupplung	*f*	solenoid-operated coupling	*n*	accouplement électromagnétique	*m*
Magnetrelaisventil	*n*	solenoid relay valve	*n*	électrovalve-relais	*f*
Magnetsteller	*n*	solenoid actuator	*n*	actionneur électromagnétique	*m*
Magnetventil	*n*	solenoid valve	*n*	électrovalve	*f*
Magnetventilblock	*m*	solenoid-valve block	*n*	bloc d'électrovalves	*m*
Magnetwicklung	*f*	solenoid winding	*n*	bobine d'électro-aimant	*f*
Manipulationsschutz	*m*	protection against manipulation	*n*	protection contre manipulation	*f*
Mantelblech (Zündspule)	*n*	metal jacket (ignition coil)	*n*	enveloppe à lamelles (bobine d'allumage)	*f*
Maßbild	*n*	dimensional drawing	*n*	croquis coté	*m*
Masse (Fahrzeugmasse)	*f*	vehicle ground	*n*	masse (du véhicule)	*f*
Masse (Gehäusemasse)	*f*	equipment ground	*n*	masse (du boîtier)	*f*
Masseelektrode	*f*	ground electrode	*n*	électrode de masse	*f*
Masseleitung	*f*	ground cable	*n*	câble de retour à la masse	*m*
Massenträgheitsmoment	*n*	mass moment of inertia	*n*	moment d'inertie	*m*
Masserückführung	*f*	ground return	*n*	retour par la masse	*m*
Masserückleitung	*f*	ground cable	*n*	câble de retour à la masse	*m*
Masseverbindung	*f*	ground connection	*n*	mise à la terre	*f*
Maximal-Mengenanschlag	*m*	full-load stop	*n*	butée de débit maximal	*f*

Deutsch		Englisch		Französisch	
mechanisch entriegelte Startmenge	*f*	mechanically controlled starting quantity	*n*	surcharge à déverrouillage mécanique	*f*
mechanische Abstellvorrichtung, MEAB	*f*	mechanical shutoff device	*n*	dispositif d'arrêt mécanique	*m*
mechanischer Regler	*m*	mechanical governor	*n*	régulateur mécanique	*m*
Mehrfachschwingrohr	*n*	multi-tract runner	*n*	collecteur d'admission multitubes	*m*
Mehrkammerleuchte	*f*	multiple-compartment lamp	*n*	feu à plusieurs compartiments	*m*
Mehrkreis-Bremsanlage	*f*	multi-circuit braking system	*n*	dispositif de freinage à circuits multiples	*m*
Mehrkreisschutzventil	*n*	multiple-circuit protection valv‹	*n*	valve de sécurité multicircuits	*f*
Mehrleitungs-Bremsanlage	*f*	multi-line braking system	*n*	dispositif de freinage à conduites multiples	*m*
Mehrlochdüse	*f*	multihole nozzle	*n*	injecteur multitrous	*m*
Mehrlochzumessung (Einspritzventil)	*f*	multi-orifice metering	*n*	dosage multitrous (injecteur)	*m*
Mehrphasenwicklung	*f*	polyphase winding	*n*	enroulement multiphases	*m*
Mehrscheibenkupplung	*f*	multiplate clutch	*n*	embrayage multidisques	*m*
Mehrstoffbetrieb	*m*	multifuel operation	*n*	fonctionnement polycarburant	*m*
Mehrstoffmotor	*m*	multifuel engine	*n*	moteur polycarburant	*m*
Mehrstoffpumpe	*f*	multifuel pump	*n*	pompe polycarburant	*f*
Mehrzylinder-Einspritzpumpe	*f*	multiple-plunger pump	*n*	pompe multicylindrique	*f*
Membrandose	*f*	diaphragm unit	*n*	capsule à membrane	*f*
Membrandruckregler	*m*	diaphragm governor	*n*	régulateur de pression à membrane	*m*
Membrankolben	*m*	diaphragm piston	*n*	piston à joint embouti	*m*
Membranplatte	*f*	diaphragm plate	*n*	plaque-membrane	*f*
Membranpumpe	*f*	diaphragm pump	*n*	pompe à membrane	*f*
Membranventil	*n*	diaphragm valve	*n*	valve à membrane	*f*
Membranzylinder	*m*	diaphragm-type cylinder	*n*	cylindre à membrane	*m*
Mengenabgleich	*m*	fuel-quantity compensation	*n*	étalonnage de débit	*m*
Mengenabstellung	*f*	fuel shutoff	*n*	suspension de débit	*f*
Mengendrift	*f*	fuel-quantity drift	*n*	dérive de débit	*f*
Mengeneingriff	*m*	fuel-quantity command	*n*	action sur débit	*f*
Mengenendstufe	*f*	fuel-quantity power stage	*n*	étage de sortie de débit	*f*
Mengeninkrement	*n*	fuel-quantity increment	*n*	incrément de débit	*m*
Mengenkennfeld	*n*	fuel-quantity map	*n*	cartographie de débit	*f*
Mengenkorrektur	*f*	injected-fuel-quantity correctio‹	*n*	correction de débit d'injection	*f*
Mengenreduzierung	*f*	reduced delivery	*n*	réduction de débit	*f*
Mengenregelung	*f*	fuel-delivery control	*n*	régulation des débits d'injection	*f*
Mengenschwellwert	*m*	fuel-quantity threshold value	*n*	valeur de seuil de débit	*f*
Mengenstellersollwert	*m*	fuel-quantity positioner setpoint value	*n*	valeur consigne de l'actionneur de débit	*f*
Mengenstellglied	*n*	fuel-quantity positioner	*n*	actionneur de débit	*m*
Mengenteiler	*m*	fuel distributor	*n*	doseur-distributeur de carburan‹	*m*
Mengenteilerblock	*m*	fuel-distributor block	*n*	groupe doseur-distributeur	*m*
Mengenüberhöhung	*f*	excess fuel quantity	*n*	surcroît de débit	*m*
Mengenwunsch	*m*	fuel-quantity demand	*n*	demande de débit	*f*

Deutsch		Englisch		Französisch	
Meß- und Steuereinheit	*f*	measuring and control unit	*n*	bloc de mesure et de command‹	*m*
Meßdatenerfassung	*f*	measuring-data acquisition	*n*	saisie des mesures	*f*
Meßelement	*n*	measuring element	*n*	élément de mesure	*m*
Meßfühler	*m*	sensor	*n*	capteur	*m*
Meßgas (Abgasprüfung)	*n*	test gas (exhaust-gas test)	*n*	gaz de mesure (émissions)	*m*
Meßgewicht	*n*	measurement weight	*n*	poids de mesure	*m*
Meßkammer (CO-Gas)	*f*	measuring chamber (exhaust-gas test)	*n*	chambre de mesure (gaz CO)	*f*
Meßküvette (Abgasprüfung)	*f*	measuring cell (exhaust-gas test)	*n*	cuvette de mesure (émissions)	*f*
Meßwertsensor (Rollenbremsprüfstand)	*m*	measuring sensor (dynamic brake analyzer)	*n*	capteur de mesure (banc d'essai)	*m*
Meßzündkerze	*f*	thermocouple spark plug	*n*	bougie thermocouple	*f*
Metallabschirmkappe	*f*	metal screening cover	*n*	blindage métallique	*m*
Metallgeflecht (Katalysator)	*n*	metal mesh (catalytic converter	*n*	grille métallique (catalyseur)	*f*
Mikro-Doppelkante (Wischgummi)	*f*	double microedge (wiper blade`	*n*	double micro-arête (raclette en caoutchouc)	*f*
Mikrocontroller, MC (Steuergerät)	*m*	microcontroller, MC (ECU)	*n*	microcontrôleur (calculateur)	*m*
Mikromechanik	*f*	micromechanics	*npl*	micromécanique	*f*
Mikrorelais	*n*	microrelay	*n*	microrelais	*m*
Mindermenge	*f*	reduced delivery	*n*	réduction de débit	*f*
Mindermengenanschlag	*m*	reduced-delivery stop	*n*	butée de réduction de débit	*f*
Mindermengeneinsteller	*m*	fuel-flow reducing device	*n*	réducteur de débit	*m*
Mindestabbremsung	*f*	minimum retardation	*n*	taux de freinage minimum	*m*
Mindestbremswirkung	*f*	minimum braking effect	*n*	freinage minimal	*m*
Mindestdrehzahl	*f*	minimum speed	*n*	vitesse de rotation minimale	*f*
Mineralöl-Bremsflüssigkeit	*f*	mineral-oil-based brake fluid	*n*	liquide de frein à base d'huile minérale	*m*
Minimalwertoperator	*m*	minimum-value operator	*n*	opérateur à valeur minimale	*m*
Minusdiode	*f*	negative diode	*n*	diode négative	*f*
Minusplatte (Batterie)	*f*	negative plate (battery)	*n*	plaque négative (batterie)	*f*
Mischölabführung	*f*	emulsion drain	*n*	évacuation des émulsions	*f*
Mischspannungsmotor	*m*	pulsating-voltage motor	*n*	moteur à tension composée	*m*
Mitnehmer (Generator)	*m*	driver (alternator)	*n*	entraîneur (alternateur)	*m*
Mitnehmerbolzen (Luftfederventil)	*m*	driver pin (height-control valve	*n*	axe d'entraînement (suspension pneumatique)	*m*
Mitteldom (Zündspule)	*m*	center tower (ignition coil)	*n*	sortie centrale (bobine d'allumage)	*f*
Mittelelektrode	*f*	center electrode	*n*	électrode centrale	*f*
Mittellamelle (Generator)	*f*	center lamination (alternator)	*n*	lamelle centrale (alternateur)	*f*
Mittelleiter	*m*	neutral conductor	*n*	conducteur neutre	*m*
Mittelschalldämpfer	*m*	exhaust-gas center silencer	*n*	silencieux médian	*m*
Mittelspannung	*f*	medium voltage, MV	*n*	tension moyenne	*f*
Mittelstellung	*f*	intermediate setting	*n*	position médiane	*f*
Mobile Kommunikation	*f*	mobile communications	*npl*	communications mobiles	*fpl*
modifizierte Individual-regelung, IRM (ABS)	*f*	modified individual control, IRM (ABS)	*n*	régulation individuelle modifiée (ABS)	*f*

Deutsch			Englisch		Französisch	
Modulationsdruck (Getriebesteuerung)		*m*	modulation pressure (transmission control)	*n*	pression de modulation (commande de boîte de vitesses)	*f*
Modultechnik		*f*	modular system	*n*	technique modulaire	*f*
Molekularfilter (Lufttrockner)		*n*	molecular filter (air drier)	*n*	filtre moléculaire (dessiccateur)	*m*
Molekularsieb (Lufttrockner)		*n*	molecular filter (air drier)	*n*	filtre moléculaire (dessiccateur)	*m*
Momentenbilanz (ASR)		*f*	torque balance (TCS)	*n*	bilan des couples des roues motrices (ASR)	*m*
Monolith (Katalysator)		*m*	monolith (catalytic converter)	*n*	support monolythique (catalyseur)	*m*
Monolithregler		*m*	monolithic regulator	*n*	régulateur monolithe	*m*
Monolithtechnik		*f*	monolithic techniques	*npl*	technique monolithe	*f*
Montageanleitung		*f*	installation instructions	*npl*	notice de montage	*f*
Montagehinweis		*m*	assembly instructions	*n*	instruction de montage	*f*
Montagezahl		*f*	assembly number	*n*	numéro de montage	*m*
Motor-Bremsanlage		*f*	exhaust brake	*n*	ralentisseur sur échappement	*m*
Motor-Oktanzahl, MOZ		*f*	motor octane number, MON	*n*	indice d'octane moteur, MON	*m*
Motoranker (Elektrokraftstoffpumpe)		*m*	motor armature (electric fuel pump)	*n*	induit du moteur (pompe électrique à carburant)	*m*
Motorbremse	x	*f*	exhaust brake	*n*	ralentisseur sur échappement	*m*
Motorbremsmoment		*n*	engine braking torque	*n*	couple de freinage du moteur	*m*
Motorbremswirkung		*f*	engine braking action	*n*	effet de frein moteur	*m*
Motordiagnose		*f*	engine diagnosis	*n*	diagnostic du moteur	*m*
Motordrehzahl		*f*	engine speed	*n*	vitesse de rotation du moteur	*f*
Motoreingriff (ASR)		*m*	engine intervention (TCS)	*n*	intervention sur le moteur (ASR)	*f*
Motorelastizität (Verbrennungsmotor)		*f*	engine flexibility	*n*	élasticité du moteur	*f*
Motorkennfeld		*n*	engine map	*n*	cartographie moteur	*f*
Motorlast		*f*	engine load	*n*	charge du moteur	*f*
Motorleistung		*f*	engine performance	*n*	puissance du moteur	*f*
Motormanagement		*f*	engine management	*n*	gestion des fonctions du moteur	*f*
Motorölkreislauf		*m*	engine lube-oil circuit	*n*	circuit de lubrification du moteur	*m*
Motorprüfstand		*m*			banc d'essai de moteurs	*m*
Motorregelkreis (ASR)		*m*	engine-control circuit (TCS)	*n*	circuit de régulation du moteur (ASR)	*m*
Motorregler (ASR)		*m*	engine controller (TCS)	*n*	régulateur du moteur (ASR)	*m*
Motorrelais (ABS)		*n*	motor relay (ABS)	*n*	relais de commande de moteur (ABS)	*m*
Motorschleppmoment		*n*	engine-drag torque	*n*	couple d'inertie du moteur	*m*
Motorschleppmoment-regelung, MSR		*f*	engine drag-torque control	*n*	régulation du couple d'inertie du moteur	*f*
Motorschmieröl-Kreislauf		*m*	engine lube-oil circuit	*n*	circuit de lubrification du moteur	*m*
Motorsteuergerät		*n*	engine control unit	*n*	centrale de commande du moteur	*f*
Motorsteuerung		*n*	engine management	*n*	gestion des fonctions du moteur	*f*
Motortemperatursensor		*m*	engine-temperature sensor	*n*	capteur de température moteur	*m*

Deutsch			Englisch		Französisch	
Motortester	x	*m*	engine analyzer	*n*	testeur pour moteur	*m*
Motortestgerät		*n*	engine analyzer	*n*	testeur pour moteur	*m*
Motorträgheit		*f*	engine inertia	*n*	inertie du moteur	*f*
Motorträgheitsmoment		*n*	engine-drag torque	*n*	couple d'inertie du moteur	*m*
Motorzylinder		*m*	engine cylinder	*n*	cylindre moteur	*m*
Motronic (elektronische Motorsteuerung)		*f*	Motronic (electronic engine management)	*n*	Motronic (système électronique de gestion du moteur)	*m*
Muffenweg (Diesel-Regler)		*m*	sliding-sleeve travel (governor)	*n*	course du manchon central (injection diesel)	*f*
Muldenwand		*f*	piston-recess wall	*n*	paroi de la cavité du piston	*f*
Multi-Focus-Reflektor, MFR		*m*	Multi-Focus-Reflector, MFR	*n*	réflecteur multifocal	*m*
multiplikativer Abgleich		*m*	multiplicative adjustment	*n*	étalonnage multiplicatif	*m*
Multiplizierstufe (elektronisches Steuergerät)		*f*	multiplying stage (ECU)	*n*	étage multiplicateur (calculateur)	*m*
Multivibrator		*m*	multivibrator	*n*	multivibrateur	*m*
Muskelkraft (Bremsbetätigung)		*f*	muscular force (brake control)	*n*	force musculaire (commande de frein)	*f*
Muskelkraft-Bremsanlage		*f*	muscular-energy braking system	*n*	dispositif de freinage à énergie musculaire	*m*
Musterbau		*m*	prototype manufacture	*n*	réalisation d'échantillons	*f*
N						
Nacheilung (Anhängerbremse)		*f*	negative offset (trailer brake)	*n*	retard de phase (frein de remorque)	*m*
Nacheinspritzung		*f*	secondary injection	*n*	injection secondaire	*f*
Nachentflammung		*f*	post-ignition	*n*	post-allumage	*m*
Nachfilter		*n*	secondary filter	*n*	filtre secondaire	*m*
Nachfördereffekt		*m*	post-delivery effect	*n*	effet de post-refoulement	*m*
Nachfördermenge		*f*	secondary delivery quantity	*n*	débit de post-refoulement	*m*
nachglühen		*v*	post-glow	*n*	post-incandescence	*f*
Nachglühzeit		*f*	post-glow time	*n*	temps de post-incandescence	*m*
Nachheizphase		*f*	hot-soak phase	*n*	phase de post-chauffage	*f*
Nachladeeffekt		*m*	boost effect	*n*	effet de "postcharge"	*m*
Nachlauf		*m*	after-run	*n*	post-fonctionnement	*m*
Nachlaufachse		*f*	trailing axle	*n*	essieu suiveur	*m*
Nachlaufbohrung (Tandemhauptzylinder)		*f*	snifter bore (tandem master cylinder)	*n*	canal d'équilibrage (maître-cylindre tandem)	*m*
Nachrüstsatz		*m*	supplementary-equipment set	*n*	jeu d'équipement ultérieur	*m*
Nachschalldämpfer		*m*	rear muffler	*n*	silencieux arrière	*m*
nachspritzen		*v*	post-injection	*n*	post-injection	*f*
Nachspritzer (Dieseleinspritzung)		*m*	dribble (diesel fuel injection)	*n*	bavage (injection diesel)	*m*
Nachstart	x	*m*	post-start phase	*n*	phase de post-démarrage	*f*
Nachstartanhebung	+	*f*	post-start enrichment	*n*	enrichissement de post-démarrage	*m*
Nachstartanreicherung		*f*	post-start enrichment	*n*	enrichissement de post-démarrage	*m*
Nachstartphase		*f*	post-start phase	*n*	phase de post-démarrage	*f*
nachtropfen		*v*	fuel dribble	*n*	bavage de carburant	*m*
Nachverbrennung		*f*	afterburning	*n*	post-combustion	*f*

Deutsch			Englisch		Französisch	
Nadelbewegungsfühler, NBF		*m*	needle-motion sensor	*n*	capteur de déplacement d'aiguille	*m*
Nadelbewegungssensor		*m*	needle-motion sensor	*n*	capteur de déplacement d'aiguille	*m*
Nadelführung		*f*	needle guide	*n*	guide-aiguille	*m*
Nadelgeschwindigkeitsfühler		*m*	needle-velocity sensor, NVS	*n*	capteur de vitesse d'aiguille	*m*
Nadelhub		*m*	needle lift	*n*	levée de l'aiguille	*f*
Nadelhubgeber		*m*	needle-lift sensor	*n*	capteur de levée d'aiguille	*m*
Nadelschließkraft		*f*	needle closing force	*n*	force de fermeture de l'aiguille	*f*
Nadelventil		*n*	needle valve	*n*	injecteur à aiguille	*m*
nageln	x	*v*	diesel knock	*n*	claquement	*m*
Nahentstörung		*f*	intensified interference suppression	*n*	antiparasitage renforcé	*m*
Napfdiode		*f*	cup diode	*n*	diode-boisseau	*f*
Naßreibwert		*m*	coefficient of wet friction	*n*	coefficient de frottement humide	*m*
Naßsiedepunkt (Bremsflüssigkeit)		*m*	wet boiling point (brake fluid)	*n*	point d'ébullition liquide humidifié (liquide de frein)	*m*
Navigationssystem		*n*	navigation system	*n*	système de navigation	*m*
Navigationssystem (Kfz)		*n*	navigation system (motor vehicle)	*n*	système de navigation (automobile)	*m*
Nebellicht	+	*n*	fog lamp	*n*	projecteur antibrouillard	*m*
Nebelscheinwerfer, NSW		*m*	fog lamp	*n*	projecteur antibrouillard	*m*
Nebelschlußleuchte		*f*	fog warning lamp	*n*	feu arrière de brouillard	*m*
Nebenaggregat		*n*	auxiliary system	*n*	groupe auxiliaire	*m*
Nebenbrennraum		*m*	whirl chamber	*n*	chambre de tourbillonnement	*f*
Nebenkammer		*f*	whirl chamber	*n*	chambre de tourbillonnement	*f*
Nebenkammermotor		*m*	turbulence-chamber engine	*n*	moteur à chambre de turbulence	*m*
Nebenschluß		*m*	shunt	*n*	dérivation	*f*
Nebenschlußfeld		*n*	shunt field	*n*	champ en dérivation	*m*
Nebenschlußmotor		*m*	shunt-wound motor	*n*	moteur à excitation shunt	*m*
Nebenschlußpfad		*m*	leakage path	*n*	chemin de fuite	*m*
Nebenschlußquerschnitt (Drosselklappe)		*m*	bypass cross-section (throttle valve)	*n*	canal en dérivation (papillon)	*m*
Nebenschlußwicklung		*f*	shunt winding	*n*	enroulement en dérivation	*m*
Nebenverbraucher (Druckluftanlage)		*mpl*	secondary loads (compressed-air system)	*npl*	récepteurs auxiliaires (dispositif de freinage à air comprimé)	*mpl*
Nebenverbraucherkreis		*m*	ancillary circuit	*n*	circuit des récepteurs auxiliaires	*m*
negative Angleichung		*f*	negative torque control	*n*	correction de débit négative	*f*
negativer Lenkrollradius		*m*	negative steering offset	*n*	déport négatif de l'axe du pivot de fusée	*m*
negativer Temperaturkoeffizient, NTC		*m*	negative temperature coefficient, NTC	*n*	coefficient de température négatif, CTN	*m*
Nehmerzylinder (Bremse)		*m*	slave cylinder (brakes)	*n*	cylindre récepteur (frein)	*m*
Neigungsschalter (Autoalarm)		*m*	tilt switch (car alarm)	*n*	contacteur d'inclinaison (alarme auto)	*m*
Neigungssensor		*m*	tilt sensor	*n*	capteur d'inclinaison	*m*

Deutsch		Englisch		Französisch	
Nenndrehmoment	*n*	nominal load torque	*n*	couple nominal	*m*
Nenndrehzahl	*f*	rated speed	*n*	vitesse de rotation nominale	*f*
Nenndruck	*m*	nominal pressure	*n*	pression nominale	*f*
Nennkapazität (Batterie)	*f*	nominal capacity (battery)	*n*	capacité nominale (batterie)	*f*
Nennlast	*f*	nominal load	*n*	charge nominale	*f*
Nennleistung (Batterie) +	*f*	nominal capacity (battery)	*n*	capacité nominale (batterie)	*f*
Nennspannung	*f*	nominal voltage	*n*	tension nominale	*f*
Nennstrom	*m*	rated current	*n*	courant de consigne	*m*
Netzstecker	*m*	mains plug	*n*	fiche secteur	*f*
neutralsteuern (Kfz)	*v*	neutral steer (motor vehicle)	*v*	neutre (conduite de véhicule en virage)	*adj*
Nickwinkel (Kfz-Dynamik)	*m*	pitch angle (vehicle dynamics)	*n*	angle de tangage (dynamique d'un véhicule)	*m*
Niederdruck-Bremsanlage	*f*	low-pressure braking system	*n*	dispositif de freinage à basse pression	*m*
Niederdruckanlage	*f*	low-pressure braking system	*n*	dispositif de freinage à basse pression	*m*
Niederdruckförderung	*f*	low-pressure delivery	*n*	refoulement basse pression	*m*
Niederdruckkreislauf	*m*	low-pressure system	*n*	circuit basse pression	*m*
Niederdruckprüfung (Radzylinder)	*f*	low-pressure test (wheel-brake cylinder)	*n*	essai de basse pression (cylindre de roue)	*m*
Niederdruckraum	*m*	low-pressure chamber	*n*	chambre basse pression	*f*
Niederdruckteil	*n*	low-pressure stage	*n*	partie basse pression	*f*
Niveaugeber (Luftfederung)	*m*	level sensor (air suspension)	*n*	capteur de niveau (suspension pneumatique)	*m*
Niveauregelung	*f*	level control	*n*	régulation électronique du niveau	*f*
Nockenablauf	*m*	cam profile	*n*	profil de came	*m*
Nockenbremse	*f*	cam brake	*n*	frein à cames	*m*
Nockenfolge	*f*	cam sequence	*n*	ordre des cames	*m*
Nockenform	*f*	cam shape	*n*	forme de came	*f*
Nockenhöhe	*f*	cam lift	*n*	course de came	*f*
Nockenhub	*m*	cam pitch	*n*	levée de came	*f*
Nockenlaufbahn	*f*	cam track	*n*	piste de came	*f*
Nockenlaufrolle	*f*	camshaft roller	*n*	galet de palpage de la came	*m*
Nockenring	*m*	cam ring	*n*	bague à cames	*f*
Nockenscheibe	*f*	cam plate	*n*	disque à cames	*m*
Nockenversatz	*m*	angular cam spacing	*n*	écart angulaire de came	*m*
Nockenversetzung	*f*	angular cam spacing	*n*	écart angulaire de came	*m*
Nockenwellen-Drehzahlsensor	*m*	camshaft speed sensor	*n*	capteur de vitesse de rotation de l'arbre à cames	*m*
Nockenwellen-Vorstehmaß	*n*	camshaft projection	*n*	cote de dépassement de l'arbre à cames	*f*
Nockenwellensteuerung	*f*	camshaft control	*n*	commande de l'arbre à cames	*f*
Nockenwellenumschaltung	*f*	camshaft lobe control	*n*	variation du calage de l'arbre à cames	*f*
Nockenwinkel	*m*	angle of cam rotation	*n*	angle de levée de came	*m*
Noniusgeber	*m*	vernier sensor	*n*	capteur vernier	*m*
Normalhorn	*n*	standard horn	*n*	avertisseur sonore standard	*m*

Deutsch			Englisch			Französisch	
Normalkraft		*f*	normal force		*n*	force normale	*f*
Normalniveau (Luftfederung)		*n*	normal level (air suspension)		*n*	niveau normal (suspension pneumatique)	*f*
Normgeber		*m*	standard sensor		*n*	capteur de référence	*m*
Notabstellung		*f*	emergency shutoff		*n*	arrêt d'urgence	*m*
Notbremsung		*f*	panic braking		*n*	freinage en situation de panique	*m*
Notfahrbetrieb		*m*	limp-home operation		*n*	fonctionnement en mode dégradé	*m*
Notfahrfunktion		*f*	limp-home function		*n*	fonction "mode dégradé"	*f*
Notfahrstellregler		*m*	limp-home position governor		*n*	régulateur de roulage en mode incidenté	*m*
Nothahn (Türbetätigung)		*m*	emergency valve (door control		*n*	robinet de secours (commande des portes)	*m*
Notlauf		*m*	limp-home	x	*n*	mode dégradé	*m*
Notlauffunktion		*f*	limp-home function		*n*	fonction "mode dégradé"	*f*
Notluft	x	*f*	limp-home air		*n*	débit d'air minimum de secours	*m*
NTC-Widerstand		*m*	NTC resistor		*n*	thermistance CTN	*f*
Nullasttdrehzahl		*f*	idle speed		*n*	vitesse de ralenti	*f*
Nullförderlinie		*f*	zero-fuel characteristic		*n*	caractéristique de débit nul	*f*
Nullförderung (Pumpenelement)		*f*	zero delivery		*n*	débit nul	*m*
Nullgas (Abgasprüftechnik)		*n*	zero gas (exhaust-gas test)		*n*	gaz neutre (émissions)	*m*
Nullmenge		*f*	zero-fuel quantity		*n*	débit nul	*m*
Nullserie		*f*	pilot run		*n*	série pilote	*f*
Nutfüllfaktor (drehende Maschinen)		*m*	slot fill factor (rotating machines)		*n*	facteur de remplissage des rainures (machines tournantes)	*m*
Nutscheibe		*f*	slotted washer		*n*	disque rainuré	*m*
Nutzfahrzeug, Nfz		*n*	commercial vehicle		*n*	véhicule utilitaire	*m*
Nutzfluß (magnetisch)		*m*	magnetic flux		*n*	flux magnétique utile	*m*
Nutzhub		*m*	effective stroke		*n*	course effective	*f*
Nutzsignal (Entstörung)		*n*	wanted signal (interference suppression)		*n*	signal utile (antiparasitage)	*m*
O							
obere Leerlaufdrehzahl		*f*	high idle speed		*n*	vitesse maximale à vide	*f*
obere Vollastdrehzahl		*f*	maximum full-load speed		*n*	vitesse maximale à pleine charge	*f*
Oberer Totpunkt, OT		*m*	top dead center, TDC		*n*	point mort haut, PMH	*m*
Oberkammer		*f*	upper chamber		*n*	chambre supérieure	*f*
Oberschwingungen		*fpl*	harmonics		*npl*	oscillations harmoniques	*fpl*
offene Bauweise		*f*	open-type design		*n*	version ouverte	*f*
Oktanzahl, OZ		*f*	octane number		*n*	indice d'octane	*m*
Onboard-Diagnose, OBD	x	*f*	on-board diagnostics, OBD		*n*	diagnostic de bord	*m*
Operationsverstärker, OPV		*m*	operational amplifier, OPA		*n*	amplificateur opérationnel	*m*
Ottokraftstoff		*m*	gasoline		*n*	essence	*f*
Ottomotor		*m*	spark-ignition engine		*n*	moteur à allumage par étincelle	*m*
Oxydationskatalysator		*m*	oxidation catalytic converter		*n*	catalyseur d'oxydation	*m*

Deutsch			Englisch		Französisch		
Ö							
Öffner (elektrischer Schalter)		*m*	NC contact (electrical switch, normally closed)	*n*	contact à ouverture (interrupteur électrique)		*m*
Öffnungsdauer (Einspritzventil)		*f*	opening time (fuel injector)	*n*	durée d'ouverture (injecteur)		*f*
Öffnungsdruck		*m*	opening pressure	*n*	pression d'ouverture		*f*
Ölabscheider		*m*	oil separator	*n*	séparateur d'huile		*m*
Ölbadluftfilter		*n*	oil-bath air filter	*n*	filtre à air à bain d'huile		*m*
Öldruckbremse	+	*f*	hydraulic-actuated brake	*n*	frein à commande hydraulique		*m*
Ölfilter		*n*	lube-oil filter	*n*	filtre à huile		*m*
Ölfiltereinsatz		*m*	lube-oil filter element	*n*	cartouche de filtre à huile		*f*
Ölrückförderpumpe		*f*	oil-return pump	*n*	pompe de retour d'huile		*f*
Ölsperre	x	*f*	oil block (fuel-injection pump)	*n*	barrage d'huile (pompe d'injection)		*m*
P							
P-Grad		*m*	speed droop	*n*	statisme		*m*
P-Verhalten	x	*n*	speed-droop characteristic	*n*	action proportionnelle		*f*
Panikalarm (Autoalarm)		*m*	panic alarm (car alarm)	*n*	alarme panique (alarme auto)		*f*
Panikbremsung		*f*	panic braking	*n*	freinage en situation de panique		*m*
Panzerschlauch (Sonderzündspule)		*m*	armored hose (special ignition coil)	*n*	flexible blindé (bobine d'allumage spéciale)		*m*
Papiereinsatz (Luftfilter)		*m*	paper element (air filter)	*n*	élément filtrant en papier (filtre à air)		*m*
Papierluftfilter		*n*	paper air filter	*n*	filtre à air en papier		*m*
Papierwickel (Kraftstoffilter)		*m*	paper element (fuel filter)	*n*	rouleau de papier (filtre à carburant)		*m*
Parallel-Diode		*f*	parallel diode	*n*	diode parallèle		*f*
Parallelbetrieb (Generatoren)		*m*	parallel operation (alternators)	*n*	couplage en parallèle (alternateurs)		*m*
Parallelfilter		*n*	parallel filter	*n*	filtre en parallèle		*m*
Parallelogramm-Wischarm		*m*	parallelogram wiper arm	*n*	bras d'essuie-glace à parallélogramme		*m*
Parallelschaltung		*f*	parallel connection	*n*	montage en parallèle		*m*
Park-Pilot		*m*	Park Pilot	*n*	guide de parcage		*m*
Parkbremse	x	*f*	hand brake	*n*	frein à main	x	*m*
Parkdose (Anhänger-ABS)	x	*f*	parking socket (trailer ABS)	*n*	prise de stationnement (ABS pour remorque)		*f*
Parkleuchte		*f*					
Parkleuchte		*f*	parking lamp	*n*	feu de stationnement		*m*
Parklicht		*n*					
Parklicht		*n*	parking lamp	*n*	feu de stationnement		*m*
Partikelemission		*f*	particulate emission	*n*	émission de particules		*f*
Pedalanschlag		*m*	pedal stop	*n*	butée d'arrêt de la pédale		*f*
Pedalstütze (Bremsenprüfung)		*f*	pedal positioner (braking-system inspection)	*n*	positionneur de pédale de frein (contrôle des freins)		*m*
Pedalwegsensor		*m*	pedal-travel sensor	*n*	capteur d'accélérateur		*m*
Pedalwertgeber		*m*	pedal-travel sensor	*n*	capteur d'accélérateur		*m*
Periodendauer		*f*	period duration	*n*	durée de période		*f*

Deutsch		Englisch		Französisch	
Peripheralpumpe	*f*	peripheral pump	*n*	pompe à accélération périphérique	*f*
Permanentfeld	*n*	permanent-magnet field	*n*	excitation permanente	*f*
Permanentmagnet	*m*	permanent magnet	*n*	aimant permanent	*m*
Permanentmagneterregung	*f*	permanent-magnet excitation	*n*	excitation par aimant permanent	*f*
Permanentmagnetfeld	*n*	permanent-magnet field	*n*	excitation permanente	*f*
PES, Poly-Ellipsoid-Scheinwerfer	*a*	PES headlamp	*n*	projecteur polyellipsoïde	*m*
Pflichtenheft	*n*	performance specs	*n*	cahier des charges	*m*
Phasenabstimmung	*f*	phase matching	*n*	ajustement des phases	*m*
Phasengeber	*m*	phase sensor	*n*	capteur de phase	*m*
Phasensensor	*m*	phase sensor	*n*	capteur de phase	*m*
Phasenstrom	*m*	phase current	*n*	courant de phase	*m*
Phasenverschiebung	*f*	phase displacement	*n*	déphasage (entre deux grandeurs sinusoïdales)	*m*
Phasenwinkel	*m*	phase angle	*n*	phase d'une grandeur sinusoïdale	*f*
piezoelektrischer Schallaufnehmer	*m*	vibration sensor	*n*	capteur de vibrations	*m*
Piezokeramikstreifen	*m*	piezo-ceramic strip	*n*	lame piézocéramique	*f*
Pintaux-Düse	*f*	Pintaux-type nozzle	*n*	injecteur Pintaux	*m*
planare Lambda Sonde	*f*	planar Lambda sensor	*n*	sonde lambda planaire	*f*
Planarsonde	*f*	planar Lambda sensor	*n*	sonde lambda planaire	*f*
Planetengetriebe	*n*	planetary gear	*n*	train épicycloïdal	*m*
Planetenrad	*n*	planet gear	*n*	roue planétaire	*f*
Planetenradsystem	*n*	planetary-gear system	*n*	système de roues planétaires	*m*
Planetenträger	*m*	planetary-gear carrier	*n*	support d'engrenage planétaire	*m*
Planlaufabweichung (Bremsscheibe)	*f*	side runout (brake disc)	*n*	voilage (disque de frein)	*m*
Platinmittelelektrode (Zündkerze)	*f*	platinum center electrode (spark plug)	*n*	électrode centrale en platine (bougie)	*f*
Plattenventil	*n*	plate valve	*n*	plaque-soupape mobile	*f*
Plattenverbinder (Batterie)	*m*	plate strap (battery)	*n*	barrette de jonction des plaques (batterie)	*f*
Pleuelstange (Verbrennungsmotor)	*f*	connecting rod (IC engine)	*n*	bielle (moteur à combustion)	*f*
plotten	*v*	plot	*v*	tracer	*v*
Plotter	*m*	plotter	*n*	traceur	*m*
Plusdiode	*f*	positive diode	*n*	diode positive	*f*
Plusplatte (Batterie)	*f*	positive plate (battery)	*n*	plaque positive (batterie)	*f*
Pneumatikbremskreis	*m*	pneumatic-brake circuit	*n*	circuit de freinage pneumatique	*m*
Pneumatikleitung	*f*	pneumatic line	*n*	conduite pneumatique	*f*
pneumatische Abstellvorrichtung, PNAB	*f*	pneumatic shutoff device	*n*	dispositif d'arrêt pneumatique	*m*
pneumatische Bremsanlage	*f*	air-brake system	*n*	dispositif de freinage pneumatique	*m*
pneumatische Fremdkraft-Bremsanlage mit hydraul. Übertragungseinrichtung	*f*	air-over-hydraulic braking system	*n*	dispositif de freinage hydraulique à commande par air comprimé	*m*

Deutsch			Englisch		Französisch	
pneumatische Hilfskraft-Bremsanlage		*f*	air-assisted braking system	*n*	dispositif de freinage hydraulique assisté par air comprimé	*m*
pneumatische Leerlaufanhebung, PLA		*f*	pneumatic idle-speed increase	*n*	accélérateur pneumatique de ralenti	*m*
Polabdeckkappe (Batterie)		*f*	terminal-post cover (battery)	*n*	capot de protection de borne (batterie)	*m*
Poldurchgang		*m*	pole pass	*n*	passage de pôle	*m*
Polfinger		*m*	pole finger	*n*	extrémité polaire	*f*
Polgehäuse		*n*	stator housing	*n*	carcasse stator	*f*
Polhälfte		*f*	claw pole	*n*	plateau à griffes	*m*
Polkern		*m*	pole body	*n*	noyau polaire	*m*
Polrad		*n*	pole wheel	*n*	roue polaire	*f*
Polradhälfte		*f*	pole-wheel half	*n*	demi-roue polaire	*f*
Polschaft		*m*	pole body	*n*	noyau polaire	*m*
Polschuh		*m*	pole shoe	*n*	épanouissement polaire	*m*
Polschutz (Batterieladung)		*m*	reverse-polarity protection (battery charge)	*n*	protection contre l'inversion de polarité (charge de batterie)	*f*
Polteilung		*f*	pole pitch	*n*	pas polaire	*m*
Poly-Ellipsoid-Scheinwerfer, PES		*m*	PES headlamp	*n*	projecteur polyellipsoïde	*m*
Poly-V-Riemen	x	*m*	ribbed V-belt	*n*	courroie trapezoïdale à nervures	*f*
Polzahl		*f*	number of poles	*n*	nombre de pôles	*m*
Porengröße (Filter)		*f*	pore size (filter)	*n*	porosité (filtre)	*f*
Porenweite (Filter)		*f*	pore size (filter)	*n*	porosité (filtre)	*f*
Positionsgeber		*m*	position sensor	*n*	capteur de position	*m*
Positionsrückmeldung (ASR-Stellmotor)		*f*	position feedback (TCS servomotor)	*n*	confirmation de positionnement (servomoteur ASR)	*f*
Positionssensor		*m*	position sensor	*n*	capteur de position	*m*
positive Angleichung		*f*	positive torque control	*n*	correction de débit positive	*f*
Potentiometer		*m*	potentiometer	*n*	potentiomètre	*m*
Potentiometerbahn		*f*	potentiometer track	*n*	piste de potentiomètre	*f*
Prallfläche (Dieseleinspritzung)		*f*	baffle surface (diesel fuel injection)	*n*	surface d'impact (injection diesel)	*f*
Prallkante		*f*	impact edge	*n*	arête de rebond	*f*
Prallkappe (Einspritzventil)		*f*	anti-erosion cap (injector)	*n*	capuchon anti-érosion (injecteur)	*m*
Prallplatte (Drucksteller)		*f*	baffle plate (pressure actuator)	*n*	déflecteur (actionneur de pression)	*m*
Prallschraube (Dieseleinspritzung)		*f*	anti-erosion screw (diesel fuel injection)	*n*	vis anti-érosion (injection diesel)	*f*
prasseln (Funkstörung)	x	*v*	patter (radio disturbance)	*v*	crépitement (perturbation)	*m*
Prellzeit (Relais)		*f*	bounce time (relay)	*n*	temps de rebondissement (relais)	*m*
Primärdruck (Bremse)		*m*	supply pressure (brakes)	*n*	pression d'alimentation (frein)	*f*
Primärleitung (Zündanlage)		*f*	primary line (ignition system)	*n*	câble de circuit primaire (allumage)	*m*
Primärmanschette		*f*	primary cup seal	*n*	manchette primaire	*f*
Primärseite		*f*	primary side	*n*	côté primaire	*m*

Deutsch		Englisch		Französisch	
Primärwicklung	f	primary winding	n	enroulement primaire	m
Primärwiderstand	m	primary resistance	n	résistance de l'enroulement primaire	f
Produktentwicklung	f	product development	n	développement des produits	m
Produkthaftung	f	product liability	n	responsabilité produit	f
Produktspezifikation	f	product specification	n	spécification du produit	f
Produzentenhaftung	f	manufacturers responsibility	n	responsabilité du fabricant	f
Programmodul	m	program module	n	module de programme	m
Projektionsoptik (Scheinwerfer	f	projection optics (headlamp)	npl	optique de projection (projecteur)	f
Projektmanagement	n	project management	n	gestion de projet	f
Proportionalgrad	m	speed droop	n	statisme	m
Proportionalitätsfaktor	m	speed droop	n	statisme	m
Proportionalventil (ASR)	n	proportioning valve (TCS)	n	valve proportionnelle (ASR)	f
Proportionalverhalten	n	speed-droop characteristic	n	action proportionnelle	f
Prüfablauf	m	test procedure	n	déroulement du contrôle	m
Prüfanleitung	f	test instructions	npl	notice d'essai	f
Prüfanschluß (Druckluftbremse)	m	pressure test connection (compressed-air brake)	n	raccord d'essai (frein à air comprimé)	m
Prüfbericht	m	test report	n	compte-rendu d'essai	m
Prüfdüse	f	calibrating nozzle	n	injecteur d'essai	m
Prüfeinrichtung	f	test equipment	n	dispositif d'essai	m
Prüfgeschwindigkeit	f	test speed	n	vitesse d'essai	f
Prüfimpuls	m	test pulse	n	impulsion de contrôle	f
Prüfleitung (Einspritzpumpen-Prüfstand)	f	test pipe (injection-pump test bench)	n	conduite d'essai (banc d'essai)	f
Prüfmotor	m	test engine	n	moteur d'essai	m
Prüföl	n	calibrating oil	n	huile d'essai	f
Prüfplakette	f	inspection tag	n	autocollant d'inspection	m
Prüfprogramm (Abgasprüfung)	n	test program (exhaust-gas test)	n	programme d'essai (émissions)	m
Prüfprotokoll	n	test record	n	procès-verbal d'essai	m
Prüfspannung	f	test voltage	n	tension d'essai	f
Prüfstand	m	test bench	n	banc d'essai	m
Prüfstellung (Feststellbremsventil)	f	test position (parking-brake valve)	n	position de contrôle (valve de frein de stationnement)	f
Prüftechnik	f	test technology	n	technique de contrôle et d'essai	f
Prüfumfang	m	extent of inspection	n	contrôles	mpl
Prüfventil	n	test valve	n	valve de contrôle	f
Prüfvorschrift	f	test regulations	npl	instructions d'essai	fpl
Prüfwerte	mpl	test specifications	npl	valeurs d'essai	fpl
Prüfzeichen	n	mark of approval	n	marque d'homologation	f
Prüfzelle (Abgasprüfung)	f	emissions test cell	n	cabine de simulation des gaz d'échappement	f
Prüfzyklus (Abgasprüfung)	m	test cycle (exhaust-gas test)	n	diagramme de test (émissions)	m
Pufferbetrieb (Batterieladung)	m	floating-mode operation (battery charge)	n	mode "tampon" (charge de batterie)	m
pulsen (Drucksteuerung)	v	pulsing (pressure control)	v	par impulsion (pilotage de pression)	loc

Deutsch		Englisch		Französisch	
pulsierend (Drucksteuerung)	*ppr*	pulse-controlled (pressure)	*pp*	par impulsions (modulation de pression)	*loc*
pulsweitenmoduliert	*adj*	pulse width modulated, PWM	*pp*	modulé en largeur d'impulsion	*pp*
pulverbeschichtet	*pp*	powder coated	*pp*	revêtement de poudre	*m*
Pulverlack	*m*	powder-based paint	*n*	laque à base de poudre	*f*
Pumpe-Düse	+ *f*	unit injector system, UIS	*n*	injecteur-pompe	*m*
Pumpe-Düse-Einheit, UIS	*f*	unit injector system, UIS	*n*	injecteur-pompe	*m*
Pumpe-Leitung-Düse, UPS	*f*	unit pump system, UPS	*n*	système pompe-conduite-injecteur	*m*
Pumpedüse	+ *f*	unit injector system, UIS	*n*	injecteur-pompe	*m*
Pumpenabtrieb	*m*	pump power take-off	*n*	côté sortie de la pompe	*m*
Pumpendruck	*m*	pump interior pressure	*n*	pression à l'intérieur de la pompe	*f*
Pumpenelement (ABS-Hydroaggregat)	*n*	pump element (ABS hydraulic modulator)	*n*	élément de pompage (groupe hydraulique ABS)	*m*
Pumpenelement (Einspritzpumpe)	*n*	plunger-and-barrel assembly (fuel-injection pump)	*n*	élément de pompage (pompe d'injection)	*m*
Pumpengehäuse	*n*	pump housing	*n*	corps de pompe	*m*
Pumpengröße	*f*	pump size	*n*	taille de pompe	*f*
Pumpenkennfeld	*n*	pump map	*n*	cartographie de pompe	*f*
Pumpenkolben (Einspritzpumpe)	*m*	pump plunger (fuel-injection pump)	*n*	piston de pompe (pompe d'injection)	*m*
Pumpenlängsachse	*f*	longitudinal pump axis	*n*	axe longitudinal de la pompe	*m*
Pumpenmotor (ABS-Hydroaggregat)	*m*	pump motor (ABS hydraulic modulator)	*n*	moteur de pompe (groupe hydraulique ABS)	
Pumpenraum	*m*	pump interior	*n*	intérieur de la pompe	*m*
Pumpensaugraum	*m*	fuel gallery (fuel-injection pump)	*n*	galerie d'alimentation (pompe d'injection)	*f*
Pumpensteuergerät	*n*	pump ECU	*n*	calculateur pompe	*m*
Pumpenzylinder (Einspritzpumpe)	*m*	pump barrel (fuel-injection pump)	*n*	cylindre de pompe (pompe d'injection)	*m*
Q					
Qualitätsabweichung	*f*	quality deviation	*n*	variation de qualité	*f*
Qualitätsbewertung	*f*	quality assessment	*n*	évaluation de la qualité	*f*
Qualitätskontrolle	*f*	quality control	*n*	contrôle de qualité	*m*
Qualitätsprüfung	*f*	quality examination	*n*	essai qualitatif	*m*
Qualitätsprüfzertifikat	*n*	quality inspection certificate	*n*	certificat du test de qualité	*m*
Qualitätssicherung	*f*	quality assurance, QA	*n*	assurance qualité	*f*
Qualitätsstand	*m*	quality level	*n*	niveau de qualité	*m*
Qualitätsüberwachung	*f*	quality surveillance	*n*	surveillance de la qualité	*f*
Qualitätsziel	*n*	quality objective	*n*	objectif qualité	*m*
Quarzoszillator	*m*	quartz oscillator	*n*	oscillateur à quartz	*m*
Quench-Zone (Luft-Kraftstoff-Gemisch)	*f*	quench zone (air-fuel mixture)	*n*	zone de coincement (mélange air-carburant)	*f*
Querbeschleunigungssensor (ESP)	*m*	lateral-acceleration sensor (ESP)	*n*	capteur d'accélération transversale (ESP)	*m*
Querbohrung	*f*	transverse passage	*n*	canal radial	*m*
Querdrossel	*f*	cross throttle	*n*	étranglement transversal	*m*

Deutsch			Englisch			Französisch		
Querempfindlichkeit (Sensor)		*f*	cross sensitivity (sensor)		*n*	sensibilité transversale (capteur)		*f*
Quergeschwindigkeit (Kfz-Dynamik)		*f*	lateral velocity (vehicle dynamics)		*n*	vitesse transversale (dynamique d'un véhicule)		*f*
Querspülung		*f*	cross flushing		*n*	balayage transversal		*m*
Querstabilitätsachse (Kfz-Dynamik)		*f*	roll axis (vehicle dynamics)		*n*	axe de roulis (dynamique d'un véhicule)		*m*
quietschen (Bremse)		*v*	squeal (brakes)		*v*	grincement (frein)		*m*
R								
Rad- und Abschleppschutz (Autoalarm)		*m*	wheel theft and tow-away protection (car alarm)		*n*	protection contre le vol des roues et le remorquage (alarme auto)		*f*
Radaufstandspunkt		*m*	wheel contact point		*n*	point de contact de la roue avec la chaussée		*m*
Radbeschleunigung		*f*	wheel acceleration		*n*	accélération périphérique des roues		*f*
Radbremsdruck		*m*	wheel brake pressure		*n*	pression de freinage sur roue		*f*
Radbremse		*f*	wheel brake		*n*	frein de roue		*m*
Radbremszylinder	+	*m*	wheel-brake cylinder		*n*	cylindre de frein de roue		*m*
Raddifferenzgeschwindigkeit		*f*	wheel-speed differential		*n*	vitesse différentielle des roues		*f*
Raddrehzahlsensor		*m*	wheel-speed sensor		*n*	capteur de vitesse de roue		*m*
Radgeschwindigkeit		*f*	wheel speed		*n*	vitesse de rotation de la roue		*f*
Radgeschwindigkeits-vergleicher (ABS)		*m*	wheel-speed comparator (ABS)		*n*	comparateur de vitesse de roues (ABS)		*m*
Radialkolben-Hochdruckpumpe		*f*	radial-piston high-pressure pump		*n*	pompe haute pression à pistons radiaux		*f*
Radialkolben-Verteilereinspritzpumpe (VR)		*f*	radial-piston pump		*n*	pompe distributrice à pistons radiaux		*f*
Radialkolben-Verteilerpumpe (VR)		*f*	radial-piston pump		*n*	pompe distributrice à pistons radiaux		*f*
Radialkolbenpumpe (VR)		*f*	radial-piston pump		*n*	pompe distributrice à pistons radiaux		*f*
Radiallüfter		*m*	radial fan		*n*	ventilateur radial		*m*
radieren (Reifen)	x	*v*	drag (tire)	x	*v*	gommer (pneu)	x	*v*
Radkastenfilter		*n*	fender-mounted air filter		*n*	filtre dans le passage de roue		*m*
Radlager		*n*	wheel bearing		*n*	roulement de roue		*m*
Radnabe		*f*	wheel hub		*n*	moyeu de roue		*m*
Radschlupf		*m*	wheel slip		*n*	glissement (roue)		*m*
Radschutz (Autoalarm)		*m*	wheel-theft protection (car alarm)		*n*	protection contre le vol des roues (alarme auto)		*f*
Radschwenkachse (Kfz-Dynamik)		*f*	wheel swivel angle (vehicle dynamics)		*n*	axe de pivotement de roue (dynamique d'un véhicule)		*m*
Radträgheitsmoment		*n*	wheel moment of inertia		*n*	couple d'inertie de la roue		*m*
Radumfangsbeschleunigung		*f*	wheel acceleration		*n*	accélération périphérique des roues		*f*
Radumfangsgeschwindigkeit		*f*	wheel speed		*n*	vitesse de rotation de la roue		*f*
Radumfangsverzögerung		*f*	wheel deceleration		*n*	décélération périphérique des roues		*f*
Radverzögerung		*f*	wheel deceleration		*n*	décélération périphérique des roues		*f*

Deutsch		Englisch		Französisch	
Radzylinder	*m*	wheel-brake cylinder	*n*	cylindre de frein de roue	*m*
Rail (Common Rail)	*n*	high-pressure accumulator (common rail)	*n*	accumulateur haute pression (Common Rail)	*m*
Raildrucksensor (Common Rail)	*m*	common-rail pressure sensor	*n*	capteur de pression "Rail"	*m*
Rampensignal	*n*	ramp signal	*n*	signal de rampe	*m*
Rampenspannung	*f*	ramp voltage	*n*	tension de rampe	*f*
Rampensteigung	*f*	ramp climb	*n*	montée de rampe	*f*
Rampenverlauf (Lambda-Regelung)	*m*	ramp progression (lambda closed-loop control)	*n*	évolution en rampe (régulation lambda)	*f*
Rapidladung (Batterie)	*f*	boost charge (battery)	*n*	charge rapide (batterie)	*f*
Rastbolzen	*m*	ratchet pin	*n*	axe d'arrêt	*m*
Rastfeder	*f*	stop-spring	*n*	ressort à cran d'arrêt	*m*
Raststellung (Ventil)	*f*	detent position (valve)	*n*	crantage (valve)	*m*
Rauchbegrenzeranschlag	*m*	smoke-limiting stop	*n*	butée de limitation de fumée	*f*
Rauchbegrenzung	*f*	smoke limitation	*n*	limitation de l'émission de fumées	*f*
Rauchgastester	*m*	smokemeter	*n*	fumimètre	*m*
Rauchgrenze	*f*	smoke limit	*n*	limite d'émission de fumées	*f*
Rauchmessung	*f*	smoke measurement	*n*	analyse des fumées diesel	*f*
Rauchprüfung	*f*	smoke emission test	*n*	test d'émission de fumées	*m*
Rauchstoß	*m*	cloud of smoke	*n*	émission de fumées	*f*
Rauchwert	*m*	smoke-emission value	*n*	valeur d'émission de fumées	*f*
rauschen (Funkstörung)	x *v*	background noise (radio disturbance)	*n*	bruit de fond (perturbation)	*m*
Reaktionsdauer (Bremsbetätigung)	*f*	reaction time (brake actuation)	*n*	temps de réaction (freinage)	*m*
Reaktionsfeder (Feststellbremsventil)	*f*	reaction spring (parking-brake valve)	*n*	ressort de rappel (valve de frein de stationnement)	*m*
Reaktionskammer	*f*	reaction chamber	*n*	chambre de réaction	*f*
Reaktionskolben	*m*	reaction piston	*n*	piston de rappel	*m*
Reaktionskraft (Bremse)	*f*	reaction force (brakes)	*n*	force de réaction (systèmes de freinage)	*f*
Reaktionsmembran	*f*	transfer diaphragm	*n*	membrane active	*f*
Reaktionsmoment (Bremsprüfung)	*n*	reaction torque (braking-system inspection)	*n*	couple de réaction (contrôle des freins)	*m*
Rechenwerk (Steuergerät)	*n*	arithmetic-logic processor (ECU)	*n*	unité de calcul (calculateur)	*f*
Rechteckimpuls (Steuergerät)	*m*	square-wave pulse (ECU)	*n*	impulsion rectangulaire (calculateur)	*f*
Rechtecksignal (Steuergerät)	*n*	square-wave signal (ECU)	*n*	signal rectangulaire (calculateur)	*m*
Rechtslauf	*m*	clockwise rotation	*n*	rotation à droite	*f*
Reduktionskatalysator	*m*	reduction catalytic converter	*n*	catalyseur de réduction	*m*
Reduziersignal (ASR)	*n*	reduction signal (TCS)	*n*	signal de réduction (ASR)	*m*
Reduzierventil	*n*	reducing valve	*n*	réducteur de pression	*m*
Referenzdruck	*m*	reference pressure	*n*	pression de référence	*f*
Referenzgas (Lambda-Regelung)	*n*	reference gas (lambda closed-loop control)	*n*	gaz de référence (régulation lambda)	*m*

Deutsch		Englisch		Französisch	
Referenzgeschwindigkeit	*f*	reference speed	*n*	vitesse de référence	*f*
Referenzkurzschlußring	*m*	reference eddy-current ring	*n*	bague inductive de référence	*f*
Referenzleitung	*f*	reference line	*n*	tuyauterie de référence	*f*
Referenzmarke	*f*	reference mark	*n*	repère de référence	*m*
Referenzpegel	*m*	reference level	*n*	niveau de référence	*m*
Reflektor	*m*	reflector	*n*	réflecteur	*m*
Reflektoroptik	*f*	reflector optics	*npl*	optique de réflexion	*f*
Reflexionsschalldämpfer	*m*	reflection muffler	*n*	silencieux à réflexion	*m*
Regelabweichung	*f*	governor deviation	*n*	écart de régulation	*m*
Regelanker	*m*	regulating armature	*n*	armature de régulation	*f*
Regelbereich	*m*	control range	*n*	plage de régulation	*f*
Regelfeder	*f*	governor spring	*n*	ressort de régulation	*m*
Regelgröße	*f*	controlled variable (closed-loop control)	*n*	grandeur réglée	*f*
Regelgruppe	*f*	flyweight assembly	*n*	bloc de régulation	*m*
Regelhebel (Diesel-Regler)	*m*	variable-fulcrum lever (governor)	*n*	levier à coulisse (régulateur diesel)	*m*
Regelhülse (Einspritzpumpe)	*f*	control sleeve (fuel-injection pump)	*n*	douille de réglage (pompe d'injection)	*f*
Regelkanal (ABS-Hydroaggregat)	*m*	control channel (ABS hydraulic modulator)	*n*	conduite de régulation (groupe hydraulique ABS)	*f*
Regelkonfiguration (ABS)	*f*	control configuration (ABS)	*n*	configuration de régulation (ABS)	*f*
Regelkontakt	*m*	regulating contact	*n*	contact de régulation	*m*
Regelkreis	*m*	closed control loop	*n*	boucle de régulation	*f*
Regellenker	*m*	control-sleeve lever (single-plunger fuel-injection pump)	*n*	biellette de réglage	*f*
Regelmembran	*f*	control diaphragm	*n*	membrane de régulation	*f*
Regelschaltung	*f*	control loop	*n*	boucle d'asservissement	*f*
Regelschieber (Verteilereinspritzpumpe)	*m*	control collar (distributor pump)	*n*	tiroir de régulation (pompe distributrice)	*m*
Regelschieberweggeber	*m*	control-collar position sensor	*n*	capteur de course du tiroir de régulation	*m*
Regelschwelle	*f*	control threshold	*n*	seuil de régulation	*m*
Regelsignal	*n*	control signal (closed loop)	*n*	signal de régulation	*m*
Regelspannung	*f*	regulator response voltage	*n*	tension de régulation	*f*
Regelstange (Reiheneinspritzpumpe)	*f*	control rack (in-line pump)	*n*	tige de réglage (pompe d'injection en ligne)	*f*
Regelstangenanschlag (Einspritzpumpe)	*m*	control-rod stop (fuel-injection pump)	*n*	butée de la tige de réglage (pompe d'injection)	*f*
Regelstangenstellung	*f*	rack position, RP	*n*	position de la tige de réglage	*f*
Regelstangenweg	*m*	control-rack travel	*n*	course de régulation	*f*
Regelstangenweggeber	*m*	rack-travel sensor	*n*	capteur de course de régulation	*m*
Regelstrecke	*f*	controlled system	*n*	système asservi	*m*
Regelteil	*n*	flyweight assembly	*n*	bloc de régulation	*m*
Regeltoleranz	*f*	control tolerance	*n*	tolérance de régulation	*f*
Regelventil	*n*	control valve (closed loop)	*n*	valve de régulation	*f*
Regelverhältnis (Bremsventil)	*n*	control ratio (brake valve)	*n*	rapport de régulation (valve de frein)	*m*

Deutsch		Englisch		Französisch	
Regelweg	*m*	control-rack travel	*n*	course de régulation	*f*
Regelweganzeige	*f*	rack-travel indication	*n*	indicateur de course de régulation	*m*
Regelwegbegrenzungs-anschlag	*m*	rack-travel limiting stop	*n*	butée de limitation de course de régulation	*f*
Regelweggeber, RWG	*m*	rack-travel sensor	*n*	capteur de course de régulation	*m*
Regelwegsensor	*m*	rack-travel sensor	*n*	capteur de course de régulation	*m*
Regelwendel	*f*	control filament	*n*	spirale de régulation	*f*
Regelwiderstand	*m*	regulating resistor	*n*	résistance de régulation	*f*
Regelzyklus	*m*	control cycle	*n*	cycle de régulation	*m*
Regeneration (Lufttrockner)	*f*	regeneration (air drier)	*n*	régénération (dessiccateur)	*f*
Regenerationsdrossel (Lufttrockner)	*f*	regeneration throttle (air drier)	*n*	étranglement de régénération (dessiccateur)	*m*
Regenerationshilfe	*f*	regeneration aid	*n*	auxiliaire de régénération	*m*
Regenerationsluftbehälter	*m*	regeneration-air tank	*n*	réservoir d'air de régénération	*m*
Regeneriergasstrom	*m*	regeneration-gas flow	*n*	flux de gaz régénérateur	*m*
Regenerierventil (Abgastechnik)	*n*	canister-purge valve (emissions control technology)	*n*	électrovalve de régénération (technique des gaz d'échappement)	*f*
Regensensor	*m*	rain sensor	*n*	capteur de pluie	*m*
Regionalgesellschaft	*f*	regional subsidiary	*n*	société régionale	*f*
Registerresonanzaufladung	*f*	register resonance pressure-charging	*n*	suralimentation par collecteur de résonance	*f*
Regler (Dieseleinspritzung)	*m*	governor (diesel fuel injection)	*n*	régulateur (injection diesel)	*m*
Regler (Generator)	*m*	voltage regulator (alternator)	*n*	régulateur de tension (alternateur)	*m*
Reglercharakteristik	*f*	governor characteristics	*n*	caractéristique du régulateur	*f*
Reglerdeckel	*m*	governor cover	*n*	couvercle de régulateur	*m*
Reglergehäuse	*n*	governor housing	*n*	carter de régulateur	*m*
Reglergestänge	*n*	governor linkage	*n*	tringlerie du régulateur	*f*
Reglergruppe	*f*	governor assembly	*n*	bloc régulateur	*m*
Reglerkennfeld	*n*	governor characteristic curves	*n*	cartographie du régulateur	*f*
Reglerkontakt	+ *m*	regulating contact	*n*	contact de régulation	*m*
Reglerlogik (Steuergerät)	*f*	controller logic (ECU)	*n*	logique de régulation (calculateur)	*f*
Reglermuffe (Diesel-Regler)	*f*	sliding sleeve (governor)	*n*	manchon central (régulateur diesel)	*m*
Reglernabe	*f*	governor hub	*n*	moyeu de régulateur	*m*
Regulierschalter (Leuchtweitenregelung)	*m*	regulator switch (headlight leveling control)	*n*	molette de correcteur de site	*f*
Reibbelag	*m*	friction lining	*n*	garniture de friction	*f*
Reibeigenschaft (Bremsbelag)	*f*	friction properties (brake lining	*n*	propriété de friction (garniture de frein)	*f*
Reibgeräusch	*n*	friction noise	*n*	bruit de friction	*m*
Reibkraft	*f*	frictional force	*n*	force de friction	*f*
Reibleistung	*f*	friction loss	*n*	perte par frottement	*f*
Reibmoment	*n*	friction moment	*n*	couple de frottement	*m*
Reibpaarung	*f*	friction pairing	*n*	couple de friction	*m*
Reibungsbremse	*f*	friction brake	*n*	frein à friction	*m*

Deutsch		Englisch		Französisch	
Reibungskraft	*f*	friction force	*n*	force de frottement	*f*
Reibungsverlust	*m*	friction loss	*n*	perte par frottement	*f*
Reibwertpaarung	*f*	friction-coefficient matching	*n*	couple d'adhérence	*m*
Reichweite (Scheinwerfer)	*f*	range (headlamp)	*n*	portée (projecteur)	*f*
Reifenarbeitspunkt	*m*	tire working point	*n*	point de travail du pneumatique	*m*
Reifenaufstandsfläche	*f*	tire contact patch	*n*	surface de contact du pneu	*f*
Reifenaufstandskraft	*f*	vertical tire force	*n*	force verticale du pneumatique	*f*
Reifenbremskraft	*f*	tire braking force	*n*	force de freinage du pneumatique	*f*
Reifendruck	*m*	tire pressure	*n*	pression du pneu	*f*
Reifenfüllanschluß	*m*	tire-inflation fitting	*n*	raccord de gonflage des pneus	*m*
Reifenfülleinrichtung	*f*	tire-inflation device	*n*	dispositif de gonflage des pneus	*m*
Reifenfüllschlauch	*m*	tire-inflation hose	*n*	flexible de gonflage des pneus	*m*
Reifenkontrollsystem	*n*	tire-pressure monitoring system	*n*	système de contrôle des pneumatiques	*m*
Reifenkraft	*f*	tire force	*n*	force de freinage au roulement des pneumatiques	*f*
Reifenquerkraft	*f*	lateral tire force	*n*	force latérale du pneumatique	*f*
Reifenschlupf	*m*	tire slip	*n*	glissement (pneu)	*m*
Reifenseitenkraft	*f*	lateral tire force	*n*	force latérale du pneumatique	*f*
Reifensteifigkeit	*f*	tire rigidity	*n*	rigidité du pneumatique	*f*
Reifenverschleiß	*m*	tire wear	*n*	usure du pneu	*f*
Reiheneinspritzpumpe (PE)	*f*	in-line fuel-injection pump (PE	*n*	pompe d'injection en ligne (PE)	*f*
Reihenpumpe (PE) x	*f*	in-line fuel-injection pump (PE	*n*	pompe d'injection en ligne (PE)	*f*
Reihenschaltung	*f*	series connection	*n*	montage en série	*m*
Reihenschlußmotor	*m*	series motor	*n*	moteur série	*m*
Reihenschlußwicklung	*f*	series winding	*n*	enroulement série	*m*
Reinigungsadditiv (Benzin)	*n*	detergent additive (gasoline)	*n*	agent détergent (essence)	*m*
Reinseite (Filter)	*f*	clean side (filter)	*n*	côté propre (filtre)	*m*
Reizleitung (Eigendiagnose)	*f*	self-diagnosis initiate line	*n*	câble d'activation de l'autodiagnostic	*m*
Relais	*n*	relay	*n*	relais	*m*
Relaiskolben	*m*	relay piston	*n*	piston-relais	*m*
Relaiskombination	*f*	relay combination	*n*	module relais	*m*
Relaisventil	*n*	relay valve	*n*	valve-relais	*f*
Relativgeschwindigkeit	*f*	relative speed	*n*	vitesse relative	*f*
Remanenz	*f*	residual magnetism	*n*	magnétisme restant	*m*
Reparaturanleitung	*f*	repair instructions	*npl*	notice de remise en état	*f*
Reparaturhandbuch	*n*	repair manual	*n*	manuel de réparation	*m*
Reparatursatz	*m*	repair kit	*n*	kit de remise en état	*m*
Research-Oktanzahl, ROZ	*f*	research octane number, RON	*n*	indice d'octane recherche, RON	*m*
Resonanzaufladung	*f*	tuned-intake pressure-charging	*n*	suralimentation par résonance	*f*
Resonanzbehälter	*m*	resonance chamber	*n*	boîte à résonance	*f*
Resonanzfrequenz	*f*	resonant frequency	*n*	fréquence de résonance	*f*
Resonanzkammer	*f*	resonance chamber	*n*	boîte à résonance	*f*
Resonanzrohr	*n*	resonance tube	*n*	tube à résonance	*m*
Restbremswirkung	*f*	residual braking	*n*	effet résiduel de freinage	*m*

Deutsch

Deutsch		Englisch		Französisch	
Restdruck	m	residual pressure	n	pression résiduelle	f
Restgas	n	residual exhaust gas	n	gaz résiduels	mpl
Resthub (Pumpenelement)	m	residual stroke (plunger-and-barrel assembly)	n	course restante (élément de pompage)	f
Restluftspalt	m	residual air gap	n	fente d'air résiduel	f
Restmagnetismus	m	residual magnetism	n	magnétisme restant	m
Restsauerstoff (Abgas)	m	exhaust-gas oxygen	n	oxygène résiduel (gaz d'échappement)	m
Restvolumen	n	dead volume	n	volume mort	m
Retarder	m	retarder	n	ralentisseur	m
Retarderrelais	n	retarder relay	n	relais du ralentisseur	m
Riemenscheibe	f	belt pulley	n	poulie	f
Riemenspanner	m	belt tensioner	n	tendeur de courroie	m
Riementrieb	m	belt drive	n	transmission à courroie	f
Riemenvorspannung	f	belt pre-tension	n	prétension de courroie	f
Ringfläche	f	ring-shaped area	n	surface annulaire	f
Ringkanal	m	annular groove	n	canal annulaire	m
Ringleitung	f	ring main	n	conduite annulaire	f
Ringmagnet	m	ring magnet	n	aimant torique	m
Ringnut	f	ring groove	n	rainure annulaire	f
Ringspalt	m	annular orifice	n	fente annulaire	f
Ringspaltzumessung (Einspritzventil)	f	ring-gap metering (fuel injector)	n	dosage par fente annulaire (injecteur)	m
Rippenkühlkörper	m	heat sink with ribs	n	refroidisseur nervuré	m
Ritzelschaft	m	pinion shaft	n	queue de pignon	f
Ritzelverdrehung	f	pinion rotation	n	rotation du pignon	f
Ritzelvorschub	m	pinion advance (starter)	n	avance du pignon (démarreur)	f
Ritzelwelle	f	pinion shaft	n	queue de pignon	f
Ritzelzahn	m	pinion tooth	n	dent du pignon	f
Rohrdichtkegel	m	pipe sealing cone	n	cône d'étanchéité du tube	m
Rohrschlange	f	coiled pipe	n	serpentin	m
Rohwert (Fahrpedalsensor)	m	raw value (accelerator-pedal sensor)	n	valeur brute (capteur d'accélérateur)	f
Rollachse (Kfz-Dynamik)	f	roll axis (vehicle dynamics)	n	axe de roulis (dynamique d'un véhicule)	m
Rollbalg (Luftfeder)	m	roll bellows (air spring)	n	soufflet en U (suspension)	m
Rollbalgfeder (Luftfeder)	f	roll bellows (air spring)	n	soufflet en U (suspension)	m
Rollenbremsprüfstand	m	dynamic brake analyzer	n	banc d'essai à rouleaux pour freins	m
Rolleneinspritzpumpe x	f	roller-type fuel-injection pump	n	pompe d'injection à galet	f
Rollenfreilauf (Starter)	m	roller-type overrunning clutch (starter)	n	dispositif de roue libre (démarreur)	m
Rollengleitkurve	f	roller race	n	rampe de travail	f
Rollenlaufbahn	f	roller path	n	surface de guidage des rouleaux	f
Rollenpaar (Rollenbremsprüfstand)	n	roller set (dynamic brake analyzer)	n	jeu de rouleaux (banc d'essai)	m
Rollenprüfstand	m	chassis dynamometer	n	banc d'essai à rouleaux	m
Rollenring	m	roller ring	n	bague porte-galets	f

Deutsch		Englisch		Französisch	
Rollensatz (Rollenbremsprüfstand)	*m*	roller set (dynamic brake analyzer)	*n*	jeu de rouleaux (banc d'essai)	*m*
Rollenschuh	*m*	roller support	*n*	talon de galet	*m*
Rollenstößel	*m*	roller tappet	*n*	poussoir à galet	*m*
Rollenstößel-Einspritzpumpe	*f*	roller-type fuel-injection pump	*n*	pompe d'injection à galet	*f*
Rollenstößelspalt	*m*	roller-tappet gap	*n*	fente du poussoir à galet	*f*
Rollenzellenpumpe	*f*	roller-cell pump	*n*	pompe multicellulaire à rouleaux	*f*
Rollreibung	*f*	rolling friction	*n*	frottement au roulement	*m*
Rollstartsperre	*f*	roll-start block	*n*	dispositif antidémarrage	*m*
Rollwiderstand	*m*	rolling resistance	*n*	résistance au roulement	*f*
Rollwiderstandsbeiwert	*m*	coefficient of rolling resistance	*n*	coefficient de résistance au roulement	*m*
Roots-Gebläse	*n*	rotary-piston blower	*n*	soufflante à piston rotatif	*f*
Roots-Lader	*m*	Roots supercharger	*n*	compresseur Roots	*m*
Rostlöser	*m*	rust remover	*n*	dissolvant antirouille	*m*
Rotationskolbenverdichter	*m*	rotary-piston supercharger	*n*	compresseur à piston rotatif	*m*
Rotor (Druckwellenlader)	*m*	rotor (pressure-wave supercharger)	*n*	rotor (échangeur de pression)	*m*
rückblasen	*v*	blowback	*n*	reflux des gaz	*m*
Ruckeldämpfung	*f*	surge damping	*n*	amortissement d'à-coups	*m*
ruckeln	*v*	buck	*v*	à-coups	*mpl*
Ruckelschwingung	*f*	bucking oscillations	*npl*	vibrations dues aux à-coups	*fpl*
Rückfahrleuchte	*f*	backup lamp	*n*	feu de marche arrière	*m*
Rückfahrscheinwerfer	*m*	backup lamp	*n*	feu de marche arrière	*m*
Rückfallspannung	*f*	dropout voltage	*n*	tension de relâchement	*f*
Rückfallzeit (Relais)	*f*	release time (relay)	*n*	temps de relâchement (relais)	*m*
Rückförderprinzip (ABS)	*n*	return principle (ABS)	*n*	principe de reflux (ABS)	*m*
Rückförderpumpe	*f*	return pump	*n*	pompe de retour	*f*
Rückführverstärkung (ESP)	*f*	return amplification (ESP)	*n*	amplification de retour (ESP)	*f*
Rückhalteventil	*n*	backup valve	*n*	valve de secours	*f*
Rückholfeder	*f*	return spring	*n*	ressort de rappel	*m*
Rückhub	*m*	return stroke	*n*	course de retour	*f*
Rückkoppelung (Regelung)	*f*	feedback (control)	*n*	réaction (régulation)	*f*
Rücklauf (ABS-Magnetventil)	*m*	return line (ABS solenoid valve)	*n*	retour (électrovalve ABS)	*m*
Rücklaufbohrung	*f*	return passage	*n*	orifice de retour	*m*
Rücklaufleitung	*f*	return line	*n*	conduite de retour	*f*
Rückmeldung (ABS-Regelung)	*f*	feedback signal (ABS control)	*n*	confirmation (régulation ABS)	*f*
Rücknahmeliste (Werksaustausch)	*f*	catalog of exchange parts (factory exchange)	*n*	liste des reprises (échange standard)	*f*
rückschärfen (Autoalarm)	*v*	reprime (car alarm)	*v*	remise en veille (alarme auto)	*f*
Rückschlagventil	*n*	non-return valve	*n*	clapet de non-retour	*m*
Rückspülung	*f*	air backflush	*n*	balayage de retour	*m*
Rückstelldruck	*m*	retraction pressure	*n*	pression de rappel	*f*
Rückstellfeder	*f*	return spring	*n*	ressort de rappel	*m*
Rückstellkraft	*f*	return force	*n*	force de rappel	*f*
Rückstellmoment	*n*	return torque	*n*	couple de rappel	*m*

Deutsch

Deutsch		Englisch		Französisch	
Rückströmdrossel, RSD	*f*	return-flow restriction	*n*	frein de réaspiration	*m*
Rückströmdrosselventil	*n*	orifice check valve	*n*	soupape de frein de réaspiratior	*f*
Rückströmrichtung	*f*	return-flow direction	*n*	sens d'écoulement inverse	*m*
Rückstromsperre (Gleichrichtung)	*f*	reverse-current block (rectification)	*n*	isolement (redressement)	*m*
Rückströmung (Überströmventil)	*f*	return flow (overflow valve)	*n*	débit de retour (valve de barrage)	*m*
Ruhespannung (Batterie)	*f*	steady-state voltage (battery)	*n*	tension au repos (batterie)	*f*
Ruhestrom	*m*	peak coil current	*n*	courant de repos	*m*
Rundlauf (Verbrennungsmotor)	*m*	smooth running (IC engine)	*n*	fonctionnement régulier (moteur à combustion)	*m*
Rundstecker	*m*	pin terminal	*n*	fiche ronde	*f*
Rundsteckerhülse	*f*	pin receptable	*n*	fiche femelle ronde	*f*
Rundumkennleuchte	*f*	rotating beacon	*n*	gyrophare	*m*
Rußabbrand	*m*	soot burn-off	*n*	combustion de la suie	*f*
Rußabbrennfilter	*m*	soot burn-off filter	*n*	filtre d'oxidation de particules	*m*
Rußabscheider	*m*	soot separator	*n*	séparateur de particules de suie	*m*
Rußbildung	*f*	soot production	*n*	formation de suie	*f*
Rußemission	*f*	soot emission	*n*	émission de particules de suie	*f*
Rußfilter	*n*	particulate filter	*n*	filtre pour particules de suie	*m*
Rußpartikel	*n*	soot particle	*n*	particules de suie	*fpl*
rutschig	*adj*	slippery	*adj*	glissant	*adj*
rüttelfest (Batterie)	*adj*	vibration-proof (battery)	*adj*	insensible aux secousses (batterie)	*loc*
S					
S-Nocken (Bremse)	*m*	S-cam (brakes)	*n*	came en S (frein)	*f*
Sackloch (Einspritzventil)	*n*	blind hole (injector)	*n*	sac d'injecteur	*m*
Sacklochdüse	*f*	blind-hole nozzle	*n*	injecteur à trou borgne	*m*
Sacklochelement	*n*	blind-hole pumping element	*n*	élément à trou borgne	*m*
Salzsprühtest	*m*	salt spray test	*n*	test au brouillard salin	*m*
Satellitenortungssystem (Navigationssystem)	*n*	satellite positioning system (navigation system)	*n*	système de localisation par satellite (système de navigation	*m*
Sattelbefestigung	*f*	cradle mounting	*n*	fixation par berceau	*f*
Sättigungsmenge (Luftfeuchtigkeit)	*f*	saturation point (water content)	*n*	quantité de saturation (humidité de l'air)	*f*
Sauerstoff-Lambda-Sonde	*f*	lambda sensor	*n*	sonde de richesse	*f*
Sauganschluß	*m*	suction connection	*n*	raccord d'aspiration	*m*
Saugbohrung	*f*	inlet port (in-line pump)	*n*	orifice d'admission (pompe d'injection en ligne)	*m*
Saugdrossel	*f*	suction throttle	*n*	gicleur d'aspiration	*m*
Saugdrosseleinheit	*f*	inlet metering unit	*n*	unité de gicleur d'aspiration	*f*
Saugdruck	*m*	suction pressure	*n*	pression d'aspiration	*f*
Saugfilter	*n*	intake filter	*n*	filtre d'aspiration	*m*
Sauggebläse	*n*	intake fan	*n*	ventilateur d'aspiration	*m*
Saughub (Verbrennungsmotor)	*m*	intake stroke (IC engine)	*n*	course d'admission (moteur à combution)	*f*
Saugleitung	*f*	intake passage	*n*	conduit d'admission	*m*

Deutsch		Englisch		Französisch	
Saugloch (Reiheneinspritzpumpe)	*n*	inlet port (in-line pump)	*n*	orifice d'admission (pompe d'injection en ligne)	*m*
Saugmotor	*m*	naturally aspirated engine	*n*	moteur à aspiration naturelle	*m*
Saugraum (Einspritzpumpe)	*m*	fuel gallery (fuel-injection pump)	*n*	galerie d'alimentation (pompe d'injection)	*f*
Saugraumspülung	*f*	fuel-gallery flushing	*n*	balayage de la galerie d'alimentation	*m*
Saugresonator	*m*	suction resonator	*n*	résonateur d'admission	*m*
Saugrohr	*n*	intake manifold	*n*	collecteur d'admission	*m*
Saugrohrdruck	*m*	intake-manifold pressure	*n*	pression d'admission	*f*
Saugrohrdrucksensor	*m*	intake-manifold pressure sensoı	*n*	capteur de pression d'admission	*m*
Saugrohrgestaltung	*f*	intake-passage design	*n*	forme du collecteur d'admissior	*f*
Saugrohrrückzündung	*f*	backfiring	*n*	retour d'allumage	*m*
Saugrohrumschaltung	*f*	variable-tract intake manifold	*n*	commande de collecteur d'admission à géométrie variable	*f*
Saugrohrvorwärmung	*f*	intake-manifold preheating	*n*	préchauffage du collecteur d'admission	*m*
Saugseite	*f*	intake	*n*	côté aspiration	*m*
Saugventil (Kraftstofförderpumpe)	*n*	suction valve (fuel-supply pump)	*n*	soupape d'aspiration (pompe d'alimentation)	*f*
Säuredichte	*f*	specific gravity of electrolyte	*n*	densité de l'électrolyte	*f*
Säurekonzentration (Batterie)	*f*	specific gravity of electrolyte	*n*	densité de l'électrolyte	*f*
Säureprüfer (Batterie)	*m*	hydrometer (battery charge)	*n*	pèse-acide (charge de batterie)	*m*
Säurewerte (Batterie)	*fpl*	electrolyte values (battery)	*npl*	indices des acides (batterie)	*mpl*
Schachbrettverippung	*f*	chequerboard ribbing	*n*	nervurage en échiquier	*m*
Schadstoffanteil	*m*	noxious constituents	*npl*	taux de polluants	*m*
Schadstoffausstoß	*m*	pollutant emission	*n*	émission de polluants	*f*
Schadstoffe (Motorabgas)	*mpl*	pollutants (exhaust gas)	*npl*	polluants (gaz d'échappement)	*mpl*
Schadstoffemission	*f*	pollutant emission	*n*	émission de polluants	*f*
Schadstoffkomponente	*f*	pollutant component	*n*	polluant	*m*
Schalldämpfer (Druckregler)	*m*	silencer (pressure regulator)	*n*	silencieux (régulateur de pression)	*m*
Schalldichte	*f*	sound density	*n*	densité acoustique	*f*
Schalldruck	*m*	sound pressure	*n*	pression acoustique	*f*
Schalldruckpegel	*m*	sound pressure level	*n*	niveau de pression acoustique	*m*
Schallgeber (Autoalarm)	*m*	sonic generator (car alarm)	*n*	générateur acoustique (alarme auto)	*m*
Schallisolierung	*f*	soundproofing	*n*	isolation acoustique	*f*
Schallquelle	*f*	acoustic source	*n*	source acoustique	*f*
Schallschnelle	*f*	acoustic velocity	*n*	célérité du son	*f*
Schalt-Ansaugsystem	*n*	variable-configuration intake manifold	*n*	système d'admission à géométrie variable	*m*
Schaltbild	*n*	symbol	*n*	symbole graphique	*m*
Schaltgerät (Zündung)	*n*	ignition trigger box	*a*	module de commande de l'allumage	*m*
Schaltgetriebe	*n*	manually shifted transmission	*n*	boîte de vitesses classique	*f*
Schaltkasten	*m*	switch box	*n*	boîte de commande	*f*
Schaltkulisse	*f*	contoured switching guide	*n*	coulisse de contact	*f*

Deutsch		Englisch		Französisch	
Schaltplan	*m*	diagram	*n*	schéma électrique	*m*
Schaltpunkt (Getriebesteuerung)	*m*	shifting point (transmission control)	*n*	point de changement de vitesse	*m*
Schaltrhythmus (Relais)	*m*	switching frequency	*n*	rythme de commutation	*m*
Schaltspanne	*f*	operating range	*n*	écart de réglage	*m*
Schaltspannung	*f*	switched voltage	*n*	tension de rupture	*f*
Schaltspiel	*n*	switching cycle	*n*	cycle de commutation	*m*
Schaltstrom	*m*	switched current	*n*	courant d'enclenchement	*m*
Schaltungsgruppe	*f*	circuit group	*n*	module de circuit	*m*
Schaltwippe	*f*	rocker	*n*	bascule de commutation	*f*
Schaltzahl	*f*	number of switching operations	*n*	nombre de cycles de commutation	*m*
Schaltzeichen	*n*	symbol	*n*	symbole graphique	*m*
schärfen (Autoalarm)	*v*	prime (car alarm)	*v*	mise en veille (alarme auto)	*f*
Scharfschaltung (Autoalarm)	*f*	priming (car alarm)	*n*	amorçage (alarme auto)	*m*
Schaufelkranz (Elektrokraftstoffpumpe)	*m*	blade ring (electric fuel pump)	*n*	couronne à palettes (pompe électrique à carburant)	*f*
Schaufelrad (hydrodynamischer Verlangsamer)	*n*	blade wheel (hydrodynamic retarder)	*n*	roue à palettes (ralentisseur hydrodynamique)	*f*
Schaufelraum (hydrodynamischer Verlangsamer)	*m*	rotor chamber (hydrodynamic retarder)	*n*	volume entre les palettes du rotor (ralentisseur hydrodynamique)	*m*
Scheibenbremsbelag	*m*	disc-brake pad	*n*	garniture de frein à disque	*f*
Scheibenbremse	*f*	disc brake	*n*	frein à disque	*m*
Scheibenläufer	*m*	disc rotor	*n*	rotor à disque	*m*
Scheibenreinigung	*f*	windshield and rear-window cleaning	*n*	nettoyage des vitres	*m*
Scheibenspüler	*m*	windshield washer	*n*	lave-glace	*m*
Scheibenspülerpumpe	*f*	windshield-washer pump	*n*	pompe de lave-glace	*f*
Scheibenwischer	*m*	windshield wiper	*n*	essuie-glace	*m*
Scheibenwischeranlage	*f*	wiper system	*n*	équipement d'essuie-glace	*m*
Scheibenwischermotor	*m*	wiper motor	*n*	moteur d'essuie-glace	*m*
Scheinwerfer	*m*	headlamp	*n*	projecteur	*m*
Scheinwerfer-Einstellprüfgerät	*n*	headlight aiming device	*n*	appareil de réglage des projecteurs	*m*
Scheinwerfer-Waschanlage	*f*	headlamp washer system	*n*	lavophare complet	*m*
Scheinwerfer-Wischeranlage	*f*	headlamp wiper system	*n*	nettoyeur de projecteurs	*m*
Scheinwerferaufnahme	*f*	headlamp-housing assembly	*n*	cuvelage de projecteur	*m*
Scheinwerfereinsatz	*m*	headlight unit	*n*	bloc optique	*m*
Scheinwerfergehäuse	*n*	headlamp housing	*n*	boîtier de projecteur	*m*
Scheinwerfersystem	*n*	headlamp system	*n*	système de projecteurs	*m*
Scheitelspannung	*f*	peak voltage	*n*	tension de crête	*f*
Schichtlademotor	*m*	stratified-charge engine	*n*	moteur à charge stratifiée	*m*
Schiebebetrieb	*m*	overrun	*n*	régime de décélération	*m*
Schiebedach	*n*	sliding sunroof	*n*	toît ouvrant	*m*
Schiebedachantrieb	*m*	power-sunroof drive unit	*n*	entraînement du toit ouvrant	*m*
schieben (Fahrzeug, beim Lenken) x	*v*	push (out to the side, vehicle)	*v*	pousser (voiture, en braquage)	*v*

Deutsch		Englisch		Französisch	
Schieber-Überströmventil	*n*	spool overflow valve	*n*	soupape de décharge du coulisseau	*f*
Schieberweg	*m*	sleeve travel	*n*	course de coulisseau	*f*
Schieberzumessung	*f*	sleeve metering	*n*	dosage par bague	*m*
schiefziehen (Bremse) x	*v*	brake "pull"	*n*	déséquilibre des freins	*m*
schirmen (Entstörung)	*v*	shield (interference suppression)	*v*	blinder (antiparasitage)	*v*
Schlauchklemme	*f*	hose clamp	*n*	collier de serrage	*m*
Schleiferabgriff	*m*	wiper tap	*n*	curseur de contact	*m*
Schleiferarm (Drosselklappengeber)	*m*	wiper arm (throttle-valve sensor)	*n*	curseur (actionneur de papillon)	*m*
Schleiferbahn	*f*	potentiometer track	*n*	piste de potentiomètre	*f*
Schleiferhebel (Potentiometer)	*m*	wiper lever (potentiometer)	*n*	levier du curseur (potentiomètre)	*m*
Schleifkohle (elektrische Maschinen)	*f*	carbon brush (rotating machines)	*n*	balai de charbon (machines tournantes)	*m*
Schleifkontakt	*m*	sliding contact	*n*	contact par curseur	*m*
Schleifring	*m*	collector ring	*n*	bague collectrice	*f*
Schleifringkapselung	*f*	collector-ring housing	*n*	encapsulage des bagues collectrices	*m*
Schleifringlagerschild (Generator)	*m*	collector-ring end shield (alternator)	*n*	flasque côté bagues collectrices (alternateur)	*m*
schleifringlos (Generator)	*adj*	brushless (alternator)	*adj*	sans bagues collectrices (alternateur)	*loc*
Schlepper	*m*	tractor vehicle	*n*	véhicule tracteur	*m*
Schleppfeder	*f*	drag spring	*n*	ressort compensateur	*m*
Schlepphebel (Ventilsteuerung)	*m*	rocker arm (valve timing)	*n*	levier oscillant (commande des soupapes)	*m*
Schleppkolben	*m*	drag piston	*n*	piston de réaction	*m*
Schleuderprüfung	*f*	overspeed test	*n*	essai de dérapage	*m*
Schließdruck	*m*	closing pressure	*n*	pression de fermeture	*f*
Schließer (elektrischer Schalter	*m*	NO contact (electrical switch, normally open)	*n*	contact à fermeture (interrupteur électrique)	*m*
Schließglied (Kupplungskopf)	*n*	shutoff element (coupling head)	*n*	obturateur (tête d'accouplement)	*m*
Schließkraft	*f*	closing force	*n*	force de fermeture	*f*
Schließwinkel	*m*	dwell angle	*n*	angle de fermeture	*m*
Schließwinkelkennfeld	*n*	dwell-angle map	*n*	cartographie de l'angle de came	*f*
Schließzeit (Zündung)	*f*	dwell period (ignition)	*n*	temps de fermeture (allumage)	*m*
Schlitzträger (Jetronic)	*m*	barrel with metering slits (Jetronic)	*n*	cylindre à fentes d'étranglement (Jetronic)	*m*
Schloßzylinder (Sonderzündspule)	*m*	lock barrel (special ignition coil)	*n*	serrure à barillet (bobine d'allumage spéciale)	*f*
Schlupf (Rad)	*m*	wheel slip	*n*	glissement (roue)	*m*
Schlupfabschaltung (Rollenbremsprüfstand)	*f*	wheel-slip shutoff device (dynamic brake analyzer)	*n*	déconnexion automatique de glissement (banc d'essai)	*f*
Schlupfdifferenz	*f*	slip-rate difference	*n*	différence de glissement	*f*
Schlupfregler (ESP)	*m*	slip controller (ESP)	*n*	régulateur de glissement (ESP)	*m*
Schlupfschaltschwelle (ABS)	*f*	slip switching threshold (ABS)	*n*	seuil de glissement (ABS)	*m*
Schlüsselschalter (Autoalarm)	*m*	key-operated switch (car alarm)	*n*	interrupteur à clé (alarme auto)	*m*

Deutsch

Deutsch		Englisch		Französisch	
Schlußleuchte	*f*	tail lamp	*n*	feu arrière	*m*
Schlußlicht	*n*	tail lamp	*n*	feu arrière	*m*
Schlußprüfung	*f*	final inspection	*n*	contrôle final	*m*
Schmalbandstörung	*f*	narrow-band interference	*n*	perturbation à bande étroite	*f*
Schmierölkreislauf	*m*	engine lube-oil circuit	*n*	circuit de lubrification du moteur	*m*
Schmierölrücklauf	*m*	lube-oil return	*n*	retour de l'huile de graissage	*m*
Schmierölzulauf	*m*	lube-oil inlet	*n*	arrivée de l'huile de graissage	*f*
Schmierpumpe	*f*	lubricating pump	*n*	pompe de graissage	*f*
Schmutzseite (Filter)	*f*	contaminated side (filter)	*n*	côté impuretés (filtre)	*m*
Schnappverbindung	*f*	snap-on connection	*n*	liaison à déclic	*f*
schnarren	*v*	chatter <to chatter>	*v*	ronfler	*v*
Schnarrgruppe	*f*	chatter group	*n*	groupe de ronflement	*m*
Schnarrverhalten	*n*	chatter <noun>	*n*	ronflement	*m*
Schnelladung (Batterie)	*f*	boost charge (battery)	*n*	charge rapide (batterie)	*f*
schnellaufend (Dieselmotor)	*ppr*	high-speed (diesel engine)	*n*	à régime rapide (moteur diesel)	*loc*
Schnellbremsung	*f*	emergency braking	*n*	freinage rapide	*m*
Schnellentlüftungsventil (Bremse)	*n*	rapid-bleeder valve (brakes)	*n*	purgeur rapide (frein)	*m*
Schnellkupplung	*f*	rapid coupling	*n*	accouplement rapide	*m*
Schnellöseventil (Bremse)	*n*	quick-release valve (brakes)	*n*	valve de desserrage rapide (frein)	*f*
Schnellstart-Satz (Dieselfahrzeuge)	*m*	rapid starting kit (diesel vehicles)	*n*	kit de démarrage rapide (véhicules diesel)	*m*
Schnellstartanlage (Dieselfahrzeuge)	*f*	rapid starting system (diesel vehicles)	*n*	dispositif de démarrage rapide (véhicules diesel)	*m*
Schnellstartlader (Batterie)	*m*	rapid-start charger (battery)	*n*	chargeur de démarrage rapide (batterie)	*m*
Schnittstelle	*f*	interface	*n*	interface	*f*
Schnittzeichnung	*f*	sectional drawing	*n*	dessin en coupe	*m*
Schnorchel (Bremsventil)	*m*	snorkel (brake valve)	*n*	reniflard (valve de frein)	*m*
Schocksensor (Autoalarm)	*m*	shock sensor (car alarm)	*n*	capteur de choc (alarme auto)	*m*
Schrägkante (Pumpenelement)	*f*	helix (plunger-and-barrel assembly)	*n*	rampe hélicoïdale (élément de pompage)	*f*
Schrägkantensteuerung	*f*	helix control	*n*	commande par rampe inclinée	*f*
Schräglaufwinkel (Kfz-Dynamik)	*m*	slip angle (vehicle dynamics)	*n*	angle de dérive (dynamique d'un véhicule)	*m*
Schrägschulter-Düse	*f*	chamfered-shoulder nozzle	*n*	injecteur à portée oblique	*m*
Schraubachse (Kfz)	*f*	axis of rotation (motor vehicle)	*n*	axe de vissage (véhicule)	*m*
Schraubendruckfeder	*f*	helical compression spring	*n*	ressort hélicoïdal de compression	*m*
Schraubenverdichter	*m*	screw-type supercharger	*n*	compresseur à vis	*m*
Schraubweg (Starter)	*m*	helical travel (starter)	*n*	déplacement hélicoïdal (démarreur)	*m*
Schreib-Lese-Speicher, RAM	*m*	random-access memory, RAM	*n*	mémoire vive à lecture/écriture, RAM	*f*
Schrittmotor	*m*	stepping motor	*n*	moteur pas à pas	*m*
Schub-Schraubtrieb-Starter	*m*	pre-engaged-drive starter	*n*	démarreur à commande positive électromécanique	*m*

Deutsch		Englisch		Französisch	
Schubabschaltung	*f*	overrun fuel cutoff	*n*	coupure d'injection en décélération	*f*
Schubabschaltventil	*n*	overrun fuel-cutoff valve	*n*	électrovalve de coupure en décélération	*f*
Schubbetrieb	+ *m*	overrun	*n*	régime de décélération	*m*
Schubtrieb-Starter	*m*	sliding-gear starter	*n*	démarreur à pignon coulissant	*m*
Schubweg	*m*	pinion travel	*n*	course d'engrènement	*f*
Schüttelbeanspruchung	*f*	vibration	*n*	contrainte de vibration	*f*
Schüttelfestigkeit	*f*	vibration strength	*n*	résistance aux secousses	*f*
Schüttgutträger (Katalysator)	*m*	pelleted substrate (catalytic converter)	*n*	support à billes (catalyseur)	*m*
Schutzart	*f*	degree of protection	*n*	degré de protection	*m*
Schutzbalg	*m*	protective bellows	*n*	soufflet de protection	*m*
Schutzeinheit (Steuergerät)	*f*	protective unit (ECU)	*n*	module de protection (calculateur)	*m*
Schutzhaube	*f*	protection hood	*n*	capot de protection	*m*
Schutzkappe	*f*	protective cap	*n*	couvercle de protection	*m*
Schutzleiter	*m*	protective conductor	*n*	conducteur de protection	*m*
Schutzrelais	*n*	protective relay	*n*	relais de protection	*m*
Schutzschaltung	*f*	protective circuit	*n*	circuit de protection	*m*
Schutzventil (Bremse)	*n*	protection valve (brakes)	*n*	valve de sécurité (frein)	*f*
Schwachstelle	*f*	problem area	*n*	point faible	*m*
Schwarzrauch	*m*	black smoke	*n*	fumées noires	*fpl*
Schwärzung	*f*	blackening	*n*	noircissement	*m*
Schwärzungszahl	*f*	smoke number	*n*	indice de noircissement	*m*
Schwelldauer (Bremsvorgang)	*f*	pressure build-up time (braking)	*n*	temps d'accroissement (freinage)	*m*
Schwellendrehzahl	*f*	threshold speed	*n*	régime de seuil	*m*
Schwellenspannung	*f*	threshold voltage	*n*	tension de seuil	*f*
Schwellzeit (Bremsvorgang)	*f*	pressure build-up time (braking)	*n*	temps de montée en pression (freinage)	*m*
Schwenkarm	*m*	swivel arm	*n*	bras pivotant	*m*
Schwenkhebel	*m*	swivelling lever	*n*	levier pivotant	*m*
Schwerpunktverlagerung	*f*	displacement of the center of gravity	*n*	déplacement du centre de gravité	*m*
Schwimmkolben	*m*	float piston	*n*	piston flotteur	*m*
Schwimmkreis (Tandemhauptzylinder)	*m*	floating circuit (tandem master cylinder)	*n*	circuit flottant (maître-cylindre tandem)	*m*
Schwimmsattel (Bremse)	*m*	floating caliper (brakes)	*n*	étrier flottant (frein)	*m*
Schwimmwinkel (Kfz-Dynamik)	*m*	float angle (vehicle dynamics)	*n*	angle de flottement (dynamique d'un véhicule)	*m*
Schwingfestigkeit	*f*	vibrational strength	*n*	résistance aux vibrations	*f*
Schwingrohr	*n*	intake runner	*n*	pipe d'admission	*f*
Schwingsaugrohr	*n*	oscillatory intake passage	*n*	collecteur d'admission à oscillation	*m*
Schwingsaugrohr-Aufladung	*f*	ram-effect supercharging	*v*	suralimentation par oscillation d'admission	*f*
Schwingtür (Omnibus)	*f*	swinging door (bus)	*n*	porte va-et-vient (autobus)	*f*
Schwingungsdämpfer	*m*	vibration damper	*n*	amortisseur de vibrations	*m*

Deutsch			Englisch		Französisch	
Schwingungsfestigkeit		*f*	resistance to vibrations	*n*	tenue aux vibrations	*f*
Schwungmasse		*f*	flywheel	*n*	volant moteur	*m*
Schwungrad		*n*	flywheel	*n*	volant moteur	*m*
Schwungradzahnkranz		*m*	ring gear (flywheel)	*n*	couronne dentée de volant	*f*
Schwungscheibe	x	*f*	flywheel	*n*	volant moteur	*m*
Seilzug (Feststellbremse)		*n*	brake cable (parking brake)	*n*	câble de frein (frein de stationnement)	*m*
Seitenairbag		*m*	side airbag	*n*	coussin gonflable latéral	*m*
Seitenelektrode (Zündkerze)		*f*	side electrode (spark plug)	*n*	électrode latérale (bougie)	*f*
Seitenführungskraft		*f*	lateral force	*n*	force de guidage latéral	*f*
Seitenkanalpumpe		*f*	side-channel pump	*n*	pompe à canal latéral	*f*
Seitenkraft		*f*	side force	*n*	force latérale	*f*
Seitenkraftbeiwert		*m*	lateral-force coefficient	*n*	coefficient de force latérale	*m*
Seitenschlag (Bremsscheibe)		*m*	side runout (brake disc)	*n*	voilage (disque de frein)	*m*
Seitenwindkraft		*f*	crosswind force	*n*	force du vent latéral	*f*
Sekundärdruck (Bremse)		*m*	secondary pressure (brakes)	*n*	pression secondaire (frein)	*f*
Sekundärkreis	x	*m*	secondary circuit	*n*	circuit secondaire	*m*
Sekundärluft		*f*	secondary air	*n*	air secondaire	*m*
Sekundärlufteinblasung		*f*	secondary-air injection	*n*	insufflation d'air secondaire	*f*
Sekundärluftpumpe		*f*	secondary-air pump	*n*	pompe à air secondaire	*f*
Sekundärluftspalt		*m*	secondary air gap	*n*	entrefer secondaire	*m*
Sekundärluftventil		*n*	secondary-air valve	*n*	électrovalve d'air secondaire	*f*
Sekundärmanschette		*f*	secondary cup seal	*n*	manchette secondaire	*f*
Sekundärseite (Druckluftgeräte)		*f*	secondary side (compressed-air components)	*n*	côté secondaire (dispositifs à air comprimé)	*m*
Sekundärspannung		*f*	secondary voltage	*n*	tension secondaire	*f*
Sekundärstrom		*m*	secondary current	*n*	courant secondaire	*m*
Sekundärwicklung		*f*	secondary winding	*n*	enroulement secondaire	*m*
Selbstadaption		*f*	self-adaptation	*n*	auto-adaptation	*f*
Selbstaufladung		*f*	self-charging	*ppr*	auto-suralimentation	*f*
Selbstdrehzahl (Verbrennungsmotor)		*f*	self-sustaining speed (IC engine)	*n*	vitesse d'entretien (moteur à combustion)	*f*
selbsteinstellend		*ppr*	self-adjusting	*ppr*	autoréglable	*adj*
Selbstentladung (Batterie)		*f*	self-discharge (battery)	*n*	décharge spontanée (batterie)	*f*
Selbsterregung (drehende Maschinen)		*f*	self-excitation (rotating machines)	*n*	auto-excitation (machines tournantes)	*f*
selbsthemmend		*adj*	self-locking	*adj*	autobloquant	*adj*
Selbstinduktion		*f*	self-induction	*n*	auto-induction	*f*
Selbstlauf		*m*	sustained operation	*n*	fonctionnement autonome	*m*
selbstregelnd		*ppr*	self-governing	*ppr*	autorégulation	*f*
selbstreinigend		*adj*	self-cleaning	*ppr*	autonettoyant	*adj*
selbstschmierend		*adj*	self-lubricating	*adj*	autolubrifiant	*adj*
selbsttätige Bremsanlage		*f*	automatic braking system	*n*	dispositif de freinage automatique	*m*
selbsttätige Bremsung		*f*	automatic braking	*n*	freinage automatique	*m*
Selbsttest		*m*	self test	*n*	test automatique	*m*
Selbstüberwachung		*f*	self-monitoring	*n*	autosurveillance	*f*

Deutsch		Englisch		Französisch	
Selbstverringerung (Bremskraft)	*f*	self-reduction (braking force)	*n*	autoréduction (force de freinage)	*f*
Selbstverstärkung (Bremskraft)	*f*	self-amplification (braking force)	*n*	auto-amplification (force de freinage)	*f*
Selbstzünder	*m*	compression-ignition (CI) engine	*n*	moteur à allumage par compression	*m*
Selbstzündpunkt	+ *m*	auto-ignition temperature	*n*	température d'autoallumage	*f*
Selbstzündtemperatur	*f*	auto-ignition temperature	*n*	température d'autoallumage	*f*
Selbstzündung	*f*	auto-ignition	*n*	auto-allumage	*m*
Selbstzündungsmotor	*m*	compression-ignition (CI) engine	*n*	moteur à allumage par compression	*m*
Select-high-Regelung, SH (ABS/ASR)	x *f*	select-high control, SH (ABS/TCS)	*n*	sélection haute (ABS/ASR)	*f*
Select-low-Regelung, SL (ABS/ASR)	x *f*	select-low control, SL (ABS/TCS)	*n*	sélection basse (ABS/ASR)	*f*
Select-smart-Regelung, SSM (ABS/ASR)	x *f*	select-smart control, SSM (ABS/TCS)	*n*	sélection idéale (ABS/ASR)	*f*
Sensor	*m*	sensor	*n*	capteur	*m*
Sensorelement	*n*	sensor element	*n*	élément sensible	*m*
Separator (Batterie)	*m*	separator (battery)	*n*	séparateur (batterie)	*m*
sequentiell	*adj*	sequential	*adj*	séquentiel	*adj*
seriell	*adj*	serial	*adj*	sériel	*adj*
Serienausführung	*f*	series fabrication type	*n*	version de série	*f*
Seriendüse	*f*	standard nozzle	*n*	injecteur de série	*m*
Servo-Bremsanlage	*f*	power-assisted braking system	*n*	dispositif de freinage assisté par énergie auxiliaire	*m*
Servobremse (Trommelbremse)	*f*	servo brake (drum brake)	*n*	servofrein (frein à tambour)	*m*
Servoeinspritzpumpe	*f*	servo fuel-injection pump	*n*	servopompe d'injection	*f*
Servolenkung	*f*	power steering	*n*	direction assistée	*f*
Servoventil	*n*	servo valve	*n*	vanne commandée par servomoteur	*f*
Shuttle-Zumessung	*f*	displacement metering	*n*	dosage par déplacement	*m*
Sicherheitsabstand (Kolbenkopf)	*m*	head clearance (piston)	*n*	jeu d'extrémité supérieure (piston)	*m*
Sicherheitselektronik	*f*	safety and security electronics	*npl*	électronique de sécurité	*f*
Sicherheitsgurt	*m*	seat belt	*n*	ceinture de sécurité	*f*
Sicherheitshinweise	*mpl*	safety instructions	*npl*	conseils de sécurité	*mpl*
Sicherheitsmodul	*m*	safety module	*n*	module de sécurité	*m*
Sicherheitsmodus	*m*	safety mode	*n*	mode "sécurité"	*m*
Sicherheitspatrone (Luftfilter)	*f*	safety element (air filter)	*n*	cartouche de sécurité (filtre à air)	*f*
Sicherheitsrelais (Steuergerät)	*n*	safety relay (ECU)	*n*	relais de sécurité (calculateur)	*m*
Sicherheitsschalter	*m*	safety switch	*n*	contacteur de sécurité	*m*
Sicherheitsschaltung	*f*	safety circuit	*n*	circuit de sécurité	*m*
Sicherheitssystem	*n*	safety and security system	*n*	système de sécurité	*m*
Sicherheitsventil (Lufttrockner)	*n*	safety valve (air drier)	*n*	valve de sécurité (dessiccateur)	*f*
Sicherheitsvorschriften	*fpl*	safety regulations	*npl*	prescriptions de sécurité	*fpl*
Sicherungsdose	*f*	fuse box	*n*	boîte à fusibles	*f*
Sicherungsdruck	*m*	safety pressure	*n*	pression de sécurité	*f*

Deutsch		Englisch		Französisch	
Sicherungsring	*m*	retainer	*n*	anneau d'arrêt	*m*
Sichtprüfung	*f*	visual examination	*n*	examen visuel	*m*
Sichttrübung	*f*	impairment of vision	*n*	manque de visibilité	*m*
Sichtweite	*f*	visual range	*n*	visibilité	*f*
Siebeffekt (Filter)	*m*	straining (filter)	*n*	effet de filtrage (filtre)	*m*
Siebfilter (Kraftstofförderpumpe)	*n*	strainer (fuel-supply pump)	*n*	crépine (pompe d'alimentation)	*f*
Siebkörper (Einspritzventil)	*m*	strainer (fuel injector)	*n*	crible (injecteur)	*m*
Siedeverlauf (Benzin)	*m*	boiling curve (gasoline)	*n*	courbe d'ébullition (essence)	*f*
Signalanlage	*f*	signaling system	*n*	dispositif de signalisation	*m*
Signalfluß	*m*	current flow	*n*	flux de signaux	*m*
Signalhorn	*n*	horn	*n*	avertisseur sonore	*m*
Signalwandler	*m*	signal transducer	*n*	convertisseur de signaux	*m*
Simplex-Trommelbremse	*f*	simplex brake	*n*	frein simplex	*m*
Simplexbremse	*f*	simplex brake	*n*	frein simplex	*m*
simultan	*adj*	simultaneous	*adj*	simultané	*adj*
Sitzbelegungserkennung	*f*	seat-occupant detection	*n*	détection d'occupation de siège	*f*
Sitzdurchmesser (Düse)	*m*	nozzle-seat diameter	*n*	diamètre du siège d'injecteur	*m*
Sitzheizung	*f*	seat heating	*n*	chauffage de siège	*m*
Sitzlochdüse	*f*	sac-less (vco) nozzle	*n*	injecteur à siège perforé	*m*
Sitzverstellung	*f*	seat adjustment	*n*	réglage des sièges	*m*
Solldrehzahl	*f*	set speed	*n*	vitesse de rotation prescrite	*f*
Sollstrom	*m*	nominal current	*n*	courant nominal	*m*
Sollwertgeber	*m*	desired-value generator	*n*	consignateur	*m*
Sonderelektrode	*f*	special electrode	*n*	électrode spéciale	*f*
Sonderuntersuchung (Bremse)	*f*	special examination (brakes)	*n*	contrôle spécifique (frein)	*m*
Sonderwerkzeug	*n*	special tool	*n*	outil spécial	*m*
Sonderzündspule	*f*	special ignition coil	*n*	bobine d'allumage spéciale	*f*
Sonnenrad	*n*	sun gear	*n*	roue solaire	*f*
Spaltfilter	*n*	edge filter	*n*	filtre à disques	*m*
Spaltlochdüse	*f*	hole-type nozzle gap	*n*	injecteur à fente	*m*
Spaltmaß (Dieseleinspritzung)	*n*	gap dimension (diesel fuel injection)	*n*	cote d'écartement (injection diesel)	*f*
Spannbügel	*m*	hold-down clamp	*n*	étrier de fixation	*m*
Spannhebel	*m*	tensioning lever	*n*	levier de tension	*m*
Spannhülse	*f*	slotted spring pin	*n*	douille de serrage	*f*
Spannkraft (Bremsbeläge)	*f*	application force (brake linings	*n*	force de serrage (garnitures de frein)	*f*
Spannmutter	*f*	retaining nut	*n*	écrou-raccord	*m*
Spannstift	*m*	locating pin	*n*	broche de positionnement	*f*
Spannungsabfall	*m*	voltage drop	*n*	chute de tension	*f*
Spannungsabgriff (Niveaugeber)	*m*	contact wiper (level sensor)	*n*	prise de tension (capteur de niveau)	*f*
Spannungsbegrenzung	*f*	voltage limitation	*n*	limitation de tension	*f*
Spannungseinbruch	*m*	voltage drop	*n*	chute de tension	*f*
Spannungsfall	*m*	voltage drop	*n*	chute de tension	*f*
spannungsfest	*adj*	surge-proof	*adj*	rigidité diélectrique	*f*

Deutsch		Englisch		Französisch	
Spannungsfestigkeit	*f*	electric strength	*n*	résistance à la tension	*f*
Spannungskonstanthalter	*m*	voltage stabilizer	*n*	stabilisateur de tension	*m*
Spannungsregelung	*f*	voltage regulation	*n*	régulation de tension	*f*
Spannungsregler (Generator)	*m*	voltage regulator (alternator)	*n*	régulateur de tension (alternateur)	*m*
Spannungsspitze	*f*	voltage peak	*n*	pointe de tension	*f*
Spannungssprung	*m*	voltage jump	*n*	saut de tension	*m*
Spannungsstabilisator	*m*	voltage stabilizer	*n*	stabilisateur de tension	*m*
Spannungsstabilisierung	*f*	voltage stabilisation	*n*	stabilisation de la tension	*f*
Spannungsteiler	*m*	voltage divider	*n*	diviseur de tension	*m*
Spannungsversorgung	*f*	power supply	*n*	alimentation en tension	*f*
Spannungsverteilung	*f*	voltage distribution	*n*	distribution de tension	*f*
Spät-Verstellsystem	*n*	late (retard) adjustment system	*n*	système de correction "retard"	*m*
Spätverstellung (Zündwinkel)	*f*	ignition retard	*n*	retard (angle d'allumage)	*m*
Speicherdruck	*m*	storage pressure	*n*	pression de l'accumulateur	*f*
Speichereinspritzpumpe	*f*	accumulator fuel-injection pump	*n*	pompe d'injection à accumulateur	*f*
Speicherkammer (ABS)	*f*	accumulator chamber (ABS)	*n*	chambre d'accumulation (ABS)	*f*
Speicherschaltung (Rollenbremsprüfstand)	*f*	memory circuit (dynamic brake analyzer)	*n*	circuit de mémorisation (banc d'essai)	*m*
Speicherüberströmventil	*n*	accumulator overflow valve	*n*	soupape de décharge de l'accumulateur	*f*
Speicherventil	*n*	compensation valve	*n*	soupape de compensation	*f*
spektrale Beschleunigungs-dichte	*f*	spectral acceleration density	*n*	densité spectrale d'accélération	*f*
Sperr-Diode	*f*	block diode	*n*	diode de barrage	*f*
Sperrdifferential	*n*	locking differential	*n*	différentiel autobloquant	*m*
Sperreffekt (Filter)	*m*	blockage (filter)	*n*	effet de barrage (filtre)	*m*
Sperrkennlinie	*f*	off-state characteristic	*n*	caractéristique à l'état bloqué	*f*
Sperrmagnet	*m*	shut-down solenoid	*n*	électro-aimant de blocage	*m*
Sperrnut	*f*	oil-block groove	*n*	rainure de barrage	*f*
Sperröl x	*n*	sealing oil	*n*	carburant de barrage	*m*
Sperrölzulaufbohrung +	*f*	blocking-oil inlet passage	*n*	orifice d'admission de carburant de barrage	*m*
Sperrspannung (Diode)	*f*	reverse voltage (diode)	*n*	tension inverse (diode)	*f*
Sperrspannung (Halbleiter)	*f*	off-state voltage (semiconductor)	*n*	tension à l'état bloqué (semi-conducteur)	*f*
Sperrventil	*n*	check valve	*n*	valve d'arrêt	*f*
Spiegelheizung	*f*	mirror heating	*n*	chauffage de rétroviseur	*m*
Spiegelverstellsystem	*n*	mirror adjusting system	*n*	système de réglage des rétroviseurs	*m*
Spiegelverstellung	*f*	mirror adjuster	*n*	réglage de rétroviseur	*m*
Spiralfeder	*f*	spiral spring	*n*	ressort hélicöidal	*m*
Spiralgehäuse	*n*	spiral housing	*n*	carter hélicoïde	*m*
Spirallader	*m*	spiral-type supercharger	*n*	compresseur à hélicoïde	*m*
Spitzenbelastung	*f*	peak load	*n*	charge de pointe	*f*
Spitzendruck	*m*	peak injection pressure	*n*	pression de pointe	*f*
Spitzenwertpegel	*m*	peak-value level	*n*	niveau de valeur de pointe	*m*

Deutsch		Englisch		Französisch	
Split-Element	*n*	stepped plunger	*n*	élément avec fente de préinjection	*m*
Spreizbacke (Trommelbremse)	*f*	wedge-type shoe (drum brake)	*n*	came d'écartement (frein)	*f*
Spreizkeil (Bremse)	*m*	wedge (brakes)	*n*	coin d'écartement (frein)	*m*
Spreizkeilbremse	*f*	wedge-actuated brake	*n*	frein à coin	*m*
Spritzbeginn	*m*	start of injection	*n*	début d'injection	*m*
Spritzbohrung	*f*	injection orifice	*n*	trou d'injection	*m*
Spritzdauer	*f*	injection time	*n*	durée d'injection	*f*
Spritzdüse (Scheibenwaschanlage)	*f*	nozzle (windshield washer)	*n*	gicleur (lavophare)	*m*
Spritzende	*n*	end of injection	*n*	fin d'injection	*f*
Spritzfolge	x *f*	injection sequence	*n*	ordre d'injection	*m*
Spritzloch	*n*	injection orifice	*n*	trou d'injection	*m*
Spritzlochkegelwinkel	*m*	spray-hole cone angle	*n*	angle des trous d'injection	*m*
Spritzrate	*f*	injection rate	*n*	taux d'injection	*m*
Spritzschutz (Wasser)	*m*	splash guard (water)	*n*	protection contre les projections d'eau	*f*
Spritzversteller	*m*	timing device	*n*	variateur d'avance	*m*
Spritzversteller-Magnetventil	*n*	timing-device solenoid valve	*n*	électrovanne de variateur d'avance	*f*
Spritzverzug	*m*	injection lag	*n*	délai d'injection	*m*
Spritzwasserschutz	*m*	splash guard (water)	*n*	protection contre les projections d'eau	*f*
Spritzwinkel	*m*	spray dispersal angle	*n*	angle du cône d'injection	*m*
Spritzzapfen	*m*	pintle	*n*	téton d'injection	*m*
Sprühelektrode	*f*	discharge electrode	*n*	électrode de diffusion	*f*
Sprühscheibenelektrode	*f*	discharge electrode	*n*	électrode de diffusion	*f*
Spulenzündung, SZ	*f*	coil ignition, CI	*n*	allumage par bobine	*m*
Spülluft	*f*	purge air	*n*	air de balayage	*m*
Spurkreisradius	*m*	turning radius	*n*	rayon du cercle de braquage	*m*
Spurtreue (Kfz)	*f*	vehicle stability (staying in lane)	*n*	trajectoire (véhicule)	*f*
Stabfilter	*n*	edge-type filter	*n*	filtre-tige	*m*
Stabilisator	*m*	stabilizer	*n*	stabilisateur	*m*
Stabilisierungssystem (Kfz)	+ *n*	electronic stability program, ESP	*n*	régulation du comportement dynamique, ESP	*f*
Stabwicklung	*f*	bar winding	*n*	enroulement-tige	*m*
Standard-Düsenhalter	*m*	standard nozzle holder	*n*	porte-injecteur standard	*m*
Standard-Kipphebel (Ventiltrieb)	*m*	standard rocker arm (valve gear)	*n*	levier culbuteur (commande de soupapes)	*m*
Standard-Zündspule	*f*	standard ignition coil	*n*	bobine d'allumage standard	*f*
Standardisierung	*f*	standardization	*n*	standardisation	*f*
Standdruck	*m*	static pressure	*n*	pression statique	*f*
Ständer (Generator)	*m*	stator (alternator)	*n*	stator (alternateur)	*m*
Ständerblechpaket (Generator)	*n*	stator lamination (alternator)	*n*	paquet de lamelles de tôle (alternateur)	*m*
Ständergehäuse	*n*	stator housing	*n*	carcasse stator	*f*
Ständerpaket (Generator)	*n*	stator lamination (alternator)	*n*	paquet de lamelles de tôle (alternateur)	*m*

Deutsch			Englisch		Französisch	
Ständerstrom		*m*	stator current	*n*	courant statorique	*m*
Ständerwicklung		*f*	stator winding	*n*	enroulement statorique	*m*
Standheizung		*f*	auxiliary heating	*n*	chauffage auxiliaire	*m*
Standheizungs-Glühkerze		*f*	glow plug for auxiliary heaters	*n*	bougie de préchauffage pour chauffage auxiliaire	*f*
Standlicht	+	*n*	side-marker lamp	*n*	feu de position	*m*
Starktonhorn		*n*	supertone horn	*n*	avertisseur surpuissant	*m*
Start-Externschalter		*m*	external start switch	*n*	commande extérieure de démarrage	*f*
Startabwurfdrehzahl		*f*	starting cutout speed	*n*	régime en fin de démarrage	*m*
Startabwurfsperrzeit		*f*	starting-cutout	*n*	verrouillage en fin de démarrage	*m*
Startanhebung		*f*	starting enrichment	*n*	signal d'enrichissement au démarrage	*m*
Startanlage		*f*	starting system	*n*	équipement de démarrage	*m*
Startbereitschaftsanzeige (Dieselmotor)		*f*	ready-to-start indicator (diesel engine)	*n*	indicateur de disponibilité de démarrage (moteur diesel)	*m*
Startbetrieb		*m*	starting operation	*n*	démarrage (opération)	*m*
Startdauer		*f*	starting time	*n*	durée de démarrage	*f*
Startdrehzahl		*f*	cranking speed	*n*	vitesse de démarrage	*f*
Startdrehzahlanhebung		*f*	cranking-speed increase	*n*	régime accéléré de démarrage	*m*
Startentriegelung	x	*f*	start-quantity release	*n*	débloqueur du débit de surcharge au démarrage	*m*
Starter		*m*	starter	*n*	démarreur	*m*
Starterbatterie		*f*	starter battery	*n*	batterie de démarrage	*f*
Starterhauptleitung		*f*	starter cable	*n*	câble principal du démarreur	*m*
Starterleitung	+	*f*	starter cable	*n*	câble principal du démarreur	*m*
Starterrelais		*m*	starting-motor relay	*n*	relais de démarreur	*m*
Starterritzel		*n*	starter pinion	*n*	pignon du démarreur	*m*
Startfeder		*f*	starting spring	*n*	ressort de démarrage	*m*
Startgrenztemperatur		*f*	minimum starting temperature	*n*	température limite de démarrage	*f*
Starthebel		*m*	starting lever	*n*	levier de démarrage	*m*
Starthilfe		*f*	start-assist measure	*n*	auxiliaire de démarrage	*m*
Starthilfesystem		*n*	start-assist system	*n*	dispositif auxiliaire de démarrage	*m*
Starthilfsanlage		*f*	start-assist system	*n*	dispositif auxiliaire de démarrage	*m*
Starthilfskabel		*n*	battery jumper cable	*n*	câble d'aide au démarrage	*m*
Startlage		*f*	start position	*n*	position de démarrage	*f*
Startleistung		*f*	starting power	*n*	puissance de démarrage	*f*
Startmagnet		*m*	starting solenoid	*n*	électro-aimant de démarrage	*m*
Startmehrmenge		*f*	excess fuel for starting	*n*	surdébit de démarrage	*m*
Startmenge		*f*	start quantity	*n*	débit de démarrage	*m*
Startmengenabgleich		*m*	starting fuel-quantity compensation	*n*	étalonnage du débit de démarrage	*m*
Startmengenanschlag		*m*	start-quantity stop	*n*	butée de débit de surcharge au démarrage	*f*

Deutsch		Englisch		Französisch	
Startmengenbegrenzung	*f*	start-quantity limitation	*n*	limitation du débit de surcharge au démarrage	*f*
Startmengenentriegelung	*f*	start-quantity release	*n*	débloqueur du débit de surcharge au démarrage	*m*
Startmengenverriegelung	*f*	start-quantity locking device	*n*	bloqueur du débit de surcharge au démarrage	*m*
Startmengenverstellweg	*m*	start-quantity stop travel	*n*	course de surcharge au démarrage	*f*
Startmengenvorrichtung	*f*	excess-fuel device	*n*	dispositif de débit de surcharge au démarrage	*m*
Startmengenvorsteuerung	*f*	excess-fuel preset	*n*	pilotage du débit de surcharge	*m*
Startmindestdrehzahl	*f*	minimum starting speed	*n*	régime minimum de démarrage	*m*
Startnut (Pumpenelement)	*f*	starting groove (plunger-and-barrel assembly)	*n*	encoche d'autoretard (élément de pompage)	*f*
Startphase	*f*	starting phase	*n*	phase de démarrage	*f*
Startregelweg	*m*	starting rack travel	*n*	course de régulation au démarrage	*f*
Startschalter	x *m*	ignition/starting switch	*n*	commutateur d'allumage-démarrage	*m*
Startspannungsanhebung	*f*	starting-voltage increase	*n*	élévation de tension au démarrage	*f*
Startsperreinrichtung	*f*	start-locking	*n*	dispositif de blocage du démarreur	*m*
Startsperrelais	*n*	start-locking relay	*n*	relais de blocage du démarreur	*m*
Startsteuerung	*f*	start control	*n*	commande de démarrage	*f*
Starttemperatur	*f*	starting temperature	*n*	température de démarrage	*f*
Starttemperaturgrenze	*f*	start-temperature limit	*n*	limite de température de démarrage	*f*
Startventil	*n*	cold-start valve	*n*	injecteur de départ à froid	*m*
Startverhalten	*n*	starting response	*n*	comportement au démarrage	*m*
Startverriegelung	*f*	starting-quantity deactivator	*n*	verrouillage du débit de surcharge	*m*
Startvorgang	*m*	start	*v*	démarrage	*m*
Startwiederholsperre	*f*	start-repeating block	*n*	anti-répétiteur de démarrage	*m*
stationäre Kreisfahrt	*f*	steady-state skidpad testing	*n*	conduite circulaire stationnaire	*f*
Stator (Generator)	*m*	stator (alternator)	*n*	stator (alternateur)	*m*
Statorwicklung	*f*	stator winding	*n*	enroulement statorique	*m*
staubgeschützt	*adj*	dust-protected	*pp*	protégé contre la poussière	*pp*
Staubmanschette	*f*	dust sleeve	*n*	garniture anti-poussière	*f*
Staubsammelbehälter (Filter)	*m*	dust bowl (filter)	*n*	collecteur de poussière (filtre)	*m*
Staubtopf (Filter)	*m*	dust bowl (filter)	*n*	collecteur de poussière (filtre)	*m*
Stauklappe (L-Jetronic)	*f*	sensor plate (L-Jetronic)	*n*	volet-sonde (L-Jetronic)	*m*
Stauscheibe (K-Jetronic)	*f*	sensor plate (K-Jetronic)	*n*	plateau-sonde (K-Jetronic)	*m*
Stechspitzenanschluß	*m*	piercing-tip terminal	*n*	connexion à pointes d'enfichage	*f*
Steckbefestigung (Wischer)	*f*	snap-in fastening (wipers)	*n*	fixation par enfichage (essuie-glace)	*f*
Steckdose	*f*	socket	*n*	prise	*f*
Stecker	*m*	connector	*n*	fiche	*f*
Steckerbuchse	*f*	plug socket	*n*	contact femelle	*m*

Deutsch		Englisch		Französisch	
Steckercodierung	*f*	plug code	*n*	codage des fiches	*m*
Steckerstift	*m*	connector pin	*n*	contact mâle	*m*
Steckhülse	*f*	receptable	*n*	fiche femelle	*f*
Steckhülsengehäuse	*n*	socket housing	*n*	boîtier pour fiches femelles	*m*
Stecklehre	*f*	plug gauge	*n*	calibre	*m*
Steckschnabelbefestigung (Wischer)	*f*	snap-in nib fastening (wipers)	*n*	fixation par bec enfichable (essuie-glace)	*f*
Steckverbindung	*f*	plug-in connection	*n*	connecteur	*m*
Stehbolzen	*m*	stud	*n*	boulon fileté	*m*
Steigstrom-Luftmengenmesser	*m*	updraft air-flow sensor	*n*	débitmètre d'air à flux ascendant	*m*
Steigungswiderstand	*m*	climbing resistance	*n*	résistance en côte	*f*
Stellbefehl (Steuergerät)	*m*	control command (ECU)	*n*	instruction de commande (calculateur)	*f*
Stelleingriff	*m*	actuator adjustment	*n*	intervention par positionnement	*f*
Stelleinrichtung (ASR)	*f*	final control element (TCS)	*n*	actionneur de réglage (ASR)	*m*
Stellelement	*n*	control element	*n*	élément de commande	*m*
Stellfenster (Leerlaufsteller)	*n*	actuator window (idle actuator)	*n*	fenêtre de régulation (actionneur de ralenti)	*f*
Stellgeschwindigkeit	*f*	positioning rate	*n*	vitesse de régulation	*f*
Stellglied	*n*	actuator	*n*	actuateur	*m*
Stellgröße	*f*	manipulated variable	*n*	grandeur réglante	*f*
Stellgrößenbegrenzung	*f*	correcting-variable limit	*n*	limitation des grandeurs de correction	*f*
Stellmagnet	*m*	actuator solenoid	*n*	électro-aimant de positionnement	*m*
Stellmotor	*m*	servomotor	*n*	servomoteur	*m*
Stellschalter	*m*	detent switch	*n*	interrupteur à retour non automatique	*m*
Stellsignal	*n*	command signal	*n*	signal de réglage	*m*
Stellwelle	*f*	actuator shaft	*n*	axe de positionnement	*m*
Stellwerk	*n*	actuator mechanism	*n*	actionneur	*m*
Stellwerkjoch	*m*	actuator fastening flange	*m*	noyau d'actionneur	*m*
Stellwerkrotor	*m*	actuator rotor	*n*	rotor d'actionneur	*m*
Stellzylinder (ASR)	*m*	positioning cylinder (TCS)	*n*	cylindre positionneur (ASR)	*m*
Sternfilterelement	*n*	radial vee-form filter element	*n*	cartouche filtrante en étoile	*f*
Sternpunkt	*m*	neutral point	*n*	point neutre	*m*
Sternschaltung	*f*	star connection	*n*	montage en étoile	*m*
Steueranschluß	*m*	control connection	*n*	raccord de commande	*m*
Steuerbefehl (Steuergerät)	*m*	control command (ECU)	*n*	instruction de commande (calculateur)	*f*
Steuerbohrung	*f*	spill port	*n*	orifice de distribution	*m*
Steuerbolzen (Luftfederventil)	*m*	control pin (height-control valve)	*n*	axe de commande (valve de nivellement)	*m*
Steuerdose	*f*	aneroid capsule	*n*	capsule de commande	*f*
Steuerdruck	*m*	control pressure	*n*	pression de commande	*f*
Steuergerät	*n*	electronic control unit, ECU	*n*	centrale de commande électronique	*f*

Deutsch		Englisch		Französisch	
Steuergerätebox	*f*	control-unit box	*n*	boîtier de centrale de commande	*m*
Steuergeräteinitialisierung	*f*	control-unit initialization	*n*	initialisation de la centrale de commande	*f*
Steuergröße	*f*	controlled variable (open-loop control)	*n*	paramètre de commande	*m*
Steuerimpuls (Steuergerät)	*m*	control pulse (ECU)	*n*	impulsion de commande (calculateur)	*f*
Steuerkammer	*f*	pilot chamber	*n*	chambre de commande	*f*
Steuerkante (Pumpenelement)	*f*	helix (plunger-and-barrel assembly)	*n*	rampe hélicoïdale (élément de pompage)	*f*
Steuerkanten-Zumessung	*f*	port-and-helix metering	*n*	dosage par rampe et trou	*m*
Steuerkegel	*m*	control cone	*n*	cône de commande	*m*
Steuerkette	*f*	open control loop	*n*	chaîne de commande	*f*
Steuerkolben	*m*	control plunger	*n*	piston de commande	*m*
Steuerleitung	*f*	control line	*n*	câble-pilote	*m*
Steuerrelais	*n*	control relay	*n*	relais de commande	*m*
Steuerschalter	*m*	control switch	*n*	contacteur de commande	*m*
Steuerschlitz	*m*	metering slot	*n*	fente d'étranglement (piston)	*f*
Steuersignal	*n*	control signal (open loop)	*n*	signal de commande	*m*
Steuerstrom	*m*	control current	*n*	courant de pilotage	*m*
Steuerteil (Lufttrockner)	*n*	control section (air drier)	*n*	module de commande (dessiccateur)	*m*
Steuerventil	*n*	control valve (open loop)	*n*	valve de commande	*f*
Steuerzeit	*f*	control time	*n*	temps de commande	*m*
Stichprobenprüfung	*f*	sampling inspection	*n*	contrôle par échantillonnage	*m*
Stiftgehäuse	*n*	pin housing	*n*	boîtier à contacts mâles	*m*
stöchiometrisch	*adj*	stoichiometric	*adj*	stœchiométrique	*adj*
Stopp-Lage	*f*	stop setting	*n*	position de stop	*f*
Stopp-Position	*f*	stop setting	*n*	position de stop	*f*
Stopp-Stellung	*f*	stop setting	*n*	position de stop	*f*
Stoppanschlag (Dieseleinspritzung)	*m*	shutoff stop (diesel fuel injection)	*n*	butée de stop (injection diesel)	*f*
Stoppbremsung	*f*	braking to a standstill	*n*	freinage d'arrêt	*m*
Stopphebel (Verteilereinspritzpumpe)	*m*	stop lever (distributor pump)	*n*	levier de stop (pompe distributrice)	*m*
Stopplichtschalter	*m*	brake-light switch	*n*	contacteur de feux de stop	*m*
Stoppnut	*f*	stop slot	*n*	rainure de stop	*f*
Störabstrahlung (EMV)	*f*	interference radiation (EMC)	*n*	rayonnement de signaux perturbateurs (CEM)	*m*
Störenergie (EMV)	*f*	interference energy (EMC)	*n*	énergie perturbatrice (CEM)	*f*
Störgröße (Regelung und Steuerung)	*f*	disturbance value (regulation and control)	*n*	grandeur perturbatrice (régulation)	*f*
Störpegel (EMV)	*m*	interference level (EMC)	*n*	niveau de perturbations (CEM)	*m*
Störquelle	*f*	radio-interference source	*n*	source de perturbations (CEM)	*f*
Störsenke (EMV)	*f*	susceptible device (EMC)	*n*	capteur de perturbations (CEM)	*m*
Störspannung (EMV)	*f*	radio interference voltage (EMC)	*n*	tension perturbatrice (CEM)	*f*

Deutsch		Englisch		Französisch	
Störstrahlung (EMV)	f	interference radiation (EMC)	n	rayonnement de signaux perturbateurs (CEM)	m
Störstrom (EMV)	m	interference current (EMC)	n	courant perturbateur (CEM)	m
Störunterdrückung	f	interference suppression	n	antiparasitage	m
Störwelle (EMV)	f	interference wave (EMC)	n	onde perturbatrice (CEM)	f
Stoßaufladung	f	pulse turbocharging	v	suralimentation pulsatoire	f
Stoßdämpfer (Kfz)	m	shock absorber (motor vehicle)	n	amortisseur (véhicule)	m
Stößel (Türbetätigung)	m	push rod (door control)	n	poussoir (commande des portes	m
Stößel (Ventiltrieb)	m	tappet (valve gear)	n	poussoir (commande de soupape)	m
Stößelkolben	m	tappet plunger	n	piston-poussoir	m
Stößelkörper	m	roller-tappet shell	n	corps de poussoir	m
Stößelrolle	f	tappet roller	n	galet de poussoir	m
Stoßsensor	m	impact sensor	n	capteur de choc	m
Strahlbild	n	spray pattern	n	aspect du jet	m
Strahldüse	f	jet	n	buse d'éjection	f
Strahlenregler	m	straight-line controller	n	correcteur à divergence	m
Strahlform (Einspritzung)	f	spray shape (injection)	n	forme du jet (injection)	f
Strahlkegelwinkel	m	spray dispersal angle	n	angle du cône d'injection	m
Strahlungsschutz	m	radiation shield	n	protection contre les radiations	f
Strahlwinkel	m	spray dispersal angle	n	angle du cône d'injection	m
Straßenmoment (ASR)	n	road torque (TCS)	n	couple de la route (ASR)	m
Streuflußverluste (magnetische)	mpl	magnetic leakage	n	pertes de flux magnétique	fpl
Streulinse	f	lens (headlamp)	n	diffuseur (projecteur)	m
Streuscheibe (Scheinwerfer)	f	lens (headlamp)	n	diffuseur (projecteur)	m
Stromabgabe (Generator)	f	current output (alternator)	n	débit (alternateur)	m
Strombegrenzer	m	current limiter	n	limiteur d'intensité	m
Strombegrenzungsventil	n	flow-limiting valve	n	limiteur de débit	m
Strombremse (Starter)	f	electric brake (starter)	n	frein électrique (démarreur)	m
Stromkreis	m	electric circuit	n	circuit électrique	m
Stromlaufplan	m	schematic diagram	n	schéma des circuits	m
Stromregelventil	n	flow-control valve	n	régulateur de débit	m
Stromregelzeit	f	current control time	n	temps de régulation du courant	m
Stromregler	m	current regulator	n	régulateur de courant	m
Stromschiene	f	bus bar	n	barre de distribution	f
Strömungsfühler (Abgasprüfung)	m	flow sensor (exhaust-gas test)	n	débitmètre (émissions)	m
Strömungsgeschwindigkeit	f	flow velocity	n	vitesse d'écoulement	f
Strömungslader	m	centrifugal turbo-compressor	n	compresseur centrifuge	m
Strömungsmaschine	f	turbo element	n	turbomachine	f
Strömungspumpe	f	flow-type pump	n	pompe centrifuge	f
Strömungsquerschnitt	m	flow cross-section	n	section de passage de flux	f
Strömungsrichtung	f	flow direction	n	sens d'écoulement	m
Strömungsverdichter	m	centrifugal turbo-compressor	n	compresseur centrifuge	m
Strömungswiderstand	m	resistance to flow	n	résistance au courant	f
Stromwender	m	commutator	n	collecteur	m
Stromwendung	f	commutation	n	commutation	f

Deutsch		Englisch		Französisch	
Stromzange	*f*	current clamp	x *n*	pince d'intensité	*f*
Stückliste	*f*	parts list	*n*	nomenclature	*f*
stufbar	*adj*	graduable	*adj*	modérable	*adj*
Stufenboxfilter	*n*	two-stage box-type filter	*n*	filtre-box à deux étages	*m*
Stufendrehzahlregler	*m*	combination governor	*n*	régulateur à échelons	*m*
Stufenfilter	*n*	multistage filter	*n*	filtre à étages	*m*
Stufenkolben	*m*	stepped piston	*n*	piston différentiel	*m*
Stufenreflektor	*m*	stepped reflector	*n*	réflecteur étagé	*m*
Stufenregler	*m*	combination governor	*n*	régulateur à échelons	*m*
Stufenschalter	*m*	step switch	*n*	commutateur à gradins	*m*
Sturzgas	x *n*	quick-gas pedal release	*n*	décélération	*f*
Sturzwinkel (Kfz-Dynamik)	*m*	camber angle (vehicle dynamics)	*n*	angle de carrossage (dynamique d'un véhicule)	*m*
Stützbetrieb (Batterieladung)	*m*	backup mode (battery charge)	*n*	mode "soutien" (charge de batterie)	*m*
Stützlager (Trommelbremse)	*n*	support bearing (drum brake)	*n*	palier d'appui (frein à tambour)	*m*
Stützplatte (Filter)	*f*	support plate (filter)	*n*	plaque-support (filtre)	*f*
Stützring	*m*	support ring	*n*	bague d'appui	*f*
Stützrippe	*f*	support rib	*n*	nervure d'appui	*f*
Stützstelle (Kennfeld)	*f*	data point (program map)	*n*	point d'appui (cartographie)	*m*
Suchscheinwerfer	*m*	spot lamp	*n*	projecteur de recherche	*m*
Summierer	*m*	adder	*n*	additionneur	*m*
Systemdruck (Jetronic)	*m*	primary pressure (Jetronic)	*n*	pression du système (Jetronic)	*f*
Systemdruckregler	*m*	primary-pressure regulator	*n*	régulateur de pression du système	*m*
Systemperipherie	*f*	system peripheral equipment	*n*	périphériques du système	*mpl*
T					
Tachogenerator	*m*	speedometer generator	*n*	transmetteur tachymétrique	*m*
Tachograph	*m*	trip recorder	*n*	tachographe	*m*
Tagfahrleuchte	*f*	daytime running lamp	*n*	feu de roulage de jour	*m*
takten (Radbremsdruck)	*v*	cyclical actuation (wheel brake-pressure)	*n*	pilotage cyclique (pression de freinage)	*m*
Taktfrequenz	*f*	timing frequency	*n*	fréquence des impulsions	*f*
Taktventil	*n*	pulse valve	*n*	électrovanne à rapport cyclique d'ouverture	*f*
Tandemhauptzylinder	*m*	tandem master cylinder	*n*	maître-cylindre tandem	*m*
Tandemzylinder	*m*	tandem master cylinder	*n*	maître-cylindre tandem	*m*
Tankeinbaueinheit	*f*	in-tank unit	*n*	unité de puisage	*f*
Tankeinbaupumpe	*f*	in-tank pump	*n*	pompe incorporée au réservoir	*f*
Tankentlüftung	*f*	tank ventilation	*n*	dégazage du réservoir	*m*
Tankentlüftungsventil	*n*	canister-purge valve (emissions control technology)	*n*	électrovalve de régénération (technique des gaz d'échappement)	*f*
Tankstandsgeber	*m*	level sensor (in-tank unit)	*n*	capteur de niveau (pompe électrique à carburant)	*m*
Taster	*m*	non-locking switch	*n*	interrupteur à touche	*m*
Tastrolle (Rollenbremsprüfstand)	*f*	sensor roller (dynamic brake analyzer)	*n*	rouleau palpeur (banc d'essai)	*m*

Deutsch		Englisch		Französisch	
Tastschalter	*m*	non-locking switch	*n*	interrupteur à touche	*m*
Tastverhältnis	*n*	on/off ratio	*n*	rapport cyclique d'impulsions	*m*
Tauchankerrelais	*n*	solenoid plunger relay	*n*	relais à noyau plongeur	*m*
Tauchstufe (ABS-Magnetventil)	*f*	recess step (ABS solenoid valve)	*n*	volume de détente (électrovalve ABS)	*m*
Technische Kundenunterlage, TKU	*f*	technical customer information	*n*	document technique client	*m*
Technische Unterrichtung (Bosch-Schriftenreihe)	*f*	Technical Instruction (Bosch publication)	*n*	Cahier technique (publication Bosch)	*m*
Teilbremsdruck	*m*	partial braking pressure	*n*	pression de freinage partielle	*f*
Teilbremsstellung	*f*	partially braked mode	*n*	position de freinage partiel	*f*
Teilbremsung	*f*	partial braking	*n*	freinage partiel	*m*
Teilchengröße (Filter)	*f*	particle size (filter)	*n*	taille de particule (filtre)	*f*
Teilesatz	*m*	parts set	*n*	kit de pièces	*m*
Teilförderung	*f*	partial delivery	*n*	débit partiel	*m*
Teilkreis (Zahnrad)	*m*	reference circle (gear)	*n*	cercle primitif de référence (engrenage)	*m*
Teillast (Verbrennungsmotor)	*f*	part load (IC engine)	*n*	charge partielle (moteur à combustion)	*f*
Teillastbereich	*m*	part-load range	*n*	plage de charge partielle	*f*
Teillastdrehzahl	*f*	part-load speed	*n*	vitesse à charge partielle	*f*
Teilspannung	*f*	partial voltage	*n*	tension partielle	*f*
teilweise durchgehende Bremsanlage	*f*	semi-continuous braking systen	*n*	dispositif de freinage semi-continu	*m*
Teleskopfederkontakt	*m*	telescopic spring contact	*n*	contact télescopique à ressort	*m*
Tellerfeder	*f*	disc spring	*n*	rondelle-ressort	*f*
Temperatur-Meßzündkerze	*f*	thermocouple spark plug	*n*	bougie thermocouple	*f*
temperaturabhängige Grenzmenge	*f*	temperature-dependent limit quantity	*n*	débit limite en fonction de la température	*m*
temperaturabhängige Leerlaufanhebung, TLA	*f*	temperature-controlled idle-speed increase	*n*	correcteur de ralenti piloté par la température	*m*
temperaturabhängige Leerlaufkorrektur	*f*	temperature-dependent low-idle correction	*n*	correction de ralenti en fonction de la température	*f*
temperaturabhängige Startmenge	*f*	temperature-dependent excess-fuel quantity	*n*	surcharge variable en fonction de la température	*f*
temperaturabhängige Vollastmenge	*f*	temperature-dependent full-load fuel delivery	*n*	débit de pleine charge dépendant de la température	*m*
temperaturabhängige Wartezeit	*f*	temperature-dependent waiting period	*n*	temps d'attente en fonction de la température	*m*
temperaturabhängiger Startanschlag, TAS	*m*	temperature-dependent starting stop	*n*	correcteur de surcharge en fonction de la température	*m*
temperaturabhängiges Mengeninkrement	*n*	temperature-dependent quantity increment	*n*	incrément de débit en fonction de la température	*m*
Temperaturbeständigkeit	*f*	temperature resistance	*n*	résistance thermique	*f*
Temperaturdrift	*f*	temperature drift	*n*	dérive de température	*f*
Temperaturfühler	*m*	temperature sensor	*n*	capteur de température	*m*
Temperaturkoeffizient	*m*	temperature coefficient	*n*	coefficient de température	*m*
Temperaturkompensation	*f*	temperature compensation	*n*	compensation thermique	*f*
Temperaturmeßfühler	*m*	temperature sensor	*n*	capteur de température	*m*
Temperaturschalter	*m*	thermostatic switch	*n*	thermocontact	*m*

Deutsch		Englisch		Französisch	
Temperaturschwelle	*f*	temperature threshold	*n*	seuil de température	*m*
Temperatursensor	*m*	temperature sensor	*n*	capteur de température	*m*
Temperaturverlauf	*m*	temperature profile	*n*	évolution de la température	*f*
Temperaturwechselfestigkeit	*f*	resistance to thermal cycling	*n*	résistance aux chocs thermiques	*f*
Tempomat	*m*	vehicle-speed controller	*n*	régulateur de vitesse de roulage	*m*
Testverbrauch	*m*	test consumption	*n*	consommation d'essai	*f*
Testzyklus (Abgasprüfung)	*m*	test cycle (exhaust-gas test)	*n*	diagramme de test (émissions)	*m*
theoretischer Luftdurchsatz	*m*	theoretical air-flow volume	*n*	débit volumétrique théorique d'air	*m*
thermischer Anwendungsbereich	*m*	temperature limits of application	*n*	plage d'application thermique	*f*
Thermoschalter	*m*	thermostatic switch	*n*	thermocontact	*m*
Thermoschock	*m*	thermal shock	*n*	choc thermique	*m*
Thermostat	*m*	thermostat	*n*	thermostat	*m*
Thermostatventil	*n*	thermostatic valve	*n*	valve thermostatique	*f*
Thermozeitschalter	*m*	thermo-time switch	*n*	thermocontact temporisé	*m*
Tiefenfilter	*n*	deep-bed filter	*n*	filtre en profondeur	*m*
Tiefentladung (Batterie)	*f*	exhaustive discharge (battery)	*n*	décharge en profondeur (batterie)	*f*
Tiefniveau (Luftfederung)	*n*	low level (air suspension)	*n*	niveau bas (suspension pneumatique)	*m*
Tiefpaßfilter (Steuergerät)	*n*	low-pass filter (ECU)	*n*	filtre passe-bas (calculateur)	*m*
Tieftemperaturviskosität	*f*	cold viscosity	*n*	viscosité à basse température	*f*
Tieftonhorn	*n*	low-tone horn	*n*	avertisseur à tonalité grave	*m*
Tochtergesellschaft	*f*	subsidiary	*n*	filiale	*f*
Toleranzbereich	*m*	range of tolerance	*n*	marge de tolérance	*f*
Tonfolgeschalter	*m*	tone-sequence control device	*n*	relais commutateur de tonalités	*m*
Topf-Generator	*m*	compact-diode-assembly alternator	*n*	alternateur à bloc redresseur compact	*m*
Topfbauart (Generator)	*f*	compact-diode-assembly model (alternator)	*n*	type à bloc redresseur compact (alternateur)	*m*
Topfmagnet	*m*	induction cup	*n*	aimant tambour	*m*
Topfmanschette (Radzylinder)	*f*	cup seal (wheel-brake cylinder)	*n*	joint embouti (cylindre de roue)	*m*
Torusbalg (Luftfeder)	*m*	toroid bellows (air spring)	*n*	ressort toroïde (suspension)	*m*
Torusbalgfeder (Luftfeder)	*f*	toroid bellows (air spring)	*n*	ressort toroïde (suspension)	*m*
Torusfeder (Luftfeder)	*f*	toroid bellows (air spring)	*n*	ressort toroïde (suspension)	*m*
Totraum	*m*	clearance volume	*n*	espace mort	*m*
Totvolumen	*n*	dead volume	*n*	volume mort	*m*
Totzeit x	*f*	response time	*n*	temps de réponse	*m*
Trägerplatte (Hall-Auslösesystem)	*f*	carrying plate (Hall triggering system)	*n*	plateau-support (système de déclenchement Hall)	*m*
Trägersystem (Katalysator)	*n*	substrate system (catalytic converter)	*n*	support (catalyseur)	*m*
Transistorzündung, TZ	*f*	transistorized ignition, TI	*n*	allumage transistorisé	*m*
Treibertransistor	*m*	driving transistor	*n*	transistor d'attaque	*m*
Trennfunken	*m*	contact-breaking spark	*n*	étincelle de rupture	*f*
Trennmanschette	*f*	separating cup seal	*n*	manchette de séparation	*f*
Trennschieber (Pumpenprüfstand)	*m*	shut-off slide (injection-pump test bench)	*n*	vanne d'isolement (banc d'essai de pompes)	*f*

Deutsch			Englisch			Französisch	
Triebachse		f	powered axle		n	essieu moteur	m
Trigger-Impulsgeber		m	pulse-generator trigger		n	capteur de synchronisme	m
triggern		v	trigger		v	piloter	v
Triggerpegel		m	trigger level		n	bascule bistable	f
Trittstufenleuchte		f	step light		n	lampe de marchepied	f
Trockenmittel (Lufttrockner)		n	desiccant (air drier)		n	déshydratant (dessiccateur)	m
Trockenmittelbox (Lufttrockner)		f	desiccant box (air drier)		n	cartouche de déshydratant (dessiccateur)	f
Trockenreibwert		m	coefficient of dry friction		n	coefficient de frottement à sec	m
Trockensiedepunkt (Bremsflüssigkeit)		m	dry boiling point (brake fluid)		n	point d'ébullition liquide sec (liquide de frein)	m
Trockenwisch-Automatik		f	automatic wash-and-wipe system		n	essuyage-séchage automatique	m
Trommel (Bremse)		f	brake drum		n	tambour de frein	m
Trommelbremse		f	drum brake		n	frein à tambour	m
Tropfkante (Spritzwasserschutz)		f	drip rim (splash resistance)		n	pare-gouttes (projections d'eau)	m
Trübung		f	opacity		n	opacité	f
Türbetätigung (Omnibus)		f	door control (bus)		n	commande des portes (autobus)	f
Türbetätigungsanlage (Omnibus)		f	door-control system (bus)		n	dispositif de commande des portes (autobus)	m
Turbinengehäuse		n	turbine housing		n	carter de turbine	m
Turbolader		m	exhaust-gas turbocharger		n	turbocompresseur	m
Turboloch	x	n	turbo lag	x	n	trou de suralimentation	m
Turbomotor		m	turbocharged engine		n	moteur à turbocompresseur	m
Turboschubbegrenzung		f	turbo overrun limiting		n	limitation de suralimentation en décélération	f
Türflügelantrieb		m	door-section drive (door control)		n	commande de vantail (commande des portes)	f
Türschloßheizung		f	door-lock heating		n	chauffage de serrure de porte	m
Typengenehmigung		f	General Certification		n	homologation générale	f
Typenschild		n	nameplate		n	plaque signalétique	f
Typformel		f	type designation		n	formule de type	f
Typschild		n	nameplate		n	plaque signalétique	f
U							
Ultraschall-Innenraumschutz (Autoalarm)		m	ultrasonic passenger-compartment protection (car alarm)		n	protection de l'habitacle par ultrasons (alarme auto)	f
Ultraschalldetektor (Autoalarm)		m	ultrasonic receiver		n	récepteur à ultrasons	m
Ultraschallfeld (Autoalarm)		n	ultrasonic field (car alarm)		n	champ ultrasonique (alarme auto)	m
Ultraschallsensor		m	ultrasonic receiver		n	récepteur à ultrasons	m
Umfangsgeschwindigkeit		f	circumferential speed		n	vitesse périphérique	f
Umfangskraft (Rad)		f	circumferential force (wheel)		n	force circonférentielle (roue)	f
Umgehungsleitung		f	bypass passage		n	canal de dérivation	m
umlaufende Einspritzpumpe		f	revolving injection pump		n	pompe d'injection rotative	f
Umlaufrad	+	n	planet gear		n	roue planétaire	f
Umlenkhebel		m	reverse-transfer lever		n	levier de renvoi	m

Deutsch		Englisch		Französisch	
ummantelt (Keilriemen)	*pp*	sheathed (V-belt)	*pp*	guipé (courroie trapézoïdale)	*pp*
Umrechnungskennfeld	*n*	conversion map	*n*	cartographie de conversion	*f*
Umschaltglied (Türbetätigung)	*n*	switching element (door control)	*n*	contact d'inversion (commande des portes)	*m*
Umschaltventil (ABS/ASR)	*n*	pilot valve (ABS, TCS)	*n*	vanne d'inversion (ABS/ASR)	*f*
Umschaltverlust	*m*	switching loss	*n*	pertes de commutation	*fpl*
Umschlingungswinkel (Keilriemen)	*m*	wrap angle (V-belt)	*n*	angle d'enroulement (courroie trapézoïdale)	*m*
Umweltbeanspruchung	*f*	environmental impact	*n*	incompatibilité avec l'environnement	*f*
Umweltbelastung	*f*	environmental impact	*n*	incompatibilité avec l'environnement	*f*
Umweltbeständigkeit	*f*	environmental resistance	*n*	résistance à l'environnement	*f*
umweltfreundlich	*adj*	non-polluting	*ppr*	compatible avec l'environnement	*loc*
umweltverträglich	*adj*	non-polluting	*ppr*	compatible avec l'environnement	*loc*
Umweltverträglichkeit	*f*	environmental compatibility	*n*	compatibilité environnementale	*f*
ungeregelter Bereich	*m*	uncontrolled range	*n*	plage non régulée	*f*
ungleiches Bremsen	*n*	uneven braking	*v*	louvoiement (freinage)	*m*
Ungleichförmigkeit (Fahrbahn)	*f*	pavement irregularity	*n*	défaut d'uniformité (route)	*m*
Unterbrecher (Zündung)	*m*	ignition contact breaker	*n*	rupteur (allumage)	*m*
Unterbrecherhebel (Zündung)	*m*	breaker lever (ignition)	*n*	linguet (rupteur)	*m*
Unterbrecherkontakt (Zündung)	*m*	distributor contact points	*npl*	contacts du rupteur (allumage)	*mpl*
Unterbrechernocken (Zündung)	*m*	breaker cam (ignition)	*n*	came de rupteur (allumage)	*f*
Unterdruck-Bremskraftverstärker	*m*	vacuum brake booster	*n*	servofrein à dépression	*m*
Unterdruck-Fremdkraft-Bremsanlage mit hydr. Übertragungseinrichtung	*f*	vacuum-over-hydraulic braking system	*n*	dispositif de freinage hydraulique à commande par dépression	*m*
Unterdruck-Hilfskraft-Bremsanlage mit hydraul. Übertragungseinrichtung	*f*	vacuum-assisted hydraulic braking system	*n*	dispositif de freinage hydraulique assisté par dépression	*m*
Unterdruckbegrenzer (Jetronic)	*m*	vacuum limiter (Jetronic)	*n*	limiteur de dépression (Jetronic)	*m*
Unterdruckgeber (Zündung)	*m*	vacuum pickup (ignition)	*n*	capteur de dépression (allumage)	*m*
Unterdruckkammer	*f*	vacuum chamber	*n*	chambre de dépression	*f*
Unterdruckpumpe	*f*	vacuum pump	*n*	pompe à dépression	*f*
Unterdruckversteller	*m*	vacuum control	*n*	correcteur à dépression	*m*
Unterdruckverstellung	*f*	vacuum advance mechanism	*n*	dispositif d'avance à dépression	*m*
Unterdruckzündversteller	*m*	vacuum advance mechanism	*n*	dispositif d'avance à dépression	*m*
untere Leerlaufdrehzahl	*f*	low-idle speed	*n*	régime minimum à vide	*m*
untere Vollastdrehzahl	*f*	minimum full-load speed	*n*	régime inférieur de pleine charge	*m*
Unterer Totpunkt, UT	*m*	bottom dead center, BDC	*n*	point mort bas, PMB	*m*
Unterkammer	*f*	lower chamber	*n*	chambre inférieure	*f*
Unternehmensbereich	*m*	business sector	*n*	secteur (entreprise)	*m*
Untersetzungsgetriebe	*n*	reduction gear	*n*	réducteur	*m*
Unterspannung	*f*	under-voltage	*n*	sous-tension	*f*

Deutsch			Englisch		Französisch	
untersteuern (Kfz)		v	understeer (motor vehicle)	v	sous-virage (véhicule)	m
Unterstützungskraft (Bremskraftverstärker)		m	assisting force (brake booster)	n	force d'assistance (servofrein)	f
unverbleit (Benzin)		pp	unleaded (gasoline)	pp	sans plomb (essence)	loc
unverlierbarer Dichtring (Zündkerze)		m	captive gasket (spark plug)	n	joint prisonnier (bougie)	m
Ü						
überbremsen		v	overbrake	v	surfreiner	v
Überdeckung (Steuerschlitze)		f	overlap (metering slits)	n	chevauchement (fentes d'étranglement)	m
überdrehen (Verbrennungsmotor)	x	v	speed up out of control (IC engine)	v	emballer <s'emballer> (moteur à combustion)	v
Überdrehschalter		m	overspeed switch	n	commande de surrégime	f
Überdrehzahl		f	overspeed	n	surrégime	m
Überdrehzahlschutz		m	overspeed protection	n	protection de surrégime	f
Überdrucknippel		m	overpressure nipple	n	raccord de surpression	m
Überfallbügelbefestigung (Wischer)		m	hasp-type fastening (wipers)	n	fixation par contre-étrier (essuie-glace)	f
überfetten (Luft-Kraftstoff-Gemisch)	x	v	over-enrich (air-fuel mixture)	v	surenrichir (mélange air-carburant)	v
Überfettung	x	f	over-enrichment	n	mélange trop riche	m
Übergangsanreicherung		f	acceleration enrichment	n	enrichissement à l'accélération	m
Übergangsphase (Abgasprüfung)		f	transition phase (exhaust-gas test)	n	phase transitoire (émissions)	f
Übergangsverhalten		n	transition response	n	réaction transitoire	f
Übergangswiderstand		m	contact resistance	n	résistance de contact	f
Überhitzungsschutz		m	overheat protection	n	protection de surchauffage	f
überladen (Batterie)		v	overcharge (battery) <to overcharge>	v	surcharger (batterie)	v
Überladung (Batterie)		f	overcharge (battery) <noun>	n	surcharge (batterie)	f
Überlaufdrossel		f	overflow restriction	n	calibrage de décharge	m
Überlaufmenge (Einspritzpumpe)		f	overflow quantity (fuel-injection pump)	n	débit de balayage (pompe d'injection)	m
Überrollbügel		m	rollover bar	n	arceau de capotage	m
Überrollsensor		m	rollover sensor	n	capteur de capotage	m
Überschlagschutz		m	rollover protection	n	protection anticapotage	f
Überschlagschutzsystem		n	rollover protection	n	protection anticapotage	f
Überschlagspannung		f	ignition voltage	n	tension d'allumage	f
Überschußkraft		f	surplus force	n	force excédentaire	f
Übersetzungsverhältnis (Windungszahl)		n	turn ratio	n	rapport de transformation (nombre de spires)	m
Übersichtsschaltplan		m	block diagram	n	schéma fonctionnel	m
Überspannungsschutz		m	overvoltage protection	n	protection contre les surtension:	f
Überspannungsschutzgerät		n	overvoltage-protection device	n	dispositif de protection contre les surtensions	m
übersteuern (Kfz)		v	oversteer (motor vehicle)	v	survirage (véhicule)	m
Überströmbohrung		f	overflow orifice	n	orifice de balayage	m
Überströmdosierventil		n	overflow metering valve	n	soupape de dosage de débit de retour	f

Deutsch		Englisch		Französisch	
Überströmdrossel	*f*	overflow restriction	*n*	calibrage de décharge	*m*
Überströmdrosselventil	*n*	overflow throttle valve	*n*	soupape de décharge à calibrage	*f*
Überströmdruckregler	*m*	overflow pressure regulator	*n*	régulateur de pression à trop-plein	*m*
Überströmleitung	*f*	overflow line	*n*	conduite de décharge	*f*
Überströmmenge (Einspritzpumpe)	*f*	overflow quantity (fuel-injection pump)	*n*	débit de balayage (pompe d'injection)	*m*
Überströmprinzip	*n*	overflow principle	*n*	principe de décharge	*m*
Überströmventil	*n*	overflow valve	*n*	valve de décharge	*f*
Übertragungseinrichtung (Bremsanlage)	*f*	transmission (braking system)	*n*	dispositif de transmission (dispositif de freinage)	*m*
Übertragungsmedium (Bremsanlage)	*n*	transmission agent (braking system)	*n*	moyen de transmission (dispositif de freinage)	*m*
Übertragungsrate (CAN)	*f*	transfer rate (CAN)	*n*	taux de transmission (multiplexage)	*m*
Übertragungsverhalten (Kfz)	*n*	response (motor vehicle)	*n*	réponse (véhicule)	*f*
Überwachungsmodul	*m*	monitoring module	*n*	module de surveillance	*m*
Überwachungsschaltung	*f*	monitoring circuit	*n*	circuit de surveillance	*m*
Überwachungssoftware	*f*	monitoring software	*n*	logiciel de surveillance	*m*
V					
V-Anordnung	*f*	vee-type	*n*	en V	*loc*
Vakuum-Bremsanlage	*f*	vacuum-brake system	*n*	dispositif de freinage à dépression	*m*
Vakuumpumpe	*f*	vacuum pump	*n*	pompe à dépression	*f*
variable Turbinengeometrie	*f*	variable turbine geometry	*n*	géométrie variable de turbine	*f*
Ventilansteuermodus	*m*	valve-triggering mode	*n*	mode de pilotage des vannes	*m*
Ventildurchlaß	*m*	valve throat	*n*	diamètre intérieur	*m*
Ventilerhebung	*f*	valve lift	*n*	lévée de soupape	*f*
Ventilfeder	*f*	valve spring	*n*	ressort de valve	*m*
ventilgesteuerte Zumessung	*f*	valve metering	*n*	dosage par valve	*m*
Ventilhub	*m*	valve lift	*n*	lévée de soupape	*f*
Ventilkegel	*m*	valve cone	*n*	cône de soupape	*m*
Ventilkolben	*m*	valve plunger	*n*	piston de soupape	*m*
Ventilkörper	*m*	valve body	*n*	corps de soupape	*m*
Ventilnadel	*f*	valve needle	*n*	aiguille de soupape	*f*
Ventilplatte (Jetronic)	*f*	valve plate (Jetronic)	*n*	plaque porte-soupape (Jetronic)	*f*
Ventilrelais (ABS)	*n*	valve relay (ABS)	*n*	relais des électrovalves (ABS)	*m*
Ventilsitz	*m*	valve seat	*n*	siège de soupape	*m*
Ventilsteuerdiagramm (Verbrennungsmotor)	*n*	valve timing diagram (IC engine)	*n*	diagramme de distribution (moteur à combustion)	*m*
Ventilsteuerkolben	*m*	valve control plunger	*n*	tige de commande d'injecteur	*f*
Ventilsteuerung (Verbrennungsmotor)	*f*	valve timing (engine design)	*n*	commande des soupapes (moteur à combustion)	*f*
Ventilsteuerzeit (Verbrennungsmotor)	*f*	valve timing (IC engine)	*n*	distribution (moteur à combustion)	*f*
Ventilstift	*m*	valve pin	*n*	tige de soupape	*f*
Ventilteller (Bremse)	*m*	valve plate (brakes)	*n*	clapet (frein)	*m*
Ventilträger	*m*	valve holder	*n*	porte-soupape	*m*

Deutsch		Englisch		Französisch	
Ventiltrieb	*m*	valve gear	*n*	distribution (commande des soupapes)	*f*
Ventilüberschneidung	*f*	valve overlap	*n*	croisement des soupapes	*m*
Venturi-Düse	*f*	venturi tube	*n*	buse venturi	*f*
Verbindungsleitung (Bremsanlage)	*f*	connecting line (braking system)	*n*	conduite de raccordement (dispositif de freinage)	*f*
Verbindungsmittel (elektrisch)	*n*	connecting devices (electrical)	*n*	matériel de connexion (électrique)	*m*
Verbindungsstange (Bremse)	*f*	connecting rod (brakes)	*n*	biellette (frein)	*f*
verbleit (Benzin)	*pp*	leaded (gasoline)	*pp*	au plomb (essence)	*loc*
Verbleiung (Zündkerze)	*f*	lead fouling (spark plug)	*n*	depôt de plomb (bougie)	*m*
Verbraucherleistung	*f*	electrical load requirements	*n*	puissance des récepteurs	*f*
Verbraucherstrom	*m*	equipment current draw	*n*	courant des récepteurs	*m*
Verbrauchsmodul	*m*	consumption meter	*n*	indicateur de consommation	*m*
Verbrennungsablauf	*m*	combustion characteristics	*npl*	processus de combustion	*m*
Verbrennungsaussetzer	*m*	combustion miss	*n*	ratés de combustion	*mpl*
Verbrennungsbeginn	*m*	combustion start	*n*	début de combustion	*m*
Verbrennungsdruck	*m*	combustion pressure	*n*	pression de combustion	*f*
Verbrennungsende	*n*	end of combustion	*n*	fin de combustion	*f*
Verbrennungsgas	*n*	combustion gas	*n*	gaz de combustion	*mpl*
Verbrennungsgeräusch	*n*	combustion noise	*n*	bruit de combustion	*m*
Verbrennungshub	*m*	working stroke	*n*	temps de combustion	*m*
Verbrennungsluft	*f*	combustion air	*n*	air de combustion	*m*
Verbrennungsmotor	*m*	internal-combustion (IC) engin	*n*	moteur à combustion interne	*m*
Verbrennungsraum	x *m*	combustion chamber	*n*	chambre de combustion	*f*
Verbrennungsrückstände	*mpl*	combustion residues	*npl*	résidus de la combustion	*mpl*
Verbrennungsverfahren	*n*	combustion system	*n*	procédé de combustion	*m*
Verbrennungswärme	*f*	combustion heat	*n*	chaleur dégagée par la combustion	*f*
Verbundbremsanlage	*f*	combination braking system	*n*	dispositif de freinage combiné	*m*
Verbundelektrode (Zündkerze)	*f*	compound electrode (spark plug)	*n*	électrode composite (bougie)	*f*
Verbundmittelelektrode (Zündkerze)	*f*	compound center electrode (spark plug)	*n*	électrode centrale composite (bougie)	*f*
Verdampferrohr	*n*	evaporator tube	*n*	tube de vaporisation	*m*
Verdampfungsmulde	*f*	evaporation recess	*n*	cellule de vaporisation	*f*
Verdampfungsverluste (Kraftstoffsystem)	*mpl*	evaporative losses (fuel system)	*npl*	pertes par évaporation (alimentation en carburant)	*fpl*
Verdichter	*m*	air compressor	*n*	compresseur d'air	*m*
Verdichtergehäuse	*n*	compressor housing	*n*	carter de compresseur	*m*
Verdichterrad	*n*	compressor wheel	*n*	roue de compresseur centrifuge	*f*
Verdichtung (Verbrennungsmotor)	*f*	compression (IC engine)	*n*	compression (moteur à combustion)	*f*
Verdichtungshub	*m*	compression stroke	*n*	course de compression	*f*
Verdichtungstakt (Verbrennungsmotor)	*m*	compression cycle (IC engine)	*n*	temps de compression (moteur à combustion)	*m*
Verdichtungsverhältnis	*n*	compression ratio	*n*	taux de compression	*m*
Verdichtungsvorgang	*m*	compression (IC engine)	*n*	compression (moteur à combustion)	*f*

Deutsch		Englisch		Französisch	
Verdränger (Aufladung)	*m*	displacer element (supercharging)	*n*	rotor excentré (suralimentation)	*m*
Verdrängerlader	*m*	positive-displacement supercharger	*n*	compresseur volumétrique	*m*
Verdrängerpumpe	*f*	positive-displacement pump	*n*	pompe volumétrique	*f*
Verdrehsicherung (Türbetätigung)	*f*	anti-rotation element (door control)	*n*	sécurité antirotation (commande des portes)	*f*
Verdünnungstunnel (CVS-Methode)	*m*	dilution tunnel (CVS method)	*n*	tunnel de dilution (méthode CVS)	*m*
Verdünnungsverfahren (CVS-Methode)	*n*	dilution prodedure (CVS method)	*n*	essai d'évaporation (méthode CVS)	*m*
Verdunstungsprüfung	*f*	evaporative-emissions test	*n*	test d'évaporation	*m*
Vereisungsschutz (Drosselklappe)	*m*	icing protection (throttle valve)	*n*	additif antigivre (papillon)	*m*
Verformungsfestigkeit	*f*	dimensional stability	*n*	résistance à la déformation	*f*
Vergaser	*m*	carburetor	*n*	carburateur	*m*
Vergußmasse (Batterie)	*f*	sealing compound (battery)	*n*	masse d'enrobage (batterie)	*f*
Verkehrsleittechnik	*f*	traffic-control engeneering	*n*	technique de radioguidage de la circulation	*f*
Verkehrstelematik	*f*	traffic-control engeneering	*n*	technique de radioguidage de la circulation	*f*
verkoken	*v*	coke	*v*	calaminer	*v*
Verkokung	*f*	coking	*n*	calaminage	*m*
verlangsamen	*v*	slow down	*v*	ralentir	*v*
Verlangsamer	*m*	retarder	*n*	ralentisseur	*m*
Verlustdauer (Bremsvorgang)	*f*	reaction time (braking action)	*n*	temps mort (effet de freinage)	*m*
Verlustwärme	*f*	heat losses	*npl*	chaleur de dissipation	*f*
Verlustweg (Bremswirkung)	*m*	pre-braking distance (braking action)	*n*	course morte (effet de freinage)	*f*
Verlustzeit (Bremsvorgang)	*f*	reaction time (braking action)	*n*	temps mort (effet de freinage)	*m*
verpolsicher	*adj*	insensitive to reverse polarity	*adj*	insensible à l'inversion de polarité	*loc*
Verpolungsschutz (Batterieladung)	*m*	reverse-polarity protection (battery charge)	*n*	protection contre l'inversion de polarité (charge de batterie)	*f*
Verpolungsschutzdiode	*f*	incorrect-polarity protection diode	*n*	diode de protection contre inversion de polarité	*f*
verpolungssicher	*adj*	insensitive to reverse polarity	*adj*	insensible à l'inversion de polarité	*loc*
Verriegelungsventil	*n*	locking valve	*n*	valve de verrouillage	*f*
Versatz	*m*	phasing	*n*	phasage	*m*
Verschiebeflansch	*m*	sliding flange	*n*	bride coulissante	*f*
verschleißfest	*adj*	wear-resistant	*adj*	résistant à l'usure	*ppr*
Verschleißkontrolle (Bremsbelag)	*f*	wear inspection (brake lining)	*n*	contrôle d'usure (garniture de frein)	*m*
Verschleißsensor (Bremsbelag)	*m*	wear sensor (brake lining)	*n*	capteur d'usure (garniture de frein)	*m*
Verschleißteil	*n*	wearing part	*n*	pièce d'usure	*f*
Verschlußfeder	*f*	sealing spring	*n*	ressort à déclic	*m*
Verschlußscheibe	*f*	sealing washer	*n*	rondelle d'obturation	*f*

Deutsch			Englisch		Französisch	
Versorgungsdruck (Jetronic)		*m*	supply pressure (Jetronic)	*n*	pression d'alimentation (Jetronic)	*f*
Versorgungsleitung		*f*	supply line	*n*	conduite d'alimentation	*f*
Versorgungsspannung		*f*	supply voltage	*n*	tension d'alimentation	*f*
Verstärkerkolben		*m*	servo-unit piston	*n*	piston amplificateur	*m*
Verstärkungsfaktor (Bremskraftverstärker)		*m*	boost factor (brake booster)	*n*	effet de renforcement de freinage (servofrein)	*m*
Verstärkungsrippe		*f*	strengthening rib	*n*	raidisseur nervuré	*m*
Verstärkungsverhältnis		*n*	amplification ratio	*n*	rapport d'amplification	*m*
Versteifungsrippe		*f*	strengthening rib	*n*	raidisseur nervuré	*m*
Verstellbolzen		*m*	sliding bolt	*n*	axe de réglage	*m*
Verstellcharakteristik		*f*	timing characteristic	*n*	caractéristique d'avance	*f*
Verstelleinheit (Leuchtweiteregelung)		*f*	adjuster (headlight vertical-aim control)	*n*	module de réglage (correcteur de site)	*m*
Verstelleinrichtung		*f*	adjusting device	*n*	dispositif de réglage	*m*
Verstellexzenter		*m*	adjusting eccentric	*n*	excentrique de réglage	*m*
Verstellfunktion		*f*	adjustment function	*n*	fonction de correction	*f*
Verstellhebel (Reiheneinspritzpumpe)		*m*	control lever (in-line pump)	*n*	levier de commande (pompe d'injection en ligne)	*m*
Verstellhebelwelle		*f*	control-lever shaft	*n*	axe du levier de commande	*m*
Verstellkraft (ABS-Magnetventil)		*f*	actuating force (ABS solenoid valve)	*n*	force de réglage (électrovalve ABS)	*f*
Verstellmotor		*m*	servomotor	*n*	servomoteur	*m*
Verstellregler	+	*m*	variable-speed governor	*n*	régulateur toutes vitesses	*m*
Verstellwelle		*f*	setting shaft	*n*	axe de correction	*m*
Verstellwinkel (Spritzversteller		*m*	advance angle (timing device)	*n*	angle d'avance (correcteur d'avance)	*m*
Verstellwinkel (Zündung)	+	*m*	advance angle (ignition)	*n*	angle de correction (allumage)	*m*
Versuchsdüse		*f*	calibrating nozzle	*n*	injecteur d'essai	*m*
Verteilerbüchse		*f*	distributor-head bushing	*n*	chemise	*f*
Verteilereinspritzpumpe (VE)		*f*	distributor injection pump	*n*	pompe d'injection distributrice	*f*
Verteilerfinger (Zündung)		*m*	distributor rotor (ignition)	*n*	rotor distributeur (allumage)	*m*
Verteilerflansch		*m*	distributor-head flange	*n*	flasque de distribution	*m*
Verteilerkappe (Zündung)		*f*	distributor cap	*n*	tête d'allumeur	*f*
Verteilerkolben		*m*	distributor plunger	*n*	piston distributeur	*m*
Verteilerkopf (Verteilereinspritzpumpe)		*m*	distributor head (distributor pump)	*n*	tête hydraulique (pompe distributrice)	*f*
Verteilerkörper (Verteilereinspritzpumpe)		*m*	distributor head (distributor pump)	*n*	tête hydraulique (pompe distributrice)	*f*
Verteilerläufer (Zündung)		*m*	distributor rotor (ignition)	*n*	rotor distributeur (allumage)	*m*
Verteilerlogik		*f*	distributor logic	*n*	logique d'allumeur	*f*
Verteilernut		*f*	distributor slot	*n*	rainure de distribution	*f*
Verteilerpumpe (VE)	x	*f*	distributor injection pump	*n*	pompe d'injection distributrice	*f*
Verteilerrohr (Einzeleinspritzung)		*n*	fuel-distribution pipe (multipoint fuel injection)	*n*	rampe d'injection (injection multipoint)	*f*
Verteilerstecker		*m*	distributor connector	*n*	connecteur d'allumeur	*m*
Verteilerwelle (Zündung)	x	*f*	ignition-distributor shaft	*n*	arbre d'allumeur	*m*
Verunreinigung		*f*	contamination	*n*	contamination	*f*
Verwirbelung		*f*	swirl effect	*n*	turbulence	*f*

Deutsch		Englisch		Französisch	
Verzögerung (Bremsvorgang) x	*f*	braking deceleration	*n*	décélération de freinage	*f*
verzögerungsabhängig (Druckminderer)	*adj*	deceleration-sensitive (brake-pressure regulating valve)	*adj*	asservi à la décélération (réducteur de pression de freinage)	*pp*
Verzögerungsabmagerung	*f*	trailing-throttle lean adjustment	*n*	appauvrissement en décélération	*m*
Verzögerungsschaltung (Startventil)	*f*	delay switch (start valve)	*n*	temporisateur (électrovanne de démarrage)	*m*
Vibrationssensor	*m*	vibration sensor	*n*	capteur de vibrations	*m*
Vielstoffmotor	*m*	multifuel engine	*n*	moteur polycarburant	*m*
Vielstoffpumpe	*f*	multifuel pump	*n*	pompe polycarburant	*f*
Vielzweckleuchte	*f*	multipurpose lamp	*n*	baladeuse	*f*
Vier-Scheinwerfer-System	*n*	four-headlamp system	*n*	système à quatre projecteurs	*m*
Vierfunken-Zündspule	*f*	four-spark ignition coil	*n*	bobine d'allumage à quatre sorties	*f*
Vierkreis-Schutzventil	*n*	four-circuit protection valve	*n*	valve de sécurité à quatre circuits	*f*
Vierradantrieb	*m*	four-wheel drive, FWD	*n*	transmission quatre roues	*f*
Viertaktprinzip	*n*	four-stroke principle	*n*	cycle à quatre temps	*m*
Viertaktverfahren	*n*	four-stroke principle	*n*	cycle à quatre temps	*m*
Vierventil-Technik	*f*	four-valve design	*n*	système à quatre soupapes par cylindre	*m*
Vierwegehahn	*m*	four-way cock	*n*	robinet à quatre voies	*m*
Viscokupplung (Allradantrieb)	*f*	viscous coupling (all-wheel drive)	*n*	visco-coupleur (transmission intégrale)	*m*
Viskosesperre (Allradantrieb)	*f*	viscous lock (all-wheel drive)	*n*	blocage par visco-coupleur (transmission intégrale)	*m*
Vollast, VL	*f*	wide-open throttle, WOT	*n*	pleine charge	*f*
Vollastangleichung	*f*	full-load torque control	*n*	correction de pleine charge	*f*
Vollastanreicherung	*f*	full-load enrichment	*n*	enrichissement de pleine charge	*m*
Vollastanschlag	*m*	full-load stop	*n*	butée de débit maximal	*f*
Vollastbegrenzung	*f*	full-load limitation	*n*	limitation du débit maximal	*f*
Vollastbeschleunigung	*f*	full-load acceleration	*n*	accélération à pleine charge	*f*
Vollastcharakteristik	*f*	full-load curve	*n*	courbe caractéristique de pleine charge	*f*
Vollastdrehzahl	*f*	full-load speed	*n*	vitesse de pleine charge	*f*
Vollasteinspritzmenge	*f*	full-load delivery	*n*	débit de pleine charge (refoulement)	*m*
Vollasteinstellschraube	*f*	full-load screw	*n*	vis de réglage de pleine charge	*f*
Vollastfördermenge	*f*	full-load delivery	*n*	débit de pleine charge (refoulement)	*m*
Vollastkennlinie	*f*	full-load curve	*n*	courbe caractéristique de pleine charge	*f*
Vollastkurve	*f*	full-load curve	*n*	courbe caractéristique de pleine charge	*f*
Vollastmenge +	*f*	full-load delivery	*n*	débit de pleine charge (refoulement)	*m*
Vollastmengenanschlag	*m*	full-load stop	*n*	butée de débit maximal	*f*
Vollastschalter	*m*	full-load switch	*n*	contacteur de pleine charge	*m*
Vollastschraube +	*f*	full-load screw	*n*	vis de réglage de pleine charge	*f*

Deutsch		Englisch		Französisch	
Vollaststellung	*f*	full-load position	*n*	position de pleine charge	*f*
Vollbremsstellung	*f*	fully braked mode	*n*	position de freinage d'urgence	*f*
Vollbremsung	*f*	full braking	*n*	freinage d'urgence	*m*
vollelektronische Zündung, VZ	*f*	distributorless semiconductor ignition	*n*	allumage électronique intégral	*m*
Vollförderung	*f*	maximum delivery	*n*	débit maximal	*m*
vollgeschirmte Zündkerze	*f*	fully-shielded spark plug	*n*	bougie totalement blindée	*f*
Vollverzögerung	*f*	fully developed deceleration	*n*	décélération totale	*f*
Vollweggleichrichtung	*f*	full-wave rectification	*n*	redressement à deux alternance:	*m*
Volumenentlastung	*f*	retraction volume (distributor pump)	*n*	décharge de volume	*f*
Volumenstrom	*m*	flow volume	*n*	débit volumique	*m*
volumetrischer Wirkungsgrad (Verbrennungsmotor)	*m*	volumetric efficiency (IC engine)	*n*	rendement volumétrique (moteur à combustion)	*m*
Vorabregelung	*f*	pre-governing	*n*	précoupure	*f*
Vorabscheider (Jetronic)	*m*	preliminary filter (Jetronic)	*n*	préséparateur (Jetronic)	*m*
Vordruck (ESP)	*m*	admission pressure (ESP)	*n*	pression d'alimentation (ESP)	*f*
Vordruckprüfung (Radzylinder)	*f*	latent-pressure test (wheel-brake cylinder)	*n*	essai de pression pilote (cylindre de roue)	*m*
Vordruckventil	*n*	admission-pressure valve	*n*	valve de pression d'admission	*f*
Voreilung (Bremsdruck)	*f*	pressure lead (braking pressure	*n*	à avance de pression	*loc*
Voreinspritzung	*f*	pilot injection	*n*	injection pilote	*f*
Voreinspritzverlauf	*m*	pre-injection characteristic	*n*	évolution de la préinjection	*f*
Vorentflammung	*f*	pre-ignition	*n*	pré-allumage	*m*
Vorentwässerung (Lufttrockner)	*f*	initial drying (air drier)	*n*	prédéshydratation (dessiccateur)	*f*
Vorerregermagnetfeld	*n*	pre-excitation magnetic field	*n*	champ magnétique d'amorçage	*m*
Vorerregerstromkreis	*m*	pre-excitation circuit	*n*	circuit d'amorçage	*m*
Vorerregung (drehende Maschinen)	*f*	pre-excitation (rotating machines)	*n*	pré-excitation (machines tournantes)	*f*
Vorfilter (Lufttrockner)	*n*	preliminary filter (air drier)	*n*	préfiltre (dessiccateur)	*m*
Vorfiltereinsatz	*m*	preliminary-filter element	*n*	cartouche filtrante primaire	*f*
Vorfördereffekt	*m*	pre-delivery effect	*n*	effet de prérefoulement	*m*
Vorfördermenge	*f*	pre-delivery quantity	*n*	débit de prérefoulement	*m*
Vorförderpumpe	*f*	presupply pump	*n*	pompe de pré-alimentation	*f*
Vorgelege	*n*	reduction gear	*n*	réducteur	*m*
Vorgelegestarter	*m*	reduction-gear starter	*n*	démarreur à réducteur	*m*
vorgespannt (Feder)	*pp*	pre-loaded (spring)	*pp*	taré (ressort)	*pp*
Vorglühanzeige	*f*	pre-glow indicator	*n*	témoin de préchauffage	*m*
Vorglühdauer	*f*	preheating time	*n*	durée de préchauffage	*f*
vorglühen	*v*	preheat	*v*	préchauffage	*m*
Vorglühgerät	*n*	pre-glow relay (diesel engine)	*n*	appareil de préchauffage (moteur diesel)	*m*
Vorglühzeit	*f*	preheating time	*n*	durée de préchauffage	*f*
Vorhub (Pumpenkolben)	*m*	plunger lift to port closing	*n*	précourse (piston de pompe)	*f*
Vorhubansteuerung	*f*	energizing LPC (lift port closing)	*n*	commande de précourse	*f*
Vorhubeinstellung	*f*	prestroke adjustment	*n*	réglage de la précourse	*m*

Deutsch		Englisch		Französisch	
Vorhubstellwerk	*n*	LPC (lift port closing) actuator	*n*	actionneur de précourse	*m*
Vorkammer	*f*	prechamber	*n*	préchambre	*f*
Vorkammermotor	*m*	prechamber engine	*n*	moteur à préchambre	*m*
Vorkontakt (Relais)	*m*	advance contact (relay)	*n*	précontact (relais)	*m*
Vorlaufachse	*f*	leading axle	*n*	essieu directeur	*m*
Vorlaufventil (Dieseleinspritzung)	*n*	forward-delivery valve (diesel fuel injection)	*n*	clapet-pilote (injection diesel)	*m*
Vorratsbehälter (Pneumatik)	*m*	compressed-air reservoir (pneumatics)	*n*	réservoir d'air comprimé (pneumatique)	*m*
Vorratsdruck (Bremse)	*m*	supply pressure (brakes)	*n*	pression d'alimentation (frein)	*f*
Vorratskreis (Druckluft)	*m*	compressed-air supply circuit	*n*	circuit d'alimentation (air comprimé)	*m*
Vorratskupplungskopf	*m*	coupling head "supply"	*n*	tête d'accouplement "alimentation"	*f*
Vorratsleitung (Zweileitungs-Bremsanlage)	*f*	supply line (two-line braking system)	*n*	conduite d'alimentation (dispositif de freinage à deux conduites)	*f*
Vorreiniger	*m*	preliminary filter (fuel-supply pump)	*n*	préfiltre (pompe d'alimentation)	*m*
Vorschalldämpfer	*m*	front muffler	*n*	silencieux avant	*m*
Vorschaltgerät (Gasentladungslampe)	*n*	ballast unit (gaseous-discharge lamp)	*n*	module de commande (lampe à décharge dans un gaz)	*m*
Vorschaltgerät (Zündung)	*n*	ballast unit (ignition)	*n*	module pilote (allumage)	*m*
Vorschaltmodul (Autoalarm)	*m*	ballast module (car alarm)	*n*	module de protection (alarme auto)	*m*
Vorspannzylinder	*m*	booster cylinder	*n*	cylindre d'assistance	*m*
Vorsteuerlogik	*f*	precontrol logic	*n*	logique de pilotage	*f*
Vorsteuerung (Nfz-ABS)	*f*	pilot control (commercial-vehicle ABS)	*n*	pilotage (ABS pour véhicules utilitaires)	*m*
Vorsteuerventil (Bremskraftregler)	*n*	pilot valve (load-sensing valve)	*n*	valve pilote (modulateur de freinage)	*f*
Vorstufe (Seitenkanalpumpe)	*f*	first stage (side-channel pump)	*n*	premier étage (pompe à canal latéral)	*m*
Vortrieb (Kfz)	*m*	accelerative force (motor vehicle)	*n*	propulsion (véhicule)	*f*
Vortriebskraft	*f*	drive force	*n*	force de propulsion	*f*
Vorverbrennung	*f*	pre-combustion	*n*	précombustion	*f*
Vorwiderstand	*m*	series resistor	*n*	résistance additionnelle	*f*
W					
Wabenkeramik (Rußabbrennfilter)	*f*	honeycomb ceramic (soot burn-off filter)	*n*	céramique en nid d'abeilles (filtre d'oxidation de particules)	*f*
Wackelkontakt	*m*	loose contact	*n*	faux contact	*m*
Wafer (Halbleiter)	x *m*	wafer (semiconductor)	*n*	tranche (semi-conducteur)	*f*
Wagenheizer	x *m*	vehicle heater	*n*	chauffage d'habitacle	*m*
Wagenheizung	*f*	vehicle heater	*n*	chauffage d'habitacle	*m*
Wälzbahn (Zündversteller)	*f*	contact path (advance mechanism)	*n*	rampe à profil (correcteur d'avance)	*f*
Wandbenetzung (Saugrohr)	*f*	manifold-wall fuel condensation	*n*	humidification des parois (collecteur d'admission)	*f*

Deutsch		Englisch		Französisch	
Wandfilmbildung (Saugrohr)	*f*	manifold-wall fuel condensation	*n*	humidification des parois (collecteur d'admission)	*f*
Wankachse (Kfz-Dynamik)	*f*	roll axis (vehicle dynamics)	*n*	axe de roulis (dynamique d'un véhicule)	*m*
Wankwinkel (Kfz-Dynamik)	*m*	roll angle (vehicle dynamics)	*n*	angle de roulis (dynamique d'un véhicule)	*m*
Wannenbefestigung	*f*	cradle mounting	*n*	fixation par berceau	*f*
Wannenpumpe	x *f*	cradle-mounted pump	*n*	pompe à fixation par berceau	*f*
Wärmeabführung	*f*	heat dissipation	*n*	dissipation de la chaleur	*f*
Wärmeableitvermögen	*n*	thermal conductivity	*n*	conductibilité thermique	*f*
Wärmeaufnahme	*f*	heat absorption	*n*	absorption de chaleur	*f*
Wärmeaufnahmevermögen	*n*	heat-absorbing property	*n*	capacité d'absorption thermique	*f*
Wärmeaustausch	*m*	heat exchange	*n*	échange de chaleur	*m*
Wärmeleitfähigkeit	*f*	thermal conductivity	*n*	conductibilité thermique	*f*
Wärmeleitpaste	*f*	thermal-conduction paste	*n*	pâte thermoconductrice	*f*
Wärmeleitung	*f*	heat conduction	*n*	conduction thermique	*f*
Wärmeleitweg	*m*	thermal conduction path	*n*	chemin de conduction de la chaleur	*m*
Wärmeschutz (Einspritzdüse)	*m*	heat shield (nozzle)	*n*	isolation thermique (injecteur)	*f*
Wärmeschutzhülse (Einspritzdüse)	*f*	thermal-protection sleeve (injection nozzle)	*n*	manchon calorifuge (injecteur)	*m*
Wärmeschutzhütchen (Einspritzdüse)	*n*	thermal-protection cap (injection nozzle)	*n*	capuchon calorifuge (injecteur)	*m*
Wärmeschutzplättchen (Einspritzdüse)	*n*	thermal-protection plate (injection nozzle)	*n*	plaquette calorifuge (injecteur)	*f*
Wärmeschutzscheibe (Einspritzdüse)	*f*	thermal-protection disc (injection nozzle)	*n*	rondelle calorifuge (injecteur)	*f*
Wärmestrahlung	*f*	heat radiation	*n*	rayonnement thermique	*m*
Wärmetauscher (hydrodynamischer Verlangsamer)	*m*	heat exchanger (hydrodynamic retarder)	*n*	échangeur de chaleur (ralentisseur hydrodynamique)	*m*
Wärmeverlust	*m*	heat losses	*npl*	chaleur de dissipation	*f*
Wärmewert (Zündkerze)	*m*	heat range (spark plug)	*n*	degré thermique (bougie)	*m*
Wärmewertkennzahl (Zündkerze)	*f*	heat-range code number (spark plug)	*n*	indice caractéristique du degré thermique (bougie)	*m*
Warmlauf	*m*	warm-up	*v*	mise en action	*f*
Warmlaufanreicherung	*f*	warm-up enrichment	*n*	enrichissement de mise en action	*m*
Warmlaufphase (Verbrennungsmotor)	*f*	warm-up period (IC engine)	*n*	période de mise en action (moteur à combustion)	*f*
Warmlaufregler	*m*	warm-up regulator	*n*	régulateur de mise en action	*m*
Warmlaufzeit (Verbrennungsmotor)	*f*	warm-up period (IC engine)	*n*	période de mise en action (moteur à combustion)	*f*
Warmschrumpfzone (Zündkerze)	*f*	heat-shrinkage zone (spark plug)	*n*	zone de contraction et de rétraction à chaud (bougie)	*f*
Warmstart	*m*	hot start	*n*	départ à chaud	*m*
Warnaufkleber (Autoalarm)	*m*	warning sticker (car alarm)	*n*	autocollant d'avertissement (alarme auto)	*m*
Warnblinkanlage	*f*	hazard-warning and turn-signal system	*n*	dispositif de signalisation direction-détresse	*m*

Deutsch		Englisch		Französisch	
warnblinken	*v*	hazard flashing	*v*	signalisation "détresse"	*f*
Warnblinker	*m*	hazard-warning and turn-signal system	*n*	dispositif de signalisation direction-détresse	*m*
Warnblinkgeber	*m*	hazard-warning and turn-signal flasher	*n*	centrale mixte de direction-détresse	*f*
Warnblinkrelais	*n*	hazard-warning and turn-signal relay	*n*	relais du signal de détresse	*m*
Warnblinkschalter	*m*	hazard-switch	*n*	commutateur des feux de détresse	*m*
Warndruckanzeiger	*m*	low-pressure indicator	*n*	indicateur-avertisseur de pression	*m*
Warndruckeinrichtung (Bremse)	*f*	low-pressure warning device (brakes)	*n*	dispositif d'alerte (frein)	*m*
Warnkontakt (Bremsbelagverschleiß)	*m*	wear sensor (brake lining)	*n*	capteur d'usure (garniture de frein)	*m*
Warnlampe	*f*	warning lamp	*n*	témoin d'alerte	*m*
Warnlichtgeber	*m*	hazard-warning signal flasher	*n*	centrale de signal de détresse	*f*
Warnsignal	*n*	warning signal	*n*	signal de détresse	*m*
Warnsummer	*m*	buzzer	*n*	vibreur	*m*
wartungsarm	*adj*	low-maintenance	*n*	à entretien minimal	*loc*
wartungsfrei	*adj*	maintenance-free	*adj*	sans entretien	*loc*
Wartungsvorschrift	*f*	maintainance instructions	*npl*	notice d'entretien	*f*
Wasserablaßschraube (Kraftstoffilter)	*f*	drain screw (fuel filter)	*n*	vis de purge d'eau (filtre à carburant)	*f*
Wasserablaßventil	*n*	drain valve	*n*	purgeur d'eau	*m*
Wasserabscheider	*m*	water separator	*n*	séparateur d'eau	*m*
Wasserdruckpumpe	*f*	water-pressure pump	*n*	pompe de refoulement d'eau	*f*
Wasserpumpe	*f*	water pump	*n*	pompe à eau	*f*
Wassersammelraum (Kraftstoffilter)	*m*	water chamber (fuel filter)	*n*	collecteur d'eau (filtre à carburant)	*m*
Wasserumwälzpumpe	*f*	water-circulating pump	*n*	pompe de circulation d'eau	*f*
Wastegate-Regelventil	*n*	waste-gate control valve	*n*	valve modulatrice de pression	*f*
Wechselaufbau	*m*	interchangeable body	*n*	carrosserie interchangeable	*f*
Wechselbox (Filter)	*f*	fuel-filter exchange box	*n*	filtre-box interchangeable	*m*
Wechselcode (Autoalarm)	*m*	changeable code (car alarm)	*n*	code interchangeable (alarme auto)	*m*
Wechselfilter	*n*	easy-change filter	*n*	filtre à rechange rapide	*m*
Wechselspannung	*f*	alternating voltage	*n*	tension alternative	*f*
Wechselstrom	*m*	alternating current, AC	*n*	courant alternatif	*m*
Wechselventil	*n*	shuttle valve	*n*	sélecteur de circuit	*m*
Wechsler (Umschaltkontakt)	*m*	changeover contact	*n*	contact bidirectionnel	*m*
Wegeventil, WGV	*n*	directional-control valve	*n*	distributeur	*m*
Wegeventilblock	*m*	directional-control-valve block	*n*	bloc-distributeur	*m*
Wegfahrsperre (Autoalarm)	*f*	vehicle immobilizer (car alarm)	*n*	dispositif antidémarrage (alarme auto)	*m*
Wegfeder	*f*	travel-limiting spring	*n*	ressort limiteur de course	*m*
Weggeber	*m*	travel sensor	*n*	capteur de déplacement	*m*
Weicheisenkern	*m*	iron core	*n*	noyau de fer	*m*
Weichverguß	*m*	soft casting	*n*	enrobage mou	*m*

Deutsch			Englisch		Französisch	
Weißrauch	x	*m*	white smoke	*n*	fumées blanches	*fpl*
Weitstrahlscheinwerfer		*m*	long-range driving lamp	*n*	projecteur longue portée	*m*
Werksaustausch (Ersatzbedarf)		*m*	factory exchange (replacement requirements)	*n*	échange standard (rechanges)	*m*
Werkstatthandbuch		*n*	workshop manual	*n*	manuel d'atelier	*m*
Werkstattlader (Batterie)		*m*	workshop charger (battery)	*n*	chargeur de garage (batterie)	*m*
Werkstattzeichnung		*f*	workshop drawing	*n*	dessin d'exécution	*m*
Werkstückträger		*m*	workpiece carrier	*n*	chariot porte-pièce	*m*
Wettbewerber		*m*	competitor	*n*	concurrent	*m*
wettbewerbsfähig		*adj*	competitive	*adj*	compétitif	*adj*
Wickeldraht		*m*	winding wire	*n*	fil de bobinage	*m*
Wickelfiltereinsatz		*m*	spiral vee-shaped filter element	*n*	cartouche filtrante en rouleau	*f*
Wickelkopf (Ständer)		*m*	winding head (stator)	*n*	tête de bobine (stator)	*f*
Wickelkörper (Filter)		*m*	paper tube (filter)	*n*	corps de filtre	*m*
Wickelkörper (Zündspule)		*m*	bobbin (ignition coil)	*n*	corps d'enroulement (bobine d'allumage)	*m*
wickeln (Spule)		*v*	wind (coil)	*v*	enrouler (bobine)	*v*
Wickelschema		*n*	winding diagram	*n*	schéma de bobinage	*m*
Wicklungsfaktor		*m*	winding factor	*n*	facteur de bobinage	*m*
Wicklungsstrang		*m*	phase winding	*n*	faisceau d'enroulements	*m*
Wicklungswiderstand		*m*	winding resistance	*n*	résistance d'enroulement	*f*
Widerstands-Zündleitung		*f*	resistance ignition cable	*n*	câble d'allumage résistif	*m*
Widerstandsbahn		*f*	potentiometer track	*n*	piste de potentiomètre	*f*
wiederschärfen (Autoalarm)		*v*	reprime (car alarm)	*v*	remise en veille (alarme auto)	*f*
Wiederstart	x	*m*	repeat start	*n*	redémarrage	*m*
Wiegekolben		*m*	rocking piston	*n*	piston à fléau	*f*
Windkanal		*m*	wind tunnel	*n*	soufflerie	*f*
Windungsschluß		*m*	coil-winding short circuit	*n*	court-circuit entre spires	*m*
Windungsverhältnis		*n*	turn ratio	*n*	rapport de transformation (nombre de spires)	*m*
Windungszahl		*f*	number of coils	*n*	nombre de tours des spires de l'enroulement	*m*
Winkelgeber (Autoalarm)		*m*	tilt sensor (car alarm)	*n*	capteur de position angulaire (alarme auto)	*m*
Winkelhebel		*m*	bell crank	*n*	levier coudé	*m*
Winkelsensor		*m*	tilt sensor (car alarm)	*n*	capteur de position angulaire (alarme auto)	*m*
Wirbelkammer		*f*	whirl chamber	*n*	chambre de tourbillonnement	*f*
Wirbelkammermotor		*m*	whirl-chamber diesel engine	*n*	moteur à chambre de tourbillonnement	*m*
Wirbelstrom		*m*	eddy current	*n*	courants de Foucault	*mpl*
Wirbelstrombremse		*f*	electrodynamic retarder	*n*	ralentisseur électromagnétique	*m*
Wirbelstromsensor		*m*	eddy-current sensor	*n*	capteur à courants de Foucault	*m*
Wirbelstromsonde		*f*	eddy-current sensor	*n*	capteur à courants de Foucault	*m*
Wirkfläche		*f*	effective area	*n*	surface utile	*f*
Wirkmembran		*f*	transfer diaphragm	*n*	membrane active	*f*
Wirkradius		*m*	effective radius	*n*	rayon actif	*m*
Wirkrichtung		*f*	force-transfer direction	*n*	sens d'action	*m*

Deutsch		Englisch		Französisch	
Wirkverbindung	*f*	mechanical linkage	*n*	liaison mécanique	*f*
Wirkwiderstand	*m*	active resistance	*n*	résistance active	*f*
Wisch-Wasch-Anlage (Scheinwerfer)	*f*	wipe/wash system (headlamp)	*n*	lave/essuie-projecteur	*m*
Wischarm (Wischeranlage)	*m*	wiper arm (windshield wiper sytem)	*n*	bras d'essuie-glace	*m*
Wischblatt	*n*	wiper blade	*n*	raclette d'essuie-glace	*f*
Wischer	*m*	windshield wiper	*n*	essuie-glace	*m*
Wischeranlage	*f*	wiper system	*n*	équipement d'essuie-glace	*m*
Wischermotor	*m*	wiper motor	*n*	moteur d'essuie-glace	*m*
Wischfeld	*n*	wipe pattern	*n*	champ de balayage	*m*
Wischgummi	*n*	wiper-blade element	*n*	lame racleuse	*f*
Wischhebel (Scheinwerfer-Reinigungsanlage)	*m*	wiper arm (headlamp cleaning system)	*n*	bras d'essuie-glace équipé (nettoyeur de projecteurs)	*m*
Wischintervallrelais	*n*	intermittent-wiper relay	*n*	relais cadenceur d'essuie-glace	*m*
Wischintervallschalter	*m*	intermittent-wiper switch	*n*	commutateur intermittent d'essuie-glace	*m*
Wischlippe	*f*	wiper-element lip	*n*	lèvre d'essuyage	*f*
Wischwinkel	*m*	wiping angle	*n*	angle de balayage	*m*
Wunschmengenanfangswert	*m*	demand-value starting point	*n*	valeur initiale de débit demandé	*f*
Z					
Zahnkranz (Motorschwungrad)	*m*	ring gear (flywheel)	*n*	couronne dentée de volant	*f*
Zahnlücke	*f*	tooth space	*n*	entredent	*m*
Zahnradkraftstoffpumpe	*f*	gear pump	*n*	pompe à engrenage	*f*
Zahnradmotor	*m*	hydraulic gear motor	*n*	moteur à engrenage	*m*
Zahnradpumpe	*f*	gear pump	*n*	pompe à engrenage	*f*
Zahnriemen	*m*	toothed belt	*n*	courroie dentée	*f*
Zahnscheibe (Zündung)	*f*	trigger wheel (ignition)	*n*	noyau synchroniseur (allumage)	*m*
Zahnsegment	*n*	control-sleeve gear	*n*	secteur denté	*m*
Zahnstange	*f*	rack	*n*	crémaillère	*f*
Zangengeber	*m*	clamp-on sensor	*n*	capteur à pince	*m*
Zapfendüse	*f*	pintle nozzle	*n*	injecteur à téton	*m*
Zeigerbremse (Rollenbremsprüfstand)	*f*	indicator lock (dynamic brake analyzer)	*n*	frein d'aiguille (afficheur de banc d'essai)	*m*
Zellenrad (Druckwellenlader)	*n*	rotor (pressure-wave supercharger)	*n*	rotor (échangeur de pression)	*m*
Zellenverbinder (Batterie)	*m*	cell connector (battery)	*n*	connexion des éléments (batterie)	*f*
Zenerdiode	*f*	Zener diode	*n*	diode Zener	*f*
Zenerspannung	*f*	Zener voltage	*n*	tension Zener	*f*
Zentral-Einspritzeinheit (Mono-Jetronic)	*f*	central injection unit (Mono-Jetronic)	*n*	unité d'injection (Mono-Jetronic)	*f*
Zentralachsanhänger	*m*	centre-axle trailer	*n*	remorque à essieu central	*f*
zentrale Einspritzeinheit (Mono-Jetronic)	*f*	central injection unit (Mono-Jetronic)	*n*	unité d'injection (Mono-Jetronic)	*f*
Zentraleinheit (Fahrdatenrechner)	*f*	central processing unit (on-board computer), CPU	*n*	unité de traitement (ordinateur de bord)	*f*

Deutsch		Englisch		Französisch	
Zentraleinspritzung	*f*	single-point fuel injection	*n*	injection monopoint	*f*
Zentralfilter	*n*	centrally located air filter	*n*	filtre central	*m*
Zentralventil	*n*	central valve	*n*	soupape centrale	*f*
Zentralverriegelung	*f*	central locking system	*n*	verrouillage centralisé	*m*
Zentrierbund	*m*	locating collar	*n*	épaulement de centrage	*m*
Zentrierstift (Rollenbremsprüfstand)	*m*	alignment pin (dynamic brake analyzer)	*n*	axe de centrage (banc d'essai)	*m*
Zertifizierung (ISO)	*f*	certification (ISO)	*n*	certification (ISO)	*f*
Zielkurve	*f*	target curve	*n*	courbe cible	*f*
Zubehörsatz	*m*	accessory set	*n*	kit d'accessoires	*m*
Zugfahrzeug	*n*	tractor vehicle	*n*	véhicule tracteur	*m*
Zugmagnet	*m*	pulling electromagnet	*n*	électro-aimant de traction	*m*
Zugmaschine	*f*	tractor vehicle	*n*	véhicule tracteur	*m*
Zugschalter	*m*	pull switch	*n*	interrupteur à tirette (alarme auto)	
Zugstange (Zündversteller)	*f*	vacuum advance arm (advance mechanism)	*n*	biellette (correcteur d'avance)	*f*
Zulaufbohrung (Einspritzdüse)	*f*	inlet passage (injection nozzle)	*n*	orifice d'admission (injecteur)	*m*
Zulaufdrossel	*f*	input throttle	*n*	étranglement d'arrivée	*m*
Zulaufmessung	*f*	inlet metering	*n*	dosage à l'admission	*m*
Zulaufquerschnitt (Verteilereinspritzpumpe)	*m*	inlet port (distributor pump)	*n*	canal d'admission (pompe distributrice)	*m*
Zulaufventil	*n*	inlet valve	*n*	soupape d'arrivée	*f*
Zumeß-Schieber	*m*	metering sleeve	*n*	bague de dosage	*f*
Zumeßfunktion	*f*	metering function	*n*	fonction de dosage	*f*
Zumeßgenauigkeit	*f*	metering accuracy	*n*	précision de dosage	*f*
Zumeßkolben (KE-Jetronic)	*m*	fuel-metering plunger (KE-Jetronic)	*n*	piston de dosage (KE-Jetronic)	*m*
Zumeßschlitz (KE-Jetronic)	*m*	fuel-metering slit (KE-Jetronic)	*n*	fente de dosage (KE-Jetronic)	*f*
Zumeßstelle	*f*	metering point	*n*	point de dosage	*m*
Zumessung (Kraftstoff)	*f*	fuel metering	*n*	dosage du carburant	*m*
Zünd-Start-Schalter	*m*	ignition/starting switch	*n*	commutateur d'allumage-démarrage	*m*
Zündabstand	*m*	angular ignition spacing	*n*	période de l'allumage	*f*
Zündanlage	*f*	ignition system	*n*	équipement d'allumage	*m*
Zündauslöser	*m*	ignition trigger	*n*	déclencheur d'allumage	*m*
Zündauslösung (Impulsgeber)	*f*	ignition triggering (pulse generator)	*n*	déclenchement de l'allumage (générateur d'impulsions)	*m*
Zündaussetzer	*m*	misfiring	*n*	ratés d'allumage	*mpl*
Zündbeginn	*m*	start of ignition	*n*	début d'inflammation	*m*
Zündenergie	*f*	ignition energy	*n*	énergie d'allumage	*f*
Zündfolge	*f*	firing sequence	*n*	ordre d'allumage	*m*
Zündfunke	*m*	ignition spark	*n*	étincelle d'allumage	*f*
Zündgrenze	*f*	ignition limit	*n*	limite d'allumage	*f*
Zündimpuls	*m*	ignition pulse	*n*	impulsion d'allumage	*f*
Zündkennfeld	*n*	ignition map	*n*	cartographie d'allumage	*f*
Zündkerze	*f*	spark plug	*n*	bougie d'allumage	*f*
Zündkerzengehäuse	*n*	spark-plug shell	*n*	culot de bougie	*m*

Deutsch		Englisch		Französisch	
Zündkerzengesichter	*npl*	spark-plug faces	*npl*	aspects de la bougie d'allumage	*mpl*
Zündkerzenlehre	*f*	spark-plug-gap gauge	*n*	jauge (bougie)	*f*
Zündkerzenmulde	*f*	spark-plug recess	*n*	logement de la bougie	*m*
Zündkerzenstecker	*m*	spark-plug connector	*n*	embout de bougie	*m*
Zündkondensator	*m*	ignition capacitor	*n*	condensateur d'allumage	*m*
Zündkontakt	*m*	distributor contact points	*npl*	contacts du rupteur (allumage)	*mpl*
Zündkontaktsatz	*m*	contact set	*n*	jeu de contacts d'allumage	*m*
Zündleitung	*f*	high-tension ignition cable	*n*	câble d'allumage	*m*
Zündleitungssatz	*m*	ignition-cable set	*n*	jeu de câbles d'allumage	*m*
Zündmarke	*f*	ignition mark	*n*	repère d'allumage	*m*
Zündmodul (Airbag)	*m*	firing module (airbag)	*n*	module de mise à feu (coussin gonflable)	*m*
Zündmodul (Luft-Kraftstoff-Gemisch)	*m*	ignition module (air-fuel mixture)	*n*	module d'allumage (mélange air-carburant)	*m*
Zündpille (Airbag)	*f*	firing pellet (airbag)	*n*	pastille explosive (coussin gonflable)	*f*
Zündschalter	*m*	ignition switch	*n*	commutateur d'allumage	*m*
Zündschaltgerät	*n*	ignition trigger box	*a*	module de commande de l'allumage	*m*
Zündsicherheit	*f*	ignition reliability	*n*	fiabilité d'allumage	*f*
Zündspannung	*f*	ignition voltage	*n*	tension d'allumage	*f*
Zündspannungsgeber	*m*	ignition-voltage pick-up	*n*	capteur de tension d'allumage	*m*
Zündspannungsreserve	*f*	voltage reserve	*n*	réserve de tension d'allumage	*f*
Zündspule	*f*	ignition coil	*n*	bobine d'allumage	*f*
Zündsystem	*n*	ignition system	*n*	équipement d'allumage	*m*
Zündtemperatur	*f*	ignition temperature	*n*	température d'inflammation	*f*
Zündtrafo	*m*	ignition tranformer	*n*	transformateur d'allumage	*m*
Zündtransistor	*m*	ignition transistor	*n*	transistor d'allumage	*m*
Zündung	*f*	ignition	*n*	allumage	*m*
Zündungseingriff	*m*	ignition adjustment	*n*	intervention sur l'allumage	*f*
Zündungsendstufe	*f*	ignition driver stage	*n*	étage de sortie d'allumage	*m*
Zündunterbrecher	*m*	ignition contact breaker	*n*	rupteur (allumage)	*m*
Zündverstellung	*f*	spark advance	*n*	correction du point d'allumage	*f*
Zündverstellwinkel	*m*	advance angle (ignition)	*n*	angle de correction (allumage)	*m*
Zündverteiler	*m*	ignition distributor	*n*	allumeur	*m*
Zündverteilerkappe	*f*	distributor cap	*n*	tête d'allumeur	*f*
Zündverteilerläufer	*m*	distributor rotor (ignition)	*n*	rotor distributeur (allumage)	*m*
Zündverteilernocken	*m*	distributor cam	*n*	came d'allumage	*f*
Zündverteilerstecker	*m*	distributor connector	*n*	connecteur d'allumeur	*m*
Zündverteilerwelle	*f*	ignition-distributor shaft	*n*	arbre d'allumeur	*m*
Zündverzug	*m*	ignition lag	*n*	délai d'inflammation	*m*
zündwillig	*adj*	ignitable	*adj*	inflammable	*adj*
Zündwilligkeit	*f*	ignition quality	*n*	inflammabilité	*f*
Zündwinkel	*f*	ignition angle	*n*	angle d'allumage	*m*
Zündwinkelkennfeld	*n*	ignition map	*n*	cartographie d'allumage	*f*
Zündwinkelsteuerung	*f*	ignition timing	*n*	commande de l'angle d'allumage	*f*
Zündzeitpunkt	*m*	moment of ignition	*n*	point d'allumage	*m*

Deutsch		Englisch		Französisch	
Zündzeitpunktsteuerung	*f*	ignition timing	*n*	commande de l'angle d'allumage	*f*
Zungenventil	*n*	reed valve	*n*	clapet à languette	*m*
Zusammenbauzeichnung	*f*	assembly drawing	*n*	plan d'assemblage	*m*
Zusatz (Kraftstoff)	*n*	additive (fuel)	*n*	additif (carburant)	*m*
Zusatz-Bremsleuchte	*f*	auxiliary stop lamp	*n*	feu stop supplémentaire	*m*
Zusatz-Fernlichtscheinwerfer	*m*	auxiliary driving lamp	*n*	projecteur route supplémentaire	*m*
Zusatzaggregat	*n*	ancillary	*n*	auxiliaire	*m*
Zusatzbremse	*f*	auxiliary brake	*n*	frein additionnel	*m*
Zusatzeinrichtung (Anhängefahrzeuge)	*f*	auxiliary device (trailers)	*n*	équipement auxiliaire (remorque)	*m*
Zusatzluftmenge	*f*	auxiliary air	*n*	volume d'air additionnel	*m*
Zusatzluftschieber	*m*	auxiliary-air device	*n*	commande d'air additionnel	*f*
Zusatzluftventil	*n*	auxiliary-air valve	*n*	valve d'air additionnel	*f*
Zusatzreflektor	*m*	supplementary reflector	*n*	réflecteur supplémentaire	*m*
Zusatzscheinwerfer, ZSW	*m*	auxiliary lamp	*n*	projecteur complémentaire	*m*
Zuspannung (Bremse)	*f*	application (brakes)	*n*	application de l'effort (frein)	*f*
Zustandsregler (ESP)	*m*	state controller (ESP)	*n*	régulateur d'état (ESP)	*m*
Zuverlässigkeitsprüfung	*f*	reliability test	*n*	essai de fiabilité	*m*
Zwangsregeneration	*f*	forced regeneration	*n*	régénération forcée	*f*
Zweifeder-Düsenhalter	*m*	two-spring nozzle holder	*n*	porte-injecteur à deux ressorts	*m*
zweiflutig (Lüfter)	*adj*	double-flow cooling (fan)	*ppr*	biflux (ventilateur)	*adj*
Zweifunken-Zündspule	*f*	dual-spark ignition coil	*n*	bobine d'allumage à deux sorties	*f*
Zweikammerbetrieb (Vakuum-Bremsanlage)	*m*	dual-chamber operation (vacuum-brake system)	*n*	système à deux chambres (dispositif de freinage à dépression)	*m*
Zweikammerleuchte	*f*	two-chamber lamp	*n*	lanterne à deux compartiments	*f*
Zweikontaktregler	*m*	double-contact regulator	*n*	régulateur bicontact	*m*
Zweikreis-Betriebsbremsventil	*n*	dual-circuit service-brake valve	*n*	valve de frein de service à double circuit	*f*
Zweikreis-Bremsanlage	*f*	dual-circuit braking system	*n*	dispositif de freinage à transmission à double circuit	*m*
Zweikreis-Bremsgerät	*n*	dual-circuit brake assembly	*n*	groupe de freinage à double circuit	*m*
Zweikreis-Schutzventil	*f*	dual-circuit protection valve (brakes)	*n*	valve de sécurité à deux circuits	*f*
Zweikreis-Vorspannzylinder	*m*	dual-circuit actuator cylinder for the brake master cylinder	*n*	cylindre d'assistance à double circuit	*m*
zweikreisig (Bremsanlage)	*adj*	dual-circuit (braking system)	*n*	à deux circuits (dispositif de freinage)	*loc*
Zweileitungs-Anhängersteuerventil	*n*	dual-line trailer-control valve	*n*	valve de commande de remorque à deux conduites	*f*
Zweileitungs-Bremsanlage	*f*	dual-line braking system	*n*	dispositif de freinage à deux conduites	*m*
Zweilochelement	*n*	two-port plunger-and-barrel assembly	*n*	élément à deux orifices	*m*
Zweimassenschwungrad	*n*	dual-mass flywheel	*n*	volant d'inertie à deux masses	*m*
Zweipunktregler (Lambda-Regelung)	*m*	two-position controller (lambda closed-loop control)	*n*	régulateur à deux positions (régulation lambda)	*m*

Deutsch		Englisch		Französisch	
Zweirechner-Prinzip (ABS-Regelung)	*n*	dual-processor principle (ABS control)	*n*	principe bicalculateur (régulation ABS)	*m*
Zweischeinwerfer-System	*n*	two-headlamp system	*n*	système à deux projecteurs	*m*
Zweischichtwicklung	*f*	two-layer winding	*n*	enroulement à deux couches	*m*
Zweischlag (Wischeranlage)	*m*	four-bar linkage (wiper system)	*n*	double battement (essuie-glace)	*m*
Zweistellungsventil	*n*	two-position valve	*n*	valve à deux positions	*f*
Zweistrahlventil	*n*	dual-stream injector	*n*	injecteur bi-jet	*m*
Zweistufen-Boxfilter	*n*	two-stage box-type filter	*n*	filtre-box à deux étages	*m*
Zweitaktverfahren	*n*	two-stroke principle	*n*	cycle à deux temps	*m*
Zweiwegeventil (ASR)	*n*	two-way directional-control valve (TCS)	*n*	distributeur à deux voies (ASR)	*m*
Zweiweggleichrichter	*m*	full-wave rectifier	*n*	redresseur pleine-onde	*m*
Zweiweggleichrichtung	*f*	full-wave rectification	*n*	redressement à deux alternance:	*m*
Zwillingsstromgehäuse	*n*	twin-flow housing	*n*	dispositif à flux jumelé	*m*
Zwischendrehzahl	*m*	intermediate speed	*n*	régime intermédiaire	*m*
Zwischendrehzahlanschlag	*m*	intermediate-speed stop	*n*	butée de vitesse intermédiaire	*f*
Zwischendrehzahlregelung	*f*	intermediate-speed regulation	*n*	régulation de vitesses intermédiaires	*f*
Zwischengehäuse	*n*	intermediate housing	*n*	boîtier intermédiaire	*m*
Zwischenkolben	*m*	intermediate piston	*n*	piston intermédiaire	*m*
Zwischenplatte	*f*	intermediate plate	*n*	plaque intermédiaire	*f*
Zwischenring	*m*	intermediate ring	*n*	disque intermédiaire	*m*
Zwischenuntersuchung, ZU (Bremse)	*f*	intermediate inspection (brakes	*n*	inspection intermédiaire (frein)	*f*
zyklenfest (Batterie)	*adj*	deep-cycle resistant (battery)	*ppr*	résistant aux cycles alternés (batterie)	*ppr*
Zyklon	*m*	cyclone	*n*	cyclone	*m*
Zyklon-Vorabscheider (Papierluftfilter)	*m*	cyclone prefilter (paper filter)	*n*	préséparateur à cyclone (filtre à air en papier)	*m*
Zylinderabschaltung	*f*	cylinder shut-off	*n*	coupure des cylindres	*f*
Zylinderanordnung	*f*	cylinder arrangement	*n*	disposition des cylindres	*f*
Zylinderboden	*m*	cylinder base	*n*	fond du cylindre	*m*
Zylinderdeckel (Luftkompressor)	*m*	cylinder head (air compressor)	*n*	culasse (compresseur d'air)	*f*
Zylinderfüllung	*f*	cylinder charge	*n*	remplissage du cylindre	*m*
Zylinderkammer	*f*	cylinder chamber	*n*	chambre du vérin	*f*
Zylinderkopf (Luftkompressor)	*m*	cylinder head (air compressor)	*n*	culasse (compresseur d'air)	*f*
Zylinderladung	*f*	cylinder charge	*n*	remplissage du cylindre	*m*
zylindrische Anordnung	*f*	cylindrical-type	*n*	en barillet	*loc*

English		German		French	
A					
A/D converter	n	Analog-Digital-Wandler	m	convertisseur analogique-numérique	m
A/F (air-fuel) ratio	n	Luft-Kraftstoff-Verhältnis	n	rapport air-carburant	m
A/F mixture	n	Luft-Kraftstoff-Gemisch	n	mélange air-carburant	m
abrasion resistance	n	Abriebfestigkeit	f	résistance à l'abrasion	f
ABS indicator lamp	n	ABS-Funktionskontrolleuchte	f	lampe témoin de fonctionnement (ABS)	f
ABS, antilock braking system	a	ABS, Antiblockiersystem	a	ABS, système antiblocage	a
ABS/ABD, automatic brake-force differential lock,	a	automatische Brems-Differentialsperre, ABS/ABD	f	blocage automatique du différentiel	m
absolute-boost-pressure-dependent full-load stop	n	absolutdruckmessender, ladedruckabhängiger Vollastanschlag	m	correcteur pneumatique à mesure de pression absolue	m
absolute-pressure sensor	n	Absolutdrucksensor	m	capteur de pression absolue	m
absorption analyzer	n	Absorptionsanalysator	m	analyseur à absorption	m
absorption band	n	Absorptionsband	n	bande d'absorption	f
AC (alternating current) voltage	n	Wechselspannung	f	tension alternative	f
ACC, adaptive cruise control	a	adaptive Fahrgeschwindigkeitsregelung, ACC	f	régulation auto-adaptative de vitesse de roulage	f
acceleration enrichment	n	Beschleunigungsanreicherung	f	enrichissement à l'accélération	m
acceleration knock	n	Beschleunigungsklopfen	n	cliquetis à l'accélération	m
acceleration sensor	n	Beschleunigungssensor	m	capteur d'accélération	m
accelerative force (motor vehicle)	n	Vortrieb (Kfz)	m	propulsion (véhicule)	f
accelerator sensor	n	Fahrpedalsensor	m	capteur d'accélérateur	m
accelerator-lever linkage	n	Gasgestänge	n	timonerie d'accélérateur	f
accelerator-pedal module	n	Fahrpedalmodul	m	module d'accélérateur	m
accessory set	n	Zubehörsatz	m	kit d'accessoires	m
accumulator chamber (ABS)	n	Speicherkammer (ABS)	f	chambre d'accumulation (ABS)	f
accumulator fuel-injection pump	n	Speichereinspritzpumpe	f	pompe d'injection à accumulateur	f
accumulator overflow valve	n	Speicherüberströmventil	n	soupape de décharge de l'accumulateur	f
acoustic source	n	Schallquelle	f	source acoustique	f
acoustic velocity	n	Schallschnelle	f	célérité du son	f
activation blocking (car alarm)	n	Aktivierungssperre (Autoalarm)	f	sécurité de mise en veille (alarme auto)	f
active braking time	n	Bremswirkungsdauer	f	temps de freinage actif	m
active materials (battery)	n	aktive Masse (Batterie)	f	matière active (batterie)	f
active resistance	n	Wirkwiderstand	m	résistance active	f
active-surge damper	n	aktiver Ruckeldämpfer	m	amortisseur actif d'à-coups	m
actual speed	n	Istdrehzahl	f	vitesse de rotation réelle	f
actuate (brakes)	v	betätigen (Bremse)	v	actionner (frein)	v
actuating device (braking system)	n	Betätigungseinrichtung (Bremsanlage)	f	commande (dispositif de freinage)	f
actuating force (ABS solenoid valve)	n	Verstellkraft (ABS-Magnetventil)	f	force de réglage (électrovalve ABS)	f

English

English		German		French	
actuating lever	*n*	Betätigungshebel	*m*	levier de manoeuvre	*m*
actuating shaft	*n*	Betätigungswelle	*f*	arbre de commande	*m*
actuating variable	*n*	Einflußgröße	*f*	paramètre d'influence	*m*
actuator	*n*	Stellglied	*n*	actuateur	*m*
actuator adjustment	*n*	Stelleingriff	*m*	intervention par positionnement	*f*
actuator fastening flange	*m*	Stellwerkjoch	*m*	noyau d'actionneur	*m*
actuator mechanism	*n*	Stellwerk	*n*	actionneur	*m*
actuator rotor	*n*	Stellwerkrotor	*m*	rotor d'actionneur	*m*
actuator shaft	*n*	Stellwelle	*f*	axe de positionnement	*m*
actuator solenoid	*n*	Stellmagnet	*m*	électro-aimant de positionnement	*m*
actuator window (idle actuator)	*n*	Stellfenster (Leerlaufsteller)	*n*	fenêtre de régulation (actionneur de ralenti)	*f*
adapter box (wipers)	*n*	Adapterbox (Wischer)	*f*	boîte d'adaptateurs (essuie-glace)	*f*
adapter lead	*n*	Adapterkabel	*n*	câble adaptateur	*m*
adapter plate (nozzle holder)	*n*	Düsenhalter-Zwischenscheibe	*f*	glace de porte-injecteur	*f*
adapter valve	*n*	Druckverhältnisventil	*n*	régulateur proportionnel de pression	*m*
adaptive cruise control, ACC	*n*	adaptive Fahrgeschwindig-keitsregelung, ACC	*f*	régulation auto-adaptative de vitesse de roulage	*f*
add-on ECU	*n*	Anbausteuergerät	*n*	calculateur adaptable	*m*
add-on module	*n*	Anpaßeinrichtung	*f*	groupe d'adaptation	*m*
adder	*n*	Summierer	*m*	additionneur	*m*
additive (fuel)	*n*	Additiv (Kraftstoff)	*m*	additif (carburant)	*m*
adhesion (tire/road)	*n*	Kraftschluß (Reifen/Straße)	*m*	adhérence (pneu/route)	*f*
adhesion/slip curve	*n*	Haftreibungs-Schlupfkurve	*f*	courbe caractéristique glissement/adhérence	*f*
adhesive label	*n*	Klebeschild	*n*	autocollant	*m*
adjuster (headlight vertical-aim control)	*n*	Verstelleinheit (Leuchtweiteregelung)	*f*	module de réglage (correcteur de site)	*m*
adjusting device	*n*	Verstelleinrichtung	*f*	dispositif de réglage	*m*
adjusting eccentric	*n*	Verstellexzenter	*m*	excentrique de réglage	*m*
adjusting potentiometer	*n*	Einstellpotentiometer	*n*	potentiomètre de réglage	*m*
adjusting screw	*n*	Einstellschraube	*f*	vis de réglage	*f*
adjusting sleeve	*n*	Einstellhülse	*f*	manchon de réglage	*m*
adjustment device	*n*	Stellelement	*n*	élément de commande	*m*
adjustment function	*n*	Verstellfunktion	*f*	fonction de correction	*f*
adjustment plate (dynamic brake analyzer)	*n*	Justierplatte (Rollenbremsprüfstand)	*f*	plateau d'ajustage (banc d'essai)	*m*
adjustment point	*n*	Einstellpunkt	*m*	point de réglage	*m*
admission pressure (ESP)	*n*	Vordruck (ESP)	*m*	pression d'alimentation (ESP)	*f*
admission-pressure valve	*n*	Vordruckventil	*n*	valve de pression d'admission	*f*
advance (start of injection)	*n*	Frühverstellung (Einspritzbeginn)	*f*	avance (début d'injection)	*f*
advance angle (ignition)	*n*	Zündverstellwinkel	*m*	angle de correction (allumage)	*m*
advance angle (timing device)	*n*	Verstellwinkel (Spritzversteller	*m*	angle d'avance (correcteur d'avance)	*m*
advance contact (relay)	*n*	Vorkontakt (Relais)	*m*	précontact (relais)	*m*

English		German		French	
advanced ignition	*n*	Frühzündung	*f*	avance à l'allumage	*f*
aerial	*n*	Antenne	*f*	antenne	*f*
aerodynamic drag	*n*	Luftwiderstand	*m*	résistance de l'air	*f*
after-run	*n*	Nachlauf	*m*	post-fonctionnement	*m*
afterburning	*n*	Nachverbrennung	*f*	post-combustion	*f*
aftermarket program	*n*	Handelsprogramm	*n*	programme Commerce	*m*
air backflush	*n*	Rückspülung	*f*	balayage de retour	*m*
air brake	*n*	Druckluftbremse	*f*	frein à air comprimé	*m*
air chamber	*n*	Luftkammer	*f*	chambre d'air	*f*
air charge	*n*	Luftfüllung	*f*	charge d'air	*f*
air cleaner	*n*	Luftreiniger	*m*	épurateur d'air	*m*
air compressor	*n*	Luftkompressor	*m*	compresseur d'air	*m*
air conditioner	*n*	Klimaanlage	*f*	climatiseur	*m*
air connection	*n*	Luftanschluß	*m*	orifice d'air	*m*
air cooling	*n*	Luftkühlung	*f*	refroidissement par air	*m*
air deficiency (air-fuel mixture)	*n*	Luftmangel (Luft-Kraftstoff-Gemisch)	*m*	déficit d'air (mélange air-carburant)	*m*
air density	*n*	Luftdichte	*f*	densité atmosphérique	*f*
air drier	*n*	Lufttrockner	*m*	dessiccateur d'air	*m*
air filter	*n*	Luftfilter	*n*	filtre à air	*m*
air force (pneumatics)	*n*	Luftkraft	*f*	force de l'air	*f*
air funnel (KE-Jetronic)	*n*	Lufttrichter (KE-Jetronic)	*m*	divergent d'air (KE-Jetronic)	*m*
air gap	*n*	Luftspalt	*m*	entrefer	*m*
air gap (spark plug)	*n*	Luftfunken (Zündkerze)	*m*	étincelle dans l'air (bougie)	*f*
air mass	*n*	Luftmasse	*f*	masse d'air	*f*
air pressure	*n*	Luftdruck	*m*	pression d'air	*f*
air pump	*n*	Luftpumpe	*f*	pompe à air	*f*
air ratio (lambda)	*n*	Luftverhältnis	*n*	coefficient d'air (lambda)	*m*
air requirement (IC engine)	*n*	Luftbedarf (Verbrennungsmotor)	*m*	débit d'air nécessaire (moteur à combustion)	*m*
air reservoir (pneumatics)	*n*	Druckluftbehälter (Pneumatik)	*m*	réservoir d'air comprimé (pneumatique)	*m*
air spring	*n*	Luftfeder	*f*	soufflet de suspension	*m*
air supply	*n*	Luftversorgung	*f*	alimentation en air	*f*
air swirl	*n*	Luftverwirbelung	*f*	turbulence de l'air	*f*
air throughput	*n*	Luftdurchsatz	*m*	débit d'air (disponible)	*m*
air turbulence	*n*	Luftverwirbelung	*f*	turbulence de l'air	*f*
air-assisted braking system	*n*	pneumatische Hilfskraft-Bremsanlage	*f*	dispositif de freinage hydraulique assisté par air comprimé	*m*
air-brake reservoir (pneumatics)	*n*	Druckluftbehälter (Pneumatik)	*m*	réservoir d'air comprimé (pneumatique)	*m*
air-brake system	*n*	pneumatische Bremsanlage	*f*	dispositif de freinage pneumatique	*m*
air-conditioner compressor	*n*	Klimakompressor	*m*	compresseur de climatiseur	*m*
air-conditioner input	*n*	Klimaeingang (Luftzufuhr Klimakompressor) x	*m*	entrée climatiseur	*f*
air-conditioning	*n*	Klimaregelung	*f*	régulateur de climatisseur	*m*
air-cooled	*pp*	luftgekühlt	*pp*	refroidi par air	*pp*

English		German		French	
air-filter element	*n*	Luftfiltereinsatz	*m*	cartouche de filtre à air	*f*
air-flow sensor	*n*	Luftmengenmesser	*m*	débitmètre d'air	*m*
air-fuel (A/F) ratio	*n*	Luft-Kraftstoff-Verhältnis	*n*	rapport air-carburant	*m*
air-fuel mixture	*n*	Luft-Kraftstoff-Gemisch	*n*	mélange air-carburant	*m*
air-fuel-mixture metering	*v*	Gemischzumessung	*f*	dosage du mélange	*m*
air-gap design (spark plug)	*n*	Luftfunkentechnik (Zündkerze)	*f*	éclateur à étincelle dans l'air (bougie)	*m*
air-intake fitting	*n*	Luftansaugstutzen	*m*	tubulure d'aspiration d'air	*f*
air-intake system (IC engine)	*n*	Ansaugsystem (Verbrennungsmotor)	*n*	système d'admission (moteur à combustion)	*m*
air-mass flow	*n*	Luftmassendurchsatz	*m*	débit massique d'air	*m*
air-mass meter	*n*	Luftmassenmesser	*m*	débitmètre massique d'air	*m*
air-over-hydraulic braking system	*n*	pneumatische Fremdkraft-Bremsanlage mit hydraul. Übertragungseinrichtung	*f*	dispositif de freinage hydraulique à commande par air comprimé	*m*
air-pressure sensor	*n*	Luftdruck-Kontrollschalter	*m*	contacteur de contrôle de pression d'air	*m*
air-quantity flow	*n*	Luftmengendurchsatz	*m*	débit volumique d'air	*m*
air-shrouding (fuel injector)	*n*	Luftumfassung (Einspritzventil)	*f*	enveloppe d'air (injecteur)	*f*
air-spring bellows	*n*	Luftfederbalg	*m*	soufflet à air	*m*
air-supply position (pressure regulator)	*n*	Luftförderungsstellung (Druckregler)	*f*	position de refoulement	*f*
air-temperature sensor, ATS	*n*	Lufttemperaturfühler	*m*	capteur de température d'air	*m*
air-tightness test	*n*	Dichtheitsprüfung	*f*	essai d'étanchéité	*m*
airbag	*n*	Airbag	*m*	coussin gonflable (système de retenue des passager)	*m*
airbag triggering unit	*n*	Airbag-Auslösegerät	*n*	déclencheur de coussin d'air	*m*
alarm horn	*n*	Alarmhorn	*n*	avertisseur d'alarme	*m*
alarm switch	*n*	Alarmschalter	*m*	commutateur d'alarme	*m*
alarm tone (car alarm)	*n*	Alarmton (Autoalarm)	*m*	tonalité d'alerte (alarme auto)	*f*
alignment mirror (lighting)	*n*	Ausrichtspiegel (Lichttechnik)	*m*	miroir d'orientation (éclairage)	*m*
alignment pin (dynamic brake analyzer)	*n*	Zentrierstift (Rollenbremsprüfstand)	*m*	axe de centrage (banc d'essai)	*m*
all-wheel drive, AWD	*n*	Allradantrieb	*m*	transmission intégrale	*f*
all-wheel-drive system	*n*	Allradsystem	*n*	système de transmission intégrale	*m*
alternating current, AC	*n*	Wechselstrom	*m*	courant alternatif	*m*
alternating voltage	*n*	Wechselspannung	*f*	tension alternative	*f*
alternator	*n*	Drehstromgenerator	*m*	alternateur triphasé	*m*
alternator output power	*n*	Generatorleistung	*f*	puissance de l'alternateur	*f*
altitude compensation	*n*	Höhenkorrektur	*f*	correction altimétrique	*f*
altitude compensator	*n*	atmosphärendruckabhängiger Vollastanschlag, ADA	*m*	correcteur altimétrique	*m*
altitude control	*n*	Höhenanschlag	*m*	correcteur altimétrique	*m*
altitude sensor	*n*	Höhensensor	*m*	capteur altimétrique	*m*
altitude-controlled full-load stop	*n*	höhengesteuerter Vollastmengenanschlag	*m*	butée de pleine charge en fonction de l'altitude	*f*
altitude-pressure compensator	*n*	atmosphärendruckabhängiger Vollastanschlag, ADA	*m*	correcteur altimétrique	*m*

English

English		German		French	
ambient-pressure-dependent port closing	*n*	atmosphärendruckabhängiger Förderbeginn	*m*	début de refoulement en fonction de la pression atmosphérique	*m*
amplification ratio	*n*	Verstärkungsverhältnis	*n*	rapport d'amplification	*m*
analog-digital converter	*n*	Analog-Digital-Wandler	*m*	convertisseur analogique-numérique	*m*
analog-value conditioning	*n*	Analogwertaufbereitung	*f*	conditionnement de valeur analogique	*m*
analog-value evaluation	*n*	Analogwertauswertung	*f*	exploitation de valeur analogique	*f*
analog-value sampling	*n*	Analogwerterfassung	*f*	saisie de valeur analogique	*f*
ancillary	*n*	Zusatzaggregat	*n*	auxiliaire	*m*
ancillary circuit	*n*	Nebenverbraucherkreis	*m*	circuit des récepteurs auxiliaires	*m*
aneroid box	*n*	Membrandose	*f*	capsule à membrane	*f*
aneroid capsule	*n*	Steuerdose	*f*	capsule de commande	*f*
angle of cam rotation	*n*	Nockenwinkel	*m*	angle de levée de came	*m*
angle of impact (crosswind)	*n*	Anströmwinkel (Seitenwind)	*m*	angle d'attaque (vent latéral)	*m*
angle of rotation sensor	*n*	Drehwinkelsensor, DWS	*m*	capteur d'angle de rotation	*m*
angular cam spacing	*n*	Nockenversatz	*m*	écart angulaire de came	*m*
angular ignition spacing	*n*	Zündabstand	*m*	période de l'allumage	*f*
angular sensor (car alarm)	*n*	Winkelgeber (Autoalarm)	*m*	capteur de position angulaire (alarme auto)	*m*
annular groove	*n*	Ringkanal	*m*	canal annulaire	*m*
annular orifice	*n*	Ringspalt	*m*	fente annulaire	*f*
anolog input	*n*	Analogeingang	*m*	entrée analogique	*f*
antenna	*n*	Antenne	*f*	antenne	*f*
anti-aging additive (gasoline)	*n*	Alterungsschutz (Kraftstoff)	*m*	protection contre le vieillissement (essence)	*f*
anti-bucking device	*n*	aktive Ruckeldämpfung, ARD	*f*	amortissement actif d'à-coups	*m*
anti-erosion cap (injector)	*n*	Prallkappe (Einspritzventil)	*f*	capuchon anti-érosion (injecteur)	*m*
anti-erosion screw (diesel fuel injection)	*n*	Prallschraube (Dieseleinspritzung)	*f*	vis anti-érosion (injection diesel)	*f*
anti-rotation element (door control)	*n*	Verdrehsicherung (Türbetätigung)	*f*	sécurité antirotation (commande des portes)	*f*
antifreeze	*n*	Frostschutzmittel	*n*	antigel	*m*
antifreeze pump	*n*	Frostschutzpumpe	*f*	pompe antigel	*f*
antifreeze unit	*n*	Frostschutzeinrichtung	*f*	dispositif antigel	*m*
antiknock agent	*n*	Antiklopfmittel	*n*	agent antidétonant	*m*
antiknock quality	*n*	Klopffestigkeit	*f*	indétonance	*f*
antilock braking system, ABS	*n*	Antiblockiersystem, ABS	*n*	système antiblocage, ABS	*m*
antiskid system	*n*	Antiblockiersystem, ABS	*n*	système antiblocage, ABS	*m*
application (brakes)	*n*	Zuspannung (Bremse)	*f*	application de l'effort (frein)	*f*
application force (brake linings	*n*	Spannkraft (Bremsbeläge)	*f*	force de serrage (garnitures de frein)	*f*
application instructions	*npl*	Applikationshinweis	*m*	notice d'application	*f*
application pressure (brake linings)	*n*	Spannkraft (Bremsbeläge)	*f*	force de serrage (garnitures de frein)	*f*

English		German		French	
applied pressure	*n*	Betätigungsdruck	*m*	pression d'actionnement	*f*
apply (brakes)	*v*	anlegen (Bremse)	*v*	appliquer (frein)	*v*
apply (braking force)	*v*	einsteuern (Bremskraft)	*v*	moduler (force de freinage)	*v*
aquaplaning (tire)	*n*	Aquaplaning (Reifen)	*n*	aquaplanage (pneu)	*m*
arc (spark plug)	*n*	Flammkern (Zündkerze)	*m*	coeur de la flamme (bougie)	*m*
arcing	*n*	Durchschlag (elektrisch)	*m*	décharge disruptive	*f*
arcing voltage	*n*	Zündspannung	*f*	tension d'allumage	*f*
arithmetic-logic processor (ECU)	*n*	Rechenwerk (Steuergerät)	*n*	unité de calcul (calculateur)	*f*
armature (ABS hydraulic modulator)	*n*	Anker (ABS-Hydroaggregat)	*m*	noyau (groupe hydraulique ABS)	*m*
armature (relays)	*n*	Anker (Relais)	*m*	armature (relais)	*f*
armature (rotating machines)	*n*	Anker (umlaufende Maschinen	*m*	induit (machines tournantes)	*m*
armature braking	*n*	Ankerabbremsung	*f*	freinage de l'induit	*m*
armature current	*n*	Ankerstrom	*m*	courant d'induit	*m*
armature reaction	*n*	Ankerrückwirkung	*f*	réaction d'induit	*f*
armature shaft	*n*	Ankerwelle	*f*	arbre d'induit	*m*
armature stack	*n*	Ankerpaket	*n*	noyau feuilleté d'induit	*m*
armature stroke	*n*	Ankerhub	*m*	course du noyau	*f*
armature winding	*n*	Ankerwicklung	*f*	enroulement d'induit	*m*
armored hose (special ignition coil)	*n*	Panzerschlauch (Sonderzündspule)	*m*	flexible blindé (bobine d'allumage spéciale)	*m*
articulated vehicle	*n*	Gelenkfahrzeug	*n*	véhicule articulé	*m*
assembly	*n*	Baugruppe	*f*	sous-ensemble	*m*
assembly drawing	*n*	Zusammenbauzeichnung	*f*	plan d'assemblage	*m*
assembly instructions	*n*	Montagehinweis	*m*	instruction de montage	*f*
assembly number	*n*	Montagezahl	*f*	numéro de montage	*m*
assisting force (brake booster)	*n*	Unterstützungskraft (Bremskraftverstärker)	*m*	force d'assistance (servofrein)	*f*
asymmetrical lower beam	*n*	asymmetrisches Abblendlicht	*n*	feu de croisement asymétrique	*m*
atmospheric-pressure sensor	*n*	Atmosphärendrucksensor	*m*	capteur de pression atmosphérique	*m*
audit calibration pump	*f*	Fördermengenhauptnormal	*n*	pompe de référence étalon	*f*
auto-ignition	*n*	Selbstzündung	*f*	auto-allumage	*m*
auto-ignition temperature	*n*	Selbstzündtemperatur	*f*	température d'autoallumage	*f*
automatic brake	*n*	automatische Bremse	*f*	frein automatique	*m*
automatic brake-force differential lock, ABS/ABD	*n*	automatische Brems-Differentialsperre, ABS/ABD	*f*	blocage automatique du différentiel	*m*
automatic braking	*n*	selbsttätige Bremsung	*f*	freinage automatique	*m*
automatic braking system	*n*	selbsttätige Bremsanlage	*f*	dispositif de freinage automatique	*m*
automatic gearbox	*n*	Automatikgetriebe	*n*	boîte de vitesses automatique	*f*
automatic heater	*n*	Heizautomatik	*f*	chauffage automatique	*m*
automatic load-sensitive braking-force metering	*n*	automatisch lastabhängige Bremskraftregelung, ALB	*f*	correction automatique de la force de freinage en fonction de la charge	*f*
automatic starting quantity	*n*	automatische Startmenge	*f*	surcharge automatique au démarrage	*f*

English		German		French	
automatic wash-and-wipe system	*n*	Trockenwisch-Automatik	*f*	essuyage-séchage automatique	*m*
automotive alarm system	*n*	Auto-Alarmanlage	*n*	alarme auto	*f*
automotive equipment	*n*	Kraftfahrzeugausrüstung	*f*	equipement automobile	*m*
Automotive Handbook (Bosch publication)	*n*	Kraftfahrtechnisches Taschenbuch (Bosch-Schriftenreihe)	*n*	Mémento de technologie automobile (publication Bosch)	*m*
automotive pneumatics	*n*	Fahrzeugpneumatik	*f*	pneumatique automobile	*f*
automotive stabilization system+	*n*	Fahrdynamikregelung, ESP	*f*	régulation du comportement dynamique, ESP	*f*
auxiliary actuating variable	*n*	Hilfssteuergröße	*f*	grandeur convergente	*f*
auxiliary air	*n*	Zusatzluftmenge	*f*	volume d'air additionnel	*m*
auxiliary brake	*n*	Zusatzbremse	*f*	frein additionnel	*m*
auxiliary chamber	*n*	Wirbelkammer	*f*	chambre de tourbillonnement	*f*
auxiliary device (trailers)	*n*	Zusatzeinrichtung (Anhängefahrzeuge)	*f*	équipement auxiliaire (remorque)	*m*
auxiliary driving lamp	*n*	Zusatz-Fernlichtscheinwerfer	*m*	projecteur route supplémentaire	*m*
auxiliary engine-speed sensor	*n*	Hilfsdrehzahlgeber	*m*	capteur auxiliaire de régime	*m*
auxiliary heating	*n*	Standheizung	*f*	chauffage auxiliaire	*m*
auxiliary idle-speed spring	*n*	Leerlauf-Zusatzfeder	*f*	ressort additionnel de ralenti	*m*
auxiliary lamp	*n*	Zusatzscheinwerfer, ZSW	*m*	projecteur complémentaire	*m*
auxiliary release device (brakes)	*n*	Hilfslöseeinrichtung (Bremse)	*f*	dispositif auxiliaire de desserrage (frein)	*m*
auxiliary stop lamp	*n*	Zusatz-Bremsleuchte	*f*	feu stop supplémentaire	*m*
auxiliary system	*n*	Nebenaggregat	*n*	groupe auxiliaire	*m*
auxiliary ventilation	*n*	Fremdbelüftung	*f*	ventilation externe	*f*
auxiliary ventilator	*n*	Hilfsgebläse	*n*	ventilateur auxiliaire	*m*
auxiliary-air device	*n*	Zusatzluftschieber	*m*	commande d'air additionnel	*f*
auxiliary-air valve	*n*	Zusatzluftventil	*n*	valve d'air additionnel	*f*
AWD, all-wheel drive	*a*	Allradantrieb	*m*	transmission intégrale	*f*
axial cam (radial-piston pump)	*n*	Axialnocken (Radialkolbenpumpe)	*m*	came axiale (pompe à pistons radiaux)	*f*
axial fan	*n*	Axiallüfter	*m*	ventilateur axial	*m*
axial runout (brake disc)	*n*	Seitenschlag (Bremsscheibe)	*m*	voilage (disque de frein)	*m*
axial-piston distributor pump	*n*	Axialkolben-Verteiler-einspritzpumpe	*f*	pompe distributrice à piston axial	*f*
axial-piston motor	*n*	Axialkolbenmotor	*m*	moteur à pistons axiaux	*m*
axial-piston pump	*n*	Axialkolben-Verteiler-einspritzpumpe	*f*	pompe distributrice à piston axial	*f*
axis of rotation (motor vehicle)	*n*	Schraubachse (Kfz)	*f*	axe de vissage (véhicule)	*m*
axis resonance	*n*	Achsresonanz	*f*	résonance des essieux	*f*
axle load	*n*	Achslast	*f*	charge (essieu)	*f*
axle weight	*n*	Achsgewicht	*n*	poids de l'essieu	*m*
axle-load distribution	*n*	Achslastverteilung	*f*	répartition de la charge par essieu	*f*
axle-load sensor	*n*	Achslastsensor	*m*	capteur de charge sur essieu	*m*
axle-load signal	*n*	Achslastsignal	*n*	signal de charge sur essieu	*m*
axle-load transfer	*n*	Achslastverlagerung	*f*	report de charge dynamique de l'essieu	*m*

English

English		German		French	
B					
back-pressure reaction	*n*	Gegendruck	*m*	réaction de contre-pression	*f*
back-up ring	*n*	Stützring	*m*	bague d'appui	*f*
backfiring	*n*	Saugrohrrückzündung	*f*	retour d'allumage	*m*
background noise (radio disturbance)	*n*	rauschen (Funkstörung) x	*v*	bruit de fond (perturbation)	*m*
backlash (gear)	*n*	Flankenspiel (Zahnrad)	*n*	jeu entre dents (engrenage)	*m*
backlite	*n*	Heckscheibe	*f*	vitre arrière	*f*
backrest adjuster	*n*	Lehnenverstellung	*f*	réglage du dossier de siège	*m*
backup lamp	*n*	Rückfahrscheinwerfer	*m*	feu de marche arrière	*m*
backup mode (battery charge)	*n*	Stützbetrieb (Batterieladung)	*m*	mode "soutien" (charge de batterie)	*m*
backup valve	*n*	Rückhalteventil	*n*	valve de secours	*f*
baffle plate (pressure actuator)	*n*	Prallplatte (Drucksteller)	*f*	déflecteur (actionneur de pression)	*m*
baffle surface (diesel fuel injection)	*n*	Prallfläche (Dieseleinspritzung)	*f*	surface d'impact (injection diesel)	*f*
ball pin	*n*	Kugelbolzen	*m*	rotule	*f*
ball pivot	*n*	Kugelzapfen	*m*	tourillon sphérique	*m*
ball valve	*n*	Kugelventil	*n*	clapet à bille	*m*
ballast module (car alarm)	*n*	Vorschaltmodul (Autoalarm)	*m*	module de protection (alarme auto)	*m*
ballast unit (gaseous-discharge lamp)	*n*	Vorschaltgerät (Gasentladungslampe)	*n*	module de commande (lampe à décharge dans un gaz)	*m*
ballast unit (ignition)	*n*	Vorschaltgerät (Zündung)	*n*	module pilote (allumage)	*m*
bandpass filter	*n*	Bandpaßfilter	*n*	filtre passe-bande	*m*
bar winding	*n*	Stabwicklung	*f*	enroulement-tige	*m*
barometric-pressure and load-dependent start of delivery	*n*	atmosphärendruck- und lastabhängiger Förderbeginn	*m*	début de refoulement en fonction de la pression atmosph. et de la charge	*m*
barrel with metering slits (Jetronic)	*n*	Schlitzträger (Jetronic)	*m*	cylindre à fentes d'étranglement (Jetronic)	*m*
barrel-and-flange-element	*n*	Flanschelement	*n*	élément de pompage à bride	*m*
barrel-and-valve assembly	*n*	Elementverband	*m*	ensemble élément-soupape	*m*
base mounted	*pp*	Flachbettbefestigung	*f*	fixation par base plane	*f*
basic injection quantity	*n*	Grundeinspritzmenge	*f*	débit d'injection de base	*m*
basic injection timing	*n*	Grundeinspritzzeit	*f*	durée d'injection de base	*f*
basic reflector	*n*	Grundreflektor	*m*	réflecteur de base	*m*
battery	*n*	Batterie	*f*	batterie d'accumulateurs	*f*
battery acid	*n*	Elektrolyt	*m*	électrolyte	*m*
battery cable	*n*	Batteriekabel	*n*	câble de batterie	*m*
battery capacity	*n*	Nennkapazität (Batterie)	*f*	capacité nominale (batterie)	*f*
battery case	*n*	Blockkasten (Batterie)	*m*	bac monobloc (batterie)	*m*
battery changeover	*n*	Batterieumschaltung	*f*	commutation de batteries	*f*
battery changeover relay	*n*	Batterieumschaltrelais	*n*	coupleur de batteries	*m*
battery charge	*n*	Ladung (Batterie)	*f*	charge (batterie)	*f*
battery charge current	*n*	Batterieladestrom	*m*	courant de charge de la batterie	*m*
battery charger	*n*	Batterieladegerät	*n*	chargeur de batterie	*m*

English

English		German		French	
battery discharge	*n*	Batterieentladung	*f*	décharge de la batterie	*f*
battery jumper cable	*n*	Starthilfskabel	*n*	câble d'aide au démarrage	*m*
battery master switch	*n*	Batterieschalter	*m*	robinet de batterie	*m*
battery set	*n*	Batterie-Set	*n*	kit batterie	*m*
battery terminal	*n*	Batterieklemme	*f*	cosse de batterie	*f*
battery tester	*n*	Batterie-Tester	*m*	testeur de batteries	*m*
battery voltage +	*n*	Ruhespannung (Batterie)	*f*	tension au repos (batterie)	*f*
battery-cable terminal	*n*	Batterieklemme	*f*	cosse de batterie	*f*
battery-cutoff relay	*n*	Batterietrennrelais	*n*	relais de découplage de batterie	*m*
beamwash	*n*	Lichtwischeranlage	*f*	lavophare	*m*
beamwash motor	*n*	Lichtwischermotor	*m*	moteur de lavophare	*m*
beamwash wiper-arm	*n*	Lichtwischerarm	*m*	bras de lavophare	*m*
beamwash wiper-blade	*n*	Lichtwischerblatt	*n*	raclette de lavophare	*f*
beamwash wiper-lever	*n*	Lichtwischerhebel	*m*	levier de lavophare	*m*
bearing cage (door control)	*n*	Kugelkäfig (Türbetätigung)	*m*	cage à billes (commande des portes)	*f*
bearing housing	*n*	Lagergehäuse	*n*	carter de palier	*m*
bearing ring	*n*	Lagerring	*m*	bague de guidage	*f*
bell crank	*n*	Winkelhebel	*m*	levier coudé	*m*
bellows pressure	*n*	Balgdruck (Luftfeder)	*m*	pression soufflet	*f*
belt drive	*n*	Riementrieb	*m*	transmission à courroie	*f*
belt pre-tension	*n*	Riemenvorspannung	*f*	prétension de courroie	*f*
belt pulley	*n*	Riemenscheibe	*f*	poulie	*f*
belt tensioner	*n*	Riemenspanner	*m*	tendeur de courroie	*m*
bifocal reflector	*n*	Bifokalreflektor	*m*	réflecteur bifocal	*m*
bipolar technology	*n*	Bipolartechnik	*f*	technique bipolaire	*f*
black smoke	*n*	Schwarzrauch	*m*	fumées noires	*fpl*
blackening	*n*	Schwärzung	*f*	noircissement	*m*
bladder accumulator	*n*	Blasenspeicher	*m*	accumulateur à vessie	*m*
blade ring (electric fuel pump)	*n*	Schaufelkranz (Elektrokraftstoffpumpe)	*m*	couronne à palettes (pompe électrique à carburant)	*f*
blade terminal	*n*	Flachstecker	*m*	fiche plate	*f*
blade terminal housing	*n*	Flachsteckergehäuse	*n*	boîtier pour fiches plates	*m*
blade wheel (hydrodynamic retarder)	*n*	Schaufelrad (hydrodynamischer Verlangsamer)	*n*	roue à palettes (ralentisseur hydrodynamique)	*f*
bleed	*v*	entlüften	*v*	dégazage	*m*
bleed screw	*n*	Entlüftungsschraube	*f*	vis de purge d'air	*f*
bleeder screw	*n*	Entlüftungsschraube	*f*	vis de purge d'air	*f*
bleeder valve	*n*	Entlüftungsventil	*n*	valve de purge air	*f*
blind hole (injector)	*n*	Sackloch (Einspritzventil)	*n*	sac d'injecteur	*m*
blind-hole nozzle	*n*	Sacklochdüse	*f*	injecteur à trou borgne	*m*
blind-hole pumping element	*n*	Sacklochelement	*n*	élément à trou borgne	*m*
blink code (self-diagnosis)	*n*	Blink Code (Eigendiagnose)	*m*	code clignotant (autodiagnostic	*m*
blinker switch	*n*	Blinkerschalter	*m*	inverseur des feux clignotants	*m*
blister pack	*n*	Blisterverpackung	*f*	emballage blister	*m*
block diagram	*n*	Übersichtsschaltplan	*m*	schéma fonctionnel	*m*
block diode	*n*	Sperr-Diode	*f*	diode de barrage	*f*

English

English		German			French	
blockage (filter)	*n*	Sperreffekt (Filter)		*m*	effet de barrage (filtre)	*m*
blocking pin	*n*	Arretierbolzen		*m*	axe de blocage	*m*
blocking-oil inlet passage	*n*	Sperrölzulaufbohrung	+	*f*	orifice d'admission de carburant de barrage	*m*
blow-off (pressure regulator)	*v*	abblasen (Druckregler)	x	*v*	échappement d'air (régulateur de pression)	*m*
blow-off fitting (pressure regulator)	*n*	Ablaßstutzen (Druckregler)		*m*	tubulure d'échappement (régulateur de pression)	*f*
blow-off noise (pressure regulator)	*n*	Abblasgeräusch (Druckregler)		*n*	bruit d'échappement (régulateur de pression)	*m*
blowback	*n*	rückblasen		*v*	reflux des gaz	*m*
blowby gas	*n*	Leckgas		*n*	gaz de fuite	*mpl*
blower	*n*	Lüfter		*m*	ventilateur	*m*
blower control unit	*n*	Gebläseregler		*m*	régulateur de ventilateur	*m*
blowout magnet (power relay)	*n*	Blasmagnet (Leistungsrelais)		*m*	aimant de soufflage (relais de puissance)	*m*
blue smoke	*n*	Blaurauch	x	*m*	fumées bleues	*fpl*
bobbin (ignition coil)	*n*	Wickelkörper (Zündspule)		*m*	corps d'enroulement (bobine d'allumage)	*m*
body electrics	*n*	Karosserie-Elektrik		*f*	électrotechnique de carrosserie	*f*
body electronics	*n*	Karosserie-Elektronik		*f*	électronique de carrosserie	*f*
boiling curve (gasoline)	*n*	Siedeverlauf (Benzin)		*m*	courbe d'ébullition (essence)	*f*
boost charge (battery)	*n*	Schnelladung (Batterie)		*f*	charge rapide (batterie)	*f*
boost effect	*n*	Nachladeeffekt		*m*	effet de "postcharge"	*m*
boost factor (brake booster)	*n*	Verstärkungsfaktor (Bremskraftverstärker)		*m*	effet de renforcement de freinage (servofrein)	*m*
boost pressure	*n*	Ladedruck		*m*	pression de suralimentation	*f*
boost ratio	*n*	Aufladegrad		*m*	degré de suralimentation	*m*
boost-pressure control	*n*	Ladedruckregelung		*f*	régulation de la pression de suralimentation	*f*
boost-pressure sensor, BPS	*n*	Ladedrucksensor		*m*	capteur de pression de suralimentation	*m*
booster cylinder	*n*	Vorspannzylinder		*m*	cylindre d'assistance	*m*
booster pump	*n*	Vorförderpumpe		*f*	pompe de pré-alimentation	*f*
bore (engine cylinder)	*n*	Bohrung (Motorzylinder)		*f*	alésage (cylindre moteur)	*m*
Bosch black-smoke number	*n*	Bosch-Schwärzungszahl, BSZ		*f*	indice de noircissement Bosch	*m*
bottom dead center, BDC	*n*	Unterer Totpunkt, UT		*m*	point mort bas, PMB	*m*
bottom rail (battery)	*n*	Bodenleiste (Batterie)		*f*	rebord de fixation (batterie)	*m*
bottom-feed injector	*n*	Einspritzventil mit radialer Zuführung ("Bottom-Feed")		*n*	injecteur à flux radial	*m*
bounce time (relay)	*n*	Prellzeit (Relais)		*f*	temps de rebondissement (relais)	*m*
box-type fuel filter	*n*	Boxfilter		*n*	filtre-box	*m*
bracket clamp (wipers)	*n*	Bügelkralle (Wischer)		*f*	griffe de palonnier (essuie-glace)	*f*
bracket system (wiper system)	*n*	Bügelsystem (Wischeranlage)		*n*	palonniers (essuie-glace)	*mpl*
brake	*v*	bremsen		*v*	freiner	*v*
brake	*n*	Bremse		*f*	frein	*m*
brake "pull"	*n*	schiefziehen (Bremse)	x	*v*	déséquilibre des freins	*m*

English

English		German		French	
brake adjustment	*n*	Bremsennachstellung	*f*	rattrapage de jeu (frein)	*m*
brake anchor plate (brakes)	*n*	Bremsträger (Bremse)	*m*	support de frein	*m*
brake application (TCS)	*n*	Bremseneingriff (ASR)	*m*	intervention sur les freins (ASR)	*f*
brake balance	*n*	Bremsenabstimmung	*f*	adaptation des freins (aux différents véhicules)	*f*
brake booster (passenger car)	*n*	Bremskraftverstärker (Pkw)	*m*	servofrein (voiture)	*m*
brake cable (parking brake)	*n*	Bremsseil (Feststellbremse)	*n*	câble de frein (frein de stationnement)	*m*
brake calibration	*n*	Bremsabstimmung	*f*	équilibrage des freins	*m*
brake caliper set	*n*	Bremssattel-Set	*n*	kit d'étrier de frein	*m*
brake cam	*n*	Bremsnocken	*m*	came de frein	*f*
brake circuit	*n*	Bremskreis	*m*	circuit de freinage	*m*
brake coefficient	*n*	Bremsenkennwert	*m*	coefficient d'autoserrage	*m*
brake connection	*n*	Bremsanschluß	*m*	raccordement de frein	*m*
brake contact	*n*	Bremskontakt	*m*	contacteur de freins	*m*
brake control circuit (TCS)	*n*	Bremsregelkreis (ASR)	*m*	circuit de régulation du freinage (ASR)	*m*
brake control system	*n*	Bremsregelung	*f*	régulation de freinage	*f*
brake controller (TCS)	*n*	Bremsregler (ASR)	*m*	régulateur de freinage (ASR)	*m*
brake cycle	*n*	Bremszyklus	*m*	cycle de freinage	*m*
brake cylinder	*n*	Bremszylinder	*m*	cylindre de frein	*m*
brake disc	*n*	Bremsscheibe	*f*	disque de frein	*m*
brake drum	*n*	Bremstrommel	*f*	tambour de frein	*m*
brake dust	*n*	Bremsabrieb	*m*	traces d'abrasion dues au freinage	*fpl*
brake dynamometer	*n*	Rollenbremsprüfstand	*m*	banc d'essai à rouleaux pour freins	*m*
brake fluid	*n*	Bremsflüssigkeit	*f*	liquide de frein	*m*
brake hose	*n*	Bremsschlauch	*m*	flexible de frein	*m*
brake intervention (TCS)	*n*	Bremseneingriff (ASR)	*m*	intervention sur les freins (ASR)	*f*
brake lever	*n*	Bremshebel	*m*	levier de frein	*m*
brake line (general)	*n*	Bremsleitung (allgemein)	*f*	conduite de frein (en général)	*f*
brake lining	*n*	Bremsbelag	*m*	garniture de frein	*f*
brake linkage	*n*	Bremsgestänge	*n*	timonerie de frein	*f*
brake master cylinder	*n*	Hauptzylinder	*m*	maître-cylindre de frein	*m*
brake pad	*n*	Bremsbelag	*m*	garniture de frein	*f*
brake pedal	*n*	Bremspedal	*n*	pédale de frein	*f*
brake repair service	*n*	Bremsendienst	*m*	service freins	*m*
brake response time	*n*	Bremsenansprechdauer	*f*	temps de réponse des freins	*m*
brake service line (dual-line braking system)	*n*	Bremsleitung (Zweileitungs-Bremsanlage)	*f*	conduite de commande (dispositif de freinage à deux conduites)	*f*
brake servo unit (passenger car)	*n*	Bremskraftverstärker (Pkw)	*m*	servofrein (voiture)	*m*
brake servo-unit cylinder (commercial vehicles)	*n*	Bremsverstärker (Nfz)	*m*	cylindre de servofrein (véhicules utilitaires)	*m*
brake shoe	*n*	Bremsbacke	*f*	segment de frein	*m*
brake slip	*n*	Bremsschlupf	*m*	glissement au freinage	*m*

English		German		French	
brake specifications	*npl*	Bremskenndaten	*npl*	caractéristiques du freinage	*fpl*
brake system	*n*	Bremsanlage	*f*	dispositif de freinage	*m*
brake test	*n*	Bremsprüfung	*f*	essai des freins	*m*
brake tester	*n*	Bremsentester	*m*	contrôleur de freins	*m*
brake testing	*n*	Bremsenprüfung	*f*	essai de freinage	*m*
brake valve	*n*	Bremsventil	*n*	valve de frein	*f*
brake winding	*n*	Bremswicklung	*f*	enroulement de freinage	*m*
brake-circuit configuration	*n*	Bremskreisaufteilung	*f*	répartition des circuits de freinage	*f*
brake-component group	*n*	Bremsgerätegruppe	*f*	groupe de freinage	*m*
brake-fluid level	*n*	Bremsflüssigkeitsstand	*m*	niveau du liquide de frein	*m*
brake-fluid reservoir	*n*	Bremsflüssigkeitsbehälter	*m*	réservoir de liquide de frein	*m*
brake-force differential lock	*n*	Brems-Differentialsperre	*f*	blocage du différentiel	*m*
brake-light switch	*n*	Bremslichtschalter	*m*	contacteur de feux de stop	*m*
brake-pressure modulation	*n*	Bremsdruckmodulation	*f*	modulation de la force de freinage	*f*
brake-pressure regulating valve	*n*	Bremsdruckminderer	*m*	réducteur de pression de freinage	*m*
brake-shoe set	*n*	Bremsbackensatz	*m*	jeu de mâchoires de frein	*m*
brakes-applied mode	*n*	Bremsstellung	*f*	position de freinage	*f*
brakes-released mode	*n*	Fahrstellung	*f*	position de roulage	*f*
braking	*n*	Bremsung	*f*	freinage	*m*
braking action	*n*	Bremsvorgang	*m*	mécanique du freinage	*f*
braking condition	*n*	Bremszustand	*m*	situation de freinage	*f*
braking deceleration	*n*	Bremsverzögerung	*f*	décélération de freinage	*f*
braking distance	*n*	Bremsweg	*m*	distance de freinage	*f*
braking during cornering	*n*	Kurvenbremsung	*f*	freinage en virage	*m*
braking effect	*n*	Bremswirkung	*f*	effet de freinage	*m*
braking energy	*n*	Bremsenergie	*f*	énergie de freinage	*f*
braking equipment	*n*	Bremsausrüstung	*f*	équipement de freinage	*m*
braking factor	*n*	Abbremsung	*f*	taux de freinage	*m*
braking fading	x *n*	Fading (Bremse)	x *n*	fading (frein)	x *m*
braking force	*n*	Bremskraft	*f*	force de freinage	*f*
braking heat	*n*	Bremswärme	*f*	chaleur de freinage	*f*
braking hysteresis	*n*	Bremshysterese	*f*	hystérésis du freinage	*f*
braking position	*n*	Bremsstellung	*f*	position de freinage	*f*
braking pressure	*n*	Bremsdruck	*m*	pression de freinage	*f*
braking ratio	*n*	Abbremsung	*f*	taux de freinage	*m*
braking response	*n*	Bremsverhalten	*n*	comportement au freinage	*m*
braking rotor	*n*	Bremsrotor	*m*	rotor de freinage	*m*
braking stator	*n*	Bremsstator	*m*	stator de freinage	*m*
braking system	*n*	Bremsanlage	*f*	dispositif de freinage	*m*
braking time	*n*	Bremsdauer	*f*	temps de freinage	*m*
braking to a standstill	*n*	Stoppbremsung	*f*	freinage d'arrêt	*m*
braking torque	*n*	Bremsmoment	*n*	couple de freinage	*m*
braking work	*n*	Bremsarbeit	*f*	travail de freinage	*m*

English		German			French	
braking-equipment test bench	*n*	Bremsaggregateprüfstand		*m*	banc d'essai pour équipement pneumatique de freinage	*m*
braking-force control	*n*	Bremskraftsteuerung		*f*	commande de la force de freinage	*f*
braking-force controller	*n*	Bremskraftsteuerer		*m*	commande de force de freinage	*f*
braking-force distribution	*n*	Bremskraftverteilung		*f*	répartition de la force de freinage	*f*
braking-force limiter	*n*	Bremskraftbegrenzer		*m*	limiteur de pression de freinage	*m*
braking-force metering	*n*	Bremskraftregelung		*f*	régulation de la force de freinage	*f*
braking-force metering device	*n*	Bremskraftverteiler		*m*	répartiteur de force de freinage	*m*
braking-force reducer	*n*	Bremskraftminderer		*m*	réducteur de freinage	*m*
braking-force regulator	*n*	Bremskraftregler		*m*	modulateur de freinage	*m*
braking-pressure control	*n*	Bremsdruckregelung		*f*	régulation de pression de freinage	*f*
braking-system design	*n*	Bremsanlagenauslegung		*f*	conception d'un dispositif de freinage	*f*
braking-system inspection	*n*	Bremsenprüfung		*f*	essai de freinage	*m*
braking-system special inspection	*n*	Bremsensonderuntersuchung, BSU		*f*	contrôle spécial des freins	*m*
braking-system-activation time	*n*	Ansprechdauer		*f*	temps de réponse initial	*m*
braking-system-application and braking time	*n*	Bremsdauer		*f*	temps de freinage	*m*
braking-value sensor	*n*	Bremswertsensor		*m*	capteur de freinage	*m*
break away (motor vehicle)	*v*	ausbrechen (Kfz)	x	*v*	chasser (véhicule)	*v*
break contact (electrical switch)	*n*	Öffner (elektrischer Schalter)		*m*	contact à ouverture (interrupteur électrique)	*m*
breakaway	*n*	Abregelbeginn		*m*	début de la coupure de débit	*m*
breakaway characteristic	*n*	Abregelverlauf		*m*	caractéristique de coupure de débit	*f*
breakaway delivery	*n*	Abregelmenge		*f*	débit au moment de la coupure	*m*
breakaway edge	*n*	Abreißkante (Spritzzapfen)		*f*	arête de rupture (téton d'injection)	*f*
breakaway range	*n*	Abregelbereich		*m*	plage de coupure de débit	*f*
breakaway speed	*n*	Abregeldrehzahl		*f*	vitesse de coupure	*f*
breakdown voltage	*n*	Durchbruchspannung		*f*	tension de claquage	*f*
breaker arm (ignition)	*n*	Unterbrecherhebel (Zündung)		*m*	linguet (rupteur)	*m*
breaker cam (ignition)	*n*	Unterbrechernocken (Zündung)		*m*	came de rupteur (allumage)	*f*
breaker lever (ignition)	*n*	Unterbrecherhebel (Zündung)		*m*	linguet (rupteur)	*m*
breaker point (ignition)	*n*	Zündkontakt		*m*	contacts du rupteur (allumage)	*mpl*
breaker-triggered	*pp*	kontaktgesteuert		*pp*	à déclenchement par rupteur	*loc*
breakerless	*adj*	kontaktlos		*adj*	sans rupteur mécanique	*loc*
breathing space (diaphragm)	*n*	Atmungsraum (Membran)	x	*m*	côté secondaire (cylindre à membrane)	*m*
bridge	*n*	Plattenverbinder (Batterie)		*m*	barrette de jonction des plaques (batterie)	*f*
bridge circuit	*n*	Brückenschaltung		*f*	circuit en pont	*m*
bridge connection	*n*	Brückenschaltung		*f*	circuit en pont	*m*
broad-band interference	*n*	Breitbandstörung		*f*	perturbation à large bande	*f*

English		German		French	
brush (rotating machines)	*n*	Kohlebürste (elektrische Maschinen)	*f*	balai de charbon (machines tournantes)	*m*
brush holder	*n*	Kohlebürstenhalter	*m*	porte-balais	*m*
brush wear	*n*	Bürstenverschleiß	*m*	usure des balais	*f*
brush-holder plate	*n*	Bürstenhalterplatte	*f*	plateau porte-balais	*m*
brushless (alternator)	*adj*	schleifringlos (Generator)	*adj*	sans bagues collectrices (alternateur)	*loc*
buck	*v*	ruckeln	*v*	à-coups	*mpl*
bucking oscillations	*npl*	Ruckelschwingung	*f*	vibrations dues aux à-coups	*fpl*
burn-off	*n*	Freibrand	*m*	autonettoyage	*m*
burn-off temperature	*n*	Freibrenntemperatur	*f*	température d'autonettoyage	*f*
burner (emissions testing)	*n*	Brennkammer (Abgastester)	*f*	chambre de combustion (émissions)	*f*
bus arbitration (CAN)	*n*	Busvergabe (CAN)	*f*	affectation du bus	*f*
bus bar	*n*	Stromschiene	*f*	barre de distribution	*f*
bus configuration (CAN)	*n*	Busstruktur (CAN)	*f*	structure du bus	*f*
bus structure (CAN)	*n*	Busstruktur (CAN)	*f*	structure du bus	*f*
bushing	*n*	Lagerbuchse	*f*	coussinet	*m*
business area	*n*	Geschäftsfeld	*n*	domaine de spécialisation	*m*
business sector	*n*	Unternehmensbereich	*m*	secteur (entreprise)	*m*
butterfly valve (engine brake)	*n*	Auspuffklappe (Motorbremse)	*f*	volet d'échappement (frein moteur)	*m*
button diode	*n*	Knopfdiode	*f*	diode-bouton	*f*
buzzer	*n*	Warnsummer	*m*	vibreur	*m*
bypass	*n*	Umgehungsleitung	*f*	canal de dérivation	*m*
bypass cross-section (throttle valve)	*n*	Nebenschlußquerschnitt (Drosselklappe)	*m*	canal en dérivation (papillon)	*m*
bypass passage	*n*	Umgehungsleitung	*f*	canal de dérivation	*m*
bypass valve	*n*	Bypassventil	*n*	valve de dérivation	*f*
C					
cab	*n*	Fahrerhaus	*n*	cabine de conduite	*f*
cable break	*n*	Kabelbruch	*m*	rupture de câble	*f*
cable cross-section	*n*	Kabelquerschnitt	*m*	section de câble	*f*
cable lead-through	*n*	Kabeldurchführung	*f*	passage de câble	*m*
cable lug	*n*	Kabelschuh	*m*	cosse	*f*
calculation of conductor sizes	*n*	Leitungsberechnung	*f*	calcul des conducteurs	*m*
calibrating gas	*n*	Kalibriergas	*n*	gaz de calibrage	*m*
calibrating nozzle	*n*	Prüfdüse	*f*	injecteur d'essai	*m*
calibrating oil	*n*	Prüföl	*n*	huile d'essai	*f*
calibrating unit	*n*	Einstellgerät	*n*	appareil de réglage	*m*
calibration pump	*n*	Fördermengennormal	*n*	pompe de référence de débit	*f*
calibration-pump test bench	*n*	Fördermengennormal-Prüfbank	*f*	banc de contrôle de pompe de référence	*m*
cam angle	*n*	Nockenwinkel	*m*	angle de levée de came	*m*
cam angle of fuel-delivery	*n*	Förderwinkel am Nocken	*m*	angle de refoulement sur la came	*m*
cam brake	*n*	Nockenbremse	*f*	frein à cames	*m*
cam contour	*n*	Nockenform	*f*	forme de came	*f*

English

English		German		French	
cam disc (braking-force regulator)	n	Kurvenscheibe (Bremskraftregler)	f	disque à cames (correcteur de freinage)	m
cam follower (breaker lever)	n	Gleitstück (Unterbrecherhebel)	n	toucheau (rupteur)	m
cam lift	n	Nockenhöhe	f	course de came	f
cam pitch	n	Nockenhub	m	levée de came	f
cam plate	n	Hubscheibe	f	disque à cames	m
cam profile	n	Nockenablauf	m	profil de came	m
cam ring	n	Nockenring	m	bague à cames	f
cam sequence	n	Nockenfolge	f	ordre des cames	m
cam shape	n	Nockenform	f	forme de came	f
cam track	n	Nockenlaufbahn	f	piste de came	f
camber angle (vehicle dynamics)	n	Sturzwinkel (Kfz-Dynamik)	m	angle de carrossage (dynamique d'un véhicule)	m
camshaft	n	Antriebsnockenwelle	f	arbre à came d'entraînement	m
camshaft control	n	Nockenwellensteuerung	f	commande de l'arbre à cames	f
camshaft lobe control	n	Nockenwellenumschaltung	f	variation du calage de l'arbre à cames	f
camshaft projection	n	Nockenwellen-Vorstehmaß	n	cote de dépassement de l'arbre à cames	f
camshaft roller	n	Nockenlaufrolle	f	galet de palpage de la came	m
camshaft speed sensor	n	Nockenwellen-Drehzahlsensor	m	capteur de vitesse de rotation de l'arbre à cames	m
camshaftless pump (PF)	n	Einzylinder-Einspritzpumpe (PF)	f	pompe d'injection monocylindrique (PF)	f
CAN, controller area network	a	CAN, Controller Area Network	a	CAN, système de multiplexage	a
canister-purge valve (emissions control technology)	n	Regenerierventil (Abgastechnik)	n	électrovalve de régénération (technique des gaz d'échappement)	f
cap (relay)	n	Grundplatte (Relais)	f	embase (relais)	f
capacitive clamp (EMC) x	n	kapazitive Zange (EMV)	f	pince capacitive (CEM)	f
capacitor	n	Kondensator	m	condensateur	m
captive gasket (spark plug)	n	unverlierbarer Dichtring (Zündkerze)	m	joint prisonnier (bougie)	m
car alarm	n	Auto-Alarmanlage	n	alarme auto	f
car heater	n	Wagenheizung	f	chauffage d'habitacle	m
carbon brush (rotating machines)	n	Kohlebürste (elektrische Maschinen)	f	balai de charbon (machines tournantes)	m
carbon canister (emissions control technology)	n	Aktivkohlebehälter (Abgastechnik)	m	bac à charbon actif (technique des gaz d'échappement)	m
carbon-brush set	n	Kohlebürstensatz	m	jeu de balais	m
carburetor	n	Vergaser	m	carburateur	m
carrying plate (Hall triggering system)	n	Trägerplatte (Hall-Auslösesystem)	f	plateau-support (système de déclenchement Hall)	m
cartridge-type brush holder	n	Köcherbürstenhalter	m	porte-balais tubulaire	m
catalog of exchange parts (factory exchange)	n	Rücknahmeliste (Werksaustausch)	f	liste des reprises (échange standard)	f
catalytic converter	n	Katalysator	m	catalyseur	m
catalytic converter window	n	Katalysatorfenster	n	créneau de pot catalytique	m
catalytic exhaust converter	n	Abgaskonverter	m	convertisseur catalytique des gaz d'échappement	m

English		German		French	
cavitation	*n*	Kavitation (Lochfraß)	*f*	cavitation (formation de cavités gazeuses)	*f*
cavitation damage	*n*	Kavitationsschaden	*m*	dommages par cavitation	*mpl*
cell connector (battery)	*n*	Zellenverbinder (Batterie)	*m*	connexion des éléments (batterie)	*f*
center electrode	*n*	Mittelelektrode	*f*	électrode centrale	*f*
center lamination (alternator)	*n*	Mittellamelle (Generator)	*f*	lamelle centrale (alternateur)	*f*
center tower (ignition coil)	*n*	Mitteldom (Zündspule)	*m*	sortie centrale (bobine d'allumage)	*f*
central injection unit (Mono-Jetronic)	*n*	Einspritzaggregat (Mono-Jetronic)	*n*	unité d'injection (Mono-Jetronic)	*f*
central locking system	*n*	Zentralverriegelung	*f*	verrouillage centralisé	*m*
central processing unit (on-board computer), CPU	*n*	Zentraleinheit (Fahrdatenrechner)	*f*	unité de traitement (ordinateur de bord)	*f*
central valve	*n*	Zentralventil	*n*	soupape centrale	*f*
centrally located air filter	*n*	Zentralfilter	*n*	filtre central	*m*
centre-axle trailer	*n*	Zentralachsanhänger	*m*	remorque à essieu central	*f*
centrifugal advance	*n*	Fliehkraftverstellung	*f*	correction centrifuge	*f*
centrifugal advance mechanism	*n*	Fliehkraftzündversteller	*m*	correcteur d'avance centrifuge	*m*
centrifugal governor	*n*	Fliehkraftregler	*m*	régulateur mécanique	*m*
centrifugal separator	*n*	Fliehkraftabscheider	*m*	séparateur centrifuge	*m*
centrifugal supercharger	*n*	Strömungslader	*m*	compresseur centrifuge	*m*
centrifugal turbo-compressor	*n*	Strömungslader	*m*	compresseur centrifuge	*m*
ceramic layer (lambda oxygen sensor)	*n*	Keramikschicht (Lambda-Sonde)	*f*	couche de céramique (sonde lambda)	*f*
ceramic substrate	*n*	Keramikträger	*m*	support en céramique	*m*
certification (ISO)	*n*	Zertifizierung (ISO)	*f*	certification (ISO)	*f*
cetane number, CN	*n*	Cetanzahl, CZ	*f*	indice de cétane	*m*
chamfered-shoulder nozzle	*n*	Schrägschulter-Düse	*f*	injecteur à portée oblique	*m*
changeable code (car alarm)	*n*	Wechselcode (Autoalarm)	*m*	code interchangeable (alarme auto)	*m*
changeover contact	*n*	Wechsler (Umschaltkontakt)	*m*	contact bidirectionnel	*m*
characteristic	*n*	Kennlinie	*f*	courbe caractéristique	*f*
charge adjustment (air supply)	*n*	Füllungsregelung (Luftversorgung)	*f*	régulation du remplissage des cylindres	*f*
charge air	*n*	Ladeluft	*f*	air de suralimentation	*m*
charge balance (battery)	*n*	Ladebilanz (Batterie)	*f*	bilan de charge (batterie)	*m*
charge cycle	*n*	Ladungswechsel	*m*	alternance de charge	*f*
charge indicator	*n*	Ladezustandsanzeige	*f*	indicateur de charge	*m*
charge stratification	*n*	Ladungsschichtung	*f*	stratification de la charge	*f*
charge voltage	*n*	Ladespannung (Batterie)	*f*	tension de charge	*f*
charge-air cooler	*n*	Ladeluftkühler	*m*	refroidisseur d'air de suralimentation	*m*
charge-air cooling	*n*	Ladeluftkühlung, LLK	*f*	refroidissement de la charge d'air	*m*
charge-air pressure	*n*	Ladedruck	*m*	pression de suralimentation	*f*
charge-cycle losses	*npl*	Gaswechselverlust	*m*	pertes au renouvellement des gaz	*fpl*
charge-indicator lamp	*n*	Generatorkontrolleuchte	*f*	lampe témoin d'alternateur	*f*

English

English		German		French	
charge-pressure actuator	*n*	Ladedrucksteller (Radialkolbenpumpe)	*m*	actionneur de pression de suralimentation (pompe à pistons radiaux)	*m*
charged carrier (spark plug)	*n*	Ladungsträger (Zündkerze)	*m*	porteur de charge (bougie)	*m*
charger (battery)	*n*	Batterieladegerät	*n*	chargeur de batterie	*m*
charging (battery)	*n*	Ladung (Batterie)	*f*	charge (batterie)	*f*
charging cable	*n*	Ladeleitung	*f*	câble de charge	*m*
charging characteristic (battery)	*n*	Ladekennlinie (Batterie)	*f*	caractéristique de charge (batterie)	*f*
charging current (battery)	*n*	Batterieladestrom	*m*	courant de charge de la batterie	*m*
charging mode (battery charge)	*n*	Ladebetrieb (Batterieladung)	*m*	mode "charge" (charge de batterie)	*m*
charging potential	*n*	Ladespannung (Batterie)	*f*	tension de charge	*f*
charging pump (EHB)	*n*	Ladepumpe (EHB)	*f*	pompe de charge	*f*
charging time (battery)	*n*	Ladezeit (Batterie)	*m*	temps de charge (batterie)	*m*
charging unit (hand-portable searchlight)	*n*	Ladesessel (Handscheinwerfer)	*m*	chargeur (projecteur portable)	*m*
charging voltage	*n*	Ladespannung (Batterie)	*f*	tension de charge	*f*
charging-piston unit (ESP)	*n*	Ladekolbeneinheit (ESP)	*f*	unité de piston de charge (ESP)	*f*
chassis dynamometer	*n*	Rollenprüfstand	*m*	banc d'essai à rouleaux	*m*
chassis number	*n*	Fahrgestellnummer	*f*	numéro de châssis	*m*
chassis system	*n*	Fahrwerksystem	*n*	système de suspension	*m*
chatter <noun>	*n*	Schnarrverhalten	*n*	ronflement	*m*
chatter <to chatter>	*v*	schnarren	*v*	ronfler	*v*
chatter group	*n*	Schnarrgruppe	*f*	groupe de ronflement	*m*
check valve	*n*	Sperrventil	*n*	valve d'arrêt	*f*
chequerboard ribbing	*n*	Schachbrettverippung	*f*	nervurage en échiquier	*m*
choke	*v*	drosseln	*v*	étrangler	*v*
CI engine	*n*	Selbstzündungsmotor	*m*	moteur à allumage par compression	*m*
circuit breaker	*n*	Leistungsschalter	*m*	interrupteur de circuit	*m*
circuit group	*n*	Schaltungsgruppe	*f*	module de circuit	*m*
circuit pressure (ESP)	*n*	Kreisdruck (ESP)	*m*	pression de circuit (ESP)	*f*
circuit safeguard (braking system)	*n*	Kreisabsicherung (Bremssystem)	*f*	protection des circuits d'alimentation (système de freinage)	*f*
circumferential force (wheel)	*n*	Umfangskraft (Rad)	*f*	force circonférentielle (roue)	*f*
circumferential speed	*n*	Umfangsgeschwindigkeit	*f*	vitesse périphérique	*f*
clamp (ignition coil)	*n*	Klemmschelle (Zündspule)	*f*	collier (bobine d'allumage)	*m*
clamp-on pickup	*n*	Aufklemmgeber	*m*	capteur à pince	*m*
clamp-on sensor	*n*	Aufklemmgeber	*m*	capteur à pince	*m*
clamping sleeve (wheel-speed sensor)	*n*	Federhülse (Drehzahlsensor)	*f*	douille élastique (capteur de vitesse)	*f*
claw (coupling head)	*n*	Klaue (Kupplungskopf)	*f*	griffe (tête d'accouplement)	*f*
claw guide (coupling head)	*n*	Klauenführung (Kupplungskopf)	*f*	glissière (tête d'accouplement)	*f*
claw pole	*n*	Klauenpol	*m*	plateau à griffes	*m*
claw-pole alternator	*n*	Klauenpolgenerator	*m*	alternateur à rotor à griffes	*m*
claw-pole chamfer	*n*	Klauenpolabhebung	*f*	chanfrein des pôles à griffes	*m*

English

English		German			French	
claw-pole rotor	*n*	Klauenpolläufer		*m*	rotor à griffes	*m*
claw-type sliding contact	*n*	Krallenschleifer		*m*	curseur à griffes	*m*
clean side (filter)	*n*	Reinseite (Filter)		*f*	côté propre (filtre)	*m*
clearance (brake shoes)	*n*	Lüftspiel (Bremsbacken)		*n*	jeu (segments de frein)	*m*
clearance volume	*n*	Totraum		*m*	espace mort	*m*
click (radio disturbance)	*v*	knacken (Funkstörung)		*v*	claquement (perturbation)	*m*
climate test bench	*n*	Klimaprüfstand		*m*	banc d'essai climatique	*m*
climbing resistance	*n*	Steigungswiderstand		*m*	résistance en côte	*f*
clockwise rotation	*n*	Rechtslauf		*m*	rotation à droite	*f*
closed control loop	*n*	Regelkreis		*m*	boucle de régulation	*f*
closed loop	*n*	Regelkreis		*m*	boucle de régulation	*f*
closed-loop position control	*n*	Lageregelung		*f*	régulation de position	*f*
closed-type design	*n*	geschlossene Bauweise		*f*	version fermée	*f*
closing element (coupling head	*n*	Absperrglied (Kupplungskopf)		*n*	obturateur (tête d'accouplement)	*m*
closing force	*n*	Schließkraft		*f*	force de fermeture	*f*
closing pressure	*n*	Schließdruck		*m*	pression de fermeture	*f*
cloud of smoke	*n*	Rauchstoß		*m*	émission de fumées	*f*
cloud point (mineral oil)	*n*	Cloudpoint (Mineralöl)	x	*m*	point de trouble (huile minérale)	*m*
clutch input	*n*	Kupplungseingang		*m*	entrée embrayage	*f*
clutch shell	*n*	Freilaufring		*m*	bague de roue libre	*f*
clutch switch	*n*	Kupplungsschalter		*m*	contacteur d'embrayage	*m*
coaxial-type starting motor	*n*	Schubtrieb-Starter		*m*	démarreur à pignon coulissant	*m*
cockpit instrument	*n*	Cockpit-Instrument		*n*	instrument du poste de pilotage	*m*
coding plug	*n*	Codierstecker		*m*	connecteur à module de codage	*m*
coefficient of dry friction	*n*	Trockenreibwert		*m*	coefficient de frottement à sec	*m*
coefficient of friction (tire/road	*n*	Haftreibungszahl (Reifen/Straße)		*f*	coefficient d'adhérence (pneu/route)	*m*
coefficient of rolling resistance	*n*	Rollwiderstandsbeiwert		*m*	coefficient de résistance au roulement	*m*
coefficient of sliding friction	*n*	Gleitreibungszahl		*f*	coefficient de frottement de glissement	*m*
coefficient of wet friction	*n*	Naßreibwert		*m*	coefficient de frottement humide	*m*
coil ignition, CI	*n*	Spulenzündung, SZ		*f*	allumage par bobine	*m*
coil-winding short circuit	*n*	Windungsschluß		*m*	court-circuit entre spires	*m*
coiled pipe	*n*	Rohrschlange		*f*	serpentin	*m*
coke	*v*	verkoken		*v*	calaminer	*v*
coking	*n*	Verkokung		*f*	calaminage	*m*
cold start	*n*	Kaltstart		*m*	démarrage à froid	*m*
cold viscosity	*n*	Tieftemperaturviskosität		*f*	viscosité à basse température	*f*
cold-running enrichment	*n*	Kaltlaufanreicherung		*f*	enrichissement au fonctionnement à froid	*m*
cold-start accelerator	*n*	Kaltstartbeschleuniger, KSB		*m*	accélérateur de démarrage à froid	*m*
cold-start aid	*n*	Kaltstarthilfe		*f*	aide au démarrage à froid	*f*
cold-start compensation	*n*	Kaltstartanpassung		*f*	adaptation au démarrage à froid	*f*

English

English		German		French	
cold-start control	*n*	Kaltstartsteuerung	*f*	pilotage de démarrage à froid	*m*
cold-start enrichment	*n*	Kaltstartanreicherung	*f*	enrichissement de départ à froic	*m*
cold-start limit	*n*	Kaltstartgrenze	*f*	limite de démarrage à froid	*f*
cold-start valve	*n*	Kaltstartventil	*n*	injecteur de départ à froid	*m*
cold-test test bench	*n*	Kälteprüfstand	*m*	banc d'essai au froid	*m*
collector ring	*n*	Schleifring	*m*	bague collectrice	*f*
collector-ring end shield (alternator)	*n*	Schleifringlagerschild (Generator)	*m*	flasque côté bagues collectrices (alternateur)	*m*
collector-ring housing	*n*	Schleifringkapselung	*f*	encapsulage des bagues collectrices	*m*
collector-track	*n*	Kollektorbahn	*f*	piste à résistance	*f*
color temperature (lighting)	*n*	Farbtemperatur (Lichttechnik)	*f*	température de couleur (éclairage)	*f*
combination brake actuator	*n*	Kombibremszylinder	*m*	cylindre de frein combiné	*m*
combination brake cylinder	*n*	Kombibremszylinder	*m*	cylindre de frein combiné	*m*
combination braking system	*n*	Kombi-Bremsanlage	*f*	dispositif de freinage combiné	*m*
combination governor	*n*	Stufendrehzahlregler	*m*	régulateur à échelons	*m*
combined transmission (braking system)	*n*	gemischte Übertragungs-einrichtung (Bremsanlage)	*f*	transmission combinée (dispositif de freinage)	*f*
combustion air	*n*	Verbrennungsluft	*f*	air de combustion	*m*
combustion chamber	*n*	Verbrennungsraum x	*m*	chambre de combustion	*f*
combustion characteristics	*npl*	Verbrennungsablauf	*m*	processus de combustion	*m*
combustion deposits	*npl*	Verbrennungsrückstände	*mpl*	résidus de la combustion	*mpl*
combustion gas	*n*	Verbrennungsgas	*n*	gaz de combustion	*mpl*
combustion heat	*n*	Verbrennungswärme	*f*	chaleur dégagée par la combustion	*f*
combustion knock	*n*	klopfende Verbrennung	*f*	combustion détonante	*f*
combustion miss	*n*	Verbrennungsaussetzer	*m*	ratés de combustion	*mpl*
combustion noise	*n*	Verbrennungsgeräusch	*n*	bruit de combustion	*m*
combustion pressure	*n*	Verbrennungsdruck	*m*	pression de combustion	*f*
combustion residues	*npl*	Verbrennungsrückstände	*mpl*	résidus de la combustion	*mpl*
combustion start	*n*	Verbrennungsbeginn	*m*	début de combustion	*m*
combustion system	*n*	Verbrennungsverfahren	*n*	procédé de combustion	*m*
combustion time (air-fuel mixture)	*n*	Brenndauer (Kraftstoff-Luft-Gemisch)	*f*	durée de combustion (mélange air-carburant)	*f*
combustion-chamber design	*n*	Brennraumgestaltung	*f*	forme de la chambre de combustion	*f*
comfort and convenience electronics	*npl*	Komfortelektronik	*f*	électronique de confort	*f*
comfort and convenience systems	*npl*	Komfortsysteme	*npl*	systèmes de confort	*mpl*
command signal	*n*	Stellsignal	*n*	signal de réglage	*m*
commercial vehicle	*n*	Nutzfahrzeug, Nfz	*n*	véhicule utilitaire	*m*
common-rail high-pressure fuel rail	*n*	Common Rail Hochdruckverteilerleiste	*f*	rampe distributrice haute pression "Common Rail"	*f*
common-rail high-pressure pump	*n*	Common Rail Hochdruckpumpe	*f*	pompe haute pression "Common Rail"	*f*
common-rail injector	*n*	Common Rail Injektor	*m*	injecteur "Common Rail"	*m*
common-rail pipe	*n*	Common Rail Leitung	*f*	tube "Common Rail"	*m*

English		German		French	
common-rail pressure sensor	*n*	Raildrucksensor (Common Rail)	*m*	capteur de pression "Rail"	*m*
common-rail pump	*n*	Common Rail Pumpe	*f*	pompe "Common Rail"	*f*
common-rail system, CR	*n*	Common Rail System, CR	*n*	système d'injection à pression modulée (Common Rail)	*m*
common-rail, CR	*n*	Common Rail System, CR	*n*	système d'injection à pression modulée (Common Rail)	*m*
commutating zone (carbon brush)	*n*	Kommutierungsszone (Kohlebürste)	*f*	partie commutateur (balai)	*f*
commutation	*n*	Kommutierung	*f*	commutation	*f*
commutator	*n*	Kommutator	*m*	collecteur	*m*
commutator end shield (alternator)	*n*	Kommutatorlager (Generator)	*n*	flasque côté collecteur (alternateur)	*m*
compact alternator	*n*	Compact-Generator	*m*	alternateur compact	*m*
compact-diode-assembly alternator	*n*	Topf-Generator	*m*	alternateur à bloc redresseur compact	*m*
compact-diode-assembly model (alternator)	*n*	Topfbauart (Generator)	*f*	type à bloc redresseur compact (alternateur)	*m*
comparator	*n*	Komparator	*m*	comparateur	*m*
compensating eccentric	*n*	Ausgleichexzenter	*m*	excentrique de compensation	*m*
compensating reservoir (brakes	*n*	Ausgleichsbehälter (Bremse)	*m*	réservoir de compensation (frein)	*m*
compensation flap	*n*	Kompensationsklappe	*f*	volet de compensation	*m*
compensation valve	*n*	Speicherventil	*n*	soupape de compensation	*f*
compensation volume	*n*	Ausgleichsvolumen	*n*	volume de compensation	*m*
competitive	*adj*	wettbewerbsfähig	*adj*	compétitif	*adj*
competitor	*n*	Wettbewerber	*m*	concurrent	*m*
component (unit)	*n*	Bauteil (Gerät)	*n*	composant (appareil)	*m*
component group (air-brake systems)	*n*	Gerätegruppe (Druckluftanlagen)	*f*	ensemble d'appareils de freinage	*m*
compound center electrode (spark plug)	*n*	Verbundmittelelektrode (Zündkerze)	*f*	électrode centrale composite (bougie)	*f*
compound electrode (spark plug)	*n*	Verbundelektrode (Zündkerze)	*f*	électrode composite (bougie)	*f*
compound motor	*n*	Doppelschlußmotor	*m*	moteur à excitation compound	*m*
compound navigation (navigation system)	*n*	Koppelortungssystem (Navigationssystem)	*n*	système de localisation à l'estime (système de navigation	*m*
compound-excited motor	*n*	Doppelschlußmotor	*m*	moteur à excitation compound	*m*
compound-wound motor	*n*	Doppelschlußmotor	*m*	moteur à excitation compound	*m*
compressed air	*n*	Druckluft	*f*	air comprimé	*m*
compressed-air brake	*n*	Druckluftbremse	*f*	frein à air comprimé	*m*
compressed-air braking system	*n*	Druckluft-Bremsanlage	*f*	dispositif de freinage à air comprimé	*m*
compressed-air circuit	*n*	Druckluftkreis	*m*	circuit d'air comprimé	*m*
compressed-air load	*n*	Druckluftverbraucher	*m*	récepteur d'air comprimé	*m*
compressed-air reserve	*n*	Druckluftvorrat	*m*	réserve d'air comprimé	*f*
compressed-air reservoir (pneumatics)	*n*	Druckluftbehälter (Pneumatik)	*m*	réservoir d'air comprimé (pneumatique)	*m*
compressed-air supply	*n*	Druckluftversorgung	*f*	alimentation en air comprimé	*f*

English

English		German		French	
compressed-air supply circuit	*n*	Druckluftvorratskreis	*m*	circuit d'alimentation (air comprimé)	*m*
compressed-air system	*n*	Druckluftanlage	*f*	dispositif à air comprimé	*m*
compressibility	*n*	Kompressibilität	*f*	compressibilité	*f*
compression (IC engine)	*n*	Verdichtung (Verbrennungsmotor)	*f*	compression (moteur à combustion)	*f*
compression cycle (IC engine)	*n*	Verdichtungstakt (Verbrennungsmotor)	*m*	temps de compression (moteur à combustion)	*m*
compression pulsating fatigue strength	*n*	Druckschwellfestigkeit	*f*	tenue aux ondes de pression	*f*
compression ratio	*n*	Verdichtungsverhältnis	*n*	taux de compression	*m*
compression spring	*f*	Druckfeder	*f*	ressort de pression	*m*
compression stroke	*n*	Verdichtungshub	*m*	course de compression	*f*
compression volume	*n*	Kompressionsvolumen	*n*	volume de compression	*m*
compression-ignition (CI) engine	*n*	Selbstzündungsmotor	*m*	moteur à allumage par compression	*m*
compressor housing	*n*	Verdichtergehäuse	*n*	carter de compresseur	*m*
compressor wheel	*n*	Verdichterrad	*n*	roue de compresseur centrifuge	*f*
Computer Aided Design, CAD	*n*	Computer Aided Design, CAD	*n*	dessin assisté par ordinateur, DAO	*m*
Computer Aided Lighting, CAL	*n*	Computer Aided Lighting, CAL	*n*	éclairage assisté par ordinateur	*m*
conductive element	*n*	Leitstück	*n*	pièce conductrice	*f*
conductive foil (angle of rotation sensor)	*n*	Leiterfolie (Drehwinkelsensor)	*f*	feuille conductrice (capteur d'angle de rotation)	*f*
conductive glass seal	*n*	Glasschmelze (elektrisch leitend)	*f*	ciment à base de verre conducteur	*m*
conductor	*n*	Leiterbahn	*f*	piste de contact	*f*
conductor cross section	*n*	Leiterquerschnitt	*m*	section du conducteur	*f*
conductor crossover	*n*	Leitungskreuzung	*f*	croisement de conducteurs	*m*
conductor loop	*n*	Leiterschleife	*f*	boucle conductrice	*f*
cone angle	*n*	Kegelwinkel	*m*	angle de cône	*m*
configure (ECU)	*v*	konfigurieren (Steuergerät)	*v*	configurer (fonction du calculateur)	*v*
conical seat	*n*	Kegeldichtsitz	*m*	siège conique	*m*
connecting cable	*n*	Anschlußleitung	*f*	câble de connexion	*m*
connecting devices (electrical)	*n*	Verbindungsmittel (elektrisch)	*n*	matériel de connexion (électrique)	*m*
connecting line (braking system)	*n*	Verbindungsleitung (Bremsanlage)	*f*	conduite de raccordement (dispositif de freinage)	*f*
connecting rod (brakes)	*n*	Verbindungsstange (Bremse)	*f*	biellette (frein)	*f*
connecting rod (IC engine)	*n*	Pleuelstange (Verbrennungsmotor)	*f*	bielle (moteur à combustion)	*f*
connection fitting	*n*	Anschlußnippel	*m*	raccord fileté	*m*
connector	*n*	Stecker	*m*	fiche	*f*
connector pin	*n*	Steckerstift	*m*	contact mâle	*m*
conrod (IC engine)	*n*	Pleuelstange (Verbrennungsmotor)	*f*	bielle (moteur à combustion)	*f*
consequential-damage protection (overvoltage)	*n*	Folgeschadenschutz (Überspannung)	*m*	protection contre les incidences (surtension)	*f*
constant field	*n*	Gleichfeld	*n*	plage neutre	*f*

English

English		German		French	
constant field pick-up	*n*	Gleichfeldeinstreuung	*f*	perturbation par champ continu	*f*
constant throttle (engine brake)	*n*	Konstantdrossel (Motorbremse)	*f*	étranglement constant (frein moteur)	*m*
constant-pressure valve	*n*	Gleichdruckventil, GDV	*n*	clapet de refoulement à pression constante	*m*
constant-volume valve	*n*	Gleichraumventil, GRV	*n*	clapet de refoulement à volume constant	*m*
consumption meter	*n*	Verbrauchsmodul	*m*	indicateur de consommation	*m*
contact bounce	*n*	Kontaktprellung	*f*	rebondissement des contacts	*m*
contact breaker (ignition)	*n*	Zündunterbrecher	*m*	rupteur (allumage)	*m*
contact chatter	*n*	Kontaktprellung	*f*	rebondissement des contacts	*m*
contact erosion	*n*	Kontaktabbrand	*m*	érosion des contacts	*f*
contact path (advance mechanism)	*n*	Wälzbahn (Zündversteller)	*f*	rampe à profil (correcteur d'avance)	*f*
contact rail (fuel rail)	*n*	Kontaktschiene (Kraftstoffverteiler)	*f*	rail de contact (rampe distributrice)	*m*
contact regulator	*n*	Kontaktregler	*m*	régulateur à vibreur	*m*
contact resistance	*n*	Übergangswiderstand	*m*	résistance de contact	*f*
contact set	*n*	Zündkontaktsatz	*m*	jeu de contacts d'allumage	*m*
contact set (ignition)	*n*	Kontaktsatz (Zündung)	*m*	jeu de contacts (allumage)	*m*
contact spring	*n*	Kontaktfeder	*f*	contact à ressort	*m*
contact surface (brake drum, brake disc)	*n*	Lauffläche (Bremstrommel, Bremsscheibe)	*f*	surface de friction (tambour, disque de frein)	*f*
contact switch	*n*	Kontaktschalter	*m*	contacteur	*m*
contact wiper (level sensor)	*n*	Spannungsabgriff (Niveaugeber)	*m*	prise de tension (capteur de niveau)	*f*
contact-breaking spark	*n*	Abreißfunke	*m*	étincelle de rupture	*f*
contaminated side (filter)	*n*	Schmutzseite (Filter)	*f*	côté impuretés (filtre)	*m*
contamination	*n*	Verunreinigung	*f*	contamination	*f*
continuous braking	*n*	Dauerbremsung	*f*	freinage prolongé	*m*
continuous braking system	*n*	durchgehende Bremsanlage	*f*	dispositif de freinage continu	*m*
continuous glowing	*v*	dauerglühen	*v*	incandescence permanente	*f*
continuous loading	*n*	Dauerbeanspruchung	*f*	contrainte permanente	*f*
continuous operation	*n*	Dauerlauf	*m*	fonctionnement continu	*m*
continuous running	*n*	Dauerlauf	*m*	fonctionnement continu	*m*
continuous tone (car alarm)	*n*	Dauerton (Autoalarm)	*m*	tonalité continue (alarme auto)	*f*
continuous torque	*n*	Dauerdrehmoment	*n*	couple permanent	*m*
continuous-operation braking system	*n*	Dauer-Bremsanlage	*f*	dispositif de freinage additionnel de ralentissement	*m*
continuous-running-duty type (electrical machines)	*n*	Dauerbetrieb (elektrische Maschinen)	*m*	fonctionnement permanent (machines électriques)	*m*
contoured switching guide	*n*	Schaltkulisse	*f*	coulisse de contact	*f*
control (braking system)	*n*	Betätigungseinrichtung (Bremsanlage)	*f*	commande (dispositif de freinage)	*f*
control channel (ABS hydraulic modulator)	*n*	Regelkanal (ABS-Hydroaggregat)	*m*	conduite de régulation (groupe hydraulique ABS)	*f*
control collar (distributor pump)	*n*	Regelschieber (Verteilereinspritzpumpe)	*m*	tiroir de régulation (pompe distributrice)	*m*

English

English		German		French	
control command (ECU)	n	Steuerbefehl (Steuergerät)	m	instruction de commande (calculateur)	f
control cone	n	Steuerkegel	m	cône de commande	m
control configuration (ABS)	n	Regelkonfiguration (ABS)	f	configuration de régulation (ABS)	f
control connection	n	Steueranschluß	m	raccord de commande	m
control current	n	Steuerstrom	m	courant de pilotage	m
control cycle	n	Regelzyklus	m	cycle de régulation	m
control diaphragm	n	Regelmembran	f	membrane de régulation	f
control dimension	n	Kontrollmaß	n	cote de contrôle	f
control edge (plunger-and-barrel assembly)	n	Steuerkante (Pumpenelement)	f	rampe hélicoïdale (élément de pompage)	f
control element	n	Stellelement	n	élément de commande	m
control filament	n	Regelwendel	f	spirale de régulation	f
control force	n	Betätigungskraft	f	force de commande	f
control lead	n	Steuerleitung	f	câble-pilote	m
control lever (distributor pump)	n	Einstellhebel (Verteilereinspritzpumpe)	m	levier de réglage (pompe distributrice)	m
control lever (in-line pump)	n	Verstellhebel (Reiheneinspritzpumpe)	m	levier de commande (pompe d'injection en ligne)	m
control line	n	Steuerleitung	f	câble-pilote	m
control loop	n	Regelschaltung	f	boucle d'asservissement	f
control pin (height-control valve)	n	Steuerbolzen (Luftfederventil)	m	axe de commande (valve de nivellement)	m
control plunger	n	Steuerkolben	m	piston de commande	m
control pressure	n	Steuerdruck	m	pression de commande	f
control pulse (ECU)	n	Steuerimpuls (Steuergerät)	m	impulsion de commande (calculateur)	f
control rack (in-line pump)	n	Regelstange (Reiheneinspritzpumpe)	f	tige de réglage (pompe d'injection en ligne)	f
control range	n	Regelbereich	m	plage de régulation	f
control ratio (brake valve)	n	Regelverhältnis (Bremsventil)	n	rapport de régulation (valve de frein)	m
control relay	n	Steuerrelais	n	relais de commande	m
control rod (in-line pump)	n	Regelstange (Reiheneinspritzpumpe)	f	tige de réglage (pompe d'injection en ligne)	f
control section (air drier)	n	Steuerteil (Lufttrockner)	n	module de commande (dessiccateur)	m
control signal (closed loop)	n	Regelsignal	n	signal de régulation	m
control signal (open loop)	n	Steuersignal	n	signal de commande	m
control sleeve	n	Hubschieber	m	ligne à tiroirs	f
control sleeve (fuel-injection pump)	n	Regelhülse (Einspritzpumpe)	f	douille de réglage (pompe d'injection)	f
control switch	n	Steuerschalter	m	contacteur de commande	m
control threshold	n	Regelschwelle	f	seuil de régulation	m
control time	n	Steuerzeit	f	temps de commande	m
control tolerance	n	Regeltoleranz	f	tolérance de régulation	f
control unit (electronic), ECU	n	elektronisches Steuergerät	n	centrale de commande électronique	f

English		German		French	
control unit (trip computer)	*n*	Bedieneinheit (Fahrdatenrechner)	*f*	unité de sélection (ordinateur de bord)	*f*
control valve (closed loop)	*n*	Regelventil	*n*	valve de régulation	*f*
control valve (open loop)	*n*	Steuerventil	*n*	valve de commande	*f*
control-collar position sensor	*n*	Regelschieberweggeber	*m*	capteur de course du tiroir de régulation	*m*
control-lever shaft	*n*	Verstellhebelwelle	*f*	axe du levier de commande	*m*
control-rack travel	*n*	Regelstangenweg	*m*	course de régulation	*f*
control-rod stop (fuel-injection pump)	*n*	Regelstangenanschlag (Einspritzpumpe)	*m*	butée de la tige de réglage (pompe d'injection)	*f*
control-sleeve actuator	*n*	Hubschieberstellwerk	*n*	actionneur de ligne à tiroirs	*m*
control-sleeve element	*n*	Hubschieberelement	*n*	élément à tiroir	*m*
control-sleeve gear	*n*	Zahnsegment	*n*	secteur denté	*m*
control-sleeve in-line fuel-injection pump (PE)	*n*	Hubschieber-Reiheneinspritzpumpe (PE)	*f*	pompe d'injection en ligne à tiroirs (PE)	*f*
control-sleeve lever (control-sleeve fuel-injection pump)	*n*	Anlenkhebel (Hubschieberpumpe)	*m*	levier de positionnement (pompe d'injection en ligne à tiroirs)	*m*
control-sleeve lever (single-plunger fuel-injection pump)	*n*	Regellenker	*m*	biellette de réglage	*f*
control-sleeve shaft	*n*	Hubschieber-Verstellwelle	*f*	arbre de déplacement des tiroirs	*m*
control-unit box	*n*	Steuergerätebox	*f*	boîtier de centrale de commande	*m*
control-unit initialization	*n*	Steuergeräteinitialisierung	*f*	initialisation de la centrale de commande	*f*
controlled sleeve damping	*n*	gesteuerte Muffendämpfung	*f*	amortisseur de manchon piloté	*m*
controlled system	*n*	Regelstrecke	*f*	système asservi	*m*
controlled variable (closed-loop control)	*n*	Regelgröße	*f*	grandeur réglée	*f*
controlled variable (open-loop control)	*n*	Steuergröße	*f*	paramètre de commande	*m*
controller logic (ECU)	*n*	Reglerlogik (Steuergerät)	*f*	logique de régulation (calculateur)	*f*
conversion map	*n*	Umrechnungskennfeld	*n*	cartographie de conversion	*f*
coolant	*n*	Kühlmittel	*n*	liquide de refroidissement	*m*
cooling	*n*	Kühlung	*f*	refroidissement	*m*
cooling air	*n*	Kühlluft	*f*	air de refroidissement	*m*
cooling channel (brake disc)	*n*	Kühlkanal (Bremsscheibe)	*m*	canal de circulation d'air (frein à disque)	*m*
cooling element	*n*	Kühlkörper	*m*	refroidisseur	*m*
cooling pip	*n*	Kühlnoppe	*f*	plateau en plastique	*m*
cooling water	*n*	Kühlwasser	*n*	eau de refroidissement	*f*
copper core (spark plug)	*n*	Kupferkern (Zündkerze)	*m*	noyau de cuivre (bougie)	*m*
copper losses (alternator)	x *npl*	Kupferverluste (Generator)	x *mpl*	pertes cuivre (alternateur)	x *fpl*
copper paste	*n*	Kupferpaste	*f*	pâte de cuivre	*f*
copper spray	*n*	Kupferspray	*m*	spray au cuivre	*m*
cornering	*ppr*	Kurvenfahrt	*f*	conduite en virage	*f*
cornering force	*n*	Seitenführungskraft	*f*	force de guidage latéral	*f*
cornering limit speed	*n*	Kurvengrenzgeschwindigkeit	*f*	vitesse limite en virage	*f*

English		German			French	
corrected air pressure	*n*	korrigierter Luftdruck		*m*	pression d'air corrigée	*f*
correcting element	*n*	Stellglied		*n*	actuateur	*m*
correcting variable	*n*	Stellgröße		*f*	grandeur réglante	*f*
correcting-variable limit	*n*	Stellgrößenbegrenzung		*f*	limitation des grandeurs de correction	*f*
correction quantity	*n*	Korrekturmenge		*f*	volume de correction	*m*
corrosion protection	*n*	Korrosionsschutz		*m*	protection anticorrosion	*f*
corrosion resistance	*n*	Korrosionsfestigkeit		*f*	résistance à la corrosion	*f*
cost center	*n*	Kostenstelle		*f*	code d'imputation	*m*
coulisse (diesel fuel injection)	*n*	Kulissenführung (Diesel-Regler)		*f*	guide-coulisse (injection diesel)	*m*
counterclockwise rotation	*n*	Linkslauf		*m*	rotation à gauche	*f*
countersteer (motor vehicle)	*v*	gegenlenken (Kfz)		*v*	contre-braquage (véhicule)	*m*
couple (EMC)	*v*	Einkopplung (EMV)		*f*	couplage (CEM)	*m*
coupling assembly	*n*	Antriebskupplung		*f*	accouplement	*m*
coupling force (electronic/compressed-air braking system)	*n*	Koppelkraft (elektronisch-pneumatisches Bremssystem)		*f*	force de couplage (dispositif de freinage électronique-pneumatique)	*f*
coupling head	*n*	Kupplungskopf		*m*	tête d'accouplement	*f*
coupling head "brakes"	*n*	Kupplungskopf "Bremse"		*m*	tête d'accouplement "frein"	*f*
coupling head "supply"	*n*	Kupplungskopf "Vorrat"		*m*	tête d'accouplement "alimentation"	*f*
coupling holder	*n*	Leerkupplung		*f*	accouplement borgne	*m*
coupling port	*n*	Kupplungsanschluß		*m*	raccord d'accouplement	*m*
coupling spring	*n*	Koppelfeder		*f*	ressort de couplage	*m*
coupling support	*n*	Leerkupplung		*f*	accouplement borgne	*m*
coupling-force sensor (electronic/compressed-air braking system)	*n*	Koppelkraftsensor (elektronisch-pneumatisches Bremssystem)		*m*	capteur de force de couplage (dispositif de freinage électro-pneumatique	*m*
course filter	*n*	Grobfilter		*n*	filtre grossier	*m*
cover (battery)	*n*	Blockdeckel (Batterie)		*m*	couvercle de batterie	*m*
cover plate	*n*	Halteplatte		*f*	platine	*f*
cover ring	*n*	Abdeckring		*m*	anneau de recouvrement	*m*
crackle (radio disturbance)	*v*	krachen (Funkstörung)	x	*v*	craquement (perturbation)	*m*
cradle mounting	*n*	Sattelbefestigung		*f*	fixation par berceau	*f*
cradle-mounted pump	*n*	Wannenpumpe	x	*f*	pompe à fixation par berceau	*f*
crank-angle sensor	*n*	Kurbelwinkelsensor		*m*	capteur d'angle vilebrequin	*m*
cranking (IC engine)	*n*	durchdrehen (Verbrennungsmotor)	x	*v*	lancement (moteur à combustion)	*m*
cranking power	*n*	Startleistung		*f*	puissance de démarrage	*f*
cranking speed	*n*	Startdrehzahl		*f*	vitesse de démarrage	*f*
cranking-speed increase	*n*	Startdrehzahlanhebung		*f*	régime accéléré de démarrage	*m*
crankshaft angle	*n*	Kurbelwinkel (Grad Kurbelwelle)		*m*	angle vilebrequin	*m*
crankshaft disturbance frequency	*n*	Kurbelwellenstörfrequenz		*f*	fréquence perturbatrice du vilebrequin	*f*
crankshaft drive	*n*	Kurbeltrieb		*m*	mécanisme d'embiellage	*m*
crankshaft speed sensor	*n*	Kurbelwellen-Drehzahlsensor		*m*	capteur de vitesse de rotation du vilebrequin	*m*

English		German		French	
crash discrimination (airbag)	*n*	Aufpralldetektion (Airbag)	*f*	détection de collision (coussin gonflable)	*f*
crash sensing (airbag)	*n*	Aufpralldetektion (Airbag)	*f*	détection de collision (coussin gonflable)	*f*
creep tendency (vehicles with automatic gearbox)	*n*	Kriechneigung (Fahrzeuge mit Automatikgetriebe)	*f*	tendance au rampement (véhicules à boîte automatique)	*f*
creepage-discharge path	*n*	Funkenbahn	*f*	éclateur	*m*
crimp	*v*	crimpen	*v*	sertir	*v*
crocodile clip	*n*	Batteriezange	*f*	pince de batterie	*f*
cross flushing	*n*	Querspülung	*f*	balayage transversal	*m*
cross sensitivity (sensor)	*n*	Querempfindlichkeit (Sensor)	*f*	sensibilité transversale (capteur)	*f*
cross throttle	*n*	Querdrossel	*f*	étranglement transversal	*m*
cross-reference	*n*	Gegenüberstellung	*f*	table de correspondance	*f*
crosswind force	*n*	Seitenwindkraft	*f*	force du vent latéral	*f*
crowning	*n*	Balligkeit	*f*	bombage	*m*
cruise control (equipment)	*n*	Fahrgeschwindigkeitsregler, FGR	*m*	régulateur de vitesse de roulage	*m*
cruise control (system)	*n*	Fahrgeschwindigkeitsregelung	*f*	régulation de la vitesse de roulage	*f*
cup diode	*n*	Napfdiode	*f*	diode-boisseau	*f*
cup seal	*n*	Dichtmanschette	*f*	garniture	*f*
cup seal (wheel-brake cylinder)	*n*	Topfmanschette (Radzylinder)	*f*	joint embouti (cylindre de roue)	*m*
current clamp x	*n*	Stromzange	*f*	pince d'intensité	*f*
current control time	*n*	Stromregelzeit	*f*	temps de régulation du courant	*m*
current flow	*n*	Signalfluß	*m*	flux de signaux	*m*
current limiter	*n*	Strombegrenzer	*m*	limiteur d'intensité	*m*
current output (alternator)	*n*	Stromabgabe (Generator)	*f*	débit (alternateur)	*m*
current regulator	*n*	Stromregler	*m*	régulateur de courant	*m*
current reversal	*n*	Kommutierung	*f*	commutation	*f*
curve braking behavior	*n*	Kurvenbremsverhalten	*n*	comportement au freinage en virage	*m*
curve profile	*n*	Kurvenprofil	*n*	profil de courbe	*m*
customer service	*n*	Kundendienst	*m*	service après-vente	*m*
customer specification	*n*	Kundenspezifikation	*f*	spécification client	*f*
cutin area	*n*	Einschaltbereich	*m*	plage d'enclenchement	*f*
cutin current	*n*	Einschaltstrom	*m*	courant de démarrage	*m*
cutin point	*n*	Einschaltpunkt	*m*	point d'enclenchement	*m*
cutin pressure	*n*	Einschaltdruck	*m*	pression d'enclenchement	*f*
cutoff bore	*n*	Absteuerquerschnitt	*m*	orifice de décharge	*m*
cutoff frequency (governor)	*n*	Grenzfrequenz (Regler)	*f*	fréquence limite (régulateur)	*f*
cutoff jet	*n*	Absteuerstrahl	*m*	jet de décharge	*m*
cutoff port	*n*	Steuerbohrung	*f*	orifice de distribution	*m*
cutoff pressure	*n*	Abschaltdruck	*m*	pression de coupure	*f*
cutoff speed	*n*	Abschaltdrehzahl	*f*	régime de coupure	*m*
cutting-in speed (alternator)	*n*	Einschaltdrehzahl (Generator)	*f*	vitesse d'amorçage (alternateur)	*f*
CVS method (exhaust-gas test)	*n*	Verdünnungsverfahren (CVS-Methode)	*n*	essai d'évaporation (méthode CVS)	*m*

English		German		French	
cycle point (brake booster)	*n*	Aussteuerpunkt (Bremskraftverstärker)	*m*	point de régulation finale (servofrein)	*m*
cycle pressure (brake booster)	*n*	Aussteuerdruck (Bremskraftverstärker)	*m*	pression maximale (servofrein)	*f*
cyclical actuation (wheel brake-pressure)	*n*	takten (Radbremsdruck)	*v*	pilotage cyclique (pression de freinage)	*m*
cyclone	*n*	Zyklon	*m*	cyclone	*m*
cyclone prefilter (paper filter)	*n*	Zyklon-Vorabscheider (Papierluftfilter)	*m*	préséparateur à cyclone (filtre à air en papier)	*m*
cylinder arrangement	*n*	Zylinderanordnung	*f*	disposition des cylindres	*f*
cylinder base	*n*	Zylinderboden	*m*	fond du cylindre	*m*
cylinder chamber	*n*	Zylinderkammer	*f*	chambre du vérin	*f*
cylinder charge	*n*	Zylinderladung	*f*	remplissage du cylindre	*m*
cylinder fill	*n*	Zylinderladung	*f*	remplissage du cylindre	*m*
cylinder head (air compressor)	*n*	Zylinderdeckel (Luftkompressor)	*m*	culasse (compresseur d'air)	*f*
cylinder shut-off	*n*	Zylinderabschaltung	*f*	coupure des cylindres	*f*
cylinder-balancing integrator	*n*	Laufruheintegrator	*m*	intégrateur de régulation poste à poste	*m*
cylinder-charge control (EGAS	*n*	Füllungssteuerung (EGAS)	*f*	commande de remplissage (EMS)	*f*
cylindrical-type	*n*	zylindrische Anordnung	*f*	en barillet	*loc*
D					
damper (ABS, TCS)	*n*	Dämpfer (ABS/ASR)	*m*	amortisseur (ABS/ASR)	*m*
damper chamber (ABS)	*n*	Dämpferkammer (ABS)	*f*	chambre d'amortissement (ABS)	*f*
damping (air suspension)	*n*	Dämpfung (Luftfederung)	*f*	amortissement (suspension pneumatique)	*m*
damping chamber (height-control valve)	*n*	Dämpfungskammer (Luftfederventil)	*f*	chambre d'amortissement (valve de nivellement)	*f*
damping restriction	*n*	Dämpfungsdrossel	*f*	orifice calibré	*m*
damping throttle	*n*	Dämpfungsdrossel	*f*	orifice calibré	*m*
damping volume	*n*	Dämpfungsvolumen	*n*	volume d'amortissement	*m*
dashboard	*n*	Armaturenbrett	*n*	tableau de bord	*m*
data acquisition	*n*	Betriebsdatenerfassung	*f*	saisie des paramètres opérationnels	*f*
data bus	*n*	Datenbus	*m*	bus de données	*m*
data frame (CAN)	*n*	Datenrahmen (CAN)	*m*	cadre de données (multiplexage)	*m*
data point (program map)	*n*	Stützstelle (Kennfeld)	*f*	point d'appui (cartographie)	*m*
data transmission	*n*	Datenübertragung	*f*	transmission de données	*f*
daytime running lamp	*n*	Tagfahrleuchte	*f*	feu de roulage de jour	*m*
DC generator	*n*	Gleichstromgenerator	*m*	génératrice de courant continu	*f*
DC motor	*n*	Gleichstrommotor	*m*	moteur à courant continu	*m*
DC relay	*n*	Gleichstromrelais	*n*	relais à courant continu	*m*
de-icing pump	*n*	Frostschutzpumpe	*f*	pompe antigel	*f*
dead time	*n*	Ansprechzeit	*f*	temps de réponse	*m*
dead volume	*n*	Totvolumen	*n*	volume mort	*m*
decay diode	*n*	Löschdiode	*f*	diode de décharge	*f*

English

English		German		French	
deceleration	*n*	Bremsverzögerung	*f*	décélération de freinage	*f*
deceleration lean adjustment	*n*	Verzögerungsabmagerung	*f*	appauvrissement en décélération	*m*
deceleration-sensitive (brake-pressure regulating valve)	*adj*	verzögerungsabhängig (Druckminderer)	*adj*	asservi à la décélération (réducteur de pression de freinage)	*pp*
decrease threshold value (accelerator-pedal sensor)	*n*	Abfallschwellwert (Fahrpedalsensor)	*m*	seuil décroissant (capteur d'accélérateur)	*m*
deep-bed filter	*n*	Tiefenfilter	*n*	filtre en profondeur	*m*
deep-cycle resistant (battery)	*ppr*	zyklenfest (Batterie)	*adj*	résistant aux cycles alternés (batterie)	*ppr*
deflection angle (air-flow sensor)	*n*	Auslenkwinkel (Luftmengenmesser)	*m*	angle de déplacement (débitmètre d'air)	*m*
deformation process (tire)	*n*	Formänderungsarbeit (Reifen)	*f*	travail de déformation (pneu)	*m*
degree of protection	*n*	Schutzart	*f*	degré de protection	*m*
degrees crankshaft (°cks)	*npl*	Kurbelwinkel (Grad Kurbelwelle)	*m*	angle vilebrequin	*m*
delay switch (start valve)	*n*	Verzögerungsschaltung (Startventil)	*f*	temporisateur (électrovanne de démarrage)	*m*
delivery capacity (air compressor)	*n*	Fördermenge (Luftkompressor)	*f*	débit du compresseur d'air	*m*
delivery direction	*n*	Förderrichtung	*f*	sens de refoulement	*m*
delivery period	*n*	Förderdauer	*f*	durée de refoulement	*f*
delivery phase	*n*	Förderphase	*f*	phase de refoulement	*f*
delivery plunger	*n*	Förderkolben	*m*	piston de refoulement	*m*
delivery pressure	*n*	Förderdruck	*m*	pression de refoulement	*f*
delivery quantity (fuel-injection pump)	*n*	Fördermenge (Einspritzpumpe)	*f*	débit de refoulement (pompe d'injection)	*m*
delivery rate	*n*	Förderrate	*f*	taux de refoulement	*m*
delivery stroke	*n*	Förderhub	*m*	course de refoulement	*f*
delivery valve (fuel-injection pump)	*n*	Druckventil (Einspritzpumpe)	*n*	clapet de refoulement (pompe d'injection)	*m*
delivery-signal sensor	*n*	Fördersignal-Sensor	*m*	capteur de signal de refoulement	*m*
delivery-stroke phase	*n*	Förderhubphase	*f*	course d'admission	*f*
delivery-valve cone	*n*	Druckventilkegel	*m*	cône de soupape de refoulemen	*m*
delivery-valve holder (fuel-injection pump)	*n*	Druckventilhalter (Einspritzpumpe)	*m*	ensemble de clapet de refoulement (pompe d'injection	*m*
delivery-valve plunger	*n*	Druckventilkolben	*m*	piston de soupape de refoulement	*m*
delivery-valve seat	*n*	Druckventilsitz	*m*	siège de soupape de refoulement	*m*
delivery-valve stem	*n*	Druckventilschaft	*m*	tige de soupape de refoulement	*f*
delivery-valve support	*n*	Druckventilträger	*m*	porte-soupape de refoulement	*m*
delivery-valve with flat	*n*	Flächendruckventil	*n*	soupape de pression à méplat	*f*
delta circuit	*n*	Dreieckschaltung	*f*	montage en triangle	*m*
delta connection	*n*	Dreieckschaltung	*f*	montage en triangle	*m*
demand-value starting point	*n*	Wunschmengenanfangswert	*m*	valeur initiale de débit demandé	*f*
demesh (starter pinion)	*v*	ausspuren (Starterritzel)	*v*	désengrènement	*m*

English		German		French	
deposit	*n*	Ablagerung	*f*	dépôt	*m*
deprime (car alarm)	*v*	entschärfen (Autoalarm)	*v*	mise hors veille (alarme auto)	*f*
desiccant (air drier)	*n*	Trockenmittel (Lufttrockner)	*n*	déshydratant (dessiccateur)	*m*
desiccant box (air drier)	*n*	Trockenmittelbox (Lufttrockner)	*f*	cartouche de déshydratant (dessiccateur)	*f*
design pressure (braking action	*n*	Berechnungsdruck (Bremswirkung)	*m*	pression calculée (effet de freinage)	*f*
desired-value generator	*n*	Sollwertgeber	*m*	consignateur	*m*
desired/setpoint speed differential	*n*	Differenzsollmoment	*n*	couple différentiel de consigne	*m*
detent element (parking-brake valve)	*n*	Kulisse (Feststellbremsventil)	*f*	coulisse (valve de frein de stationnement)	*f*
detent position (valve)	*n*	Raststellung (Ventil)	*f*	crantage (valve)	*m*
detent switch	*n*	Stellschalter	*m*	interrupteur à retour non automatique	*m*
detergent additive (gasoline)	*n*	Reinigungsadditiv (Benzin)	*n*	agent détergent (essence)	*m*
dew point (air drying)	*n*	Drucktaupunkt (Lufttrocknung)	*m*	point de rosée sous pression (dessiccation de l'air)	*m*
DI engine	*n*	Direkteinspritzmotor	*m*	moteur à injection directe	*m*
DI, direct injection	*a*	Direkteinspritzung (Dieselmotor)	*f*	injection directe	*f*
diagnosis cable	*n*	Diagnoseleitung	*f*	câble de diagnostic	*m*
diagnosis connection	*n*	Diagnoseanschluß	*m*	connexion de diagnostic	*f*
diagnosis display	*n*	Diagnoseanzeige	*f*	affichage diagnostic	*m*
diagnosis initiate cable	*n*	Eigendiagnose-Reizleitung	*f*	câble d'activation de l'autodiagnostic	*m*
diagnosis interface (electronic systems)	*n*	Diagnoseschnittstelle (elektronische Systeme)	*f*	interface de diagnostic (systèmes électroniques)	*f*
diagnosis lamp	*n*	Diagnoselampe	*f*	lampe de diagnostic	*f*
diagnosis module	*n*	Diagnosemodul	*m*	module de diagnostic	*m*
diagnosis output	*n*	Diagnoseausgabe	*f*	sortie de diagnostic	*f*
diagnosis socket	*n*	Diagnosesteckdose	*f*	prise de diagnostic	*f*
diagnosis tester	*n*	Diagnosetestgerät	*n*	testeur de diagnostic	*m*
diagnosis tool	*n*	Diagnosewerkzeug	*n*	outil de diagnostic	*m*
diagnostics system	*n*	Diagnosesystem	*n*	système de diagnostic	*m*
diagram	*n*	Schaltplan	*m*	schéma électrique	*m*
diaphragm actuator	*n*	Membranzylinder	*m*	cylindre à membrane	*m*
diaphragm governor	*n*	Membrandruckregler	*m*	régulateur de pression à membrane	*m*
diaphragm piston	*n*	Membrankolben	*m*	piston à joint embouti	*m*
diaphragm plate	*n*	Membranplatte	*f*	plaque-membrane	*f*
diaphragm pump	*n*	Membranpumpe	*f*	pompe à membrane	*f*
diaphragm unit	*n*	Membrandose	*f*	capsule à membrane	*f*
diaphragm valve	*n*	Membranventil	*n*	valve à membrane	*f*
diaphragm-type cylinder	*n*	Membranzylinder	*m*	cylindre à membrane	*m*
diesel direct injection	*n*	Dieseldirekteinspritzung	*f*	injection directe diesel	*f*
diesel fuel	*n*	Dieselkraftstoff	*m*	gazole	*m*
diesel fuel injection, DFI	*n*	Dieseleinspritzung	*f*	injection diesel	*f*
diesel fuel-injection pump	*n*	Dieseleinspritzpumpe	*f*	pompe d'injection diesel	*f*

English		German			French	
diesel knock	*n*	nageln	x	*v*	claquement	*m*
diesel smoke	*n*	Dieselrauch	x	*m*	fumées diesel	*fpl*
diesel theft deterrent	*n*	Dieseldiebstahlschutz, DDS		*m*	antivol diesel	*m*
diesel-fuel resistant	*ppr*	dieselbeständig		*adj*	résistant au gazole	*ppr*
differential brake	*n*	Getriebedifferentialbremse		*f*	frein de différentiel	*m*
differential lock	*n*	Differentialsperre		*f*	blocage des différentiels	*m*
differential pressure	*n*	Differenzdruck		*m*	pression différentielle	*f*
differential ratio (nozzle needle	*n*	Druckstufe (Düsennadel)		*f*	différentiel d'aiguille	*m*
differential-pressure sensor	*n*	Differenzdrucksensor		*m*	capteur de pression différentielle	*m*
differential-pressure valve	*n*	Differenzdruckventil		*n*	régulateur de pression différentielle	*m*
diffusion (filter)	*n*	Diffusionseffekt (Filter)		*m*	effet de diffusion (filtre)	*m*
dilution prodedure (CVS method)	*n*	Verdünnungsverfahren (CVS-Methode)		*n*	essai d'évaporation (méthode CVS)	*m*
dilution tunnel (CVS method)	*n*	Verdünnungstunnel (CVS-Methode)		*m*	tunnel de dilution (méthode CVS)	*m*
dimensional drawing	*n*	Maßbild		*n*	croquis coté	*m*
dimensional stability	*n*	Verformungsfestigkeit		*f*	résistance à la déformation	*f*
diode module	*n*	Diodenmodul		*m*	module de diodes	*m*
diode plate (alternator)	*n*	Diodenträger (Generator)		*m*	porte-diodes (alternateur)	*m*
dipped beam	*n*	Abblendlicht		*n*	feu de croisement	*m*
dipped-beam headlamp	*n*	Abblendscheinwerfer		*m*	projecteur code	*m*
direct current	*n*	Gleichstrom		*m*	courant continu	*m*
direct injection, DI	*n*	Direkteinspritzung (Dieselmotor)		*f*	injection directe	*f*
direct-current generator	*n*	Gleichstromgenerator		*m*	génératrice de courant continu	*f*
direct-injection (DI) engine	*n*	Direkteinspritzmotor		*m*	moteur à injection directe	*m*
direct-injection (DI) process	*n*	Direkteinspritzverfahren		*n*	procédé d'injection directe	*m*
direction indicator	*n*	Fahrtrichtungsanzeiger		*m*	feu indicateur de direction	*m*
direction of rotation	*n*	Drehrichtung		*f*	sens de rotation	*m*
direction-indicator lamp	*n*	Fahrtrichtungsanzeiger		*m*	feu indicateur de direction	*m*
direction-indicator signal	*n*	Fahrtrichtungsblinken		*n*	indication de changement de direction	*f*
directional stability (driveability)	*n*	Fahrtrichtungsstabilität (Kfz)		*f*	stabilité directionnelle (comportement de roulage)	*f*
directional-control valve	*n*	Wegeventil, WGV		*n*	distributeur	*m*
directional-control-valve block	*n*	Wegeventilblock		*m*	bloc-distributeur	*m*
disc (armature core)	*n*	Blechlamelle (Anker)		*f*	disque de tôle (induit)	*m*
disc brake	*n*	Scheibenbremse		*f*	frein à disque	*m*
disc filter	*n*	Spaltfilter		*n*	filtre à disques	*m*
disc rotor	*n*	Scheibenläufer		*m*	rotor à disque	*m*
disc spring	*n*	Tellerfeder		*f*	rondelle-ressort	*f*
disc-brake caliper	*n*	Bremssattel		*m*	étrier de frein à disque	*m*
disc-brake pad	*n*	Scheibenbremsbelag		*m*	garniture de frein à disque	*f*
discharge (battery) <noun>	*n*	Entladung (Batterie)		*f*	décharge (batterie)	*f*
discharge (battery) <to discharge>	*v*	entladen (Batterie)		*v*	décharger (batterie)	*v*

English		German		French	
discharge chamber (gaseous-discharge lamp)	*n*	Entladungsraum (Gasentladungslampe)	*m*	cellule de décharge (lampe à décharge)	*f*
discharge current	*n*	Entladestrom	*m*	courant de décharge	*m*
discharge electrode	*n*	Sprühelektrode	*f*	électrode de diffusion	*f*
discharge valve	*n*	Entlüftungsventil	*n*	valve de purge air	*f*
discharge-valve seat	*n*	Auslaßventilsitz	*m*	siège d'échappement	*m*
displacement metering	*n*	Shuttle-Zumessung	*f*	dosage par déplacement	*m*
displacement of the center of gravity	*n*	Schwerpunktverlagerung	*f*	déplacement du centre de gravité	*m*
displacer element (supercharging)	*n*	Verdränger (Aufladung)	*m*	rotor excentré (suralimentation)	*m*
display diode	*n*	Anzeigediode	*f*	diode d'affichage	*f*
display unit (dynamic brake analyzer)	*n*	Anzeigegerät (Rollenbremsprüfstand)	*n*	afficheur (banc d'essai)	*m*
display unit (trip computer)	*n*	Anzeigeeinheit (Fahrdatenrechner)	*f*	unité d'affichage (ordinateur de bord)	*f*
disposable bowl and element	*n*	Wechselfilter	*n*	filtre à rechange rapide	*m*
disruptive discharge	*n*	Durchschlag (elektrisch)	*m*	décharge disruptive	*f*
distributor cam	*n*	Zündverteilernocken	*m*	came d'allumage	*f*
distributor cap	*n*	Zündverteilerkappe	*f*	tête d'allumeur	*f*
distributor connector	*n*	Zündverteilerstecker	*m*	connecteur d'allumeur	*m*
distributor contact points	*npl*	Zündkontakt	*m*	contacts du rupteur (allumage)	*mpl*
distributor head (distributor pump)	*n*	Verteilerkörper (Verteilereinspritzpumpe)	*m*	tête hydraulique (pompe distributrice)	*f*
distributor injection pump	*n*	Verteilereinspritzpumpe (VE)	*f*	pompe d'injection distributrice	*f*
distributor logic	*n*	Verteilerlogik	*f*	logique d'allumeur	*f*
distributor plunger	*n*	Verteilerkolben	*m*	piston distributeur	*m*
distributor pump	*n*	Verteilereinspritzpumpe (VE)	*f*	pompe d'injection distributrice	*f*
distributor rotor (ignition)	*n*	Zündverteilerläufer	*m*	rotor distributeur (allumage)	*m*
distributor shaft	*n*	Zündverteilerwelle	*f*	arbre d'allumeur	*m*
distributor slot	*n*	Verteilernut	*f*	rainure de distribution	*f*
distributor-head bushing	*n*	Verteilerbüchse	*f*	chemise	*f*
distributor-head flange	*n*	Verteilerflansch	*m*	flasque de distribution	*m*
distributor-type fuel-injection pump	*n*	Verteilereinspritzpumpe (VE)	*f*	pompe d'injection distributrice	*f*
distributorless semiconductor ignition	*n*	vollelektronische Zündung, VZ	*f*	allumage électronique intégral	*m*
disturbance value (regulation and control)	*n*	Störgröße (Regelung und Steuerung)	*f*	grandeur perturbatrice (régulation)	*f*
division (business)	*n*	Geschäftsbereich	*m*	division (entreprise)	*f*
division control multivibrator	*n*	Divisions-Steuer-Multivibrator	*m*	multivibrateur-diviseur de commande	*m*
door control (bus)	*n*	Türbetätigung (Omnibus)	*f*	commande des portes (autobus)	*f*
door operation (bus)	*n*	Türbetätigung (Omnibus)	*f*	commande des portes (autobus)	*f*
door-control system (bus)	*n*	Türbetätigungsanlage (Omnibus)	*f*	dispositif de commande des portes (autobus)	*m*
door-lock heating	*n*	Türschloßheizung	*f*	chauffage de serrure de porte	*m*
door-section drive (door control)	*n*	Türflügelantrieb	*m*	commande de vantail (commande des portes)	*f*

English		German		French	
double ignition	*n*	Doppelzündung	*f*	système d'allumage double	*m*
double microedge (wiper blade)	*n*	Mikro-Doppelkante (Wischgummi)	*f*	double micro-arête (raclette en caoutchouc)	*f*
double seal	*n*	Doppeldichtung	*f*	double joint	*m*
double solenoid-operated valve	*n*	Doppelmagnetventil	*n*	électrovalve double	*f*
double-acting (working cylinder)	*ppr*	doppeltwirkend (Arbeitszylinder)	*ppr*	à double effet (vérin)	*loc*
double-contact regulator	*n*	Zweikontaktregler	*m*	régulateur bicontact	*m*
double-flow cooling (fan)	*ppr*	zweiflutig (Lüfter)	*adj*	biflux (ventilateur)	*adj*
double-seat valve	*n*	Doppelsitzventil	*n*	valve à double siège	*f*
downdraft air-flow sensor	*n*	Fallstrom-Luftmengenmesser	*m*	débitmètre d'air à flux inversé	*m*
downforce	*n*	Anpreßkraft	*f*	force d'application	*f*
downgrade force	*n*	Hangabtriebskraft	*f*	force de déclivité	*f*
draft drawing	*n*	Entwicklungszeichnung	*f*	plan de développement	*m*
drag (tire)	x *v*	radieren (Reifen)	x *v*	gommer (pneu)	x *v*
drag coefficient	*n*	Luftwiderstandsbeiwert	*m*	coefficient de pénétration dans l'air	*m*
drag piston	*n*	Schleppkolben	*m*	piston de réaction	*m*
drag spring	*n*	Schleppfeder	*f*	ressort compensateur	*m*
drain (drain)	*v*	entwässern (Filter)	*v*	drainer (filtre)	*v*
drain screw (fuel filter)	*n*	Wasserablaßschraube (Kraftstoffilter)	*f*	vis de purge d'eau (filtre à carburant)	*f*
drain valve	*n*	Entwässerungsventil	*n*	purgeur d'eau	*m*
draw bar trailer	*n*	Gelenk-Deichselanhänger	*m*	remorque à timon articulé	*f*
drawbar	*n*	Deichsel	*f*	timon (remorque)	*m*
dribble	*v*	Nachspritzer (Dieseleinspritzung)	*m*	bavage (injection diesel)	*m*
dribble (diesel fuel injection)	*n*	Nachspritzer (Dieseleinspritzung)	*m*	bavage (injection diesel)	*m*
drip rim (splash resistance)	*n*	Tropfkante (Spritzwasserschutz)	*f*	pare-gouttes (projections d'eau)	*m*
drive assembly	*n*	Antriebsvorrichtung	*f*	transmission	*f*
drive belt	*n*	Antriebsriemen	*m*	courroie d'entraînement	*f*
drive eccentric	*n*	Antriebsexzenter	*m*	excentrique d'entraînement	*m*
drive electronics	*npl*	Ansteuerungselektronik	*f*	électronique de commande	*f*
drive element (braking force regulator)	*n*	Antrieb (Bremskraftregler)	*m*	transmission (correcteur de freinage)	*f*
drive end shield (alternator)	*n*	Antriebslagerschild (Generator)	*m*	flasque côté entraînement (alternateur)	*m*
drive force	*n*	Vortriebskraft	*f*	force de propulsion	*f*
drive power	*n*	Antriebsleistung	*f*	puissance motrice	*f*
drive program (exhaust-gas test)	*n*	Fahrzyklus (Abgasprüfung)	*m*	cycle de conduite (émissions)	*m*
drive roller (dynamic brake analyzer)	*n*	Antriebsrolle (Rollenbremsprüfstand)	*f*	rouleau d'entraînement (banc d'essai)	*m*
drive shaft	*n*	Antriebswelle	*f*	arbre d'entraînement	*m*
drive slip (driven wheel)	*n*	Antriebsschlupf	*m*	antipatinage à la traction	*m*
drive torque	*n*	Antriebsmoment	*n*	couple de traction	*m*

English

English		German		French	
drive unit (dynamic brake analyzer)	*n*	Antriebseinheit (Rollenbremsprüfstand)	*f*	unité d'entraînement (banc d'essai)	*f*
drive-by-wire	*n*	elektronische Motorfüllungs-steuerung, EGAS	*f*	commande électronique du moteur	*f*
drive-control switch	*n*	Fahrreglerschalter	*m*	commutateur régulateur de marche	*m*
drive-slip controller	*n*	Antriebsschlupfregelung, ASR	*f*	régulation d'antipatinage à la traction, ASR	*f*
driveability (motor vehicle)	*n*	Fahrverhalten (Kfz)	*n*	comportement de roulage (véhicule)	*m*
driven shaft	*n*	Abtriebswelle	*f*	arbre de sortie	*m*
driven wheel (motor vehicle)	*n*	Antriebsrad (Kfz)	*n*	roue motrice (véhicule)	*f*
driver (alternator)	*n*	Mitnehmer (Generator)	*m*	entraîneur (alternateur)	*m*
driver airbag	*n*	Fahrerairbag	*m*	coussin gonflable côté conducteur	*m*
driver pin (height-control valve	*n*	Mitnehmerbolzen (Luftfederventil)	*m*	axe d'entraînement (suspension pneumatique)	*m*
driver stage (ECU)	*n*	Leistungsendstufe (Steuergerät)	*f*	étage de sortie (calculateur)	*m*
driver-information system	*n*	Fahrerinformationssystem	*n*	système d'information de l'automobiliste	*m*
driver-input engine torque	*n*	Fahrervorgabemotormoment	*n*	couple moteur sélectionné par le conducteur	*m*
driver-selected torque	*n*	Fahrervorgabemoment	*n*	couple sélectionné par le conducteur	*m*
driver-stage defect recognition (ECU)	*n*	Endstufenfehlererkennung (Steuergerät)	*f*	détection de défaut à l'étage de sortie (calculateur)	*f*
driver-stage processing (ECU)	*n*	Endstufenbearbeitung (Steuergerät)	*f*	traitement à l'étage de sortie (calculateur)	*m*
drivetrain	*n*	Antriebsstrang	*m*	chaîne cinématique	*f*
driving (non-braked) mode	*n*	Fahrstellung	*f*	position de roulage	*f*
driving curve	*n*	Fahrkurve	*f*	caractéristique de conduite	*f*
driving cycle (exhaust-gas test)	*n*	Fahrzyklus (Abgasprüfung)	*m*	cycle de conduite (émissions)	*m*
driving gear	*n*	Antriebsrad (Elektrokraftstoffpumpe)	*n*	roue menante	*f*
driving lamp	*n*	Fernscheinwerfer	*m*	projecteur route	*m*
driving schedule (exhaust-gas test)	*n*	Fahrzyklus (Abgasprüfung)	*m*	cycle de conduite (émissions)	*m*
driving smoothness	*n*	Fahrkomfort	*m*	confort de conduite	*m*
driving speed	*n*	Fahrgeschwindigkeit	*f*	vitesse de roulage	*f*
driving switch	*n*	Fahrtschalter	*m*	commutateur de marche	*m*
driving transistor	*n*	Treibertransistor	*m*	transistor d'attaque	*m*
driving wheel	*n*	Antriebsrad (Elektrokraftstoffpumpe)	*n*	roue menante	*f*
drop-proof	*adj*	fallbeständig	*adj*	résistant aux chutes	*ppr*
dropout voltage	*n*	Rückfallspannung	*f*	tension de relâchement	*f*
dropping resistor	*n*	Vorwiderstand	*m*	résistance additionnelle	*f*
drum brake	*n*	Trommelbremse	*f*	frein à tambour	*m*
dry boiling point (brake fluid)	*n*	Trockensiedepunkt (Bremsflüssigkeit)	*m*	point d'ébullition liquide sec (liquide de frein)	*m*
dual cone (nozzle)	*n*	Doppelkonus (Einspritzdüse)	*m*	cône double (injecteur)	*m*

English		German		French	
dual exhaust system	*n*	Doppel-Auspuffanlage	*f*	système à double pot d'échappement	*m*
dual ignition	*n*	Doppelzündung	*f*	système d'allumage double	*m*
dual-bed catalytic converter	*n*	Doppelbettkatalysator	*m*	catalyseur à double lit	*m*
dual-chamber brake cylinder	*n*	Zweikreis-Vorspannzylinder	*m*	cylindre d'assistance à double circuit	*m*
dual-chamber operation (vacuum-brake system)	*n*	Zweikammerbetrieb (Vakuum-Bremsanlage)	*m*	système à deux chambres (dispositif de freinage à dépression)	*m*
dual-circuit (braking system)	*n*	zweikreisig (Bremsanlage)	*adj*	à deux circuits (dispositif de freinage)	*loc*
dual-circuit actuator cylinder for the brake master cylinder	*n*	Zweikreis-Vorspannzylinder	*m*	cylindre d'assistance à double circuit	*m*
dual-circuit brake assembly	*n*	Zweikreis-Bremsgerät	*n*	groupe de freinage à double circuit	*m*
dual-circuit brake valve	*n*	Zweikreis-Betriebsbremsventil	*n*	valve de frein de service à double circuit	*f*
dual-circuit braking system	*n*	Zweikreis-Bremsanlage	*f*	dispositif de freinage à transmission à double circuit	*m*
dual-circuit protection valve (brakes)	*n*	Zweikreis-Schutzventil	*f*	valve de sécurité à deux circuits	*f*
dual-circuit safety valve (brakes)	*n*	Zweikreis-Schutzventil	*f*	valve de sécurité à deux circuits	*f*
dual-circuit service-brake valve	*n*	Zweikreis-Betriebsbremsventil	*n*	valve de frein de service à double circuit	*f*
dual-line braking system	*n*	Zweileitungs-Bremsanlage	*f*	dispositif de freinage à deux conduites	*m*
dual-line trailer-control valve	*n*	Zweileitungs-Anhängersteuerventil	*n*	valve de commande de remorque à deux conduites	*f*
dual-mass flywheel	*n*	Zweimassenschwungrad	*n*	volant d'inertie à deux masses	*m*
dual-processor principle (ABS control)	*n*	Zweirechner-Prinzip (ABS-Regelung)	*n*	principe bicalculateur (régulation ABS)	*m*
dual-spark ignition coil	*n*	Zweifunken-Zündspule	*f*	bobine d'allumage à deux sorties	*f*
dual-stream injector	*n*	Zweistrahlventil	*n*	injecteur bi-jet	*m*
duo-duplex brake	*n*	Duo-Duplexbremse	*f*	frein duo-duplex	*m*
duo-servo brake	*n*	Duo-Servobremse	*f*	servofrein duo	*m*
duplex brake	*n*	Duplexbremse	*f*	frein duplex	*m*
duration of application	*n*	Betätigungsdauer	*f*	durée d'actionnement	*f*
duration of injection	*n*	Einspritzzeit	*f*	durée d'injection	*f*
dust bowl (filter)	*n*	Staubsammelbehälter (Filter)	*m*	collecteur de poussière (filtre)	*m*
dust sleeve	*n*	Staubmanschette	*f*	garniture anti-poussière	*f*
dust-protected	*pp*	staubgeschützt	*adj*	protégé contre la poussière	*pp*
dwell angle	*n*	Schließwinkel	*m*	angle de fermeture	*m*
dwell period (ignition)	*n*	Schließzeit (Zündung)	*f*	temps de fermeture (allumage)	*m*
dwell-angle map	*n*	Schließwinkelkennfeld	*n*	cartographie de l'angle de came	*f*
dynamic axle load	*n*	dynamische Achslast	*f*	charge dynamique par essieu	*f*
dynamic brake analyzer	*n*	Rollenbremsprüfstand	*m*	banc d'essai à rouleaux pour freins	*m*
dynamic braking response	*n*	Bremsdynamik	*f*	dynamique du freinage	*f*

English		German		French	
dynamic functional range, DFR	*n*	dynamischer Funktionsbereich	*m*	plage de fonctionnement dynamique	*f*
dynamic load-sensing valve (brakes)	*n*	Knickregler (Bremse)	x *m*	régulateur à caractéristique coudée (frein)	*m*
dynamic pilot control	*n*	dynamische Vorsteuerung	*f*	pilotage dynamique	*m*
dynamic plausibility	*n*	dynamische Plausibilität	*f*	plausibilité dynamique	*f*
dynamic supercharging	*v*	dynamische Aufladung	*f*	suralimentation dynamique	*f*
dynamic timing adjustment	*n*	dynamische Förderbeginn-Einstellung	*f*	calage dynamique du début de refoulement	*m*
dynamic weight transfer	*n*	dynamische Gewichtsverlagerung	*f*	report de charge dynamique	*m*
dynamics of lateral motion (motor vehicle)	*n*	Fahrzeugquerdynamik	*f*	dynamique transversale d'un véhicule	*f*
dynamics of linear motion (motor vehicle)	*n*	Fahrzeuglängsdynamik	*f*	dynamique longitudinale d'un véhicule	*f*
dynamics of vehicular operatioı	*n*	Fahrdynamik	*f*	dynamique des véhicules à moteur	*f*
dynamo	+ *n*	Gleichstromgenerator	*m*	génératrice de courant continu	*f*
E					
early (advance) adjustment system	*n*	Früh-Verstellsystem	*n*	système de correction "avance"	*m*
easy-change filter	*n*	Wechselfilter	*n*	filtre à rechange rapide	*m*
eccentric cam (common rail)	*n*	Exzenternocken (Common Rail)	*m*	came à excentrique (Common Rail)	*f*
eccentric element (parking-brake valve)	*n*	Exzenter (Feststellbremsventil)	*m*	excentrique (valve de frein de stationnement)	*m*
eccentric lift	*n*	Exzenterhub	*m*	levée d'excentrique	*f*
eccentric ring	*n*	Exzenterring	*m*	bague excentrique	*f*
ECU, electronic control unit	*a*	elektronisches Steuergerät	*n*	centrale de commande électronique	*f*
EDC, electronic diesel control	*a*	elektronische Dieselregelung, EDC	*f*	régulation électronique diesel, RED	*f*
eddy current	*n*	Wirbelstrom	*m*	courants de Foucault	*mpl*
eddy-current brake	*n*	elektrodynamischer Verlangsamer	*m*	ralentisseur électromagnétique	*m*
eddy-current sensor	*n*	Wirbelstromsensor	*m*	capteur à courants de Foucault	*m*
eddy-current travel sensor	*n*	Kurzschlußringsensor	*m*	capteur à bague de court-circuitage	*m*
edge cam	*n*	Kurvenplatte	*f*	plaque à came	*f*
edge filter	*n*	Spaltfilter	*n*	filtre à disques	*m*
edge-type filter	*n*	Stabfilter	*n*	filtre-tige	*m*
effective area	*n*	Wirkfläche	*f*	surface utile	*f*
effective braking time	*n*	Bremswirkungsdauer	*f*	temps de freinage actif	*m*
effective radius	*n*	Wirkradius	*m*	rayon actif	*m*
effective stroke	*n*	Nutzhub	*m*	course effective	*f*
effectiveness of hot brakes	*n*	Heißbremswirkung	*f*	effet de freinage à chaud	*m*
EFI engine	*n*	Einspritzmotor	*m*	moteur à injection	*m*
EFI, electronic fuel injection	*a*	Jetronic (elektronische Benzineinspritzung)	*f*	Jetronic (injection électronique d'essence)	*m*

English		German		French	
EGR positioner	*n*	Abgasrückführsteller	*m*	actionneur de recyclage des gaz d'échappement	*m*
EGR, exhaust-gas recirculation	*a*	Abgasrückführung, AGR	*f*	recyclage des gaz d'échappement	*m*
EHB, electrohydraulic braking system	*a*	elektrohydraulische Bremse, EHB	*f*	frein électrohydraulique, EHB	*m*
ejector	*n*	Auswerfer	*m*	éjecteur	*m*
elapsed-time electronics	*n*	Laufzeitelektronik	*f*	horamètre électronique	*m*
elastomer swelling (brake fluid)	*n*	Elastomerquellung (Bremsflüssigkeit)	*f*	gonflement des élastomères (liquide de frein)	*m*
ELB, electronically controlled braking system	*a*	elektronisch geregelte Bremsanlage, ELB	*f*	dispositif de freinage à régulation électronique	*m*
electric brake (starter)	*n*	Strombremse (Starter)	*f*	frein électrique (démarreur)	*m*
electric circuit	*n*	Stromkreis	*m*	circuit électrique	*m*
electric compressor	*n*	Elektrokompressor	*m*	compresseur électrique	*m*
electric fuel pump	*n*	Elektrokraftstoffpumpe, EKP	*f*	pompe électrique à carburant	*f*
electric fuel-supply pump	*n*	Elektrokraftstoffpumpe, EKP	*f*	pompe électrique à carburant	*f*
electric generator	*n*	Generator	*m*	génératrice	*f*
electric motor	*n*	Elektromotor	*m*	moteur électrique	*m*
electric strength	*n*	Spannungsfestigkeit	*f*	résistance à la tension	*f*
electric supply pump	*n*	Elektroförderpumpe	*f*	pompe d'alimentation électrique	*f*
electric vehicle, EV	*n*	Elektrofahrzeug (Straßenfahrzeug)	*n*	véhicule électrique	*m*
electrical load requirements	*n*	Verbraucherleistung	*f*	puissance des récepteurs	*f*
electrical power dissipation	*n*	elektrische Verlustleistung	*f*	pertes de puissance	*fpl*
electrical power loss	*n*	elektrische Verlustleistung	*f*	pertes de puissance	*fpl*
electrical separator	*n*	Elektroabscheider	*m*	séparateur électrique	*m*
electrical sheet steel	*n*	Elektroblech	*n*	tôle magnétique	*f*
electrical shutoff device	*n*	elektrische Abstellvorrichtung, ELAB	*f*	dispositif d'arrêt électrique	*m*
electro-hydraulic pressure actuator	*n*	elektrohydraulischer Drucksteller	*m*	actionneur de pression électrohydraulique	*m*
electro-hydraulic pump	*n*	elektro-hydraulische Pumpe	*f*	groupe électropompe	*m*
electrode	*n*	Elektrode	*f*	électrode	*f*
electrode composition	*n*	Elektrodenwerkstoffe	*mpl*	matériaux des électrodes	*mpl*
electrode gap (spark plug)	*n*	Elektrodenabstand (Zündkerze)	*m*	écartement des électrodes (bougie)	*m*
electrode materials	*npl*	Elektrodenwerkstoffe	*mpl*	matériaux des électrodes	*mpl*
electrode shape (spark plug)	*n*	Elektrodenform (Zündkerze)	*f*	forme des électrodes	*f*
electrode wear	*n*	Elektrodenverschleiß	*m*	usure des électrodes	*f*
electrodynamic retarder	*n*	elektrodynamischer Verlangsamer	*m*	ralentisseur électromagnétique	*m*
electrohydraulic braking system, EHB	*n*	elektrohydraulische Bremse, EHB	*f*	frein électrohydraulique, EHB	*m*
electrohydraulic shutoff device	*n*	elektrohydraulische Abstellvorrichtung, EHAB	*f*	dispositif d'arrêt électrohydraulique	*m*
electrolyte	*n*	Elektrolyt	*m*	électrolyte	*m*
electrolyte density (battery)	*n*	Säuredichte	*f*	densité de l'électrolyte	*f*
electrolyte level (battery)	*n*	Füllungsgrad (Batterie)	*m*	taux de remplissage (batterie)	*m*

English

English		German		French	
electrolyte values (battery)	*npl*	Säurewerte (Batterie)	*fpl*	indices des acides (batterie)	*mpl*
electrolytic capacitor	*n*	Elektrolytkondensator	*m*	condensateur électrolytique	*m*
electromagnetic compatibility, EMC	*n*	elektromagnetische Verträglichkeit, EMV	*f*	compatibilité électromagnétique, CEM	*f*
electromotive shutoff device	*n*	elektromotorische Abstellvorrichtung, EMAB	*f*	dispositif d'arrêt électromotoris‹	*m*
electronic braking-pressure control, EPC	*n*	elektronische Bremsdruckregelung, EPC	*f*	régulation électronique de pression de freinage, EPC	*f*
electronic charger (battery)	*n*	Elektroniklader (Batterie)	*m*	chargeur électronique (batterie)	*m*
electronic control unit, ECU	*n*	elektronisches Steuergerät	*n*	centrale de commande électronique	*f*
electronic diesel control, EDC	*n*	elektronische Dieselregelung, EDC	*f*	régulation électronique diesel, RED	*f*
electronic engine-management system, Motronic	*n*	elektronische Motorsteuerung, Motronic	*f*	système électronique de gestion du moteur, Motronic	*m*
electronic engine-power control, ETC	*n*	elektronische Motorfüllungs-steuerung, EGAS	*f*	commande électronique du moteur	*f*
electronic fuel injection, EFI	*n*	Jetronic (elektronische Benzineinspritzung)	*f*	Jetronic (injection électronique d'essence)	*m*
electronic idle-speed control	*n*	elektronische Leerlaufregelung, ELR	*f*	régulation électronique du ralenti	*f*
electronic stability program, ESP	*n*	Fahrdynamikregelung, ESP	*f*	régulation du comportement dynamique, ESP	*f*
electronic throttle control, ETC	*n*	elektronische Motorfüllungs-steuerung, EGAS	*f*	commande électronique du moteur	*f*
electronically controlled braking system, ELB	*n*	elektronisch geregelte Bremsanlage, ELB	*f*	dispositif de freinage à régulation électronique	*m*
electronically controlled gasoline fuel-injection system, Jetronic	*n*	Jetronic (elektronische Benzineinspritzung)	*f*	Jetronic (injection électronique d'essence)	*m*
electronically controlled pneumatic suspension, ELF	*n*	elektronisch geregelte Luftfederung, ELF	*f*	suspension pneumatique à régulation électronique, ELF	*f*
electropneumatic braking system	*n*	elektro-pneumatische Bremsanlage	*f*	dispositif de freinage électro-pneumatique	*m*
electropneumatic converter	*n*	elektropneumatischer Wandler	*m*	convertisseur électropneumatique	*m*
element chamber (common rail	*n*	Elementraum (Common Rail)	*m*	chambre d'élément (Common Rail)	*f*
element cutoff valve	*n*	Element-Abschaltventil	*n*	soupape de coupure d'élément	*f*
element switchoff valve (common rail)	*n*	Elementabschaltventil (Common Rail)	*n*	électrovanne de désactivation d'élément	*f*
EMC, electromagnetic compatibility	*a*	elektromagnetische Verträglichkeit, EMV	*f*	compatibilité électromagnétique, CEM	*f*
emergency braking	*n*	Schnellbremsung	*f*	freinage rapide	*m*
emergency function	*n*	Notfahrfunktion	*f*	fonction "mode dégradé"	*f*
emergency shutoff	*n*	Notabstellung	*f*	arrêt d'urgence	*m*
emergency valve (door control	*n*	Nothahn (Türbetätigung)	*m*	robinet de secours (commande des portes)	*m*
emergency-brake application	*n*	Panikbremsung	*f*	freinage en situation de paniqu‹	*m*
emergency-brake system	*n*	Hilfs-Bremsanlage	*f*	dispositif de freinage de secour:	*m*
emergency-brake valve	*n*	Hilfsbremsventil	*n*	valve de frein de secours	*f*

English		German		French	
emergency-running mode	n	Notfahrbetrieb	m	fonctionnement en mode dégradé	m
emission limits	n	Abgasgrenzwert	m	valeur limite d'émission	f
emission regulations	npl	Abgasgesetzgebung	f	législation antipollution	f
emission values	npl	Emissionswerte	mpl	valeurs d'émission	fpl
emission-control legislation	n	Abgasgesetzgebung	f	législation antipollution	f
emissions test cell	n	Abgasprüfzelle	f	cabine de simulation des gaz d'échappement	f
emissions-control technology	n	Abgastechnik	f	technique des gaz d'échappement	f
emulsion drain	n	Mischölabführung	f	évacuation des émulsions	f
end gas	n	Restgas	n	gaz résiduels	mpl
end of braking	n	Bremsende	n	fin de freinage	f
end of breakaway	n	Abregelende	n	fin de coupure de débit	f
end of combustion	n	Verbrennungsende	n	fin de combustion	f
end of delivery	n	Absteuerung	f	coupure progressive	f
end of injection	n	Spritzende	n	fin d'injection	f
end of pump delivery	n	Förderende (Einspritzpumpe)	n	fin de refoulement (pompe d'injection)	f
end position	n	Endlage	f	position de fin de course	f
end-of-delivery control	n	Förderenderegelung	f	régulation de la fin de refoulement	f
endurance test	n	Dauerlauferprobung	f	essai d'endurance	m
energize	v	ansteuern	v	piloter	v
energizing LPC (lift port closing)	n	Vorhubansteuerung	f	commande de précourse	f
energy accumulator	n	Energiespeicher	m	accumulateur d'énergie	m
energy balance (motor vehicle)	n	Energiehaushalt (Kfz)	m	bilan énergétique (automobile)	m
energy conversion	n	Energieumsetzung	f	conversion d'énergie	f
energy input	n	Energiezufluß	m	arrivée d'énergie	f
energy output	n	Energieabfluß	m	départ d'énergie	m
energy reserve (airbag triggering system)	n	Energiereserve (Airbag)	f	réserve d'énergie (coussin d'air)	f
energy storage	n	Energiespeicherung	f	accumulation de l'énergie	f
energy supply	n	Energieversorgung	f	génération d'énergie	f
energy-assisted braking system	n	Hilfskraft-Bremsanlage	f	dispositif de freinage assisté par énergie auxiliaire	m
energy-supply system	n	Energieversorgungs-einrichtung	f	dispositif d'alimentation en énergie	m
engagement lever (starter)	n	Einrückhebel (Starter)	m	fourchette d'engrènement (démarreur)	f
engagement linkage (starter)	n	Einrückstange (Starter)	f	tige d'engrènement (démarreur)	f
engagement rod (starter)	n	Einrückstange (Starter)	f	tige d'engrènement (démarreur)	f
engaging system	n	Einspursystem	n	système d'engrènement	m
engine analyzer	n	Motortestgerät	n	testeur pour moteur	m
engine brake	n	Auspuffverlangsamer	m	ralentisseur sur échappement	m
engine braking action	n	Motorbremswirkung	f	effet de frein moteur	m
engine braking torque	n	Motorbremsmoment	n	couple de freinage du moteur	m

English

English		German		French	
engine control unit	*n*	Motorsteuergerät	*n*	centrale de commande du moteur	*f*
engine controller (TCS)	*n*	Motorregler (ASR)	*m*	régulateur du moteur (ASR)	*m*
engine cylinder	*n*	Motorzylinder	*m*	cylindre moteur	*m*
engine diagnosis	*n*	Motordiagnose	*f*	diagnostic du moteur	*m*
engine drag-torque control	*n*	Motorschleppmoment-regelung, MSR	*f*	régulation du couple d'inertie du moteur	*f*
engine flexibility	*n*	Motorelastizität (Verbrennungsmotor)	*f*	élasticité du moteur	*f*
engine inertia	*n*	Motorträgheit	*f*	inertie du moteur	*f*
engine intervention (TCS)	*n*	Motoreingriff (ASR)	*m*	intervention sur le moteur (ASR)	*f*
engine load	*n*	Motorlast	*f*	charge du moteur	*f*
engine lube-oil circuit	*n*	Schmierölkreislauf	*m*	circuit de lubrification du moteur	*m*
engine management	*n*	Motormanagement	*f*	gestion des fonctions du moteur	*f*
engine map	*n*	Motorkennfeld	*n*	cartographie moteur	*f*
engine moment of inertia	*n*	Motorschleppmoment	*n*	couple d'inertie du moteur	*m*
engine performance	*n*	Motorleistung	*f*	puissance du moteur	*f*
engine speed	*n*	Motordrehzahl	*f*	vitesse de rotation du moteur	*f*
engine tester	*n*	Motortestgerät	*n*	testeur pour moteur	*m*
engine-control circuit (TCS)	*n*	Motorregelkreis (ASR)	*m*	circuit de régulation du moteur (ASR)	*m*
engine-drag torque	*n*	Motorschleppmoment	*n*	couple d'inertie du moteur	*m*
engine-speed advance	*n*	Drehzahlverstellung	*f*	correction en fonction du régime	*f*
engine-speed limitation	*n*	Drehzahlbegrenzung	*f*	limitation de la vitesse de rotation	*f*
engine-speed threshold	*n*	Drehzahlschwelle	*f*	seuil de régime	*m*
engine-temperature sensor	*n*	Motortemperatursensor	*m*	capteur de température moteur	*m*
enrich (air-fuel mixture)	*v*	anfetten (Luft-Kraftstoff-Gemisch)	*v*	enrichir (mélange air-carburant)	*v*
enrichment factor (air-fuel mixture)	*n*	Anreicherungsfaktor (Luft-Kraftstoff-Gemisch)	*m*	facteur d'enrichissement (mélange air-carburant)	*m*
enrichment quantity	*n*	Anreicherungsrate	*f*	taux d'enrichissement	*m*
enrichment solenoid	*n*	Fettzugmagnet	*m*	électro-aimant d'enrichissement	*m*
envelope	*n*	Hüllkurve	*f*	enveloppe	*f*
environmental compatibility	*n*	Umweltverträglichkeit	*f*	compatibilité environnementale	*f*
environmental impact	*n*	Umweltbelastung	*f*	incompatibilité avec l'environnement	*f*
environmental resistance	*n*	Umweltbeständigkeit	*f*	résistance à l'environnement	*f*
environmentally acceptable	*adj*	umweltfreundlich	*adj*	compatible avec l'environnement	*loc*
epicycloidal gear train	*n*	Planetengetriebe	*n*	train épicycloïdal	*m*
equipment current draw	*n*	Verbraucherstrom	*m*	courant des récepteurs	*m*
equipment ground	*n*	Masse (Gehäusemasse)	*f*	masse (du boîtier)	*f*
equivalent resistance	*n*	Wirkwiderstand	*m*	résistance active	*f*
error diagnosis	*n*	Fehlerdiagnose	*f*	diagnostic de défauts	*m*
error signal	*n*	Fehlersignal	*n*	signal de défaut	*m*

English

English		German		French	
error simulation	*n*	Fehlersimulation	*f*	simulation des défauts	*f*
error storage	*n*	Fehlerabspeicherung	*f*	mémorisation des défauts	*f*
error-code (self-diagnosis)	*n*	Fehlercode (Eigendiagnose)	*m*	code de défaut (autodiagnostic)	*m*
ESP, electronic stability program	*a*	Fahrdynamikregelung, ESP	*f*	régulation du comportement dynamique, ESP	*f*
ETC, electronic throttle control	*a*	EGAS, elektronische Motorleistungssteuerung	*a*	EMS, commande électronique du moteur	*a*
euro-pallet	*n*	Europalette	*f*	palette Europe	*f*
evaluation circuit	*n*	Auswertschaltung	*f*	circuit d'exploitation	*m*
evaluation electronics	*npl*	Auswertelektronik	*f*	circuit électronique de décodag‹	*m*
evaporation recess	*n*	Verdampfungsmulde	*f*	cellule de vaporisation	*f*
evaporative losses (fuel system)	*npl*	Verdampfungsverluste (Kraftstoffsystem)	*mpl*	pertes par évaporation (alimentation en carburant)	*fpl*
evaporative-emissions control system	*n*	Kraftstoffverdunstungs-Rückhaltesystem	*n*	système de retenue des vapeurs de carburant	*m*
evaporative-emissions test	*n*	Verdunstungsprüfung	*f*	test d'évaporation	*m*
evaporator tube	*n*	Verdampferrohr	*n*	tube de vaporisation	*m*
even mixture distribution (air-fuel mixture)	*n*	Gleichverteilung (Luft-Kraftstoff-Gemisch)	*f*	répartition uniforme (mélange air-carburant)	*f*
event-driven	*pp*	ereignisgesteuert	*pp*	commandé par évènements	*pp*
excess air	*n*	Luftüberschuß	*m*	excès d'air	*m*
excess fuel	*n*	Kraftstoff-Mehrmenge	*f*	surdébit de carburant	*m*
excess fuel for starting	*n*	Startmehrmenge	*f*	surdébit de démarrage	*m*
excess fuel quantity	*n*	Mengenüberhöhung	*f*	surcroît de débit	*m*
excess start quantity	*n*	Startmehrmenge	*f*	surdébit de démarrage	*m*
excess-air factor (lambda)	*n*	Luftverhältnis	*n*	coefficient d'air (lambda)	*m*
excess-fuel device	*n*	Startmengenvorrichtung	*f*	dispositif de débit de surcharge au démarrage	*m*
excess-fuel preset	*n*	Startmengenvorsteuerung	*f*	pilotage du débit de surcharge	*m*
exchange alternator	*n*	Austauschgenerator	*m*	alternateur d'échange standard	*m*
exchange product	*n*	Austausch-Erzeugnis	*n*	produit d'échange standard	*m*
exchange program (factory exchange)	*n*	Austauschprogramm (Werksaustausch)	*n*	programme d'échange standard	*m*
excitation circuit	*n*	Erregerstromkreis	*m*	circuit d'excitation	*m*
excitation diode	*n*	Erregerdiode	*f*	diode d'excitation	*f*
excitation field	*n*	Erregerfeld	*n*	champ d'excitation	*m*
excitation losses	*npl*	Erregerverluste	*mpl*	pertes d'excitation	*fpl*
excitation system	*n*	Erregersystem	*n*	système d'excitation	*m*
excitation voltage	*n*	Erregerspannung	*f*	tension d'excitation	*f*
excitation winding	*n*	Erregerwicklung	*f*	enroulement d'excitation	*m*
excitation-diode plate	*n*	Erregerdiodenplatte	*f*	plaque à diodes d'excitation	*f*
exciting current	*n*	Erregerstrom	*m*	courant d'excitation	*m*
excursion (oscillation)	*n*	Auslenkung (Schwingung)	*f*	amplitude (oscillation)	*f*
exhaust brake	*n*	Auspuffverlangsamer	*m*	ralentisseur sur échappement	*m*
exhaust camshaft	*n*	Auslaßnockenwelle	*f*	arbre à cames côté admission	*m*
exhaust cycle	*n*	Ausstoßtakt	*m*	échappement (moteur à combustion)	*m*
exhaust gas	*n*	Abgas	*n*	gaz d'échappement	*mpl*

English

English		German		French	
exhaust manifold	*n*	Abgaskrümmer	*m*	collecteur d'échappement	*m*
exhaust passage	*n*	Abgasleitung	*f*	conduite d'échappement	*f*
exhaust pipe	*n*	Abgasrohr	*n*	tuyau d'échappement	*m*
exhaust retarder	*n*	Auspuffverlangsamer	*m*	ralentisseur sur échappement	*m*
exhaust treatment	*n*	Abgasreinigung	*f*	dépollution des gaz d'échappement	*f*
exhaust turbo-supercharging	*n*	Abgasturboaufladung	*f*	suralimentation par turbocompresseur	*f*
exhaust valve (IC engine)	*n*	Auslaßventil (Verbrennungsmotor)	*n*	soupape d'échappement (moteur à combustion)	*f*
exhaust-gas analysis techniques	*npl*	Abgasprüftechnik	*f*	technique d'analyse des gaz d'échappement	*f*
exhaust-gas analyzer	*n*	Abgasmeßgerät	*n*	appareil de mesure des gaz d'échappement	*m*
exhaust-gas back pressure	*n*	Abgasgegendruck	*m*	contre-pression des gaz d'échappement	*f*
exhaust-gas center silencer	*n*	Mittelschalldämpfer	*m*	silencieux médian	*m*
exhaust-gas component	*n*	Abgasbestandteil	*m*	composant des gaz d'échappement	*m*
exhaust-gas composition	*n*	Abgaszusammensetzung	*f*	composition des gaz d'échappement	*f*
exhaust-gas constituent	*n*	Abgasbestandteil	*m*	composant des gaz d'échappement	*m*
exhaust-gas emission	*n*	Abgasemission	*f*	émission de gaz d'échappement	*f*
exhaust-gas legislation	*n*	Abgasgesetzgebung	*f*	législation antipollution	*f*
exhaust-gas measuring techniques	*npl*	Abgasmeßtechnik	*f*	technique de mesure des gaz d'échappement	*f*
exhaust-gas oxygen	*n*	Restsauerstoff (Abgas)	*m*	oxygène résiduel (gaz d'échappement)	*m*
exhaust-gas partial flow	*n*	Abgasteilstrom	*m*	flux partiel de gaz d'échappement	*m*
exhaust-gas rear silencer	*n*	Nachschalldämpfer	*m*	silencieux arrière	*m*
exhaust-gas recirculation (EGR) control	*n*	Abgasrückführregelung	*f*	régulation du recyclage des gaz d'échappement	*f*
exhaust-gas recirculation (EGR) positioner	*n*	Abgasrückführsteller	*m*	actionneur de recyclage des gaz d'échappement	*m*
exhaust-gas recirculation (EGR) rate	*n*	Abgasrückführrate	*f*	taux de recyclage des gaz d'échappement	*m*
exhaust-gas recirculation (EGR) valve	*n*	Abgasrückführventil	*n*	électrovalve de recyclage des gaz d'échappement	*f*
exhaust-gas recirculation, EGR	*n*	Abgasrückführung, AGR	*f*	recyclage des gaz d'échappement	*m*
exhaust-gas system	*n*	Abgasanlage	*f*	système d'échappement	*m*
exhaust-gas temperature sensor	*n*	Abgastemperaturfühler	*m*	capteur de température des gaz d'échappement	*m*
exhaust-gas test	*n*	Abgastest	*m*	test des gaz d'échappement	*m*
exhaust-gas treatment	*n*	Abgasnachbehandlung	*f*	traitement secondaire des gaz d'échappement	*m*
exhaust-gas turbine	*n*	Abgasturbine	*f*	turbine à gaz d'échappement	*f*
exhaust-gas turbocharger	*n*	Abgasturbolader	*m*	turbocompresseur	*m*

English		German			French	
exhaust-gas turbocharging	*n*	Abgasturboaufladung		*f*	suralimentation par turbocompresseur	*f*
exhaust-gas volume	*n*	Abgasvolumen		*n*	volume des gaz d'échappement	*m*
exhaust-sample probe	*n*	Entnahmesonde		*f*	sonde de prélèvement	*f*
exhaustive discharge (battery)	*n*	Tiefentladung (Batterie)		*f*	décharge en profondeur (batterie)	*f*
expansion element	*n*	Dehnstoffelement		*n*	élément thermostatique	*m*
expansion phase (IC engine)	*n*	Expansionsphase (Verbrennungsmotor)		*f*	phase de détente (moteur à combustion interne)	*f*
experimental nozzle	*n*	Prüfdüse		*f*	injecteur d'essai	*m*
exposed annular area (nozzle needle)	*n*	Druckschulter (Düsennadel)		*f*	cône d'attaque (aiguille d'injecteur)	*m*
extent of inspection	*n*	Prüfumfang		*m*	contrôles	*mpl*
external drive	*n*	Fremdantrieb		*m*	entraînement extérieur	*m*
external exitation (rotating machines)	*n*	Fremderregung (drehende Maschinen)		*f*	excitation extérieure (machines tournantes)	*f*
external force (brake control)	*n*	Fremdkraft (Bremsbetätigung)		*f*	énergie étrangère (commande de frein)	*f*
external start switch	*n*	Start-Externschalter		*m*	commande extérieure de démarrage	*f*
external-fitting headlamp	*n*	Anbauscheinwerfer		*m*	projecteur extérieur	*m*
externally supplied ignition	*n*	Fremdzündung		*f*	allumage par appareillage externe	*m*
extractor fan	*n*	Ansauggebläse		*n*	ventilateur d'aspiration	*m*
extruded	*pp*	fließgepreßt		*pp*	extrudé	*pp*
F						
face cam	*n*	Hubscheibe		*f*	disque à cames	*m*
factory exchange (replacement requirements)	*n*	Werksaustausch (Ersatzbedarf)		*m*	échange standard (rechanges)	*m*
fading (brakes)	*n*	Fading (Bremse)	x	*n*	fading (frein) x	*m*
failure cause	*n*	Fehlerursache		*f*	cause du défaut	*f*
failure mechanism	*n*	Ausfallmechanismus		*m*	mécanisme de la défaillance (de l'incident)	*m*
failure mode	*n*	Fehlerart		*f*	type de défaut	*m*
failure mode and effects analysis, FMEA	*n*	Fehlermöglichkeits- und Fehlereinfluß-Analyse, FMEA		*f*	analyse des modes de défaillance et de leurs effets	*f*
failure protection (car alarm)	*n*	Ausfallsperre (Autoalarm)		*f*	sécurité en cas de panne (alarme auto)	*f*
fan	*n*	Lüfter		*m*	ventilateur	*m*
fan blade	*n*	Lüfterschaufel		*f*	ailette	*f*
fan motor	*n*	Lüftermotor		*m*	moteur de soufflante	*m*
fan-type piston (braking-force regulator)	*n*	Fächerkolben (Bremskraftregler)		*m*	piston à palettes (correcteur de freinage)	*m*
fanfare horn	*n*	Fanfare		*f*	fanfare	*f*
fastening clamp (ignition coil)	*n*	Klemmschelle (Zündspule)		*f*	collier (bobine d'allumage)	*m*
fault detection	*n*	Fehlererkennung		*f*	détection des défauts	*f*
fault display	*n*	Fehleranzeige		*f*	affichage de défauts	*m*
fault memory	*n*	Fehlerspeicher		*m*	mémoire de défauts	*f*
fault store	*n*	Fehlerspeicher		*m*	mémoire de défauts	*f*

English		German		French	
feedback (control)	n	Rückkoppelung (Regelung)	f	réaction (régulation)	f
feedback loop	n	Regelkreis	m	boucle de régulation	f
feedback signal (ABS control)	n	Rückmeldung (ABS-Regelung)	f	confirmation (régulation ABS)	f
fender-mounted air filter	n	Radkastenfilter	n	filtre dans le passage de roue	m
field displacement	n	Feldverzerrung	f	distorsion du champ d'excitation	f
field frame	n	Polgehäuse	n	carcasse stator	f
field of force	n	Kraftlinienfeld	n	champ de lignes de force	m
field resistor	n	Feldwiderstand	m	impédance de champ	f
fifth wheel	n	Königszapfen	m	pivot central	m
fifthwheel coupling	n	Aufsattelkupplung	f	sellette de semi-remorque	f
fill factor (rotating machines)	n	Nutfüllfaktor (drehende Maschinen)	m	facteur de remplissage des rainures (machines tournantes)	m
filler piece	n	Füllstück	n	cale	f
filling phase	n	Füllphase	f	phase de remplissage	f
filling powder (sheathed-element glow plug)	n	Füllpulver (Glühstiftkerze)	n	poudre isolante (bougie-crayon de préchauffage)	f
filter cake	n	Filterkuchen	m	gâteau de filtre x	m
filter cartridge	n	Filtereinsatz	m	cartouche filtrante	f
filter case	n	Filtergehäuse	n	carter de filtre	m
filter clogging	n	Filterverstopfung	f	bouchage du filtre	m
filter cover	n	Filterdeckel	m	couvercle de filtre	m
filter effect	n	Filterwirkung	f	effet de filtration	m
filter element	n	Filtereinsatz	m	cartouche filtrante	f
filter head	n	Filterdeckel	m	couvercle de filtre	m
filter heating	n	Filteraufheizung	f	réchauffage du filtre	m
filter service life	n	Filterstandzeit	f	durabilité du filtre	f
filter strainer	n	Filtersieb	n	crépine	f
filtration efficiency	n	Abscheidegüte (Filter)	f	qualité de séparation (filtre)	f
filtration separator	n	Filtrationsabscheider	m	séparateur à filtration	m
final control element (TCS)	n	Stelleinrichtung (ASR)	f	actionneur de réglage (ASR)	m
final controlling element	n	Stellglied	n	actuateur	m
final drive (motor vehicle)	n	Achsantrieb (Kfz)	m	essieu moteur (véhicule)	m
final inspection	n	Endkontrolle	f	contrôle final	m
final operating temperature	n	Enderwärmung	f	température finale de fonctionnement	f
final position	n	Abschlußstellung	f	position d'arrêt	f
final test	n	Endkontrolle	f	contrôle final	m
fine filter	n	Feinfilter	n	filtre fin	m
fine-filter element	n	Feinfiltereinsatz	m	cartouche filtrante fine	f
firing interval	n	Zündabstand	m	période de l'allumage	f
firing module (airbag)	n	Zündmodul (Airbag)	m	module de mise à feu (coussin gonflable)	m
firing order	n	Zündfolge	f	ordre d'allumage	m
firing pellet (airbag)	n	Zündpille (Airbag)	f	pastille explosive (coussin gonflable)	f
firing sequence	n	Zündfolge	f	ordre d'allumage	m

English		German		French	
firing squib (airbag)	*n*	Zündpille (Airbag)	*f*	pastille explosive (coussin gonflable)	*f*
firing voltage	*n*	Zündspannung	*f*	tension d'allumage	*f*
first stage (side-channel pump)	*n*	Vorstufe (Seitenkanalpumpe)	*f*	premier étage (pompe à canal latéral)	*m*
first start	*n*	Erststart	*m*	premier démarrage	*m*
fitting	*n*	Anschlußstutzen	*m*	raccord	*m*
fitting ring	*n*	Einpaßring	*m*	bague de centrage	*f*
fixed caliper (brakes)	*n*	Festsattel (Bremse)	*m*	étrier fixe (frein)	*m*
fixed cam	*n*	Festnocken	*m*	came solidaire	*f*
fixed resistor	*n*	Festwiderstand	*m*	résistance électrique fixe	*f*
fixed restriction (pressure actuator)	*n*	Festdrossel (Drucksteller)	*f*	étranglement fixe (actionneur de pression)	*m*
fixed throttle	*n*	feste Drossel	*f*	étranglement fixe	*m*
fixing hole	*n*	Befestigungsloch	*n*	trou de fixation	*m*
flame front	*n*	Flammenfront	*f*	front de flamme	*m*
flame glow plug	*n*	Flammkerze	*f*	bougie de préchauffage à flamme	*f*
flame ionization detection analyzer, FID	*n*	Flammen-Ionisations-Detektor, FID	*m*	détecteur d'ionisation à flamme, FID	*m*
flame primer	*n*	Flammstartanlage	*f*	dispositif de démarrage à flamme	*m*
flame start	*n*	Flammstart	*m*	démarrage par flamme	*m*
flame starting system	*n*	Flammstartanlage	*f*	dispositif de démarrage à flamme	*m*
flame travel	*n*	Flammenweg	*m*	course de flamme	*f*
flame-front propagation time	*n*	Entflammungsdauer	*f*	durée d'inflammation	*f*
flange bushing	*n*	Flanschbuchse	*f*	manchon à bride	*m*
flange cylinder	*n*	Flanschzylinder	*m*	vérin à bride	*m*
flange mounting	*n*	Flanschbefestigung	*f*	fixation par bride	*f*
flash frequency	*n*	Blinkfrequenz	*f*	fréquence de clignotement	*f*
flashing adapter (trailer ABS)	*n*	Blinkadapter (Anhänger-ABS)	*m*	adaptateur clignotant (ABS pour remorques)	*m*
flashing signal	*n*	Blinksignal	*n*	signal clignotant	*m*
flashover (at electrodes)	*n*	Funkenüberschlag (an den Elektroden)	*m*	éclatement de l'étincelle (aux électrodes)	*m*
flat motor	*n*	Flachmotor	*m*	moteur plat	*m*
flat seat	*n*	Flachdichtsitz	*m*	siège plat	*m*
flat spot	*n*	Beschleunigungsloch x	*n*	trou à l'accélération	*m*
flat-seat valve	*n*	Flachsitzventil	*n*	soupape à siège plan	*f*
flatbed mounting	*n*	Flachbettbefestigung	*f*	fixation par base plane	*f*
flatted pintle nozzle	*n*	Flächenzapfendüse	*f*	injecteur à téton plan	*m*
flexible line	*n*	flexible Leitung	*f*	tuyau flexible	*m*
flexible strip	*n*	Federschiene	*f*	lame-ressort	*f*
flexural sensor (dynamic brake analyzer)	*n*	Biegebalken (Rollenbremsprüfstand)	*m*	balancier (banc d'essai)	*m*
flipflop	*n*	Multivibrator	*m*	multivibrateur	*m*
float angle (vehicle dynamics)	*n*	Schwimmwinkel (Kfz-Dynamik)	*m*	angle de flottement (dynamique d'un véhicule)	*m*

English		German		French	
float piston	n	Schwimmkolben	m	piston flotteur	m
floating block	n	Kulissenstein	m	coulisseau	m
floating caliper (brakes)	n	Faustsattel (Bremse)	m	étrier flottant (frein)	m
floating circuit (tandem master cylinder)	n	Schwimmkreis (Tandemhauptzylinder)	m	circuit flottant (maître-cylindre tandem)	m
floating-mode operation (battery charge)	n	Pufferbetrieb (Batterieladung)	m	mode "tampon" (charge de batterie)	m
floodlamp	n	Arbeitsscheinwerfer	m	projecteur de travail	m
floodlight	n	Flutlichtstrahler	m	projecteur d'ambiance	m
flow cross-section	n	Strömungsquerschnitt	m	section de passage de flux	f
flow direction	n	Strömungsrichtung	f	sens d'écoulement	m
flow limiter	n	Durchflußbegrenzer	m	limiteur d'écoulement	m
flow medium	n	Fördermedium	n	fluide de refoulement	m
flow of energy	n	Energiefluß	m	flux d'énergie	m
flow sensor (exhaust-gas test)	n	Strömungsfühler (Abgasprüfung)	m	débitmètre (émissions)	m
flow sensor (hot-film air-mass meter)	n	Durchflußsensor (Heißfilm-Luftmassenmesser)	m	capteur de flux d'écoulement (débitmètre massique à film chaud)	m
flow throttle	n	Durchflußdrossel	f	étrangleur	m
flow velocity	n	Strömungsgeschwindigkeit	f	vitesse d'écoulement	f
flow volume	n	Volumenstrom	m	débit volumique	m
flow-control valve	n	Stromregelventil	n	régulateur de débit	m
flow-limiting valve	n	Strombegrenzungsventil	n	limiteur de débit	m
flow-type pump	n	Strömungspumpe	f	pompe centrifuge	f
flush-fitting headlamp	n	Einbauscheinwerfer	m	projecteur encastrable	m
flushing method	n	Durchspülungsverfahren	n	méthode de balayage	f
flyweight	n	Fliehgewicht	n	masselotte	f
flyweight assembly	n	Regelgruppe	f	bloc de régulation	m
flyweight bolt	n	Fliehgewichtsbolzen	m	axe de masselottes	m
flyweight governor	n	Fliehkraftregler	m	régulateur mécanique	m
flyweight mount	n	Fliehgewichtsträger	m	porte-masselottes	m
flyweight speed-sensing elemer	n	Fliehgewichtsmeßwerk	n	mécanisme de détection à masselottes	m
flyweight travel	n	Fliehgewichtsweg	m	course des masselottes	f
flywheel	n	Schwungrad	n	volant moteur	m
focal length (headlamp)	n	Brennweite (Scheinwerfer)	f	distance focale (projecteur)	f
focal point (headlamp)	n	Brennpunkt (Scheinwerfer)	m	foyer (projecteur)	m
fog lamp	n	Nebelscheinwerfer, NSW	m	projecteur antibrouillard	m
fog light +	n	Nebelscheinwerfer, NSW	m	projecteur antibrouillard	m
fog warning lamp	n	Nebelschlußleuchte	f	feu arrière de brouillard	m
follow-up spark	n	Folgefunken	m	trains d'étincelles	mpl
foot brake	n	Betriebs-Bremsanlage	f	dispositif de freinage de service	m
force-distribution control (wiper system)	n	Auflagekraftsteuerung (Wischeranlage)	f	commande de la force d'appui (essuie-glace)	f
force-transfer direction	n	Wirkrichtung	f	sens d'action	m
forced regeneration	n	Zwangsregeneration	f	régénération forcée	f
fork head	n	Gabelkopf	m	chape	f

English

English		German		French	
fork lever (starter)	*n*	Gabelhebel (Starter)	*m*	levier à fourche (démarreur)	*m*
forward voltage (rectifier diode	*n*	Durchlaßspannung (Gleichrichterdiode)	*f*	tension à l'état passant (diode redresseuse)	*f*
forward-delivery valve (diesel fuel injection)	*n*	Vorlaufventil (Dieseleinspritzung)	*n*	clapet-pilote (injection diesel)	*m*
four-bar linkage (wiper system)	*n*	Zweischlag (Wischeranlage)	*m*	double battement (essuie-glace)	*m*
four-circuit protection valve	*n*	Vierkreis-Schutzventil	*n*	valve de sécurité à quatre circuits	*f*
four-circuit safety valve	*n*	Vierkreis-Schutzventil	*n*	valve de sécurité à quatre circuits	*f*
four-headlamp system	*n*	Vier-Scheinwerfer-System	*n*	système à quatre projecteurs	*m*
four-spark ignition coil	*n*	Vierfunken-Zündspule	*f*	bobine d'allumage à quatre sorties	*f*
four-stroke cycle	*n*	Viertaktverfahren	*n*	cycle à quatre temps	*m*
four-stroke principle	*n*	Viertaktverfahren	*n*	cycle à quatre temps	*m*
four-valve design	*n*	Vierventil-Technik	*f*	système à quatre soupapes par cylindre	*m*
four-way cock	*n*	Vierwegehahn	*m*	robinet à quatre voies	*m*
four-wheel drive, FWD	*n*	Vierradantrieb	*m*	transmission quatre roues	*f*
frame or chassis connection	*n*	Masse (Gehäusemasse)	*f*	masse (du boîtier)	*f*
free-wheeling diode	*n*	Freilaufdiode	*f*	diode de récupération	*f*
frequency divider	*n*	Frequenzteiler	*m*	diviseur de fréquence	*m*
frequency modulation, FM	*n*	Frequenzmodulation	*f*	modulation de fréquence	*f*
fresh A/F mixture (IC engine)	*n*	Frischgas (Verbrennungsmotor)	*n*	gaz frais (moteur à combustion)	*mpl*
fresnel optics	*npl*	Fresneloptik	*f*	optique de Fresnel	*f*
friction brake	*n*	Reibungsbremse	*f*	frein à friction	*m*
friction force	*n*	Reibungskraft	*f*	force de frottement	*f*
friction lining	*n*	Reibbelag	*m*	garniture de friction	*f*
friction loss	*n*	Reibungsverlust	*m*	perte par frottement	*f*
friction moment	*n*	Reibmoment	*n*	couple de frottement	*m*
friction noise	*n*	Reibgeräusch	*n*	bruit de friction	*m*
friction pairing	*n*	Reibpaarung	*f*	couple de friction	*m*
friction properties (brake lining	*n*	Reibeigenschaft (Bremsbelag)	*f*	propriété de friction (garniture de frein)	*f*
friction washer (starter)	*n*	Anlaufscheibe (Starter)	*f*	rondelle de friction (démarreur)	*f*
friction-coefficient matching	*n*	Reibwertpaarung	*f*	couple d'adhérence	*m*
frictional force	*n*	Reibkraft	*f*	force de friction	*f*
front airbag	*n*	Frontairbag	*m*	coussin gonflable avant	*m*
front electrode (spark plug)	*n*	Dachelektrode (Zündkerze)	*f*	électrode frontale (bougie)	*f*
front lamp	*n*	Frontleuchte	*f*	feu avant	*m*
front muffler	*n*	Vorschalldämpfer	*m*	silencieux avant	*m*
front screen (headlamp)	*n*	Frontblende (Scheinwerfer)	*f*	cache avant (projecteur)	*m*
front wiper blade	*n*	Front-Wischblatt	*n*	raclette de pare-brise	*f*
front-wheel drive	*n*	Frontantrieb	*m*	traction avant	*f*
fuel accumulator	*n*	Kraftstoffspeicher	*m*	accumulateur de carburant	*m*
fuel atomization	*n*	Kraftstoffzerstäubung	*f*	pulvérisation du carburant	*f*
fuel chamber (fuel-pressure regulator)	*n*	Kraftstoffkammer (Kraftstoffdruckregler)	*f*	chambre à carburant (amortisseur de pression du carburant)	*f*

English

English		German		French	
fuel consumption	*n*	Kraftstoffverbrauch	*m*	consommation de carburant	*f*
fuel consumption by mass	*n*	Kraftstoff-Massenverbrauch	*m*	consommation massique de carburant	*f*
fuel distribution	*n*	Kraftstoffverteilung	*f*	répartition du carburant	*f*
fuel distributor	*n*	Kraftstoffmengenteiler	*m*	doseur-distributeur de carburant	*m*
fuel dribble	*n*	nachtropfen	*v*	bavage de carburant	*m*
fuel droplet	*n*	Kraftstofftröpfchen	*n*	gouttelette de carburant	*f*
fuel filter	*n*	Kraftstoffilter	*n*	filtre à carburant	*m*
fuel gallery (fuel-injection pump)	*n*	Saugraum (Einspritzpumpe)	*m*	galerie d'alimentation (pompe d'injection)	*f*
fuel gauge	*n*	Kraftstoffanzeiger	*m*	jauge à carburant	*f*
fuel injection	*n*	Kraftstoffeinspritzung	*f*	injection de carburant	*f*
fuel injector	*n*	Einspritzventil	*n*	injecteur	*m*
fuel inlet	*n*	Kraftstoffzulauf	*m*	arrivée de carburant	*f*
fuel intake	*n*	Kraftstoffzulauf	*m*	arrivée de carburant	*f*
fuel line	*n*	Kraftstoffleitung	*f*	conduite de carburant	*f*
fuel metering	*n*	Kraftstoffzumessung	*f*	dosage du carburant	*m*
fuel prefilter	*n*	Kraftstoffvorreiniger	*m*	préfiltre à carburant	*m*
fuel rail	*n*	Kraftstoffverteiler	*m*	rampe distributrice de carburant	*f*
fuel reduction	*n*	Mindermenge	*f*	réduction de débit	*f*
fuel shutoff	*n*	Mengenabstellung	*f*	suspension de débit	*f*
fuel spinner	*n*	Dralltopf	*m*	pot de giration	*m*
fuel spray	*n*	Düsenstrahl (aufgelöst)	*m*	jet pulvérisé	*m*
fuel supply	*n*	Kraftstoffversorgung	*f*	alimentation en carburant	*f*
fuel supply and delivery	*n*	Kraftstofförderung	*f*	refoulement du carburant	*m*
fuel system	*n*	Kraftstoffsystem	*n*	système d'alimentation en carburant	*m*
fuel tank	*n*	Kraftstoffbehälter	*m*	réservoir de carburant	*m*
fuel vaporization	*n*	Kraftstoffverdampfung	*f*	vaporisation du carburant	*f*
fuel-air separator	*n*	Kraftstoffluftabscheider	*m*	séparateur d'air du carburant	*m*
fuel-delivery characteristics	*npl*	Fördermengenverlauf	*m*	courbe du débit d'injection	*f*
fuel-delivery control	*n*	Fördermengenregelung	*f*	régulation des débits d'injection	*f*
fuel-delivery curve	*n*	Fördermengen-Kennlinie	*f*	courbe caractéristique des débits	*f*
fuel-delivery measurement device	*n*	Fördermengenmeßgerät	*n*	appareil de mesure du débit	*m*
fuel-delivery rate	*n*	Förderrate	*f*	taux de refoulement	*m*
fuel-delivery termination (diesel fuel injection)	*n*	absteuern (Dieseleinspritzung)	*v*	fin de refoulement (injection diesel)	*f*
fuel-distribution pipe (multipoint fuel injection)	*n*	Kraftstoffverteilerstück (Einzeleinspritzung)	*n*	rampe d'injection (injection multipoint)	*f*
fuel-distributor block	*n*	Mengenteilerblock	*m*	groupe doseur-distributeur	*m*
fuel-filter exchange box	*n*	Wechselbox (Filter)	*f*	filtre-box interchangeable	*m*
fuel-flow reducing device	*n*	Mindermengeneinsteller	*m*	réducteur de débit	*m*
fuel-gallery flushing	*n*	Saugraumspülung	*f*	balayage de la galerie d'alimentation	*m*
fuel-injection engine	*n*	Einspritzmotor	*m*	moteur à injection	*m*
fuel-injection equipment	*n*	Einspritzausrüstung	*f*	équipement d'injection	*m*

English		German		French	
fuel-injection installation	*n*	Einspritzanlage	*f*	dispositif d'injection	*m*
fuel-injection pump	*n*	Kraftstoffeinspritzpumpe	*f*	pompe d'injection	*f*
fuel-injection system	*n*	Einspritzanlage	*f*	dispositif d'injection	*m*
fuel-injection tubing	*n*	Druckleitung	*f*	tuyau de refoulement	*m*
fuel-level indicator	*n*	Füllstandsanzeige	*f*	jauge de niveau	*f*
fuel-mass sensor	*n*	Kraftstoffmasse-Sensor	*m*	capteur de masse de combustible	*m*
fuel-metering plunger (KE-Jetronic)	*n*	Zumeßkolben (KE-Jetronic)	*m*	piston de dosage (KE-Jetronic)	*m*
fuel-metering slit (KE-Jetronic)	*n*	Zumeßschlitz (KE-Jetronic)	*m*	fente de dosage (KE-Jetronic)	*f*
fuel-pressure attenuator (Jetronic)	*n*	Kraftstoffdruckdämpfer (Jetronic)	*m*	amortisseur de pression du carburant (Jetronic)	*m*
fuel-pressure regulator	*n*	Kraftstoffdruckregler	*m*	régulateur de pression de carburant	*m*
fuel-pressure sensor	*n*	Kraftstoffdrucksensor	*m*	capteur de pression du carburant	*m*
fuel-quantity command	*n*	Mengeneingriff	*m*	action sur débit	*f*
fuel-quantity compensation	*n*	Mengenabgleich	*m*	étalonnage de débit	*m*
fuel-quantity correction	*n*	Kraftstoffmengenkorrektur	*f*	correction de débit de carburant	*f*
fuel-quantity demand	*n*	Mengenwunsch	*m*	demande de débit	*f*
fuel-quantity drift	*n*	Mengendrift	*f*	dérive de débit	*f*
fuel-quantity increment	*n*	Mengeninkrement	*n*	incrément de débit	*m*
fuel-quantity map	*n*	Mengenkennfeld	*n*	cartographie de débit	*f*
fuel-quantity positioner	*n*	Mengenstellglied	*n*	actionneur de débit	*m*
fuel-quantity positioner setpoint value	*n*	Mengenstellersollwert	*m*	valeur consigne de l'actionneur de débit	*f*
fuel-quantity power stage	*n*	Mengenendstufe	*f*	étage de sortie de débit	*f*
fuel-quantity reduction	*n*	Mindermenge	*f*	réduction de débit	*f*
fuel-quantity threshold value	*n*	Mengenschwellwert	*m*	valeur de seuil de débit	*f*
fuel-recirculation valve	*n*	Kraftstoffrückführventil	*n*	vanne de recyclage de carburan	*f*
fuel-return line	*n*	Kraftstoffrückleitung	*f*	conduite de retour du carburant	*f*
fuel-supply pump	*n*	Kraftstofförderpumpe	*f*	pompe d'alimentation (carburant)	*f*
fuel-water separator	*n*	Kraftstoffwasserabscheider	*m*	séparateur d'eau du carburant	*m*
fuel/air mix	*n*	Luft-Kraftstoff-Gemisch	*n*	mélange air-carburant	*m*
fulcrum (brake shoe)	*n*	Abstützpunkt (Bremsbacke)	*m*	point d'appui (frein)	*m*
full braking	*n*	Vollbremsung	*f*	freinage d'urgence	*m*
full load	*n*	Vollast, VL	*f*	pleine charge	*f*
full-load acceleration	*n*	Vollastbeschleunigung	*f*	accélération à pleine charge	*f*
full-load characteristic	*n*	Vollastkennlinie	*f*	courbe caractéristique de pleine charge	*f*
full-load curve	*n*	Vollastkennlinie	*f*	courbe caractéristique de pleine charge	*f*
full-load delivery	*n*	Vollastfördermenge	*f*	débit de pleine charge (refoulement)	*m*
full-load enrichment	*n*	Vollastanreicherung	*f*	enrichissement de pleine charge	*m*
full-load fuel quantity	*n*	Vollastfördermenge	*f*	débit de pleine charge (refoulement)	*m*
full-load limitation	*n*	Vollastbegrenzung	*f*	limitation du débit maximal	*f*

English		German		French	
full-load position	n	Vollaststellung	f	position de pleine charge	f
full-load screw	n	Vollasteinstellschraube	f	vis de réglage de pleine charge	f
full-load speed	n	Vollastdrehzahl	f	vitesse de pleine charge	f
full-load speed regulation (fuel-injection pump)	n	Endabregelung (Einspritzpumpe)	f	coupure de vitesse maximale (pompe d'injection)	f
full-load stop	n	Vollastanschlag	m	butée de débit maximal	f
full-load switch	n	Vollastschalter	m	contacteur de pleine charge	m
full-load torque control	n	Vollastangleichung	f	correction de pleine charge	f
full-wave rectification	n	Zweiweggleichrichtung	f	redressement à deux alternances	m
full-wave rectifier	n	Zweiweggleichrichter	m	redresseur pleine-onde	m
fully braked mode	n	Vollbremsstellung	f	position de freinage d'urgence	f
fully developed deceleration	n	Vollverzögerung	f	décélération totale	f
fully-shielded spark plug	n	vollgeschirmte Zündkerze	f	bougie totalement blindée	f
function lamp	n	Funktionskontrolleuchte	f	témoin de fonctionnement	m
function module (ECU)	n	Funktionsblock (Steuergerät)	m	bloc fonctionnel (calculateur)	m
functional security	n	Betriebssicherheit	f	sécurité de fonctionnement	f
fuse box	n	Sicherungsdose	f	boîte à fusibles	f
G					
gaiter seal	n	Faltenbalg	m	soufflet	m
gap dimension (diesel fuel injection)	n	Spaltmaß (Dieseleinspritzung)	n	cote d'écartement (injection diesel)	f
garage-door drive	n	Garagentor-Antrieb	m	commande de porte pour garages	f
gas exchange	n	Gaswechsel	m	renouvellement des gaz	m
gas generator (airbag)	n	Gasgenerator (Airbag)	m	générateur de gaz (coussin gonflable)	m
gas inflator (airbag)	n	Gasgenerator (Airbag)	m	générateur de gaz (coussin gonflable)	m
gas travel time (lambda closed-loop control)	n	Gaslaufzeit (Lambda-Regelung)	f	temps de transit des gaz (régulation lambda)	m
gas-filled shock absorber	n	Gasdruck-Stoßdämpfer	m	amortisseur à pression de gaz	m
gaseous-discharge lamp, GDL	n	Gasentladungslampe	f	lampe à décharge dans un gaz	f
gasoline	n	Ottokraftstoff	m	essence	f
gasoline direct injection	n	Benzindirekteinspritzung, BDE	f	injection directe essence	f
gasoline injection	n	Benzineinspritzung	f	injection d'essence	f
gasoline/diesel stop	n	Benzin-Diesel-Anschlag	m	butée essence/gazole	f
gassing voltage	n	Gasungsspannung	f	tension de dégagement gazeux	f
gear pump	n	Zahnradpumpe	f	pompe à engrenage	f
gear selection	n	Fahrstufe	f	rapport de roulage	m
gear switch	n	Gangschalter	m	commande de changement de vitesse	f
gear-indicator switch	n	Ganganzeigeschalter	m	interrupteur-témoin de rapport de vitesse	m
gear-preselector switch	n	Gangvorwahlschalter	m	présélecteur de vitesses	m
gearbox intervention	n	Getriebesteuerung	f	commande de boîte de vitesses	f
gearbox stage	n	Getriebefahrstufe	f	rapport de vitesse	m
gearbox step-up ratio	n	Getriebeübersetzung	f	rapport de transmission de la boîte de vitesses	m

English

English		German		French	
General Certification	*n*	Allgemeine Betriebserlaubnis, ABE	*f*	homologation générale	*f*
general inspection	*n*	Hauptuntersuchung, HU	*f*	contrôle technique	*m*
general-service lamp	*n*	Arbeitsscheinwerfer	*m*	projecteur de travail	*m*
generator	*n*	Generator	*m*	génératrice	*f*
generator circuit (alternator)	*n*	Generatorstromkreis	*m*	circuit principal (alternateur)	*m*
generator regulator (alternator)	*n*	Spannungsregler (Generator)	*m*	régulateur de tension (alternateur)	*m*
geomagnetic sensor (navigation system)	*n*	Erdmagnetfeldsonde (Navigationssystem)	*f*	sonde de champ magnétique terrestre (système de navigation)	*f*
geometric range (headlamp)	*n*	geometrische Reichweite (Scheinwerfer)	*f*	portée géométrique (projecteur)	*f*
gladhand	*n*	Kupplungskopf	*m*	tête d'accouplement	*f*
glare (headlamp)	*n*	Blendung (Scheinwerfer)	*f*	éblouissement (projecteur)	*m*
glare effect (headlamp)	*n*	Blendwirkung (Scheinwerfer)	*f*	effet d'éblouissement (projecteur)	*m*
glass-breakage detector (car alarm)	*n*	Glasbruchmelder (Autoalarm)	*m*	détecteur de bris de glaces (alarme auto)	*m*
glow control unit	*n*	Glühzeitsteuergerät, GZS	*n*	module de commande du temps de préchauffage	*m*
glow discharge	*n*	Glimmentladung	*f*	décharge d'arc	*f*
glow duration	*n*	Glühdauer	*f*	durée d'incandescence	*f*
glow element	*n*	Glühstift	*m*	crayon de préchauffage	*m*
glow indicator	*n*	Glühüberwacher	*m*	contrôleur d'incandescence	*m*
glow plug	*n*	Glühkerze	*f*	bougie de préchauffage	*f*
glow plug for auxiliary heaters	*n*	Standheizungs-Glühkerze	*f*	bougie de préchauffage pour chauffage auxiliaire	*f*
glow time	*n*	Vorglühdauer	*f*	durée de préchauffage	*f*
glow tube	*n*	Glührohr	*n*	tube incandescent	*m*
glow-plug and starter switch	*n*	Glüh-Start-Schalter	*m*	commutateur de préchauffage-démarrage	*m*
glow-plug tip	*n*	Glühkörper	*m*	corps chauffant (crayon)	*m*
glycol-based brake fluid	*n*	Glykol-Bremsflüssigkeit	*f*	liquide de frein à base de glycol	*m*
go/no-go gauge	*n*	Gut-Schlechtlehre	*f*	jauge "bon/mauvais"	*f*
governing (diesel engine)	*n*	Dieselregelung	*f*	régulation diesel	*f*
governor (diesel fuel injection)	*n*	Drehzahlregler (Dieseleinspritzung)	*m*	régulateur (injection diesel)	*m*
governor assembly	*n*	Reglergruppe	*f*	bloc régulateur	*m*
governor characteristic curves	*n*	Reglerkennfeld	*n*	cartographie du régulateur	*f*
governor characteristics	*n*	Reglercharakteristik	*f*	caractéristique du régulateur	*f*
governor cover	*n*	Reglerdeckel	*m*	couvercle de régulateur	*m*
governor deviation	*n*	Regelabweichung	*f*	écart de régulation	*m*
governor housing	*n*	Reglergehäuse	*n*	carter de régulateur	*m*
governor hub	*n*	Reglernabe	*f*	moyeu de régulateur	*m*
governor linkage	*n*	Reglergestänge	*n*	tringlerie du régulateur	*f*
governor spring	*n*	Regelfeder	*f*	ressort de régulation	*m*
graded start quantity	*n*	gestufte Startmenge, GST	*f*	surcharge étagée	*f*
graduable	*adj*	abstufbar	*adj*	modérable	*adj*

English		German		French	
granulate (air drier)	n	Trockenmittel (Lufttrockner)	n	déshydratant (dessiccateur)	m
gravity braking system	n	Fall-Bremsanlage	f	dispositif de freinage à commande par gravité	m
gravity-feed fuel-tank operation	n	Falltankbetrieb	m	réservoir en charge	m
grip x	n	Bodenhaftung	f	adhérence au sol	f
grip ring (brakes)	n	Greifring (Bremse)	m	bague d'attaque (frein)	f
grooved toothing	n	Kerbverzahnung	f	cannelure	f
ground cable	n	Masserückleitung	f	câble de retour à la masse	m
ground clearance (motor vehicle)	n	Bodenfreiheit (Kfz)	f	garde au sol (véhicule)	f
ground connection	n	Masseverbindung	f	mise à la terre	f
ground electrode	n	Masseelektrode	f	électrode de masse	f
ground return	n	Masserückführung	f	retour par la masse	m
group injection	n	Gruppeneinspritzung	f	injection groupée	f
guide block	n	Kulissenstein	m	coulisseau	m
guide bushing	n	Führungsbuchse	f	douille de guidage	f
guide lever	n	Führungshebel	m	levier de guidage	m
guide pin	n	Führungsstift	m	axe de guidage	m
guide slot	n	Führungsschlitz	m	rainure de guidage	f
H					
half-wave rectifier	n	Einweggleichrichter	m	redresseur demi-onde	m
Hall effect	n	Hall-Effekt	m	effet Hall	m
Hall element	n	Hall-Element	n	élément Hall	m
Hall generator	n	Hall-Sensor	m	générateur de Hall	m
Hall layer	n	Hall-Schicht	f	couche Hall	f
Hall triggering system	n	Hall-Auslösesystem	n	système de déclenchement Hall	m
Hall vane switch	n	Hall-Schranke	f	barrière Hall	f
Hall voltage	n	Hall-Spannung	f	tension Hall	f
halogen lamp	n	Halogenlampe	f	lampe à halogène	f
halogen-gas light	n	Halogenlicht	n	éclairage par lampe à halogène	m
hand brake	n	Handbremse	f	frein à main x	m
hand primer pump	n	Handpumpe	f	pompe à main	f
hand pump	n	Handpumpe	f	pompe à main	f
hand throttle	n	Handfahrgeber	m	accélérateur manuel	m
hand transmitter (car alarm)	n	Handsender (Autoalarm)	m	émetteur manuel (alarme auto)	m
hand-brake lever	n	Handbremshebel	m	levier du frein à main	m
hand-brake shoe	n	Handbremsbacke	f	mâchoire de frein à main	f
hand-brake valve	n	Handbremsventil	n	valve de frein à main	f
hand-portable searchlight	n	Handscheinwerfer	m	projecteur portable	m
harmonics	npl	Oberschwingungen	fpl	oscillations harmoniques	fpl
hasp-type fastening (wipers)	n	Überfallbügelbefestigung (Wischer)	m	fixation par contre-étrier (essuie-glace)	f
hazard flashing	v	warnblinken	v	signalisation "détresse"	f
hazard-switch	n	Warnblinkschalter	m	commutateur des feux de détresse	m
hazard-warning and turn-signal flasher	n	Warnblinkgeber	m	centrale mixte de direction-détresse	f

English

English		German		French	
hazard-warning and turn-signal relay	*n*	Warnblinkrelais	*n*	relais du signal de détresse	*m*
hazard-warning and turn-signal system	*n*	Warnblinkanlage	*f*	dispositif de signalisation direction-détresse	*m*
hazard-warning signal flasher	*n*	Warnlichtgeber	*m*	centrale de signal de détresse	*f*
head clearance (piston)	*n*	Sicherheitsabstand (Kolbenkopf)	*m*	jeu d'extrémité supérieure (piston)	*m*
head clearance (plunger-and-barrel assembly)	*n*	Kopfspiel (Pumpenelement)	*n*	jeu en tête (élément de pompage)	*m*
headlamp	*n*	Scheinwerfer	*m*	projecteur	*m*
headlamp flasher	*n*	Lichthupe	*f*	signal optique	*m*
headlamp housing	*n*	Scheinwerfergehäuse	*n*	boîtier de projecteur	*m*
headlamp system	*n*	Scheinwerfersystem	*n*	système de projecteurs	*m*
headlamp washer system	*n*	Scheinwerfer-Waschanlage	*f*	lavophare complet	*m*
headlamp wiper	*n*	Lichtwischer	*m*	lavophare	*m*
headlamp wiper system	*n*	Scheinwerfer-Wischeranlage	*f*	nettoyeur de projecteurs	*m*
headlamp-housing assembly	*n*	Scheinwerferaufnahme	*f*	cuvelage de projecteur	*m*
headlight	*n*	Scheinwerfer	*m*	projecteur	*m*
headlight aiming device	*n*	Scheinwerfer-Einstellprüfgerät	*n*	appareil de réglage des projecteurs	*m*
headlight leveling (manually operated)	*n*	Leuchtweiteeinstellung	*f*	correction de la portée d'éclairement	*f*
headlight leveling control	*n*	Leuchtweitenregelung, LWR	*f*	correcteur de site des projecteurs	*m*
headlight leveling control	*n*	Leuchtweiteregler, LWR	*m*	correcteur de site	*m*
headlight range control	*n*	Leuchtweitenregelung, LWR	*f*	correcteur de site des projecteurs	*m*
headlight setter	*n*	Scheinwerfer-Einstellprüfgerät	*n*	appareil de réglage des projecteurs	*m*
headlight unit	*n*	Scheinwerfereinsatz	*m*	bloc optique	*m*
headlight-range adjustment	*n*	Leuchtweiteeinstellung	*f*	correction de la portée d'éclairement	*f*
heat absorption	*n*	Wärmeaufnahme	*f*	absorption de chaleur	*f*
heat conduction	*n*	Wärmeleitung	*f*	conduction thermique	*f*
heat dissipation	*n*	Wärmeabführung	*f*	dissipation de la chaleur	*f*
heat exchange	*n*	Wärmeaustausch	*m*	échange de chaleur	*m*
heat exchanger (hydrodynamic retarder)	*n*	Wärmetauscher (hydrodynamischer Verlangsamer)	*m*	échangeur de chaleur (ralentisseur hydrodynamique)	*m*
heat losses	*npl*	Verlustwärme	*f*	chaleur de dissipation	*f*
heat radiation	*n*	Wärmestrahlung	*f*	rayonnement thermique	*m*
heat range (spark plug)	*n*	Wärmewert (Zündkerze)	*m*	degré thermique (bougie)	*m*
heat rating (spark plug)	*n*	Wärmewert (Zündkerze)	*m*	degré thermique (bougie)	*m*
heat shield (nozzle)	*n*	Wärmeschutz (Einspritzdüse)	*m*	isolation thermique (injecteur)	*f*
heat sink	*n*	Kühlkörper	*m*	refroidisseur	*m*
heat sink with ribs	*n*	Rippenkühlkörper	*m*	refroidisseur nervuré	*m*
heat-absorbing property	*n*	Wärmeaufnahmevermögen	*n*	capacité d'absorption thermique	*f*
heat-range code number (spark plug)	*n*	Wärmewertkennzahl (Zündkerze)	*f*	indice caractéristique du degré thermique (bougie)	*m*

English

English		German		French	
heat-shrinkage zone (spark plug)	n	Warmschrumpfzone (Zündkerze)	f	zone de contraction et de rétraction à chaud (bougie)	f
heated lambda sensor, LSH	n	beheizte Lambda-Sonde, LSH	f	sonde de richesse chauffée	f
heater blower	n	Heizergebläse	n	ventilateur de chaufferette	m
heater element	n	Heizelement	n	élément chauffant	m
heater plug	n	Flammkerze	f	bougie de préchauffage à flamme	f
heater system	n	Heizungsanlage	f	chauffage	m
heating element (air drier)	n	Heizstab (Lufttrockner)	m	tige chauffante (dessiccateur)	f
heating flange	n	Heizflansch	m	bride de réchauffage	f
heating regulator	n	Heizungsregelung	f	régulation du chauffage	f
heating tube	n	Heizrohr	n	tube chauffant	m
height-control valve	n	Luftfederventil	n	valve de nivellement	f
height-control-valve unit	n	Luftfeder-Ventileinheit	f	bloc-valves (suspension pneumatique)	m
helical compression spring	n	Schraubendruckfeder	f	ressort hélicoïdal de compression	m
helical heating wire	n	Heizwendel	f	filament chauffant hélicoïdal	m
helical travel (starter)	n	Schraubweg (Starter)	m	déplacement hélicoïdal (démarreur)	m
helix (plunger-and-barrel assembly)	n	Steuerkante (Pumpenelement)	f	rampe hélicoïdale (élément de pompage)	f
helix control	n	Schrägkantensteuerung	f	commande par rampe inclinée	f
high beam	n	Fernlicht	n	feu de route	m
high idle speed	n	obere Leerlaufdrehzahl	f	vitesse maximale à vide	f
high level (air suspension)	n	Hochniveau (Luftfederung)	n	niveau haut (suspension pneumatique)	f
high wheel (ABS)	n	High-Rad (ABS) x	n	roue à sélection "haute" (ABS)	f
high-frequency inductive senso	n	Hochfrequenzinduktivgeber	m	capteur inductif haute fréquence	m
high-mounted stop lamp	n	Zusatz-Bremsleuchte	f	feu stop supplémentaire	m
high-performance ignition coil	n	Hochleistungs-Zündspule	f	bobine d'allumage à hautes performances	f
high-pressure accumulator (common rail)	n	Hochdruckspeicher (Common Rail)	m	accumulateur haute pression (Common Rail)	m
high-pressure braking system	n	Hochdruck-Bremsanlage	f	dispositif de freinage à haute pression	m
high-pressure chamber (fuel-injection pump)	n	Druckraum (Einspritzpumpe)	m	chambre de refoulement (pompe d'injection)	f
high-pressure charge pump (TCS)	n	Hochdruckladepumpe (ASR)	f	pompe de suralimentation haute pression (ASR)	f
high-pressure delivery	n	Hochdruckförderung	f	refoulement haute pression	m
high-pressure delivery line	n	Hochdruckleitung	f	tuyauterie haute pression	f
high-pressure fuel injection	n	Hochdruckeinspritzung	f	injection haute pression	f
high-pressure pump	n	Hochdruckpumpe	f	pompe à haute pression	f
high-pressure solenoid valve	n	Hochdruckmagnetventil	n	électrovanne haute pression	f
high-pressure stage	n	Hochdruckteil	n	partie haute pression	f
high-pressure test	n	Hochdruckprüfung	f	essai de haute pression	m
high-speed (diesel engine)	n	schnellaufend (Dieselmotor)	ppr	à régime rapide (moteur diesel)	loc

English

English		German		French	
high-speed knock	*n*	Hochgeschwindigkeitsklopfen	*n*	cliquetis à haut régime	*m*
high-tension ignition cable	*n*	Zündleitung	*f*	câble d'allumage	*m*
high-tone horn	*n*	Hochtonhorn	*n*	avertisseur à tonalité aiguë	*m*
high-voltage cable	*n*	Hochspannungsleitung	*f*	câble haute tension	*m*
high-voltage distributor	*n*	Hochspannungsverteiler	*m*	distributeur haute tension	*m*
hinged housing	*n*	Klappgehäuse	*n*	boîtier rabattable	*m*
hinged-armature relay	*n*	Klappankerrelais	*n*	relais à armature battante	*m*
hold-down clamp	*n*	Spannbügel	*m*	étrier de fixation	*m*
hold-in winding	*n*	Haltewicklung	*f*	enroulement de maintien	*m*
holding current	*n*	Haltestrom	*m*	courant de maintien	*m*
holding voltage	*n*	Haltespannung	*f*	tension de maintien	*f*
holding winding	*n*	Haltewicklung	*f*	enroulement de maintien	*m*
hole angle	*n*	Strahlkegelwinkel	*m*	angle du cône d'injection	*m*
hole pintle nozzle	*n*	Lochzapfendüse	*f*	injecteur à téton perforé	*m*
hole-type nozzle	*n*	Lochdüse	*f*	injecteur à trou(s)	*m*
hole-type nozzle gap	*n*	Spaltlochdüse	*f*	injecteur à fente	*m*
hole-type perforated-seat nozzle	*n*	Sitzlochdüse	*f*	injecteur à siège perforé	*m*
hollow axle	*n*	Hohlachse	*f*	axe creux	*m*
hollow screw	*n*	Hohlschraube	*f*	vis creuse	*f*
hollow shaft	*n*	Hohlwelle	*f*	arbre creux	*m*
homofocal reflector	*n*	Homofokal-Reflektor	*m*	réflecteur homofocal	*m*
homologation	*n*	Homologation	*f*	homologation	*f*
homologation approval	*n*	Allgemeine Betriebserlaubnis, ABE	*f*	homologation générale	*f*
honeycomb ceramic (soot burn-off filter)	*n*	Wabenkeramik (Rußabbrennfilter)	*f*	céramique en nid d'abeilles (filtre d'oxidation de particules)	*f*
hook fastening (wipers)	*n*	Hakeneinhängung (Wischer)	*f*	fixation par crochet (essuie-glace)	*f*
hook mounting (wipers)	*n*	Hakeneinhängung (Wischer)	*f*	fixation par crochet (essuie-glace)	*f*
hook-type fastening (wipers)	*n*	Hakeneinhängung (Wischer)	*f*	fixation par crochet (essuie-glace)	*f*
horn	*n*	Signalhorn	*n*	avertisseur sonore	*m*
hose clamp	*n*	Schlauchklemme	*f*	collier de serrage	*m*
hot start	*n*	Heißstart	*m*	départ à chaud	*m*
hot test (exhaust-gas test)	*n*	Heißtest (Abgasprüfung)	*m*	cycle départ à chaud (émissions)	*m*
hot wire (air-mass meter)	*n*	Hitzdraht (Luftmassenmesser)	*m*	fil chaud (débitmètre massique)	*m*
hot-engine driving response	*n*	Heißlaufverhalten (Verbrennungsmotor)	*n*	comportement en surchauffe (moteur à combustion)	*m*
hot-film air-mass meter	*n*	Heißfilm-Luftmassenmesser, HMM	*m*	débitmètre massique à film chaud	*m*
hot-film air-mass sensor	*n*	Heißfilm-Luftmassenmesser	*m*	débitmètre d'air à film chaud	*m*
hot-film sensor	*n*	Heißfilmsensor	*m*	capteur à film chaud	*m*
hot-fuel delivery	*n*	Heißförderung	*f*	refoulement à chaud	*m*
hot-fuel handling characteristics	*npl*	Heißbenzinverhalten x	*n*	comportement avec carburant chaud	*m*
hot-soak phase	*n*	Nachheizphase	*f*	phase de post-chauffage	*f*
hot-start fuel quantity	*n*	Heißstartmenge	*f*	débit de démarrage à chaud	*m*

English		German		French	
hot-start response	*n*	Heißstartverhalten	*f*	comportement au démarrage à chaud	*m*
hot-water valve	*n*	Heizwasserventil	*n*	vanne d'eau chaude	*f*
hot-wire air-mass meter	*n*	Hitzdraht-Luftmassenmesser, HLM	*m*	débitmètre massique à fil chaud	*m*
hot-wire anemometer	*n*	Hitzdrahtanemometer	*m*	anémomètre à fil chaud	*m*
housing (lamps)	*n*	Gehäuse (Leuchtkörper)	*n*	boîtier (lampes)	*m*
housing mounting	*n*	Gehäusebefestigung	*f*	fixation sur carter	*f*
housing stop	*n*	Gehäuseanschlag	*m*	butée sur carter	*f*
hum (radio disturbance)	*v*	brummen (Funkstörung)	*v*	ronflement (perturbation)	*m*
HV distributor	*n*	Hochspannungsverteiler	*m*	distributeur haute tension	*m*
hybrid circuit	*n*	Hybridschaltung	*f*	circuit hybride	*m*
hybrid regulator	*n*	Hybridregler	*m*	régulateur hybride	*m*
hybrid technology	*n*	Hybridtechnik	*f*	technique hybride	*f*
hydraulic accumulator	*n*	Hydrospeicher	*m*	accumulateur hydraulique	*m*
hydraulic brake	*n*	hydraulische Bremse	*f*	frein à commande hydraulique	*m*
hydraulic brake booster	*n*	Hydraulik-Bremskraftverstärker	*m*	servofrein hydraulique	*m*
hydraulic brake circuit	*n*	Hydraulikbremskreis	*m*	circuit de freinage hydraulique	*m*
hydraulic fluid	*n*	Hydraulikflüssigkeit	*f*	fluide hydraulique	*m*
hydraulic fluid reservoir	*n*	Hydraulikbehälter	+ *m*	réservoir de fluide hydraulique	*m*
hydraulic gear motor	*n*	Zahnradmotor	*m*	moteur à engrenage	*m*
hydraulic head (distributor pump)	*n*	Verteilerkörper (Verteilereinspritzpumpe)	*m*	tête hydraulique (pompe distributrice)	*f*
hydraulic line	*n*	Hydraulikleitung	*f*	conduite hydraulique	*f*
hydraulic modulator (ABS)	*n*	Hydroaggregat (ABS)	*n*	groupe hydraulique (ABS)	*m*
hydraulic pump	*n*	Hydropumpe	*f*	pompe hydraulique	*f*
hydraulic shutoff device	*n*	hydraulische Abstellvorrichtung, HYAB	*f*	dispositif d'arrêt hydraulique	*m*
hydraulic-actuated brake	*n*	hydraulische Bremse	*f*	frein à commande hydraulique	*m*
hydraulically controlled torque control	*n*	hydraulisch betätigte Angleichung, HBA	*f*	correcteur hydraulique de débit	*m*
hydrodynamic retarder	*n*	hydrodynamischer Verlangsamer	*m*	ralentisseur hydrodynamique	*m*
hydrometer (battery charge)	*n*	Säureprüfer (Batterie)	*m*	pèse-acide (charge de batterie)	*m*
hysteresis test	*n*	Hysterese-Prüfung	*f*	contrôle d'hystérésis	*m*
I					
IC engine	*n*	Verbrennungsmotor	*m*	moteur à combustion interne	*m*
icing protection (throttle valve)	*n*	Vereisungsschutz (Drosselklappe)	*m*	additif antigivre (papillon)	*m*
identification lamp	*n*	Kennleuchte	*f*	feu spécial d'avertissement	*m*
IDI engine	*n*	Kammermotor	*m*	moteur à injection indirecte	*m*
IDI, indirect injection	*a*	indirekte Einspritzung, IDI	*f*	injection indirecte	*f*
idle	*n*	Leerlauf	*m*	ralenti	*m*
idle (pressure regulator)	*v*	Leerlaufbetrieb (Druckregler)	*m*	fonctionnement à vide (régulateur de pression)	*m*
idle actuator	*n*	Leerlaufsteller	*m*	actionneur de ralenti	*m*
idle contact	*n*	Leerlaufkontakt	*m*	contact de ralenti	*m*

English		German		French	
idle controller	n	Leerlaufregler	m	correcteur de ralenti	m
idle delivery	n	Leerlauf-Fördermenge	f	débit de ralenti	m
idle piston (air drier)	n	Leerlaufkolben (Lufttrockner)	m	piston de marche à vide (dessiccateur)	m
idle speed	n	Leerlaufdrehzahl	f	vitesse de ralenti	f
idle stabilization	n	Leerlaufstabilisierung	f	stabilisation du ralenti	f
idle valve	n	Leerlaufventil	n	soupape de marche à vide	f
idle-speed adjustment point	n	Leerlaufeinstellpunkt	m	point de réglage de ralenti	m
idle-speed control	n	Leerlaufregelung, LLR	f	régulation de la vitesse de ralenti	f
idle-speed controller	n	Leerlaufregler	m	correcteur de ralenti	m
idle-speed increase	n	Leerlaufanhebung	f	ralenti accéléré	m
idle-speed regulation	n	Leerlaufregelung, LLR	f	régulation de la vitesse de ralenti	f
idle-speed spring	n	Leerlauffeder	f	ressort de ralenti	m
idle-speed spring attached to governor housing	n	gehäusefeste Leerlauffeder, LFG x	f	ressort de ralenti solidaire du corps de pompe	m
idle-speed stage	n	Leerlaufstufe	f	étage de ralenti	m
idle-speed stop screw	n	Leerlaufanschlagschraube	f	vis de butée de ralenti	f
idling	n	Leerlauf	m	ralenti	m
ignitable	adj	zündwillig	adj	inflammable	adj
ignition	n	Zündung	f	allumage	m
ignition adjustment	n	Zündungseingriff	m	intervention sur l'allumage	f
ignition advance	n	Frühverstellung (Zündwinkel)	f	avance (angle d'allumage)	f
ignition advance angle	n	Zündwinkel	f	angle d'allumage	m
ignition and starting switch	n	Zünd-Start-Schalter	m	commutateur d'allumage-démarrage	m
ignition angle	n	Zündwinkel	f	angle d'allumage	m
ignition cable	n	Zündleitung	f	câble d'allumage	m
ignition capacitor	n	Zündkondensator	m	condensateur d'allumage	m
ignition coil	n	Zündspule	f	bobine d'allumage	f
ignition condenser	n	Zündkondensator	m	condensateur d'allumage	m
ignition contact breaker	n	Zündunterbrecher	m	rupteur (allumage)	m
ignition distributor	n	Zündverteiler	m	allumeur	m
ignition driver stage	n	Zündungsendstufe	f	étage de sortie d'allumage	m
ignition energy	n	Zündenergie	f	énergie d'allumage	f
ignition lag	n	Zündverzug	m	délai d'inflammation	m
ignition limit	n	Zündgrenze	f	limite d'allumage	f
ignition map	n	Zündwinkelkennfeld	n	cartographie d'allumage	f
ignition mark	n	Zündmarke	f	repère d'allumage	m
ignition miss	n	Entflammungsaussetzer	m	ratés d'inflammation	mpl
ignition module (air-fuel mixture)	n	Zündmodul (Luft-Kraftstoff-Gemisch)	m	module d'allumage (mélange air-carburant)	m
ignition point	n	Zündzeitpunkt	m	point d'allumage	m
ignition pulse	n	Zündimpuls	m	impulsion d'allumage	f
ignition quality	n	Zündwilligkeit	f	inflammabilité	f
ignition reliability	n	Zündsicherheit	f	fiabilité d'allumage	f
ignition retard	n	Spätverstellung (Zündwinkel)	f	retard (angle d'allumage)	m

English

English		German		French	
ignition sequence	*n*	Zündfolge	*f*	ordre d'allumage	*m*
ignition spark	*n*	Zündfunke	*m*	étincelle d'allumage	*f*
ignition switch	*n*	Zündschalter	*m*	commutateur d'allumage	*m*
ignition system	*n*	Zündanlage	*f*	équipement d'allumage	*m*
ignition temperature	*n*	Zündtemperatur	*f*	température d'inflammation	*f*
ignition timing	*n*	Zündwinkelsteuerung	*f*	commande de l'angle d'allumage	*f*
ignition tranformer	*n*	Zündtrafo	*m*	transformateur d'allumage	*m*
ignition transistor	*n*	Zündtransistor	*m*	transistor d'allumage	*m*
ignition trigger	*n*	Zündauslöser	*m*	déclencheur d'allumage	*m*
ignition trigger box	*a*	Zündschaltgerät	*n*	module de commande de l'allumage	*m*
ignition triggering (pulse generator)	*n*	Zündauslösung (Impulsgeber)	*f*	déclenchement de l'allumage (générateur d'impulsions)	*m*
ignition voltage	*n*	Zündspannung	*f*	tension d'allumage	*f*
ignition-cable set	*n*	Zündleitungssatz	*m*	jeu de câbles d'allumage	*m*
ignition-distributor shaft	*n*	Zündverteilerwelle	*f*	arbre d'allumeur	*m*
ignition-voltage pick-up	*n*	Zündspannungsgeber	*m*	capteur de tension d'allumage	*m*
ignition/starting switch	*n*	Zünd-Start-Schalter	*m*	commutateur d'allumage-démarrage	*m*
illumination	*n*	Ausleuchtung	*f*	éclairement	*m*
illumination meter	*n*	Luxmeter	*n*	luxmètre	*m*
impact (filter)	*n*	Aufpralleffekt (Filter)	*m*	effet d'impact (filtre)	*m*
impact detection (airbag)	*n*	Aufpralldetektion (Airbag)	*f*	détection de collision (coussin gonflable)	*f*
impact edge	*n*	Prallkante	*f*	arête de rebond	*f*
impact sensor	*n*	Stoßsensor	*m*	capteur de choc	*m*
impairment of vision	*n*	Sichttrübung	*f*	manque de visibilité	*m*
impeller blade (electric fuel pump)	*n*	Laufradschaufel (Elektrokraftstoffpumpe)	*f*	ailette de rotor (pompe électrique à carburant)	*f*
impeller ring (peripheral pump)	*n*	Laufrad (Peripheralpumpe)	*n*	rotor (pompe à accélération périphérique)	*m*
impulse control	*n*	Impulssteuerung	*f*	commande à impulsions	*f*
in-house production	*n*	Eigenfertigung	*f*	production propre	*f*
in-line fuel-injection pump (PE	*n*	Reiheneinspritzpumpe (PE)	*f*	pompe d'injection en ligne (PE)	*f*
in-line pump (fuel injection)	*n*	Reiheneinspritzpumpe (PE)	*f*	pompe d'injection en ligne (PE)	*f*
in-line pump (fuel supply)	*n*	Leitungseinbaupumpe	*f*	pompe sur conduite	*f*
in-tank pump	*n*	Tankeinbaupumpe	*f*	pompe incorporée au réservoir	*f*
in-tank unit	*n*	Tankeinbaueinheit	*f*	unité de puisage	*f*
incident radiation (EMC)	*n*	Einstrahlung (EMV)	*f*	rayonnement incident (CEM)	*m*
incipient lock (wheel)	*n*	Blockierneigung (Rad)	*f*	tendance au blocage (roue)	*f*
incorrect-polarity protection diode	*n*	Verpolungsschutzdiode	*f*	diode de protection contre inversion de polarité	*f*
increase threshold value (accelerator-pedal sensor)	*n*	Anstiegsschwellwert (Fahrpedalsensor)	*m*	seuil croissant (capteur d'accélérateur)	*m*
increment-angle-time system	*n*	Inkremental-Winkel-Zeit-System	*n*	système incrémentiel angle-temps	*m*
indicated torque	*n*	indiziertes Motormoment	*n*	couple indiqué	*m*
indicator lamp	*n*	Informationslampe	*f*	lampe de signalisation	*f*

English			German			French	
indicator lock (dynamic brake analyzer)		*n*	Zeigerbremse (Rollenbremsprüfstand)		*f*	frein d'aiguille (afficheur de banc d'essai)	*m*
indirect injection, IDI		*n*	indirekte Einspritzung, IDI		*f*	injection indirecte	*f*
indirect-injection (IDI) engine		*n*	Kammermotor		*m*	moteur à injection indirecte	*m*
individual control, IR (ABS)		*n*	Einzelradregelung (ABS)		*f*	régulation individuelle (ABS)	*f*
individual runner		*n*	Einzelschwingrohr		*n*	tubulure d'admission	*f*
induction coil		*n*	Induktionswicklung		*f*	enroulement d'induction	*m*
induction cup		*n*	Topfmagnet		*m*	aimant tambour	*m*
induction stroke		*n*	Ansaugtakt		*m*	admission	*f*
induction system (IC engine)		*n*	Ansaugsystem (Verbrennungsmotor)		*n*	système d'admission (moteur à combustion)	*m*
induction tube		*n*	Saugrohr		*n*	collecteur d'admission	*m*
induction voltage		*n*	Induktionsspannung		*f*	tension d'induction	*f*
induction-type pulse-generator (ignition)		*n*	Induktionsgeber (Zündung)		*m*	générateur à induction (allumage)	*m*
inductive ignition		*n*	Spulenzündung, SZ		*f*	allumage par bobine	*m*
inert-gas light		*n*	Edelgaslicht		*n*	éclairage par lampe à gaz rare	*m*
inertia braking system		*n*	Auflauf-Bremsanlage		*f*	dispositif de freinage à inertie	*m*
info display (ABS)		*n*	Informationsanzeige, INA (ABS)	+	*f*	visuel d'information (ABS)	*m*
info lamp	x	*n*	Informationslampe		*f*	lampe de signalisation	*f*
infrared analyzer		*n*	Infrarot-Analysator		*m*	enregistreur infrarouge à absorption	*m*
infrared hand transmitter (car alarm)		*n*	Infrarot-Handsender (Autoalarm)		*m*	émetteur manuel infrarouge (alarme auto)	*m*
initial braking		*n*	Anbremsvorgang		*m*	évolution du freinage	*f*
initial delay time		*n*	Ansprechdauer		*f*	temps de réponse initial	*m*
initial drying (air drier)		*n*	Vorentwässerung (Lufttrockner)		*f*	prédéshydratation (dessiccateur)	*f*
initial response time		*n*	Ansprechdauer		*f*	temps de réponse initial	*m*
initial spring tension		*n*	Federvorspannung		*f*	tension initiale du ressort	*f*
initialization error		*n*	Initialisierungsfehler		*m*	erreur d'initialisation	*f*
injected fuel quantity		*n*	Einspritzmenge		*f*	débit d'injection	*m*
injected fuel volume		*n*	Einspritzvolumen		*n*	volume de carburant injecté	*m*
injected-fuel-quantity control		*n*	Fördermengenregelung		*f*	régulation des débits d'injection	*f*
injected-fuel-quantity correctioı		*n*	Mengenkorrektur		*f*	correction de débit d'injection	*f*
injected-fuel-quantity indicator		*n*	Einspritzmengenindikator		*m*	débitmètre instantané	*m*
injected-fuel-quantity scatter		*n*	Einspritzmengenstreuung		*f*	dispersion de débit	*f*
injection		*n*	Kraftstoffeinspritzung		*f*	injection de carburant	*f*
injection adaption		*n*	Einspritzanpassung		*f*	adaptation de l'injection	*f*
injection blank-out period (Jetronic)		*n*	Einspritzausblendungszeit (Jetronic)		*f*	temps d'interruption de l'injection (Jetronic)	*m*
injection cam		*n*	Einspritznocken		*m*	came d'injection	*f*
injection cycle		*n*	Einspritztakt		*m*	cycle d'injection	*m*
injection direction		*n*	Einspritzrichtung		*f*	sens d'injection	*m*
injection jet		*n*	Einspritzstrahl		*m*	jet d'injection	*m*
injection lag		*n*	Spritzverzug		*m*	délai d'injection	*m*
injection mass		*n*	Einspritzmasse		*f*	masse injectée	*f*

English		German		French	
injection orifice	*n*	Spritzloch	*n*	trou d'injection	*m*
injection pressure	*n*	Einspritzdruck	*m*	pression d'injection	*f*
injection process	*n*	Einspritzvorgang	*m*	injection (opération)	*f*
injection pulse	*n*	Einspritzimpuls	*m*	impulsion d'injection	*f*
injection pump	*n*	Kraftstoffeinspritzpumpe	*f*	pompe d'injection	*f*
injection rate	*n*	Spritzrate	*f*	taux d'injection	*m*
injection sequence	*n*	Einspritzfolge	*f*	ordre d'injection	*m*
injection time	*n*	Einspritzzeit	*f*	durée d'injection	*f*
injection valve	*n*	Einspritzventil	*n*	injecteur	*m*
injection-pump assembly	*n*	Einspritzpumpen-Kombination	*f*	ensemble de pompe d'injection	*m*
injection-pump delivery	*n*	Fördermenge (Einspritzpumpe)	*f*	débit de refoulement (pompe d'injection)	*m*
injection-pump test bench	*n*	Einspritzpumpen-Prüfstand	*m*	banc d'essai pour pompes d'injection	*m*
injection-valve group	*n*	Einspritzventilgruppe	*f*	groupe d'injecteurs	*m*
injector (common rail)	*n*	Injektor (Common Rail)	*m*	injecteur (système "Common Rail")	*m*
inlet manifold	*n*	Saugrohr	*n*	collecteur d'admission	*m*
inlet metering	*n*	Zulaufmessung	*f*	dosage à l'admission	*m*
inlet metering unit	*n*	Saugdrosseleinheit	*f*	unité de gicleur d'aspiration	*f*
inlet passage (distributor pump)	*n*	Einlaßquerschnitt (Verteilereinspritzpumpe)	*m*	canal d'arrivée (pompe distributrice)	*m*
inlet passage (injection nozzle)	*n*	Zulaufbohrung (Einspritzdüse)	*f*	orifice d'admission (injecteur)	*m*
inlet port (distributor pump)	*n*	Zulaufquerschnitt (Verteilereinspritzpumpe)	*m*	canal d'admission (pompe distributrice)	*m*
inlet port (in-line pump)	*n*	Saugloch (Reiheneinspritzpumpe)	*n*	orifice d'admission (pompe d'injection en ligne)	*m*
inlet restriction	*n*	Zulaufdrossel	*f*	étranglement d'arrivée	*m*
inlet valve	*n*	Zulaufventil	*n*	soupape d'arrivée	*f*
input amplifier (ECU)	*n*	Eingangsverstärker (Steuergerät)	*m*	amplificateur d'entrée (calculateur)	*m*
input circuit (ECU)	*n*	Eingangsbeschaltung (Steuergerät)	*f*	circuit d'entrée (calculateur)	*m*
input filter	*n*	Eingangsfilter	*n*	filtre d'entrée	*m*
input restriction	*n*	Zulaufdrossel	*f*	étranglement d'arrivée	*m*
input throttle	*n*	Zulaufdrossel	*f*	étranglement d'arrivée	*m*
input variable	*n*	Eingangsgröße	*f*	grandeur d'entrée	*f*
insensitive to reverse polarity	*adj*	verpolungssicher	*adj*	insensible à l'inversion de polarité	*loc*
insensitive to short-circuit	*adj*	kurzschlußsicher	*adj*	insensible au court-circuit	*loc*
inspection tag	*n*	Prüfplakette	*f*	autocollant d'inspection	*m*
installation instructions	*npl*	Montageanleitung	*f*	notice de montage	*f*
installation position	*n*	Einbaulage	*f*	position de montage	*f*
instantaneous braking power	*n*	Bremsleistung	*f*	puissance instantanée de freinage	*f*
instrument panel	*n*	Armaturenbrett	*n*	tableau de bord	*m*
instrument-panel lamp	*n*	Instrumentenleuchte	*f*	lampe de tableau de bord	*f*
insulating cover (ignition distributor)	*n*	Isolierdeckel (Zündverteiler)	*m*	couvercle isolant (allumeur)	*m*

English		German		French	
insulating paper	*n*	Isolierpapier	*n*	papier isolant	*m*
insulating tubing	*n*	Isolierschlauch	*m*	gaine isolante	*f*
insulating washer	*n*	Isolierscheibe	*m*	rondelle isolante	*f*
insulation	*n*	Isolierung	*f*	isolation	*f*
insulator (ignition coil)	*n*	Isolierkörper (Zündspule)	*m*	isolateur (bobine d'allumage)	*m*
insulator (spark plug)	*n*	Isolator (Zündkerze)	*m*	isolant (bougie)	*m*
insulator flashover (spark-plug)	*n*	Kriechstrom (Zündkerze)	*m*	courant de fuite (bougie)	*m*
insulator nose (spark plug)	*n*	Isolatorfuß (Zündkerze)	*m*	bec d'isolant (bougie)	*m*
intake	*n*	Saugseite	*f*	côté aspiration	*m*
intake air	*n*	Ansaugluft	*f*	air d'admission	*m*
intake camshaft	*n*	Einlaßnockenwelle	*f*	arbre à cames côté échappemen	*m*
intake chamber (CO tester)	*n*	Empfängerkammer (Abgastester)	*f*	collecteur (gaz CO)	*m*
intake cover	*n*	Luftansaugdeckel	*m*	capot d'aération	*m*
intake fan	*n*	Ansauggebläse	*n*	ventilateur d'aspiration	*m*
intake filter	*n*	Ansaugfilter	*n*	filtre d'aspiration	*m*
intake line	*n*	Saugleitung	*f*	conduit d'admission	*m*
intake manifold	*n*	Saugrohr	*n*	collecteur d'admission	*m*
intake noise	*n*	Ansauggeräusch	*n*	bruit d'aspiration	*m*
intake passage	*n*	Saugleitung	*f*	conduit d'admission	*m*
intake port	*n*	Ansaugkanal	*m*	canal d'admission	*m*
intake runner	*n*	Schwingrohr	*n*	pipe d'admission	*f*
intake stroke	*n*	Ansaugtakt	*m*	admission	*f*
intake stroke (IC engine)	*n*	Ansaughub (Verbrennungsmotor)	*m*	course d'admission (moteur à combution)	*f*
intake swirl (intake manifold)	*n*	Einlaßdrall (Saugrohr)	*m*	tourbillon à l'admission	*m*
intake system (IC engine)	*n*	Ansaugsystem (Verbrennungsmotor)	*n*	système d'admission (moteur à combustion)	*m*
intake tract	*n*	Ansaugkanal	*m*	canal d'admission	*m*
intake valve	*n*	Einlaßventil	*n*	valve d'admission	*f*
intake-air adjustment	*n*	Luftsteuerung (Ansaugluft)	*f*	commande de l'air d'admission	*f*
intake-manifold preheating	*n*	Saugrohrvorwärmung	*f*	préchauffage du collecteur d'admission	*m*
intake-manifold pressure	*n*	Saugrohrdruck	*m*	pression d'admission	*f*
intake-manifold pressure sensoı	*n*	Saugrohrdrucksensor	*m*	capteur de pression d'admission	*m*
intake-passage design	*n*	Saugrohrgestaltung	*f*	forme du collecteur d'admissior	*f*
intake-valve seat (IC engine)	*n*	Einlaßventilsitz (Verbrennungsmotor)	*m*	siège d'admission (moteur à combustion)	*m*
integral braking system	*n*	Kombi-Bremsanlage	*f*	dispositif de freinage combiné	*m*
integrated circuit, IC	*n*	integrierter Schaltkreis, IC	*m*	circuit intégré, C.I.	*m*
integrated diagnostics	*n*	integrierte Diagnose	*f*	diagnostic intégré	*m*
intensified interference suppression	*n*	Nahentstörung	*f*	antiparasitage renforcé	*m*
inter-axle lock (all-wheel drive)	*n*	Längssperre (Allradantrieb)	*f*	blocage longitudinal (transmission intégrale)	*m*
interchangeable	*adj*	einbaugleich	*adj*	de montage identique	*loc*
interchangeable body	*n*	Wechselaufbau	*m*	carrosserie interchangeable	*f*
interconnected braking system	*n*	Kombi-Bremsanlage	*f*	dispositif de freinage combiné	*m*

English

English		German		French	
intercooler	*n*	Ladeluftkühler	*m*	refroidisseur d'air de suralimentation	*m*
intercooling	*n*	Ladeluftkühlung, LLK	*f*	refroidissement de la charge d'air	*m*
interface	*n*	Schnittstelle	*f*	interface	*f*
interference current (EMC)	*n*	Störstrom (EMV)	*m*	courant perturbateur (CEM)	*m*
interference energy (EMC)	*n*	Störenergie (EMV)	*f*	énergie perturbatrice (CEM)	*f*
interference level (EMC)	*n*	Funkstörspannungspegel (EMV)	*m*	niveau de perturbations (CEM)	*m*
interference radiation (EMC)	*n*	Störstrahlung (EMV)	*f*	rayonnement de signaux perturbateurs (CEM)	*m*
interference resistor	*n*	Entstörwiderstand	*m*	résistance d'antiparasitage	*f*
interference suppression	*n*	Funkentstörung	*f*	antiparasitage	*m*
interference wave (EMC)	*n*	Störwelle (EMV)	*f*	onde perturbatrice (CEM)	*f*
interference-suppression category	*n*	Entstörklasse	*m*	classe d'antiparasitage	*f*
interference-suppression choke	*n*	Entstördrossel	*f*	self d'antiparasitage	*f*
interference-suppression level	*n*	Entstörgrad	*n*	degré d'antiparasitage	*m*
interference-suppression resisto	*n*	Entstörwiderstand	*m*	résistance d'antiparasitage	*f*
interference-suppressor	*n*	Entstörmittel	*n*	dispositifs d'antiparasitage	*mpl*
interior light	*n*	Innenleuchte	*f*	éclairage intérieur	*m*
intermediate housing	*n*	Zwischengehäuse	*n*	boîtier intermédiaire	*m*
intermediate inspection (brakes	*n*	Zwischenuntersuchung, ZU (Bremse)	*f*	inspection intermédiaire (frein)	*f*
intermediate piston	*n*	Zwischenkolben	*m*	piston intermédiaire	*m*
intermediate plate	*n*	Zwischenplatte	*f*	plaque intermédiaire	*f*
intermediate ring	*n*	Zwischenring	*m*	disque intermédiaire	*m*
intermediate setting	*n*	Mittelstellung	*f*	position médiane	*f*
intermediate speed	*n*	Zwischendrehzahl	*m*	régime intermédiaire	*m*
intermediate transmission +	*n*	Vorgelege	*n*	réducteur	*m*
intermediate-speed regulation	*n*	Zwischendrehzahlregelung	*f*	régulation de vitesses intermédiaires	*f*
intermediate-speed stop	*n*	Zwischendrehzahlanschlag	*m*	butée de vitesse intermédiaire	*f*
intermittent fuel injection	*n*	intermittierende Kraftstoffeinspritzung	*f*	injection intermittente de carburant	*f*
intermittent-periodic duty (electrical machines)	*n*	Aussetzbetrieb (elektrische Maschinen)	*m*	fonctionnement intermittent (machines électriques)	*m*
intermittent-wiper relay	*n*	Wischintervallrelais	*n*	relais cadenceur d'essuie-glace	*m*
intermittent-wiper switch	*n*	Wischintervallschalter	*m*	commutateur intermittent d'essuie-glace	*m*
internal gear (ring gear)	*n*	Hohlrad	*n*	roue à denture intérieure	*f*
internal-combustion (IC) engin(	*n*	Verbrennungsmotor	*m*	moteur à combustion interne	*m*
internal-gear pump	*n*	Innenzahnradpumpe	*f*	pompe à engrenage intérieur	*f*
internal-shoe brake	*n*	Innenbackenbremse	*f*	frein à segments à expansion interne	*m*
internally ventilated (brake disc)	*pp*	innenbelüftet (Bremsscheibe)	*pp*	ventilation interne (disque de frein)	*f*
intrusion detection (motor vehicle)	*n*	Innenraumüberwachung (Kfz)		surveillance de l'habitacle (véhicule)	*f*

English		German		French	
ionic current	*n*	Ionenstrom	*m*	courant ionique	*m*
iron core	*n*	Eisenkern	*m*	noyau de fer	*m*
iron losses (alternator)	x *npl*	Eisenverluste (Generator)	x *mpl*	pertes fer (alternateur)	x *fpl*
iron yoke (idle actuator)	*n*	Eisenjoch (Leerlaufsteller)	*n*	culasse de fer (actionneur de ralenti)	*f*
isodromous governor	*n*	Isodromregler	*m*	régulateur isodromique	*m*
J					
jacknife (semitrailer unit)	*v*	einknicken (Sattelzug)	*v*	phénomène de mise en "portefeuille" (semi-remorque)	x *m*
jet	*n*	Strahldüse	*f*	buse d'éjection	*f*
Jetronic (electronic fuel injection)	*n*	Jetronic (elektronische Benzineinspritzung)	*f*	Jetronic (injection électronique d'essence)	*m*
K					
key-operated switch (car alarm)	*n*	Schlüsselschalter (Autoalarm)	*m*	interrupteur à clé (alarme auto)	*m*
keyboard	*n*	Bedientastatur	*f*	clavier de commande	*m*
kick-down switch	*n*	Kickdown-Schalter	*m*	contacteur de kickdown	*m*
kinetic energy	*n*	Bewegungsenergie	*f*	énergie cinétique	*f*
kingpin load	*n*	Aufsatteldruck (Sattelschlepper)	*m*	pression d'accouplement	*f*
knee point (characteristic curve)	*n*	Knickpunkt (Kennlinie)	*m*	coude (courbe caractéristique)	*m*
kneeling level (air suspension)	*n*	Kneeling-Niveau (Luftfederung)	x *n*	niveau d'inclinaison (suspension pneumatique)	*m*
kneeling-function (air suspension)	*n*	Kneeling-Funktion (Luftfederung)	x *f*	fonction d'inclinaison (suspension pneumatique)	*f*
knock (IC engine)	*v*	klopfen (Verbrennungsmotor)	x *v*	cliquetis (moteur à combustion)	*m*
knock control	*n*	Klopfregelung	*f*	régulation du cliquetis	*f*
knock inhibitor	*n*	Antiklopfmittel	*n*	agent antidétonant	*m*
knock limit	*n*	Klopfgrenze	*f*	limite de cliquetis	*f*
knock sensor	*n*	Klopfsensor	*m*	capteur de cliquetis	*m*
knock-resistant (fuel)	*adj*	klopffest (Kraftstoff)	*adj*	antidétonant (carburant)	*adj*
L					
laden state (motor vehicle)	*n*	Beladungszustand (Kfz)	*m*	chargement (véhicule)	*m*
lambda closed-loop control	*n*	Lambda-Regelung	*f*	régulation de richesse	*f*
lambda oxygen sensor	*n*	Lambda-Sonde	*f*	sonde de richesse	*f*
lambda program map	*n*	Lambda-Kennfeld	*n*	cartographie de richesse (lambda)	*f*
lambda sensor	*n*	Lambda-Sonde	*f*	sonde de richesse	*f*
laminated armature core	*n*	Ankerpaket	*n*	noyau feuilleté d'induit	*m*
lamination contact	*n*	Lamellenkontakt	*m*	contact à lamelles	*m*
lamp	*n*	Leuchte	*f*	feu	*m*
lamp housing	*n*	Leuchtengehäuse	*n*	boîtier de feu	*m*
lane	*n*	Fahrspur	*f*	trajectoire	*f*
late (retard) adjustment system	*n*	Spät-Verstellsystem	*n*	système de correction "retard"	*m*
latent-pressure test (wheel-brake cylinder)	*n*	Vordruckprüfung (Radzylinder)	*f*	essai de pression pilote (cylindre de roue)	*m*
lateral force	*n*	Seitenführungskraft	*f*	force de guidage latéral	*f*
lateral tire force	*n*	Reifenseitenkraft	*f*	force latérale du pneumatique	*f*

English		German			French	
lateral velocity (vehicle dynamics)	*n*	Quergeschwindigkeit (Kfz-Dynamik)		*f*	vitesse transversale (dynamique d'un véhicule)	*f*
lateral-acceleration sensor (ESP)	*n*	Querbeschleunigungssensor (ESP)		*m*	capteur d'accélération transversale (ESP)	*m*
lateral-force coefficient	*n*	Seitenkraftbeiwert		*m*	coefficient de force latérale	*m*
lead fouling (spark plug)	*n*	Verbleiung (Zündkerze)		*f*	depôt de plomb (bougie)	*m*
lead grid (battery)	*n*	Bleigitter (Batterie)		*n*	grille de plomb (batterie)	*f*
lead storage battery	*n*	Bleibatterie		*f*	accumulateur au plomb	*m*
lead-acid battery	*n*	Bleibatterie		*f*	accumulateur au plomb	*m*
lead-calcium battery	*n*	Blei-Kalzium-Batterie		*f*	batterie plomb-calcium	*f*
leaded (gasoline)	*pp*	verbleit (Benzin)		*pp*	au plomb (essence)	*loc*
leading axle	*n*	Vorlaufachse		*f*	essieu directeur	*m*
leading shoe	*n*	auflaufende Bremsbacke		*f*	mâchoire primaire	*f*
leaf spring	*n*	Blattfeder		*f*	ressort à lames	*m*
leak fuel	*n*	Leckkraftstoff		*m*	carburant de fuite	*m*
leak-fuel quantity	*n*	Leckmenge		*f*	débit de carburant de fuite	*m*
leak-off	*n*	Leckkraftstoff		*m*	carburant de fuite	*m*
leakage	*n*	Leckage	x	*f*	fuite	*f*
leakage current (spark-plug)	*n*	Kriechstrom (Zündkerze)		*m*	courant de fuite (bougie)	*m*
leakage flow	*n*	Leckstrom		*m*	courant de fuite	*m*
leakage losses	*npl*	Leckverlust		*m*	pertes par fuites	*fpl*
leakage path	*n*	Kriechweg		*m*	chemin de fuite	*m*
leakage return	*n*	Leckkraftstoff-Rückführung		*f*	canal de retour des fuites	*m*
leakage-fuel connection	*n*	Leckölanschluß		*m*	raccord d'huile de fuite	*m*
leakage-return duct	*n*	Leckkraftstoff-Rückführung		*f*	canal de retour des fuites	*m*
leakage-return slot	*n*	Leckrückführnut		*f*	rainure de retour des fuites	*f*
lean (air-fuel-mixture)	*adj*	mager (Luft-Kraftstoff-Gemisch)		*adj*	pauvre (mélange air-carburant)	*adj*
lean adjustment (air-fuel mixture)	*n*	Gemischabmagerung		*f*	appauvrissement du mélange	*m*
lean misfire limit, LML	*n*	Laufgrenze		*f*	limite de stabilité du moteur	*f*
lean-burn concept	*n*	Magerkonzept		*n*	concept à mélange pauvre	*m*
lean-burn engine	*n*	Magermotor		*m*	moteur pour mélange pauvre	*m*
lean-off (air-fuel mixture)	*v*	abmagern (Luft-Kraftstoff-Gemisch)		*v*	appauvrir (mélange air-carburant)	*v*
legal requirements	*npl*	gesetzliche Vorschriften		*fpl*	législation	*f*
lens (headlamp)	*n*	Streuscheibe (Scheinwerfer)		*f*	diffuseur (projecteur)	*m*
lens (lamp)	*n*	Lichtscheibe (Leuchte)		*f*	glace de diffusion (feu)	*f*
lens aperture area (lighting)	*n*	Lichtaustrittsfläche (Lichttechnik)		*f*	surface de sortie de la lumière (éclairage)	*f*
level control	*n*	Niveauregelung		*f*	régulation électronique du niveau	*f*
level sensor (air suspension)	*n*	Niveaugeber (Luftfederung)		*m*	capteur de niveau (suspension pneumatique)	*m*
level sensor (in-tank unit)	*n*	Füllstandsgeber (Elektrokraftstoffpumpe)		*m*	capteur de niveau (pompe électrique à carburant)	*m*
lever assembly	*n*	Hebelverband		*m*	groupe de leviers	*m*
license-plate lamp	*n*	Kennzeichenleuchte		*f*	feu d'éclairage de plaque d'immatriculation	*m*

English

English			German			French	
lift-stop		n	Hubanschlag		m	butée de course	f
lifting axle		n	Liftachse		f	essieu relevable	m
lifting gear assembly		n	Hubgetriebe		n	réducteur à course de levée	m
light deflection		n	Lichtablenkung		f	déviation de la lumière	f
light distribution (lighting)		n	Lichtverteilung (Lichttechnik)		f	répartition de la lumière (éclairage)	f
light filter		n	Lichtfilter		n	filtre (projecteur)	m
light pattern (lighting)		n	Lichtverteilung (Lichttechnik)		f	répartition de la lumière (éclairage)	f
light source		n	Leuchtkörper		m	lampe	f
light-dark cutoff (headlamp)		n	Hell-Dunkel-Grenze, HDG (Scheinwerfer)		f	limite entre la clarté et l'obcurité (projecteur)	f
light-dark cutoff contrast (headlamp)		n	Hell-Dunkel-Kontrast (Scheinwerfer)		m	contraste entre clarté et obscurité (projecteur)	m
light-metal housing		n	Leichtmetallgehäuse		n	carter en alliage léger	m
lighting (motor vehicle)		n	Beleuchtung (Kfz)		f	éclairage (automobile)	m
lighting techniques		n	Lichttechnik		f	technique d'éclairage	f
lighting-strip unit		n	Lichtbandeinheit		f	bande d'éclairage	f
limit quantity		n	Grenzmenge		f	débit limite	m
limit speed		n	Grenzdrehzahl		f	régime limite	m
limit stress		n	Grenzbeanspruchung		f	contrainte limite	f
limit temperature		n	Grenztemperatur		f	température limite	f
limp-home	x	n	Notlauf		m	mode dégradé	m
limp-home air		n	Notluft	x	f	débit d'air minimum de secours	m
limp-home function		n	Notfahrfunktion		f	fonction "mode dégradé"	f
limp-home operation		n	Notfahrbetrieb		m	fonctionnement en mode dégradé	m
limp-home position governor		n	Notfahrstellregler		m	régulateur de roulage en mode incidenté	m
line break (braking system)		n	Leitungsbruch (Bremssystem)		m	rupture de conduite (système de freinage)	f
line filter		n	Leitungsfilter		n	filtre de conduite	m
line pressure		n	Leitungsdruck		m	pression dans conduite	f
linear actuator (TCS)		n	Linearsteller (ASR)		m	actionneur linéaire (ASR)	m
lining load		n	Belagbelastung (Bremsbelag)		f	pression d'appui (garniture de frein)	f
lining wear		n	Belagverschleiß		m	usure de garniture de frein	f
lining-wear sensor		n	Verschleißsensor (Bremsbelag)		m	capteur d'usure (garniture de frein)	m
link fork		n	Gelenkgabel		f	fourchette d'articulation	f
linkage (braking system)		n	Übertragungseinrichtung (Bremsanlage)		f	dispositif de transmission (dispositif de freinage)	m
linkage lever		n	Lenkhebel		m	levier articulé	m
Litronic (headlamp system with gaseous-discharge lamp)		n	Litronic (Scheinwerfer mit Gasentladungslampe)		f	Litronic (projecteur avec lampe à décharge)	m
load adjustment		n	Lastverstellung		f	correction à dépression	f
load changes		npl	Lastwechsel		m	variation de la charge	f
load condition		n	Lastzustand		m	état de charge du moteur	m
load control		n	Laststeuerung		f	commande de la charge	f

English		German		French	
load current	*n*	Laststrom	*m*	courant en charge	*m*
load dump (vehicle electrical system)	*n*	Lastabwurf (Bordnetz)	*m*	délestage (circuit de bord)	*m*
load moment	*n*	Lastmoment	*n*	couple de charge	*m*
load sensor (chassis)	*n*	Achslastsensor	*m*	capteur de charge sur essieu	*m*
load sensor (dynamic brake analyzer)	*n*	Kraftmeßeinrichtung (Rollenbremsprüfstand)	*f*	dynamomètre (banc d'essai)	*m*
load sensor (engine management)	*n*	Lastsensor (Motor)	*m*	capteur de charge (moteur)	*m*
load signal	*n*	Lastsignal	*n*	signal de charge	*m*
load switch	*n*	Lastschalter	*m*	commutateur de charge	*m*
load value (braking-force metering)	*n*	Lastgröße (Bremskraftregelung)	*f*	charge (correction automatique de la force de feinage)	*f*
load valve (TCS)	*n*	Lastventil (ASR)	*n*	valve asservie à la charge (ASR)	*f*
load-dependent start of delivery	*n*	lastabhängiger Förderbeginn, LFB	*m*	initiateur de refoulement	*m*
load-dependent start of injection	*n*	lastabhängiger Spritzbeginn	*m*	début d'injection variable en fonction de la charge	*m*
load-proportioning valve	*n*	Last-Leer-Ventil	*n*	valve vide-charge	*f*
load-reversal damping	*n*	Lastschlagdämpfung	*f*	amortissement des à-coups de charge	*m*
load-sensing valve	*n*	Bremskraftregler	*m*	modulateur de freinage	*m*
load-sensitive	*adj*	lastabhängig	*adj*	asservi à la charge	*pp*
locating collar	*n*	Zentrierbund	*m*	épaulement de centrage	*m*
locating pin	*n*	Fixierstift	*m*	broche de positionnement	*f*
lock barrel (special ignition coil)	*n*	Schloßzylinder (Sonderzündspule)	*m*	serrure à barillet (bobine d'allumage spéciale)	*f*
locking differential	*n*	Sperrdifferential	*n*	différentiel autobloquant	*m*
locking point (brakes)	*n*	Blockierdruck	*m*	pression de blocage (frein)	*f*
locking pressure (brakes)	*n*	Blockierdruck	*m*	pression de blocage (frein)	*f*
locking valve	*n*	Verriegelungsventil	*n*	valve de verrouillage	*f*
long-distance interference suppression	*n*	Fernentstörung	*f*	antiparasitage simple	*m*
long-range driving lamp	*n*	Weitstrahlscheinwerfer	*m*	projecteur longue portée	*m*
longitudinal lock (all-wheel-drive)	*n*	Längssperre (Allradantrieb)	*f*	blocage longitudinal (transmission intégrale)	*m*
longitudinal passage	*n*	Längsbohrung	*f*	canal axial	*m*
longitudinal pump axis	*n*	Pumpenlängsachse	*f*	axe longitudinal de la pompe	*m*
longitudinal train (all-wheel drive)	*n*	Längsstrang (Allradantrieb)	*m*	train longitudinal (système de transmission intégrale)	*m*
longitudinal velocity (vehicle dynamics)	*n*	Längsgeschwindigkeit (Kfz-Dynamik)	*f*	vitesse longitudinale (dynamique d'un véhicule)	*f*
loose contact	*n*	Wackelkontakt	*m*	faux contact	*m*
lost time (braking action)	*n*	Verlustzeit (Bremsvorgang)	*f*	temps mort (effet de freinage)	*m*
low beam	*n*	Abblendlicht	*n*	feu de croisement	*m*
low level (air suspension)	*n*	Tiefniveau (Luftfederung)	*n*	niveau bas (suspension pneumatique)	*m*
low stretch (V-belt)	*n*	dehnungsarm (Keilriemen)	*adj*	peu extensible (courroie trapézoïdale)	*loc*

English		German		French	
low wheel (ABS)	*n*	Low-Rad (ABS) x	*n*	roue à sélection "basse" (ABS)	*f*
low-beam headlamp	*n*	Abblendscheinwerfer	*m*	projecteur code	*m*
low-idle integrator	*n*	Leerlaufintegrator	*m*	intégrateur de ralenti	*m*
low-idle setpoint speed	*n*	Leerlauf-Solldrehzahl	*f*	régime consigne de ralenti	*m*
low-idle speed	*n*	untere Leerlaufdrehzahl	*f*	régime minimum à vide	*m*
low-idle stop	*n*	Leerlaufanschlag	*m*	butée de ralenti	*f*
low-idle switch	*n*	Leergasschalter	*m*	contacteur de ralenti	*m*
low-maintenance	*n*	wartungsarm	*adj*	à entretien minimal	*loc*
low-pass filter (ECU)	*n*	Tiefpaßfilter (Steuergerät)	*n*	filtre passe-bas (calculateur)	*m*
low-pressure braking system	*n*	Niederdruck-Bremsanlage	*f*	dispositif de freinage à basse pression	*m*
low-pressure chamber	*n*	Niederdruckraum	*m*	chambre basse pression	*f*
low-pressure delivery	*n*	Niederdruckförderung	*f*	refoulement basse pression	*m*
low-pressure indicator	*n*	Warndruckanzeiger	*m*	indicateur-avertisseur de pression	*m*
low-pressure stage	*n*	Niederdruckteil	*n*	partie basse pression	*f*
low-pressure system	*n*	Niederdruckkreislauf	*m*	circuit basse pression	*m*
low-pressure test (wheel-brake cylinder)	*n*	Niederdruckprüfung (Radzylinder)	*f*	essai de basse pression (cylindre de roue)	*m*
low-pressure warning device (brakes)	*n*	Warndruckeinrichtung (Bremse)	*f*	dispositif d'alerte (frein)	*m*
low-temperature test current (battery)	*n*	Batteriekälteprüfstrom	*m*	courant d'essai au froid (batterie)	*m*
low-temperature viscosity	*n*	Tieftemperaturviskosität	*f*	viscosité à basse température	*f*
low-tone horn	*n*	Tieftonhorn	*n*	avertisseur à tonalité grave	*m*
lower chamber	*n*	Unterkammer	*f*	chambre inférieure	*f*
LPC (lift port closing) actuator	*n*	Vorhubstellwerk	*n*	actionneur de précourse	*m*
LSI circuit (large scale integration)	*n*	Großschaltkreis (Steuergerät)	*m*	circuit à haute intégration (calculateur)	*m*
lube-oil filter	*n*	Ölfilter	*n*	filtre à huile	*m*
lube-oil filter element	*n*	Ölfiltereinsatz	*m*	cartouche de filtre à huile	*f*
lube-oil inlet	*n*	Schmierölzulauf	*m*	arrivée de l'huile de graissage	*f*
lube-oil return	*n*	Schmierölrücklauf	*m*	retour de l'huile de graissage	*m*
lube-oil seal (fuel-injection pump)	*n*	Leckkraftstoffsperre (Einspritzpumpe)	*f*	barrage d'huile (pompe d'injection)	*m*
lubricating pump	*n*	Schmierpumpe	*f*	pompe de graissage	*f*
luminance (lighting)	*n*	Leuchtdichte (Lichttechnik)	*f*	luminance (éclairage)	*f*
luminosity controller (headlamp)	*n*	Helligkeitsregler (Scheinwerfer	*m*	régulateur de luminosité (projecteur)	*m*
luminous flux	*n*	Lichtstrom	*m*	flux lumineux	*m*
luminous intensity	*n*	Lichtstärke	*f*	intensité lumineuse	*f*
luxmeter	*n*	Luxmeter	*n*	luxmètre	*m*
M					
magnet armature	*n*	Magnetanker	*m*	armature d'électro-aimant	*f*
magnetic circuit	*n*	Magnetkreis	*m*	circuit magnétique	*m*
magnetic field	*n*	Magnetfeld	*n*	champ magnétique	*m*
magnetic flux	*n*	Nutzfluß (magnetisch)	*m*	flux magnétique utile	*m*
magnetic leakage	*n*	Streuflußverluste (magnetische	*mpl*	pertes de flux magnétique	*fpl*

English

English		German		French	
magnetic-field sensor	*n*	Magnetfeldsensor	*m*	capteur de champ magnétique	*m*
magnetization loss	*n*	Magnetisierungsverlust	*m*	pertes d'aimantation	*fpl*
magnetizing current	*n*	Erregerstrom	*m*	courant d'excitation	*m*
magnetoresistive sensor	*n*	Feldplattensensor	*m*	capteur magnétorésistif	*m*
main beam	*n*	Fernlicht	*n*	feu de route	*m*
main circuit (alternator)	*n*	Generatorstromkreis	*m*	circuit principal (alternateur)	*m*
main combustion chamber	*n*	Hauptverbrennungsraum	*m*	chambre de combustion principale	*f*
main contact (relay)	*n*	Hauptkontakt (Relais)	*m*	contact principal (relais)	*m*
main injection	*n*	Haupteinspritzung	*f*	injection principale	*f*
main relay	*n*	Hauptrelais	*n*	relais principal	*m*
main stage (peripheral pump)	*n*	Hauptstufe (Peripheralpumpe)	*f*	étage principal (pompe à accélération périphérique)	*m*
main terminal	*n*	Hauptanschluß	*m*	connexion principale	*f*
main-program running time	*n*	Hauptprogrammlaufzeit	*f*	temps opérationnel du programme principal	*m*
main-relay test	*n*	Hauptrelaistest	*m*	test du relais principal	*m*
mains plug	*n*	Netzstecker	*m*	fiche secteur	*f*
maintainance instructions	*npl*	Wartungsvorschrift	*f*	notice d'entretien	*f*
maintenance-free	*adj*	wartungsfrei	*adj*	sans entretien	*loc*
make contact (electrical switch, normally open)	*n*	Schließer (elektrischer Schalter	*m*	contact à fermeture (interrupteur électrique)	*m*
manifold pressure	*n*	Saugrohrdruck	*m*	pression d'admission	*f*
manifold-pressure compensator	*n*	ladedruckabhängiger Vollastanschlag, LDA	*m*	limiteur de richesse	*m*
manifold-wall fuel condensation	*n*	Wandfilmbildung (Saugrohr)	*f*	humidification des parois (collecteur d'admission)	*f*
manipulated variable	*n*	Stellgröße	*f*	grandeur réglante	*f*
manipulated-variable limit	*n*	Stellgrößenbegrenzung	*f*	limitation des grandeurs de correction	*f*
manual	*n*	Handbuch	*n*	manuel	*m*
manual electric control unit, MECU	*n*	Handsteuergerät	*n*	boîtier de commande manuel	*m*
manually shifted transmission	*n*	Handschalt-Getriebe	*n*	boîte de vitesses classique	*f*
manufacturers responsibility	*n*	Produzentenhaftung	*f*	responsabilité du fabricant	*f*
manufacturing date	*n*	Fertigungsdatum	*n*	date de fabrication	*f*
manufacturing defect	*n*	Fertigungsfehler	*m*	défaut de fabrication	*m*
manufacturing information	*n*	Fertigungshinweis	*m*	information de production	*f*
manufacturing release	*n*	Fertigungsfreigabe	*f*	autorisation de fabrication	*f*
map-based control	*n*	Kennfeldregelung	*f*	régulation cartographique	*f*
map-controlled (ignition)	*pp*	kennfeldgesteuert (Zündung)	*pp*	piloté par cartographie (allumage)	*pp*
map-controlled ignition	*n*	Kennfeldzündung	*f*	allumage cartographique	*m*
mark of approval	*n*	Prüfzeichen	*n*	marque d'homologation	*f*
mass moment of inertia	*n*	Massenträgheitsmoment	*n*	moment d'inertie	*m*
master cylinder	*n*	Hauptzylinder	*m*	maître-cylindre de frein	*m*
master cylinder (brakes)	*n*	Geberzylinder (Bremse)	*m*	cylindre capteur (frein)	*m*
master pump	*n*	Förderbeginn-Normal (Einspritzpumpe)	*n*	pompe de référence de début de refoulement	*f*

English

English		German		French	
maximum delivery	*n*	Vollförderung	*f*	débit maximal	*m*
maximum fuel stop	*n*	Vollastanschlag	*m*	butée de débit maximal	*f*
maximum full-load speed	*n*	obere Vollastdrehzahl	*f*	vitesse maximale à pleine charge	*f*
maximum no-load speed	*n*	obere Leerlaufdrehzahl	*f*	vitesse maximale à vide	*f*
maximum sampling time	*n*	Abtastzeitmaxima	*npl*	temps maximum de détection (régulateur)	*m*
maximum speed	*n*	obere Leerlaufdrehzahl	*f*	vitesse maximale à vide	*f*
maximum-speed governor	*n*	Enddrehzahlregler	*m*	régulateur de vitesse maximale	*m*
maximum-speed regulation (fuel-injection pump)	*n*	Endabregelung (Einspritzpumpe)	*f*	coupure de vitesse maximale (pompe d'injection)	*f*
maximum-speed spring	*n*	Endregelfeder	*f*	ressort de régulation de vitesse maximale	*m*
measurement weight	*n*	Meßgewicht	*n*	poids de mesure	*m*
measuring and control unit	*n*	Meß- und Steuereinheit	*f*	bloc de mesure et de command‹	*m*
measuring cell (exhaust-gas test)	*n*	Meßküvette (Abgasprüfung)	*f*	cuvette de mesure (émissions)	*f*
measuring chamber (exhaust-gas test)	*n*	Meßkammer (CO-Gas)	*f*	chambre de mesure (gaz CO)	*f*
measuring element	*n*	Meßelement	*n*	élément de mesure	*m*
measuring sensor (dynamic brake analyzer)	*n*	Meßwertsensor (Rollenbremsprüfstand)	*m*	capteur de mesure (banc d'essai)	*m*
measuring-data acquisition	*n*	Meßdatenerfassung	*f*	saisie des mesures	*f*
mechanical connection	*n*	Wirkverbindung	*f*	liaison mécanique	*f*
mechanical governor	*n*	Fliehkraftregler	*m*	régulateur mécanique	*m*
mechanical linkage	*n*	Wirkverbindung	*f*	liaison mécanique	*f*
mechanical release (spring-type brake actuator)	*n*	Löseeinrichtung (Federspeicherzylinder)	*f*	dispositif de desserrage (cylindre à accumulateur élastique)	*m*
mechanical shutoff device	*n*	mechanische Abstellvorrichtung, MEAB	*f*	dispositif d'arrêt mécanique	*m*
mechanically controlled starting quantity	*n*	mechanisch entriegelte Startmenge	*f*	surcharge à déverrouillage mécanique	*f*
medium voltage, MV	*n*	Mittelspannung	*f*	tension moyenne	*f*
memory circuit (dynamic brake analyzer)	*n*	Speicherschaltung (Rollenbremsprüfstand)	*f*	circuit de mémorisation (banc d'essai)	*m*
mesh (starter pinion)	*v*	einspuren (Starterritzel)	*v*	engrènement (pignon)	*m*
meshed container	*n*	Gitterbox	*f*	conteneur à claire-voie	*m*
meshing drive	*n*	Einspurgetriebe	*n*	lanceur	*m*
meshing resistance (starter)	*n*	Einrückwiderstand (Starter)	*m*	résistance à l'engrènement (démarreur)	*f*
meshing spring	*n*	Einspurfeder	*f*	ressort d'engrènement	*m*
meshing system	*n*	Einspursystem	*n*	système d'engrènement	*m*
message format (CAN)	*n*	Botschaftsformat (CAN)	*n*	format de message (multiplexage)	*m*
metal jacket (ignition coil)	*n*	Mantelblech (Zündspule)	*n*	enveloppe à lamelles (bobine d'allumage)	*f*
metal mesh (catalytic converter	*n*	Metallgeflecht (Katalysator)	*n*	grille métallique (catalyseur)	*f*
metal screening cover	*n*	Metallabschirmkappe	*f*	blindage métallique	*m*
meter	*v*	Dosierung	*f*	dosage	*m*

English

English		German		French	
metering accuracy	*n*	Zumeßgenauigkeit	*f*	précision de dosage	*f*
metering function	*n*	Zumeßfunktion	*f*	fonction de dosage	*f*
metering point	*n*	Zumeßstelle	*f*	point de dosage	*m*
metering sleeve	*n*	Zumeß-Schieber	*m*	bague de dosage	*f*
metering slot	*n*	Steuerschlitz	*m*	fente d'étranglement (piston)	*f*
metering spill (fuel-injection pump)	*n*	Auslaßventil (Einspritzpumpe)	*n*	soupape de dosage (pompe d'injection)	*f*
microcontroller, MC (ECU)	*n*	Mikrocontroller, MC (Steuergerät)	*m*	microcontrôleur (calculateur)	*m*
micromechanics	*npl*	Mikromechanik	*f*	micromécanique	*f*
microprocessor, MP (ECU)	*n*	Mikrocontroller, MC (Steuergerät)	*m*	microcontrôleur (calculateur)	*m*
microrelay	*n*	Mikrorelais	*n*	microrelais	*m*
mineral-oil-based brake fluid	*n*	Mineralöl-Bremsflüssigkeit	*f*	liquide de frein à base d'huile minérale	*m*
minimum braking effect	*n*	Mindestbremswirkung	*f*	freinage minimal	*m*
minimum full-load speed	*n*	untere Vollastdrehzahl	*f*	régime inférieur de pleine charge	*m*
minimum retardation	*n*	Mindestabbremsung	*f*	taux de freinage minimum	*m*
minimum speed	*n*	Mindestdrehzahl	*f*	vitesse de rotation minimale	*f*
minimum starting speed	*n*	Startmindestdrehzahl	*f*	régime minimum de démarrage	*m*
minimum starting temperature	*n*	Startgrenztemperatur	*f*	température limite de démarrage	*f*
minimum-maximum-speed governor	*n*	Leerlauf- und Enddrehzahlregler	*m*	régulateur mini-maxi	*m*
minimum-value operator	*n*	Minimalwertoperator	*m*	opérateur à valeur minimale	*m*
minirelay	*n*	Kleinrelais	*n*	petit relais	*m*
mirror adjuster	*n*	Spiegelverstellung	*f*	réglage de rétroviseur	*m*
mirror adjusting system	*n*	Spiegelverstellsystem	*n*	système de réglage des rétroviseurs	*m*
mirror heating	*n*	Spiegelheizung	*f*	chauffage de rétroviseur	*m*
misfiring	*n*	Zündaussetzer	*m*	ratés d'allumage	*mpl*
mixture adaptation	*n*	Gemischanpassung	*f*	adaptation du mélange	*f*
mixture composition	*n*	Gemischzusammensetzung	*f*	composition du mélange	*f*
mixture distribution	*n*	Gemischverteilung	*f*	répartition du mélange	*f*
mixture enrichment	*n*	Gemischanreicherung	*f*	enrichissement du mélange	*m*
mixture formation	*n*	Gemischaufbereitung	*f*	préparation du mélange	*f*
mixture ignition point	*n*	Entflammungszeitpunkt	*m*	point d'inflammation	*m*
mixture turbulence	*n*	Gemischturbulenz	*f*	turbulence du mélange	*f*
mixture-control unit (Jetronic)	*n*	Gemischregler (Jetronic)	*m*	régulateur de mélange (Jetronic)	*m*
mobile communications	*npl*	Mobile Kommunikation	*f*	communications mobiles	*fpl*
modified individual control, IRM (ABS)	*n*	modifizierte Individual-regelung, IRM (ABS)	*f*	régulation individuelle modifiée (ABS)	*f*
modular system	*n*	Modultechnik	*f*	technique modulaire	*f*
modulation pressure (transmission control)	*n*	Modulationsdruck (Getriebesteuerung)	*m*	pression de modulation (commande de boîte de vitesses)	*f*
molecular filter (air drier)	*n*	Molekularfilter (Lufttrockner)	*n*	filtre moléculaire (dessiccateur)	*m*

English		German		French	
moment of ignition	*n*	Zündzeitpunkt	*m*	point d'allumage	*m*
momentary switch	*n*	Tastschalter	*m*	interrupteur à touche	*m*
monitoring circuit	*n*	Überwachungsschaltung	*f*	circuit de surveillance	*m*
monitoring module	*n*	Überwachungsmodul	*m*	module de surveillance	*m*
monitoring software	*n*	Überwachungssoftware	*f*	logiciel de surveillance	*m*
monolith (catalytic converter)	*n*	Monolith (Katalysator)	*m*	support monolythique (catalyseur)	*m*
monolithic regulator	*n*	Monolithregler	*m*	régulateur monolithe	*m*
monolithic techniques	*npl*	Monolithtechnik	*f*	technique monolithe	*f*
motion detector (car alarm)	*n*	Bewegungsdetektor (Autoalarm)	*m*	détecteur de mouvement (alarme auto)	*m*
motive force	*n*	Antriebskraft	*f*	force motrice	*f*
motor armature (electric fuel pump)	*n*	Motoranker (Elektrokraftstoffpumpe)	*m*	induit du moteur (pompe électrique à carburant)	*m*
motor octane number, MON	*n*	Motor-Oktanzahl, MOZ	*f*	indice d'octane moteur, MON	*m*
motor relay (ABS)	*n*	Motorrelais (ABS)	*n*	relais de commande de moteur (ABS)	*m*
motor-and-gear assembly	*n*	Getriebemotor	*m*	motoréducteur	*m*
motor-vehicle brakes	*npl*	Kraftfahrzeugbremsen	*fpl*	freins d'un véhicule à moteur	*mpl*
motor-vehicle lamp	*n*	Kraftfahrzeugleuchte	*f*	feu (véhicule automobile)	*m*
Motronic (electronic engine management)	*n*	Motronic (elektronische Motorsteuerung)	*f*	Motronic (système électronique de gestion du moteur)	*m*
mounting bracket	*n*	Befestigungslasche	*f*	patte de fixation	*f*
mounting flange	*n*	Befestigungsflansch	*m*	bride de fixation	*f*
moving iron actuator	*n*	Dreheisenstellwerk	*n*	commande à noyau de ferrite rotatif	*f*
multi-circuit braking system	*n*	Mehrkreis-Bremsanlage	*f*	dispositif de freinage à circuits multiples	*m*
Multi-Focus-Reflector, MFR	*n*	Multi-Focus-Reflektor, MFR	*m*	réflecteur multifocal	*m*
multi-line braking system	*n*	Mehrleitungs-Bremsanlage	*f*	dispositif de freinage à conduites multiples	*m*
multi-orifice metering	*n*	Mehrlochzumessung (Einspritzventil)	*f*	dosage multitrous (injecteur)	*m*
multi-orifice nozzle	*n*	Mehrlochdüse	*f*	injecteur multitrous	*m*
multi-plunger pump	*n*	Mehrzylinder-Einspritzpumpe	*f*	pompe multicylindrique	*f*
multi-tract runner	*n*	Mehrfachschwingrohr	*n*	collecteur d'admission multitubes	*m*
multifuel engine	*n*	Mehrstoffmotor	*m*	moteur polycarburant	*m*
multifuel operation	*n*	Mehrstoffbetrieb	*m*	fonctionnement polycarburant	*m*
multifuel pump	*n*	Mehrstoffpumpe	*f*	pompe polycarburant	*f*
multihole nozzle	*n*	Mehrlochdüse	*f*	injecteur multitrous	*m*
multiplate clutch	*n*	Lamellenkupplung	*f*	embrayage multidisques	*m*
multiple-circuit protection valve	*n*	Mehrkreisschutzventil	*n*	valve de sécurité multicircuits	*f*
multiple-compartment lamp	*n*	Mehrkammerleuchte	*f*	feu à plusieurs compartiments	*m*
multiple-disc clutch	*n*	Lamellenkupplung	*f*	embrayage multidisques	*m*
multiple-plunger pump	*n*	Mehrzylinder-Einspritzpumpe	*f*	pompe multicylindrique	*f*
multiplicative adjustment	*n*	multiplikativer Abgleich	*m*	étalonnage multiplicatif	*m*
multiplying stage (ECU)	*n*	Multiplizierstufe (elektronisches Steuergerät)	*f*	étage multiplicateur (calculateur)	*m*

English		German		French	
multipoint fuel injection, MPI	*n*	Einzeleinspritzung	*f*	injection multipoint	*f*
multipoint injection, MPI	*n*	Einzeleinspritzung	*f*	injection multipoint	*f*
multipurpose lamp	*n*	Vielzweckleuchte	*f*	baladeuse	*f*
multistage filter	*n*	Stufenfilter	*n*	filtre à étages	*m*
multivibrator	*n*	Multivibrator	*m*	multivibrateur	*m*
muscular force (brake control)	*n*	Muskelkraft (Bremsbetätigung)	*f*	force musculaire (commande de frein)	*f*
muscular-energy braking system	*n*	Muskelkraft-Bremsanlage	*f*	dispositif de freinage à énergie musculaire	*m*
N					
nameplate	*n*	Typenschild	*n*	plaque signalétique	*f*
narrow-band interference	*n*	Schmalbandstörung	*f*	perturbation à bande étroite	*f*
natural frequency	*n*	Eigenfrequenz	*f*	fréquence propre	*f*
naturally aspirated engine	*n*	Saugmotor	*m*	moteur à aspiration naturelle	*m*
navigation system	*n*	Navigationssystem	*n*	système de navigation	*m*
navigation system (motor vehicle)	*n*	Navigationssystem (Kfz)	*n*	système de navigation (automobile)	*m*
NC contact (electrical switch, normally closed)	*n*	Öffner (elektrischer Schalter)	*m*	contact à ouverture (interrupteur électrique)	*m*
needle closing force	*n*	Nadelschließkraft	*f*	force de fermeture de l'aiguille	*f*
needle guide	*n*	Nadelführung	*f*	guide-aiguille	*m*
needle lift	*n*	Nadelhub	*m*	levée de l'aiguille	*f*
needle valve	*n*	Nadelventil	*n*	injecteur à aiguille	*m*
needle valve (in a closed nozzle)	*n*	Düsennadel	*f*	aiguille d'injecteur	*f*
needle-lift sensor	*n*	Nadelhubgeber	*m*	capteur de levée d'aiguille	*m*
needle-motion sensor	*n*	Nadelbewegungssensor	*m*	capteur de déplacement d'aiguille	*m*
needle-movement sensor	*n*	Nadelbewegungssensor	*m*	capteur de déplacement d'aiguille	*m*
needle-velocity sensor, NVS	*n*	Nadelgeschwindigkeitsfühler	*m*	capteur de vitesse d'aiguille	*m*
negative diode	*n*	Minusdiode	*f*	diode négative	*f*
negative electrode (battery)	*n*	Minusplatte (Batterie)	*f*	plaque négative (batterie)	*f*
negative offset (trailer brake)	*n*	Nacheilung (Anhängerbremse)	*f*	retard de phase (frein de remorque)	*m*
negative plate (battery)	*n*	Minusplatte (Batterie)	*f*	plaque négative (batterie)	*f*
negative steering offset	*n*	negativer Lenkrollradius	*m*	déport négatif de l'axe du pivot de fusée	*m*
negative temperature coefficient, NTC	*n*	negativer Temperaturkoeffizient, NTC	*m*	coefficient de température négatif, CTN	*m*
negative torque control	*n*	negative Angleichung	*f*	correction de débit négative	*f*
neutral conductor	*n*	Mittelleiter	*m*	conducteur neutre	*m*
neutral point	*n*	Sternpunkt	*m*	point neutre	*m*
neutral steer (motor vehicle)	*v*	neutralsteuern (Kfz)	*v*	neutre (conduite de véhicule en virage)	*adj*
NO contact (electrical switch, normally open)	*n*	Schließer (elektrischer Schalter	*m*	contact à fermeture (interrupteur électrique)	*m*
no-follow speed	*n*	Abspringdrehzahl	*f*	régime de décrochage	*m*
no-load charcteristic	*n*	Leerlaufkennlinie	*f*	caractéristique à vide	*f*

English		German		French	
noise encapsulation	*n*	Geräuschkapselung	*f*	encapsulage antibruit	*m*
noise level	*n*	Geräuschpegel	*m*	niveau de bruit	*m*
noise suppression	*n*	Geräuschminderung	*f*	atténuation du bruit	*f*
noise-emission level (fan)	*n*	Abstrahlgrad (Lüfter)	*m*	degré de rayonnement sonore (ventilateur)	*m*
noise-level test	*n*	Geräuschprüfung	*f*	essai de niveau sonore	*m*
noise-level test bench	*n*	Geräuschprüfstand	*m*	banc d'essai acoustique	*m*
nominal capacity (battery)	*n*	Nennkapazität (Batterie)	*f*	capacité nominale (batterie)	*f*
nominal current	*n*	Sollstrom	*m*	courant nominal	*m*
nominal load	*n*	Nennlast	*f*	charge nominale	*f*
nominal load torque	*n*	Nenndrehmoment	*n*	couple nominal	*m*
nominal pressure	*n*	Nenndruck	*m*	pression nominale	*f*
nominal rpm	*n*	Nenndrehzahl	*f*	vitesse de rotation nominale	*f*
nominal voltage	*n*	Nennspannung	*f*	tension nominale	*f*
non-Bosch product	*n*	Fremderzeugnis	*n*	produit d'autre marque	*m*
non-governed range	*n*	ungeregelter Bereich	*m*	plage non régulée	*f*
non-leak-off nozzle	*n*	lecköllose Düse	*f*	injecteur sans retour de fuite	*m*
non-locking switch	*n*	Tastschalter	*m*	interrupteur à touche	*m*
non-muscular-energy braking system	*n*	Fremdkraft-Bremsanlage	*f*	dispositif de freinage à énergie non musculaire	*m*
non-polluting	*ppr*	umweltfreundlich	*adj*	compatible avec l'environnement	*loc*
non-return valve	*n*	Rückschlagventil	*n*	clapet de non-retour	*m*
normal force	*n*	Normalkraft	*f*	force normale	*f*
normal level (air suspension)	*n*	Normalniveau (Luftfederung)	*n*	niveau normal (suspension pneumatique)	*f*
normally closed (NC) contact	*n*	Öffner (elektrischer Schalter)	*m*	contact à ouverture (interrupteur électrique)	*m*
normally open (NO) contact	*n*	Schließer (elektrischer Schalter	*m*	contact à fermeture (interrupteur électrique)	*m*
noxious constituents	*npl*	Schadstoffanteil	*m*	taux de polluants	*m*
noxious substances (exhaust gas)	*npl*	Schadstoffe (Motorabgas)	*mpl*	polluants (gaz d'échappement)	*mpl*
nozzle (diesel fuel injection)	*n*	Einspritzdüse	*f*	injecteur (injection diesel)	*m*
nozzle (windshield washer)	*n*	Spritzdüse (Scheibenwaschanlage)	*f*	gicleur (lavophare)	*m*
nozzle axis	*n*	Düsenachse	*f*	axe d'injecteur	*m*
nozzle body	*n*	Düsenkörper	*m*	corps d'injecteur	*m*
nozzle chamber	*n*	Düsenraum	*m*	chambre d'injecteur	*f*
nozzle coking	*n*	Düsenverkokung	*f*	calaminage des injecteurs	*m*
nozzle cone	*n*	Düsenkuppe	*f*	buse d'injecteur	*f*
nozzle holder	*n*	Düsenhalter	*m*	porte-injecteur	*m*
nozzle hole	*n*	Spritzloch	*n*	trou d'injection	*m*
nozzle jet	*n*	Düsenstrahl (vor der Auflösung)	*m*	jet	*m*
nozzle needle	*n*	Düsennadel	*f*	aiguille d'injecteur	*f*
nozzle pressure chamber	*n*	Druckkammer (Einspritzdüse)	*f*	chambre de pression (injecteur)	*f*
nozzle seat	*n*	Düsensitz	*m*	siège d'injecteur	*m*
nozzle spring	*n*	Düsenfeder	*f*	ressort d'injecteur	*m*

English

English		German		French	
nozzle stem	n	Düsenschaft	m	fût d'injecteur	m
nozzle-and-holder assembly	n	Düsenhalterkombination, DHK	f	ensemble injecteur/porte-injecteur	m
nozzle-holder assembly	n	Düsenhalter	m	porte-injecteur	m
nozzle-needle seat	n	Düsennadelsitz	m	siège de l'aiguille d'injecteur	m
nozzle-opening pressure	n	Düsenöffnungsdruck	m	pression d'ouverture de l'injecteur	f
nozzle-retaining nut	n	Düsenspannmutter	f	écrou-raccord d'injecteur	m
nozzle-seat diameter	n	Sitzdurchmesser (Düse)	m	diamètre du siège d'injecteur	m
nozzle-valve opening pressure	n	Düsenöffnungsdruck	m	pression d'ouverture de l'injecteur	f
NTC resistor	n	NTC-Widerstand	m	thermistance CTN	f
number of coils	n	Windungszahl	f	nombre de tours des spires de l'enroulement	m
number of poles	n	Polzahl	f	nombre de pôles	m
number of switching operations	n	Schaltzahl	f	nombre de cycles de commutation	m
number-plate lamp	n	Kennzeichenleuchte	f	feu d'éclairage de plaque d'immatriculation	m
O					
occupant-protection system	n	Insassenschutzsystem	n	système de protection des passagers	m
octane number	n	Oktanzahl, OZ	f	indice d'octane	m
off-state characteristic	n	Sperrkennlinie	f	caractéristique à l'état bloqué	f
off-state voltage (semiconductor)	n	Sperrspannung (Halbleiter)	f	tension à l'état bloqué (semi-conducteur)	f
oil block (fuel-injection pump)	n	Leckkraftstoffsperre (Einspritzpumpe)	f	barrage d'huile (pompe d'injection)	m
oil separator	n	Ölabscheider	m	séparateur d'huile	m
oil-bath air filter	n	Ölbadluftfilter	n	filtre à air à bain d'huile	m
oil-block groove	n	Sperrnut	f	rainure de barrage	f
oil-return pump	n	Ölrückförderpumpe	f	pompe de retour d'huile	f
on period	n	Einschaltdauer	f	durée d'enclenchement	f
on-board computer	n	Bordcomputer	m	ordinateur de bord	m
on-board diagnostics, OBD	n	Onboard-Diagnose, OBD x	f	diagnostic de bord	m
on-state characteristic (rectifier diode)	n	Durchlaßkennlinie (Gleichrichterdiode)	f	caractéristique tension-courant à l'état passant (diode redresseuse)	f
on/off ratio	n	Tastverhältnis	n	rapport cyclique d'impulsions	m
one-piece cover (battery)	n	Blockdeckel (Batterie)	m	couvercle de batterie	m
opacimeter	n	Lichtabsorptionsmeßgerät	n	opacimètre	m
opacity	n	Trübung	f	opacité	f
open control loop	n	Steuerkette	f	chaîne de commande	f
open flank (V-belt)	n	flankenoffen (Keilriemen)	adj	à flanc ouvert (courroie trapézoïdale)	loc
open-type design	n	offene Bauweise	f	version ouverte	f
opening pressure	n	Öffnungsdruck	m	pression d'ouverture	f
opening time (fuel injector)	n	Öffnungsdauer (Einspritzventil)	f	durée d'ouverture (injecteur)	f
operating frequency	n	Betriebsfrequenz	f	fréquence d'utilisation	f

English		German		French	
operating instructions	*npl*	Bedienungsanleitung	*f*	notice d'utilisation	*f*
operating limits	*n*	Betriebsgrenzwert	*m*	valeurs limites de fonctionnement	*fpl*
operating parameter	*n*	Betriebsparameter	*m*	paramètre de fonctionnement	*m*
operating pressure	*n*	Betriebsdruck	*m*	pression de service	*f*
operating range	*n*	Schaltspanne	*f*	écart de réglage	*m*
operating speed	*n*	Betriebsdrehzahl	*f*	vitesse de fonctionnement	*f*
operating state	*n*	Betriebszustand	*m*	conditions de fonctionnement	*fpl*
operating temperature	*n*	Betriebstemperatur	*f*	température normale de fonctionnement	*f*
operating time	*n*	Einschaltdauer	*f*	durée d'enclenchement	*f*
operating valve	*n*	Steuerventil	*n*	valve de commande	*f*
operating voltage	*n*	Betriebsspannung	*f*	tension de service	*f*
operating-data module	*n*	Datenmodul	*m*	module de données	*m*
operating-data processing	*n*	Betriebsdatenverarbeitung	*f*	traitement des paramètres de fonctionnement	*m*
operational amplifier, OPA	*n*	Operationsverstärker, OPV	*m*	amplificateur opérationnel	*m*
operator unit	*n*	Bedienteil	*n*	clavier opérateur	*m*
opposed-pattern wiper system	*n*	Gegenlaufsystem (Scheibenwischer)	*n*	système antagoniste (essuie-glace)	*m*
optical waveguide	*n*	Lichtwellenleiter	*m*	fibre optique	*f*
orifice check valve	*n*	Rückströmdrosselventil	*n*	soupape de frein de réaspiratior	*f*
orifice plate	*n*	Lochplatte	*f*	pastille perforée	*f*
oscillatory intake passage	*n*	Schwingsaugrohr	*n*	collecteur d'admission à oscillation	*m*
otto engine	*n*	Ottomotor	*m*	moteur à allumage par étincelle	*m*
out-sourcing	*n*	Fremdbezug	*m*	origine étrangère	*f*
outer rim (headlamp)	*n*	Abdeckrahmen (Scheinwerfer)	*m*	collerette (projecteur)	*f*
outer tower (ignition distributor)	*n*	Außendom (Zündverteiler)	*m*	cheminée (allumeur)	*f*
outlet	*n*	Auslaß	*m*	sortie	*f*
outlet bore (electric fuel pump)	*n*	Abflußbohrung (Elektrokraftstoffpumpe)	*f*	canal de sortie (pompe électrique à carburant)	*m*
outlet cross-section	*n*	Ausflußquerschnitt	*m*	section d'écoulement	*f*
output (braking force)	*v*	aussteuern (Bremskraft)	*v*	piloter (force de freinage)	*v*
output circuit (ECU)	*n*	Ausgangsschaltung (Steuergerät)	*f*	circuit de sortie (calculateur)	*m*
output pressure (brake booster)	*n*	Aussteuerdruck (Bremskraftverstärker)	*m*	pression maximale (servofrein)	*f*
output stage (ECU)	*n*	Leistungsendstufe (Steuergerät)	*f*	étage de sortie (calculateur)	*m*
output throttle	*n*	Ablaufdrossel	*f*	étranglement de sortie	*m*
output voltage	*n*	Ausgangsspannung	*f*	tension de sortie	*f*
over-enrich (air-fuel mixture)	*v*	überfetten (Luft-Kraftstoff-Gemisch)	x *v*	surenrichir (mélange air-carburant)	*v*
over-enrichment	*n*	Überfettung	x *f*	mélange trop riche	*m*
overbrake	*v*	überbremsen	*v*	surfreiner	*v*
overcharge (battery) <noun>	*n*	Überladung (Batterie)	*f*	surcharge (batterie)	*f*
overcharge (battery) <to overcharge>	*v*	überladen (Batterie)	*v*	surcharger (batterie)	*v*

English		German			French	
overflow line	*n*	Überströmleitung		*f*	conduite de décharge	*f*
overflow metering valve	*n*	Überströmdosierventil		*n*	soupape de dosage de débit de retour	*f*
overflow orifice	*n*	Überströmbohrung		*f*	orifice de balayage	*m*
overflow pressure regulator	*n*	Überströmdruckregler		*m*	régulateur de pression à trop-plein	*m*
overflow principle	*n*	Überströmprinzip		*n*	principe de décharge	*m*
overflow quantity (fuel-injection pump)	*n*	Überlaufmenge (Einspritzpumpe)		*f*	débit de balayage (pompe d'injection)	*m*
overflow restriction	*n*	Überströmdrossel		*f*	calibrage de décharge	*m*
overflow throttle valve	*n*	Überströmdrosselventil		*n*	soupape de décharge à calibrage	*f*
overflow valve	*n*	Überströmventil		*n*	valve de décharge	*f*
overheat (brakes)	*v*	heißfahren (Bremse)		*v*	surchauffer (frein)	*v*
overheat protection	*n*	Überhitzungsschutz		*m*	protection de surchauffage	*f*
overheat-protection quantity	*n*	Kochschutzmenge		*f*	volume de protection anti-ébullition	*m*
overlap (metering slits)	*n*	Überdeckung (Steuerschlitze)		*f*	chevauchement (fentes d'étranglement)	*m*
overpressure nipple	*n*	Überdrucknippel		*m*	raccord de surpression	*m*
overrun	*n*	Schiebebetrieb		*m*	régime de décélération	*m*
overrun braking system	*n*	Auflauf-Bremsanlage		*f*	dispositif de freinage à inertie	*m*
overrun fuel cutoff	*n*	Schubabschaltung		*f*	coupure d'injection en décélération	*f*
overrun fuel-cutoff valve	*n*	Schubabschaltventil		*n*	électrovalve de coupure en décélération	*f*
overrunning clutch (starter)	*n*	Freilaufgetriebe (Starter)		*n*	lanceur (à roue libre)	*m*
overspeed	*n*	Überdrehzahl		*f*	surrégime	*m*
overspeed (IC engine)	*v*	durchgehen (Verbrennungsmotor)	x	*v*	emballer <s'emballer> (moteur à combustion)	*v*
overspeed protection	*n*	Überdrehzahlschutz		*m*	protection de surrégime	*f*
overspeed switch	*n*	Überdrehschalter		*m*	commande de surrégime	*f*
overspeed test	*n*	Schleuderprüfung		*f*	essai de dérapage	*m*
oversteer (motor vehicle)	*v*	übersteuern (Kfz)		*v*	survirage (véhicule)	*m*
overvoltage protection	*n*	Überspannungsschutz		*m*	protection contre les surtension:	*f*
overvoltage-protection device	*n*	Überspannungsschutzgerät		*n*	dispositif de protection contre les surtensions	*m*
oxidation catalytic converter	*n*	Oxydationskatalysator		*m*	catalyseur d'oxydation	*m*
oxygen sensor	*n*	Lambda-Sonde		*f*	sonde de richesse	*f*
P						
panic alarm (car alarm)	*n*	Panikalarm (Autoalarm)		*m*	alarme panique (alarme auto)	*f*
panic braking	*n*	Panikbremsung		*f*	freinage en situation de panique	*m*
panic stop	*n*	Panikbremsung		*f*	freinage en situation de panique	*m*
paper air filter	*n*	Papierluftfilter		*n*	filtre à air en papier	*m*
paper element (air filter)	*n*	Papiereinsatz (Luftfilter)		*m*	élément filtrant en papier (filtre à air)	*m*
paper element (fuel filter)	*n*	Papierwickel (Kraftstoffilter)		*m*	rouleau de papier (filtre à carburant)	*m*
paper tube (filter)	*n*	Wickelkörper (Filter)		*m*	corps de filtre	*m*

English

English		German			French	
parallel connection	n	Parallelschaltung		f	montage en parallèle	m
parallel diode	n	Parallel-Diode		f	diode parallèle	f
parallel filter	n	Parallelfilter		n	filtre en parallèle	m
parallel operation (alternators)	n	Parallelbetrieb (Generatoren)		m	couplage en parallèle (alternateurs)	m
parallelogram wiper arm	n	Parallelogramm-Wischarm		m	bras d'essuie-glace à parallélogramme	m
park braking system	n	Feststell-Bremsanlage		f	dispositif de freinage de stationnement	m
Park Pilot	n	Park-Pilot		m	guide de parcage	m
parking lamp	n	Parkleuchte		f	feu de stationnement	m
parking lamp	n	Parklicht		n		
parking socket (trailer ABS)	n	Parkdose (Anhänger-ABS)	x	f	prise de stationnement (ABS pour remorque)	f
parking-brake circuit	n	Feststellbremskreis		m	circuit de freinage de stationnement	m
parking-brake system	n	Feststell-Bremsanlage		f	dispositif de freinage de stationnement	m
parking-brake valve	n	Feststellbremsventil		n	valve de frein de stationnement	f
parking-brake-applied position	n	Feststellbremsstellung		f	position de freinage de stationnement	f
part load (IC engine)	n	Teillast (Verbrennungsmotor)		f	charge partielle (moteur à combustion)	f
part number	n	Bestellnummer		f	référence	f
part-load range	n	Teillastbereich		m	plage de charge partielle	f
part-load speed	n	Teillastdrehzahl		f	vitesse à charge partielle	f
part-throttle operation (IC engine)	n	Teillast (Verbrennungsmotor)		f	charge partielle (moteur à combustion)	f
partial braking	n	Teilbremsung		f	freinage partiel	m
partial braking pressure	n	Teilbremsdruck		m	pression de freinage partielle	f
partial delivery	n	Teilförderung		f	débit partiel	m
partial voltage	n	Teilspannung		f	tension partielle	f
partially braked mode	n	Teilbremsstellung		f	position de freinage partiel	f
particle size (filter)	n	Teilchengröße (Filter)		f	taille de particule (filtre)	f
particulate emission	n	Partikelemission		f	émission de particules	f
particulate filter	n	Rußfilter		n	filtre pour particules de suie	m
particulates test result (diesel smoke)	n	Feststoff-Testergebnis (Dieselrauch)		n	résultat du test de particules (fumées diesel)	m
parts list	n	Stückliste		f	nomenclature	f
parts set	n	Teilesatz		m	kit de pièces	m
passenger airbag	n	Beifahrerairbag		m	coussin gonflable côté passager	m
patter (radio disturbance)	v	prasseln (Funkstörung)	x	v	crépitement (perturbation)	m
pavement irregularity	n	Ungleichförmigkeit (Fahrbahn)		f	défaut d'uniformité (route)	m
PC board	n	Leiterplatte		f	carte à circuit imprimé	f
PC-board relay	n	Leiterplattenrelais		n	relais pour cartes imprimées	m
peak coil current	n	Ruhestrom		m	courant de repos	m
peak injection pressure	n	Spitzendruck		m	pression de pointe	f
peak load	n	Spitzenbelastung		f	charge de pointe	f
peak voltage	n	Scheitelspannung		f	tension de crête	f

English

English		German		French	
peak-value level	*n*	Spitzenwertpegel	*m*	niveau de valeur de pointe	*m*
pedal positioner (braking-system inspection)	*n*	Pedalstütze (Bremsenprüfung)	*f*	positionneur de pédale de frein (contrôle des freins)	*m*
pedal stop	*n*	Pedalanschlag	*m*	butée d'arrêt de la pédale	*f*
pedal-position sensor	*n*	Fahrpedalsensor	*m*	capteur d'accélérateur	*m*
pedal-travel sensor	*n*	Fahrpedalsensor	*m*	capteur d'accélérateur	*m*
pelleted substrate (catalytic converter)	*n*	Schüttgutträger (Katalysator)	*m*	support à billes (catalyseur)	*m*
perforated plate (auxiliary-air device)	*n*	Lochblende (Zusatzluftschieber)	*f*	diaphragme (commande d'air additionnel)	*m*
performance drop	*n*	Leistungsverlust	*m*	perte de puissance	*f*
performance specs	*n*	Pflichtenheft	*n*	cahier des charges	*m*
period duration	*n*	Periodendauer	*f*	durée de période	*f*
period of use	*n*	Betriebsdauer	*f*	durée de fonctionnement	*f*
peripheral pump	*n*	Peripheralpumpe	*f*	pompe à accélération périphérique	*f*
permanent load	*n*	Dauerverbraucher	*m*	récepteur permanent	*m*
permanent magnet	*n*	Permanentmagnet	*m*	aimant permanent	*m*
permanent-magnet excitation	*n*	Permanentmagneterregung	*f*	excitation par aimant permanent	*f*
permanent-magnet field	*n*	Permanentfeld	*n*	excitation permanente	*f*
permissible total weight	*n*	Gesamtgewichtskraft	*f*	poids total admissible	*m*
PES headlamp	*n*	Poly-Ellipsoid-Scheinwerfer, PES	*m*	projecteur polyellipsoïde	*m*
petrol	*n*	Ottokraftstoff	*m*	essence	*f*
phase angle	*n*	Phasenwinkel	*m*	phase d'une grandeur sinusoïdale	*f*
phase current	*n*	Phasenstrom	*m*	courant de phase	*m*
phase displacement	*n*	Phasenverschiebung	*f*	déphasage (entre deux grandeurs sinusoïdales)	*m*
phase matching	*n*	Phasenabstimmung	*f*	ajustement des phases	*m*
phase sensor	*n*	Phasensensor	*m*	capteur de phase	*m*
phase winding	*n*	Wicklungsstrang	*m*	faisceau d'enroulements	*m*
phasing	*n*	Versatz	*m*	phasage	*m*
phasing (plunger-and-barrel assembly)	*n*	Förderabstand (Pumpenelement)	*m*	phasage (élément de pompage)	*m*
pickoff brush (potentiometer)	*n*	Bürstenschleifer (Potentiometer)	*m*	balai de captage (potentiomètre	*m*
pickup	*n*	Sensor	*m*	capteur	*m*
pickup time (fuel injector)	*n*	Anzugszeit (Einspritzventil)	*f*	durée d'attraction (injecteur)	*f*
piercing-tip terminal	*n*	Stechspitzenanschluß	*m*	connexion à pointes d'enfichage	*f*
piezo-ceramic strip	*n*	Piezokeramikstreifen	*m*	lame piézocéramique	*f*
piezoelectric sensor	*n*	Vibrationssensor	*m*	capteur de vibrations	*m*
pilot chamber	*n*	Steuerkammer	*f*	chambre de commande	*f*
pilot control (commercial-vehicle ABS)	*n*	Vorsteuerung (Nfz-ABS)	*f*	pilotage (ABS pour véhicules utilitaires)	*m*
pilot injection	*n*	Voreinspritzung	*f*	injection pilote	*f*
pilot run	*n*	Nullserie	*f*	série pilote	*f*
pilot valve (ABS, TCS)	*n*	Umschaltventil (ABS/ASR)	*n*	vanne d'inversion (ABS/ASR)	*f*

English		German		French	
pilot valve (constant-pressure valve)	*n*	Vorlaufventil (Dieseleinspritzung)	*n*	clapet-pilote (injection diesel)	*m*
pilot valve (load-sensing valve)	*n*	Vorsteuerventil (Bremskraftregler)	*n*	valve pilote (modulateur de freinage)	*f*
pin housing	*n*	Stiftgehäuse	*n*	boîtier à contacts mâles	*m*
pin receptable	*n*	Rundsteckerhülse	*f*	fiche femelle ronde	*f*
pin terminal	*n*	Rundstecker	*m*	fiche ronde	*f*
pinion advance (starter)	*n*	Ritzelvorschub	*m*	avance du pignon (démarreur)	*f*
pinion rotation	*n*	Ritzelverdrehung	*f*	rotation du pignon	*f*
pinion shaft	*n*	Ritzelschaft	*m*	queue de pignon	*f*
pinion tooth	*n*	Ritzelzahn	*m*	dent du pignon	*f*
pinion travel	*n*	Einspurhub	*m*	course d'engrènement	*f*
pinion-engaging drive	*n*	Einspurgetriebe	*n*	lanceur	*m*
Pintaux-type nozzle	*n*	Pintaux-Düse	*f*	injecteur Pintaux	*m*
pintle	*n*	Spritzzapfen	*m*	téton d'injection	*m*
pintle nozzle	*n*	Zapfendüse	*f*	injecteur à téton	*m*
pipe sealing cone	*n*	Rohrdichtkegel	*m*	cône d'étanchéité du tube	*m*
piston (disc brake)	*n*	Druckkolben (Scheibenbremse)	*m*	piston (frein à disque)	*m*
piston accumulator	*n*	Kolbenspeicher	*m*	accumulateur à piston	*m*
piston cylinder	*n*	Kolbenzylinder	*m*	cylindre à piston	*m*
piston displacement (IC engine)	*n*	Hubvolumen (Verbrennungsmotor)	*n*	cylindrée (moteur à combustion)	*f*
piston force	*n*	Kolbenkraft	*f*	force de piston	*f*
piston gas accumulator (TCS)	*n*	Gaskolbenspeicher (ASR)	*m*	accumulateur de gaz à piston (ASR)	*m*
piston injection pump	*n*	Hubkolbeneinspritzpumpe	*f*	pompe d'injection à piston	*f*
piston recess	*n*	Kolbenmulde	*f*	cavité du piston	*f*
piston rod	*n*	Kolbenstange	*f*	tige de piston	*f*
piston seizure	*n*	Kolbenfresser	*m*	grippage de piston	*m*
piston-recess wall	*n*	Muldenwand	*f*	paroi de la cavité du piston	*f*
piston-ring groove	*n*	Kolbenringnut	*f*	rainure annulaire de piston	*f*
pitch (motor vehicle)	*v*	aufschaukeln (Kfz)	*v*	oscillation croissante (véhicule)	*f*
pitch angle (vehicle dynamics)	*n*	Nickwinkel (Kfz-Dynamik)	*m*	angle de tangage (dynamique d'un véhicule)	*m*
pitting	*n*	Kontaktabbrand	*m*	érosion des contacts	*f*
pivot	*n*	Drehpunkt	*m*	centre de rotation	*m*
pivoting armature	*n*	Drehanker	*m*	induit rotatif	*m*
planar Lambda sensor	*n*	planare Lambda Sonde	*f*	sonde lambda planaire	*f*
planet gear	*n*	Planetenrad	*n*	roue planétaire	*f*
planetary gear	*n*	Planetengetriebe	*n*	train épicycloïdal	*m*
planetary-gear carrier	*n*	Planetenträger	*m*	support d'engrenage planétaire	*m*
planetary-gear system	*n*	Planetenradsystem	*n*	système de roues planétaires	*m*
plate cam	*n*	Kurvenplatte	*f*	plaque à came	*f*
plate strap (battery)	*n*	Plattenverbinder (Batterie)	*m*	barrette de jonction des plaques (batterie)	*f*
plate valve	*n*	Plattenventil	*n*	plaque-soupape mobile	*f*
platinum center electrode (spark plug)	*n*	Platinmittelelektrode (Zündkerze)	*f*	électrode centrale en platine (bougie)	*f*

English

English		German		French	
plot	*v*	plotten	*v*	tracer	*v*
plotter	*n*	Plotter	*m*	traceur	*m*
plug code	*n*	Steckercodierung	*f*	codage des fiches	*m*
plug connector	*n*	Steckverbindung	*f*	connecteur	*m*
plug gap	*n*	Elektrodenabstand (Zündkerze)	*m*	écartement des électrodes (bougie)	*m*
plug gauge	*n*	Stecklehre	*f*	calibre	*m*
plug socket	*n*	Steckerbuchse	*f*	contact femelle	*m*
plug-in connection	*n*	Steckverbindung	*f*	connecteur	*m*
plunger chamber (fuel-injection pump)	*n*	Druckraum (Einspritzpumpe)	*m*	chambre de refoulement (pompe d'injection)	*f*
plunger control arm	*n*	Kolbenfahne (Pumpenkolben)	*f*	entraîneur (piston de pompe)	*m*
plunger lift	*n*	Kolbenhub	*m*	course du piston	*f*
plunger lift to cutoff port closing	*n*	Kolbenhub bis Förderbeginn (Vorhub des Pumpenkolbens)	*m*	précourse du piston (jusqu'au début de refoulement)	*f*
plunger lift to port closing	*n*	Vorhub (Pumpenkolben)	*m*	précourse (piston de pompe)	*f*
plunger lift to spill-port opening	*n*	Kolbenhub bis Förderende (Pumpenkolben)	*m*	course du piston en fin de refoulement (piston de pompe)	*f*
plunger passage	*n*	Kolbenbohrung (Pumpenkolben)	*f*	alésage de piston (piston de pompe)	*m*
plunger return spring	*n*	Kolbenfeder (Pumpenkolben)	*f*	ressort de rappel du piston (piston de pompe)	*m*
plunger return stroke	*n*	Kolbenrücklauf (Pumpenkolben)	*m*	course de retour du piston (piston de pompe)	*f*
plunger travel	*n*	Kolbenhub	*m*	course du piston	*f*
plunger-and-barrel assembly (fuel-injection pump)	*n*	Pumpenelement (Einspritzpumpe)	*n*	élément de pompage (pompe d'injection)	*m*
plunger-and-barrel head	*n*	Elementkopf (Pumpenelement)	*m*	tête de l'élément de pompage	*f*
plunger-type pressure regulator	*n*	Kolbendruckregler	*m*	régulateur de pression à piston	*m*
plunger-type valve	*n*	Kolbenventil (Pumpenkolben)	*n*	soupape à piston (piston de pompe)	*f*
pneumatic idle-speed increase	*n*	pneumatische Leerlaufanhebung, PLA	*f*	accélérateur pneumatique de ralenti	*m*
pneumatic line	*n*	Pneumatikleitung	*f*	conduite pneumatique	*f*
pneumatic shutoff device	*n*	pneumatische Abstellvorrichtung, PNAB	*f*	dispositif d'arrêt pneumatique	*m*
pneumatic suspension	*n*	Luftfederanlage	*f*	dispositif de suspension pneumatique	*m*
pneumatic suspension	*n*	Luftfederung	*f*	suspension pneumatique	*f*
pneumatic-brake circuit	*n*	Pneumatikbremskreis	*m*	circuit de freinage pneumatique	*m*
pneumatic-brake system	*n*	pneumatische Bremsanlage	*f*	dispositif de freinage pneumatique	*m*
point of injection	*n*	Abspritzstelle	*f*	point d'injection	*m*
pole body	*n*	Polkern	*m*	noyau polaire	*m*
pole core	*n*	Polkern	*m*	noyau polaire	*m*
pole finger	*n*	Polfinger	*m*	extrémité polaire	*f*
pole half	*n*	Klauenpol	*m*	plateau à griffes	*m*
pole pass	*n*	Poldurchgang	*m*	passage de pôle	*m*
pole pitch	*n*	Polteilung	*f*	pas polaire	*m*

English

English		German		French	
pole shoe	*n*	Polschuh	*m*	épanouissement polaire	*m*
pole wheel	*n*	Polrad	*n*	roue polaire	*f*
pole-wheel half	*n*	Polradhälfte	*f*	demi-roue polaire	*f*
pollutant component	*n*	Schadstoffkomponente	*f*	polluant	*m*
pollutant emission	*n*	Schadstoffausstoß	*m*	émission de polluants	*f*
pollutants (exhaust gas)	*npl*	Schadstoffe (Motorabgas)	*mpl*	polluants (gaz d'échappement)	*mpl*
polyphase winding	*n*	Mehrphasenwicklung	*f*	enroulement multiphases	*m*
pore size (filter)	*n*	Porengröße (Filter)	*f*	porosité (filtre)	*f*
port opening (fuel-injection pump)	*n*	Förderende (Einspritzpumpe)	*n*	fin de refoulement (pompe d'injection)	*f*
port-and-helix control	*n*	Schrägkantensteuerung	*f*	commande par rampe inclinée	*f*
port-and-helix metering	*n*	Steuerkanten-Zumessung	*f*	dosage par rampe et trou	*m*
port-closing sensor	*n*	Förderbeginngeber, FBG	*m*	capteur de début de refoulemen	*m*
position control loop (throttle)	*n*	Lageregelkreis (Drosselklappe)	*m*	circuit de régulation de position (papillon)	*m*
position feedback (TCS servomotor)	*n*	Positionsrückmeldung (ASR-Stellmotor)	*f*	confirmation de positionnement (servomoteur ASR)	*f*
position pick-up	*n*	Lagesensor	*m*	capteur de position	*m*
position sensor	*n*	Lagesensor	*m*	capteur de position	*m*
positioning cylinder (TCS)	*n*	Stellzylinder (ASR)	*m*	cylindre positionneur (ASR)	*m*
positioning rate	*n*	Stellgeschwindigkeit	*f*	vitesse de régulation	*f*
positive diode	*n*	Plusdiode	*f*	diode positive	*f*
positive electrode (battery)	*n*	Plusplatte (Batterie)	*f*	plaque positive (batterie)	*f*
positive plate (battery)	*n*	Plusplatte (Batterie)	*f*	plaque positive (batterie)	*f*
positive torque control	*n*	positive Angleichung	*f*	correction de débit positive	*f*
positive-displacement pump	*n*	Verdrängerpumpe	*f*	pompe volumétrique	*f*
positive-displacement supercharger	*n*	Verdrängerlader	*m*	compresseur volumétrique	*m*
post-delivery effect	*n*	Nachfördereffekt	*m*	effet de post-refoulement	*m*
post-glow	*n*	nachglühen	*v*	post-incandescence	*f*
post-glow time	*n*	Nachglühzeit	*f*	temps de post-incandescence	*m*
post-ignition	*n*	Nachentflammung	*f*	post-allumage	*m*
post-injection	*n*	nachspritzen	*v*	post-injection	*f*
post-start enrichment	*n*	Nachstartanreicherung	*f*	enrichissement de post-démarrage	*m*
post-start phase	*n*	Nachstartphase	*f*	phase de post-démarrage	*f*
potentiometer	*n*	Potentiometer	*m*	potentiomètre	*m*
potentiometer track	*n*	Potentiometerbahn	*f*	piste de potentiomètre	*f*
powder coated	*pp*	pulverbeschichtet	*pp*	revêtement de poudre	*m*
powder-based paint	*n*	Pulverlack	*m*	laque à base de poudre	*f*
power cycle	*n*	Arbeitstakt	*m*	temps moteur	*m*
power demand	*n*	Verbraucherleistung	*f*	puissance des récepteurs	*f*
power diode	*n*	Leistungsdiode	*f*	diode de puissance	*f*
power input	*n*	Leistungsaufnahme	*f*	puissance absorbée	*f*
power module	*n*	Leistungsmodul	*m*	module de puissance	*m*
power on/off damper	*n*	Lastschlag-Dämpfer	*m*	amortisseur d'à-coups de charge	*m*

English		German		French	
power output (electrical machines)	n	Leistungsabgabe (elektrische Maschinen)	f	puissance débitée (machines électriques)	f
power relay	n	Leistungsrelais	n	relais de puissance	m
power section (ignition system)	n	Leistungsteil (Zündsystem)	n	bloc de puissance (allumage)	m
power stage (ECU)	n	Leistungsstufe (Steuergerät)	f	étage de puissance (calculateur)	m
power steering	n	Servolenkung	f	direction assistée	f
power supply	n	Spannungsversorgung	f	alimentation en tension	f
power transistor	n	Leistungstransistor	m	transistor de puissance	m
power zone (carbon brush)	n	Leistungszone (Kohlebürste)	f	partie puissance (balai)	f
power-assisted braking system	n	Hilfskraft-Bremsanlage	f	dispositif de freinage assisté par énergie auxiliaire	m
power-brake system	n	Fremdkraft-Bremsanlage	f	dispositif de freinage à énergie non musculaire	m
power-steering pump	n	Lenkhilfpumpe	f	pompe de direction assistée	f
power-sunroof drive	n	Schiebedachantrieb	m	entraînement du toit ouvrant	m
power-sunroof drive unit	n	Schiebedachantrieb	m	entraînement du toit ouvrant	m
power-window control	n	Fensterhebersteuerung	f	commande de lève-vitres	f
power-window drive	n	Fensterantrieb	m	entraînement de lève-vitre	m
power-window motor	n	Fensterhebermotor	m	moteur de lève-vitre	m
power-window unit	n	Fensterheber	m	lève-vitre	m
power/space ratio (winding technique)	n	Ausnutzungsgrad (Wickeltechnik)	m	rendement (technique d'enroulement)	m
powered axle	n	Antriebsachse	f	essieu moteur	m
powered wheel (motor vehicle)	n	Antriebsrad (Kfz)	n	roue motrice (véhicule)	f
pre-braking distance (braking action)	n	Verlustweg (Bremswirkung)	m	course morte (effet de freinage)	f
pre-combustion	n	Vorverbrennung	f	précombustion	f
pre-delivery effect	n	Vorfördereffekt	m	effet de prérefoulement	m
pre-delivery quantity	n	Vorfördermenge	f	débit de prérefoulement	m
pre-engaged-drive starter	n	Schub-Schraubtrieb-Starter	m	démarreur à commande positive électromécanique	m
pre-excitation (rotating machines)	n	Vorerregung (drehende Maschinen)	f	pré-excitation (machines tournantes)	f
pre-excitation circuit	n	Vorerregerstromkreis	m	circuit d'amorçage	m
pre-excitation magnetic field	n	Vorerregermagnetfeld	n	champ magnétique d'amorçage	m
pre-filter	n	Vorfilter (Lufttrockner)	n	préfiltre (dessiccateur)	m
pre-glow indicator	n	Vorglühanzeige	f	témoin de préchauffage	m
pre-glow relay (diesel engine)	n	Vorglühgerät	n	appareil de préchauffage (moteur diesel)	m
pre-governing	n	Vorabregelung	f	précoupure	f
pre-heating rate	n	Aufheizgeschwindigkeit	m	vitesse de chauffe	f
pre-ignition	n	Vorentflammung	f	pré-allumage	m
pre-injection characteristic	n	Voreinspritzverlauf	m	évolution de la préinjection	f
pre-loaded (spring)	pp	vorgespannt (Feder)	pp	taré (ressort)	pp
prechamber	n	Vorkammer	f	préchambre	f
prechamber engine	n	Vorkammermotor	m	moteur à préchambre	m
precombustion chamber	n	Vorkammer	f	préchambre	f
precombustion-chamber engine	n	Vorkammermotor	m	moteur à préchambre	m

English		German		French	
precontrol logic	*n*	Vorsteuerlogik	*f*	logique de pilotage	*f*
preheat	*v*	vorglühen	*v*	préchauffage	*m*
preheating curve	*n*	Aufheizkurve	*f*	courbe de chauffe	*f*
preheating sequence	*n*	Glühzeitablauf	*m*	période de préchauffage	*f*
preheating time	*n*	Vorglühdauer	*f*	durée de préchauffage	*f*
preinjection	*n*	Voreinspritzung	*f*	injection pilote	*f*
preliminary filter (air drier)	*n*	Vorfilter (Lufttrockner)	*n*	préfiltre (dessiccateur)	*m*
preliminary filter (fuel-supply pump)	*n*	Vorreiniger	*m*	préfiltre (pompe d'alimentation)	*m*
preliminary filter (Jetronic)	*n*	Vorabscheider (Jetronic)	*m*	préséparateur (Jetronic)	*m*
preliminary-filter element	*n*	Vorfiltereinsatz	*m*	cartouche filtrante primaire	*f*
press-in diode	*n*	Einpreßdiode	*f*	diode emmanchée	*f*
pressure actuator	*n*	Drucksteller	*m*	actionneur manométrique	*m*
pressure area	*n*	Druckbereich	*m*	plage de pression	*f*
pressure build-up time (braking)	*n*	Schwelldauer (Bremsvorgang)	*f*	temps d'accroissement (freinage)	*m*
pressure build-up time (braking)	*n*	Schwellzeit (Bremsvorgang)	*f*	temps de montée en pression (freinage)	*m*
pressure buildup	*n*	Druckaufbau	*m*	montée en pression	*f*
pressure chamber (brakes)	*n*	Druckraum (Bremse)	*m*	chambre de compression (frein)	*f*
pressure chamber (fuel-pressure regulator)	*n*	Federkammer (Kraftstoffdruckregler)	*f*	chambre à ressort (amortisseur de pression du carburant)	*f*
pressure chamber (injection nozzle)	*n*	Druckkammer (Einspritzdüse)	*f*	chambre de pression (injecteur)	*f*
pressure characteristic	*n*	Druckverlauf	*m*	courbe de pression	*f*
pressure compensation	*n*	Druckausgleich	*m*	compensation de pression	*f*
pressure connection	*n*	Druckanschluß	*m*	raccord de pression	*m*
pressure connection (fuel-injection pump)	*n*	Druckanschluß (Einspritzpumpe)	*m*	raccord de refoulement (pompe d'injection)	*m*
pressure control	*n*	Druckregelung	*f*	régulation de pression	*f*
pressure damper (Jetronic)	*n*	Kraftstoffdruckdämpfer (Jetronic)	*m*	amortisseur de pression du carburant (Jetronic)	*m*
pressure delivery (compressed air)	*n*	Druckförderung (Druckluft)	*f*	refoulement (air comprimé)	*m*
pressure diecasting	*v*	druckgießen	*v*	mouler sous pression	*v*
pressure differential	*n*	Druckdifferenz	*f*	différence de pression	*f*
pressure drop	*n*	Druckabbau	*m*	chute de pression	*f*
pressure drop (fuel)	*n*	Druckgefälle (Kraftstoff)	*n*	perte de charge (carburant)	*f*
pressure gauge	*n*	Druckmesser	*m*	manomètre	*m*
pressure generator (TCS)	*n*	Druckversorgung (ASR)	*f*	générateur de pression (ASR)	*m*
pressure hose	*n*	Druckschlauch	*m*	flexible de pression	*m*
pressure lead (braking pressure)	*n*	Voreilung (Bremsdruck)	*f*	à avance de pression	*loc*
pressure limiter	*n*	Druckbegrenzer	*m*	limiteur de pression	*m*
pressure loss	*n*	Druckverlust	*m*	perte de pression	*f*
pressure modulation	*n*	Bremsdruckmodulation	*f*	modulation de la force de freinage	*f*
pressure modulator (ABS)	*n*	Druckmodulator (ABS)	*m*	modulateur de pression (ABS)	*m*
pressure outlet (filter)	*n*	Druckseite (Filter)	*f*	côté refoulement (filtre)	*m*
pressure passage	*n*	Druckkanal	*m*	canal de refoulement	*m*

English		German		French	
pressure pin	*n*	Druckbolzen	*m*	tige-poussoir	*f*
pressure pin (throttling-pintle nozzle)	*n*	Druckzapfen (Drosselzapfendüse)	*m*	téton de pression (injecteur à téton et étranglement)	*m*
pressure pin (two-spring nozzle holder)	*n*	Druckstift (Zweifeder-Düsenhalter)	*m*	poussoir (porte-injecteur à deux ressorts)	*m*
pressure plate (brakes)	*n*	Druckplatte (Bremse)	*f*	plateau de pression (frein)	*m*
pressure point (crosswind)	*n*	Druckpunkt (Seitenwind)	*m*	centre de pression (vent latéral)	*m*
pressure point (parking-brake valve)	*n*	Druckpunkt (Feststellbremsventil)	*m*	point de pression (valve de frein de stationnement)	*m*
pressure pulsation	*n*	Druckschwingung	*f*	pulsation de pression	*f*
pressure pump (windshield washer)	*n*	Druckpumpe (Scheibenspüler)	*f*	pompe de refoulement (lave-glace)	*f*
pressure reduction	*n*	Druckabbau	*m*	chute de pression	*f*
pressure regulating valve (ABS)	*n*	Drucksteuerventil (ABS)	*n*	valve modulatrice de pression (ABS)	*f*
pressure regulator	*n*	Druckregler	*m*	régulateur de pression	*m*
pressure relief	*n*	Druckentlastung	*f*	délestage de pression	*m*
pressure relief valve	*n*	Druckablaßventil	*n*	soupape de décharge	*f*
pressure rise	*n*	Druckaufbau	*m*	montée en pression	*f*
pressure roller (wedge brake)	*n*	Druckrolle (Keilbremse)	*f*	galet de pression (frein à coin)	*m*
pressure sensor	*n*	Drucksensor	*m*	capteur de pression	*m*
pressure switch	*n*	Druckschalter	*m*	manocontact	*m*
pressure test connection (compressed-air brake)	*n*	Prüfanschluß (Druckluftbremse)	*m*	raccord d'essai (frein à air comprimé)	*m*
pressure transmitter	*n*	Drucksensor	*m*	capteur de pression	*m*
pressure variation	*n*	Druckschwankung	*f*	variation de pression	*f*
pressure wave	*n*	Druckwelle	*f*	onde de pression	*f*
pressure-buildup valve (ELB)	*n*	Hochtaktventil (ELB)	*n*	valve à impulsions progressives (ELB)	*f*
pressure-charge fuel-delivery quantity	*n*	Lademenge	*f*	débit de suralimentation	*m*
pressure-charging (IC engine)	*n*	Aufladung (Verbrennungsmotor)	*f*	suralimentation (moteur à combustion)	*f*
pressure-charging regulator	*n*	Ladedruckregler	*m*	régulateur de pression de suralimentation	*m*
pressure-compensation disc (nozzle)	*n*	Druckausgleichscheibe (Einspritzdüse)	*f*	cale de réglage de pression (injecteur)	*f*
pressure-contact switch	*n*	Drucksprungschalter	*m*	contacteur à bond de pression	*m*
pressure-control module	*n*	Druckregelmodul, DRM	*m*	modulateur de pression	*m*
pressure-control valve	*n*	Druckregelventil	*n*	soupape modulatrice de pression	*f*
pressure-control valve (ABS)	*n*	Drucksteuerventil (ABS)	*n*	valve modulatrice de pression (ABS)	*f*
pressure-correction map	*n*	Druckkorrekturkennfeld	*n*	cartographie de correction de pression	*f*
pressure-equalization element	*n*	Druckausgleichselement	*n*	compensateur de pression	*m*
pressure-holding phase (ABS)	*n*	Druckhaltephase (ABS)	*f*	stade de maintien de la pression (ABS)	*m*
pressure-holding valve (ABS)	*n*	Halteventil (ABS)	*n*	valve de maintien (ABS)	*f*

English		German		French	
pressure-holding valve (diesel fuel injection)	*n*	Druckhalteventil (Dieseleinspritzung)	*n*	soupape de maintien de la pression (injection diesel)	*f*
pressure-limiting valve	*n*	Druckbegrenzer	*m*	limiteur de pression	*m*
pressure-reduction step (ABS)	*n*	Druckabbaustufe (ABS)	*f*	palier de baisse de pression (ABS)	*m*
pressure-regulator valve block	*n*	Druckregler-Ventilblock	*m*	bloc-valves de régulateur de pression	*m*
pressure-relief element	*n*	Druckbegrenzer	*m*	limiteur de pression	*m*
pressure-sensitive	*adj*	druckabhängig	*adj*	asservi à la pression	*pp*
pressure-valve stem	*n*	Kolbenschaft (Druckventil)	*m*	tige de piston (clapet de refoulement)	*f*
pressure-wave supercharger	*n*	Druckwellenlader	*m*	échangeur de pression	*m*
pressure-wave supercharging	*n*	Druckwellenaufladung	*f*	suralimentation par ondes de pression	*f*
prestroke	*n*	Vorhub (Pumpenkolben)	*m*	précourse (piston de pompe)	*f*
prestroke adjustment	*n*	Vorhubeinstellung	*f*	réglage de la précourse	*m*
presupply pump	*n*	Vorförderpumpe	*f*	pompe de pré-alimentation	*f*
primary cup seal	*n*	Primärmanschette	*f*	manchette primaire	*f*
primary current (alternator)	*n*	Hauptstrom (Generator)	*m*	courant principal (alternateur)	*m*
primary line (ignition system)	*n*	Primärleitung (Zündanlage)	*f*	câble de circuit primaire (allumage)	*m*
primary pressure (brakes)	*n*	Vorratsdruck (Bremse)	*m*	pression d'alimentation (frein)	*f*
primary pressure (Jetronic)	*n*	Systemdruck (Jetronic)	*m*	pression du système (Jetronic)	*f*
primary resistance	*n*	Primärwiderstand	*m*	résistance de l'enroulement primaire	*f*
primary side	*n*	Primärseite	*f*	côté primaire	*m*
primary winding	*n*	Primärwicklung	*f*	enroulement primaire	*m*
primary-pressure regulator	*n*	Systemdruckregler	*m*	régulateur de pression du système	*m*
prime (car alarm)	*v*	schärfen (Autoalarm)	*v*	mise en veille (alarme auto)	*f*
priming (car alarm)	*n*	Scharfschaltung (Autoalarm)	*f*	amorçage (alarme auto)	*m*
printed-circuit board	*n*	Leiterplatte	*f*	carte à circuit imprimé	*f*
problem area	*n*	Schwachstelle	*f*	point faible	*m*
product development	*n*	Produktentwicklung	*f*	développement des produits	*m*
product liability	*n*	Produkthaftung	*f*	responsabilité produit	*f*
product specification	*n*	Produktspezifikation	*f*	spécification du produit	*f*
production location	*n*	Fertigungsstandort	*m*	lieu de production	*m*
program map	*n*	Kennfeld	*n*	cartographie	*f*
program module	*n*	Programmodul	*m*	module de programme	*m*
project drawing	*n*	Angebotszeichnung	*f*	plan d'offre	*m*
project management	*n*	Projektmanagement	*n*	gestion de projet	*f*
projection optics (headlamp)	*npl*	Projektionsoptik (Scheinwerfer	*f*	optique de projection (projecteur)	*f*
proportionality factor	*n*	Proportionalgrad	*m*	statisme	*m*
proportioning valve (brakes)	*n*	Bremsdruckminderer	*m*	réducteur de pression de freinage	*m*
proportioning valve (TCS)	*n*	Proportionalventil (ASR)	*n*	valve proportionnelle (ASR)	*f*
propshaft torque	*n*	Kardanwellenmoment	*n*	couple de l'arbre à cardan	*m*
protection against manipulation	*n*	Manipulationsschutz	*m*	protection contre manipulation	*f*

English

English		German		French	
protection hood	*n*	Schutzhaube	*f*	capot de protection	*m*
protection valve (brakes)	*n*	Schutzventil (Bremse)	*n*	valve de sécurité (frein)	*f*
protective bellows	*n*	Schutzbalg	*m*	soufflet de protection	*m*
protective cap	*n*	Schutzkappe	*f*	couvercle de protection	*m*
protective circuit	*n*	Schutzschaltung	*f*	circuit de protection	*m*
protective conductor	*n*	Schutzleiter	*m*	conducteur de protection	*m*
protective relay	*n*	Schutzrelais	*n*	relais de protection	*m*
protective unit (ECU)	*n*	Schutzeinheit (Steuergerät)	*f*	module de protection (calculateur)	*m*
proteted against polarity reversal	*pp*	verpolungssicher	*adj*	insensible à l'inversion de polarité	*loc*
prototype manufacture	*n*	Musterbau	*m*	réalisation d'échantillons	*f*
pull switch	*n*	Zugschalter	*m*	interrupteur à tirette (alarme auto)	
pull-in technique (winding)	*n*	Einziehtechnik (Wicklung)	*f*	tréfilage (enroulement)	*m*
pull-in winding	*n*	Einzugswicklung	*f*	enroulement d'appel	*m*
pull-off force	*n*	Abzugskraft	*f*	force d'extraction	*f*
pulling electromagnet	*n*	Zugmagnet	*m*	électro-aimant de traction	*m*
pulsating-voltage motor	*n*	Mischspannungsmotor	*m*	moteur à tension composée	*m*
pulse divider	*n*	Impulsteiler	*m*	diviseur d'impulsions	*m*
pulse generator	*n*	Impulsgeber	*m*	générateur d'impulsions	*m*
pulse shaper	*n*	Impulsformer	*m*	conformateur d'impulsions	*m*
pulse turbocharging	*v*	Stoßaufladung	*f*	suralimentation pulsatoire	*f*
pulse valve	*n*	Taktventil	*n*	électrovanne à rapport cyclique d'ouverture	*f*
pulse width modulated, PWM	*pp*	pulsweitenmoduliert	*adj*	modulé en largeur d'impulsion	*pp*
pulse-controlled (pressure)	*pp*	pulsierend (Drucksteuerung)	*ppr*	par impulsions (modulation de pression)	*loc*
pulse-generator trigger	*n*	Trigger-Impulsgeber	*m*	capteur de synchronisme	*m*
pulse-generator voltage	*n*	Geberspannung	*f*	tension du générateur d'impulsions	*f*
pulse-shaping circuit	*n*	Impulsformer	*m*	conformateur d'impulsions	*m*
pulsing (pressure control)	*v*	pulsen (Drucksteuerung)	*v*	par impulsion (pilotage de pression)	*loc*
pump barrel (fuel-injection pump)	*n*	Pumpenzylinder (Einspritzpumpe)	*m*	cylindre de pompe (pompe d'injection)	*m*
pump ECU	*n*	Pumpensteuergerät	*n*	calculateur pompe	*m*
pump element (ABS hydraulic modulator)	*n*	Pumpenelement (ABS-Hydroaggregat)	*n*	élément de pompage (groupe hydraulique ABS)	*m*
pump housing	*n*	Pumpengehäuse	*n*	corps de pompe	*m*
pump interior	*n*	Pumpenraum	*m*	intérieur de la pompe	*m*
pump interior pressure	*n*	Pumpendruck	*m*	pression à l'intérieur de la pompe	*f*
pump map	*n*	Pumpenkennfeld	*n*	cartographie de pompe	*f*
pump motor (ABS hydraulic modulator)	*n*	Pumpenmotor (ABS-Hydroaggregat)	*m*	moteur de pompe (groupe hydraulique ABS)	
pump plunger (fuel-injection pump)	*n*	Pumpenkolben (Einspritzpumpe)	*m*	piston de pompe (pompe d'injection)	*m*
pump power take-off	*n*	Pumpenabtrieb	*m*	côté sortie de la pompe	*m*

English		German			French	
pump size	*n*	Pumpengröße		*f*	taille de pompe	*f*
pump-side pressure	*n*	Elementdruck		*m*	pression dans l'élément	*f*
pumping element	*n*	Pumpenelement (Einspritzpumpe)		*n*	élément de pompage (pompe d'injection)	*m*
pumping-assembly barrel	*n*	Elementzylinder		*m*	cylindre d'élément de pompage	*m*
pumping-element plunger	*n*	Elementkolben		*m*	piston d'élément de pompage	*m*
pumping-element bushing	*n*	Elementbuchse		*f*	douille d'élément de pompage	*f*
pumping-element head	*n*	Elementkopf (Pumpenelement)		*m*	tête de l'élément de pompage	*f*
purge	*v*	entlüften		*v*	dégazage	*m*
purge air	*n*	Spülluft		*f*	air de balayage	*m*
push (out to the side, vehicle)	*v*	schieben (Fahrzeug, beim Lenken)	x	*v*	pousser (voiture, en braquage)	*v*
push rod (brake booster)	*n*	Druckstange (Bremskraftverstärker)		*f*	tige de poussoir (servofrein)	*f*
push rod (door control)	*n*	Stößel (Türbetätigung)		*m*	poussoir (commande des portes	*m*
push-button valve	*n*	Druckknopfventil		*n*	distributeur à bouton-poussoir	*m*
push-in fuse (motor vehicle)	*n*	Einklemmsicherung (Kfz)		*f*	dispositif anti-pincement (véhicule)	*m*
push-rod piston	*n*	Druckstangenkolben		*m*	piston à tige-poussoir	*m*
pushing electromagnet	*n*	Druckmagnet		*m*	électro-aimant de poussée	*m*
Q						
quality assessment	*n*	Qualitätsbewertung		*f*	évaluation de la qualité	*f*
quality assurance, QA	*n*	Qualitätssicherung		*f*	assurance qualité	*f*
quality control	*n*	Qualitätskontrolle		*f*	contrôle de qualité	*m*
quality deviation	*n*	Qualitätsabweichung		*f*	variation de qualité	*f*
quality examination	*n*	Qualitätsprüfung		*f*	essai qualitatif	*m*
quality factor	*n*	Gütefaktor		*m*	facteur de qualité	*m*
quality inspection certificate	*n*	Qualitätsprüfzertifikat		*n*	certificat du test de qualité	*m*
quality level	*n*	Qualitätsstand		*m*	niveau de qualité	*m*
quality objective	*n*	Qualitätsziel		*n*	objectif qualité	*m*
quality surveillance	*n*	Qualitätsüberwachung		*f*	surveillance de la qualité	*f*
quartz oscillator	*n*	Quarzoszillator		*m*	oscillateur à quartz	*m*
quench zone (air-fuel mixture)	*n*	Quench-Zone (Luft-Kraftstoff-Gemisch)		*f*	zone de coincement (mélange air-carburant)	*f*
quick-connect coupling	*n*	Schnellkupplung		*f*	accouplement rapide	*m*
quick-gas pedal release	*n*	Sturzgas	x	*n*	décélération	*f*
quick-release coupling	*n*	Schnellkupplung		*f*	accouplement rapide	*m*
quick-release valve (brakes)	*n*	Schnellöseventil (Bremse)		*n*	valve de desserrage rapide (frein)	*f*
quiet running (IC engine)	*n*	Laufruhe (Verbrennungsmotor)		*f*	fonctionnement régulier (moteur à combustion)	*m*
R						
race (IC engine)	*v*	durchgehen (Verbrennungsmotor)	x	*v*	emballer <s'emballer> (moteur à combustion)	*v*
rack	*n*	Zahnstange		*f*	crémaillère	*f*
rack position, RP	*n*	Regelstangenstellung		*f*	position de la tige de réglage	*f*
rack travel, RT	*n*	Regelstangenweg		*m*	course de régulation	*f*

English

English		German		French	
rack-travel indication	*n*	Regelweganzeige	*f*	indicateur de course de régulation	*m*
rack-travel limiting stop	*n*	Regelwegbegrenzungs-anschlag	*m*	butée de limitation de course de régulation	*f*
rack-travel sensor	*n*	Regelwegsensor	*m*	capteur de course de régulation	*m*
radial fan	*n*	Radiallüfter	*m*	ventilateur radial	*m*
radial plunger distributor pump	*n*	Radialkolbenpumpe (VR)	*f*	pompe distributrice à pistons radiaux	*f*
radial vee-form filter element	*n*	Sternfilterelement	*n*	cartouche filtrante en étoile	*f*
radial-piston distributor pump	*n*	Radialkolbenpumpe (VR)	*f*	pompe distributrice à pistons radiaux	*f*
radial-piston high-pressure pump	*n*	Radialkolben-Hochdruckpumpe	*f*	pompe haute pression à pistons radiaux	*f*
radial-piston pump	*n*	Radialkolbenpumpe (VR)	*f*	pompe distributrice à pistons radiaux	*f*
radiation (EMC)	*n*	Abstrahlung (EMV)	*f*	rayonnement (CEM)	*m*
radiation shield	*n*	Strahlungsschutz	*m*	protection contre les radiations	*f*
radiator blower	*n*	Kühlergebläse	*n*	ventilateur de radiateur	*m*
radiator fan	*n*	Kühlergebläse	*n*	ventilateur de radiateur	*m*
radio disturbance	*n*	Funkstörung (Ursache)	*f*	perturbation radioélectrique	*f*
radio hand transmitter (car alarm)	*n*	Funk-Handsender (Autoalarm)	*m*	émetteur manuel radio (alarme auto)	*m*
radio interference	*n*	Funkstörung (Wirkung)	*f*	brouillage radioélectrique	*m*
radio interference voltage (EMC)	*n*	Funkstörspannung (EMV)	*f*	tension perturbatrice (CEM)	*f*
radio remote control	*n*	Funk-Fernbedienung	*f*	radiocommande	*f*
radio remote control	*n*	Funkfernbedienung	*f*	télécommande radio	*f*
radio-interference source	*n*	Störquelle	*f*	source de perturbations (CEM)	*f*
radius of bend (road)	*n*	Kurvenradius (Fahrbahn)	*m*	rayon de courbure (virage)	*m*
rain sensor	*n*	Regensensor	*m*	capteur de pluie	*m*
ram tube	*n*	Schwingsaugrohr	*n*	collecteur d'admission à oscillation	*m*
ram-effect supercharging	*v*	Schwingsaugrohr-Aufladung	*f*	suralimentation par oscillation d'admission	*f*
ramp climb	*n*	Rampensteigung	*f*	montée de rampe	*f*
ramp progression (lambda closed-loop control)	*n*	Rampenverlauf (Lambda-Regelung)	*m*	évolution en rampe (régulation lambda)	*f*
ramp signal	*n*	Rampensignal	*n*	signal de rampe	*m*
ramp slope	*n*	Rampensteigung	*f*	montée de rampe	*f*
ramp voltage	*n*	Rampenspannung	*f*	tension de rampe	*f*
random-access memory, RAM	*n*	Schreib-Lese-Speicher, RAM	*m*	mémoire vive à lecture/écriture, RAM	*f*
range (headlamp)	*n*	Reichweite (Scheinwerfer)	*f*	portée (projecteur)	*f*
range of spring	*n*	Federweg	*m*	course du ressort	*f*
range of tolerance	*n*	Toleranzbereich	*m*	marge de tolérance	*f*
rapid coupling	*n*	Schnellkupplung	*f*	accouplement rapide	*m*
rapid starting kit (diesel vehicles)	*n*	Schnellstart-Satz (Dieselfahrzeuge)	*m*	kit de démarrage rapide (véhicules diesel)	*m*
rapid starting system (diesel vehicles)	*n*	Schnellstartanlage (Dieselfahrzeuge)	*f*	dispositif de démarrage rapide (véhicules diesel)	*m*

English		German		French	
rapid-bleeder valve (brakes)	*n*	Schnellentlüftungsventil (Bremse)	*n*	purgeur rapide (frein)	*m*
rapid-start charger (battery)	*n*	Schnellstartlader (Batterie)	*m*	chargeur de démarrage rapide (batterie)	*m*
ratchet pin	*n*	Rastbolzen	*m*	axe d'arrêt	*m*
rate of air flow	*n*	Luftdurchsatz	*m*	débit d'air (disponible)	*m*
rate of injection	*n*	Einspritzverlauf	*m*	loi d'injection	*f*
rate-of-discharge curve	*n*	Einspritzverlauf	*m*	loi d'injection	*f*
rated capacity (battery)	*v*	Nennkapazität (Batterie)	*f*	capacité nominale (batterie)	*f*
rated current	*n*	Nennstrom	*m*	courant de consigne	*m*
rated speed	*n*	Nenndrehzahl	*f*	vitesse de rotation nominale	*f*
rated voltage	*n*	Nennspannung	*f*	tension nominale	*f*
rating plate	*n*	Typenschild	*n*	plaque signalétique	*f*
raw value (accelerator-pedal sensor)	*n*	Rohwert (Fahrpedalsensor)	*m*	valeur brute (capteur d'accélérateur)	*f*
reaction chamber	*n*	Reaktionskammer	*f*	chambre de réaction	*f*
reaction force (brakes)	*n*	Reaktionskraft (Bremse)	*f*	force de réaction (systèmes de freinage)	*f*
reaction piston	*n*	Reaktionskolben	*m*	piston de rappel	*m*
reaction spring (parking-brake valve)	*n*	Reaktionsfeder (Feststellbremsventil)	*f*	ressort de rappel (valve de frein de stationnement)	*m*
reaction time (brake actuation)	*n*	Reaktionsdauer (Bremsbetätigung)	*f*	temps de réaction (freinage)	*m*
reaction time (braking action)	*n*	Verlustzeit (Bremsvorgang)	*f*	temps mort (effet de freinage)	*m*
reaction torque (braking-system inspection)	*n*	Reaktionsmoment (Bremsprüfung)	*n*	couple de réaction (contrôle des freins)	*m*
read out (error code)	*v*	auslesen (Fehlercode)	x *v*	visualiser (code de défaut)	*v*
read-only memory, ROM	*n*	Festwertspeicher, ROM	*f*	mémoire de valeurs fixes, ROM	*f*
reading lamp	*n*	Leseleuchte	*f*	lampe de lecture	*f*
ready-to-start indicator (diesel engine)	*n*	Startbereitschaftsanzeige (Dieselmotor)	*f*	indicateur de disponibilité de démarrage (moteur diesel)	*m*
rear lamp	*n*	Schlußleuchte	*f*	feu arrière	*m*
rear muffler	*n*	Nachschalldämpfer	*m*	silencieux arrière	*m*
rear window	*n*	Heckscheibe	*f*	vitre arrière	*f*
rear wiper	*n*	Heckwischer	*m*	essuie-glace arrière	*m*
rear-axle differential	*n*	Hinterachsdifferential	*n*	différentiel de l'essieu arrière	*m*
rear-axle lock	*n*	Hinterachssperre	*f*	blocage de l'essieu arrière	*m*
rear-window wiper blade	*n*	Heck-Wischblatt	*n*	raclette de lunette arrière	*f*
receiver transducer (car alarm)	*n*	Empfänger-Wandler (Autoalarm)	*m*	transducteur-récepteur (alarme auto)	*m*
receiving chamber (CO test)	*n*	Empfängerkammer (Abgastester)	*f*	collecteur (gaz CO)	*m*
receptable	*n*	Steckhülse	*f*	fiche femelle	*f*
recess step (ABS solenoid valve)	*n*	Tauchstufe (ABS-Magnetventil)	*f*	volume de détente (électrovalve ABS)	*m*
reciprocating fuel-injection pump	*n*	Kolben-Einspritzpumpe	*f*	pompe d'injection alternative	*f*
reciprocating solenoid	*m*	Hubmagnet	*m*	électro-aimant de commande	*m*
reciprocating-piston engine	*n*	Hubkolbenmotor	*m*	moteur à pistons alternatifs	*m*

English		German		French	
reciprocating-piston supercharger	n	Hubkolbenverdichter	m	compresseur à piston	m
recirculating-ball device (door control, steering system)	n	Kugelumlauf (Türbetätigung, Lenkung)	m	rampe à billes (commande des portes, direction)	f
rectification (alternating current)	n	Gleichrichtung (Wechselstrom)	f	redressement (courant alternatif)	m
rectifier (alternator)	n	Gleichrichter (Generator)	m	redresseur (alternateur)	m
rectifier diode	n	Gleichrichterdiode	f	diode redresseuse	f
rectifier losses	npl	Gleichrichterverluste	mpl	pertes redresseurs	fpl
reduced delivery	n	Mindermenge	f	réduction de débit	f
reduced-delivery stop	n	Mindermengenanschlag	m	butée de réduction de débit	f
reducing valve	n	Reduzierventil	n	réducteur de pression	m
reduction catalytic converter	n	Reduktionskatalysator	m	catalyseur de réduction	m
reduction gear	n	Vorgelege	n	réducteur	m
reduction signal (TCS)	n	Reduziersignal (ASR)	n	signal de réduction (ASR)	m
reduction-gear starter	n	Vorgelegestarter	m	démarreur à réducteur	m
reed valve	n	Zungenventil	n	clapet à languette	m
reference circle (gear)	n	Teilkreis (Zahnrad)	m	cercle primitif de référence (engrenage)	m
reference eddy-current ring	n	Referenzkurzschlußring	m	bague inductive de référence	f
reference gas (lambda closed-loop control)	n	Referenzgas (Lambda-Regelung)	n	gaz de référence (régulation lambda)	m
reference ground (vehicle electrical system)	n	Bezugsmasse (Bordnetz)	f	masse de référence (circuit de bord)	f
reference level	n	Referenzpegel	m	niveau de référence	m
reference line	n	Referenzleitung	f	tuyauterie de référence	f
reference mark	n	Bezugsmarke	f	repère de référence	m
reference pressure	n	Referenzdruck	m	pression de référence	f
reference speed	n	Referenzgeschwindigkeit	f	vitesse de référence	f
reference-mark sensor (ignition	n	Bezugsmarkensensor (Zündung)	m	capteur de repère de consigne (allumage)	m
reflection muffler	n	Reflexionsschalldämpfer	m	silencieux à réflexion	m
reflector	n	Reflektor	m	réflecteur	m
reflector optics	npl	Reflektoroptik	f	optique de réflexion	f
regeneration (air drier)	n	Regeneration (Lufttrockner)	f	régénération (dessiccateur)	f
regeneration aid	n	Regenerationshilfe	f	auxiliaire de régénération	m
regeneration throttle (air drier)	n	Regenerationsdrossel (Lufttrockner)	f	étranglement de régénération (dessiccateur)	m
regeneration-air tank	n	Regenerationsluftbehälter	m	réservoir d'air de régénération	m
regeneration-gas flow	n	Regeneriergasstrom	m	flux de gaz régénérateur	m
regional subsidiary	n	Regionalgesellschaft	f	société régionale	f
register resonance pressure-charging	n	Registerresonanzaufladung	f	suralimentation par collecteur de résonance	f
regulate (diesel fuel injection)	v	abregeln (Dieseleinspritzung)	v	fin de régulation (injection diesel)	f
regulated voltage	n	Regelspannung	f	tension de régulation	f
regulating armature	n	Regelanker	m	armature de régulation	f
regulating contact	n	Regelkontakt	m	contact de régulation	m
regulating resistor	n	Regelwiderstand	m	résistance de régulation	f

English

English		German		French	
regulator contact	*n*	Regelkontakt	*m*	contact de régulation	*m*
regulator response voltage	*n*	Regelspannung	*f*	tension de régulation	*f*
regulator switch (headlight leveling control)	*n*	Regulierschalter (Leuchtweitenregelung)	*m*	molette de correcteur de site	*f*
relative speed	*n*	Relativgeschwindigkeit	*f*	vitesse relative	*f*
relay	*n*	Relais	*n*	relais	*m*
relay combination	*n*	Relaiskombination	*f*	module relais	*m*
relay piston	*n*	Relaiskolben	*m*	piston-relais	*m*
relay set	*n*	Relaiskombination	*f*	module relais	*m*
relay valve	*n*	Relaisventil	*n*	valve-relais	*f*
release (emergency valve)	*n*	Entriegelung (Nothahn)	*f*	déverrouillage (robinet de secours)	*m*
release (manufacturing)	*n*	Freigabe (Fertigung)	*f*	autorisation (fabrication)	*f*
release position	*n*	Lösestellung	*f*	position de desserrage	*f*
release pressure	*n*	Lösedruck	*m*	pression de desserrage	*f*
release time (brakes)	*n*	Lösedauer (Bremse)	*f*	temps de desserrage (frein)	*m*
release time (fuel injector)	*n*	Abfallzeit (Einspritzventil)	*f*	temps de fermeture (injecteur)	*m*
release time (relay)	*n*	Rückfallzeit (Relais)	*f*	temps de relâchement (relais)	*m*
release valve	*n*	Löseventil	*n*	valve de desserrage	*f*
reliability test	*n*	Zuverlässigkeitsprüfung	*f*	essai de fiabilité	*m*
relief collar	*n*	Entlastungsbund	*m*	épaulement de détente	*m*
relief piston	*n*	Entlastungskolben	*m*	piston de détente	*m*
relief valve	*n*	Überströmventil	*n*	valve de décharge	*f*
remanence	*n*	Restmagnetismus	*m*	magnétisme restant	*m*
remote-control line (battery charge)	*n*	Fernstartleitung (Batterieladung)	*f*	câble de télécommande (charge de batterie)	*m*
repair instructions	*npl*	Reparaturanleitung	*f*	notice de remise en état	*f*
repair kit	*n*	Reparatursatz	*m*	kit de remise en état	*m*
repair manual	*n*	Reparaturhandbuch	*n*	manuel de réparation	*m*
repairing	*n*	Instandsetzung	*f*	remise en état	*f*
repeat start	*n*	Wiederstart x	*m*	redémarrage	*m*
reprime (car alarm)	*v*	rückschärfen (Autoalarm)	*v*	remise en veille (alarme auto)	*f*
research octane number, RON	*n*	Research-Oktanzahl, ROZ	*f*	indice d'octane recherche, RON	*m*
residual air gap	*n*	Restluftspalt	*m*	fente d'air résiduel	*f*
residual braking	*n*	Restbremswirkung	*f*	effet résiduel de freinage	*m*
residual exhaust gas	*n*	Restgas	*n*	gaz résiduels	*mpl*
residual magnetism	*n*	Restmagnetismus	*m*	magnétisme restant	*m*
residual oxygen	*n*	Restsauerstoff (Abgas)	*m*	oxygène résiduel (gaz d'échappement)	*m*
residual pressure	*n*	Restdruck	*m*	pression résiduelle	*f*
residual stroke (plunger-and-barrel assembly)	*n*	Resthub (Pumpenelement)	*m*	course restante (élément de pompage)	*f*
resistance ignition cable	*n*	Widerstands-Zündleitung	*f*	câble d'allumage résistif	*m*
resistance to flow	*n*	Strömungswiderstand	*m*	résistance au courant	*f*
resistance to incident radiation (EMC)	*n*	Einstrahlfestigkeit (EMV)	*f*	tenue au rayonnement incident (CEM)	*f*
resistance to pressure	*n*	Druckfestigkeit	*f*	résistance à la pression	*f*

English		German		French	
resistance to rotation (IC engine)	*n*	Durchdrehwiderstand (Verbrennungsmotor)	*m*	résistance de lancement du moteur	*f*
resistance to thermal cycling	*n*	Temperaturwechselfestigkeit	*f*	résistance aux chocs thermique:	*f*
resistance to vibrations	*n*	Schwingungsfestigkeit	*f*	tenue aux vibrations	*f*
resistive suppressor	*n*	Entstörwiderstand	*m*	résistance d'antiparasitage	*f*
resonance chamber	*n*	Resonanzbehälter	*m*	boîte à résonance	*f*
resonance tube	*n*	Resonanzrohr	*n*	tube à résonance	*m*
resonant frequency	*n*	Resonanzfrequenz	*f*	fréquence de résonance	*f*
response (motor vehicle)	*n*	Übertragungsverhalten (Kfz)	*n*	réponse (véhicule)	*f*
response delay	*n*	Ansprechverzögerung	*f*	délai de réponse	*m*
response pressure	*n*	Ansprechdruck	*m*	pression de réponse	*f*
response threshold	*n*	Ansprechschwelle	*f*	seuil de réponse	*m*
response time	*n*	Ansprechzeit	*f*	temps de réponse	*m*
response travel	*n*	Ansprechweg	*m*	course de réponse	*f*
response voltage	*n*	Ansprechspannung	*f*	tension de réponse	*f*
restriction	*n*	Drosselwirkung	*f*	effet d'étranglement	*m*
restriction bore	*n*	Drosselbohrung	*f*	orifice d'étranglement	*m*
restriction passage	*n*	Durchflußdrossel	*f*	étrangleur	*m*
retainer	*n*	Sicherungsring	*m*	anneau d'arrêt	*m*
retaining nut	*n*	Spannmutter	*f*	écrou-raccord	*m*
retardation	*n*	Abbremsung	*f*	taux de freinage	*m*
retarder	*n*	Verlangsamer	*m*	ralentisseur	*m*
retarder relay	*n*	Dauerbremsrelais, DBR	*n*	relais du ralentisseur	*m*
retarding force (chassis dynamometer)	*n*	Bremslast (Rollenprüfstand)	*f*	charge de freinage (banc d'essai)	*f*
retention efficiency (filter)	*n*	Abscheidegüte (Filter)	*f*	qualité de séparation (filtre)	*f*
retractable headlight	*n*	Klappscheinwerfer	*m*	projecteur escamotable	*m*
retraction lift	*n*	Entlastungshub	*m*	course de détente	*f*
retraction piston	*n*	Entlastungskolben	*m*	piston de détente	*m*
retraction pressure	*n*	Rückstelldruck	*m*	pression de rappel	*f*
retraction volume (distributor pump)	*n*	Volumenentlastung	*f*	décharge de volume	*f*
retraction volume (in-line pump)	*n*	Entlastungsvolumen	*n*	volume de réaspiration	*m*
return amplification (ESP)	*n*	Rückführverstärkung (ESP)	*f*	amplification de retour (ESP)	*f*
return flow (overflow valve)	*n*	Rückströmung (Überströmventil)	*f*	débit de retour (valve de barrage)	*m*
return force	*n*	Rückstellkraft	*f*	force de rappel	*f*
return line	*n*	Rücklaufleitung	*f*	conduite de retour	*f*
return line (ABS solenoid valve)	*n*	Rücklauf (ABS-Magnetventil)	*m*	retour (électrovalve ABS)	*m*
return passage	*n*	Rücklaufbohrung	*f*	orifice de retour	*m*
return principle (ABS)	*n*	Rückförderprinzip (ABS)	*n*	principe de reflux (ABS)	*m*
return pump	*n*	Rückförderpumpe	*f*	pompe de retour	*f*
return spring	*n*	Rückholfeder	*f*	ressort de rappel	*m*
return stroke	*n*	Rückhub	*m*	course de retour	*f*
return torque	*n*	Rückstellmoment	*n*	couple de rappel	*m*
return-flow direction	*n*	Rückströmrichtung	*f*	sens d'écoulement inverse	*m*

English		German		French	
return-flow restriction	*n*	Rückströmdrossel, RSD	*f*	frein de réaspiration	*m*
revcounter (motor vehicle)	*n*	Drehzahlmesser (Kfz)	*m*	compte-tours (véhicule)	*m*
reverse voltage (diode)	*n*	Sperrspannung (Diode)	*f*	tension inverse (diode)	*f*
reverse-current block (rectification)	*n*	Rückstromsperre (Gleichrichtung)	*f*	isolement (redressement)	*m*
reverse-polarity protection (battery charge)	*n*	Verpolungsschutz (Batterieladung)	*m*	protection contre l'inversion de polarité (charge de batterie)	*f*
reverse-transfer lever	*n*	Umlenkhebel	*m*	levier de renvoi	*m*
reversing lamp	+ *n*	Rückfahrscheinwerfer	*m*	feu de marche arrière	*m*
revolving injection pump	*n*	umlaufende Einspritzpumpe	*f*	pompe d'injection rotative	*f*
ribbed V-belt	*n*	Keilrippenriemen	*m*	courroie trapezoïdale à nervures	*f*
rich (air-fuel mixture)	*adj*	fett (Luft-Kraftstoff-Gemisch)	*adj*	riche (mélange air-carburant)	*adj*
ring gap	*n*	Ringspalt	*m*	fente annulaire	*f*
ring gear (flywheel)	*n*	Zahnkranz (Motorschwungrad)	*m*	couronne dentée de volant	*f*
ring groove	*n*	Ringnut	*f*	rainure annulaire	*f*
ring magnet	*n*	Ringmagnet	*m*	aimant torique	*m*
ring main	*n*	Ringleitung	*f*	conduite annulaire	*f*
ring-gap metering (fuel injector)	*n*	Ringspaltzumessung (Einspritzventil)	*f*	dosage par fente annulaire (injecteur)	*m*
ring-shaped area	*n*	Ringfläche	*f*	surface annulaire	*f*
road condition	*n*	Fahrbahnbeschaffenheit	*f*	état de la chaussée	*m*
road frictional torque	*n*	Fahrbahrbahnreibmoment	*n*	couple de frottement de la chaussée	*m*
road torque (TCS)	*n*	Straßenmoment (ASR)	*n*	couple de la route (ASR)	*m*
road-speed limitation	*n*	Fahrgeschwindigkeits-begrenzung	*f*	limitation de vitesse de roulage	*f*
road-surface adhesion	*n*	Bodenhaftung	*f*	adhérence au sol	*f*
rocker	*n*	Schaltwippe	*f*	bascule de commutation	*f*
rocker arm (valve timing)	*n*	Schlepphebel (Ventilsteuerung)	*m*	levier oscillant (commande des soupapes)	*m*
rocking piston	*n*	Wiegekolben	*m*	piston à fléau	*f*
rod adjuster	*n*	Gestängesteller (Radbremse)	*m*	dispositif automatique de rattrapage de jeu (freins des roues)	*f*
roll angle (vehicle dynamics)	*n*	Wankwinkel (Kfz-Dynamik)	*m*	angle de roulis (dynamique d'un véhicule)	*m*
roll axis (vehicle dynamics)	*n*	Rollachse (Kfz-Dynamik)	*f*	axe de roulis (dynamique d'un véhicule)	*m*
roll bellows (air spring)	*n*	Rollbalgfeder (Luftfeder)	*f*	soufflet en U (suspension)	*m*
roll-start block	*n*	Rollstartsperre	*f*	dispositif antidémarrage	*m*
rolled-on	*pp*	aufgewalzt	*pp*	appliqué par laminage	*pp*
roller fuel-injection pump	*n*	Rollenstößel-Einspritzpumpe	*f*	pompe d'injection à galet	*f*
roller path	*n*	Rollenlaufbahn	*f*	surface de guidage des rouleaux	*f*
roller race	*n*	Rollengleitkurve	*f*	rampe de travail	*f*
roller ring	*n*	Rollenring	*m*	bague porte-galets	*f*
roller set (dynamic brake analyzer)	*n*	Rollensatz (Rollenbremsprüfstand)	*m*	jeu de rouleaux (banc d'essai)	*m*
roller support	*n*	Rollenschuh	*m*	talon de galet	*m*
roller tappet	*n*	Rollenstößel	*m*	poussoir à galet	*m*

English		German		French	
roller-cell pump	*n*	Rollenzellenpumpe	*f*	pompe multicellulaire à rouleaux	*f*
roller-tappet gap	*n*	Rollenstößelspalt	*m*	fente du poussoir à galet	*f*
roller-tappet shell	*n*	Stößelkörper	*m*	corps de poussoir	*m*
roller-type fuel-injection pump	*n*	Rollenstößel-Einspritzpumpe	*f*	pompe d'injection à galet	*f*
roller-type overrunning clutch (starter)	*n*	Rollenfreilauf (Starter)	*m*	dispositif de roue libre (démarreur)	*m*
roller-type pump	*n*	Rollenzellenpumpe	*f*	pompe multicellulaire à rouleaux	*f*
roller-type test stand	*n*	Rollenprüfstand	*m*	banc d'essai à rouleaux	*m*
rolling friction	*n*	Rollreibung	*f*	frottement au roulement	*m*
rolling movement	*n*	Abrollbewegung	*f*	mouvement de rotation	*m*
rolling resistance	*n*	Rollwiderstand	*m*	résistance au roulement	*f*
rollover bar	*n*	Überrollbügel	*m*	arceau de capotage	*m*
rollover protection	*n*	Überschlagschutz	*m*	protection anticapotage	*f*
rollover sensor	*n*	Überrollsensor	*m*	capteur de capotage	*m*
Roots blower	*n*	Drehkolben-Gebläse	*n*	soufflante à piston rotatif	*f*
Roots supercharger	*n*	Roots-Lader	*m*	compresseur Roots	*m*
rotary actuator (door control)	*n*	Drehantrieb (Türbetätigung)	*m*	commande de pivotement des portes	*f*
rotary actuator (KE-Jetronic)	*n*	Drehsteller (KE-Jetronic)	*m*	actionneur rotatif (KE-Jetronic)	*m*
rotary idle actuator	*n*	Leerlaufdrehsteller	*m*	actionneur rotatif de ralenti	*m*
rotary oscillation	*n*	Drehschwingung	*f*	vibration due à la torsion	*f*
rotary potentiometer	*n*	Drehpotentiometer	*n*	potentiomètre rotatif	*m*
rotary slider	*n*	Drehschieber	*m*	tiroir rotatif	*m*
rotary valve	*n*	Drehschieber	*m*	tiroir rotatif	*m*
rotary-knob valve	*n*	Drehknopfventil	*n*	valve à bouton rotatif	*f*
rotary-piston blower	*n*	Drehkolben-Gebläse	*n*	soufflante à piston rotatif	*f*
rotary-piston supercharger	*n*	Rotationskolbenverdichter	*m*	compresseur à piston rotatif	*m*
rotating armature	*n*	Drehanker	*m*	induit rotatif	*m*
rotating armature relay	*n*	Drehankerrelais	*n*	relais à armature pivotante	*m*
rotating beacon	*n*	Rundumkennleuchte	*f*	gyrophare	*m*
rotating shoe (drum brake)	*n*	Drehbacke (Trommelbremse)	*f*	mâchoire pivotante (frein à tambour)	*f*
rotating slide	*n*	Drehschieber	*m*	tiroir rotatif	*m*
rotating-reciprocating movement	*n*	Dreh-Hub-Bewegung	*f*	mouvement alternatif et rotatif	*m*
rotating-solenoid actuator	*n*	Drehmagnetstellwerk	*n*	commande à aimant rotatif	*f*
rotational angle	*n*	Drehwinkel	*m*	angle de rotation	*m*
rotational-speed control	*n*	Drehzahlregelung	*f*	régulation de la vitesse de rotation	*f*
rotor (pressure-wave supercharger)	*n*	Rotor (Druckwellenlader)	*m*	rotor (échangeur de pression)	*m*
rotor arm (ignition)	*n*	Zündverteilerläufer	*m*	rotor distributeur (allumage)	*m*
rotor chamber (hydrodynamic retarder)	*n*	Schaufelraum (hydrodynamischer Verlangsamer)	*m*	volume entre les palettes du rotor (ralentisseur hydrodynamique)	*m*
rotor plate (roller-cell pump)	*n*	Läuferscheibe (Rollenzellenpumpe)	*f*	rotor à cages (pompe multicellulaire à rouleaux)	*m*

English

English		German			French	
rotor shaft	*n*	Läuferwelle		*f*	arbre de rotor	*m*
rotor winding	*n*	Läuferwicklung		*f*	enroulement rotorique	*m*
RT sensor	*n*	Regelwegsensor		*m*	capteur de course de régulation	*m*
rubber bellows	*n*	Gummirollbalg		*m*	soufflet en caoutchouc	*m*
rubber grommet	*n*	Gummitülle		*f*	passe-fil caoutchouc	*m*
rubber sleeve	*n*	Gummimanschette		*f*	douille en caoutchouc	*f*
rubbing block (breaker lever)	*n*	Gleitstück (Unterbrecherhebel)		*n*	toucheau (rupteur)	*m*
run-up to speed (IC engine)	*v*	hochlaufen (Verbrennungsmotor)	x	*v*	montée en régime (moteur à combustion)	*f*
running noise	*n*	Laufgeräusch		*n*	bruits de fonctionnement	*mpl*
running refinement	*n*	Fahrkomfort		*m*	confort de conduite	*m*
running-up time	*n*	Hochlaufdauer		*f*	temps de montée en régime	*m*
rust remover	*n*	Rostlöser		*m*	dissolvant antirouille	*m*
S						
S-cam (brakes)	*n*	S-Nocken (Bremse)		*m*	came en S (frein)	*f*
sac hole (injector)	*n*	Sackloch (Einspritzventil)		*n*	sac d'injecteur	*m*
sac-less (vco) nozzle	*n*	Sitzlochdüse		*f*	injecteur à siège perforé	*m*
safety and security electronics	*npl*	Sicherheitselektronik		*f*	électronique de sécurité	*f*
safety and security system	*n*	Sicherheitssystem		*n*	système de sécurité	*m*
safety circuit	*n*	Sicherheitsschaltung		*f*	circuit de sécurité	*m*
safety element (air filter)	*n*	Sicherheitspatrone (Luftfilter)		*f*	cartouche de sécurité (filtre à air)	*f*
safety instructions	*npl*	Sicherheitshinweise		*mpl*	conseils de sécurité	*mpl*
safety mode	*n*	Sicherheitsmodus		*m*	mode "sécurité"	*m*
safety module	*n*	Sicherheitsmodul		*m*	module de sécurité	*m*
safety pressure	*n*	Sicherungsdruck		*m*	pression de sécurité	*f*
safety regulations	*npl*	Sicherheitsvorschriften		*fpl*	prescriptions de sécurité	*fpl*
safety relay (ECU)	*n*	Sicherheitsrelais (Steuergerät)		*n*	relais de sécurité (calculateur)	*m*
safety switch	*n*	Sicherheitsschalter		*m*	contacteur de sécurité	*m*
safety valve (air drier)	*n*	Sicherheitsventil (Lufttrockner)		*n*	valve de sécurité (dessiccateur)	*f*
salient-pole generator	*n*	Einzelpolgenerator		*m*	alternateur à pôles saillants	*m*
salient-pole rotor	*n*	Einzelpolläufer		*m*	rotor à pôles saillants	*m*
salt spray test	*n*	Salzsprühtest		*m*	test au brouillard salin	*m*
sampling inspection	*n*	Stichprobenprüfung		*f*	contrôle par échantillonnage	*m*
satellite positioning system (navigation system)	*n*	Satellitenortungssystem (Navigationssystem)		*n*	système de localisation par satellite (système de navigation	*m*
saturation point (brake booster)	*n*	Aussteuerpunkt (Bremskraftverstärker)		*m*	point de régulation finale (servofrein)	*m*
saturation point (water content)	*n*	Sättigungsmenge (Luftfeuchtigkeit)		*f*	quantité de saturation (humidité de l'air)	*f*
schematic diagram	*n*	Stromlaufplan		*m*	schéma des circuits	*m*
scoring (brake drum, brake disc)	*n*	Einlaufstelle (Bremstrommel, Bremsscheibe)		*f*	trace d'usure (tambour, frein à disque)	*f*
screen	*n*	Abschirmung		*f*	blindage	*m*
screened	*pp*	geschirmt		*pp*	blindé	*pp*
screw-type supercharger	*n*	Schraubenverdichter		*m*	compresseur à vis	*m*
screwed socket	*n*	Einschraubstutzen		*m*	manchon fileté	*m*
seal	*v*	abdichten		*v*	étancher	*v*

English		German			French	
seal piece	n	Dichtstück		n	pièce d'étanchement	f
seal seat	n	Dichtsitz		m	siège d'étanchéité	m
sealing cap (wheel-brake cylinder)	n	Abdichtstulpe (Radzylinder)		f	manchon d'étanchéité (cylindre de roue)	m
sealing compound (battery)	n	Vergußmasse (Batterie)		f	masse d'enrobage (batterie)	f
sealing cone	n	Dichtkegel		m	cône d'étanchéité	m
sealing gasket	n	Dichtrahmen		m	cadre d'étanchéité	m
sealing oil	n	Sperröl	x	n	carburant de barrage	m
sealing spring	n	Verschlußfeder		f	ressort à déclic	m
sealing washer	n	Verschlußscheibe		f	rondelle d'obturation	f
seat adjustment	n	Sitzverstellung		f	réglage des sièges	m
seat belt	n	Sicherheitsgurt		m	ceinture de sécurité	f
seat heating	n	Sitzheizung		f	chauffage de siège	m
seat-belt brake	n	Gurtbremse (Sicherheitsgurt)		f	frein de ceinture de sécurité	m
seat-belt extender	n	Gurtbringer		m	serveur de ceinture	m
seat-belt locking	n	Gurtverriegelung (Sicherheitsgurt)		f	verrouillage de ceinture de sécurité	m
seat-belt slack	n	Gurtlose (Sicherheitsgurt)	x	f	jeu de ceinture de sécurité	m
seat-belt tightener	n	Gurtstraffer (Sicherheitsgurt)		m	prétensionneur de ceinture	m
seat-belt-tightener trigger unit	n	Gurtstraffer-Auslösegerät		n	déclencheur de prétensionneur	m
seat-hole nozzle	n	Sitzlochdüse		f	injecteur à siège perforé	m
seat-occupant detection	n	Sitzbelegungserkennung		f	détection d'occupation de siège	f
secondary air	n	Sekundärluft		f	air secondaire	m
secondary air gap	n	Sekundärluftspalt		m	entrefer secondaire	m
secondary braking effect	n	Hilfsbremswirkung		f	effet de freinage auxiliaire	m
secondary circuit	n	Sekundärkreis	x	m	circuit secondaire	m
secondary cup seal	n	Sekundärmanschette		f	manchette secondaire	f
secondary current	n	Sekundärstrom		m	courant secondaire	m
secondary delivery quantity	n	Nachfördermenge		f	débit de post-refoulement	m
secondary filter	n	Nachfilter		n	filtre secondaire	m
secondary injection	n	Nacheinspritzung		f	injection secondaire	f
secondary loads (compressed-air system)	npl	Nebenverbraucher (Druckluftanlage)		mpl	récepteurs auxiliaires (dispositif de freinage à air comprimé)	mpl
secondary pressure (brakes)	n	Sekundärdruck (Bremse)		m	pression secondaire (frein)	f
secondary roller (dynamic brake analyzer)	n	Auflaufrolle (Rollenbremsprüfstand)		f	rouleau suiveur (banc d'essai)	m
secondary shoe	n	ablaufende Bremsbacke		f	mâchoire secondaire	f
secondary side (compressed-air components)	n	Sekundärseite (Druckluftgeräte)		f	côté secondaire (dispositifs à air comprimé)	m
secondary voltage	n	Sekundärspannung		f	tension secondaire	f
secondary winding	n	Sekundärwicklung		f	enroulement secondaire	m
secondary-air injection	n	Sekundärlufteinblasung		f	insufflation d'air secondaire	f
secondary-air pump	n	Sekundärluftpumpe		f	pompe à air secondaire	f
secondary-air valve	n	Sekundärluftventil		n	électrovalve d'air secondaire	f
secondary-brake line	n	Hilfsbremsleitung		f	conduite de secours	f
secondary-brake system	n	Hilfs-Bremsanlage		f	dispositif de freinage de secour:	m
secondary-brake valve	n	Hilfsbremsventil		n	valve de frein de secours	f

English		German			French	
secondary-load circuit	*n*	Nebenverbraucherkreis		*m*	circuit des récepteurs auxiliaires	*m*
sectional drawing	*n*	Schnittzeichnung		*f*	dessin en coupe	*m*
segregation process	*n*	Entmischungsvorgang		*m*	phénomène de démixtion	*m*
select-high control, SH (ABS/TCS)	*n*	Select-high-Regelung, SH (ABS/ASR)	x	*f*	sélection haute (ABS/ASR)	*f*
select-low control, SL (ABS/TCS)	*n*	Select-low-Regelung, SL (ABS/ASR)	x	*f*	sélection basse (ABS/ASR)	*f*
select-smart control, SSM (ABS/TCS)	*n*	Select-smart-Regelung, SSM (ABS/ASR)	x	*f*	sélection idéale (ABS/ASR)	*f*
selector lever	*n*	Getriebewählhebel		*m*	sélecteur de rapport de vitesse	*m*
self test	*n*	Selbsttest		*m*	test automatique	*m*
self-adaptation	*n*	Selbstadaption		*f*	auto-adaptation	*f*
self-adjusting	*ppr*	selbsteinstellend		*ppr*	autoréglable	*adj*
self-amplification (braking force)	*n*	Selbstverstärkung (Bremskraft)		*f*	auto-amplification (force de freinage)	*f*
self-charging	*ppr*	Selbstaufladung		*f*	auto-suralimentation	*f*
self-cleaning	*ppr*	selbstreinigend		*adj*	autonettoyant	*adj*
self-cleaning temperature	*n*	Freibrenntemperatur		*f*	température d'autonettoyage	*f*
self-diagnosis	*n*	Eigendiagnose		*f*	autodiagnostic	*m*
self-diagnosis initiate line	*n*	Eigendiagnose-Reizleitung		*f*	câble d'activation de l'autodiagnostic	*m*
self-discharge (battery)	*n*	Selbstentladung (Batterie)		*f*	décharge spontanée (batterie)	*f*
self-excitation (rotating machines)	*n*	Selbsterregung (drehende Maschinen)		*f*	auto-excitation (machines tournantes)	*f*
self-excitation speed (rotating machines)	*n*	Angehdrehzahl (drehende Maschinen)	x	*f*	vitesse d'auto-excitation (machines tournantes)	*f*
self-governing	*ppr*	selbstregelnd		*ppr*	autorégulation	*f*
self-ignition	*n*	Selbstzündung		*f*	auto-allumage	*m*
self-induction	*n*	Selbstinduktion		*f*	auto-induction	*f*
self-locking	*adj*	selbsthemmend		*adj*	autobloquant	*adj*
self-lubricating	*adj*	selbstschmierend		*adj*	autolubrifiant	*adj*
self-monitoring	*n*	Selbstüberwachung		*f*	autosurveillance	*f*
self-parking (wiper motor)	*n*	Endabstellung (Wischermotor)		*f*	arrêt en fin de course (moteur d'essuie-glace)	*m*
self-reduction (braking force)	*n*	Selbstverringerung (Bremskraft)		*f*	autoréduction (force de freinage)	*f*
self-steering properties	*npl*	Eigenlenkverhalten		*n*	comportement directionnel propre	*m*
self-sustaining speed (IC engine)	*n*	Selbstdrehzahl (Verbrennungsmotor)		*f*	vitesse d'entretien (moteur à combustion)	*f*
semi-continuous braking systen	*n*	teilweise durchgehende Bremsanlage		*f*	dispositif de freinage semi-continu	*m*
semi-surface gap (spark plug)	*n*	Luftgleitfunkenstrecke (Zündkerze)		*f*	distance d'éclatement et de glissement (bougie)	*f*
semi-trailer coupling	*n*	Aufliegerkupplung		*f*	accouplement de semi-remorque	*m*
semiconductor wafer	*n*	Halbleiterplättchen		*n*	plaquette semi-conductrice	*f*
sensing roller (dynamic brake analyzer)	*n*	Tastrolle (Rollenbremsprüfstand)		*f*	rouleau palpeur (banc d'essai)	*m*

English		German		French	
sensor	*n*	Sensor	*m*	capteur	*m*
sensor characteristic	*n*	Geberkennlinie	*f*	courbe caractéristique de capteur	*f*
sensor element	*n*	Sensorelement	*n*	élément sensible	*m*
sensor ID	*n*	Geberkennwort	*n*	identificateur de capteur	*m*
sensor plate (K-Jetronic)	*n*	Stauscheibe (K-Jetronic)	*f*	plateau-sonde (K-Jetronic)	*m*
sensor plate (L-Jetronic)	*n*	Stauklappe (L-Jetronic)	*f*	volet-sonde (L-Jetronic)	*m*
sensor ring (ABS/TCS)	*n*	Impulsring (ABS/ASR)	*m*	disque d'impulsion (ABS/ASR)	*m*
sensor roller (dynamic brake analyzer)	*n*	Tastrolle (Rollenbremsprüfstand)	*f*	rouleau palpeur (banc d'essai)	*m*
separating cup seal	*n*	Trennmanschette	*f*	manchette de séparation	*f*
separation arc	*n*	Abreißfunke	*m*	étincelle de rupture	*f*
separator (battery)	*n*	Separator (Batterie)	*m*	séparateur (batterie)	*m*
separator (filter)	*n*	Abscheider (Filter)	*m*	séparateur (filtre)	*m*
sequential	*adj*	sequentiell	*adj*	séquentiel	*adj*
serial	*adj*	seriell	*adj*	sériel	*adj*
series	*n*	Baureihe	*f*	série	*f*
series connection	*n*	Reihenschaltung	*f*	montage en série	*m*
series fabrication type	*n*	Serienausführung	*f*	version de série	*f*
series motor	*n*	Reihenschlußmotor	*m*	moteur série	*m*
series resistor	*n*	Vorwiderstand	*m*	résistance additionnelle	*f*
series winding	*n*	Reihenschlußwicklung	*f*	enroulement série	*m*
service	*n*	Kundendienst	*m*	service après-vente	*m*
service braking system	*n*	Betriebs-Bremsanlage	*f*	dispositif de freinage de service	*m*
service life	*n*	Dauerstandfestigkeit	*f*	durabilité	*f*
service-brake application	*n*	Betriebsbremsung	*f*	freinage de service	*m*
service-brake circuit	*n*	Betriebsbremskreis	*m*	circuit de freinage de service	*m*
service-brake system	*n*	Betriebs-Bremsanlage	*f*	dispositif de freinage de service	*m*
service-brake valve	*n*	Betriebsbremsventil	*n*	valve de frein de service	*f*
service-line hose coupler	*n*	Kupplungskopf "Bremse"	*m*	tête d'accouplement "frein"	*f*
servo brake (drum brake)	*n*	Servobremse (Trommelbremse)	*f*	servofrein (frein à tambour)	*m*
servo fuel-injection pump	*n*	Servoeinspritzpumpe	*f*	servopompe d'injection	*f*
servo valve	*n*	Servoventil	*n*	vanne commandée par servomoteur	*f*
servo-unit piston	*n*	Verstärkerkolben	*m*	piston amplificateur	*m*
servomotor	*n*	Stellmotor	*m*	servomoteur	*m*
set speed	*n*	Solldrehzahl	*f*	vitesse de rotation prescrite	*f*
setpoint braking torque	*n*	Bremssollmoment	*n*	couple de freinage de consigne	*m*
setting shaft	*n*	Verstellwelle	*f*	axe de correction	*m*
setting sleeve	*n*	Einstellhülse	*f*	manchon de réglage	*m*
settling time	*n*	Ausregelzeit	*f*	délai de régulation	*m*
sheathed (V-belt)	*pp*	ummantelt (Keilriemen)	*pp*	guipé (courroie trapézoïdale)	*pp*
sheathed-element flame glow plug	*n*	Flammglühstiftkerze	*f*	bougie-crayon de préchauffage à flamme	*f*
sheathed-element glow plug	*n*	Glühstiftkerze, GSK	*f*	bougie-crayon de préchauffage	*f*
shield	*n*	Abschirmung	*f*	blindage	*m*
shield (interference suppression)	*v*	schirmen (Entstörung)	*v*	blinder (antiparasitage)	*v*

English		German		French	
shielded	*pp*	geschirmt	*pp*	blindé	*pp*
shielding cover (ignition distributor)	*n*	Abschirmhaube (Zündverteiler)	*f*	calotte de blindage (allumeur)	*f*
shielding sleeve	*n*	Abschirmhülse	*f*	manchon de blindage	*m*
shift lever	*n*	Einrückhebel (Starter)	*m*	fourchette d'engrènement (démarreur)	*f*
shifting point (transmission control)	*n*	Schaltpunkt (Getriebesteuerung)	*m*	point de changement de vitesse	*m*
shim (delivery-valve holder)	*n*	Ausgleichscheibe	*f*	cale de réglage	*f*
shim (nozzle-holder assembly)	*n*	Einstellscheibe	*f*	rondelle de réglage	*f*
shim plate	*n*	Ausgleichsplatte	*f*	plaque de réglage	*f*
shock absorber (motor vehicle)	*n*	Stoßdämpfer (Kfz)	*m*	amortisseur (véhicule)	*m*
shock sensor (car alarm)	*n*	Schocksensor (Autoalarm)	*m*	capteur de choc (alarme auto)	*m*
shoe brake	*n*	Backenbremse	*f*	frein à mâchoires	*m*
shoe factor (brakes)	*n*	Backenkennwert (Bremse)	*m*	facteur de mâchoire (frein)	*m*
short-circuit <noun>	*n*	Kurzschluß	*m*	court-circuit	*m*
short-circuit <to short-circuit>	*v*	kurzschließen	*v*	court-circuiter	*v*
short-circuit current	*n*	Kurzschlußstrom	*m*	courant de court-circuit	*m*
short-circuit resistant	*adj*	kurzschlußfest	*adj*	résistant aux courts-circuits	*ppr*
short-circuit shim	*n*	Kurzschlußscheibe	*f*	rondelle court-circuit	*f*
short-circuit-ring sensor	*n*	Kurzschlußringsensor	*m*	capteur à bague de court-circuitage	*m*
short-circuiting ring	*n*	Kurzschlußring	*m*	bague de court-circuitage	*f*
short-term behaviour	*n*	Kurzzeitverhalten	*n*	comportement à court terme	*m*
short-term load	*n*	Kurzzeitverbraucher	*m*	récepteur à fonctionnement de courte durée	*m*
short-time-duty type (electrical machines)	*n*	Kurzzeitbetrieb (elektrische Maschinen)	*m*	fonctionnement de courte durée (machines électriques)	*m*
shunt	*n*	Nebenschluß	*m*	dérivation	*f*
shunt field	*n*	Nebenschlußfeld	*n*	champ en dérivation	*m*
shunt path	*n*	Kriechweg	*m*	chemin de fuite	*m*
shunt winding	*n*	Nebenschlußwicklung	*f*	enroulement en dérivation	*m*
shunt-wound motor	*n*	Nebenschlußmotor	*m*	moteur à excitation shunt	*m*
shut-down solenoid	*n*	Sperrmagnet	*m*	électro-aimant de blocage	*m*
shut-off slide (injection-pump test bench)	*n*	Trennschieber (Pumpenprüfstand)	*m*	vanne d'isolement (banc d'essai de pompes)	*f*
shut-off threshold	*n*	Ausschaltschwelle	*f*	seuil de coupure	*m*
shutoff (governor)	*n*	Abschaltung (Regler)	*f*	coupure (régulateur)	*f*
shutoff device	*n*	Abstellvorrichtung	*f*	dispositif d'arrêt	*m*
shutoff element (coupling head)	*n*	Absperrglied (Kupplungskopf)	*n*	obturateur (tête d'accouplement)	*m*
shutoff position	*n*	Stopp-Stellung	*f*	position de stop	*f*
shutoff stop	*n*	Absperrhahn	*m*	robinet d'arrêt	*m*
shutoff stop (diesel fuel injection)	*n*	Stoppanschlag (Dieseleinspritzung)	*m*	butée de stop (injection diesel)	*f*
shutoff valve	*n*	Absperrventil	*n*	valve de barrage	*f*
shuttle valve	*n*	Wechselventil	*n*	sélecteur de circuit	*m*
SI (spark ignition) engine	*n*	Ottomotor	*m*	moteur à allumage par étincelle	*m*
side airbag	*n*	Seitenairbag	*m*	coussin gonflable latéral	*m*

English		German		French	
side electrode (spark plug)	*n*	Seitenelektrode (Zündkerze)	*f*	électrode latérale (bougie)	*f*
side force	*n*	Seitenkraft	*f*	force latérale	*f*
side runout (brake disc)	*n*	Seitenschlag (Bremsscheibe)	*m*	voilage (disque de frein)	*m*
side-channel pump	*n*	Seitenkanalpumpe	*f*	pompe à canal latéral	*f*
side-marker lamp	*n*	Begrenzungsleuchte	*f*	feu de position	*m*
signal transducer	*n*	Signalwandler	*m*	convertisseur de signaux	*m*
signal transformer	*n*	Signalwandler	*m*	convertisseur de signaux	*m*
signal-evaluation module	*n*	Auswertschaltgerät	*n*	module électronique d'exploitation	*m*
signaling system	*n*	Signalanlage	*f*	dispositif de signalisation	*m*
silencer	*n*	Geräuschdämpfer	*m*	amortisseur de bruit	*m*
silencer (pressure regulator)	*n*	Schalldämpfer (Druckregler)	*m*	silencieux (régulateur de pression)	*m*
simplex brake	*n*	Simplexbremse	*f*	frein simplex	*m*
simplex drum brake	*n*	Simplexbremse	*f*	frein simplex	*m*
simultaneous	*adj*	simultan	*adj*	simultané	*adj*
single-arm wiper system	*n*	Einhebelsystem (Scheibenwischer)	*n*	système monobras (essuie-glace)	*m*
single-bed catalytic converter	*n*	Einbettkatalysator	*m*	catalyseur à une voie	*m*
single-circuit (braking system)	*n*	einkreisig (Bremsanlage)	*adj*	à un circuit (dispositif de freinage)	*loc*
single-circuit braking system	*n*	Einkreis-Bremsanlage	*f*	dispositif de freinage à transmission à circuit unique	*m*
single-contact regulator	*n*	Einkontaktregler	*m*	régulateur monocontact	*m*
single-flow (fan)	*n*	einflutig (Lüfter)	*adj*	monoflux (ventilateur)	*adj*
single-function lamp	*n*	Einfunktionsleuchte	*f*	feu à fonction unique	*m*
single-hole nozzle	*n*	Einstrahldüse	*f*	injecteur monotrou	*m*
single-jet throttling-pintle nozzle	*n*	Einstrahl-Drosselzapfendüse	*f*	injecteur monojet à téton et étranglement	*m*
single-line braking system	*n*	Einleitungs-Bremsanlage	*f*	dispositif de freinage à conduite unique	*m*
single-orifice metering	*n*	Einlochzumessung (Einspritzventil)	*f*	dosage monotrou (injecteur)	*m*
single-plunger fuel-injection pump (PF)	*n*	Einzylinder-Einspritzpumpe (PF)	*f*	pompe d'injection monocylindrique (PF)	*f*
single-point fuel injection	*n*	Zentraleinspritzung	*f*	injection monopoint	*f*
single-port plunger-and-barrel assembly	*n*	Einlochelement	*n*	élément à un orifice	*m*
single-spark ignition coil	*n*	Einzelfunken-Zündspule	*f*	bobine d'allumage à une sortie	*f*
single-spring nozzle holder	*n*	Einfeder-Düsenhalter	*m*	porte-injecteur à un ressort	*m*
single-stage filter	*n*	Einfachfilter	*n*	filtre à un étage	*m*
single-wheel control (ABS)	*n*	Einzelradregelung (ABS)	*f*	régulation individuelle (ABS)	*f*
slack adjuster (wheel brake)	*n*	Gestängesteller (Radbremse)	*m*	dispositif automatique de rattrapage de jeu (freins des roues)	*f*
slave cylinder (brakes)	*n*	Nehmerzylinder (Bremse)	*m*	cylindre récepteur (frein)	*m*
sleeve metering	*n*	Schieberzumessung	*f*	dosage par bague	*m*
sleeve travel	*n*	Schieberweg	*m*	course de coulisseau	*f*

English		German		French	
sleeve-metering fuel-injection pump (PE)	*n*	Hubschieber-Reiheneinspritzpumpe (PE)	*f*	pompe d'injection en ligne à tiroirs (PE)	*f*
slider	*n*	Gleitstein	*m*	tête coulissante	*f*
slider (brake cylinder)	*n*	Gleitstück (Bremszylinder)	*n*	coulisseau (cylindre de frein)	*m*
sliding block	*n*	Gleitstein	*m*	tête coulissante	*f*
sliding bolt	*n*	Verstellbolzen	*m*	axe de réglage	*m*
sliding contact	*n*	Schleifkontakt	*m*	contact par curseur	*m*
sliding flange	*n*	Verschiebeflansch	*m*	bride coulissante	*f*
sliding friction	*n*	Gleitreibung	*f*	frottement de glissement	*m*
sliding sleeve (governor)	*n*	Reglermuffe (Diesel-Regler)	*f*	manchon central (régulateur diesel)	*m*
sliding sunroof	*n*	Schiebedach	*n*	toît ouvrant	*m*
sliding tappet	*n*	Gleitstößel	*m*	poussoir coulissant	*m*
sliding-block guide (governor)	*n*	Kulissenführung (Diesel-Regler)	*f*	guide-coulisse (injection diesel)	*m*
sliding-gear starter	*n*	Schubtrieb-Starter	*m*	démarreur à pignon coulissant	*m*
sliding-gear starting motor	*n*	Schubtrieb-Starter	*m*	démarreur à pignon coulissant	*m*
sliding-sleeve travel (governor)	*n*	Muffenweg (Diesel-Regler)	*m*	course du manchon central (injection diesel)	*f*
sliding-vane supercharger	*n*	Flügelzellenlader	*m*	compresseur à palettes	*m*
slip	*n*	Gleitvorgang	*m*	glissement	*m*
slip angle (vehicle dynamics)	*n*	Schräglaufwinkel (Kfz-Dynamik)	*m*	angle de dérive (dynamique d'un véhicule)	*m*
slip controller (ESP)	*n*	Schlupfregler (ESP)	*m*	régulateur de glissement (ESP)	*m*
slip paste	*n*	Gleitpaste	*f*	pâte antigrippage	*f*
slip resistance (dynamic brake analyzer)	*n*	Gleitwiderstand (Rollenbremsprüfstand)	*m*	résistance de glissement (banc d'essai)	*f*
slip ring	*n*	Schleifring	*m*	bague collectrice	*f*
slip switching threshold (ABS)	*n*	Schlupfschaltschwelle (ABS)	*f*	seuil de glissement (ABS)	*m*
slip-rate difference	*n*	Schlupfdifferenz	*f*	différence de glissement	*f*
slip-ring end frame	*n*	Schleifringlagerschild (Generator)	*m*	flasque côté bagues collectrices (alternateur)	*m*
slippery	*adj*	rutschig	*adj*	glissant	*adj*
slit-shaped metering port	*n*	Steuerschlitz	*m*	fente d'étranglement (piston)	*f*
slot fill factor (rotating machines)	*n*	Nutfüllfaktor (drehende Maschinen)	*m*	facteur de remplissage des rainures (machines tournantes)	*m*
slotted spring pin	*n*	Spannhülse	*f*	douille de serrage	*f*
slotted washer	*n*	Nutscheibe	*f*	disque rainuré	*m*
slow down	*v*	verlangsamen	*v*	ralentir	*v*
small charger (battery)	*n*	Kleinlader (Batterie)	*m*	chargeur compact (batterie)	*m*
smoke emission test	*n*	Rauchprüfung	*f*	test d'émission de fumées	*m*
smoke limit	*n*	Rauchgrenze	*f*	limite d'émission de fumées	*f*
smoke limitation	*n*	Rauchbegrenzung	*f*	limitation de l'émission de fumées	*f*
smoke measurement	*n*	Rauchmessung	*f*	analyse des fumées diesel	*f*
smoke number	*n*	Schwärzungszahl	*f*	indice de noircissement	*m*
smoke-emission value	*n*	Rauchwert	*m*	valeur d'émission de fumées	*f*
smoke-limiting stop	*n*	Rauchbegrenzeranschlag	*m*	butée de limitation de fumée	*f*
smokemeter	*n*	Rauchgastester	*m*	fumimètre	*m*

English		German		French	
smooth running (IC engine)	*n*	Laufruhe (Verbrennungsmotor)	*f*	fonctionnement régulier (moteur à combustion)	*m*
smooth-idle device	*n*	Leiselaufvorrichtung	*f*	dispositif d'injection différée	*m*
smooth-running control	*n*	Laufruheregelung	*f*	régulation de la stabilité de fonctionnement	*f*
smooth-running regulator	*n*	Laufruheregler	*m*	régulateur de la stabilité de fonctionnement	*m*
snap-in fastening (wipers)	*n*	Steckbefestigung (Wischer)	*f*	fixation par enfichage (essuie-glace)	*f*
snap-in nib fastening (wipers)	*n*	Steckschnabelbefestigung (Wischer)	*f*	fixation par bec enfichable (essuie-glace)	*f*
snap-on connection	*n*	Schnappverbindung	*f*	liaison à déclic	*f*
snap-ring groove	*n*	Ringnut	*f*	rainure annulaire	*f*
snifter bore (tandem master cylinder)	*n*	Nachlaufbohrung (Tandemhauptzylinder)	*f*	canal d'équilibrage (maître-cylindre tandem)	*m*
snorkel (brake valve)	*n*	Schnorchel (Bremsventil)	*m*	reniflard (valve de frein)	*m*
socket	*n*	Steckdose	*f*	prise	*f*
socket housing	*n*	Steckhülsengehäuse	*n*	boîtier pour fiches femelles	*m*
soft casting	*n*	Weichverguß	*m*	enrobage mou	*m*
solenoid actuator	*n*	Magnetsteller	*n*	actionneur électromagnétique	*m*
solenoid armature	*n*	Magnetanker	*m*	armature d'électro-aimant	*f*
solenoid plunger relay	*n*	Tauchankerrelais	*n*	relais à noyau plongeur	*m*
solenoid relay valve	*n*	Magnetrelaisventil	*n*	électrovalve-relais	*f*
solenoid switch (starter)	*n*	Einrückrelais (Starter)	*n*	contacteur électromagnétique (démarreur)	*m*
solenoid valve	*n*	Magnetventil	*n*	électrovalve	*f*
solenoid winding	*n*	Magnetwicklung	*f*	bobine d'électro-aimant	*f*
solenoid-operated coupling	*n*	Magnetkupplung	*f*	accouplement électromagnétique	*m*
solenoid-operated shutoff	*n*	elektrische Abstellvorrichtung, ELAB	*f*	dispositif d'arrêt électrique	*m*
solenoid-valve block	*n*	Magnetventilblock	*m*	bloc d'électrovalves	*m*
sonic generator (car alarm)	*n*	Schallgeber (Autoalarm)	*m*	générateur acoustique (alarme auto)	*m*
soot burn-off	*n*	Rußabbrand	*m*	combustion de la suie	*f*
soot burn-off filter	*n*	Rußabbrennfilter	*m*	filtre d'oxidation de particules	*m*
soot emission	*n*	Rußemission	*f*	émission de particules de suie	*f*
soot filter	*n*	Rußfilter	*n*	filtre pour particules de suie	*m*
soot particle	*n*	Rußpartikel	*n*	particules de suie	*fpl*
soot production	*n*	Rußbildung	*f*	formation de suie	*f*
soot separator	*n*	Rußabscheider	*m*	séparateur de particules de suie	*m*
sound density	*n*	Schalldichte	*f*	densité acoustique	*f*
sound pressure	*n*	Schalldruck	*m*	pression acoustique	*f*
sound pressure level	*n*	Schalldruckpegel	*m*	niveau de pression acoustique	*m*
soundproofing	*n*	Schallisolierung	*f*	isolation acoustique	*f*
source of energy	*n*	Energiequelle	*f*	source d'énergie	*f*
spacer ring	*n*	Distanzring	*m*	bague-entretoise	*f*
spark advance	*n*	Zündverstellung	*f*	correction du point d'allumage	*f*
spark air gap (spark plug)	*n*	Luftfunkenstrecke (Zündkerze)	*f*	éclateur dans l'air (bougie)	*m*

English		German		French	
spark current	*n*	Funkenstrom	*m*	courant d'arc	*m*
spark discharge (at electrodes)	*n*	Funkenüberschlag (an den Elektroden)	*m*	éclatement de l'étincelle (aux électrodes)	*m*
spark duration	*n*	Funkendauer	*f*	durée de l'étincelle	*f*
spark erosion	*n*	Funkenerosion	*f*	érosion ionique	*f*
spark gap	*n*	Funkenstrecke	*f*	distance d'éclatement	*f*
spark head	*n*	Funkenkopf	*m*	tête de l'étincelle	*f*
spark length	*n*	Funkenlänge	*f*	longueur d'étincelle	*f*
spark plug	*n*	Zündkerze	*f*	bougie d'allumage	*f*
spark position	*n*	Funkenlage	*f*	position de l'éclateur	*f*
spark tail	*n*	Funkenschwanz	*m*	queue de l'étincelle	*f*
spark voltage (spark plug)	*n*	Brennspannung (Zündkerze)	*f*	tension d'arc (bougie)	*f*
spark-advance angle (ignition)	*n*	Zündverstellwinkel	*m*	angle de correction (allumage)	*m*
spark-ignition engine	*n*	Ottomotor	*m*	moteur à allumage par étincelle	*m*
spark-plug connector	*n*	Zündkerzenstecker	*m*	embout de bougie	*m*
spark-plug faces	*npl*	Zündkerzengesichter	*npl*	aspects de la bougie d'allumage	*mpl*
spark-plug gap	*n*	Elektrodenabstand (Zündkerze)	*m*	écartement des électrodes (bougie)	*m*
spark-plug recess	*n*	Zündkerzenmulde	*f*	logement de la bougie	*m*
spark-plug shell	*n*	Zündkerzengehäuse	*n*	culot de bougie	*m*
spark-plug-gap gauge	*n*	Zündkerzenlehre	*f*	jauge (bougie)	*f*
sparking rate	*n*	Funkenzahl	*f*	nombre d'étincelles	*m*
special electrode	*n*	Sonderelektrode	*f*	électrode spéciale	*f*
special examination (brakes)	*n*	Sonderuntersuchung (Bremse)	*f*	contrôle spécifique (frein)	*m*
special ignition coil	*n*	Sonderzündspule	*f*	bobine d'allumage spéciale	*f*
special tool	*n*	Sonderwerkzeug	*n*	outil spécial	*m*
specially ground pintle	*n*	Anschliff (Spritzzapfen)	*m*	chanfrein (téton d'injection)	*m*
specific gravity of electrolyte	*n*	Säuredichte	*f*	densité de l'électrolyte	*f*
spectral acceleration density	*n*	spektrale Beschleunigungs-dichte	*f*	densité spectrale d'accélération	*f*
speed droop	*n*	Proportionalgrad	*m*	statisme	*m*
speed limiting	*n*	Geschwindigkeitsbegrenzung	*f*	limitation de vitesse	*f*
speed path	*n*	Drehzahlpfad	*m*	piste de régime	*f*
speed range	*n*	Drehzahlbereich	*m*	plage de vitesses de rotation	*f*
speed regulation breakaway	*n*	Abregelung	*f*	coupure de débit	*f*
speed sensor	*n*	Drehzahlsensor	*m*	capteur de vitesse de rotation	*m*
speed up out of control (IC engine)	*v*	durchgehen (Verbrennungsmotor) x	*v*	emballer <s'emballer> (moteur à combustion)	*v*
speed-droop characteristic	*n*	Proportionalverhalten	*n*	action proportionnelle	*f*
speed-preselect, SP	*n*	Geschwindigkeits-Sollgeber	*m*	capteur de vitesse de consigne	*m*
speedometer generator	*n*	Tachogenerator	*m*	transmetteur tachymétrique	*m*
spherical pin	*n*	Kugelstift x	*m*	axe à profil sphérique	*m*
spill (fuel-injection pump)	*n*	Förderende (Einspritzpumpe)	*n*	fin de refoulement (pompe d'injection)	*f*
spill port	*n*	Steuerbohrung	*f*	orifice de distribution	*m*
spindle	*n*	Druckbolzen	*m*	tige-poussoir	*f*
spiral housing	*n*	Spiralgehäuse	*n*	carter hélicoïde	*m*
spiral spring	*n*	Spiralfeder	*f*	ressort hélicöidal	*m*

English		German		French	
spiral vee-shaped filter element	*n*	Wickelfiltereinsatz	*m*	cartouche filtrante en rouleau	*f*
spiral-type supercharger	*n*	Spirallader	*m*	compresseur à hélicoïde	*m*
splash guard (water)	*n*	Spritzschutz (Wasser)	*m*	protection contre les projections d'eau	*f*
splash protection (water)	*n*	Spritzschutz (Wasser)	*m*	protection contre les projections d'eau	*f*
spontaneous-ignition temperature	*n*	Selbstzündtemperatur	*f*	température d'autoallumage	*f*
spool overflow valve	*n*	Schieber-Überströmventil	*n*	soupape de décharge du coulisseau	*f*
spot lamp	*n*	Suchscheinwerfer	*m*	projecteur de recherche	*m*
spray	*n*	Düsenstrahl (aufgelöst)	*m*	jet pulvérisé	*m*
spray angle	*n*	Strahlkegelwinkel	*m*	angle du cône d'injection	*m*
spray direction	*n*	Düsenstrahlrichtung	*f*	direction du jet d'injecteur	*f*
spray dispersal angle	*n*	Strahlkegelwinkel	*m*	angle du cône d'injection	*m*
spray duration	*n*	Einspritzzeit	*f*	durée d'injection	*f*
spray orifice	*n*	Spritzloch	*n*	trou d'injection	*m*
spray pattern	*n*	Strahlbild	*n*	aspect du jet	*m*
spray shape (injection)	*n*	Strahlform (Einspritzung)	*f*	forme du jet (injection)	*f*
spray-hole cone angle	*n*	Spritzlochkegelwinkel	*m*	angle des trous d'injection	*m*
spray-hole length	*n*	Lochlänge	*f*	longueur des trous d'injection	*f*
spray-hole shape (injector)	*n*	Lochform (Einspritzdüse)	*f*	forme des trous d'injection	*f*
spring assembly	*n*	Federpaket	*n*	jeu de ressorts	*m*
spring chamber	*n*	Federraum	*m*	chambre de ressort(s)	*f*
spring characteristic	*n*	Federkennlinie	*f*	courbe caractéristique de ressor	*f*
spring compression	*n*	Einfederung	*f*	compression du ressort	*f*
spring contact	*n*	Federkontakt	*m*	ressort de contact	*m*
spring force	*n*	Federkraft	*f*	force du ressort	*f*
spring pack	*n*	Federpaket	*n*	jeu de ressorts	*m*
spring piston (height-control valve)	*n*	Federkolben (Luftfederventil)	*m*	piston (valve de nivellement)	*m*
spring plate	*n*	Federteller	*m*	cuvette de ressort	*f*
spring rate	*n*	Federrate	*f*	raideur de ressort	*f*
spring retainer	*n*	Federkapsel	*f*	coupelle	*f*
spring seat	*n*	Federteller	*m*	cuvette de ressort	*f*
spring sleeve (wheel-speed sensor)	*n*	Federhülse (Drehzahlsensor)	*f*	douille élastique (capteur de vitesse)	*f*
spring strip	*n*	Federschiene	*f*	lame-ressort	*f*
spring strut	*n*	Federbein	*n*	jambe de suspension	*f*
spring strut insert	*n*	Federbeineinsatz	*m*	insert de jambe de suspension	*m*
spring-loaded	*pp*	federbelastet	*pp*	taré par ressort	*pp*
spring-loaded idle-speed stop	*n*	federnder Leerlaufanschlag	*m*	butée élastique de ralenti	*f*
spring-type brake actuator	*n*	Federspeicher	*m*	accumulateur élastique	*m*
spring-type brake cylinder	*n*	Federspeicherzylinder (Bremse	*m*	cylindre de frein à accumulateur élastique	*m*
sprung weight	*n*	gefederte Masse	*f*	masse suspendue	*f*
square-wave pulse (ECU)	*n*	Rechteckimpuls (Steuergerät)	*m*	impulsion rectangulaire (calculateur)	*f*

English

English		German			French	
square-wave signal (ECU)	n	Rechtecksignal (Steuergerät)		n	signal rectangulaire (calculateur)	m
squeal (brakes)	v	quietschen (Bremse)		v	grincement (frein)	m
stabilizer	n	Stabilisator		m	stabilisateur	m
stack-type directional control valve	n	Blockwegeventil		n	bloc-distributeurs	m
standard horn	n	Normalhorn		n	avertisseur sonore standard	m
standard ignition coil	n	Standard-Zündspule		f	bobine d'allumage standard	f
standard nozzle	n	Seriendüse		f	injecteur de série	m
standard nozzle holder	n	Standard-Düsenhalter		m	porte-injecteur standard	m
standard rocker arm (valve gear)	n	Standard-Kipphebel (Ventiltrieb)		m	levier culbuteur (commande de soupapes)	m
standard sensor	n	Normgeber		m	capteur de référence	m
standardization	n	Standardisierung		f	standardisation	f
star connection	n	Sternschaltung		f	montage en étoile	m
star point	n	Sternpunkt		m	point neutre	m
star-shaped bracket (electromagnetic retarder)	n	Haltestern (Wirbelstrombremse)		m	support en forme d'étoile (frein à courants de Foucault)	m
start	v	Startvorgang		m	démarrage	m
start (IC engine)	v	anspringen (Verbrennungsmotor)	x	v	démarrer (moteur à combustion)	m
start control	n	Startsteuerung		f	commande de démarrage	f
start of braking	n	Bremsbeginn		m	début du freinage	m
start of combustion	n	Verbrennungsbeginn		m	début de combustion	m
start of delivery (fuel-injection pump)	n	Förderbeginn (Einspritzpumpe)		m	début de refoulement (pompe d'injection)	m
start of ignition	n	Zündbeginn		m	début d'inflammation	m
start of injection	n	Einspritzbeginn		m	début d'injection	m
start of lock-up (ABS)	n	Blockierbeginn (ABS)		m	début du blocage (ABS)	m
start of speed regulation	n	Abregelbeginn		m	début de la coupure de débit	m
start position	n	Startlage		f	position de démarrage	f
start quantity	n	Startmenge		f	débit de démarrage	m
start valve	n	Kaltstartventil		n	injecteur de départ à froid	m
start-assist measure	n	Starthilfe		f	auxiliaire de démarrage	m
start-assist system	n	Starthilfsanlage		f	dispositif auxiliaire de démarrage	m
start-locking	n	Startsperreinrichtung		f	dispositif de blocage du démarreur	m
start-locking relay	n	Startsperrelais		n	relais de blocage du démarreur	m
start-of-delivery control	n	Förderbeginnregelung		f	régulation du début de refoulement	f
start-of-delivery offset	n	Förderbeginnversatz		m	décalage du début de refoulement	m
start-of-delivery sensor	n	Förderbeginngeber, FBG		m	capteur de début de refoulemen	m
start-quantity limitation	n	Startmengenbegrenzung		f	limitation du débit de surcharge au démarrage	f
start-quantity lock	n	Startmengenverriegelung		f	bloqueur du débit de surcharge au démarrage	m

English

English		German		French	
start-quantity locking device	*n*	Startmengenverriegelung	*f*	bloqueur du débit de surcharge au démarrage	*m*
start-quantity release	*n*	Startmengenentriegelung	*f*	débloqueur du débit de surcharge au démarrage	*m*
start-quantity stop	*n*	Startmengenanschlag	*m*	butée de débit de surcharge au démarrage	*f*
start-quantity stop travel	*n*	Startmengenverstellweg	*m*	course de surcharge au démarrage	*f*
start-repeating block	*n*	Startwiederholsperre	*f*	anti-répétiteur de démarrage	*m*
start-temperature limit	*n*	Starttemperaturgrenze	*f*	limite de température de démarrage	*f*
starter	*n*	Starter	*m*	démarreur	*m*
starter battery	*n*	Starterbatterie	*f*	batterie de démarrage	*f*
starter cable	*n*	Starterhauptleitung	*f*	câble principal du démarreur	*m*
starter pinion	*n*	Starterritzel	*n*	pignon du démarreur	*m*
starting aid	*n*	Starthilfsanlage	*f*	dispositif auxiliaire de démarrage	*m*
starting cutout speed	*n*	Startabwurfdrehzahl	*f*	régime en fin de démarrage	*m*
starting enrichment	*n*	Startanhebung	*f*	signal d'enrichissement au démarrage	*m*
starting fuel delivery	*n*	Startmenge	*f*	débit de démarrage	*m*
starting fuel-quantity compensation	*n*	Startmengenabgleich	*m*	étalonnage du débit de démarrage	*m*
starting groove (plunger-and-barrel assembly)	*n*	Startnut (Pumpenelement)	*f*	encoche d'autoretard (élément de pompage)	*f*
starting lever	*n*	Starthebel	*m*	levier de démarrage	*m*
starting motor	*n*	Starter	*m*	démarreur	*m*
starting nozzle	*n*	Kaltstartdüse	*f*	gicleur de départ à froid	*m*
starting operation	*n*	Startbetrieb	*m*	démarrage (opération)	*m*
starting phase	*n*	Startphase	*f*	phase de démarrage	*f*
starting power	*n*	Startleistung	*f*	puissance de démarrage	*f*
starting rack travel	*n*	Startregelweg	*m*	course de régulation au démarrage	*f*
starting response	*n*	Startverhalten	*n*	comportement au démarrage	*m*
starting solenoid	*n*	Startmagnet	*m*	électro-aimant de démarrage	*m*
starting spring	*n*	Startfeder	*f*	ressort de démarrage	*m*
starting system	*n*	Startanlage	*f*	équipement de démarrage	*m*
starting temperature	*n*	Starttemperatur	*f*	température de démarrage	*f*
starting time	*n*	Startdauer	*f*	durée de démarrage	*f*
starting-cutout	*n*	Startabwurfsperrzeit	*f*	verrouillage en fin de démarrage	*m*
starting-motor relay	*n*	Starterrelais	*m*	relais de démarreur	*m*
starting-motor solenoid (starter)	*n*	Einrückmagnet (Starter)	*m*	électro-aimant d'engrènement (démarreur)	*m*
starting-quantity deactivator	*n*	Startverriegelung	*f*	verrouillage du débit de surcharge	*m*
starting-voltage increase	*n*	Startspannungsanhebung	*f*	élévation de tension au démarrage	*f*
state controller (ESP)	*n*	Zustandsregler (ESP)	*m*	régulateur d'état (ESP)	*m*
state of charge (battery)	*n*	Batterieladezustand	*m*	état de charge de la batterie	*m*

English		German		French	
static friction	*n*	Haftreibung	*f*	frottement statique (adhérence)	*m*
static pressure	*n*	Standdruck	*m*	pression statique	*f*
stator (alternator)	*n*	Stator (Generator)	*m*	stator (alternateur)	*m*
stator core (alternator)	*n*	Lamellenpaket (Generator)	*n*	paquet de lamelles de tôle (alternateur)	*m*
stator current	*n*	Ständerstrom	*m*	courant statorique	*m*
stator frame	*n*	Polgehäuse	*n*	carcasse stator	*f*
stator housing	*n*	Polgehäuse	*n*	carcasse stator	*f*
stator lamination (alternator)	*n*	Lamellenpaket (Generator)	*n*	paquet de lamelles de tôle (alternateur)	*m*
stator winding	*n*	Ständerwicklung	*f*	enroulement statorique	*m*
steady-state skidpad testing	*n*	stationäre Kreisfahrt	*f*	conduite circulaire stationnaire	*f*
steady-state speed	*n*	Beharrungsdrehzahl	*f*	vitesse d'équilibre	*f*
steady-state voltage (battery)	*n*	Ruhespannung (Batterie)	*f*	tension au repos (batterie)	*f*
steerability	*n*	Lenkbarkeit	*f*	dirigeabilité	*f*
steerable (motor vehicle)	*adj*	lenkbar (Kfz)	*adj*	dirigeable (véhicule)	*adj*
steering angle (vehicle dynamics)	*n*	Lenkwinkel (Kfz-Dynamik)	*m*	angle de braquage (dynamique d'un véhicule)	*m*
steering axis	*n*	Lenkdrehachse	*f*	axe de pivotement de la direction	*m*
steering-angle characteristic	*n*	Lenkwinkelverlauf	*m*	évolution de l'angle de braquage	*f*
steering-wheel angle sensor (ESP)	*n*	Lenkradwinkelsensor (ESP)	*m*	capteur d'angle de braquage (ESP)	*m*
steering-wheel force (vehicle dynamics)	*n*	Lenkradmoment (Kfz-Dynamik)	*n*	couple appliqué au volant de direction (dynamique d'un véhicule)	*m*
steering-wheel positioner	*n*	Lenkradverstellung	*f*	positionneur de volant	*m*
step light	*n*	Trittstufenleuchte	*f*	lampe de marchepied	*f*
step switch	*n*	Stufenschalter	*m*	commutateur à gradins	*m*
stepped	*pp*	abstufbar	*adj*	modérable	*adj*
stepped piston	*n*	Stufenkolben	*m*	piston différentiel	*m*
stepped plunger	*n*	Split-Element	*n*	élément avec fente de préinjection	*m*
stepped reflector	*n*	Stufenreflektor	*m*	réflecteur étagé	*m*
stepped spill port	*n*	gestufter Absteuerquerschnitt	*m*	trou de fin d'injection étagé	*m*
stepping motor	*n*	Schrittmotor	*m*	moteur pas à pas	*m*
sticker	*n*	Klebeschild	*n*	autocollant	*m*
stiffening element	*n*	Versteifungsrippe	*f*	raidisseur nervuré	*m*
stimulation characteristic value	*n*	Anregungskennwert	*m*	valeur d'excitation	*f*
stimulation frequency	*n*	Anregungsfrequenz	*f*	fréquence d'excitation	*f*
stoichiometric	*adj*	stöchiometrisch	*adj*	stœchiométrique	*adj*
stop (shutoff) lever	*n*	Abstellhebel	*m*	levier d'arrêt	*m*
stop adjustment mechanism	*n*	Anschlagstellwerk	*m*	commande de butée	*f*
stop disc	*n*	Anschlagscheibe	*f*	disque de butée	*m*
stop lamp	*n*	Bremsleuchte	*f*	feu de stop	*m*
stop lever (distributor pump)	*n*	Stopphebel (Verteilereinspritzpumpe)	*m*	levier de stop (pompe distributrice)	*m*

English		German		French	
stop lever (in-line pump)	*n*	Anschlaghebel (Reiheneinspritzpumpe)	*m*	levier de butée (pompe d'injection en ligne)	*m*
stop lug	*n*	Anschlagnase	*f*	bossage-butée	*m*
stop pin	*n*	Anschlagbolzen	*m*	axe de butée	*m*
stop position	*n*	Stopp-Stellung	*f*	position de stop	*f*
stop screw	*n*	Anschlagschraube	*f*	vis de butée	*f*
stop setting	*n*	Stopp-Stellung	*f*	position de stop	*f*
stop sleeve	*n*	Anschlaghülse	*f*	douille de butée	*f*
stop slot	*n*	Stoppnut	*f*	rainure de stop	*f*
stop strap	*n*	Anschlaglasche	*f*	patte de butée	*f*
stop surface	*n*	Anschlagfläche	*f*	surface d'arrêt	*f*
stop-lamp switch	*n*	Bremslichtschalter	*m*	contacteur de feux de stop	*m*
stop-light switch	*n*	Bremslichtschalter	*m*	contacteur de feux de stop	*m*
stop-spring	*n*	Rastfeder	*f*	ressort à cran d'arrêt	*m*
stopcock	*n*	Absperrhahn	*m*	robinet d'arrêt	*m*
stopping distance	*n*	Gesamtbremsweg	*m*	distance totale de freinage	*f*
stopping time (braking)	*n*	Anhaltezeit (Bremsvorgang)	*f*	temps d'arrêt (freinage)	*m*
storage pressure	*n*	Speicherdruck	*m*	pression de l'accumulateur	*f*
straight-ahead running stability (motor vehicle)	*n*	Geradeauslauf (Kfz)	*m*	trajectoire rectiligne (véhicule)	*f*
straight-line controller	*n*	Strahlenregler	*m*	correcteur à divergence	*m*
strain gage	*n*	Dehnmeßstreifen	*m*	jauge de contrainte	*f*
strainer (fuel injector)	*n*	Siebkörper (Einspritzventil)	*m*	crible (injecteur)	*m*
strainer (fuel-supply pump)	*n*	Siebfilter (Kraftstofförderpumpe)	*n*	crépine (pompe d'alimentation)	*f*
straining (filter)	*n*	Siebeffekt (Filter)	*m*	effet de filtrage (filtre)	*m*
stratified-charge engine	*n*	Schichtlademotor	*m*	moteur à charge stratifiée	*m*
strengthening rib	*n*	Versteifungsrippe	*f*	raidisseur nervuré	*m*
strip the insulation	*v*	abisolieren	*v*	dénuder	*v*
stroke at end of delivery	*n*	Hub am Förderende	*m*	course en fin de refoulement	*f*
stroke limitation	*n*	Hubkontrolle	*f*	limiteur de course	*m*
stroke limiter	*n*	Hubkontrolle	*f*	limiteur de course	*m*
stroke phase	*n*	Hubphase	*f*	série de courses	*f*
stroke-counting mechanism	*n*	Hub-Drehzähler	*m*	compte-tours et compte-coups	*m*
structure-borne noise	*n*	Körperschall	*m*	bruits d'impact	*mpl*
stud	*n*	Stehbolzen	*m*	boulon fileté	*m*
subsidiary	*n*	Tochtergesellschaft	*f*	filiale	*f*
substitute quantity curve	*n*	Ersatzmengenkennlinie	*f*	courbe de débit substitutif	*f*
substrate system (catalytic converter)	*n*	Trägersystem (Katalysator)	*n*	support (catalyseur)	*m*
suck in	*v*	ansaugen	*v*	aspirer	*v*
suction capacity	*n*	Ansaugleistung	*f*	capacité d'aspiration	*f*
suction connection	*n*	Sauganschluß	*m*	raccord d'aspiration	*m*
suction gallery	*n*	Saugraum (Einspritzpumpe)	*m*	galerie d'alimentation (pompe d'injection)	*f*
suction pressure	*n*	Saugdruck	*m*	pression d'aspiration	*f*
suction resonator	*n*	Saugresonator	*m*	résonateur d'admission	*m*
suction side	*n*	Saugseite	*f*	côté aspiration	*m*

English		German		French	
suction throttle	*n*	Saugdrossel	*f*	gicleur d'aspiration	*m*
suction valve (ABS/ABD)	*n*	Ansaugventil, ASV (ABS/ABD)	*n*	vanne d'aspiration (ABS/ABD)	*f*
suction valve (fuel-supply pump)	*n*	Saugventil (Kraftstofförderpumpe)	*n*	soupape d'aspiration (pompe d'alimentation)	*f*
sudden steering input (vehicle dynamics)	*n*	Lenkwinkelsprung (Kfz-Dynamik)	*m*	réaction transitoire de lacet (dynamique d'un véhicule)	*f*
sun gear	*n*	Sonnenrad	*n*	roue solaire	*f*
supercharge (IC engine)	*v*	aufladen (Verbrennungsmotor)	*v*	suralimenter (moteur à combustion)	*v*
supercharger	*n*	Lader	*m*	compresseur (suralimentation)	*m*
supercharging process	*n*	Aufladeverfahren	*n*	procédé de suralimentation	*m*
supertone horn	*n*	Starktonhorn	*n*	avertisseur surpuissant	*m*
supplementary reflector	*n*	Zusatzreflektor	*m*	réflecteur supplémentaire	*m*
supplementary-equipment set	*n*	Nachrüstsatz	*m*	jeu d'équipement ultérieur	*m*
supply line	*n*	Versorgungsleitung	*f*	conduite d'alimentation	*f*
supply line (two-line braking system)	*n*	Vorratsleitung (Zweileitungs-Bremsanlage)	*f*	conduite d'alimentation (dispositif de freinage à deux conduites)	*f*
supply pressure (brakes)	*n*	Vorratsdruck (Bremse)	*m*	pression d'alimentation (frein)	*f*
supply pressure (Jetronic)	*n*	Versorgungsdruck (Jetronic)	*m*	pression d'alimentation (Jetronic)	*f*
supply pump (fuel)	*n*	Kraftstofförderpumpe	*f*	pompe d'alimentation (carburant)	*f*
supply voltage	*n*	Versorgungsspannung	*f*	tension d'alimentation	*f*
supply-pump pressure	*n*	Förderpumpendruck	*m*	pression de transfert (pompe d'alimentation)	*f*
support bearing (drum brake)	*n*	Stützlager (Trommelbremse)	*n*	palier d'appui (frein à tambour)	*m*
support plate (filter)	*n*	Stützplatte (Filter)	*f*	plaque-support (filtre)	*f*
support plate (ignition-advance mechanism)	*n*	Achsplatte (Zündversteller)	*f*	plateau-support (correcteur d'avance)	*m*
support rib	*n*	Stützrippe	*f*	nervure d'appui	*f*
support ring	*n*	Stützring	*m*	bague d'appui	*f*
suppression capacitor	*n*	Entstörkondensator	*m*	condensateur d'antiparasitage	*m*
suppression filter	*n*	Entstörfilter	*n*	filtre d'antiparasitage	*m*
suppressor	*n*	Entstörstecker	*m*	embout d'antiparasitage	*m*
surface air-gap (spark plug)	*n*	Luftgleitfunken (Zündkerze)	*m*	étincelle glissante (bougie)	*f*
surface-gap spark plug	*n*	Gleitfunkenzündkerze	*f*	bougie à étincelle glissante	*f*
surge damping	*n*	Ruckeldämpfung	*f*	amortissement d'à-coups	*m*
surge damping control	*n*	aktive Ruckeldämpfung, ARD	*f*	amortissement actif d'à-coups	*m*
surge-proof	*adj*	spannungsfest	*adj*	rigidité diélectrique	*f*
surplus force	*n*	Überschußkraft	*f*	force excédentaire	*f*
susceptible device (EMC)	*n*	Störsenke (EMV)	*f*	capteur de perturbations (CEM)	*m*
suspension element (air suspension)	*n*	Federelement (Luftfederung)	*n*	élément de suspension (suspension pneumatique)	*m*
sustained braking pressure	*n*	Dauerbremsdruck	*m*	pression de freinage continue	*f*
sustained operation	*n*	Selbstlauf	*m*	fonctionnement autonome	*m*
swept volume (IC engine)	*n*	Hubvolumen (Verbrennungsmotor)	*n*	cylindrée (moteur à combustion)	*f*

English		German		French	
swinging door (bus)	*n*	Schwingtür (Omnibus)	*f*	porte va-et-vient (autobus)	*f*
swirl	*v*	Drall	*m*	tourbillon	*m*
swirl actuator (radial-piston pump)	*n*	Drallsteller (Radialkolbenpumpe)	*m*	actionneur à effet giratoire (pompe à pistons radiaux)	*m*
swirl chamber	*n*	Wirbelkammer	*f*	chambre de tourbillonnement	*f*
swirl control	*n*	Drallniveausteuerung	*f*	commande de niveau de giration	*f*
swirl effect	*n*	Verwirbelung	*f*	turbulence	*f*
swirl nozzle	*n*	Dralldüse	*f*	buse à effet giratoire	*f*
swirl plate	*n*	Dralltopf	*m*	pot de giration	*m*
switch box	*n*	Schaltkasten	*m*	boîte de commande	*f*
switch-on threshold	*n*	Einschaltschwelle	*f*	seuil d'enclenchement	*m*
switched current	*n*	Schaltstrom	*m*	courant d'enclenchement	*m*
switched voltage	*n*	Schaltspannung	*f*	tension de rupture	*f*
switching cycle	*n*	Schaltspiel	*n*	cycle de commutation	*m*
switching element (door control)	*n*	Umschaltglied (Türbetätigung)	*n*	contact d'inversion (commande des portes)	*m*
switching frequency	*n*	Schaltrhythmus (Relais)	*m*	rythme de commutation	*m*
switching frequency (multivibrator)	*n*	Kippfrequenz (Multivibrator)	*f*	fréquence d'oscillation (multivibrateur)	*f*
switching loss	*n*	Umschaltverlust	*m*	pertes de commutation	*fpl*
swivel arm	*n*	Schwenkarm	*m*	bras pivotant	*m*
swivel cover (coupling head)	*n*	Drehdeckel (Kupplungskopf)	*m*	couvercle pivotant (tête d'accouplement)	*m*
swivelling lever	*n*	Schwenkhebel	*m*	levier pivotant	*m*
symbol	*n*	Schaltzeichen	*n*	symbole graphique	*m*
system peripheral equipment	*n*	Systemperipherie	*f*	périphériques du système	*mpl*
system pressure (gasoline injection)	*n*	Systemdruck (Jetronic)	*m*	pression du système (Jetronic)	*f*
T					
tachograph	*n*	Fahrtschreiber	*m*	tachographe	*m*
tachograph chart	*n*	Diagrammscheibe (Tachograph)	*f*	disque d'enregistrement (tachographe)	*m*
tachometer (general term)	*n*	Drehzahlmesser (allgemein)	*m*	tachymètre (terme général)	*m*
tail lamp	*n*	Schlußleuchte	*f*	feu arrière	*m*
tandem master cylinder	*n*	Tandemhauptzylinder	*m*	maître-cylindre tandem	*m*
tandem-pattern wiper system	*n*	Gleichlaufsystem (Scheibenwischer)	*n*	système tandem (essuie-glace)	*m*
tank installation assembly	*n*	Tankeinbaueinheit	*f*	unité de puisage	*f*
tank ventilation	*n*	Tankentlüftung	*f*	dégazage du réservoir	*m*
tapered spray	*n*	Kegelstrahl	*m*	jet conique	*m*
tappet (valve gear)	*n*	Stößel (Ventiltrieb)	*m*	poussoir (commande de soupape)	*m*
tappet plunger	*n*	Stößelkolben	*m*	piston-poussoir	*m*
tappet roller	*n*	Stößelrolle	*f*	galet de poussoir	*m*
target curve	*n*	Zielkurve	*f*	courbe cible	*f*
TBI unit (Mono-Jetronic)	*n*	Einspritzaggregat (Mono-Jetronic)	*n*	unité d'injection (Mono-Jetronic)	*f*
TBI, throttle-body injection	*n*	Zentraleinspritzung	*f*	injection monopoint	*f*

English		German		French	
TCS lock valve	n	ASR-Sperrventil	n	valve de barrage ASR	f
TCS, traction control system	a	Antriebsschlupfregelung, ASR	f	régulation d'antipatinage à la traction, ASR	f
technical customer information	n	Technische Kundenunterlage, TKU	f	document technique client	m
Technical Instruction (Bosch publication)	n	Technische Unterrichtung (Bosch-Schriftenreihe)	f	Cahier technique (publication Bosch)	m
telescopic spring contact	n	Teleskopfederkontakt	m	contact télescopique à ressort	m
temperature coefficient	n	Temperaturkoeffizient	m	coefficient de température	m
temperature compensation	n	Temperaturkompensation	f	compensation thermique	f
temperature drift	n	Temperaturdrift	f	dérive de température	f
temperature limits of application	n	thermischer Anwendungsbereich	m	plage d'application thermique	f
temperature profile	n	Temperaturverlauf	m	évolution de la température	f
temperature resistance	n	Temperaturbeständigkeit	f	résistance thermique	f
temperature sensor	n	Temperatursensor	m	capteur de température	m
temperature switch	n	Thermoschalter	m	thermocontact	m
temperature threshold	n	Temperaturschwelle	f	seuil de température	m
temperature-controlled idle-speed increase	n	temperaturabhängige Leerlaufanhebung, TLA	f	correcteur de ralenti piloté par la température	m
temperature-dependent excess-fuel quantity	n	temperaturabhängige Startmenge	f	surcharge variable en fonction de la température	f
temperature-dependent full-load fuel delivery	n	temperaturabhängige Vollastmenge	f	débit de pleine charge dépendant de la température	m
temperature-dependent limit quantity	n	temperaturabhängige Grenzmenge	f	débit limite en fonction de la température	m
temperature-dependent low-idle correction	n	temperaturabhängige Leerlaufkorrektur	f	correction de ralenti en fonction de la température	f
temperature-dependent quantity increment	n	temperaturabhängiges Mengeninkrement	n	incrément de débit en fonction de la température	m
temperature-dependent starting stop	n	temperaturabhängiger Startanschlag, TAS	m	correcteur de surcharge en fonction de la température	m
temperature-dependent waiting period	n	temperaturabhängige Wartezeit	f	temps d'attente en fonction de la température	m
temperature-measuring spark plug	n	Temperatur-Meßzündkerze	f	bougie thermocouple	f
template	n	Kulissenplatte	f	coulisse	f
tendency to knock	n	Klopfneigung	f	tendance au cliquetis	f
tendency to lock (wheel)	n	Blockierneigung (Rad)	f	tendance au blocage (roue)	f
tensioning lever	n	Spannhebel	m	levier de tension	m
terminal designation	n	Klemmenbezeichnung	f	identification des bornes	f
terminal diagram	n	Anschlußplan	m	schéma de connexion	m
terminal location (circuit diagram)	n	Anschlußpunkt (Schaltplan)	m	borne (schéma)	f
terminal nut (spark plug)	n	Anschlußmutter (Zündkerze)	f	écrou de connexion (bougie)	m
terminal post (battery)	n	Endpol (Batterie)	m	borne (batterie)	f
terminal screw	n	Anschlußbolzen	m	tige de connexion	f
terminal stud	n	Anschlußbolzen	m	tige de connexion	f
terminal voltage	n	Klemmenspannung	f	tension aux bornes	f

English		German		French	
terminal-post cover (battery)	*n*	Polabdeckkappe (Batterie)	*f*	capot de protection de borne (batterie)	*m*
test bench	*n*	Prüfstand	*m*	banc d'essai	*m*
test consumption	*n*	Testverbrauch	*m*	consommation d'essai	*f*
test cycle (exhaust-gas test)	*n*	Fahrkurve (Abgasprüfung)	*f*	diagramme de test (émissions)	*m*
test engine	*n*	Prüfmotor	*m*	moteur d'essai	*m*
test equipment	*n*	Prüfeinrichtung	*f*	dispositif d'essai	*m*
test gas (exhaust-gas test)	*n*	Meßgas (Abgasprüfung)	*n*	gaz de mesure (émissions)	*m*
test instructions	*npl*	Prüfanleitung	*f*	notice d'essai	*f*
test pipe (injection-pump test bench)	*n*	Prüfleitung (Einspritzpumpen-Prüfstand)	*f*	conduite d'essai (banc d'essai)	*f*
test position (parking-brake valve)	*n*	Prüfstellung (Feststellbremsventil)	*f*	position de contrôle (valve de frein de stationnement)	*f*
test procedure	*n*	Prüfablauf	*m*	déroulement du contrôle	*m*
test program (exhaust-gas test)	*n*	Prüfprogramm (Abgasprüfung)	*n*	programme d'essai (émissions)	*m*
test pulse	*n*	Prüfimpuls	*m*	impulsion de contrôle	*f*
test record	*n*	Prüfprotokoll	*n*	procès-verbal d'essai	*m*
test regulations	*npl*	Prüfvorschrift	*f*	instructions d'essai	*fpl*
test report	*n*	Prüfbericht	*m*	compte-rendu d'essai	*m*
test specifications	*npl*	Prüfwerte	*mpl*	valeurs d'essai	*fpl*
test speed	*n*	Prüfgeschwindigkeit	*f*	vitesse d'essai	*f*
test technology	*n*	Prüftechnik	*f*	technique de contrôle et d'essai	*f*
test values	*npl*	Prüfwerte	*mpl*	valeurs d'essai	*fpl*
test valve	*n*	Prüfventil	*n*	valve de contrôle	*f*
test voltage	*n*	Prüfspannung	*f*	tension d'essai	*f*
theft-deterrence feature	*n*	Diebstahlschutz	*m*	dispositif antivol	*m*
theft-deterrent system	*n*	Auto-Alarmanlage	*n*	alarme auto	*f*
theoretical air-flow volume	*n*	theoretischer Luftdurchsatz	*m*	débit volumétrique théorique d'air	*m*
thermal conduction path	*n*	Wärmeleitweg	*m*	chemin de conduction de la chaleur	*m*
thermal conductivity	*n*	Wärmeleitfähigkeit	*f*	conductibilité thermique	*f*
thermal shock	*n*	Thermoschock	*m*	choc thermique	*m*
thermal value (spark plug)	*n*	Wärmewert (Zündkerze)	*m*	degré thermique (bougie)	*m*
thermal-conduction paste	*n*	Wärmeleitpaste	*f*	pâte thermoconductrice	*f*
thermal-protection cap (injection nozzle)	*n*	Wärmeschutzhütchen (Einspritzdüse)	*n*	capuchon calorifuge (injecteur)	*m*
thermal-protection disc (injection nozzle)	*n*	Wärmeschutzscheibe (Einspritzdüse)	*f*	rondelle calorifuge (injecteur)	*f*
thermal-protection plate (injection nozzle)	*n*	Wärmeschutzplättchen (Einspritzdüse)	*n*	plaquette calorifuge (injecteur)	*f*
thermal-protection sleeve (injection nozzle)	*n*	Wärmeschutzhülse (Einspritzdüse)	*f*	manchon calorifuge (injecteur)	*m*
thermo-switch	*n*	Thermoschalter	*m*	thermocontact	*m*
thermo-time switch	*n*	Thermozeitschalter	*m*	thermocontact temporisé	*m*
thermocouple spark plug	*n*	Temperatur-Meßzündkerze	*f*	bougie thermocouple	*f*
thermostat	*n*	Thermostat	*m*	thermostat	*m*
thermostatic switch	*n*	Thermoschalter	*m*	thermocontact	*m*
thermostatic valve	*n*	Thermostatventil	*n*	valve thermostatique	*f*

English		German		French	
thick-film diaphragm	*n*	Dickschicht-Membran	*f*	membrane à couches épaisses	*f*
thick-film techniques	*npl*	Dickschichttechnik	*f*	technique à couches épaisses	*f*
thin-film techniques	*npl*	Dünnschichttechnik	*f*	technique à couches minces	*f*
threaded port	*n*	Gewindeanschluß	*m*	orifice taraudé	*m*
threaded sleeve	*n*	Gewindehülse	*f*	corps fileté	*m*
threaded-neck mounting	*n*	Gewindehalsbefestigung	*f*	fixation par bague filetée	*f*
three-chamber lamp	*n*	Dreikammerleuchte	*f*	lanterne à trois compartiments	*f*
three-phase current	*n*	Drehstrom	*m*	courant triphasé	*m*
three-phase winding	*n*	Drehstromwicklung	*f*	enroulement triphasé	*m*
three-position valve	*n*	Dreistellungsventil	*n*	valve à trois positions	*f*
three-way catalytic converter, TWC	*n*	Dreiwegekatalysator	*m*	catalyseur trois voies	*m*
threshold speed	*n*	Schwellendrehzahl	*f*	régime de seuil	*m*
threshold voltage	*n*	Schwellenspannung	*f*	tension de seuil	*f*
throttle actuator	*n*	Drosselklappensteller	*m*	actionneur de papillon	*m*
throttle bore	*n*	Drosselbohrung	*f*	orifice d'étranglement	*m*
throttle device	*n*	Drosselvorrichtung	*f*	dispositif d'étranglement	*m*
throttle linkage	*n*	Gasgestänge	*n*	timonerie d'accélérateur	*f*
throttle pin	*n*	Drosselbolzen	*m*	axe d'étranglement	*m*
throttle response (IC engine)	*n*	Gasannahme (Verbrennungsmotor) x	*f*	admission des gaz (moteur à combustion)	*f*
throttle screw	*n*	Drosselschraube	*f*	vis-pointeau	*f*
throttle unit	*n*	Drosselvorrichtung	*f*	dispositif d'étranglement	*m*
throttle valve (door control)	*n*	Drosselventil (Türbetätigung)	*n*	valve d'amortissement (pivotement des portes)	*f*
throttle valve (IC engine)	*n*	Drosselklappe	*f*	papillon des gaz (moteur à combustion)	*m*
throttle-body injection, TBI	*n*	Zentraleinspritzung	*f*	injection monopoint	*f*
throttle-type non-return valve	*n*	Drosselrückschlagventil	*n*	clapet de non-retour à étranglement	*m*
throttle-valve actuator	*n*	Drosselklappensteller	*m*	actionneur de papillon	*m*
throttle-valve angle	*n*	Drosselklappenwinkel	*m*	angle de papillon	*m*
throttle-valve assembly	*n*	Drosselklappenstutzen	*m*	boîtier de papillon	*m*
throttle-valve intervention (TCS)	*n*	Drosselklappeneingriff (ASR)	*m*	intervention sur le papillon (ASR)	*f*
throttle-valve position	*n*	Drosselklappenstellung	*f*	position du papillon	*f*
throttle-valve potentiometer	*n*	Drosselklappenpotentiometer	*n*	potentiomètre de papillon	*m*
throttle-valve sensor	*n*	Drosselklappensensor	*m*	capteur de papillon	*m*
throttle-valve shaft	*n*	Drosselklappenwelle	*f*	axe de papillon	*m*
throttle-valve switch	*n*	Drosselklappenschalter	*m*	contacteur de papillon	*m*
throttling effect	*n*	Drosselwirkung	*f*	effet d'étranglement	*m*
throttling gap	*n*	Drosselspalt	*m*	fente d'étranglement (injecteur)	*f*
throttling pintle	*n*	Drosselzapfen	*m*	téton d'étranglement	*m*
throttling pintle nozzle	*n*	Drosselzapfendüse	*f*	injecteur à téton et étranglemen	*m*
throttling point	*n*	Drosselstelle	*f*	point d'étranglement	*m*
throttling stroke	*n*	Drosselhub	*m*	plage d'étranglement	*f*
throughflow principle	*n*	Durchströmprinzip	*n*	principe de transfert	*m*

English		German		French	
thrust block (dynamic brake analyzer)	*n*	Drucklager (Rollenbremsprüfstand)	*n*	butée (banc d'essai)	*f*
thrust member (coupling head)	*n*	Druckstück (Kupplungskopf)	*n*	pièce de pression (tête d'accouplement)	*f*
tightening torque	*n*	Anzugsdrehmoment	*n*	couple initial de démarrage	*m*
tilt sensor	*n*	Neigungssensor	*m*	capteur d'inclinaison	*m*
tilt sensor (car alarm)	*n*	Winkelgeber (Autoalarm)	*m*	capteur de position angulaire (alarme auto)	*m*
tilt switch (car alarm)	*n*	Neigungsschalter (Autoalarm)	*m*	contacteur d'inclinaison (alarme auto)	*m*
time loss (braking action)	*n*	Verlustzeit (Bremsvorgang)	*f*	temps mort (effet de freinage)	*m*
timer core (ignition)	*n*	Impulsgeberrad (Zündung)	*n*	noyau synchroniseur (allumage)	*m*
timing characteristic	*n*	Verstellcharakteristik	*f*	caractéristique d'avance	*f*
timing device	*n*	Spritzversteller	*m*	variateur d'avance	*m*
timing frequency	*n*	Taktfrequenz	*f*	fréquence des impulsions	*f*
timing valve	*n*	Taktventil	*n*	électrovanne à rapport cyclique d'ouverture	*f*
timing-device solenoid valve	*n*	Spritzversteller-Magnetventil	*n*	électrovanne de variateur d'avance	*f*
tip circle (gear)	*n*	Kopfkreis (Zahnrad)	*m*	cercle de tête (engrenage)	*m*
tire braking force	*n*	Reifenbremskraft	*f*	force de freinage du pneumatique	*f*
tire contact area	*n*	Reifenaufstandsfläche	*f*	surface de contact du pneu	*f*
tire contact patch	*n*	Reifenaufstandsfläche	*f*	surface de contact du pneu	*f*
tire force	*n*	Reifenkraft	*f*	force de freinage au roulement des pneumatiques	*f*
tire grip	*n*	Griffigkeit (Reifen)	*f*	adhérence (pneu)	*f*
tire pressure	*n*	Reifendruck	*m*	pression du pneu	*f*
tire rigidity	*n*	Reifensteifigkeit	*f*	rigidité du pneumatique	*f*
tire slip	*n*	Reifenschlupf	*m*	glissement (pneu)	*m*
tire wear	*n*	Reifenverschleiß	*m*	usure du pneu	*f*
tire working point	*n*	Reifenarbeitspunkt	*m*	point de travail du pneumatique	*m*
tire-inflation device	*n*	Reifenfülleinrichtung	*f*	dispositif de gonflage des pneus	*m*
tire-inflation fitting	*n*	Reifenfüllanschluß	*m*	raccord de gonflage des pneus	*m*
tire-inflation hose	*n*	Reifenfüllschlauch	*m*	flexible de gonflage des pneus	*m*
tire-pressure monitoring system	*n*	Reifenkontrollsystem	*n*	système de contrôle des pneumatiques	*m*
tire-road-interface friction coefficient	*n*	Haftreibungszahl (Reifen/Straße)	*f*	coefficient d'adhérence (pneu/route)	*m*
toggle lever	*n*	Kniehebel	*m*	levier à rotule	*m*
tone-sequence control device	*n*	Tonfolgeschalter	*m*	relais commutateur de tonalités	*m*
tooth space	*n*	Zahnlücke	*f*	entredent	*m*
toothed belt	*n*	Zahnriemen	*m*	courroie dentée	*f*
top dead center, TDC	*n*	Oberer Totpunkt, OT	*m*	point mort haut, PMH	*m*
top-feed injector	*n*	Einspritzventil mit axialer Zuführung ("Top-Feed")	*n*	injecteur à flux axial	*m*
toroid bellows (air spring)	*n*	Torusbalgfeder (Luftfeder)	*f*	ressort toroïde (suspension)	*m*

English

English		German		French	
torque balance (TCS)	n	Momentenbilanz (ASR)	f	bilan des couples des roues motrices (ASR)	m
torque control	n	Angleichung	f	correction de débit	f
torque curve	n	Drehmomentverlauf	m	courbe du couple	f
torque lever (dynamic brake analyzer)	n	Drehmomenthebel (Rollenbremsprüfstand)	m	levier dynamométrique (banc d'essai)	m
torque limitation	n	Drehmomentbegrenzung	f	limitation de couple	f
torque sensor	n	Drehmomentsensor	m	capteur de couple	m
torque-control bar	n	Angleichlasche	f	patte de correction	f
torque-control characteristic	n	Angleichverlauf	m	caractéristique de correction de débit	f
torque-control lever	n	Angleichhebel	m	levier de correction de débit	m
torque-control mechanism	n	Angleichvorrichtung	f	correcteur de débit	m
torque-control quantity	n	Angleichmenge	f	débit correcteur	m
torque-control range	n	Angleichbereich	m	plage de correction de débit	f
torque-control rate	n	Angleichrate	f	taux de correction de débit	m
torque-control shaft	n	Angleichbolzen	m	axe de correction de débit	m
torque-control spring	n	Angleichfeder	f	ressort correcteur de débit	m
torque-control travel	n	Angleichweg	m	course de correction de débit	f
torque-control valve	n	Angleichventil	n	soupape de correction de débit	f
total braking distance	n	Gesamtbremsweg	m	distance totale de freinage	f
total braking force	n	gesamte Bremskraft	f	force de freinage totale	f
total braking time	n	Gesamtbremsdauer	f	temps total de freinage	m
total running resistance	n	Gesamtfahrwiderstand	m	résistance totale à l'avancement	f
tow-away protection (car alarm)	n	Abschleppschutz (Autoalarm)	m	protection contre le remorquage (alarme auto)	f
towed vehicle	n	Anhängefahrzeug	n	véhicule tracté	m
towing vehicle	n	Zugfahrzeug	n	véhicule tracteur	m
traction control system, TCS	n	Antriebsschlupfregelung, ASR	f	régulation d'antipatinage à la traction, ASR	f
traction slip	n	Antriebsschlupf	m	antipatinage à la traction	m
tractive force	n	Vortriebskraft	f	force de propulsion	f
tractive solenoid	n	Hubmagnet	m	électro-aimant de commande	m
tractor vehicle	n	Zugfahrzeug	n	véhicule tracteur	m
traffic-control engeneering	n	Verkehrsleittechnik	f	technique de radioguidage de la circulation	f
trailer	n	Anhängefahrzeug	n	véhicule tracté	m
trailer brake	n	Anhängerbremse	f	frein de remorque	m
trailer brake line	n	Anhängerbremsleitung	f	conduite de frein de remorque	f
trailer braking equipment	n	Anhängerbremsausrüstung	f	équipement de freinage de la remorque	m
trailer circuit (compressed-air system)	n	Anhängerkreis (Druckluftanlage)	m	circuit de commande de la remorque (dispositif à air comprimé)	m
trailer control	n	Anhängersteuerung	f	commande de remorque	f
trailer control module, TCM	n	Anhängersteuermodul, ASM	m	module de commande remorque	m
trailer hitch	n	Anhängerkupplung	f	accouplement de remorque	m
trailer operation	n	Anhängerbetrieb	m	exploitation avec remorque	f
trailer pilot control	n	Anhängeransteuerung	f	pilotage de la remorque	m

English		German		French	
trailer power supply	*n*	Anhängerversorgung	*f*	alimentation de la remorque	*f*
trailer recognition (ABS)	*n*	Anhängererkennung (ABS)	*f*	détection de la fonction "remorque" (ABS)	*f*
trailer relay valve	*n*	Anhängerrelaisventil	*n*	valve-relais de remorque	*f*
trailer-brake system	*n*	Anhänger-Bremsanlage	*f*	dispositif de freinage de remorque	*m*
trailer-brake valve	*n*	Anhängerbremsventil	*n*	valve de frein de remorque	*f*
trailer-control valve	*n*	Anhängersteuerventil	*n*	valve de commande de remorque	*f*
trailing axle	*n*	Nachlaufachse	*f*	essieu suiveur	*m*
trailing shoe	*n*	ablaufende Bremsbacke	*f*	mâchoire secondaire	*f*
trailing throttle	*n*	Schiebebetrieb	*m*	régime de décélération	*m*
trailing-throttle lean adjustment	*n*	Verzögerungsabmagerung	*f*	appauvrissement en décélération	*m*
transfer diaphragm	*n*	Wirkmembran	*f*	membrane active	*f*
transfer rate (CAN)	*n*	Übertragungsrate (CAN)	*f*	taux de transmission (multiplexage)	*m*
transfer rod (level sensor)	*n*	Antriebshebel (Niveaugeber)	*m*	levier de transmission (capteur de niveau)	*m*
transformation ratio (number of coils)	*n*	Windungsverhältnis	*n*	rapport de transformation (nombre de spires)	*m*
transient response	*n*	Übergangsverhalten	*n*	réaction transitoire	*f*
transistorized ignition, TI	*n*	Transistorzündung, TZ	*f*	allumage transistorisé	*m*
transition phase (exhaust-gas test)	*n*	Übergangsphase (Abgasprüfung)	*f*	phase transitoire (émissions)	*f*
transition response	*n*	Übergangsverhalten	*n*	réaction transitoire	*f*
transmission (braking system)	*n*	Übertragungseinrichtung (Bremsanlage)	*f*	dispositif de transmission (dispositif de freinage)	*m*
transmission agent (braking system)	*n*	Übertragungsmedium (Bremsanlage)	*n*	moyen de transmission (dispositif de freinage)	*m*
transmission-shift control	*n*	Getriebesteuerung	*f*	commande de boîte de vitesses	*f*
transverse passage	*n*	Querbohrung	*f*	canal radial	*m*
transversely jointed linkage (wiper system)	*n*	Kreuzlenker (Wischeranlage)	*m*	articulation en croix (essuie-glace)	*f*
travel sensor	*n*	Weggeber	*m*	capteur de déplacement	*m*
travel-limiting spring	*n*	Wegfeder	*f*	ressort limiteur de course	*m*
trickle charging (battery charge)	*n*	Dauerladung (Batterieladung)	*f*	charge permanente (charge de batterie)	*f*
trigger	*v*	ansteuern	*v*	piloter	*v*
trigger box (ignition)	*n*	Zündschaltgerät	*n*	module de commande de l'allumage	*m*
trigger level	*n*	Triggerpegel	*m*	bascule bistable	*f*
trigger threshold	*n*	Auslöseschwelle	*f*	seuil de déclenchement	*m*
trigger unit (belt tightener)	*n*	Gurtstraffer-Auslösegerät	*n*	déclencheur de prétensionneur	*m*
trigger wheel (ignition)	*n*	Impulsgeberrad (Zündung)	*n*	noyau synchroniseur (allumage)	*m*
triggering (ABS control)	*n*	Ansteuerung (ABS-Regelung)	*f*	pilotage (régulation ABS)	*m*
triggering criterion	*n*	Auslösekriterium	*n*	critère de déclenchement	*m*
triggering signal	*n*	Ansteuersignal	*n*	signal pilote	*m*
triggering system	*n*	Auslösessystem	*m*	système de déclenchement	*m*

English

English			German			French	
trip computer		n	Bordcomputer		m	ordinateur de bord	m
trip recorder		n	Fahrtschreiber		m	tachographe	m
triple directional-control-valve block		n	Dreifach-Wegeventilblock		m	bloc-distributeur triple	m
triple-circuit protection valve		n	Dreikreis-Schutzventil		n	valve de sécurité à trois circuits	f
triple-fluted valve		n	Dreiflügelventil		n	soupape à trois ailettes	f
trunk protection (car alarm)		n	Kofferraumsicherung (Autoalarm)		f	protection du coffre (alarme auto)	f
tuned-intake pressure-charging		n	Resonanzaufladung		f	suralimentation par résonance	f
turbine housing		n	Turbinengehäuse		n	carter de turbine	m
turbo element		n	Strömungsmaschine		f	turbomachine	f
turbo lag	x	n	Turboloch	x	n	trou de suralimentation	m
turbo overrun limiting		n	Turboschubbegrenzung		f	limitation de suralimentation en décélération	f
turbocharge		v	Abgasturboaufladung		f	suralimentation par turbocompresseur	f
turbocharged engine		n	Turbomotor		m	moteur à turbocompresseur	m
turbocharger		n	Abgasturbolader		m	turbocompresseur	m
turbulence		n	Verwirbelung		f	turbulence	f
turbulence-chamber engine		n	Nebenkammermotor		m	moteur à chambre de turbulence	m
turn ratio		n	Windungsverhältnis		n	rapport de transformation (nombre de spires)	m
turn signal		n	Blinklicht		n	feu clignotant	m
turn-signal flasher		n	Blinkgeber		m	centrale clignotante	f
turn-signal lamp		n	Blinkleuchte		f	clignotant	m
turn-signal switch		n	Blinkerschalter		m	inverseur des feux clignotants	m
turn-signal unit		n	Blinklichteinsatz		m	module de feu clignotant	m
turning radius		n	Spurkreisradius		m	rayon du cercle de braquage	m
twin plunger accumulator (TCS)		n	Doppelkolbenspeicher (ASR)		m	accumulateur à double pression (ASR)	m
twin-axle module (trailer)		n	Doppelachsmodul (Anhänger)		m	module d'essieu double (remorque)	m
twin-flow housing		n	Zwillingsstromgehäuse		n	dispositif à flux jumelé	m
twin-needle nozzle		n	Doppelnadeldüse		f	injecteur à deux aiguilles	m
two-chamber lamp		n	Zweikammerleuchte		f	lanterne à deux compartiments	f
two-headlamp system		n	Zweischeinwerfer-System		n	système à deux projecteurs	m
two-layer winding		n	Zweischichtwicklung		f	enroulement à deux couches	m
two-port plunger-and-barrel assembly		n	Zweilochelement		n	élément à deux orifices	m
two-position controller (lambda closed-loop control)		n	Zweipunktregler (Lambda-Regelung)		m	régulateur à deux positions (régulation lambda)	m
two-position valve		n	Zweistellungsventil		n	valve à deux positions	f
two-spark ignition coil		n	Zweifunken-Zündspule		f	bobine d'allumage à deux sorties	f
two-spring nozzle holder		n	Zweifeder-Düsenhalter		m	porte-injecteur à deux ressorts	m
two-stage box-type filter		n	Stufenboxfilter		n	filtre-box à deux étages	m
two-stroke principle		n	Zweitaktverfahren		n	cycle à deux temps	m

English

English		German		French	
two-way directional-control valve (TCS)	*n*	Zweiwegeventil (ASR)	*n*	distributeur à deux voies (ASR)	*m*
type code	*n*	Ausführungskennzahl	*f*	code d'exécution	*m*
type designation	*n*	Typformel	*f*	formule de type	*f*
type of protection	*n*	Schutzart	*f*	degré de protection	*m*
U					
U-bellows (air spring)	*n*	Rollbalgfeder (Luftfeder)	*f*	soufflet en U (suspension)	*m*
ultrasonic detector (car alarm)	*n*	Ultraschallsensor	*m*	récepteur à ultrasons	*m*
ultrasonic field (car alarm)	*n*	Ultraschallfeld (Autoalarm)	*n*	champ ultrasonique (alarme auto)	*m*
ultrasonic passenger-compartment protection (car alarm)	*n*	Ultraschall-Innenraumschutz (Autoalarm)	*m*	protection de l'habitacle par ultrasons (alarme auto)	*f*
ultrasonic receiver	*n*	Ultraschallsensor	*m*	récepteur à ultrasons	*m*
uncontrolled range	*n*	ungeregelter Bereich	*m*	plage non régulée	*f*
under-voltage	*n*	Unterspannung	*f*	sous-tension	*f*
understeer (motor vehicle)	*v*	untersteuern (Kfz)	*v*	sous-virage (véhicule)	*m*
uneven braking	*v*	ungleiches Bremsen	*n*	louvoiement (freinage)	*m*
uneven running	*v*	Laufunruhe	*f*	instabilité de fonctionnement	*f*
uniform deceleration	*n*	gleichförmige Verzögerung	*f*	décélération uniforme	*f*
uniformity of fuel delivery	*n*	Gleichförderung	*f*	égalisation des débits	*f*
unit injector	+ *n*	Pumpe-Düse-Einheit, UIS	*f*	injecteur-pompe	*m*
unit injector system, UIS	*n*	Pumpe-Düse-Einheit, UIS	*f*	injecteur-pompe	*m*
unit pump	+ *n*	Pumpe-Leitung-Düse, UPS	*f*	système pompe-conduite-injecteur	*m*
unit pump system, UPS	*n*	Pumpe-Leitung-Düse, UPS	*f*	système pompe-conduite-injecteur	*m*
unleaded (gasoline)	*pp*	bleifrei (Benzin)	*adj*	sans plomb (essence)	*loc*
unlocking device for starting	*n*	Startmengenentriegelung	*f*	débloqueur du débit de surcharge au démarrage	*m*
unsteerable (motor vehicle)	*adj*	lenkunfähig (Kfz)	*adj*	incontrôlable (véhicule)	*adj*
updraft air-flow sensor	*n*	Steigstrom-Luftmengenmesser	*m*	débitmètre d'air à flux ascendant	*m*
upper beam	*n*	Fernlicht	*n*	feu de route	*m*
upper chamber	*n*	Oberkammer	*f*	chambre supérieure	*f*
upper-beam headlamp	*n*	Fernscheinwerfer	*m*	projecteur route	*m*
V					
V-belt	*n*	Keilriemen	*m*	courroie trapézoïdale	*f*
vacuum advance	*n*	Unterdruckzündversteller	*m*	dispositif d'avance à dépression	*m*
vacuum advance arm (advance mechanism)	*n*	Zugstange (Zündversteller)	*f*	biellette (correcteur d'avance)	*f*
vacuum advance mechanism	*n*	Unterdruckzündversteller	*m*	dispositif d'avance à dépression	*m*
vacuum brake booster	*n*	Unterdruck-Bremskraftverstärker	*m*	servofrein à dépression	*m*
vacuum chamber	*n*	Unterdruckkammer	*f*	chambre de dépression	*f*
vacuum control	*n*	Unterdruckversteller	*m*	correcteur à dépression	*m*
vacuum converter	*n*	Druckwandler	*m*	convertisseur de pression	*m*
vacuum limiter (Jetronic)	*n*	Unterdruckbegrenzer (Jetronic)	*m*	limiteur de dépression (Jetronic)	*m*

English		German		French	
vacuum pickup (ignition)	n	Unterdruckgeber (Zündung)	m	capteur de dépression (allumage)	m
vacuum pump	n	Unterdruckpumpe	f	pompe à dépression	f
vacuum unit	n	Druckdose	f	capsule manométrique	f
vacuum-assisted hydraulic braking system	n	Unterdruck-Hilfskraft-Bremsanlage mit hydraul. Übertragungseinrichtung	f	dispositif de freinage hydraulique assisté par dépression	m
vacuum-brake system	n	Vakuum-Bremsanlage	f	dispositif de freinage à dépression	m
vacuum-over-hydraulic braking system	n	Unterdruck-Fremdkraft-Bremsanlage mit hydr. Übertragungseinrichtung	f	dispositif de freinage hydraulique à commande par dépression	m
valve body	n	Ventilkörper	m	corps de soupape	m
valve cone	n	Ventilkegel	m	cône de soupape	m
valve control plunger	n	Ventilsteuerkolben	m	tige de commande d'injecteur	f
valve gear	n	Ventiltrieb	m	distribution (commande des soupapes)	f
valve holder	n	Ventilträger	m	porte-soupape	m
valve lift	n	Ventilhub	m	lévée de soupape	f
valve metering	n	ventilgesteuerte Zumessung	f	dosage par valve	m
valve needle	n	Ventilnadel	f	aiguille de soupape	f
valve overlap	n	Ventilüberschneidung	f	croisement des soupapes	m
valve pin	n	Ventilstift	m	tige de soupape	f
valve plate (brakes)	n	Ventilteller (Bremse)	m	clapet (frein)	m
valve plate (Jetronic)	n	Ventilplatte (Jetronic)	f	plaque porte-soupape (Jetronic)	f
valve plunger	n	Ventilkolben	m	piston de soupape	m
valve relay (ABS)	n	Ventilrelais (ABS)	n	relais des électrovalves (ABS)	m
valve seat	n	Ventilsitz	m	siège de soupape	m
valve spring	n	Ventilfeder	f	ressort de valve	m
valve throat	n	Ventildurchlaß	m	diamètre intérieur	m
valve timing (engine design)	n	Ventilsteuerung (Verbrennungsmotor)	f	commande des soupapes (moteur à combustion)	f
valve timing (IC engine)	n	Ventilsteuerzeit (Verbrennungsmotor)	f	distribution (moteur à combustion)	f
valve timing diagram (IC engine)	n	Ventilsteuerdiagramm (Verbrennungsmotor)	n	diagramme de distribution (moteur à combustion)	m
valve-triggering mode	n	Ventilansteuermodus	m	mode de pilotage des vannes	m
vane-type supply pump	n	Flügelzellen-Förderpumpe	f	pompe d'alimentation à palettes	f
vapor pressure (gasoline)	n	Dampfdruck (Benzin)	m	pression de vapeur (essence)	f
vapor-bubble formation	n	Dampfblasenbildung	f	percolation	f
variable turbine geometry	n	variable Turbinengeometrie	f	géométrie variable de turbine	f
variable-configuration intake manifold	n	Schalt-Ansaugsystem	n	système d'admission à géométrie variable	m
variable-fulcrum lever (governor)	n	Regelhebel (Diesel-Regler)	m	levier à coulisse (régulateur diesel)	m
variable-speed governor	n	Alldrehzahlregler	m	régulateur toutes vitesses	m
variable-tract intake manifold	n	Saugrohrumschaltung	f	commande de collecteur d'admission à géométrie variable	f
varnished copper wire	n	Kupferlackdraht	m	fil de cuivre laqué	m

English		German		French	
vee-type	*n*	V-Anordnung	*f*	en V	*loc*
vehicle acceleration	*n*	Fahrzeugbeschleunigung	*f*	accélération du véhicule	*f*
vehicle body	*n*	Fahrzeugaufbau	*m*	carrosserie du véhicule	*f*
vehicle category	*n*	Fahrzeugklasse	*f*	catégorie de véhicule	*f*
vehicle class	*n*	Fahrzeugklasse	*f*	catégorie de véhicule	*f*
vehicle combination	*n*	Fahrzeugkombination	*f*	ensemble de véhicules	*m*
vehicle deceleration	*n*	Fahrzeugverzögerung	*f*	décélération du véhicule	*f*
vehicle dynamics controller	*n*	Fahrdynamikregler	*m*	régulateur de dynamique de roulage	*m*
vehicle electrical system	*n*	Bordnetz	*n*	circuit de bord	*m*
vehicle ground	*n*	Masse (Fahrzeugmasse)	*f*	masse (du véhicule)	*f*
vehicle handling	*n*	Fahrzeugführung	*f*	guidage du véhicule	*m*
vehicle heater	*n*	Wagenheizung	*f*	chauffage d'habitacle	*m*
vehicle immobilizer (car alarm)	*n*	Wegfahrsperre (Autoalarm)	*f*	dispositif antidémarrage (alarme auto)	*m*
vehicle lateral acceleration	*n*	Fahrzeugquerbeschleunigung	*f*	accélération transversale (véhicule)	*f*
vehicle longitudinal acceleration	*n*	Fahrzeuglängsbeschleunigung	*f*	accélération longitudinale (véhicule)	*f*
vehicle longitudinal deceleration	*n*	Fahrzeuglängsverzögerung	*f*	décélération longitudinale du véhicule	*f*
vehicle manufacturer	*n*	Fahrzeughersteller	*m*	constructeur automobile	*m*
vehicle navigation	*n*	Fahrzeugnavigation	*f*	navigation automobile	*f*
vehicle operation	*n*	Fahrbetrieb	*m*	conduite véhicule	*f*
vehicle rollover	*n*	Fahrzeugüberschlag	*m*	capotage du véhicule	*m*
vehicle security system	*n*	Fahrzeug-Sicherungssystem	*n*	système de protection des véhicules	*m*
vehicle speed	*n*	Fahrzeuggeschwindigkeit	*f*	vitesse du véhicule	*f*
vehicle stability (driveability)	*n*	Fahrtrichtungsstabilität (Kfz)	*f*	stabilité directionnelle (comportement de roulage)	*f*
vehicle stability (during braking)	*n*	Fahrzeugstabilität (beim Bremsen)	*f*	stabilité du véhicule (au freinage)	*f*
vehicle stability (staying in lane)	*n*	Spurtreue (Kfz)	*f*	trajectoire (véhicule)	*f*
vehicle system voltage	*n*	Bordnetzspannung	*f*	tension du circuit de bord	*f*
vehicle type	*n*	Fahrzeugtyp	*m*	type de véhicule	*m*
vehicle vertical axis	*n*	Fahrzeughochachse	*f*	axe vertical du véhicule	*m*
vehicle yaw-moment setpoint	*n*	Fahrzeuggiersollmoment	*n*	moment de lacet de consigne du véhicule	*m*
vehicle-operator command	*n*	Fahrerwunsch	*m*	demande du conducteur	*f*
vehicle-speed controller	*n*	Fahrgeschwindigkeitsregler, FGR	*m*	régulateur de vitesse de roulage	*m*
vehicle-speed limiter	*n*	Fahrgeschwindigkeits-begrenzer, FGB	*m*	limiteur de vitesse de roulage	*m*
vehicle-speed measurement	*n*	Fahrgeschwindigkeitsmessung	*f*	mesure de la vitesse de roulage	*f*
vehicle-speed ramp	*n*	Geschwindigkeitsrampe x	*f*	rampe de vitesse	*f*
vehicle-speed sensor	*n*	Fahrgeschwindigkeitssensor	*m*	capteur de vitesse de roulage	*m*
velocity diagram	*n*	Geschwindigkeitsdiagramm	*n*	diagramme des vitesses	*m*
vent	*v*	entlüften	*v*	dégazage	*m*

English		German		French	
vent bore	*n*	Entlüftungsbohrung	*f*	orifice de purge d'air	*m*
vent connection	*n*	Entlüftungsstutzen	*m*	tubulure de mise à l'atmosphère	*f*
vent screw	*n*	Entlüftungsschraube	*f*	vis de purge d'air	*f*
ventilated disc brake	*n*	innenbelüftete Scheibenbremse	*f*	frein à disque ventilé	*m*
ventilation	*n*	Lüftung	*f*	ventilation	*f*
ventilation opening (battery)	*n*	Entgasungsöffnung (Batterie)	*f*	orifice de dégazage (batterie)	*m*
venturi tube	*n*	Venturi-Düse	*f*	buse venturi	*f*
vernier sensor	*n*	Noniusgeber	*m*	capteur vernier	*m*
vertical groove (pump plunger)	*n*	Längsnut (Pumpenkolben)	*f*	rainure verticale (piston de pompe)	*f*
vertical tire force	*n*	Reifenaufstandskraft	*f*	force verticale du pneumatique	*f*
vibration	*n*	Schüttelbeanspruchung	*f*	contrainte de vibration	*f*
vibration damper	*n*	Schwingungsdämpfer	*m*	amortisseur de vibrations	*m*
vibration sensor	*n*	Vibrationssensor	*m*	capteur de vibrations	*m*
vibration strength	*n*	Schüttelfestigkeit	*f*	résistance aux secousses	*f*
vibration-proof (battery)	*adj*	rüttelfest (Batterie)	*adj*	insensible aux secousses (batterie)	*loc*
vibrational strength	*n*	Schwingfestigkeit	*f*	résistance aux vibrations	*f*
viscous coupling (all-wheel drive)	*n*	Viscokupplung (Allradantrieb)	*f*	visco-coupleur (transmission intégrale)	*m*
viscous lock (all-wheel drive)	*n*	Viskosesperre (Allradantrieb)	*f*	blocage par visco-coupleur (transmission intégrale)	*m*
visual examination	*n*	Sichtprüfung	*f*	examen visuel	*m*
visual range	*n*	Sichtweite	*f*	visibilité	*f*
visual signal	*n*	Lichtsignal	*n*	signal lumineux	*m*
volatility (gasoline)	*n*	Flüchtigkeit (Benzin)	*f*	volatibilité (essence)	*f*
voltage distribution	*n*	Spannungsverteilung	*f*	distribution de tension	*f*
voltage divider	*n*	Spannungsteiler	*m*	diviseur de tension	*m*
voltage drop	*n*	Spannungsfall	*m*	chute de tension	*f*
voltage jump	*n*	Spannungssprung	*m*	saut de tension	*m*
voltage limitation	*n*	Spannungsbegrenzung	*f*	limitation de tension	*f*
voltage loss	*n*	Spannungsfall	*m*	chute de tension	*f*
voltage peak	*n*	Spannungsspitze	*f*	pointe de tension	*f*
voltage regulation	*n*	Spannungsregelung	*f*	régulation de tension	*f*
voltage regulator (alternator)	*n*	Spannungsregler (Generator)	*m*	régulateur de tension (alternateur)	*m*
voltage reserve	*n*	Zündspannungsreserve	*f*	réserve de tension d'allumage	*f*
voltage stabilisation	*n*	Spannungsstabilisierung	*f*	stabilisation de la tension	*f*
voltage stabilizer	*n*	Spannungsstabilisator	*m*	stabilisateur de tension	*m*
volumetric efficiency (IC engine)	*n*	Liefergrad (Verbrennungsmotor)	*m*	rendement volumétrique (moteur à combustion)	*m*
volumetric flow	*n*	Volumenstrom	*m*	débit volumique	*m*
W					
wafer (semiconductor)	*n*	Wafer (Halbleiter) x	*m*	tranche (semi-conducteur)	*f*
wanted signal (interference suppression)	*n*	Nutzsignal (Entstörung)	*n*	signal utile (antiparasitage)	*m*
warm start	*n*	Heißstart	*m*	départ à chaud	*m*
warm-up	*v*	Warmlauf	*m*	mise en action	*f*

English

English		German		French	
warm-up enrichment	*n*	Warmlaufanreicherung	*f*	enrichissement de mise en action	*m*
warm-up period (IC engine)	*n*	Warmlaufphase (Verbrennungsmotor)	*f*	période de mise en action (moteur à combustion)	*f*
warm-up regulator	*n*	Warmlaufregler	*m*	régulateur de mise en action	*m*
warming-up	*n*	Warmlauf	*m*	mise en action	*f*
warming-up period (IC engine)	*n*	Warmlaufphase (Verbrennungsmotor)	*f*	période de mise en action (moteur à combustion)	*f*
warning lamp	*n*	Warnlampe	*f*	témoin d'alerte	*m*
warning signal	*n*	Warnsignal	*n*	signal de détresse	*m*
warning sticker (car alarm)	*n*	Warnaufkleber (Autoalarm)	*m*	autocollant d'avertissement (alarme auto)	*m*
waste-gate control valve	*n*	Wastegate-Regelventil	*n*	valve modulatrice de pression	*f*
wastegate	*n*	Bypassventil	*n*	valve de dérivation	*f*
water chamber (fuel filter)	*n*	Wassersammelraum (Kraftstoffilter)	*m*	collecteur d'eau (filtre à carburant)	*m*
water port	*n*	Kühlwasseranschluß	*m*	raccord d'eau de refroidissemen	*m*
water pump	*n*	Wasserpumpe	*f*	pompe à eau	*f*
water separator	*n*	Wasserabscheider	*m*	séparateur d'eau	*m*
water-circulating pump	*n*	Wasserumwälzpumpe	*f*	pompe de circulation d'eau	*f*
water-drainage valve	*n*	Entwässerungsventil	*n*	purgeur d'eau	*m*
water-pressure pump	*n*	Wasserdruckpumpe	*f*	pompe de refoulement d'eau	*f*
wear inspection (brake lining)	*n*	Verschleißkontrolle (Bremsbelag)	*f*	contrôle d'usure (garniture de frein)	*m*
wear sensor (brake lining)	*n*	Verschleißsensor (Bremsbelag)	*m*	capteur d'usure (garniture de frein)	*m*
wear-resistant	*adj*	verschleißfest	*adj*	résistant à l'usure	*ppr*
wearing part	*n*	Verschleißteil	*n*	pièce d'usure	*f*
wedge (brakes)	*n*	Spreizkeil (Bremse)	*m*	coin d'écartement (frein)	*m*
wedge-actuated brake	*n*	Keilbremse	*f*	frein à coin	*m*
wedge-type shoe (drum brake)	*n*	Spreizbacke (Trommelbremse)	*f*	came d'écartement (frein)	*f*
weight (force)	*n*	Gewichtskraft	*f*	poids	*m*
weight distribution (brakes)	*n*	Gewichtsverteilung (Bremse)	*f*	répartition du poids (frein)	*f*
weight transfer (brakes)	*n*	Gewichtsverlagerung (Bremse)	*f*	report de charge (frein)	*m*
weighted emissions	*n*	gewichtete Schadstoffemission	*f*	émission quantifiée de polluant:	*f*
wet boiling point (brake fluid)	*n*	Naßsiedepunkt (Bremsflüssigkeit)	*m*	point d'ébullition liquide humidifié (liquide de frein)	*m*
wheel acceleration	*n*	Radumfangsbeschleunigung	*f*	accélération périphérique des roues	*f*
wheel bearing	*n*	Radlager	*n*	roulement de roue	*m*
wheel brake	*n*	Radbremse	*f*	frein de roue	*m*
wheel brake pressure	*n*	Radbremsdruck	*m*	pression de freinage sur roue	*f*
wheel contact point	*n*	Radaufstandspunkt	*m*	point de contact de la roue avec la chaussée	*m*
wheel deceleration	*n*	Radumfangsverzögerung	*f*	décélération périphérique des roues	*f*
wheel hub	*n*	Radnabe	*f*	moyeu de roue	*m*
wheel lock	*n*	blockieren (Rad)	*v*	blocage (roue)	*m*
wheel lockup	*n*	blockieren (Rad)	*v*	blocage (roue)	*m*

English		German			French	
wheel moment of inertia	*n*	Radträgheitsmoment		*n*	couple d'inertie de la roue	*m*
wheel slip	*n*	Schlupf (Rad)		*m*	glissement (roue)	*m*
wheel speed	*n*	Radgeschwindigkeit		*f*	vitesse de rotation de la roue	*f*
wheel spin	*n*	durchdrehen (Antriebsrad)	x	*v*	patiner (roue motrice)	*v*
wheel swivel angle (vehicle dynamics)	*n*	Radschwenkachse (Kfz-Dynamik)		*f*	axe de pivotement de roue (dynamique d'un véhicule)	*m*
wheel theft and tow-away protection (car alarm)	*n*	Rad- und Abschleppschutz (Autoalarm)		*m*	protection contre le vol des roues et le remorquage (alarme auto)	*f*
wheel-brake cylinder	*n*	Radzylinder		*m*	cylindre de frein de roue	*m*
wheel-lock limit	*n*	Blockiergrenze (Rad)		*f*	limite de blocage (roues)	*f*
wheel-slip shutoff device (dynamic brake analyzer)	*n*	Schlupfabschaltung (Rollenbremsprüfstand)		*f*	déconnexion automatique de glissement (banc d'essai)	*f*
wheel-speed comparator (ABS)	*n*	Radgeschwindigkeits-vergleicher (ABS)		*m*	comparateur de vitesse de roues (ABS)	*m*
wheel-speed differential	*n*	Raddifferenzgeschwindigkeit		*f*	vitesse différentielle des roues	*f*
wheel-speed sensor	*n*	Raddrehzahlsensor		*m*	capteur de vitesse de roue	*m*
wheel-theft protection (car alarm)	*n*	Radschutz (Autoalarm)		*m*	protection contre le vol des roues (alarme auto)	*f*
wheelbase (vehicle)	*n*	Achsabstand (Fahrzeug)		*m*	empattement (véhicule)	*m*
whirl chamber	*n*	Wirbelkammer		*f*	chambre de tourbillonnement	*f*
whirl-chamber diesel engine	*n*	Wirbelkammermotor		*m*	moteur à chambre de tourbillonnement	*m*
white smoke	*n*	Weißrauch	x	*m*	fumées blanches	*fpl*
wide-open throttle, WOT	*n*	Vollast, VL		*f*	pleine charge	*f*
wind (coil)	*v*	wickeln (Spule)		*v*	enrouler (bobine)	*v*
wind tunnel	*n*	Windkanal		*m*	soufflerie	*f*
winding diagram	*n*	Wickelschema		*n*	schéma de bobinage	*m*
winding factor	*n*	Wicklungsfaktor		*m*	facteur de bobinage	*m*
winding head (stator)	*n*	Wickelkopf (Ständer)		*m*	tête de bobine (stator)	*f*
winding resistance	*n*	Wicklungswiderstand		*m*	résistance d'enroulement	*f*
winding wire	*n*	Wickeldraht		*m*	fil de bobinage	*m*
windingless rotor (alternator)	*n*	Leitstückläufer (Generator)		*m*	rotor à pièce conductrice (alternateur)	*m*
windshield	*n*	Frontscheibe		*f*	pare-brise	*m*
windshield and rear-window cleaning	*n*	Scheibenreinigung		*f*	nettoyage des vitres	*m*
windshield washer	*n*	Scheibenspüler		*m*	lave-glace	*m*
windshield wiper	*n*	Scheibenwischer		*m*	essuie-glace	*m*
windshield-washer pump	*n*	Scheibenspülerpumpe		*f*	pompe de lave-glace	*f*
wipe pattern	*n*	Wischfeld		*n*	champ de balayage	*m*
wipe/wash system (headlamp)	*n*	Wisch-Wasch-Anlage (Scheinwerfer)		*f*	lave/essuie-projecteur	*m*
wiper	*n*	Scheibenwischer		*m*	essuie-glace	*m*
wiper arm (headlamp cleaning system)	*n*	Wischhebel (Scheinwerfer-Reinigungsanlage)		*m*	bras d'essuie-glace équipé (nettoyeur de projecteurs)	*m*
wiper arm (throttle-valve sensor)	*n*	Schleiferarm (Drosselklappengeber)		*m*	curseur (actionneur de papillon)	*m*

English

English		German		French	
wiper arm (windshield wiper sytem)	*n*	Wischarm (Wischeranlage)	*m*	bras d'essuie-glace	*m*
wiper arm-and-blade assembly (headlamp cleaning system)	*n*	Wischhebel (Scheinwerfer-Reinigungsanlage)	*m*	bras d'essuie-glace équipé (nettoyeur de projecteurs)	*m*
wiper blade	*n*	Wischblatt	*n*	raclette d'essuie-glace	*f*
wiper lever (potentiometer)	*n*	Schleiferhebel (Potentiometer)	*m*	levier du curseur (potentiomètre)	*m*
wiper motor	*n*	Wischermotor	*m*	moteur d'essuie-glace	*m*
wiper system	*n*	Wischeranlage	*f*	équipement d'essuie-glace	*m*
wiper tap	*n*	Schleiferabgriff	*m*	curseur de contact	*m*
wiper track	*n*	Potentiometerbahn	*f*	piste de potentiomètre	*f*
wiper-blade element	*n*	Wischgummi	*n*	lame racleuse	*f*
wiper-element lip	*n*	Wischlippe	*f*	lèvre d'essuyage	*f*
wiping angle	*n*	Wischwinkel	*m*	angle de balayage	*m*
wire loop (car alarm)	*n*	Lichtleitring (Autoalarm)	*m*	câble en boucle (alarme auto)	*m*
wire-type flame glow plug	*n*	Flammglühdrahtkerze	*f*	bougie d'inflammation à filament	*f*
wiring harness	*n*	Kabelbaum	*m*	faisceau de câbles	*m*
working air gap (ABS solenoid valve)	*n*	Arbeitsluftspalt (ABS-Magnetventil)	*m*	entrefer (électrovalve ABS)	*m*
working chamber (brake booster)	*n*	Arbeitskammer (Bremskraftverstärker)	*f*	chambre de travail (servofrein)	*f*
working cycle (IC engine)	*n*	Arbeitszyklus (Verbrennungsmotor)	*m*	cycle de travail (moteur à combustion)	*m*
working cylinder	*n*	Arbeitszylinder	*m*	vérin	*m*
working lamp	*n*	Arbeitsleuchte	*f*	lampe de travail	*f*
working piston	*n*	Arbeitskolben	*m*	piston de travail	*m*
working stroke	*n*	Arbeitshub	*m*	temps de combustion	*m*
workpiece carrier	*n*	Werkstückträger	*m*	chariot porte-pièce	*m*
workshop charger (battery)	*n*	Werkstattlader (Batterie)	*m*	chargeur de garage (batterie)	*m*
workshop drawing	*n*	Fertigungszeichnung	*f*	dessin d'exécution	*m*
workshop manual	*n*	Werkstatthandbuch	*n*	manuel d'atelier	*m*
wrap angle (V-belt)	*n*	Umschlingungswinkel (Keilriemen)	*m*	angle d'enroulement (courroie trapézoïdale)	*m*
Y					
Y-connection	*n*	Sternschaltung	*f*	montage en étoile	*m*
yaw (motor vehicle)	*v*	gieren (Kfz) x	*v*	lacet (véhicule)	*m*
yaw angle	*n*	Gierwinkel	*m*	angle d'embardée	*m*
yaw moment	*n*	Giermoment	*n*	moment de lacet	*m*
yaw moment buildup delay	*n*	Giermomentaufbau-verzögerung, GMA	*f*	temporisation de la formation du couple de lacet	*f*
yaw motion	*n*	Gierbewegung	*f*	mouvement de lacet	*m*
yaw sensor (ESP)	*n*	Drehratensensor (ESP)	*m*	capteur de taux de rotation (ESP)	*m*
yaw velocity (vehicle dynamics)	*n*	Giergeschwindigkeit (Kfz-Dynamik)	*f*	vitesse de braquage (dynamique d'un véhicule)	*f*
yaw-moment build-up	*n*	Giermomentaufbau	*m*	formation du moment de lacet	*f*
yaw-moment limitation	*n*	Giermomentbegrenzung	*f*	limitation du moment de lacet	*f*
yoke	*n*	Kreuzscheibe	*f*	croisillon	*m*

English

English		German		French	
Z					
Zener diode	*n*	Zenerdiode	*f*	diode Zener	*f*
Zener voltage	*n*	Zenerspannung	*f*	tension Zener	*f*
zero air (exhaust-gas test)	*n*	Nullgas (Abgasprüftechnik)	*n*	gaz neutre (émissions)	*m*
zero delivery	*n*	Nullförderung (Pumpenelement)	*f*	débit nul	*m*
zero gas (exhaust-gas test)	*n*	Nullgas (Abgasprüftechnik)	*n*	gaz neutre (émissions)	*m*
zero-fuel characteristic	*n*	Nullförderlinie	*f*	caractéristique de débit nul	*f*
zero-fuel quantity	*n*	Nullmenge	*f*	débit nul	*m*

Français		Allemand		Anglais	
A					
ABS, système antiblocage	*a*	ABS, Antiblockiersystem	*a*	ABS, antilock braking system	*a*
absorption de chaleur	*f*	Wärmeaufnahme	*f*	heat absorption	*n*
accélérateur de démarrage à froid	*m*	Kaltstartbeschleuniger, KSB	*m*	cold-start accelerator	*n*
accélérateur électronique	*m*	elektronische Motorfüllungs-steuerung, EGAS	*f*	electronic throttle control, ETC	*n*
accélérateur manuel	*m*	Handfahrgeber	*m*	hand throttle	*n*
accélérateur pneumatique de ralenti	*m*	pneumatische Leerlaufanhebung, PLA	*f*	pneumatic idle-speed increase	*n*
accélération à pleine charge	*f*	Vollastbeschleunigung	*f*	full-load acceleration	*n*
accélération du véhicule	*f*	Fahrzeugbeschleunigung	*f*	vehicle acceleration	*n*
accélération longitudinale (véhicule)	*f*	Fahrzeuglängsbeschleunigung	*f*	vehicle longitudinal acceleration	*n*
accélération périphérique des roues	*f*	Radumfangsbeschleunigung	*f*	wheel acceleration	*n*
accélération transversale (véhicule)	*f*	Fahrzeugquerbeschleunigung	*f*	vehicle lateral acceleration	*n*
accéléromètre	*m*	Beschleunigungssensor	*m*	acceleration sensor	*n*
accouplement	*m*	Antriebskupplung	*f*	coupling assembly	*n*
accouplement à roue libre (démarreur)	*m*	Rollenfreilauf (Starter)	*m*	roller-type overrunning clutch (starter)	*n*
accouplement borgne	*m*	Leerkupplung	*f*	coupling holder	*n*
accouplement de remorque	*m*	Anhängerkupplung	*f*	trailer hitch	*n*
accouplement de semi-remorque	*m*	Aufliegerkupplung	*f*	semi-trailer coupling	*n*
accouplement électromagnétique	*m*	Magnetkupplung	*f*	solenoid-operated coupling	*n*
accouplement rapide	*m*	Schnellkupplung	*f*	rapid coupling	*n*
accrochage (essuie-glace)	*m*	Hakeneinhängung (Wischer)	*f*	hook-type fastening (wipers)	*n*
accumulateur à double pression (ASR)	*m*	Doppelkolbenspeicher (ASR)	*m*	twin plunger accumulator (TCS)	*n*
accumulateur à piston	*m*	Kolbenspeicher	*m*	piston accumulator	*n*
accumulateur à vessie	*m*	Blasenspeicher	*m*	bladder accumulator	*n*
accumulateur au plomb	*m*	Bleibatterie	*f*	lead storage battery	*n*
accumulateur d'énergie	*m*	Energiespeicher	*m*	energy accumulator	*n*
accumulateur de carburant	*m*	Kraftstoffspeicher	*m*	fuel accumulator	*n*
accumulateur de gaz à piston (ASR)	*m*	Gaskolbenspeicher (ASR)	*m*	piston gas accumulator (TCS)	*n*
accumulateur élastique	*m*	Federspeicher	*m*	spring-type brake actuator	*n*
accumulateur haute pression (Common Rail)	*m*	Hochdruckspeicher (Common Rail)	*m*	high-pressure accumulator (common rail)	*n*
accumulateur hydraulique	*m*	Hydrospeicher	*m*	hydraulic accumulator	*n*
accumulation de l'énergie	*f*	Energiespeicherung	*f*	energy storage	*n*
acide pour accumulateurs	*m*	Elektrolyt	*m*	electrolyte	*n*
action proportionnelle	*f*	Proportionalverhalten	*n*	speed-droop characteristic	*n*
action sur débit	*f*	Mengeneingriff	*m*	fuel-quantity command	*n*
actionner (frein)	*v*	betätigen (Bremse)	*v*	actuate (brakes)	*v*
actionneur	*m*	Stellwerk	*n*	actuator mechanism	*n*

Français		Allemand		Anglais	
actionneur à effet giratoire (pompe à pistons radiaux)	*m*	Drallsteller (Radialkolbenpumpe)	*m*	swirl actuator (radial-piston pump)	*n*
actionneur de débit	*m*	Mengenstellglied	*n*	fuel-quantity positioner	*n*
actionneur de ligne à tiroirs	*m*	Hubschieberstellwerk	*n*	control-sleeve actuator	*n*
actionneur de papillon	*m*	Drosselklappensteller	*m*	throttle-valve actuator	*n*
actionneur de précourse	*m*	Vorhubstellwerk	*n*	LPC (lift port closing) actuator	*n*
actionneur de pression de suralimentation (pompe à pistons radiaux)	*m*	Ladedrucksteller (Radialkolbenpumpe)	*m*	charge-pressure actuator	*n*
actionneur de pression électrohydraulique	*m*	elektrohydraulischer Drucksteller	*m*	electro-hydraulic pressure actuator	*n*
actionneur de ralenti	*m*	Leerlaufsteller	*m*	idle actuator	*n*
actionneur de recyclage des gaz d'échappement	*m*	Abgasrückführsteller	*m*	exhaust-gas recirculation (EGR) positioner	*n*
actionneur de réglage (ASR)	*m*	Stelleinrichtung (ASR)	*f*	final control element (TCS)	*n*
actionneur électromagnétique	*m*	Magnetsteller	*n*	solenoid actuator	*n*
actionneur linéaire (ASR)	*m*	Linearsteller (ASR)	*m*	linear actuator (TCS)	*n*
actionneur manométrique	*m*	Drucksteller	*m*	pressure actuator	*n*
actionneur rotatif (KE-Jetronic)	*m*	Drehsteller (KE-Jetronic)	*m*	rotary actuator (KE-Jetronic)	*n*
actionneur rotatif de ralenti	*m*	Leerlaufdrehsteller	*m*	rotary idle actuator	*n*
actuateur	*m*	Stellglied	*n*	actuator	*n*
actuateur de pression	*m*	Drucksteller	*m*	pressure actuator	*n*
actuateur électromagnétique	*m*	Magnetsteller	*n*	solenoid actuator	*n*
adaptateur clignotant (ABS pour remorques)	*m*	Blinkadapter (Anhänger-ABS)	*m*	flashing adapter (trailer ABS)	*n*
adaptation au démarrage à froid	*f*	Kaltstartanpassung	*f*	cold-start compensation	*n*
adaptation de l'injection	*f*	Einspritzanpassung	*f*	injection adaption	*n*
adaptation des freins (aux différents véhicules)	*f*	Bremsenabstimmung	*f*	brake balance	*n*
adaptation du mélange	*f*	Gemischanpassung	*f*	mixture adaptation	*n*
additif (carburant)	*m*	Additiv (Kraftstoff)	*m*	additive (fuel)	*n*
additif antidétonant	*m*	Antiklopfmittel	*n*	knock inhibitor	*n*
additif antigivre (papillon)	*m*	Vereisungsschutz (Drosselklappe)	*m*	icing protection (throttle valve)	*n*
additionneur	*m*	Summierer	*m*	adder	*n*
adhérence (pneu)	*f*	Griffigkeit (Reifen)	*f*	tire grip	*n*
adhérence (pneu/route)	*f*	Kraftschluß (Reifen/Straße)	*m*	adhesion (tire/road)	*n*
adhérence au sol	*f*	Bodenhaftung	*f*	road-surface adhesion	*n*
admission	*f*	Ansaugtakt	*m*	induction stroke	*n*
admission des gaz (moteur à combustion)	*f*	Gasannahme (Verbrennungsmotor) x	*f*	throttle response (IC engine)	*n*
affectation du bus	*f*	Busvergabe (CAN)	*f*	bus arbitration (CAN)	*n*
affichage de défauts	*m*	Fehleranzeige	*f*	fault display	*n*
affichage diagnostic	*m*	Diagnoseanzeige	*f*	diagnosis display	*n*
afficheur (banc d'essai)	*m*	Anzeigegerät (Rollenbremsprüfstand)	*n*	display unit (dynamic brake analyzer)	*n*
agent antidétonant	*m*	Antiklopfmittel	*n*	knock inhibitor	*n*
agent d'addition (carburant)	*m*	Additiv (Kraftstoff)	*m*	additive (fuel)	*n*
agent détergent (essence)	*m*	Reinigungsadditiv (Benzin)	*n*	detergent additive (gasoline)	*n*

Français

Français		Allemand		Anglais	
aide au démarrage à froid	*f*	Kaltstarthilfe	*f*	cold-start aid	*n*
aiguille d'injecteur	*f*	Düsennadel	*f*	nozzle needle	*n*
aiguille de soupape	*f*	Ventilnadel	*f*	valve needle	*n*
ailette	*f*	Lüfterschaufel	*f*	fan blade	*n*
ailette de rotor (pompe électrique à carburant)	*f*	Laufradschaufel (Elektrokraftstoffpumpe)	*f*	impeller blade (electric fuel pump)	*n*
aimant	*m*	Permanentmagnet	*m*	permanent magnet	*n*
aimant de soufflage (relais de puissance)	*m*	Blasmagnet (Leistungsrelais)	*m*	blowout magnet (power relay)	*n*
aimant permanent	*m*	Permanentmagnet	*m*	permanent magnet	*n*
aimant tambour	*m*	Topfmagnet	*m*	induction cup	*n*
aimant torique	*m*	Ringmagnet	*m*	ring magnet	*n*
air aspiré	*m*	Ansaugluft	*f*	intake air	*n*
air comprimé	*m*	Druckluft	*f*	compressed air	*n*
air d'admission	*m*	Ansaugluft	*f*	intake air	*n*
air de balayage	*m*	Spülluft	*f*	purge air	*n*
air de combustion	*m*	Verbrennungsluft	*f*	combustion air	*n*
air de refroidissement	*m*	Kühlluft	*f*	cooling air	*n*
air de suralimentation	*m*	Ladeluft	*f*	charge air	*n*
air secondaire	*m*	Sekundärluft	*f*	secondary air	*n*
airbag (système de retenue des + passagers)	*m*	Airbag	*m*	airbag	*n*
ajustement des phases	*m*	Phasenabstimmung	*f*	phase matching	*n*
alarme auto	*f*	Auto-Alarmanlage	*n*	car alarm	*n*
alarme panique (alarme auto)	*f*	Panikalarm (Autoalarm)	*m*	panic alarm (car alarm)	*n*
alésage (cylindre moteur)	*m*	Bohrung (Motorzylinder)	*f*	bore (engine cylinder)	*n*
alésage d'étranglement	*m*	Drosselbohrung	*f*	throttle bore	*n*
alésage de piston (piston de pompe)	*m*	Kolbenbohrung (Pumpenkolben)	*f*	plunger passage	*n*
alimentation de la remorque	*f*	Anhängerversorgung	*f*	trailer power supply	*n*
alimentation en air	*f*	Luftversorgung	*f*	air supply	*n*
alimentation en air comprimé	*f*	Druckluftversorgung	*f*	compressed-air supply	*n*
alimentation en carburant	*f*	Kraftstoffversorgung	*f*	fuel supply	*n*
alimentation en combustible	*f*	Kraftstoffversorgung	*f*	fuel supply	*n*
alimentation en tension	*f*	Spannungsversorgung	*f*	power supply	*n*
allumage	*m*	Zündung	*f*	ignition	*n*
allumage cartographique	*m*	Kennfeldzündung	*f*	map-controlled ignition	*n*
allumage commandé	*m*	Fremdzündung	*f*	externally supplied ignition	*n*
allumage électronique intégral	*m*	vollelektronische Zündung, VZ	*f*	distributorless semiconductor ignition	*n*
allumage par appareillage externe	*m*	Fremdzündung	*f*	externally supplied ignition	*n*
allumage par bobine	*m*	Spulenzündung, SZ	*f*	coil ignition, CI	*n*
allumage spontané	*m*	Selbstzündung	*f*	auto-ignition	*n*
allumage transistorisé	*m*	Transistorzündung, TZ	*f*	transistorized ignition, TI	*n*
allumeur	*m*	Zündverteiler	*m*	ignition distributor	*n*
alternance de charge	*f*	Ladungswechsel	*m*	charge cycle	*n*
alternateur	*m*	Drehstromgenerator	*m*	alternator	*n*

Français		Allemand		Anglais	
alternateur à bloc redresseur compact	*m*	Topf-Generator	*m*	compact-diode-assembly alternator	*n*
alternateur à pôles saillants	*m*	Einzelpolgenerator	*m*	salient-pole generator	*n*
alternateur à rotor à griffes	*m*	Klauenpolgenerator	*m*	claw-pole alternator	*n*
alternateur compact	*m*	Compact-Generator	*m*	compact alternator	*n*
alternateur d'échange standard	*m*	Austauschgenerator	*m*	exchange alternator	*n*
alternateur triphasé	*m*	Drehstromgenerator	*m*	alternator	*n*
alvéole de la bougie	*f*	Zündkerzenmulde	*f*	spark-plug recess	*n*
amorçage (alarme auto)	*m*	Scharfschaltung (Autoalarm)	*f*	priming (car alarm)	*n*
amortissement (suspension pneumatique)	*m*	Dämpfung (Luftfederung)	*f*	damping (air suspension)	*n*
amortissement actif d'à-coups	*m*	aktive Ruckeldämpfung, ARD	*f*	surge damping control	*n*
amortissement d'à-coups	*m*	Ruckeldämpfung	*f*	surge damping	*n*
amortissement des à-coups de charge	*m*	Lastschlagdämpfung	*f*	load-reversal damping	*n*
amortisseur (ABS/ASR)	*m*	Dämpfer (ABS/ASR)	*m*	damper (ABS, TCS)	*n*
amortisseur (véhicule)	*m*	Stoßdämpfer (Kfz)	*m*	shock absorber (motor vehicle)	*n*
amortisseur à pression de gaz	*m*	Gasdruck-Stoßdämpfer	*m*	gas-filled shock absorber	*n*
amortisseur actif d'à-coups	*m*	aktiver Ruckeldämpfer	*m*	active-surge damper	*n*
amortisseur d'à-coups de charge	*m*	Lastschlag-Dämpfer	*m*	power on/off damper	*n*
amortisseur de bruit	*m*	Geräuschdämpfer	*m*	silencer	*n*
amortisseur de manchon piloté	*m*	gesteuerte Muffendämpfung	*f*	controlled sleeve damping	*n*
amortisseur de pression du carburant (Jetronic)	*m*	Kraftstoffdruckdämpfer (Jetronic)	*m*	fuel-pressure attenuator (Jetronic)	*n*
amortisseur de vibrations	*m*	Schwingungsdämpfer	*m*	vibration damper	*n*
amplificateur d'entrée (calculateur)	*m*	Eingangsverstärker (Steuergerät)	*m*	input amplifier (ECU)	*n*
amplificateur opérationnel	*m*	Operationsverstärker, OPV	*m*	operational amplifier, OPA	*n*
amplification de retour (ESP)	*f*	Rückführverstärkung (ESP)	*f*	return amplification (ESP)	*n*
amplitude (oscillation)	*f*	Auslenkung (Schwingung)	*f*	excursion (oscillation)	*n*
analyse des fumées diesel	*f*	Rauchmessung	*f*	smoke measurement	*n*
analyse des gaz d'échappement	*f*	Abgastest	*m*	exhaust-gas test	*n*
analyse des modes de défaillance et de leurs effets	*f*	Fehlermöglichkeits- und Fehlereinfluß-Analyse, FMEA	*f*	failure mode and effects analysis, FMEA	*n*
analyseur à absorption	*m*	Absorptionsanalysator	*m*	absorption analyzer	*n*
analyseur de gaz d'échappemen	*m*	Abgasmeßgerät	*n*	exhaust-gas analyzer	*n*
ancrage (frein)	*m*	Zuspannung (Bremse)	*f*	application (brakes)	*n*
anémomètre à fil chaud	*m*	Hitzdrahtanemometer	*m*	hot-wire anemometer	*n*
angle d'allumage	*m*	Zündwinkel	*f*	ignition angle	*n*
angle d'attaque (vent latéral)	*m*	Anströmwinkel (Seitenwind)	*m*	angle of impact (crosswind)	*n*
angle d'avance (correcteur d'avance)	*m*	Verstellwinkel (Spritzversteller	*m*	advance angle (timing device)	*n*
angle d'embardée	*m*	Gierwinkel	*m*	yaw angle	*n*
angle d'enroulement (courroie trapézoïdale)	*m*	Umschlingungswinkel (Keilriemen)	*m*	wrap angle (V-belt)	*n*
angle de balayage	*m*	Wischwinkel	*m*	wiping angle	*n*
angle de braquage (dynamique d'un véhicule)	*m*	Lenkwinkel (Kfz-Dynamik)	*m*	steering angle (vehicle dynamics)	*n*
angle de came	*m*	Schließwinkel	*m*	dwell angle	*n*

Français		Allemand		Anglais	
angle de carrossage (dynamique d'un véhicule)	*m*	Sturzwinkel (Kfz-Dynamik)	*m*	camber angle (vehicle dynamics)	*n*
angle de cône	*m*	Kegelwinkel	*m*	cone angle	*n*
angle de correction (allumage)	*m*	Zündverstellwinkel	*m*	advance angle (ignition)	*n*
angle de déplacement (débitmètre d'air)	*m*	Auslenkwinkel (Luftmengenmesser)	*m*	deflection angle (air-flow sensor)	*n*
angle de dérive (dynamique d'un véhicule)	*m*	Schräglaufwinkel (Kfz-Dynamik)	*m*	slip angle (vehicle dynamics)	*n*
angle de fermeture	*m*	Schließwinkel	*m*	dwell angle	*n*
angle de flottement (dynamique d'un véhicule)	*m*	Schwimmwinkel (Kfz-Dynamik)	*m*	float angle (vehicle dynamics)	*n*
angle de jet	*m*	Strahlkegelwinkel	*m*	spray dispersal angle	*n*
angle de levée de came	*m*	Nockenwinkel	*m*	angle of cam rotation	*n*
angle de papillon	*m*	Drosselklappenwinkel	*m*	throttle-valve angle	*n*
angle de pause	*m*	Schließwinkel	*m*	dwell angle	*n*
angle de refoulement sur la came	*m*	Förderwinkel am Nocken	*m*	cam angle of fuel-delivery	*n*
angle de rotation	*m*	Drehwinkel	*m*	rotational angle	*n*
angle de roulis (dynamique d'un véhicule)	*m*	Wankwinkel (Kfz-Dynamik)	*m*	roll angle (vehicle dynamics)	*n*
angle de tangage (dynamique d'un véhicule)	*m*	Nickwinkel (Kfz-Dynamik)	*m*	pitch angle (vehicle dynamics)	*n*
angle des trous d'injection	*m*	Spritzlochkegelwinkel	*m*	spray-hole cone angle	*n*
angle du cône d'injection	*m*	Strahlkegelwinkel	*m*	spray dispersal angle	*n*
angle du jet d'injection	*m*	Strahlkegelwinkel	*m*	spray dispersal angle	*n*
angle vilebrequin	*m*	Kurbelwinkel (Grad Kurbelwelle)	*m*	crankshaft angle	*n*
anneau d'arrêt	*m*	Sicherungsring	*m*	retainer	*n*
anneau de recouvrement	*m*	Abdeckring	*m*	cover ring	*n*
anneau polaire à griffes	*m*	Klauenpol	*m*	claw pole	*n*
antenne	*f*	Antenne	*f*	antenna	*n*
anti-répétiteur de démarrage	*m*	Startwiederholsperre	*f*	start-repeating block	*n*
antidémarrage	*m*	Wegfahrsperre (Autoalarm)	*f*	vehicle immobilizer (car alarm)	*n*
antidétonant (carburant)	*adj*	klopffest (Kraftstoff)	*adj*	knock-resistant (fuel)	*adj*
antigel	*m*	Frostschutzmittel	*n*	antifreeze	*n*
antiparasitage	*m*	Funkentstörung	*f*	interference suppression	*n*
antiparasitage renforcé	*m*	Nahentstörung	*f*	intensified interference suppression	*n*
antiparasitage simple	*m*	Fernentstörung	*f*	long-distance interference suppression	*n*
antipatinage à la traction	*m*	Antriebsschlupf	*m*	drive slip (driven wheel)	*n*
antivol diesel	*m*	Dieseldiebstahlschutz, DDS	*m*	diesel theft deterrent	*n*
appareil de mesure des gaz d'échappement	*m*	Abgasmeßgerät	*n*	exhaust-gas analyzer	*n*
appareil de mesure du débit	*m*	Fördermengenmeßgerät	*n*	fuel-delivery measurement device	*n*
appareil de préchauffage (moteur diesel)	*m*	Vorglühgerät	*n*	pre-glow relay (diesel engine)	*n*
appareil de réglage	*m*	Einstellgerät	*n*	calibrating unit	*n*

Français		Allemand		Anglais	
appareil de réglage des projecteurs	*m*	Scheinwerfer-Einstellprüfgerät	*n*	headlight aiming device	*n*
appauvrir (mélange air-carburant)	*v*	abmagern (Luft-Kraftstoff-Gemisch)	*v*	lean-off (air-fuel mixture)	*v*
appauvrissement du mélange	*m*	Gemischabmagerung	*f*	lean adjustment (air-fuel mixture)	*n*
appauvrissement en décélération	*m*	Verzögerungsabmagerung	*f*	trailing-throttle lean adjustment	*n*
application de l'effort (frein)	*f*	Zuspannung (Bremse)	*f*	application (brakes)	*n*
appliqué par laminage	*pp*	aufgewalzt	*pp*	rolled-on	*pp*
appliquer (frein)	*v*	anlegen (Bremse)	*v*	apply (brakes)	*v*
aquaplanage (pneu)	*m*	Aquaplaning (Reifen)	*n*	aquaplaning (tire)	*n*
arbre à came d'entraînement	*m*	Antriebsnockenwelle	*f*	camshaft	*n*
arbre à cames côté admission	*m*	Auslaßnockenwelle	*f*	exhaust camshaft	*n*
arbre à cames côté échappemen	*m*	Einlaßnockenwelle	*f*	intake camshaft	*n*
arbre creux	*m*	Hohlwelle	*f*	hollow shaft	*n*
arbre d'allumeur	*m*	Zündverteilerwelle	*f*	ignition-distributor shaft	*n*
arbre d'entraînement	*m*	Antriebswelle	*f*	drive shaft	*n*
arbre d'induit	*m*	Ankerwelle	*f*	armature shaft	*n*
arbre de commande	*m*	Betätigungswelle	*f*	actuating shaft	*n*
arbre de déplacement des tiroirs	*m*	Hubschieber-Verstellwelle	*f*	control-sleeve shaft	*n*
arbre de pignon	*m*	Ritzelschaft	*m*	pinion shaft	*n*
arbre de réglage	*m*	Stellwelle	*f*	actuator shaft	*n*
arbre de rotor	*m*	Läuferwelle	*f*	rotor shaft	*n*
arbre de sortie	*m*	Abtriebswelle	*f*	driven shaft	*n*
arceau de capotage	*m*	Überrollbügel	*m*	rollover bar	*n*
architecture de la chambre de combustion	*f*	Brennraumgestaltung	*f*	combustion-chamber design	*n*
arête de commande	*f*	Steuerkante (Pumpenelement)	*f*	helix (plunger-and-barrel assembly)	*n*
arête de rebond	*f*	Prallkante	*f*	impact edge	*n*
arête de rupture (téton d'injection)	*f*	Abreißkante (Spritzzapfen)	*f*	breakaway edge	*n*
armature (relais)	*f*	Anker (Relais)	*m*	armature (relays)	*n*
armature d'électro-aimant	*f*	Magnetanker	*m*	solenoid armature	*n*
armature de régulation	*f*	Regelanker	*m*	regulating armature	*n*
armature pivotante	*f*	Drehanker	*m*	rotating armature	*n*
arrêt (régulateur)	*m*	Abschaltung (Regler)	*f*	shutoff (governor)	*n*
arrêt d'urgence	*m*	Notabstellung	*f*	emergency shutoff	*n*
arrêt en fin de course (moteur d'essuie-glace)	*m*	Endabstellung (Wischermotor)	*f*	self-parking (wiper motor)	*n*
arrêt fixe (moteur d'essuie-glace)	*m*	Endabstellung (Wischermotor)	*f*	self-parking (wiper motor)	*n*
arrivée d'énergie	*f*	Energiezufluß	*m*	energy input	*n*
arrivée de carburant	*f*	Kraftstoffzulauf	*m*	fuel inlet	*n*
arrivée de combustible	*f*	Kraftstoffzulauf	*m*	fuel inlet	*n*
arrivée de l'huile de graissage	*f*	Schmierölzulauf	*m*	lube-oil inlet	*n*
articulation en croix (essuie-glace)	*f*	Kreuzlenker (Wischeranlage)	*m*	transversely jointed linkage (wiper system)	*n*

Français		Allemand		Anglais	
aspect du jet	*m*	Strahlbild	*n*	spray pattern	*n*
aspects de la bougie d'allumage	*mpl*	Zündkerzengesichter	*npl*	spark-plug faces	*npl*
aspirer	*v*	ansaugen	*v*	suck in	*v*
ASR, régulation d'antipatinage à la traction	*a*	Antriebsschlupfregelung, ASR	*f*	traction control system, TCS	*n*
asservi à la charge	*pp*	lastabhängig	*adj*	load-sensitive	*adj*
asservi à la décélération (réducteur de pression de freinage)	*pp*	verzögerungsabhängig (Druckminderer)	*adj*	deceleration-sensitive (brake-pressure regulating valve)	*adj*
asservi à la pression	*pp*	druckabhängig	*adj*	pressure-sensitive	*adj*
assurance qualité	*f*	Qualitätssicherung	*f*	quality assurance, QA	*n*
atténuation du bruit	*f*	Geräuschminderung	*f*	noise suppression	*n*
au plomb (essence)	*loc*	verbleit (Benzin)	*pp*	leaded (gasoline)	*pp*
augmentation de pression	*f*	Druckaufbau	*m*	pressure rise	*n*
auto-adaptation	*f*	Selbstadaption	*f*	self-adaptation	*n*
auto-allumage	*m*	Selbstzündung	*f*	auto-ignition	*n*
auto-allumage anticipé	*m*	Vorentflammung	*f*	pre-ignition	*n*
auto-amplification (force de freinage)	*f*	Selbstverstärkung (Bremskraft)	*f*	self-amplification (braking force)	*n*
auto-excitation (machines tournantes)	*f*	Selbsterregung (drehende Maschinen)	*f*	self-excitation (rotating machines)	*n*
auto-induction	*f*	Selbstinduktion	*f*	self-induction	*n*
auto-suralimentation	*f*	Selbstaufladung	*f*	self-charging	*ppr*
autobloquant	*adj*	selbsthemmend	*adj*	self-locking	*adj*
autocollant	*m*	Klebeschild	*n*	adhesive label	*n*
autocollant d'avertissement (alarme auto)	*m*	Warnaufkleber (Autoalarm)	*m*	warning sticker (car alarm)	*n*
autocollant d'inspection	*m*	Prüfplakette	*f*	inspection tag	*n*
autocontrôle	*m*	Selbstüberwachung	*f*	self-monitoring	*n*
autodiagnostic	*m*	Eigendiagnose	*f*	self-diagnosis	*n*
autolubrifiant	*adj*	selbstschmierend	*adj*	self-lubricating	*adj*
autonettoyage	*m*	Freibrand	*m*	burn-off	*n*
autonettoyant	*adj*	selbstreinigend	*adj*	self-cleaning	*ppr*
autoréduction (force de freinage)	*f*	Selbstverringerung (Bremskraft)	*f*	self-reduction (braking force)	*n*
autoréglable	*adj*	selbsteinstellend	*ppr*	self-adjusting	*ppr*
autorégulation	*f*	selbstregelnd	*ppr*	self-governing	*ppr*
autorisation (fabrication)	*f*	Freigabe (Fertigung)	*f*	release (manufacturing)	*n*
autorisation de fabrication	*f*	Fertigungsfreigabe	*f*	manufacturing release	*n*
autosurveillance	*f*	Selbstüberwachung	*f*	self-monitoring	*n*
auxiliaire	*m*	Zusatzaggregat	*n*	ancillary	*n*
auxiliaire de démarrage	*m*	Starthilfe	*f*	start-assist measure	*n*
auxiliaire de régénération	*m*	Regenerationshilfe	*f*	regeneration aid	*n*
avance (angle d'allumage)	*f*	Frühverstellung (Zündwinkel)	*f*	ignition advance	*n*
avance (début d'injection)	*f*	Frühverstellung (Einspritzbeginn)	*f*	advance (start of injection)	*n*
avance à dépression	*f*	Unterdruckzündversteller	*m*	vacuum advance mechanism	*n*
avance à l'allumage	*f*	Frühzündung	*f*	advanced ignition	*n*

Français		Allemand		Anglais	
avance centrifuge	*f*	Fliehkraftverstellung	*f*	centrifugal advance	*n*
avance du pignon (démarreur)	*f*	Ritzelvorschub	*m*	pinion advance (starter)	*n*
avertisseur	*m*	Signalhorn	*n*	horn	*n*
avertisseur à tonalité aiguë	*m*	Hochtonhorn	*n*	high-tone horn	*n*
avertisseur à tonalité grave	*m*	Tieftonhorn	*n*	low-tone horn	*n*
avertisseur d'alarme	*m*	Alarmhorn	*n*	alarm horn	*n*
avertisseur optique	*m*	Lichthupe	*f*	headlamp flasher	*n*
avertisseur sonore	*m*	Signalhorn	*n*	horn	*n*
avertisseur sonore standard	*m*	Normalhorn	*n*	standard horn	*n*
avertisseur surpuissant	*m*	Starktonhorn	*n*	supertone horn	*n*
axe à profil sphérique	*m*	Kugelstift x	*m*	spherical pin	*n*
axe creux	*m*	Hohlachse	*f*	hollow axle	*n*
axe d'arrêt	*m*	Rastbolzen	*m*	ratchet pin	*n*
axe d'entraînement (suspension pneumatique)	*m*	Mitnehmerbolzen (Luftfederventil)	*m*	driver pin (height-control valve)	*n*
axe d'étranglement	*m*	Drosselbolzen	*m*	throttle pin	*n*
axe d'injecteur	*m*	Düsenachse	*f*	nozzle axis	*n*
axe de blocage	*m*	Arretierbolzen	*m*	blocking pin	*n*
axe de butée	*m*	Anschlagbolzen	*m*	stop pin	*n*
axe de centrage (banc d'essai)	*m*	Zentrierstift (Rollenbremsprüfstand)	*m*	alignment pin (dynamic brake analyzer)	*n*
axe de commande (valve de nivellement)	*m*	Steuerbolzen (Luftfederventil)	*m*	control pin (height-control valve)	*n*
axe de correction	*m*	Verstellwelle	*f*	setting shaft	*n*
axe de correction de débit	*m*	Angleichbolzen	*m*	torque-control shaft	*n*
axe de guidage	*m*	Führungsstift	*m*	guide pin	*n*
axe de masselottes	*m*	Fliehgewichtsbolzen	*m*	flyweight bolt	*n*
axe de papillon	*m*	Drosselklappenwelle	*f*	throttle-valve shaft	*n*
axe de pivotement de la direction	*m*	Lenkdrehachse	*f*	steering axis	*n*
axe de pivotement de roue (dynamique d'un véhicule)	*m*	Radschwenkachse (Kfz-Dynamik)	*f*	wheel swivel angle (vehicle dynamics)	*n*
axe de positionnement	*m*	Stellwelle	*f*	actuator shaft	*n*
axe de réglage	*m*	Verstellbolzen	*m*	sliding bolt	*n*
axe de roulis (dynamique d'un véhicule)	*m*	Rollachse (Kfz-Dynamik)	*f*	roll axis (vehicle dynamics)	*n*
axe de vissage (véhicule)	*m*	Schraubachse (Kfz)	*f*	axis of rotation (motor vehicle)	*n*
axe du levier de commande	*m*	Verstellhebelwelle	*f*	control-lever shaft	*n*
axe instantané de rotation (dynamique d'un véhicule)	*m*	Rollachse (Kfz-Dynamik)	*f*	roll axis (vehicle dynamics)	*n*
axe longitudinal de la pompe	*m*	Pumpenlängsachse	*f*	longitudinal pump axis	*n*
axe vertical du véhicule	*m*	Fahrzeughochachse	*f*	vehicle vertical axis	*n*
À					
à avance de pression	*loc*	Voreilung (Bremsdruck)	*f*	pressure lead (braking pressure)	*n*
à commande par contacts	*loc*	kontaktgesteuert	*pp*	breaker-triggered	*pp*
à déclenchement par rupteur	*loc*	kontaktgesteuert	*pp*	breaker-triggered	*pp*
à deux circuits (dispositif de freinage)	*loc*	zweikreisig (Bremsanlage)	*adj*	dual-circuit (braking system)	*n*

Français		Allemand		Anglais	
à double effet (vérin)	*loc*	doppeltwirkend (Arbeitszylinder)	*ppr*	double-acting (working cylinder)	*ppr*
à entretien minimal	*loc*	wartungsarm	*adj*	low-maintenance	*n*
à faible entretien	*loc*	wartungsarm	*adj*	low-maintenance	*n*
à flanc nu (courroie trapézoïdale)	*loc*	flankenoffen (Keilriemen)	*adj*	open flank (V-belt)	*n*
à flanc ouvert (courroie trapézoïdale)	*loc*	flankenoffen (Keilriemen)	*adj*	open flank (V-belt)	*n*
à régime rapide (moteur diesel)	*loc*	schnellaufend (Dieselmotor)	*ppr*	high-speed (diesel engine)	*n*
à un circuit (dispositif de freinage)	*loc*	einkreisig (Bremsanlage)	*adj*	single-circuit (braking system)	*n*
à-coups	*mpl*	ruckeln	*v*	buck	*v*
B					
bac à charbon actif (technique des gaz d'échappement)	*m*	Aktivkohlebehälter (Abgastechnik)	*m*	carbon canister (emissions control technology)	*n*
bac de batterie	*m*	Blockkasten (Batterie)	*m*	battery case	*n*
bac monobloc (batterie)	*m*	Blockkasten (Batterie)	*m*	battery case	*n*
bac multiple (batterie)	*m*	Blockkasten (Batterie)	*m*	battery case	*n*
bague à cames	*f*	Nockenring	*m*	cam ring	*n*
bague collectrice	*f*	Schleifring	*m*	collector ring	*n*
bague d'appui	*f*	Stützring	*m*	support ring	*n*
bague d'attaque (frein)	*f*	Greifring (Bremse)	*m*	grip ring (brakes)	*n*
bague de centrage	*f*	Einpaßring	*m*	fitting ring	*n*
bague de court-circuitage	*f*	Kurzschlußring	*m*	short-circuiting ring	*n*
bague de dosage	*f*	Zumeß-Schieber	*m*	metering sleeve	*n*
bague de guidage	*f*	Lagerring	*m*	bearing ring	*n*
bague de réglage	*f*	Zumeß-Schieber	*m*	metering sleeve	*n*
bague de roue libre	*f*	Freilaufring	*m*	clutch shell	*n*
bague excentrique	*f*	Exzenterring	*m*	eccentric ring	*n*
bague filetée	*f*	Gewindehülse	*f*	threaded sleeve	*n*
bague inductive de référence	*f*	Referenzkurzschlußring	*m*	reference eddy-current ring	*n*
bague porte-galets	*f*	Rollenring	*m*	roller ring	*n*
bague-entretoise	*f*	Distanzring	*m*	spacer ring	*n*
bague-support des galets	*f*	Rollenring	*m*	roller ring	*n*
baladeuse	*f*	Vielzweckleuchte	*f*	multipurpose lamp	*n*
balai (machines tournantes)	*m*	Kohlebürste (elektrische Maschinen)	*f*	carbon brush (rotating machines)	*n*
balai d'essuie-glace	*m*	Wischblatt	*n*	wiper blade	*n*
balai de captage (potentiomètre	*m*	Bürstenschleifer (Potentiometer)	*m*	pickoff brush (potentiometer)	*n*
balai de charbon (machines tournantes)	*m*	Kohlebürste (elektrische Maschinen)	*f*	carbon brush (rotating machines)	*n*
balai de prise	*m*	Bürstenschleifer (Potentiometer)	*m*	pickoff brush (potentiometer)	*n*
balancier (banc d'essai)	*m*	Biegebalken (Rollenbremsprüfstand)	*m*	flexural sensor (dynamic brake analyzer)	*n*
balayage de la galerie d'alimentation	*m*	Saugraumspülung	*f*	fuel-gallery flushing	*n*
balayage de retour	*m*	Rückspülung	*f*	air backflush	*n*

Français

Français		Allemand		Anglais	
balayage transversal	*m*	Querspülung	*f*	cross flushing	*n*
banc d'essai	*m*	Prüfstand	*m*	test bench	*n*
banc d'essai à rouleaux	*m*	Rollenprüfstand	*m*	chassis dynamometer	*n*
banc d'essai à rouleaux pour freins	*m*	Rollenbremsprüfstand	*m*	dynamic brake analyzer	*n*
banc d'essai acoustique	*m*	Geräuschprüfstand	*m*	noise-level test bench	*n*
banc d'essai au froid	*m*	Kälteprüfstand	*m*	cold-test test bench	*n*
banc d'essai climatique	*m*	Klimaprüfstand	*m*	climate test bench	*n*
banc d'essai de moteurs	*m*	Motorprüfstand	*m*		
banc d'essai pour équipement pneumatique de freinage	*m*	Bremsaggregateprüfstand	*m*	braking-equipment test bench	*n*
banc d'essai pour freinage	*m*	Rollenbremsprüfstand	*m*	dynamic brake analyzer	*n*
banc d'essai pour pompes d'injection	*m*	Einspritzpumpen-Prüfstand	*m*	injection-pump test bench	*n*
banc de contrôle de pompe de référence	*m*	Fördermengennormal-Prüfbank	*f*	calibration-pump test bench	*n*
bande d'absorption	*f*	Absorptionsband	*n*	absorption band	*n*
bande d'éclairage	*f*	Lichtbandeinheit	*f*	lighting-strip unit	*n*
barrage d'huile (pompe d'injection)	*m*	Leckkraftstoffsperre (Einspritzpumpe)	*f*	oil block (fuel-injection pump)	*n*
barre de distribution	*f*	Stromschiene	*f*	bus bar	*n*
barre de traction (correcteur d'avance)	*f*	Zugstange (Zündversteller)	*f*	vacuum advance arm (advance mechanism)	*n*
barrette de connexion (batterie)	*f*	Zellenverbinder (Batterie)	*m*	cell connector (battery)	*n*
barrette de jonction des plaques (batterie)	*f*	Plattenverbinder (Batterie)	*m*	plate strap (battery)	*n*
barrière Hall	*f*	Hall-Schranke	*f*	Hall vane switch	*n*
barrière magnétique	*f*	Hall-Schranke	*f*	Hall vane switch	*n*
bascule bistable	*f*	Triggerpegel	*m*	trigger level	*n*
bascule de commutation	*f*	Schaltwippe	*f*	rocker	*n*
batterie au plomb	*f*	Bleibatterie	*f*	lead storage battery	*n*
batterie d'accumulateurs	*f*	Batterie	*f*	battery	*n*
batterie d'accumulateurs au plomb	*f*	Bleibatterie	*f*	lead storage battery	*n*
batterie de démarrage	*f*	Starterbatterie	*f*	starter battery	*n*
batterie plomb-calcium	*f*	Blei-Kalzium-Batterie	*f*	lead-calcium battery	*n*
bavage (injection diesel)	*m*	Nachspritzer (Dieseleinspritzung)	*m*	dribble (diesel fuel injection)	*n*
bavage de carburant	*m*	nachtropfen	*v*	fuel dribble	*n*
bec d'isolant (bougie)	*m*	Isolatorfuß (Zündkerze)	*m*	insulator nose (spark plug)	*n*
bielle (moteur à combustion)	*f*	Pleuelstange (Verbrennungsmotor)	*f*	connecting rod (IC engine)	*n*
biellette (correcteur d'avance)	*f*	Zugstange (Zündversteller)	*f*	vacuum advance arm (advance mechanism)	*n*
biellette (frein)	*f*	Verbindungsstange (Bremse)	*f*	connecting rod (brakes)	*n*
biellette de réglage	*f*	Regellenker	*m*	control-sleeve lever (single-plunger fuel-injection pump)	*n*
biflux (ventilateur)	*adj*	zweiflutig (Lüfter)	*adj*	double-flow cooling (fan)	*ppr*
bilan de charge (batterie)	*m*	Ladebilanz (Batterie)	*f*	charge balance (battery)	*n*

Français		Allemand		Anglais	
bilan des couples des roues motrices (ASR)	*m*	Momentenbilanz (ASR)	*f*	torque balance (TCS)	*n*
bilan énergétique (automobile)	*m*	Energiehaushalt (Kfz)	*m*	energy balance (motor vehicle)	*n*
blindage	*m*	Abschirmung	*f*	shield	*n*
blindage métallique	*m*	Metallabschirmkappe	*f*	metal screening cover	*n*
blindé	*pp*	geschirmt	*pp*	shielded	*pp*
blinder (antiparasitage)	*v*	schirmen (Entstörung)	*v*	shield (interference suppression)	*v*
bloc d'électrovalves	*m*	Magnetventilblock	*m*	solenoid-valve block	*n*
bloc de mesure et de command(	*m*	Meß- und Steuereinheit	*f*	measuring and control unit	*n*
bloc de puissance (allumage)	*m*	Leistungsteil (Zündsystem)	*n*	power section (ignition system)	*n*
bloc de régulation	*m*	Regelgruppe	*f*	flyweight assembly	*n*
bloc de ressorts	*m*	Federpaket	*n*	spring assembly	*n*
bloc fonctionnel (calculateur)	*m*	Funktionsblock (Steuergerät)	*m*	function module (ECU)	*n*
bloc optique	*m*	Scheinwerfereinsatz	*m*	headlight unit	*n*
bloc régulateur	*m*	Reglergruppe	*f*	governor assembly	*n*
bloc-distributeur	*m*	Wegeventilblock	*m*	directional-control-valve block	*n*
bloc-distributeur triple	*m*	Dreifach-Wegeventilblock	*m*	triple directional-control-valve block	*n*
bloc-distributeurs	*m*	Blockwegeventil	*n*	stack-type directional control valve	*n*
bloc-valves (suspension pneumatique)	*m*	Luftfeder-Ventileinheit	*f*	height-control-valve unit	*n*
bloc-valves de régulateur de pression	*m*	Druckregler-Ventilblock	*m*	pressure-regulator valve block	*n*
blocage (roue)	*m*	blockieren (Rad)	*v*	wheel lock	*n*
blocage automatique du différentiel	*m*	automatische Brems-Differentialsperre, ABS/ABD	*f*	automatic brake-force differential lock, ABS/ABD	*n*
blocage de l'essieu arrière	*m*	Hinterachssperre	*f*	rear-axle lock	*n*
blocage des différentiels	*m*	Differentialsperre	*f*	differential lock	*n*
blocage du différentiel	*m*	Brems-Differentialsperre	*f*	brake-force differential lock	*n*
blocage longitudinal (transmission intégrale)	*m*	Längssperre (Allradantrieb)	*f*	inter-axle lock (all-wheel drive)	*n*
blocage par visco-coupleur (transmission intégrale)	*m*	Viskosesperre (Allradantrieb)	*f*	viscous lock (all-wheel drive)	*n*
bloqueur du débit de surcharge au démarrage	*m*	Startmengenverriegelung	*f*	start-quantity locking device	*n*
bobinage d'attraction	*m*	Einzugswicklung	*f*	pull-in winding	*n*
bobinage de maintien	*m*	Haltewicklung	*f*	hold-in winding	*n*
bobine d'allumage	*f*	Zündspule	*f*	ignition coil	*n*
bobine d'allumage à deux sorties	*f*	Zweifunken-Zündspule	*f*	dual-spark ignition coil	*n*
bobine d'allumage à hautes performances	*f*	Hochleistungs-Zündspule	*f*	high-performance ignition coil	*n*
bobine d'allumage à quatre sorties	*f*	Vierfunken-Zündspule	*f*	four-spark ignition coil	*n*
bobine d'allumage à une sortie	*f*	Einzelfunken-Zündspule	*f*	single-spark ignition coil	*n*
bobine d'allumage spéciale	*f*	Sonderzündspule	*f*	special ignition coil	*n*
bobine d'allumage standard	*f*	Standard-Zündspule	*f*	standard ignition coil	*n*

Français		Allemand		Anglais	
bobine d'électro-aimant	*f*	Magnetwicklung	*f*	solenoid winding	*n*
bobine de maintien	*f*	Haltewicklung	*f*	hold-in winding	*n*
boîte à fusibles	*f*	Sicherungsdose	*f*	fuse box	*n*
boîte à résonance	*f*	Resonanzbehälter	*m*	resonance chamber	*n*
boîte d'adaptateurs (essuie-glace)	*f*	Adapterbox (Wischer)	*f*	adapter box (wipers)	*n*
boîte de commande	*f*	Schaltkasten	*m*	switch box	*n*
boîte de vitesses à commande manuelle	*f*	Handschalt-Getriebe	*n*	manually shifted transmission	*n*
boîte de vitesses automatique	*f*	Automatikgetriebe	*n*	automatic gearbox	*n*
boîte de vitesses classique	*f*	Handschalt-Getriebe	*n*	manually shifted transmission	*n*
boîtier (lampes)	*m*	Gehäuse (Leuchtkörper)	*n*	housing (lamps)	*n*
boîtier à contacts mâles	*m*	Stiftgehäuse	*n*	pin housing	*n*
boîtier de centrale de commande	*m*	Steuergerätebox	*f*	control-unit box	*n*
boîtier de commande manuel	*m*	Handsteuergerät	*n*	manual electric control unit, MECU	*n*
boîtier de feu	*m*	Leuchtengehäuse	*n*	lamp housing	*n*
boîtier de palier	*m*	Lagergehäuse	*n*	bearing housing	*n*
boîtier de papillon	*m*	Drosselklappenstutzen	*m*	throttle-valve assembly	*n*
boîtier de projecteur	*m*	Scheinwerfergehäuse	*n*	headlamp housing	*n*
boîtier électronique	*m*	elektronisches Steuergerät	*n*	electronic control unit, ECU	*n*
boîtier intermédiaire	*m*	Zwischengehäuse	*n*	intermediate housing	*n*
boîtier pour fiches femelles	*m*	Steckhülsengehäuse	*n*	socket housing	*n*
boîtier pour fiches plates	*m*	Flachsteckergehäuse	*n*	blade terminal housing	*n*
boîtier rabattable	*m*	Klappgehäuse	*n*	hinged housing	*n*
bombage	*m*	Balligkeit	*f*	crowning	*n*
borne (batterie)	*f*	Endpol (Batterie)	*m*	terminal post (battery)	*n*
borne (schéma)	*f*	Anschlußpunkt (Schaltplan)	*m*	terminal location (circuit diagram)	*n*
bossage-butée	*m*	Anschlagnase	*f*	stop lug	*n*
bouchage du filtre	*m*	Filterverstopfung	*f*	filter clogging	*n*
boucle conductrice	*f*	Leiterschleife	*f*	conductor loop	*n*
boucle d'asservissement	*f*	Regelschaltung	*f*	control loop	*n*
boucle de régulation	*f*	Regelkreis	*m*	closed control loop	*n*
bougie à étincelle glissante	*f*	Gleitfunkenzündkerze	*f*	surface-gap spark plug	*n*
bougie d'allumage	*f*	Zündkerze	*f*	spark plug	*n*
bougie d'allumage de mesure	*f*	Temperatur-Meßzündkerze	*f*	thermocouple spark plug	*n*
bougie d'inflammation à filament	*f*	Flammglühdrahtkerze	*f*	wire-type flame glow plug	*n*
bougie de préchauffage	*f*	Glühkerze	*f*	glow plug	*n*
bougie de préchauffage à flamme	*f*	Flammkerze	*f*	flame glow plug	*n*
bougie de préchauffage pour chauffage auxiliaire	*f*	Standheizungs-Glühkerze	*f*	glow plug for auxiliary heaters	*n*
bougie thermocouple	*f*	Temperatur-Meßzündkerze	*f*	thermocouple spark plug	*n*
bougie totalement blindée	*f*	vollgeschirmte Zündkerze	*f*	fully-shielded spark plug	*n*
bougie-crayon de préchauffage	*f*	Glühstiftkerze, GSK	*f*	sheathed-element glow plug	*n*

Français

Français		Allemand			Anglais	
bougie-crayon de préchauffage à flamme	*f*	Flammglühstiftkerze		*f*	sheathed-element flame glow plug	*n*
bougie-étalon	*f*	Temperatur-Meßzündkerze		*f*	thermocouple spark plug	*n*
boulon fileté	*m*	Stehbolzen		*m*	stud	*n*
bouton-poussoir diagnostic	*m*	Diagnose-Taster		*m*		
brai (batterie)	*m*	Vergußmasse (Batterie)		*f*	sealing compound (battery)	*n*
bras d'essuie-glace	*m*	Wischarm (Wischeranlage)		*m*	wiper arm (windshield wiper sytem)	*n*
bras d'essuie-glace à parallélogramme	*m*	Parallelogramm-Wischarm		*m*	parallelogram wiper arm	*n*
bras d'essuie-glace équipé (nettoyeur de projecteurs)	*m*	Wischhebel (Scheinwerfer-Reinigungsanlage)		*m*	wiper arm (headlamp cleaning system)	*n*
bras de lavophare	*m*	Lichtwischerarm		*m*	beamwash wiper-arm	*n*
bras pivotant	*m*	Schwenkarm		*m*	swivel arm	*n*
brassage	*m*	Verwirbelung		*f*	swirl effect	*n*
bride coulissante	*f*	Verschiebeflansch		*m*	sliding flange	*n*
bride de fixation	*f*	Befestigungsflansch		*m*	mounting flange	*n*
bride de réchauffage	*f*	Heizflansch		*m*	heating flange	*n*
broche de positionnement	*f*	Fixierstift		*m*	locating pin	*n*
brouillage radioélectrique	*m*	Funkstörung (Wirkung)		*f*	radio interference	*n*
bruit d'aspiration	*m*	Ansauggeräusch		*n*	intake noise	*n*
bruit d'échappement (régulateur de pression)	*m*	Abblasgeräusch (Druckregler)		*n*	blow-off noise (pressure regulator)	*n*
bruit de combustion	*m*	Verbrennungsgeräusch		*n*	combustion noise	*n*
bruit de fond (perturbation)	*m*	rauschen (Funkstörung)	x	*v*	background noise (radio disturbance)	*n*
bruit de friction	*m*	Reibgeräusch		*n*	friction noise	*n*
bruits d'impact	*mpl*	Körperschall		*m*	structure-borne noise	*n*
bruits de fonctionnement	*mpl*	Laufgeräusch		*n*	running noise	*n*
bus de données	*m*	Datenbus		*m*	data bus	*n*
buse à effet giratoire	*f*	Dralldüse		*f*	swirl nozzle	*n*
buse d'éjection	*f*	Strahldüse		*f*	jet	*n*
buse d'injecteur	*f*	Düsenkuppe		*f*	nozzle cone	*n*
buse venturi	*f*	Venturi-Düse		*f*	venturi tube	*n*
butée (banc d'essai)	*f*	Drucklager (Rollenbremsprüfstand)		*n*	thrust block (dynamic brake analyzer)	*n*
butée d'arrêt de la pédale	*f*	Pedalanschlag		*m*	pedal stop	*n*
butée de course	*f*	Hubanschlag		*m*	lift-stop	*n*
butée de débit de surcharge au démarrage	*f*	Startmengenanschlag		*m*	start-quantity stop	*n*
butée de débit maximal	*f*	Vollastanschlag		*m*	full-load stop	*n*
butée de la tige de réglage (pompe d'injection)	*f*	Regelstangenanschlag (Einspritzpumpe)		*m*	control-rod stop (fuel-injection pump)	*n*
butée de limitation de course de régulation	*f*	Regelwegbegrenzungs-anschlag		*m*	rack-travel limiting stop	*n*
butée de limitation de fumée	*f*	Rauchbegrenzeranschlag		*m*	smoke-limiting stop	*n*
butée de pleine charge	*f*	Vollastanschlag		*m*	full-load stop	*n*
butée de pleine charge en fonction de l'altitude	*f*	höhengesteuerter Vollastmengenanschlag		*m*	altitude-controlled full-load stop	*n*

Français

Français		Allemand		Anglais	
butée de ralenti	*f*	Leerlaufanschlag	*m*	low-idle stop	*n*
butée de réduction de débit	*f*	Mindermengenanschlag	*m*	reduced-delivery stop	*n*
butée de stop (injection diesel)	*f*	Stoppanschlag (Dieseleinspritzung)	*m*	shutoff stop (diesel fuel injection)	*n*
butée de vitesse intermédiaire	*f*	Zwischendrehzahlanschlag	*m*	intermediate-speed stop	*n*
butée élastique de ralenti	*f*	federnder Leerlaufanschlag	*m*	spring-loaded idle-speed stop	*n*
butée essence/gazole	*f*	Benzin-Diesel-Anschlag	*m*	gasoline/diesel stop	*n*
butée sur carter	*f*	Gehäuseanschlag	*m*	housing stop	*n*
C					
cabine de conduite	*f*	Fahrerhaus	*n*	cab	*n*
cabine de simulation des gaz d'échappement	*f*	Abgasprüfzelle	*f*	emissions test cell	*n*
câble adaptateur	*m*	Adapterkabel	*n*	adapter lead	*n*
câble d'activation de l'autodiagnostic	*m*	Eigendiagnose-Reizleitung	*f*	self-diagnosis initiate line	*n*
câble d'aide au démarrage	*m*	Starthilfskabel	*n*	battery jumper cable	*n*
câble d'allumage	*m*	Zündleitung	*f*	high-tension ignition cable	*n*
câble d'allumage résistif	*m*	Widerstands-Zündleitung	*f*	resistance ignition cable	*n*
câble de batterie	*m*	Batteriekabel	*n*	battery cable	*n*
câble de charge	*m*	Ladeleitung	*f*	charging cable	*n*
câble de circuit primaire (allumage)	*m*	Primärleitung (Zündanlage)	*f*	primary line (ignition system)	*n*
câble de commande	*m*	Steuerleitung	*f*	control line	*n*
câble de connexion	*m*	Anschlußleitung	*f*	connecting cable	*n*
câble de diagnostic	*m*	Diagnoseleitung	*f*	diagnosis cable	*n*
câble de frein (frein de stationnement)	*m*	Bremsseil (Feststellbremse)	*n*	brake cable (parking brake)	*n*
câble de retour à la masse	*m*	Masserückleitung	*f*	ground cable	*n*
câble de télécommande (charge de batterie)	*m*	Fernstartleitung (Batterieladung)	*f*	remote-control line (battery charge)	*n*
câble en boucle (alarme auto)	*m*	Lichtleitring (Autoalarm)	*m*	wire loop (car alarm)	*n*
câble haute tension	*m*	Hochspannungsleitung	*f*	high-voltage cable	*n*
câble principal du démarreur	*m*	Starterhauptleitung	*f*	starter cable	*n*
câble-pilote	*m*	Steuerleitung	*f*	control line	*n*
cache avant (projecteur)	*m*	Frontblende (Scheinwerfer)	*f*	front screen (headlamp)	*n*
cadre d'étanchéité	*m*	Dichtrahmen	*m*	sealing gasket	*n*
cadre de données (multiplexage)	*m*	Datenrahmen (CAN)	*m*	data frame (CAN)	*n*
cage à billes (commande des portes)	*f*	Kugelkäfig (Türbetätigung)	*m*	bearing cage (door control)	*n*
cage de transmission planétaire	*f*	Planetenträger	*m*	planetary-gear carrier	*n*
cahier des charges	*m*	Pflichtenheft	*n*	performance specs	*n*
Cahier technique (publication Bosch)	*m*	Technische Unterrichtung (Bosch-Schriftenreihe)	*f*	Technical Instruction (Bosch publication)	*n*
caisse du véhicule	*f*	Fahrzeugaufbau	*m*	vehicle body	*n*
calage dynamique du début de refoulement	*m*	dynamische Förderbeginn-Einstellung	*f*	dynamic timing adjustment	*n*
calaminage	*m*	Verkokung	*f*	coking	*n*
calaminage des injecteurs	*m*	Düsenverkokung	*f*	nozzle coking	*n*

Français		Allemand		Anglais	
calaminer	*v*	verkoken	*v*	coke	*v*
calcul des conducteurs	*m*	Leitungsberechnung	*f*	calculation of conductor sizes	*n*
calculateur adaptable	*m*	Anbausteuergerät	*n*	add-on ECU	*n*
calculateur électronique	*m*	elektronisches Steuergerät	*n*	electronic control unit, ECU	*n*
calculateur pompe	*m*	Pumpensteuergerät	*n*	pump ECU	*n*
cale	*f*	Füllstück	*n*	filler piece	*n*
cale de réglage	*f*	Ausgleichscheibe	*f*	shim (delivery-valve holder)	*n*
cale de réglage de pression (injecteur)	*f*	Druckausgleichscheibe (Einspritzdüse)	*f*	pressure-compensation disc (nozzle)	*n*
calibrage amortisseur	*m*	Dämpfungsdrossel	*f*	damping throttle	*n*
calibrage de décharge	*m*	Überströmdrossel	*f*	overflow restriction	*n*
calibre	*m*	Stecklehre	*f*	plug gauge	*n*
calibreur	*m*	Durchflußdrossel	*f*	flow throttle	*n*
calotte de blindage (allumeur)	*f*	Abschirmhaube (Zündverteiler)	*f*	shielding cover (ignition distributor)	*n*
came à excentrique (Common Rail)	*f*	Exzenternocken (Common Rail)	*m*	eccentric cam (common rail)	*n*
came axiale (pompe à pistons radiaux)	*f*	Axialnocken (Radialkolbenpumpe)	*m*	axial cam (radial-piston pump)	*n*
came d'allumage	*f*	Zündverteilernocken	*m*	distributor cam	*n*
came d'écartement (frein)	*f*	Spreizbacke (Trommelbremse)	*f*	wedge-type shoe (drum brake)	*n*
came d'injection	*f*	Einspritznocken	*m*	injection cam	*n*
came de frein	*f*	Bremsnocken	*m*	brake cam	*n*
came de rupteur (allumage)	*f*	Unterbrechernocken (Zündung)	*m*	breaker cam (ignition)	*n*
came en S (frein)	*f*	S-Nocken (Bremse)	*m*	S-cam (brakes)	*n*
came solidaire	*f*	Festnocken	*m*	fixed cam	*n*
came-plaque	*f*	Kurvenplatte	*f*	plate cam	*n*
CAN, système de multiplexage	*a*	CAN, Controller Area Network	*a*	CAN, controller area network	*a*
canal annulaire	*m*	Ringkanal	*m*	annular groove	*n*
canal axial	*m*	Längsbohrung	*f*	longitudinal passage	*n*
canal by-pass	*m*	Umgehungsleitung	*f*	bypass passage	*n*
canal d'admission	*m*	Ansaugkanal	*m*	intake port	*n*
canal d'admission (pompe distributrice)	*m*	Zulaufquerschnitt (Verteilereinspritzpumpe)	*m*	inlet port (distributor pump)	*n*
canal d'arrivée (pompe distributrice)	*m*	Einlaßquerschnitt (Verteilereinspritzpumpe)	*m*	inlet passage (distributor pump)	*n*
canal d'équilibrage (maître-cylindre tandem)	*m*	Nachlaufbohrung (Tandemhauptzylinder)	*f*	snifter bore (tandem master cylinder)	*n*
canal de circulation d'air (frein à disque)	*m*	Kühlkanal (Bremsscheibe)	*m*	cooling channel (brake disc)	*n*
canal de décharge	*m*	Überströmbohrung	*f*	overflow orifice	*n*
canal de dérivation	*m*	Umgehungsleitung	*f*	bypass passage	*n*
canal de fin d'injection	*m*	Steuerbohrung	*f*	spill port	*n*
canal de refoulement	*m*	Druckkanal	*m*	pressure passage	*n*
canal de retour d'huile de fuite	*m*	Leckkraftstoff-Rückführung	*f*	leakage-return duct	*n*
canal de retour des fuites	*m*	Leckkraftstoff-Rückführung	*f*	leakage-return duct	*n*
canal de sortie (pompe électrique à carburant)	*m*	Abflußbohrung (Elektrokraftstoffpumpe)	*f*	outlet bore (electric fuel pump)	*n*

Français		Allemand		Anglais	
canal en dérivation (papillon)	*m*	Nebenschlußquerschnitt (Drosselklappe)	*m*	bypass cross-section (throttle valve)	*n*
canal radial	*m*	Querbohrung	*f*	transverse passage	*n*
canalisation de retour	*f*	Rücklaufleitung	*f*	return line	*n*
cannelure	*f*	Kerbverzahnung	*f*	grooved toothing	*n*
caoutchouc d'essuie-glace	*m*	Wischgummi	*n*	wiper-blade element	*n*
capacité d'absorption thermique	*f*	Wärmeaufnahmevermögen	*n*	heat-absorbing property	*n*
capacité d'aspiration	*f*	Ansaugleistung	*f*	suction capacity	*n*
capacité de batterie	*f*	Nennkapazität (Batterie)	*f*	nominal capacity (battery)	*n*
capacité nominale (batterie)	*f*	Nennkapazität (Batterie)	*f*	nominal capacity (battery)	*n*
capot d'aération	*m*	Luftansaugdeckel	*m*	intake cover	*n*
capot de protection	*m*	Schutzhaube	*f*	protection hood	*n*
capot de protection de borne (batterie)	*m*	Polabdeckkappe (Batterie)	*f*	terminal-post cover (battery)	*n*
capotage du véhicule	*m*	Fahrzeugüberschlag	*m*	vehicle rollover	*n*
capsule à membrane	*f*	Membrandose	*f*	diaphragm unit	*n*
capsule barométrique	*f*	Membrandose	*f*	diaphragm unit	*n*
capsule de commande	*f*	Steuerdose	*f*	aneroid capsule	*n*
capsule manométrique	*f*	Druckdose	*f*	vacuum unit	*n*
capteur	*m*	Sensor	*m*	sensor	*n*
capteur à bague de court-circuitage	*m*	Kurzschlußringsensor	*m*	short-circuit-ring sensor	*n*
capteur à courants de Foucault	*m*	Wirbelstromsensor	*m*	eddy-current sensor	*n*
capteur à film chaud	*m*	Heißfilmsensor	*m*	hot-film sensor	*n*
capteur à pince	*m*	Aufklemmgeber	*m*	clamp-on sensor	*n*
capteur à ultrasons (alarme auto)	*m*	Ultraschallsensor	*m*	ultrasonic receiver	*n*
capteur altimétrique	*m*	Höhensensor	*m*	altitude sensor	*n*
capteur auxiliaire de régime	*m*	Hilfsdrehzahlgeber	*m*	auxiliary engine-speed sensor	*n*
capteur d'accélérateur	*m*	Fahrpedalsensor	*m*	pedal-travel sensor	*n*
capteur d'accélération	*m*	Beschleunigungssensor	*m*	acceleration sensor	*n*
capteur d'accélération transversale (ESP)	*m*	Querbeschleunigungssensor (ESP)	*m*	lateral-acceleration sensor (ESP)	*n*
capteur d'angle de braquage (ESP)	*m*	Lenkradwinkelsensor (ESP)	*m*	steering-wheel angle sensor (ESP)	*n*
capteur d'angle de rotation	*m*	Drehwinkelsensor, DWS	*m*	angle of rotation sensor	*n*
capteur d'angle vilebrequin	*m*	Kurbelwinkelsensor	*m*	crank-angle sensor	*n*
capteur d'inclinaison	*m*	Neigungssensor	*m*	tilt sensor	*n*
capteur d'usure (garniture de frein)	*m*	Verschleißsensor (Bremsbelag)	*m*	wear sensor (brake lining)	*n*
capteur de capotage	*m*	Überrollsensor	*m*	rollover sensor	*n*
capteur de champ magnétique	*m*	Magnetfeldsensor	*m*	magnetic-field sensor	*n*
capteur de charge (châssis)	*m*	Achslastsensor	*m*	axle-load sensor	*n*
capteur de charge (moteur)	*m*	Lastsensor (Motor)	*m*	load sensor (engine management)	*n*
capteur de charge sur essieu	*m*	Achslastsensor	*m*	axle-load sensor	*n*
capteur de choc	*m*	Stoßsensor	*m*	impact sensor	*n*
capteur de choc (alarme auto)	*m*	Schocksensor (Autoalarm)	*m*	shock sensor (car alarm)	*n*

Français

Français		Allemand		Anglais	
capteur de cliquetis	*m*	Klopfsensor	*m*	knock sensor	*n*
capteur de couple	*m*	Drehmomentsensor	*m*	torque sensor	*n*
capteur de course d'accélérateui	*m*	Fahrpedalsensor	*m*	pedal-travel sensor	*n*
capteur de course d'aiguille	*m*	Nadelbewegungssensor	*m*	needle-motion sensor	*n*
capteur de course de régulation	*m*	Regelwegsensor	*m*	rack-travel sensor	*n*
capteur de course du tiroir de régulation	*m*	Regelschieberweggeber	*m*	control-collar position sensor	*n*
capteur de début de refoulemen	*m*	Förderbeginngeber, FBG	*m*	port-closing sensor	*n*
capteur de déplacement	*m*	Weggeber	*m*	travel sensor	*n*
capteur de déplacement (suspension pneumatique)	*m*	Niveaugeber (Luftfederung)	*m*	level sensor (air suspension)	*n*
capteur de déplacement d'aiguille	*m*	Nadelbewegungssensor	*m*	needle-motion sensor	*n*
capteur de dépression (allumage)	*m*	Unterdruckgeber (Zündung)	*m*	vacuum pickup (ignition)	*n*
capteur de flux d'écoulement (débitmètre massique à film chaud)	*m*	Durchflußsensor (Heißfilm-Luftmassenmesser)	*m*	flow sensor (hot-film air-mass meter)	*n*
capteur de force de couplage (dispositif de freinage électro-pneumatique	*m*	Koppelkraftsensor (elektronisch-pneumatisches Bremssystem)	*m*	coupling-force sensor (electronic/compressed-air braking system)	*n*
capteur de freinage	*m*	Bremswertsensor	*m*	braking-value sensor	*n*
capteur de la course de la tige de réglage	*m*	Regelwegsensor	*m*	rack-travel sensor	*n*
capteur de levée d'aiguille	*m*	Nadelhubgeber	*m*	needle-lift sensor	*n*
capteur de masse de combustible	*m*	Kraftstoffmasse-Sensor	*m*	fuel-mass sensor	*n*
capteur de mesure	*m*	Sensor	*m*	sensor	*n*
capteur de mesure (banc d'essai)	*m*	Meßwertsensor (Rollenbremsprüfstand)	*m*	measuring sensor (dynamic brake analyzer)	*n*
capteur de niveau (pompe électrique à carburant)	*m*	Füllstandsgeber (Elektrokraftstoffpumpe)	*m*	level sensor (in-tank unit)	*n*
capteur de niveau (suspension pneumatique)	*m*	Niveaugeber (Luftfederung)	*m*	level sensor (air suspension)	*n*
capteur de papillon	*m*	Drosselklappensensor	*m*	throttle-valve sensor	*n*
capteur de perturbations (CEM)	*m*	Störsenke (EMV)	*f*	susceptible device (EMC)	*n*
capteur de phase	*m*	Phasensensor	*m*	phase sensor	*n*
capteur de pluie	*m*	Regensensor	*m*	rain sensor	*n*
capteur de position	*m*	Lagesensor	*m*	position sensor	*n*
capteur de position angulaire	*f*	Drehwinkelsensor, DWS	*m*	angle of rotation sensor	*n*
capteur de position angulaire (alarme auto)	*m*	Winkelgeber (Autoalarm)	*m*	tilt sensor (car alarm)	*n*
capteur de pression	*m*	Drucksensor	*m*	pressure sensor	*n*
capteur de pression "Rail"	*m*	Raildrucksensor (Common Rail)	*m*	common-rail pressure sensor	*n*
capteur de pression absolue	*m*	Absolutdrucksensor	*m*	absolute-pressure sensor	*n*
capteur de pression atmosphérique	*m*	Atmosphärendrucksensor	*m*	atmospheric-pressure sensor	*n*
capteur de pression d'admission	*m*	Saugrohrdrucksensor	*m*	intake-manifold pressure sensoı	*n*

Français		Allemand		Anglais	
capteur de pression de suralimentation	*m*	Ladedrucksensor	*m*	boost-pressure sensor, BPS	*n*
capteur de pression différentielle	*m*	Differenzdrucksensor	*m*	differential-pressure sensor	*n*
capteur de pression du carburant	*m*	Kraftstoffdrucksensor	*m*	fuel-pressure sensor	*n*
capteur de référence	*m*	Normgeber	*m*	standard sensor	*n*
capteur de repère de consigne (allumage)	*m*	Bezugsmarkensensor (Zündung)	*m*	reference-mark sensor (ignition	*n*
capteur de signal de refoulement	*m*	Fördersignal-Sensor	*m*	delivery-signal sensor	*n*
capteur de synchronisme	*m*	Trigger-Impulsgeber	*m*	pulse-generator trigger	*n*
capteur de taux de rotation (ESP)	*m*	Drehratensensor (ESP)	*m*	yaw sensor (ESP)	*n*
capteur de température	*m*	Temperatursensor	*m*	temperature sensor	*n*
capteur de température d'air	*m*	Lufttemperaturfühler	*m*	air-temperature sensor, ATS	*n*
capteur de température des gaz d'échappement	*m*	Abgastemperaturfühler	*m*	exhaust-gas temperature sensor	*n*
capteur de température moteur	*m*	Motortemperatursensor	*m*	engine-temperature sensor	*n*
capteur de tension d'allumage	*m*	Zündspannungsgeber	*m*	ignition-voltage pick-up	*n*
capteur de vibrations	*m*	Vibrationssensor	*m*	vibration sensor	*n*
capteur de vitesse	*m*	Fahrgeschwindigkeitssensor	*m*	vehicle-speed sensor	*n*
capteur de vitesse d'aiguille	*m*	Nadelgeschwindigkeitsfühler	*m*	needle-velocity sensor, NVS	*n*
capteur de vitesse de consigne	*m*	Geschwindigkeits-Sollgeber	*m*	speed-preselect, SP	*n*
capteur de vitesse de mise en lacet (ESP)	*m*	Drehratensensor (ESP)	*m*	yaw sensor (ESP)	*n*
capteur de vitesse de rotation	*m*	Drehzahlsensor	*m*	speed sensor	*n*
capteur de vitesse de rotation de l'arbre à cames	*m*	Nockenwellen-Drehzahlsensor	*m*	camshaft speed sensor	*n*
capteur de vitesse de rotation du vilebrequin	*m*	Kurbelwellen-Drehzahlsensor	*m*	crankshaft speed sensor	*n*
capteur de vitesse de roue	*m*	Raddrehzahlsensor	*m*	wheel-speed sensor	*n*
capteur de vitesse de roulage	*m*	Fahrgeschwindigkeitssensor	*m*	vehicle-speed sensor	*n*
capteur inductif	*m*	Induktionsgeber (Zündung)	*m*	induction-type pulse-generator (ignition)	*n*
capteur inductif haute fréquence	*m*	Hochfrequenzinduktivgeber	*m*	high-frequency inductive sensor	*n*
capteur magnétorésistif	*m*	Feldplattensensor	*m*	magnetoresistive sensor	*n*
capteur vernier	*m*	Noniusgeber	*m*	vernier sensor	*n*
capuchon anti-érosion (injecteur)	*m*	Prallkappe (Einspritzventil)	*f*	anti-erosion cap (injector)	*n*
capuchon calorifuge (injecteur)	*m*	Wärmeschutzhütchen (Einspritzdüse)	*n*	thermal-protection cap (injection nozzle)	*n*
caractéristique à l'état bloqué	*f*	Sperrkennlinie	*f*	off-state characteristic	*n*
caractéristique à vide	*f*	Leerlaufkennlinie	*f*	no-load charcteristic	*n*
caractéristique d'avance	*f*	Verstellcharakteristik	*f*	timing characteristic	*n*
caractéristique de charge (batterie)	*f*	Ladekennlinie (Batterie)	*f*	charging characteristic (battery)	*n*
caractéristique de conduite	*f*	Fahrkurve	*f*	driving curve	*n*

Français		Allemand		Anglais	
caractéristique de correction de débit	*f*	Angleichverlauf	*m*	torque-control characteristic	*n*
caractéristique de coupure de débit	*f*	Abregelverlauf	*m*	breakaway characteristic	*n*
caractéristique de débit nul	*f*	Nullförderlinie	*f*	zero-fuel characteristic	*n*
caractéristique de pleine charge	*f*	Vollastkennlinie	*f*	full-load curve	*n*
caractéristique du régulateur	*f*	Reglercharakteristik	*f*	governor characteristics	*n*
caractéristique tension-courant à l'état passant (diode redresseuse)	*f*	Durchlaßkennlinie (Gleichrichterdiode)	*f*	on-state characteristic (rectifier diode)	*n*
caractéristiques du freinage	*fpl*	Bremskenndaten	*npl*	brake specifications	*npl*
carburant de barrage	*m*	Sperröl	*n*	sealing oil	*n*
carburant de fuite	*m*	Leckkraftstoff	*m*	leak fuel	*n*
carburant diesel	*m*	Dieselkraftstoff	*m*	diesel fuel	*n*
carburateur	*m*	Vergaser	*m*	carburetor	*n*
carcasse polaire	*f*	Polgehäuse	*n*	stator housing	*n*
carcasse stator	*f*	Polgehäuse	*n*	stator housing	*n*
carrosserie du véhicule	*f*	Fahrzeugaufbau	*m*	vehicle body	*n*
carrosserie interchangeable	*f*	Wechselaufbau	*m*	interchangeable body	*n*
carte à circuit imprimé	*f*	Leiterplatte	*f*	printed-circuit board	*n*
carte imprimée	*f*	Leiterplatte	*f*	printed-circuit board	*n*
carter de compresseur	*m*	Verdichtergehäuse	*n*	compressor housing	*n*
carter de filtre	*m*	Filtergehäuse	*n*	filter case	*n*
carter de palier	*m*	Lagergehäuse	*n*	bearing housing	*n*
carter de pompe	*m*	Pumpengehäuse	*n*	pump housing	*n*
carter de régulateur	*m*	Reglergehäuse	*n*	governor housing	*n*
carter de turbine	*m*	Turbinengehäuse	*n*	turbine housing	*n*
carter en alliage léger	*m*	Leichtmetallgehäuse	*n*	light-metal housing	*n*
carter hélicoïde	*m*	Spiralgehäuse	*n*	spiral housing	*n*
cartographie	*f*	Kennfeld	*n*	program map	*n*
cartographie d'allumage	*f*	Zündwinkelkennfeld	*n*	ignition map	*n*
cartographie de conversion	*f*	Umrechnungskennfeld	*n*	conversion map	*n*
cartographie de correction de pression	*f*	Druckkorrekturkennfeld	*n*	pressure-correction map	*n*
cartographie de débit	*f*	Mengenkennfeld	*n*	fuel-quantity map	*n*
cartographie de l'angle de came	*f*	Schließwinkelkennfeld	*n*	dwell-angle map	*n*
cartographie de pompe	*f*	Pumpenkennfeld	*n*	pump map	*n*
cartographie de richesse (lambda)	*f*	Lambda-Kennfeld	*n*	lambda program map	*n*
cartographie du régulateur	*f*	Reglerkennfeld	*n*	governor characteristic curves	*n*
cartographie moteur	*f*	Motorkennfeld	*n*	engine map	*n*
cartouche de déshydratant (dessiccateur)	*f*	Trockenmittelbox (Lufttrockner)	*f*	desiccant box (air drier)	*n*
cartouche de filtre à air	*f*	Luftfiltereinsatz	*m*	air-filter element	*n*
cartouche de filtre à huile	*f*	Ölfiltereinsatz	*m*	lube-oil filter element	*n*
cartouche de sécurité (filtre à air)	*f*	Sicherheitspatrone (Luftfilter)	*f*	safety element (air filter)	*n*
cartouche filtrante	*f*	Filtereinsatz	*m*	filter element	*n*

Français		Allemand		Anglais	
cartouche filtrante en étoile	*f*	Sternfilterelement	*n*	radial vee-form filter element	*n*
cartouche filtrante en rouleau	*f*	Wickelfiltereinsatz	*m*	spiral vee-shaped filter element	*n*
cartouche filtrante fine	*f*	Feinfiltereinsatz	*m*	fine-filter element	*n*
cartouche filtrante primaire	*f*	Vorfiltereinsatz	*m*	preliminary-filter element	*n*
catalyseur	*m*	Katalysator	*m*	catalytic converter	*n*
catalyseur à double lit	*m*	Doppelbettkatalysator	*m*	dual-bed catalytic converter	*n*
catalyseur à une voie	*m*	Einbettkatalysator	*m*	single-bed catalytic converter	*n*
catalyseur d'oxydation	*m*	Oxydationskatalysator	*m*	oxidation catalytic converter	*n*
catalyseur de réduction	*m*	Reduktionskatalysator	*m*	reduction catalytic converter	*n*
catalyseur trifonctionnel	*m*	Dreiwegekatalysator	*m*	three-way catalytic converter, TWC	*n*
catalyseur trois voies	*m*	Dreiwegekatalysator	*m*	three-way catalytic converter, TWC	*n*
catégorie de véhicule	*f*	Fahrzeugklasse	*f*	vehicle category	*n*
cause du défaut	*f*	Fehlerursache	*f*	failure cause	*n*
cavitation (formation de cavités gazeuses)	*f*	Kavitation (Lochfraß)	*f*	cavitation	*n*
cavité du piston	*f*	Kolbenmulde	*f*	piston recess	*n*
ceinture de sécurité	*f*	Sicherheitsgurt	*m*	seat belt	*n*
célérité du son	*f*	Schallschnelle	*f*	acoustic velocity	*n*
cellule de décharge (lampe à décharge)	*f*	Entladungsraum (Gasentladungslampe)	*m*	discharge chamber (gaseous-discharge lamp)	*n*
cellule de mesure	*f*	Meßkammer (CO-Gas)	*f*	measuring chamber (exhaust-gas test)	*n*
cellule de pression	*f*	Druckkammer (Einspritzdüse)	*f*	pressure chamber (injection nozzle)	*n*
cellule de vaporisation	*f*	Verdampfungsmulde	*f*	evaporation recess	*n*
cellule réceptrice (gaz CO)	*f*	Empfängerkammer (Abgastester)	*f*	receiving chamber (CO test)	*n*
CEM, compatibilité électromagnétique	*a*	elektromagnetische Verträglichkeit, EMV	*f*	electromagnetic compatibility, EMC	*n*
centrale clignotante	*f*	Blinkgeber	*m*	turn-signal flasher	*n*
centrale de commande du moteur	*f*	Motorsteuergerät	*n*	engine control unit	*n*
centrale de commande électronique	*f*	elektronisches Steuergerät	*n*	electronic control unit, ECU	*n*
centrale de signal de détresse	*f*	Warnlichtgeber	*m*	hazard-warning signal flasher	*n*
centrale mixte de direction-détresse	*f*	Warnblinkgeber	*m*	hazard-warning and turn-signal flasher	*n*
centre de pression (vent latéral)	*m*	Druckpunkt (Seitenwind)	*m*	pressure point (crosswind)	*n*
centre de rotation	*m*	Drehpunkt	*m*	pivot	*n*
céramique en nid d'abeilles (filtre d'oxidation de particules)	*f*	Wabenkeramik (Rußabbrennfilter)	*f*	honeycomb ceramic (soot burn-off filter)	*n*
cercle de tête (engrenage)	*m*	Kopfkreis (Zahnrad)	*m*	tip circle (gear)	*n*
cercle primitif de référence (engrenage)	*m*	Teilkreis (Zahnrad)	*m*	reference circle (gear)	*n*
certificat du test de qualité	*m*	Qualitätsprüfzertifikat	*n*	quality inspection certificate	*n*
certification (ISO)	*f*	Zertifizierung (ISO)	*f*	certification (ISO)	*n*
chaîne cinématique	*f*	Antriebsstrang	*m*	drivetrain	*n*

Français		Allemand		Anglais	
chaîne de commande	*f*	Steuerkette	*f*	open control loop	*n*
chaîne de transmission	*f*	Antriebsstrang	*m*	drivetrain	*n*
chaleur de dissipation	*f*	Verlustwärme	*f*	heat losses	*npl*
chaleur de freinage	*f*	Bremswärme	*f*	braking heat	*n*
chaleur dégagée par la combustion	*f*	Verbrennungswärme	*f*	combustion heat	*n*
chambre à carburant (amortisseur de pression du carburant)	*f*	Kraftstoffkammer (Kraftstoffdruckregler)	*f*	fuel chamber (fuel-pressure regulator)	*n*
chambre à ressort (amortisseur de pression du carburant)	*f*	Federkammer (Kraftstoffdruckregler)	*f*	pressure chamber (fuel-pressure regulator)	*n*
chambre basse pression	*f*	Niederdruckraum	*m*	low-pressure chamber	*n*
chambre d'accumulation (ABS)	*f*	Speicherkammer (ABS)	*f*	accumulator chamber (ABS)	*n*
chambre d'air	*f*	Luftkammer	*f*	air chamber	*n*
chambre d'amortissement (ABS)	*f*	Dämpferkammer (ABS)	*f*	damper chamber (ABS)	*n*
chambre d'amortissement (valve de nivellement)	*f*	Dämpfungskammer (Luftfederventil)	*f*	damping chamber (height-control valve)	*n*
chambre d'élément (Common Rail)	*f*	Elementraum (Common Rail)	*m*	element chamber (common rail	*n*
chambre d'injecteur	*f*	Düsenraum	*m*	nozzle chamber	*n*
chambre de combustion	*f*	Verbrennungsraum x	*m*	combustion chamber	*n*
chambre de combustion (émissions)	*f*	Brennkammer (Abgastester)	*f*	burner (emissions testing)	*n*
chambre de combustion principale	*f*	Hauptverbrennungsraum	*m*	main combustion chamber	*n*
chambre de commande	*f*	Steuerkammer	*f*	pilot chamber	*n*
chambre de compression (frein)	*f*	Druckraum (Bremse)	*m*	pressure chamber (brakes)	*n*
chambre de dépression	*f*	Unterdruckkammer	*f*	vacuum chamber	*n*
chambre de mesure (gaz CO)	*f*	Meßkammer (CO-Gas)	*f*	measuring chamber (exhaust-gas test)	*n*
chambre de pompage	*f*	Saugraum (Einspritzpumpe)	*m*	fuel gallery (fuel-injection pump)	*n*
chambre de précombustion	*f*	Vorkammer	*f*	prechamber	*n*
chambre de pression (injecteur)	*f*	Druckkammer (Einspritzdüse)	*f*	pressure chamber (injection nozzle)	*n*
chambre de pression d'injecteur	*f*	Druckkammer (Einspritzdüse)	*f*	pressure chamber (injection nozzle)	*n*
chambre de réaction	*f*	Reaktionskammer	*f*	reaction chamber	*n*
chambre de refoulement (pompe d'injection)	*f*	Druckraum (Einspritzpumpe)	*m*	plunger chamber (fuel-injection pump)	*n*
chambre de ressort(s)	*f*	Federraum	*m*	spring chamber	*n*
chambre de tourbillonnement	*f*	Wirbelkammer	*f*	whirl chamber	*n*
chambre de travail (servofrein)	*f*	Arbeitskammer (Bremskraftverstärker)	*f*	working chamber (brake booster)	*n*
chambre de turbulence	*f*	Wirbelkammer	*f*	whirl chamber	*n*
chambre du vérin	*f*	Zylinderkammer	*f*	cylinder chamber	*n*
chambre haute pression	*f*	Druckraum (Einspritzpumpe)	*m*	plunger chamber (fuel-injection pump)	*n*
chambre inférieure	*f*	Unterkammer	*f*	lower chamber	*n*

Français		Allemand		Anglais	
chambre réceptrice (gaz CO)	*f*	Empfängerkammer (Abgastester)	*f*	receiving chamber (CO test)	*n*
chambre supérieure	*f*	Oberkammer	*f*	upper chamber	*n*
champ d'excitation	*m*	Erregerfeld	*n*	excitation field	*n*
champ de balayage	*m*	Wischfeld	*n*	wipe pattern	*n*
champ de lignes de force	*m*	Kraftlinienfeld	*n*	field of force	*n*
champ en dérivation	*m*	Nebenschlußfeld	*n*	shunt field	*n*
champ magnétique	*m*	Magnetfeld	*n*	magnetic field	*n*
champ magnétique d'amorçage	*m*	Vorerregermagnetfeld	*n*	pre-excitation magnetic field	*n*
champ permanent	*m*	Permanentfeld	*n*	permanent-magnet field	*n*
champ ultrasonique (alarme auto)	*m*	Ultraschallfeld (Autoalarm)	*n*	ultrasonic field (car alarm)	*n*
chanfrein (téton d'injection)	*m*	Anschliff (Spritzzapfen)	*m*	specially ground pintle	*n*
chanfrein des pôles à griffes	*m*	Klauenpolabhebung	*f*	claw-pole chamfer	*n*
chape	*f*	Gabelkopf	*m*	fork head	*n*
chapeau de filtre	*m*	Filterdeckel	*m*	filter cover	*n*
charge (batterie)	*f*	Ladung (Batterie)	*f*	charging (battery)	*n*
charge (correction automatique de la force de feinage)	*f*	Lastgröße (Bremskraftregelung)	*f*	load value (braking-force metering)	*n*
charge (essieu)	*f*	Achslast	*f*	axle load	*n*
charge d'air	*f*	Luftfüllung	*f*	air charge	*n*
charge de freinage (banc d'essai)	*f*	Bremslast (Rollenprüfstand)	*f*	retarding force (chassis dynamometer)	*n*
charge de pointe	*f*	Spitzenbelastung	*f*	peak load	*n*
charge du cylindre	*f*	Zylinderladung	*f*	cylinder charge	*n*
charge du moteur	*f*	Motorlast	*f*	engine load	*n*
charge dynamique par essieu	*f*	dynamische Achslast	*f*	dynamic axle load	*n*
charge nominale	*f*	Nennlast	*f*	nominal load	*n*
charge partielle (moteur à combustion)	*f*	Teillast (Verbrennungsmotor)	*f*	part load (IC engine)	*n*
charge permanente (charge de batterie)	*f*	Dauerladung (Batterieladung)	*f*	trickle charging (battery charge)	*n*
charge rapide (batterie)	*f*	Schnelladung (Batterie)	*f*	boost charge (battery)	*n*
chargement (véhicule)	*m*	Beladungszustand (Kfz)	*m*	laden state (motor vehicle)	*n*
chargeur (batterie)	*m*	Batterieladegerät	*n*	battery charger	*n*
chargeur (projecteur portable)	*m*	Ladesessel (Handscheinwerfer)	*m*	charging unit (hand-portable searchlight)	*n*
chargeur compact (batterie)	*m*	Kleinlader (Batterie)	*m*	small charger (battery)	*n*
chargeur de batterie	*m*	Batterieladegerät	*n*	battery charger	*n*
chargeur de démarrage rapide (batterie)	*m*	Schnellstartlader (Batterie)	*m*	rapid-start charger (battery)	*n*
chargeur de garage (batterie)	*m*	Werkstattlader (Batterie)	*m*	workshop charger (battery)	*n*
chargeur électronique (batterie)	*m*	Elektroniklader (Batterie)	*m*	electronic charger (battery)	*n*
chariot porte-pièce	*m*	Werkstückträger	*m*	workpiece carrier	*n*
chasser (véhicule)	*v*	ausbrechen (Kfz) x	*v*	break away (motor vehicle)	*v*
chauffage	*m*	Heizungsanlage	*f*	heater system	*n*
chauffage automatique	*m*	Heizautomatik	*f*	automatic heater	*n*
chauffage auxiliaire	*m*	Standheizung	*f*	auxiliary heating	*n*

Français		Allemand		Anglais	
chauffage d'habitacle	*m*	Wagenheizung	*f*	vehicle heater	*n*
chauffage de rétroviseur	*m*	Spiegelheizung	*f*	mirror heating	*n*
chauffage de serrure de porte	*m*	Türschloßheizung	*f*	door-lock heating	*n*
chauffage de siège	*m*	Sitzheizung	*f*	seat heating	*n*
chemin de conduction de la chaleur	*m*	Wärmeleitweg	*m*	thermal conduction path	*n*
chemin de fuite	*m*	Kriechweg	*m*	leakage path	*n*
cheminée (allumeur)	*f*	Außendom (Zündverteiler)	*m*	outer tower (ignition distributor)	*n*
chemise	*f*	Verteilerbüchse	*f*	distributor-head bushing	*n*
chevauchement (fentes d'étranglement)	*m*	Überdeckung (Steuerschlitze)	*f*	overlap (metering slits)	*n*
choc thermique	*m*	Thermoschock	*m*	thermal shock	*n*
chute de potentiel	*f*	Spannungsfall	*m*	voltage drop	*n*
chute de pression	*f*	Druckabbau	*m*	pressure drop	*n*
chute de tension	*f*	Spannungsfall	*m*	voltage drop	*n*
ciment à base de verre conducteur	*m*	Glasschmelze (elektrisch leitend)	*f*	conductive glass seal	*n*
circlips	*m*	Sicherungsring	*m*	retainer	*n*
circuit	*m*	Stromkreis	*m*	electric circuit	*n*
circuit à haute intégration (calculateur)	*m*	Großschaltkreis (Steuergerät)	*m*	LSI circuit (large scale integration)	*n*
circuit astable	*m*	Multivibrator	*m*	multivibrator	*n*
circuit basse pression	*m*	Niederdruckkreislauf	*m*	low-pressure system	*n*
circuit d'air comprimé	*m*	Druckluftkreis	*m*	compressed-air circuit	*n*
circuit d'alimentation (air comprimé)	*m*	Druckluftvorratskreis	*m*	compressed-air supply circuit	*n*
circuit d'amorçage	*m*	Vorerregerstromkreis	*m*	pre-excitation circuit	*n*
circuit d'entrée (calculateur)	*m*	Eingangsbeschaltung (Steuergerät)	*f*	input circuit (ECU)	*n*
circuit d'excitation	*m*	Erregerstromkreis	*m*	excitation circuit	*n*
circuit d'exploitation	*m*	Auswertschaltung	*f*	evaluation circuit	*n*
circuit de bord	*m*	Bordnetz	*n*	vehicle electrical system	*n*
circuit de commande de la remorque (dispositif à air comprimé)	*m*	Anhängerkreis (Druckluftanlage)	*m*	trailer circuit (compressed-air system)	*n*
circuit de freinage	*m*	Bremskreis	*m*	brake circuit	*n*
circuit de freinage de service	*m*	Betriebsbremskreis	*m*	service-brake circuit	*n*
circuit de freinage de stationnement	*m*	Feststellbremskreis	*m*	parking-brake circuit	*n*
circuit de freinage hydraulique	*m*	Hydraulikbremskreis	*m*	hydraulic brake circuit	*n*
circuit de freinage pneumatique	*m*	Pneumatikbremskreis	*m*	pneumatic-brake circuit	*n*
circuit de lubrification du moteur	*m*	Schmierölkreislauf	*m*	engine lube-oil circuit	*n*
circuit de mémorisation (banc d'essai)	*m*	Speicherschaltung (Rollenbremsprüfstand)	*f*	memory circuit (dynamic brake analyzer)	*n*
circuit de mise en forme	*m*	Impulsformer	*m*	pulse shaper	*n*
circuit de protection	*m*	Schutzschaltung	*f*	protective circuit	*n*
circuit de régulation	*m*	Regelkreis	*m*	closed control loop	*n*

Français		Allemand		Anglais	
circuit de régulation de position (papillon)	*m*	Lageregelkreis (Drosselklappe)	*m*	position control loop (throttle)	*n*
circuit de régulation du freinage (ASR)	*m*	Bremsregelkreis (ASR)	*m*	brake control circuit (TCS)	*n*
circuit de régulation du moteur (ASR)	*m*	Motorregelkreis (ASR)	*m*	engine-control circuit (TCS)	*n*
circuit de sécurité	*m*	Sicherheitsschaltung	*f*	safety circuit	*n*
circuit de sortie (calculateur)	*m*	Ausgangsschaltung (Steuergerät)	*f*	output circuit (ECU)	*n*
circuit de surveillance	*m*	Überwachungsschaltung	*f*	monitoring circuit	*n*
circuit des récepteurs auxiliaires	*m*	Nebenverbraucherkreis	*m*	ancillary circuit	*n*
circuit électrique	*m*	Stromkreis	*m*	electric circuit	*n*
circuit électronique de décodag	*m*	Auswertelektronik	*f*	evaluation electronics	*npl*
circuit en pont	*m*	Brückenschaltung	*f*	bridge circuit	*n*
circuit flottant (maître-cylindre tandem)	*m*	Schwimmkreis (Tandemhauptzylinder)	*m*	floating circuit (tandem master cylinder)	*n*
circuit hybride	*m*	Hybridschaltung	*f*	hybrid circuit	*n*
circuit inducteur	*m*	Erregerstromkreis	*m*	excitation circuit	*n*
circuit intégré, C.I.	*m*	integrierter Schaltkreis, IC	*m*	integrated circuit, IC	*n*
circuit magnétique	*m*	Magnetkreis	*m*	magnetic circuit	*n*
circuit principal (alternateur)	*m*	Generatorstromkreis	*m*	main circuit (alternator)	*n*
circuit secondaire	*m*	Sekundärkreis	x *m*	secondary circuit	*n*
clapet (frein)	*m*	Ventilteller (Bremse)	*m*	valve plate (brakes)	*n*
clapet à bille	*m*	Kugelventil	*n*	ball valve	*n*
clapet à languette	*m*	Zungenventil	*n*	reed valve	*n*
clapet antiretour	*m*	Rückschlagventil	*n*	non-return valve	*n*
clapet d'aspiration (pompe d'alimentation)	*m*	Saugventil (Kraftstofförderpumpe)	*n*	suction valve (fuel-supply pump)	*n*
clapet de non-retour	*m*	Rückschlagventil	*n*	non-return valve	*n*
clapet de non-retour à étranglement	*m*	Drosselrückschlagventil	*n*	throttle-type non-return valve	*n*
clapet de réaspiration (pompe d'injection)	*m*	Druckventil (Einspritzpumpe)	*n*	delivery valve (fuel-injection pump)	*n*
clapet de refoulement (pompe d'injection)	*m*	Druckventil (Einspritzpumpe)	*n*	delivery valve (fuel-injection pump)	*n*
clapet de refoulement à pression constante	*m*	Gleichdruckventil, GDV	*n*	constant-pressure valve	*n*
clapet de refoulement à volume constant	*m*	Gleichraumventil, GRV	*n*	constant-volume valve	*n*
clapet-pilote (injection diesel)	*m*	Vorlaufventil (Dieseleinspritzung)	*n*	forward-delivery valve (diesel fuel injection)	*n*
claquement	*m*	nageln	x *v*	diesel knock	*n*
claquement (perturbation)	*m*	knacken (Funkstörung)	*v*	click (radio disturbance)	*v*
classe d'antiparasitage	*f*	Entstörklasse	*m*	interference-suppression category	*n*
clavier de commande	*m*	Bedientastatur	*f*	keyboard	*n*
clavier opérateur	*m*	Bedienteil	*n*	operator unit	*n*
clignotant	*m*	Blinkleuchte	*f*	turn-signal lamp	*n*
climatiseur	*m*	Klimaanlage	*f*	air conditioner	*n*

Français		Allemand		Anglais	
cliquetis (moteur à combustion)	m	klopfen (Verbrennungsmotor) x	v	knock (IC engine)	v
cliquetis à grande vitesse	m	Hochgeschwindigkeitsklopfen	n	high-speed knock	n
cliquetis à haut régime	m	Hochgeschwindigkeitsklopfen	n	high-speed knock	n
cliquetis à l'accélération	m	Beschleunigungsklopfen	n	acceleration knock	n
codage des fiches	m	Steckercodierung	f	plug code	n
code clignotant (autodiagnostic	m	Blink Code (Eigendiagnose)	m	blink code (self-diagnosis)	n
code d'exécution	m	Ausführungskennzahl	f	type code	n
code d'imputation	m	Kostenstelle	f	cost center	n
code de défaut (autodiagnostic)	m	Fehlercode (Eigendiagnose)	m	error-code (self-diagnosis)	n
code interchangeable (alarme auto)	m	Wechselcode (Autoalarm)	m	changeable code (car alarm)	n
coefficient d'adhérence (pneu/route)	m	Haftreibungszahl (Reifen/Straße)	f	coefficient of friction (tire/road	n
coefficient d'air (lambda)	m	Luftverhältnis	n	excess-air factor (lambda)	n
coefficient d'autoserrage	m	Bremsenkennwert	m	brake coefficient	n
coefficient de force latérale	m	Seitenkraftbeiwert	m	lateral-force coefficient	n
coefficient de frottement à sec	m	Trockenreibwert	m	coefficient of dry friction	n
coefficient de frottement de glissement	m	Gleitreibungszahl	f	coefficient of sliding friction	n
coefficient de frottement humide	m	Naßreibwert	m	coefficient of wet friction	n
coefficient de pénétration dans l'air	m	Luftwiderstandsbeiwert	m	drag coefficient	n
coefficient de résistance au roulement	m	Rollwiderstandsbeiwert	m	coefficient of rolling resistance	n
coefficient de température	m	Temperaturkoeffizient	m	temperature coefficient	n
coefficient de température négatif, CTN	m	negativer Temperaturkoeffizient, NTC	m	negative temperature coefficient, NTC	n
coefficient thermométrique	m	Temperaturkoeffizient	m	temperature coefficient	n
coeur de la flamme (bougie)	m	Flammkern (Zündkerze)	m	arc (spark plug)	n
coin d'écartement (frein)	m	Spreizkeil (Bremse)	m	wedge (brakes)	n
collecteur	m	Kommutator	m	commutator	n
collecteur (gaz CO)	m	Empfängerkammer (Abgastester)	f	receiving chamber (CO test)	n
collecteur à lames	m	Kommutator	m	commutator	n
collecteur d'admission	m	Saugrohr	n	intake manifold	n
collecteur d'admission à oscillation	m	Schwingsaugrohr	n	oscillatory intake passage	n
collecteur d'admission multitubes	m	Mehrfachschwingrohr	n	multi-tract runner	n
collecteur d'eau (filtre à carburant)	m	Wassersammelraum (Kraftstoffilter)	m	water chamber (fuel filter)	n
collecteur d'échappement	m	Abgaskrümmer	m	exhaust manifold	n
collecteur de poussière (filtre)	m	Staubsammelbehälter (Filter)	m	dust bowl (filter)	n
collerette (projecteur)	f	Abdeckrahmen (Scheinwerfer)	m	outer rim (headlamp)	n
collier (bobine d'allumage)	m	Klemmschelle (Zündspule)	f	clamp (ignition coil)	n
collier d'accouplement	m	Kupplungskopf	m	coupling head	n
collier de fixation (bobine d'allumage)	m	Klemmschelle (Zündspule)	f	clamp (ignition coil)	n

Français		Allemand		Anglais	
collier de serrage	*m*	Schlauchklemme	*f*	hose clamp	*n*
combustible de fuite	*m*	Leckkraftstoff	*m*	leak fuel	*n*
combustion	*f*	Verbrennungsablauf	*m*	combustion characteristics	*npl*
combustion de la suie	*f*	Rußabbrand	*m*	soot burn-off	*n*
combustion détonante	*f*	klopfende Verbrennung	*f*	combustion knock	*n*
combustion et détente	*f*	Arbeitstakt	*m*	power cycle	*n*
commande (dispositif de freinage)	*f*	Betätigungseinrichtung (Bremsanlage)	*f*	control (braking system)	*n*
commande à aimant rotatif	*f*	Drehmagnetstellwerk	*n*	rotating-solenoid actuator	*n*
commande à impulsions	*f*	Impulssteuerung	*f*	impulse control	*n*
commande à noyau de ferrite rotatif	*f*	Dreheisenstellwerk	*n*	moving iron actuator	*n*
commande d'air additionnel	*f*	Zusatzluftschieber	*m*	auxiliary-air device	*n*
commande de boîte de vitesse	*f*	Getriebesteuerung	*f*	transmission-shift control	*n*
commande de boîte de vitesses	*f*	Getriebesteuerung	*f*	transmission-shift control	*n*
commande de butée	*f*	Anschlagstellwerk	*m*	stop adjustment mechanism	*n*
commande de changement de vitesse	*f*	Gangschalter	*m*	gear switch	*n*
commande de collecteur d'admission à géométrie variable	*f*	Saugrohrumschaltung	*f*	variable-tract intake manifold	*n*
commande de démarrage	*f*	Startsteuerung	*f*	start control	*n*
commande de force de freinage	*f*	Bremskraftsteuerer	*m*	braking-force controller	*n*
commande de l'air d'admission	*f*	Luftsteuerung (Ansaugluft)	*f*	intake-air adjustment	*n*
commande de l'angle d'allumage	*f*	Zündwinkelsteuerung	*f*	ignition timing	*n*
commande de l'arbre à cames	*f*	Nockenwellensteuerung	*f*	camshaft control	*n*
commande de la charge	*f*	Laststeuerung	*f*	load control	*n*
commande de la force d'appui (essuie-glace)	*f*	Auflagekraftsteuerung (Wischeranlage)	*f*	force-distribution control (wiper system)	*n*
commande de la force de freinage	*f*	Bremskraftsteuerung	*f*	braking-force control	*n*
commande de lève-vitres	*f*	Fensterhebersteuerung	*f*	power-window control	*n*
commande de niveau de giration	*f*	Drallniveausteuerung	*f*	swirl control	*n*
commande de pivotement des portes	*f*	Drehantrieb (Türbetätigung)	*m*	rotary actuator (door control)	*n*
commande de porte pour garages	*f*	Garagentor-Antrieb	*m*	garage-door drive	*n*
commande de précourse	*f*	Vorhubansteuerung	*f*	energizing LPC (lift port closing)	*n*
commande de remorque	*f*	Anhängersteuerung	*f*	trailer control	*n*
commande de remplissage (EMS)	*f*	Füllungssteuerung (EGAS)	*f*	cylinder-charge control (EGAS	*n*
commande de surrégime	*f*	Überdrehschalter	*m*	overspeed switch	*n*
commande de vantail (commande des portes)	*f*	Türflügelantrieb	*m*	door-section drive (door control)	*n*
commande des portes (autobus)	*f*	Türbetätigung (Omnibus)	*f*	door control (bus)	*n*
commande des soupapes (moteur à combustion)	*f*	Ventilsteuerung (Verbrennungsmotor)	*f*	valve timing (engine design)	*n*

Français		Allemand		Anglais	
commande électronique du moteur	*f*	elektronische Motorfüllungs-steuerung, EGAS	*f*	electronic throttle control, ETC	*n*
commande extérieure de démarrage	*f*	Start-Externschalter	*m*	external start switch	*n*
commandé par évènements	*pp*	ereignisgesteuert	*pp*	event-driven	*pp*
commande par rampe hélicoïdale	*f*	Schrägkantensteuerung	*f*	helix control	*n*
commande par rampe inclinée	*f*	Schrägkantensteuerung	*f*	helix control	*n*
communications mobiles	*fpl*	Mobile Kommunikation	*f*	mobile communications	*npl*
commutateur à gradins	*m*	Stufenschalter	*m*	step switch	*n*
commutateur d'alarme	*m*	Alarmschalter	*m*	alarm switch	*n*
commutateur d'allumage	*m*	Zündschalter	*m*	ignition switch	*n*
commutateur d'allumage-démarrage	*m*	Zünd-Start-Schalter	*m*	ignition/starting switch	*n*
commutateur de batteries	*m*	Batterieumschaltrelais	*n*	battery changeover relay	*n*
commutateur de charge	*m*	Lastschalter	*m*	load switch	*n*
commutateur de marche	*m*	Fahrtschalter	*m*	driving switch	*n*
commutateur de préchauffage-démarrage	*m*	Glüh-Start-Schalter	*m*	glow-plug and starter switch	*n*
commutateur des feux de détresse	*m*	Warnblinkschalter	*m*	hazard-switch	*n*
commutateur intermittent d'essuie-glace	*m*	Wischintervallschalter	*m*	intermittent-wiper switch	*n*
commutateur régulateur de marche	*m*	Fahrreglerschalter	*m*	drive-control switch	*n*
commutateur-cadenceur d'essuie-glace	*m*	Wischintervallschalter	*m*	intermittent-wiper switch	*n*
commutation	*f*	Kommutierung	*f*	commutation	*n*
commutation de batteries	*f*	Batterieumschaltung	*f*	battery changeover	*n*
comparateur	*m*	Komparator	*m*	comparator	*n*
comparateur de vitesse de roues (ABS)	*m*	Radgeschwindigkeits-vergleicher (ABS)	*m*	wheel-speed comparator (ABS)	*n*
compatibilité électromagnétique, CEM	*f*	elektromagnetische Verträglichkeit, EMV	*f*	electromagnetic compatibility, EMC	*n*
compatibilité environnementale	*f*	Umweltverträglichkeit	*f*	environmental compatibility	*n*
compatible avec l'environnement	*loc*	umweltfreundlich	*adj*	non-polluting	*ppr*
compensateur de pression	*m*	Druckausgleichselement	*n*	pressure-equalization element	*n*
compensation de pression	*f*	Druckausgleich	*m*	pressure compensation	*n*
compensation thermique	*f*	Temperaturkompensation	*f*	temperature compensation	*n*
compétitif	*adj*	wettbewerbsfähig	*adj*	competitive	*adj*
comportement à court terme	*m*	Kurzzeitverhalten	*n*	short-term behaviour	*n*
comportement au démarrage	*m*	Startverhalten	*n*	starting response	*n*
comportement au démarrage à chaud	*m*	Heißstartverhalten	*f*	hot-start response	*n*
comportement au freinage	*m*	Bremsverhalten	*n*	braking response	*n*
comportement au freinage en virage	*m*	Kurvenbremsverhalten	*n*	curve braking behavior	*n*
comportement avec carburant chaud	*m*	Heißbenzinverhalten x	*n*	hot-fuel handling characteristic:	*npl*

Français		Allemand		Anglais	
comportement de roulage (véhicule)	m	Fahrverhalten (Kfz)	n	driveability (motor vehicle)	n
comportement directionnel propre	m	Eigenlenkverhalten	n	self-steering properties	npl
comportement en surchauffe (moteur à combustion)	m	Heißlaufverhalten (Verbrennungsmotor)	n	hot-engine driving response	n
comportement routier (véhicule)	m	Fahrverhalten (Kfz)	n	driveability (motor vehicle)	n
composant (appareil)	m	Bauteil (Gerät)	n	component (unit)	n
composant des gaz d'échappement	m	Abgasbestandteil	m	exhaust-gas component	n
composition des gaz d'échappement	f	Abgaszusammensetzung	f	exhaust-gas composition	n
composition du mélange	f	Gemischzusammensetzung	f	mixture composition	n
compresseur (suralimentation)	m	Lader	m	supercharger	n
compresseur (dispositif à air comprimé)	m	Luftkompressor	m	air compressor	n
compresseur à hélicoïde	m	Spirallader	m	spiral-type supercharger	n
compresseur à palettes	m	Flügelzellenlader	m	sliding-vane supercharger	n
compresseur à piston	m	Hubkolbenverdichter	m	reciprocating-piston supercharger	n
compresseur à piston rotatif	m	Rotationskolbenverdichter	m	rotary-piston supercharger	n
compresseur à vis	m	Schraubenverdichter	m	screw-type supercharger	n
compresseur centrifuge	m	Strömungslader	m	centrifugal turbo-compressor	n
compresseur d'air	m	Luftkompressor	m	air compressor	n
compresseur de climatiseur	m	Klimakompressor	m	air-conditioner compressor	n
compresseur électrique	m	Elektrokompressor	m	electric compressor	n
compresseur Roots	m	Roots-Lader	m	Roots supercharger	n
compresseur volumétrique	m	Verdrängerlader	m	positive-displacement supercharger	n
compressibilité	f	Kompressibilität	f	compressibility	n
compression (moteur à combustion)	f	Verdichtung (Verbrennungsmotor)	f	compression (IC engine)	n
compression du ressort	f	Einfederung	f	spring compression	n
compte-rendu d'essai	m	Prüfbericht	m	test report	n
compte-tours (véhicule)	m	Drehzahlmesser (Kfz)	m	revcounter (motor vehicle)	n
compte-tours et compte-coups	m	Hub-Drehzähler	m	stroke-counting mechanism	n
concept à mélange pauvre	m	Magerkonzept	n	lean-burn concept	n
conception d'un dispositif de freinage	f	Bremsanlagenauslegung	f	braking-system design	n
concurrent	m	Wettbewerber	m	competitor	n
condensateur	m	Kondensator	m	capacitor	n
condensateur d'allumage	m	Zündkondensator	m	ignition capacitor	n
condensateur d'antiparasitage	m	Entstörkondensator	m	suppression capacitor	n
condensateur électrolytique	m	Elektrolytkondensator	m	electrolytic capacitor	n
conditionnement de valeur analogique	m	Analogwertaufbereitung	f	analog-value conditioning	n
conditions de fonctionnement	fpl	Betriebszustand	m	operating state	n
conducteur de protection	m	Schutzleiter	m	protective conductor	n

Français		Allemand		Anglais	
conducteur médian	*m*	Mittelleiter	*m*	neutral conductor	*n*
conducteur neutre	*m*	Mittelleiter	*m*	neutral conductor	*n*
conductibilité thermique	*f*	Wärmeleitfähigkeit	*f*	thermal conductivity	*n*
conduction thermique	*f*	Wärmeleitung	*f*	heat conduction	*n*
conduit d'admission	*m*	Saugleitung	*f*	intake passage	*n*
conduite annulaire	*f*	Ringleitung	*f*	ring main	*n*
conduite circulaire	*f*	Ringleitung	*f*	ring main	*n*
conduite circulaire stationnaire	*f*	stationäre Kreisfahrt	*f*	steady-state skidpad testing	*n*
conduite d'alimentation	*f*	Versorgungsleitung	*f*	supply line	*n*
conduite d'alimentation (dispositif de freinage à deux conduites)	*f*	Vorratsleitung (Zweileitungs-Bremsanlage)	*f*	supply line (two-line braking system)	*n*
conduite d'aspiration	*f*	Saugleitung	*f*	intake passage	*n*
conduite d'échappement	*f*	Abgasleitung	*f*	exhaust passage	*n*
conduite d'essai (banc d'essai)	*f*	Prüfleitung (Einspritzpumpen-Prüfstand)	*f*	test pipe (injection-pump test bench)	*n*
conduite de carburant	*f*	Kraftstoffleitung	*f*	fuel line	*n*
conduite de commande	*f*	Steuerleitung	*f*	control line	*n*
conduite de commande (dispositif de freinage à deux conduites)	*f*	Bremsleitung (Zweileitungs-Bremsanlage)	*f*	brake service line (dual-line braking system)	*n*
conduite de décharge	*f*	Überströmleitung	*f*	overflow line	*n*
conduite de frein (d'un dispositif de freinage à deux conduites)	*f*	Bremsleitung (Zweileitungs-Bremsanlage)	*f*	brake service line (dual-line braking system)	*n*
conduite de frein (en général)	*f*	Bremsleitung (allgemein)	*f*	brake line (general)	*n*
conduite de frein de remorque	*f*	Anhängerbremsleitung	*f*	trailer brake line	*n*
conduite de raccordement (dispositif de freinage)	*f*	Verbindungsleitung (Bremsanlage)	*f*	connecting line (braking system)	*n*
conduite de régulation (groupe hydraulique ABS)	*f*	Regelkanal (ABS-Hydroaggregat)	*m*	control channel (ABS hydraulic modulator)	*n*
conduite de retour	*f*	Rücklaufleitung	*f*	return line	*n*
conduite de retour du carburant	*f*	Kraftstoffrückleitung	*f*	fuel-return line	*n*
conduite de secours	*f*	Hilfsbremsleitung	*f*	secondary-brake line	*n*
conduite de trop-plein	*f*	Überströmleitung	*f*	overflow line	*n*
conduite en virage	*f*	Kurvenfahrt	*f*	cornering	*ppr*
conduite hydraulique	*f*	Hydraulikleitung	*f*	hydraulic line	*n*
conduite pneumatique	*f*	Pneumatikleitung	*f*	pneumatic line	*n*
conduite véhicule	*f*	Fahrbetrieb	*m*	vehicle operation	*n*
cône d'attaque (aiguille d'injecteur)	*m*	Druckschulter (Düsennadel)	*f*	exposed annular area (nozzle needle)	*n*
cône d'étanchéité	*m*	Dichtkegel	*m*	sealing cone	*n*
cône d'étanchéité du tube	*m*	Rohrdichtkegel	*m*	pipe sealing cone	*n*
cône de commande	*m*	Steuerkegel	*m*	control cone	*n*
cône de soulèvement (aiguille d'injecteur)	*m*	Druckschulter (Düsennadel)	*f*	exposed annular area (nozzle needle)	*n*
cône de soupape	*m*	Ventilkegel	*m*	valve cone	*n*
cône de soupape de refoulemen	*m*	Druckventilkegel	*m*	delivery-valve cone	*n*
cône double (injecteur)	*m*	Doppelkonus (Einspritzdüse)	*m*	dual cone (nozzle)	*n*

Français		Allemand		Anglais	
configuration de régulation (ABS)	*f*	Regelkonfiguration (ABS)	*f*	control configuration (ABS)	*n*
configuration du bus	*f*	Busstruktur (CAN)	*f*	bus configuration (CAN)	*n*
configurer (fonction du calculateur)	*v*	konfigurieren (Steuergerät)	*v*	configure (ECU)	*v*
confirmation (régulation ABS)	*f*	Rückmeldung (ABS-Regelung)	*f*	feedback signal (ABS control)	*n*
confirmation de positionnement (servomoteur ASR)	*f*	Positionsrückmeldung (ASR-Stellmotor)	*f*	position feedback (TCS servomotor)	*n*
conformateur d'impulsions	*m*	Impulsformer	*m*	pulse shaper	*n*
confort de conduite	*m*	Fahrkomfort	*m*	driving smoothness	*n*
connecteur	*m*	Steckverbindung	*f*	plug-in connection	*n*
connecteur à module de codage	*m*	Codierstecker	*m*	coding plug	*n*
connecteur d'allumeur	*m*	Zündverteilerstecker	*m*	distributor connector	*n*
connexion (batterie)	*f*	Zellenverbinder (Batterie)	*m*	cell connector (battery)	*n*
connexion à pointes d'enfichage	*f*	Stechspitzenanschluß	*m*	piercing-tip terminal	*n*
connexion de diagnostic	*f*	Diagnoseanschluß	*m*	diagnosis connection	*n*
connexion de test	*f*	Diagnoseanschluß	*m*	diagnosis connection	*n*
connexion des éléments (batterie)	*f*	Zellenverbinder (Batterie)	*m*	cell connector (battery)	*n*
connexion en étoile	*f*	Sternschaltung	*f*	star connection	*n*
connexion principale	*f*	Hauptanschluß	*m*	main terminal	*n*
conseils de sécurité	*mpl*	Sicherheitshinweise	*mpl*	safety instructions	*npl*
consignateur	*m*	Sollwertgeber	*m*	desired-value generator	*n*
consommation d'essai	*f*	Testverbrauch	*m*	test consumption	*n*
consommation de carburant	*f*	Kraftstoffverbrauch	*m*	fuel consumption	*n*
consommation massique de carburant	*f*	Kraftstoff-Massenverbrauch	*m*	fuel consumption by mass	*n*
constructeur automobile	*m*	Fahrzeughersteller	*m*	vehicle manufacturer	*n*
contact à fermeture (interrupteur électrique)	*m*	Schließer (elektrischer Schalter	*m*	NO contact (electrical switch, normally open)	*n*
contact à lamelles	*m*	Lamellenkontakt	*m*	lamination contact	*n*
contact à ouverture (interrupteur électrique)	*m*	Öffner (elektrischer Schalter)	*m*	NC contact (electrical switch, normally closed)	*n*
contact à ressort	*m*	Kontaktfeder	*f*	contact spring	*n*
contact bidirectionnel	*m*	Wechsler (Umschaltkontakt)	*m*	changeover contact	*n*
contact d'inversion (commande des portes)	*m*	Umschaltglied (Türbetätigung)	*n*	switching element (door control)	*n*
contact de ralenti	*m*	Leerlaufkontakt	*m*	idle contact	*n*
contact de régulation	*m*	Regelkontakt	*m*	regulating contact	*n*
contact de repos (interrupteur électrique)	*m*	Öffner (elektrischer Schalter)	*m*	NC contact (electrical switch, normally closed)	*n*
contact du régulateur	*m*	Regelkontakt	*m*	regulating contact	*n*
contact femelle	*m*	Steckerbuchse	*f*	plug socket	*n*
contact fermé au repos (interrupteur électrique)	*m*	Öffner (elektrischer Schalter)	*m*	NC contact (electrical switch, normally closed)	*n*
contact glissant	*m*	Schleifkontakt	*m*	sliding contact	*n*
contact mâle	*m*	Steckerstift	*m*	connector pin	*n*

Français		Allemand		Anglais	
contact ouvert au repos (interrupteur électrique)	*m*	Schließer (elektrischer Schalter	*m*	NO contact (electrical switch, normally open)	*n*
contact par curseur	*m*	Schleifkontakt	*m*	sliding contact	*n*
contact principal (relais)	*m*	Hauptkontakt (Relais)	*m*	main contact (relay)	*n*
contact télescopique à ressort	*m*	Teleskopfederkontakt	*m*	telescopic spring contact	*n*
contacteur	*m*	Kontaktschalter	*m*	contact switch	*n*
contacteur à bond de pression	*m*	Drucksprungschalter	*m*	pressure-contact switch	*n*
contacteur à solénoïde	*m*	Einrückrelais (Starter)	*n*	solenoid switch (starter)	*n*
contacteur d'allumage	*m*	Zündschalter	*m*	ignition switch	*n*
contacteur d'embrayage	*m*	Kupplungsschalter	*m*	clutch switch	*n*
contacteur d'inclinaison (alarme auto)	*m*	Neigungsschalter (Autoalarm)	*m*	tilt switch (car alarm)	*n*
contacteur de commande	*m*	Steuerschalter	*m*	control switch	*n*
contacteur de contrôle de pression d'air	*m*	Luftdruck-Kontrollschalter	*m*	air-pressure sensor	*n*
contacteur de feux de stop	*m*	Bremslichtschalter	*m*	brake-light switch	*n*
contacteur de freins	*m*	Bremskontakt	*m*	brake contact	*n*
contacteur de kickdown	*m*	Kickdown-Schalter	*m*	kick-down switch	*n*
contacteur de papillon	*m*	Drosselklappenschalter	*m*	throttle-valve switch	*n*
contacteur de pleine charge	*m*	Vollastschalter	*m*	full-load switch	*n*
contacteur de préchauffage-démarrage	*m*	Glüh-Start-Schalter	*m*	glow-plug and starter switch	*n*
contacteur de ralenti	*m*	Leergasschalter	*m*	low-idle switch	*n*
contacteur de sécurité	*m*	Sicherheitsschalter	*m*	safety switch	*n*
contacteur électromagnétique (démarreur)	*m*	Einrückrelais (Starter)	*n*	solenoid switch (starter)	*n*
contacteur thermique temporisé	*m*	Thermozeitschalter	*m*	thermo-time switch	*n*
contacts du rupteur (allumage)	*mpl*	Zündkontakt	*m*	distributor contact points	*npl*
contamination	*f*	Verunreinigung	*f*	contamination	*n*
conteneur à claire-voie	*m*	Gitterbox	*f*	meshed container	*n*
contrainte de vibration	*f*	Schüttelbeanspruchung	*f*	vibration	*n*
contrainte limite	*f*	Grenzbeanspruchung	*f*	limit stress	*n*
contrainte permanente	*f*	Dauerbeanspruchung	*f*	continuous loading	*n*
contraste clair/obscur (projecteur)	*m*	Hell-Dunkel-Kontrast (Scheinwerfer)	*m*	light-dark cutoff contrast (headlamp)	*n*
contraste entre clarté et obscurité (projecteur)	*m*	Hell-Dunkel-Kontrast (Scheinwerfer)	*m*	light-dark cutoff contrast (headlamp)	*n*
contre-braquage (véhicule)	*m*	gegenlenken (Kfz)	*v*	countersteer (motor vehicle)	*v*
contre-pression des gaz d'échappement	*f*	Abgasgegendruck	*m*	exhaust-gas back pressure	*n*
contrôle d'hystérésis	*m*	Hysterese-Prüfung	*f*	hysteresis test	*n*
contrôle d'usure (garniture de frein)	*m*	Verschleißkontrolle (Bremsbelag)	*f*	wear inspection (brake lining)	*n*
contrôle de la course	*m*	Hubkontrolle	*f*	stroke limiter	*n*
contrôle de qualité	*m*	Qualitätskontrolle	*f*	quality control	*n*
contrôle des freins	*m*	Bremsenprüfung	*f*	brake testing	*n*
contrôle final	*m*	Endkontrolle	*f*	final inspection	*n*
contrôle final	*m*	Endkontrolle	*f*	final inspection	*n*

Français		Allemand		Anglais	
contrôle intermédiaire (frein)	*m*	Zwischenuntersuchung, ZU (Bremse)	*f*	intermediate inspection (brakes	*n*
contrôle par échantillonnage	*m*	Stichprobenprüfung	*f*	sampling inspection	*n*
contrôle spécial des freins	*m*	Bremsensonderuntersuchung, BSU	*f*	braking-system special inspection	*n*
contrôle spécifique (frein)	*m*	Sonderuntersuchung (Bremse)	*f*	special examination (brakes)	*n*
contrôle technique	*m*	Hauptuntersuchung, HU	*f*	general inspection	*n*
contrôle visuel	*m*	Sichtprüfung	*f*	visual examination	*n*
contrôles	*mpl*	Prüfumfang	*m*	extent of inspection	*n*
contrôleur d'incandescence	*m*	Glühüberwacher	*m*	glow indicator	*n*
contrôleur de freins	*m*	Bremsentester	*m*	brake tester	*n*
conversion d'énergie	*f*	Energieumsetzung	*f*	energy conversion	*n*
convertisseur A/N	*m*	Analog-Digital-Wandler	*m*	analog-digital converter	*n*
convertisseur analogique-numérique	*m*	Analog-Digital-Wandler	*m*	analog-digital converter	*n*
convertisseur catalytique des gaz d'échappement	*m*	Abgaskonverter	*m*	catalytic exhaust converter	*n*
convertisseur de pression	*m*	Druckwandler	*m*	vacuum converter	*n*
convertisseur de signaux	*m*	Signalwandler	*m*	signal transducer	*n*
convertisseur électropneumatique	*m*	elektropneumatischer Wandler	*m*	electropneumatic converter	*n*
corps chauffant (crayon)	*m*	Glühkörper	*m*	glow-plug tip	*n*
corps d'enroulement (bobine d'allumage)	*m*	Wickelkörper (Zündspule)	*m*	bobbin (ignition coil)	*n*
corps d'injecteur	*m*	Düsenkörper	*m*	nozzle body	*n*
corps de filtre	*m*	Wickelkörper (Filter)	*m*	paper tube (filter)	*n*
corps de pompe	*m*	Pumpengehäuse	*n*	pump housing	*n*
corps de poussoir	*m*	Stößelkörper	*m*	roller-tappet shell	*n*
corps de soupape	*m*	Ventilkörper	*m*	valve body	*n*
corps de valve	*m*	Ventilkörper	*m*	valve body	*n*
corps distributeur	*m*	Verteilerkörper (Verteilereinspritzpumpe)	*m*	distributor head (distributor pump)	*n*
corps fileté	*m*	Gewindehülse	*f*	threaded sleeve	*n*
correcteur à dépression	*m*	Unterdruckversteller	*m*	vacuum control	*n*
correcteur à divergence	*m*	Strahlenregler	*m*	straight-line controller	*n*
correcteur altimétrique	*m*	atmosphärendruckabhängiger Vollastanschlag, ADA	*m*	altitude-pressure compensator	*n*
correcteur altimétrique	*m*	Höhenanschlag	*m*	altitude control	*n*
correcteur d'avance à dépression	*m*	Unterdruckzündversteller	*m*	vacuum advance mechanism	*n*
correcteur d'avance centrifuge	*m*	Fliehkraftzündversteller	*m*	centrifugal advance mechanism	*n*
correcteur de couple	*m*	Angleichvorrichtung	*f*	torque-control mechanism	*n*
correcteur de débit	*m*	Angleichvorrichtung	*f*	torque-control mechanism	*n*
correcteur de freinage	*m*	Bremskraftregler	*m*	load-sensing valve	*n*
correcteur de portée d'éclairement	*m*	Leuchtweitenregelung, LWR	*f*	headlight leveling control	*n*
correcteur de ralenti	*m*	Leerlaufregler	*m*	idle controller	*n*
correcteur de ralenti piloté par la température	*m*	temperaturabhängige Leerlaufanhebung, TLA	*f*	temperature-controlled idle-speed increase	*n*

Français		Allemand		Anglais	
correcteur de site	*m*	Leuchtweiteregler, LWR	*m*	headlight leveling control	*n*
correcteur de site des projecteurs	*m*	Leuchtweitenregelung, LWR	*f*	headlight leveling control	*n*
correcteur de surcharge en fonction de la température	*m*	temperaturabhängiger Startanschlag, TAS	*m*	temperature-dependent starting stop	*n*
correcteur hydraulique de débit	*m*	hydraulisch betätigte Angleichung, HBA	*f*	hydraulically controlled torque control	*n*
correcteur pneumatique	*m*	ladedruckabhängiger Vollastanschlag, LDA	*m*	manifold-pressure compensator	*n*
correcteur pneumatique à mesure de pression absolue	*m*	absolutdruckmessender, ladedruckabhängiger Vollastanschlag	*m*	absolute-boost-pressure-dependent full-load stop	*n*
correction à dépression	*f*	Lastverstellung	*f*	load adjustment	*n*
correction altimétrique	*f*	Höhenkorrektur	*f*	altitude compensation	*n*
correction automatique de la force de freinage en fonction de la charge	*f*	automatisch lastabhängige Bremskraftregelung, ALB	*f*	automatic load-sensitive braking-force metering	*n*
correction centrifuge	*f*	Fliehkraftverstellung	*f*	centrifugal advance	*n*
correction de débit	*f*	Angleichung	*f*	torque control	*n*
correction de débit d'injection	*f*	Mengenkorrektur	*f*	injected-fuel-quantity correction	*n*
correction de débit de carburant	*f*	Kraftstoffmengenkorrektur	*f*	fuel-quantity correction	*n*
correction de débit négative	*f*	negative Angleichung	*f*	negative torque control	*n*
correction de débit positive	*f*	positive Angleichung	*f*	positive torque control	*n*
correction de la portée d'éclairement	*f*	Leuchtweiteeinstellung	*f*	headlight leveling (manually operated)	*n*
correction de pleine charge	*f*	Vollastangleichung	*f*	full-load torque control	*n*
correction de ralenti en fonction de la température	*f*	temperaturabhängige Leerlaufkorrektur	*f*	temperature-dependent low-idle correction	*n*
correction du point d'allumage	*f*	Zündverstellung	*f*	spark advance	*n*
correction en fonction du régime	*f*	Drehzahlverstellung	*f*	engine-speed advance	*n*
cosse	*f*	Kabelschuh	*m*	cable lug	*n*
cosse de batterie	*f*	Batterieklemme	*f*	battery-cable terminal	*n*
côté aspiration	*m*	Saugseite	*f*	intake	*n*
cote d'écartement (injection diesel)	*f*	Spaltmaß (Dieseleinspritzung)	*n*	gap dimension (diesel fuel injection)	*n*
cote de contrôle	*f*	Kontrollmaß	*n*	control dimension	*n*
cote de dépassement de l'arbre à cames	*f*	Nockenwellen-Vorstehmaß	*n*	camshaft projection	*n*
côté impuretés (filtre)	*m*	Schmutzseite (Filter)	*f*	contaminated side (filter)	*n*
côté primaire	*m*	Primärseite	*f*	primary side	*n*
côté propre (filtre)	*m*	Reinseite (Filter)	*f*	clean side (filter)	*n*
côté refoulement (filtre)	*m*	Druckseite (Filter)	*f*	pressure outlet (filter)	*n*
côté secondaire (cylindre à membrane)	*m*	Atmungsraum (Membran) x	*m*	breathing space (diaphragm)	*n*
côté secondaire (dispositifs à air comprimé)	*m*	Sekundärseite (Druckluftgeräte)	*f*	secondary side (compressed-air components)	*n*
côté sortie de la pompe	*m*	Pumpenabtrieb	*m*	pump power take-off	*n*
couche de céramique (sonde lambda)	*f*	Keramikschicht (Lambda-Sonde)	*f*	ceramic layer (lambda oxygen sensor)	*n*

Français		Allemand		Anglais	
couche Hall	*f*	Hall-Schicht	*f*	Hall layer	*n*
coude (courbe caractéristique)	*m*	Knickpunkt (Kennlinie)	*m*	knee point (characteristic curve)	*n*
coulisse	*f*	Kulissenplatte	*f*	template	*n*
coulisse (valve de frein de stationnement)	*f*	Kulisse (Feststellbremsventil)	*f*	detent element (parking-brake valve)	*n*
coulisse de contact	*f*	Schaltkulisse	*f*	contoured switching guide	*n*
coulisse-guide (injection diesel)	*f*	Kulissenführung (Diesel-Regler)	*f*	sliding-block guide (governor)	*n*
coulisseau	*m*	Kulissenstein	*m*	guide block	*n*
coulisseau (cylindre de frein)	*m*	Gleitstück (Bremszylinder)	*n*	slider (brake cylinder)	*n*
coupelle	*f*	Federkapsel	*f*	spring retainer	*n*
coupelle de ressort	*f*	Federteller	*m*	spring seat	*n*
couplage (CEM)	*m*	Einkopplung (EMV)	*f*	couple (EMC)	*v*
couplage en parallèle (alternateurs)	*m*	Parallelbetrieb (Generatoren)	*m*	parallel operation (alternators)	*n*
couplage en série	*m*	Reihenschaltung	*f*	series connection	*n*
couplage en triangle	*m*	Dreieckschaltung	*f*	delta connection	*n*
couple appliqué au volant de direction (dynamique d'un véhicule)	*m*	Lenkradmoment (Kfz-Dynamik)	*n*	steering-wheel force (vehicle dynamics)	*n*
couple d'adhérence	*m*	Reibwertpaarung	*f*	friction-coefficient matching	*n*
couple d'inertie de la roue	*m*	Radträgheitsmoment	*n*	wheel moment of inertia	*n*
couple d'inertie du moteur	*m*	Motorschleppmoment	*n*	engine-drag torque	*n*
couple de charge	*m*	Lastmoment	*n*	load moment	*n*
couple de freinage	*m*	Bremsmoment	*n*	braking torque	*n*
couple de freinage de consigne	*m*	Bremssollmoment	*n*	setpoint braking torque	*n*
couple de freinage du moteur	*m*	Motorbremsmoment	*n*	engine braking torque	*n*
couple de friction	*m*	Reibpaarung	*f*	friction pairing	*n*
couple de frottement	*m*	Reibmoment	*n*	friction moment	*n*
couple de frottement de la chaussée	*m*	Fahrbahrbahnreibmoment	*n*	road frictional torque	*n*
couple de l'arbre à cardan	*m*	Kardanwellenmoment	*n*	propshaft torque	*n*
couple de la route (ASR)	*m*	Straßenmoment (ASR)	*n*	road torque (TCS)	*n*
couple de rappel	*m*	Rückstellmoment	*n*	return torque	*n*
couple de réaction (contrôle des freins)	*m*	Reaktionsmoment (Bremsprüfung)	*n*	reaction torque (braking-system inspection)	*n*
couple de traction	*m*	Antriebsmoment	*n*	drive torque	*n*
couple différentiel de consigne	*m*	Differenzsollmoment	*n*	desired/setpoint speed differential	*n*
couple indiqué	*m*	indiziertes Motormoment	*n*	indicated torque	*n*
couple initial de démarrage	*m*	Anzugsdrehmoment	*n*	tightening torque	*n*
couple moteur sélectionné par le conducteur	*m*	Fahrervorgabemotormoment	*n*	driver-input engine torque	*n*
couple nominal	*m*	Nenndrehmoment	*n*	nominal load torque	*n*
couple permanent	*m*	Dauerdrehmoment	*n*	continuous torque	*n*
couple sélectionné par le conducteur	*m*	Fahrervorgabemoment	*n*	driver-selected torque	*n*
coupleur	*m*	Steckverbindung	*f*	plug-in connection	*n*

Français

Français		Allemand		Anglais	
coupleur de batteries	*m*	Batterieumschaltrelais	*n*	battery changeover relay	*n*
coupleur rapide	*m*	Schnellkupplung	*f*	rapid coupling	*n*
coupure (régulateur)	*f*	Abschaltung (Regler)	*f*	shutoff (governor)	*n*
coupure d'injection en décélération	*f*	Schubabschaltung	*f*	overrun fuel cutoff	*n*
coupure de débit	*f*	Abregelung	*f*	speed regulation breakaway	*n*
coupure de vitesse maximale (pompe d'injection)	*f*	Endabregelung (Einspritzpumpe)	*f*	full-load speed regulation (fuel-injection pump)	*n*
coupure des cylindres	*f*	Zylinderabschaltung	*f*	cylinder shut-off	*n*
coupure progressive	*f*	Absteuerung	*f*	end of delivery	*n*
courant alternatif	*m*	Wechselstrom	*m*	alternating current, AC	*n*
courant continu	*m*	Gleichstrom	*m*	direct current	*n*
courant d'arc	*m*	Funkenstrom	*m*	spark current	*n*
courant d'enclenchement	*m*	Schaltstrom	*m*	switched current	*n*
courant d'essai au froid (batterie)	*m*	Batteriekälteprüfstrom	*m*	low-temperature test current (battery)	*n*
courant d'excitation	*m*	Erregerstrom	*m*	exciting current	*n*
courant d'induit	*m*	Ankerstrom	*m*	armature current	*n*
courant de champ	*m*	Erregerstrom	*m*	exciting current	*n*
courant de charge de la batterie	*m*	Batterieladestrom	*m*	battery charge current	*n*
courant de consigne	*m*	Nennstrom	*m*	rated current	*n*
courant de court-circuit	*m*	Kurzschlußstrom	*m*	short-circuit current	*n*
courant de décharge	*m*	Entladestrom	*m*	discharge current	*n*
courant de démarrage	*m*	Einschaltstrom	*m*	cutin current	*n*
courant de fuite	*m*	Leckstrom	*m*	leakage flow	*n*
courant de fuite (bougie)	*m*	Kriechstrom (Zündkerze)	*m*	insulator flashover (spark-plug)	*n*
courant de maintien	*m*	Haltestrom	*m*	holding current	*n*
courant de phase	*m*	Phasenstrom	*m*	phase current	*n*
courant de pilotage	*m*	Steuerstrom	*m*	control current	*n*
courant de repos	*m*	Ruhestrom	*m*	peak coil current	*n*
courant des récepteurs	*m*	Verbraucherstrom	*m*	equipment current draw	*n*
courant en charge	*m*	Laststrom	*m*	load current	*n*
courant ionique	*m*	Ionenstrom	*m*	ionic current	*n*
courant nominal	*m*	Sollstrom	*m*	nominal current	*n*
courant perturbateur (CEM)	*m*	Störstrom (EMV)	*m*	interference current (EMC)	*n*
courant principal (alternateur)	*m*	Hauptstrom (Generator)	*m*	primary current (alternator)	*n*
courant secondaire	*m*	Sekundärstrom	*m*	secondary current	*n*
courant statorique	*m*	Ständerstrom	*m*	stator current	*n*
courant triphasé	*m*	Drehstrom	*m*	three-phase current	*n*
courants de Foucault	*mpl*	Wirbelstrom	*m*	eddy current	*n*
courbe caractéristique	*f*	Kennlinie	*f*	characteristic	*n*
courbe caractéristique de capteur	*f*	Geberkennlinie	*f*	sensor characteristic	*n*
courbe caractéristique de pleine charge	*f*	Vollastkennlinie	*f*	full-load curve	*n*
courbe caractéristique de ressor	*f*	Federkennlinie	*f*	spring characteristic	*n*
courbe caractéristique des débits	*f*	Fördermengen-Kennlinie	*f*	fuel-delivery curve	*n*

Français		Allemand		Anglais	
courbe caractéristique glissement/adhérence	*f*	Haftreibungs-Schlupfkurve	*f*	adhesion/slip curve	*n*
courbe cible	*f*	Zielkurve	*f*	target curve	*n*
courbe d'ébullition (essence)	*f*	Siedeverlauf (Benzin)	*m*	boiling curve (gasoline)	*n*
courbe de charge	*f*	Ladekennlinie (Batterie)	*f*	charging characteristic (battery)	*n*
courbe de chauffe	*f*	Aufheizkurve	*f*	preheating curve	*n*
courbe de débit substitutif	*f*	Ersatzmengenkennlinie	*f*	substitute quantity curve	*n*
courbe de pleine charge	*f*	Vollastkennlinie	*f*	full-load curve	*n*
courbe de pression	*f*	Druckverlauf	*m*	pressure characteristic	*n*
courbe du couple	*f*	Drehmomentverlauf	*m*	torque curve	*n*
courbe du débit d'injection	*f*	Fördermengenverlauf	*m*	fuel-delivery characteristics	*npl*
couronne à palettes (pompe électrique à carburant)	*f*	Schaufelkranz (Elektrokraftstoffpumpe)	*m*	blade ring (electric fuel pump)	*n*
couronne dentée de volant	*f*	Zahnkranz (Motorschwungrad)	*m*	ring gear (flywheel)	*n*
courroie crantée	*f*	Zahnriemen	*m*	toothed belt	*n*
courroie d'entraînement	*f*	Antriebsriemen	*m*	drive belt	*n*
courroie dentée	*f*	Zahnriemen	*m*	toothed belt	*n*
courroie trapézoïdale	*f*	Keilriemen	*m*	V-belt	*n*
courroie trapezoïdale à nervures	*f*	Keilrippenriemen	*m*	ribbed V-belt	*n*
course d'admission	*f*	Förderhubphase	*f*	delivery-stroke phase	*n*
course d'admission (moteur à combution)	*f*	Ansaughub (Verbrennungsmotor)	*m*	intake stroke (IC engine)	*n*
course d'engrènement	*f*	Einspurhub	*m*	pinion travel	*n*
course de came	*f*	Nockenhöhe	*f*	cam lift	*n*
course de compression	*f*	Verdichtungshub	*m*	compression stroke	*n*
course de correction de débit	*f*	Angleichweg	*m*	torque-control travel	*n*
course de coulisseau	*f*	Schieberweg	*m*	sleeve travel	*n*
course de détente	*f*	Entlastungshub	*m*	retraction lift	*n*
course de flamme	*f*	Flammenweg	*m*	flame travel	*n*
course de l'aiguille	*f*	Nadelhub	*m*	needle lift	*n*
course de la tige de réglage	*f*	Regelstangenweg	*m*	control-rack travel	*n*
course de levée	*f*	Nockenhöhe	*f*	cam lift	*n*
course de refoulement	*f*	Förderhub	*m*	delivery stroke	*n*
course de régulation	*f*	Regelstangenweg	*m*	control-rack travel	*n*
course de régulation au démarrage	*f*	Startregelweg	*m*	starting rack travel	*n*
course de réponse	*f*	Ansprechweg	*m*	response travel	*n*
course de retour	*f*	Rückhub	*m*	return stroke	*n*
course de retour du piston (piston de pompe)	*f*	Kolbenrücklauf (Pumpenkolben)	*m*	plunger return stroke	*n*
course de surcharge au démarrage	*f*	Startmengenverstellweg	*m*	start-quantity stop travel	*n*
course des masselottes	*f*	Fliehgewichtsweg	*m*	flyweight travel	*n*
course du manchon central (injection diesel)	*f*	Muffenweg (Diesel-Regler)	*m*	sliding-sleeve travel (governor)	*n*
course du noyau	*f*	Ankerhub	*m*	armature stroke	*n*
course du piston	*f*	Kolbenhub	*m*	plunger lift	*n*

Français

Français		Allemand		Anglais	
course du piston en fin de refoulement (piston de pompe)	*f*	Kolbenhub bis Förderende (Pumpenkolben)	*m*	plunger lift to spill-port opening	*n*
course du ressort	*f*	Federweg	*m*	range of spring	*n*
course effective	*f*	Nutzhub	*m*	effective stroke	*n*
course en fin de refoulement	*f*	Hub am Förderende	*m*	stroke at end of delivery	*n*
course morte (effet de freinage)	*f*	Verlustweg (Bremswirkung)	*m*	pre-braking distance (braking action)	*n*
course motrice	*f*	Arbeitshub	*m*	working stroke	*n*
course restante (élément de pompage)	*f*	Resthub (Pumpenelement)	*m*	residual stroke (plunger-and-barrel assembly)	*n*
course utile	*f*	Nutzhub	*m*	effective stroke	*n*
court-circuit	*m*	Kurzschluß	*m*	short-circuit <noun>	*n*
court-circuit entre spires	*m*	Windungsschluß	*m*	coil-winding short circuit	*n*
court-circuiter	*v*	kurzschließen	*v*	short-circuit <to short-circuit>	*v*
coussin d'air (système de retenue des passagers)	*m*	Airbag	*m*	airbag	*n*
coussin gonflable (système de retenue des passager)	*m*	Airbag	*m*	airbag	*n*
coussin gonflable avant	*m*	Frontairbag	*m*	front airbag	*n*
coussin gonflable côté conducteur	*m*	Fahrerairbag	*m*	driver airbag	*n*
coussin gonflable côté passager	*m*	Beifahrerairbag	*m*	passenger airbag	*n*
coussin gonflable latéral	*m*	Seitenairbag	*m*	side airbag	*n*
coussinet	*m*	Lagerbuchse	*f*	bushing	*n*
couvercle bloc (batterie)	*m*	Blockdeckel (Batterie)	*m*	cover (battery)	*n*
couvercle d'allumeur	*m*	Zündverteilerkappe	*f*	distributor cap	*n*
couvercle de batterie	*m*	Blockdeckel (Batterie)	*m*	cover (battery)	*n*
couvercle de borne (batterie)	*m*	Polabdeckkappe (Batterie)	*f*	terminal-post cover (battery)	*n*
couvercle de filtre	*m*	Filterdeckel	*m*	filter cover	*n*
couvercle de protection	*m*	Schutzkappe	*f*	protective cap	*n*
couvercle de régulateur	*m*	Reglerdeckel	*m*	governor cover	*n*
couvercle isolant (allumeur)	*m*	Isolierdeckel (Zündverteiler)	*m*	insulating cover (ignition distributor)	*n*
couvercle pivotant (tête d'accouplement)	*m*	Drehdeckel (Kupplungskopf)	*m*	swivel cover (coupling head)	*n*
crantage (valve)	*m*	Raststellung (Ventil)	*f*	detent position (valve)	*n*
craquement (perturbation)	*m*	krachen (Funkstörung) x	*v*	crackle (radio disturbance)	*v*
crayon de préchauffage	*m*	Glühstift	*m*	glow element	*n*
crémaillère	*f*	Zahnstange	*f*	rack	*n*
créneau de pot catalytique	*m*	Katalysatorfenster	*n*	catalytic converter window	*n*
crépine	*f*	Filtersieb	*n*	filter strainer	*n*
crépine (pompe d'alimentation)	*f*	Siebfilter (Kraftstofförderpumpe)	*n*	strainer (fuel-supply pump)	*n*
crépitement (perturbation)	*m*	prasseln (Funkstörung) x	*v*	patter (radio disturbance)	*v*
crible (injecteur)	*m*	Siebkörper (Einspritzventil)	*m*	strainer (fuel injector)	*n*
crible moléculaire (dessiccateur)	*m*	Molekularfilter (Lufttrockner)	*n*	molecular filter (air drier)	*n*
critère de déclenchement	*m*	Auslösekriterium	*n*	triggering criterion	*n*

Français		Allemand		Anglais	
croisement (fente d'étranglement)	m	Überdeckung (Steuerschlitze)	f	overlap (metering slits)	n
croisement de conducteurs	m	Leitungskreuzung	f	conductor crossover	n
croisement des soupapes	m	Ventilüberschneidung	f	valve overlap	n
croisillon	m	Kreuzscheibe	f	yoke	n
croquis coté	m	Maßbild	n	dimensional drawing	n
culasse (compresseur d'air)	f	Zylinderdeckel (Luftkompressor)	m	cylinder head (air compressor)	n
culasse de fer (actionneur de ralenti)	f	Eisenjoch (Leerlaufsteller)	n	iron yoke (idle actuator)	n
culbuteur (système mécanique des soupapes)	m	Standard-Kipphebel (Ventiltrieb)	m	standard rocker arm (valve gear)	n
culot de bougie	m	Zündkerzengehäuse	n	spark-plug shell	n
curseur (actionneur de papillon)	m	Schleiferarm (Drosselklappengeber)	m	wiper arm (throttle-valve sensor)	n
curseur à griffes	m	Krallenschleifer	m	claw-type sliding contact	n
curseur de contact	m	Schleiferabgriff	m	wiper tap	n
cuvelage de projecteur	m	Scheinwerferaufnahme	f	headlamp-housing assembly	n
cuvette de mesure (émissions)	f	Meßküvette (Abgasprüfung)	f	measuring cell (exhaust-gas test)	n
cuvette de ressort	f	Federteller	m	spring seat	n
cycle à deux temps	m	Zweitaktverfahren	n	two-stroke principle	n
cycle à quatre temps	m	Viertaktverfahren	n	four-stroke principle	n
cycle d'essais (émissions)	m	Fahrkurve (Abgasprüfung)	f	test cycle (exhaust-gas test)	n
cycle d'injection	m	Einspritztakt	m	injection cycle	n
cycle de commutation	m	Schaltspiel	n	switching cycle	n
cycle de conduite (émissions)	m	Fahrzyklus (Abgasprüfung)	m	driving schedule (exhaust-gas test)	n
cycle de freinage	m	Bremszyklus	m	brake cycle	n
cycle de régulation	m	Regelzyklus	m	control cycle	n
cycle de travail (moteur à combustion)	m	Arbeitszyklus (Verbrennungsmotor)	m	working cycle (IC engine)	n
cycle départ à chaud (émissions)	m	Heißtest (Abgasprüfung)	m	hot test (exhaust-gas test)	n
cycle test (émissions)	m	Fahrkurve (Abgasprüfung)	f	test cycle (exhaust-gas test)	n
cyclone	m	Zyklon	m	cyclone	n
cylindre à accumulateur élastique (frein)	m	Federspeicherzylinder (Bremse)	m	spring-type brake cylinder	n
cylindre à accumulateur élastique combiné	m	Kombibremszylinder	m	combination brake cylinder	n
cylindre à fentes d'étranglement (Jetronic)	m	Schlitzträger (Jetronic)	m	barrel with metering slits (Jetronic)	n
cylindre à membrane	m	Membranzylinder	m	diaphragm-type cylinder	n
cylindre à piston	m	Kolbenzylinder	m	piston cylinder	n
cylindre capteur (frein)	m	Geberzylinder (Bremse)	m	master cylinder (brakes)	n
cylindre d'assistance	m	Vorspannzylinder	m	booster cylinder	n
cylindre d'assistance à double circuit	m	Zweikreis-Vorspannzylinder	m	dual-circuit actuator cylinder for the brake master cylinder	n
cylindre d'élément de pompage	m	Elementzylinder	m	pumping-assembly barrel	n

Français

Français		Allemand		Anglais	
cylindre de frein	*m*	Bremszylinder	*m*	brake cylinder	*n*
cylindre de frein à accumulateur élastique	*m*	Federspeicherzylinder (Bremse)	*m*	spring-type brake cylinder	*n*
cylindre de frein combiné	*m*	Kombibremszylinder	*m*	combination brake cylinder	*n*
cylindre de frein de roue	*m*	Radzylinder	*m*	wheel-brake cylinder	*n*
cylindre de pompe (pompe d'injection)	*m*	Pumpenzylinder (Einspritzpumpe)	*m*	pump barrel (fuel-injection pump)	*n*
cylindre de roue de frein hydraulique	*m*	Radzylinder	*m*	wheel-brake cylinder	*n*
cylindre de servofrein (véhicules utilitaires)	*m*	Bremsverstärker (Nfz)	*m*	brake servo-unit cylinder (commercial vehicles)	*n*
cylindre moteur	*m*	Motorzylinder	*m*	engine cylinder	*n*
cylindre positionneur (ASR)	*m*	Stellzylinder (ASR)	*m*	positioning cylinder (TCS)	*n*
cylindre récepteur (frein)	*m*	Nehmerzylinder (Bremse)	*m*	slave cylinder (brakes)	*n*
cylindrée (moteur à combustion)	*f*	Hubvolumen (Verbrennungsmotor)	*n*	piston displacement (IC engine)	*n*

D

Français		Allemand		Anglais	
date de fabrication	*f*	Fertigungsdatum	*n*	manufacturing date	*n*
de montage identique	*loc*	einbaugleich	*adj*	interchangeable	*adj*
débit (alternateur)	*m*	Stromabgabe (Generator)	*f*	current output (alternator)	*n*
débit au moment de la coupure	*m*	Abregelmenge	*f*	breakaway delivery	*n*
débit correcteur	*m*	Angleichmenge	*f*	torque-control quantity	*n*
débit d'air (disponible)	*m*	Luftdurchsatz	*m*	air throughput	*n*
débit d'air minimum de secours	*m*	Notluft x	*f*	limp-home air	*n*
débit d'air nécessaire (moteur à combustion)	*m*	Luftbedarf (Verbrennungsmotor)	*m*	air requirement (IC engine)	*n*
débit d'entretien	*m*	Leerlauf-Fördermenge	*f*	idle delivery	*n*
débit d'injection	*m*	Einspritzmenge	*f*	injected fuel quantity	*n*
débit d'injection de base	*m*	Grundeinspritzmenge	*f*	basic injection quantity	*n*
débit de balayage (pompe d'injection)	*m*	Überlaufmenge (Einspritzpumpe)	*f*	overflow quantity (fuel-injection pump)	*n*
débit de carburant (pompe d'injection)	*m*	Fördermenge (Einspritzpumpe)	*f*	delivery quantity (fuel-injection pump)	*n*
débit de carburant de fuite	*m*	Leckmenge	*f*	leak-fuel quantity	*n*
débit de démarrage	*m*	Startmenge	*f*	start quantity	*n*
débit de démarrage à chaud	*m*	Heißstartmenge	*f*	hot-start fuel quantity	*n*
débit de fuite x	*m*	Leckmenge	*f*	leak-fuel quantity	*n*
débit de pleine charge (refoulement)	*m*	Vollastfördermenge	*f*	full-load delivery	*n*
débit de pleine charge dépendant de la température	*m*	temperaturabhängige Vollastmenge	*f*	temperature-dependent full-load fuel delivery	*n*
débit de post-refoulement	*m*	Nachfördermenge	*f*	secondary delivery quantity	*n*
débit de prérefoulement	*m*	Vorfördermenge	*f*	pre-delivery quantity	*n*
débit de ralenti	*m*	Leerlauf-Fördermenge	*f*	idle delivery	*n*
débit de refoulement (pompe d'injection)	*m*	Fördermenge (Einspritzpumpe)	*f*	delivery quantity (fuel-injection pump)	*n*
débit de refoulement variable en fonction de la charge	*m*	lastabhängiger Förderbeginn, LFB	*m*	load-dependent start of delivery	*n*

Français		Allemand		Anglais	
débit de retour (valve de barrage)	*m*	Rückströmung (Überströmventil)	*f*	return flow (overflow valve)	*n*
débit de suralimentation	*m*	Lademenge	*f*	pressure-charge fuel-delivery quantity	*n*
débit de surcharge (pompe d'injection)	*m*	Überlaufmenge (Einspritzpumpe)	*f*	overflow quantity (fuel-injection pump)	*n*
débit de surcharge au démarrage	*m*	Startmehrmenge	*f*	excess fuel for starting	*n*
débit du compresseur d'air	*m*	Fördermenge (Luftkompressor)	*f*	delivery capacity (air compressor)	*n*
débit limite	*m*	Grenzmenge	*f*	limit quantity	*n*
débit limite en fonction de la température	*m*	temperaturabhängige Grenzmenge	*f*	temperature-dependent limit quantity	*n*
débit massique d'air	*m*	Luftmassendurchsatz	*m*	air-mass flow	*n*
débit maximal	*m*	Vollförderung	*f*	maximum delivery	*n*
débit maximal de pleine charge	*m*	Vollastfördermenge	*f*	full-load delivery	*n*
débit nul	*m*	Nullförderung (Pumpenelement)	*f*	zero delivery	*n*
débit nul	*m*	Nullmenge	*f*	zero-fuel quantity	*n*
débit partiel	*m*	Teilförderung	*f*	partial delivery	*n*
débit volumétrique théorique d'air	*m*	theoretischer Luftdurchsatz	*m*	theoretical air-flow volume	*n*
débit volumique	*m*	Volumenstrom	*m*	flow volume	*n*
débit volumique d'air	*m*	Luftmengendurchsatz	*m*	air-quantity flow	*n*
débitmètre (émissions)	*m*	Strömungsfühler (Abgasprüfung)	*m*	flow sensor (exhaust-gas test)	*n*
débitmètre d'air	*m*	Luftmengenmesser	*m*	air-flow sensor	*n*
débitmètre d'air à film chaud	*m*	Heißfilm-Luftmassenmesser	*m*	hot-film air-mass sensor	*n*
débitmètre d'air à flux ascendant	*m*	Steigstrom-Luftmengenmesser	*m*	updraft air-flow sensor	*n*
débitmètre d'air à flux inversé	*m*	Fallstrom-Luftmengenmesser	*m*	downdraft air-flow sensor	*n*
débitmètre instantané	*m*	Einspritzmengenindikator	*m*	injected-fuel-quantity indicator	*n*
débitmètre massique à fil chaud	*m*	Hitzdraht-Luftmassenmesser, HLM	*m*	hot-wire air-mass meter	*n*
débitmètre massique à film chaud	*m*	Heißfilm-Luftmassenmesser, HMM	*m*	hot-film air-mass meter	*n*
débitmètre massique d'air	*m*	Luftmassenmesser	*m*	air-mass meter	*n*
débloqueur du débit de surcharge au démarrage	*m*	Startmengenentriegelung	*f*	start-quantity release	*n*
début d'inflammation	*m*	Zündbeginn	*m*	start of ignition	*n*
début d'injection	*m*	Einspritzbeginn	*m*	start of injection	*n*
début d'injection variable en fonction de la charge	*m*	lastabhängiger Spritzbeginn	*m*	load-dependent start of injectio	*n*
début de combustion	*m*	Verbrennungsbeginn	*m*	combustion start	*n*
début de la coupure de débit	*m*	Abregelbeginn	*m*	start of speed regulation	*n*
début de refoulement (pompe d'injection)	*m*	Förderbeginn (Einspritzpumpe)	*m*	start of delivery (fuel-injection pump)	*n*
début de refoulement en fonction de la pression atmosph. et de la charge	*m*	atmosphärendruck- und lastabhängiger Förderbeginn	*m*	barometric-pressure and load-dependent start of delivery	*n*

Français

Français		Allemand		Anglais	
début de refoulement en fonction de la pression atmosphérique	*m*	atmosphärendruckabhängiger Förderbeginn	*m*	ambient-pressure-dependent port closing	*n*
début du blocage (ABS)	*m*	Blockierbeginn (ABS)	*m*	start of lock-up (ABS)	*n*
début du freinage	*m*	Bremsbeginn	*m*	start of braking	*n*
décalage du début de refoulement	*m*	Förderbeginnversatz	*m*	start-of-delivery offset	*n*
décélération	*f*	Sturzgas	x *n*	quick-gas pedal release	*n*
décélération <régime de décélération>	*m*	Schiebebetrieb	*m*	overrun	*n*
décélération de freinage	*f*	Bremsverzögerung	*f*	braking deceleration	*n*
décélération du véhicule	*f*	Fahrzeugverzögerung	*f*	vehicle deceleration	*n*
décélération longitudinale du véhicule	*f*	Fahrzeuglängsverzögerung	*f*	vehicle longitudinal deceleration	*n*
décélération périphérique des roues	*f*	Radumfangsverzögerung	*f*	wheel deceleration	*n*
décélération totale	*f*	Vollverzögerung	*f*	fully developed deceleration	*n*
décélération uniforme	*f*	gleichförmige Verzögerung	*f*	uniform deceleration	*n*
décharge (batterie)	*f*	Entladung (Batterie)	*f*	discharge (battery) <noun>	*n*
décharge d'arc	*f*	Glimmentladung	*f*	glow discharge	*n*
décharge de la batterie	*f*	Batterieentladung	*f*	battery discharge	*n*
décharge de volume	*f*	Volumenentlastung	*f*	retraction volume (distributor pump)	*n*
décharge disruptive	*f*	Durchschlag (elektrisch)	*m*	arcing	*n*
décharge en profondeur (batterie)	*f*	Tiefentladung (Batterie)	*f*	exhaustive discharge (battery)	*n*
décharge spontanée (batterie)	*f*	Selbstentladung (Batterie)	*f*	self-discharge (battery)	*n*
décharger (batterie)	*v*	entladen (Batterie)	*v*	discharge (battery) <to discharge>	*v*
déclenchement de l'allumage (générateur d'impulsions)	*m*	Zündauslösung (Impulsgeber)	*f*	ignition triggering (pulse generator)	*n*
déclencher	*v*	ansteuern	*v*	trigger	*v*
déclencheur (prétensionneur)	*m*	Gurtstraffer-Auslösegerät	*n*	seat-belt-tightener trigger unit	*n*
déclencheur d'allumage	*m*	Zündauslöser	*m*	ignition trigger	*n*
déclencheur de coussin d'air	*m*	Airbag-Auslösegerät	*n*	airbag triggering unit	*n*
déclencheur de prétensionneur	*m*	Gurtstraffer-Auslösegerät	*n*	seat-belt-tightener trigger unit	*n*
déconnexion automatique de glissement (banc d'essai)	*f*	Schlupfabschaltung (Rollenbremsprüfstand)	*f*	wheel-slip shutoff device (dynamic brake analyzer)	*n*
défaut d'uniformité (route)	*m*	Ungleichförmigkeit (Fahrbahn)	*f*	pavement irregularity	*n*
défaut de fabrication	*m*	Fertigungsfehler	*m*	manufacturing defect	*n*
déficit d'air (mélange air-carburant)	*m*	Luftmangel (Luft-Kraftstoff-Gemisch)	*m*	air deficiency (air-fuel mixture)	*n*
déflecteur (actionneur de pression)	*m*	Prallplatte (Drucksteller)	*f*	baffle plate (pressure actuator)	*n*
dégazage	*m*	entlüften	*v*	bleed	*v*
dégazage du réservoir	*m*	Tankentlüftung	*f*	tank ventilation	*n*
degré d'antiparasitage	*m*	Entstörgrad	*n*	interference-suppression level	*n*
degré de protection	*m*	Schutzart	*f*	degree of protection	*n*
degré de rayonnement sonore (ventilateur)	*m*	Abstrahlgrad (Lüfter)	*m*	noise-emission level (fan)	*n*

Français		Allemand		Anglais	
degré de suralimentation	*m*	Aufladegrad	*m*	boost ratio	*n*
degré thermique (bougie)	*m*	Wärmewert (Zündkerze)	*m*	heat range (spark plug)	*n*
degrés vilebrequin	*mpl*	Kurbelwinkel (Grad Kurbelwelle)	*m*	crankshaft angle	*n*
délai d'inflammation	*m*	Zündverzug	*m*	ignition lag	*n*
délai d'injection	*m*	Spritzverzug	*m*	injection lag	*n*
délai de régulation	*m*	Ausregelzeit	*f*	settling time	*n*
délai de réponse	*m*	Ansprechverzögerung	*f*	response delay	*n*
délestage (circuit de bord)	*m*	Lastabwurf (Bordnetz)	*m*	load dump (vehicle electrical system)	*n*
délestage de pression	*m*	Druckentlastung	*f*	pressure relief	*n*
demande de débit	*f*	Mengenwunsch	*m*	fuel-quantity demand	*n*
demande du conducteur	*f*	Fahrerwunsch	*m*	vehicle-operator command	*n*
démarrage	*m*	Startvorgang	*m*	start	*v*
démarrage (opération)	*m*	Startbetrieb	*m*	starting operation	*n*
démarrage à chaud	*m*	Heißstart	*m*	hot start	*n*
démarrage à froid	*m*	Kaltstart	*m*	cold start	*n*
démarrage par flamme	*m*	Flammstart	*m*	flame start	*n*
démarrer (moteur à combustion)	*m*	anspringen (Verbrennungsmotor)	x *v*	start (IC engine)	*v*
démarreur	*m*	Starter	*m*	starter	*n*
démarreur à commande positive électromécanique	*m*	Schub-Schraubtrieb-Starter	*m*	pre-engaged-drive starter	*n*
démarreur à pignon coulissant	*m*	Schubtrieb-Starter	*m*	sliding-gear starter	*n*
démarreur à réducteur	*m*	Vorgelegestarter	*m*	reduction-gear starter	*n*
demi-roue polaire	*f*	Polradhälfte	*f*	pole-wheel half	*n*
densité acoustique	*f*	Schalldichte	*f*	sound density	*n*
densité atmosphérique	*f*	Luftdichte	*f*	air density	*n*
densité de l'acide	*f*	Säuredichte	*f*	specific gravity of electrolyte	*n*
densité de l'électrolyte	*f*	Säuredichte	*f*	specific gravity of electrolyte	*n*
densité spectrale d'accélération	*f*	spektrale Beschleunigungs-dichte	*f*	spectral acceleration density	*n*
dent du pignon	*f*	Ritzelzahn	*m*	pinion tooth	*n*
dénuder	*v*	abisolieren	*v*	strip the insulation	*v*
départ à chaud	*m*	Heißstart	*m*	hot start	*n*
départ à froid	*m*	Kaltstart	*m*	cold start	*n*
départ d'énergie	*m*	Energieabfluß	*m*	energy output	*n*
déphasage (entre deux grandeurs sinusoïdales)	*m*	Phasenverschiebung	*f*	phase displacement	*n*
déplacement axial	*m*	Einspurhub	*m*	pinion travel	*n*
déplacement du centre de gravité	*m*	Schwerpunktverlagerung	*f*	displacement of the center of gravity	*n*
déplacement du piston	*m*	Kolbenhub	*m*	plunger lift	*n*
déplacement hélicoïdal (démarreur)	*m*	Schraubweg (Starter)	*m*	helical travel (starter)	*n*
dépollution des gaz d'échappement	*f*	Abgasreinigung	*f*	exhaust treatment	*n*
déport négatif de l'axe du pivot de fusée	*m*	negativer Lenkrollradius	*m*	negative steering offset	*n*

Français

Français		Allemand			Anglais	
dépôt	*m*	Ablagerung		*f*	deposit	*n*
depôt de plomb (bougie)	*m*	Verbleiung (Zündkerze)		*f*	lead fouling (spark plug)	*n*
dépôts calcinés	*mpl*	Verbrennungsrückstände		*mpl*	combustion residues	*npl*
dérivation	*f*	Nebenschluß		*m*	shunt	*n*
dérive de débit	*f*	Mengendrift		*f*	fuel-quantity drift	*n*
dérive de température	*f*	Temperaturdrift		*f*	temperature drift	*n*
déroulement du contrôle	*m*	Prüfablauf		*m*	test procedure	*n*
désengrènement	*m*	ausspuren (Starterritzel)		*v*	demesh (starter pinion)	*v*
déséquilibre des freins	*m*	schiefziehen (Bremse)	x	*v*	brake "pull"	*n*
déshydratant (dessiccateur)	*m*	Trockenmittel (Lufttrockner)		*n*	desiccant (air drier)	*n*
dessiccateur d'air	*m*	Lufttrockner		*m*	air drier	*n*
dessin assisté par ordinateur, DAO	*m*	Computer Aided Design, CAD		*n*	Computer Aided Design, CAD	*n*
dessin d'atelier	*m*	Fertigungszeichnung		*f*	workshop drawing	*n*
dessin d'exécution	*m*	Fertigungszeichnung		*f*	workshop drawing	*n*
dessin en coupe	*m*	Schnittzeichnung		*f*	sectional drawing	*n*
détecteur d'ionisation à flamme, FID	*m*	Flammen-Ionisations-Detektor, FID		*m*	flame ionization detection analyzer, FID	*n*
détecteur de bris de glaces (alarme auto)	*m*	Glasbruchmelder (Autoalarm)		*m*	glass-breakage detector (car alarm)	*n*
détecteur de mouvement (alarme auto)	*m*	Bewegungsdetektor (Autoalarm)		*m*	motion detector (car alarm)	*n*
détecteur de phase	*m*	Phasensensor		*m*	phase sensor	*n*
détecteur piezoélectrique	*m*	Vibrationssensor		*m*	vibration sensor	*n*
détection d'occupation de siège	*f*	Sitzbelegungserkennung		*f*	seat-occupant detection	*n*
détection de collision (coussin gonflable)	*f*	Aufpralldetektion (Airbag)		*f*	crash sensing (airbag)	*n*
détection de défaut à l'étage de sortie (calculateur)	*f*	Endstufenfehlererkennung (Steuergerät)		*f*	driver-stage defect recognition (ECU)	*n*
détection de la fonction "remorque" (ABS)	*f*	Anhängererkennung (ABS)		*f*	trailer recognition (ABS)	*n*
détection des défauts	*f*	Fehlererkennung		*f*	fault detection	*n*
détendeur	*m*	Bremsdruckminderer		*m*	proportioning valve (brakes)	*n*
détonation (moteur à combustion)	*f*	klopfen (Verbrennungsmotor)	x	*v*	knock (IC engine)	*v*
développement des produits	*m*	Produktentwicklung		*f*	product development	*n*
déverrouillage (robinet de secours)	*m*	Entriegelung (Nothahn)		*f*	release (emergency valve)	*n*
déviation de la lumière	*f*	Lichtablenkung		*f*	light deflection	*n*
diagnostic de bord	*m*	Onboard-Diagnose, OBD	x	*f*	on-board diagnostics, OBD	*n*
diagnostic de défauts	*m*	Fehlerdiagnose		*f*	error diagnosis	*n*
diagnostic du moteur	*m*	Motordiagnose		*f*	engine diagnosis	*n*
diagnostic embarqué	*m*	Onboard-Diagnose, OBD	x	*f*	on-board diagnostics, OBD	*n*
diagnostic intégré	*m*	integrierte Diagnose		*f*	integrated diagnostics	*n*
diagramme de conduite (émissions)	*m*	Fahrzyklus (Abgasprüfung)		*m*	driving schedule (exhaust-gas test)	*n*
diagramme de distribution (moteur à combustion)	*m*	Ventilsteuerdiagramm (Verbrennungsmotor)		*n*	valve timing diagram (IC engine)	*n*
diagramme de test (émissions)	*m*	Fahrkurve (Abgasprüfung)		*f*	test cycle (exhaust-gas test)	*n*

Français		Allemand		Anglais	
diagramme des vitesses	*m*	Geschwindigkeitsdiagramm	*n*	velocity diagram	*n*
diamètre du siège d'injecteur	*m*	Sitzdurchmesser (Düse)	*m*	nozzle-seat diameter	*n*
diamètre intérieur	*m*	Ventildurchlaß	*m*	valve throat	*n*
diaphragme (commande d'air additionnel)	*m*	Lochblende (Zusatzluftschieber)	*f*	perforated plate (auxiliary-air device)	*n*
différence de glissement	*f*	Schlupfdifferenz	*f*	slip-rate difference	*n*
différence de pression	*f*	Druckdifferenz	*f*	pressure differential	*n*
différentiel autobloquant	*m*	Sperrdifferential	*n*	locking differential	*n*
différentiel d'aiguille	*m*	Druckstufe (Düsennadel)	*f*	differential ratio (nozzle needle	*n*
différentiel de l'essieu arrière	*m*	Hinterachsdifferential	*n*	rear-axle differential	*n*
diffuseur (projecteur)	*m*	Streuscheibe (Scheinwerfer)	*f*	lens (headlamp)	*n*
diode d'affichage	*f*	Anzeigediode	*f*	display diode	*n*
diode d'excitation	*f*	Erregerdiode	*f*	excitation diode	*n*
diode d'isolement	*f*	Sperr-Diode	*f*	block diode	*n*
diode de barrage	*f*	Sperr-Diode	*f*	block diode	*n*
diode de décharge	*f*	Löschdiode	*f*	decay diode	*n*
diode de protection contre inversion de polarité	*f*	Verpolungsschutzdiode	*f*	incorrect-polarity protection diode	*n*
diode de puissance	*f*	Leistungsdiode	*f*	power diode	*n*
diode de récupération	*f*	Freilaufdiode	*f*	free-wheeling diode	*n*
diode de redressement	*f*	Gleichrichterdiode	*f*	rectifier diode	*n*
diode emmanchée	*f*	Einpreßdiode	*f*	press-in diode	*n*
diode négative	*f*	Minusdiode	*f*	negative diode	*n*
diode parallèle	*f*	Parallel-Diode	*f*	parallel diode	*n*
diode positive	*f*	Plusdiode	*f*	positive diode	*n*
diode redresseuse	*f*	Gleichrichterdiode	*f*	rectifier diode	*n*
diode Zener	*f*	Zenerdiode	*f*	Zener diode	*n*
diode-boisseau	*f*	Napfdiode	*f*	cup diode	*n*
diode-bouton	*f*	Knopfdiode	*f*	button diode	*n*
direction assistée	*f*	Servolenkung	*f*	power steering	*n*
direction du jet d'injecteur	*f*	Düsenstrahlrichtung	*f*	spray direction	*n*
directives antipollution	*fpl*	Abgasgesetzgebung	*f*	emission-control legislation	*n*
dirigeabilité	*f*	Lenkbarkeit	*f*	steerability	*n*
dirigeable (véhicule)	*adj*	lenkbar (Kfz)	*adj*	steerable (motor vehicle)	*adj*
dispersion de débit	*f*	Einspritzmengenstreuung	*f*	injected-fuel-quantity scatter	*n*
dispositif à air comprimé	*m*	Druckluftanlage	*f*	compressed-air system	*n*
dispositif à flux jumelé	*m*	Zwillingsstromgehäuse	*n*	twin-flow housing	*n*
dispositif anti-pincement (véhicule)	*m*	Einklemmsicherung (Kfz)	*f*	push-in fuse (motor vehicle)	*n*
dispositif antidémarrage	*m*	Rollstartsperre	*f*	roll-start block	*n*
dispositif antidémarrage (alarme auto)	*m*	Wegfahrsperre (Autoalarm)	*f*	vehicle immobilizer (car alarm)	*n*
dispositif antigel	*m*	Frostschutzeinrichtung	*f*	antifreeze unit	*n*
dispositif antivol	*m*	Diebstahlschutz	*m*	theft-deterrence feature	*n*
dispositif automatique de rattrapage de jeu (freins des roues)	*f*	Gestängesteller (Radbremse)	*m*	slack adjuster (wheel brake)	*n*

Français

Français		Allemand		Anglais	
dispositif auxiliaire de démarrage	*m*	Starthilfsanlage	*f*	start-assist system	*n*
dispositif auxiliaire de desserrage (frein)	*m*	Hilfslöseeinrichtung (Bremse)	*f*	auxiliary release device (brakes)	*n*
dispositif correcteur d'orientation des projecteurs	*m*	Leuchtweitenregelung, LWR	*f*	headlight leveling control	*n*
dispositif d'alerte (frein)	*m*	Warndruckeinrichtung (Bremse)	*f*	low-pressure warning device (brakes)	*n*
dispositif d'alimentation en énergie	*m*	Energieversorgungs-einrichtung	*f*	energy-supply system	*n*
dispositif d'allumage	*m*	Zündanlage	*f*	ignition system	*n*
dispositif d'arrêt	*m*	Abstellvorrichtung	*f*	shutoff device	*n*
dispositif d'arrêt électrique	*m*	elektrische Abstellvorrichtung, ELAB	*f*	solenoid-operated shutoff	*n*
dispositif d'arrêt électrohydraulique	*m*	elektrohydraulische Abstellvorrichtung, EHAB	*f*	electrohydraulic shutoff device	*n*
dispositif d'arrêt électromagnétique	*m*	elektrische Abstellvorrichtung, ELAB	*f*	solenoid-operated shutoff	*n*
dispositif d'arrêt électromotoris	*m*	elektromotorische Abstellvorrichtung, EMAB	*f*	electromotive shutoff device	*n*
dispositif d'arrêt hydraulique	*m*	hydraulische Abstellvorrichtung, HYAB	*f*	hydraulic shutoff device	*n*
dispositif d'arrêt mécanique	*m*	mechanische Abstellvorrichtung, MEAB	*f*	mechanical shutoff device	*n*
dispositif d'arrêt pneumatique	*m*	pneumatische Abstellvorrichtung, PNAB	*f*	pneumatic shutoff device	*n*
dispositif d'avance à dépression	*m*	Unterdruckzündversteller	*m*	vacuum advance mechanism	*n*
dispositif d'avance à l'injection	*m*	Spritzversteller	*m*	timing device	*n*
dispositif d'essai	*m*	Prüfeinrichtung	*f*	test equipment	*n*
dispositif d'étranglement	*m*	Drosselvorrichtung	*f*	throttle device	*n*
dispositif d'injection	*m*	Einspritzanlage	*f*	fuel-injection installation	*n*
dispositif d'injection différée	*m*	Leiselaufvorrichtung	*f*	smooth-idle device	*n*
dispositif de blocage du démarreur	*m*	Startsperreinrichtung	*f*	start-locking	*n*
dispositif de commande des portes (autobus)	*m*	Türbetätigungsanlage (Omnibus)	*f*	door-control system (bus)	*n*
dispositif de débit de surcharge au démarrage	*m*	Startmengenvorrichtung	*f*	excess-fuel device	*n*
dispositif de démarrage à flamme	*m*	Flammstartanlage	*f*	flame starting system	*n*
dispositif de démarrage rapide (véhicules diesel)	*m*	Schnellstartanlage (Dieselfahrzeuge)	*f*	rapid starting system (diesel vehicles)	*n*
dispositif de desserrage (cylindre à accumulateur élastique)	*m*	Löseeinrichtung (Federspeicherzylinder)	*f*	mechanical release (spring-type brake actuator)	*n*
dispositif de déverrouillage au démarrage	*m*	Startmengenentriegelung	*f*	start-quantity release	*n*
dispositif de freinage	*m*	Bremsanlage	*f*	braking system	*n*
dispositif de freinage à air comprimé	*m*	Druckluft-Bremsanlage	*f*	compressed-air braking system	*n*

Français

Français		Allemand		Anglais	
dispositif de freinage à basse pression	*m*	Niederdruck-Bremsanlage	*f*	low-pressure braking system	*n*
dispositif de freinage à circuits multiples	*m*	Mehrkreis-Bremsanlage	*f*	multi-circuit braking system	*n*
dispositif de freinage à commande par gravité	*m*	Fall-Bremsanlage	*f*	gravity braking system	*n*
dispositif de freinage à conduite unique	*m*	Einleitungs-Bremsanlage	*f*	single-line braking system	*n*
dispositif de freinage à conduites multiples	*m*	Mehrleitungs-Bremsanlage	*f*	multi-line braking system	*n*
dispositif de freinage à dépression	*m*	Vakuum-Bremsanlage	*f*	vacuum-brake system	*n*
dispositif de freinage à deux conduites	*m*	Zweileitungs-Bremsanlage	*f*	dual-line braking system	*n*
dispositif de freinage à énergie musculaire	*m*	Muskelkraft-Bremsanlage	*f*	muscular-energy braking system	*n*
dispositif de freinage à énergie non musculaire	*m*	Fremdkraft-Bremsanlage	*f*	power-brake system	*n*
dispositif de freinage à haute pression	*m*	Hochdruck-Bremsanlage	*f*	high-pressure braking system	*n*
dispositif de freinage à inertie	*m*	Auflauf-Bremsanlage	*f*	inertia braking system	*n*
dispositif de freinage à régulation électronique	*m*	elektronisch geregelte Bremsanlage, ELB	*f*	electronically controlled braking system, ELB	*n*
dispositif de freinage à transmission à circuit unique	*m*	Einkreis-Bremsanlage	*f*	single-circuit braking system	*n*
dispositif de freinage à transmission à double circuit	*m*	Zweikreis-Bremsanlage	*f*	dual-circuit braking system	*n*
dispositif de freinage additionnel de ralentissement	*m*	Dauer-Bremsanlage	*f*	continuous-operation braking system	*n*
dispositif de freinage assisté par énergie auxiliaire	*m*	Hilfskraft-Bremsanlage	*f*	power-assisted braking system	*n*
dispositif de freinage automatique	*m*	selbsttätige Bremsanlage	*f*	automatic braking system	*n*
dispositif de freinage avec amplificateur	*m*	Hilfskraft-Bremsanlage	*f*	power-assisted braking system	*n*
dispositif de freinage combiné	*m*	Kombi-Bremsanlage	*f*	combination braking system	*n*
dispositif de freinage continu	*m*	durchgehende Bremsanlage	*f*	continuous braking system	*n*
dispositif de freinage de remorque	*m*	Anhänger-Bremsanlage	*f*	trailer-brake system	*n*
dispositif de freinage de secour:	*m*	Hilfs-Bremsanlage	*f*	secondary-brake system	*n*
dispositif de freinage de service	*m*	Betriebs-Bremsanlage	*f*	service-brake system	*n*
dispositif de freinage de stationnement	*m*	Feststell-Bremsanlage	*f*	parking-brake system	*n*
dispositif de freinage électro-pneumatique	*m*	elektro-pneumatische Bremsanlage	*f*	electropneumatic braking system	*n*
dispositif de freinage hydraulique assisté par air comprimé	*m*	pneumatische Hilfskraft-Bremsanlage	*f*	air-assisted braking system	*n*
dispositif de freinage hydraulique à commande par air comprimé	*m*	pneumatische Fremdkraft-Bremsanlage mit hydraul. Übertragungseinrichtung	*f*	air-over-hydraulic braking system	*n*

Français		Allemand		Anglais	
dispositif de freinage hydraulique à commande par dépression	*m*	Unterdruck-Fremdkraft-Bremsanlage mit hydr. Übertragungseinrichtung	*f*	vacuum-over-hydraulic braking system	*n*
dispositif de freinage hydraulique assisté par dépression	*m*	Unterdruck-Hilfskraft-Bremsanlage mit hydraul. Übertragungseinrichtung	*f*	vacuum-assisted hydraulic braking system	*n*
dispositif de freinage pneumatique	*m*	pneumatische Bremsanlage	*f*	air-brake system	*n*
dispositif de freinage semi-continu	*m*	teilweise durchgehende Bremsanlage	*f*	semi-continuous braking systen	*n*
dispositif de gonflage des pneu:	*m*	Reifenfülleinrichtung	*f*	tire-inflation device	*n*
dispositif de lancement	*m*	Einspurgetriebe	*n*	pinion-engaging drive	*n*
dispositif de papillon	*m*	Drosselvorrichtung	*f*	throttle device	*n*
dispositif de protection contre les surtensions	*m*	Überspannungsschutzgerät	*n*	overvoltage-protection device	*n*
dispositif de réglage	*m*	Verstelleinrichtung	*f*	adjusting device	*n*
dispositif de roue libre (démarreur)	*m*	Rollenfreilauf (Starter)	*m*	roller-type overrunning clutch (starter)	*n*
dispositif de signalisation	*m*	Signalanlage	*f*	signaling system	*n*
dispositif de signalisation direction-détresse	*m*	Warnblinkanlage	*f*	hazard-warning and turn-signal system	*n*
dispositif de suspension pneumatique	*m*	Luftfederanlage	*f*	pneumatic suspension	*n*
dispositif de transmission (dispositif de freinage)	*m*	Übertragungseinrichtung (Bremsanlage)	*f*	transmission (braking system)	*n*
dispositifs auxiliaires de démarrage	*mpl*	Starthilfsanlage	*f*	start-assist system	*n*
dispositifs d'antiparasitage	*mpl*	Entstörmittel	*n*	interference-suppressor	*n*
disposition des cylindres	*f*	Zylinderanordnung	*f*	cylinder arrangement	*n*
disque à cames	*m*	Hubscheibe	*f*	cam plate	*n*
disque à cames (correcteur de freinage)	*m*	Kurvenscheibe (Bremskraftregler)	*f*	cam disc (braking-force regulator)	*n*
disque d'enregistrement (tachographe)	*m*	Diagrammscheibe (Tachograph)	*f*	tachograph chart	*n*
disque d'impulsion (ABS/ASR)	*m*	Impulsring (ABS/ASR)	*m*	sensor ring (ABS/TCS)	*n*
disque de butée	*m*	Anschlagscheibe	*f*	stop disc	*n*
disque de frein	*m*	Bremsscheibe	*f*	brake disc	*n*
disque de tôle (induit)	*m*	Blechlamelle (Anker)	*f*	disc (armature core)	*n*
disque intermédiaire	*m*	Zwischenring	*m*	intermediate ring	*n*
disque mobile	*m*	Drehschieber	*m*	rotating slide	*n*
disque rainuré	*m*	Nutscheibe	*f*	slotted washer	*n*
disque-cible (allumage)	*m*	Impulsgeberrad (Zündung)	*n*	trigger wheel (ignition)	*n*
dissipation de la chaleur	*f*	Wärmeabführung	*f*	heat dissipation	*n*
dissolvant antirouille	*m*	Rostlöser	*m*	rust remover	*n*
distance d'arrêt	*f*	Gesamtbremsweg	*m*	total braking distance	*n*
distance d'éclatement	*f*	Funkenstrecke	*f*	spark gap	*n*
distance d'éclatement et de glissement (bougie)	*f*	Luftgleitfunkenstrecke (Zündkerze)	*f*	semi-surface gap (spark plug)	*n*
distance de freinage	*f*	Bremsweg	*m*	braking distance	*n*
distance focale (projecteur)	*f*	Brennweite (Scheinwerfer)	*f*	focal length (headlamp)	*n*

Français		Allemand		Anglais	
distance totale de freinage	*f*	Gesamtbremsweg	*m*	total braking distance	*n*
distorsion du champ d'excitation	*f*	Feldverzerrung	*f*	field displacement	*n*
distributeur	*m*	Wegeventil, WGV	*n*	directional-control valve	*n*
distributeur à bouton-poussoir	*m*	Druckknopfventil	*n*	push-button valve	*n*
distributeur à deux voies (ASR)	*m*	Zweiwegeventil (ASR)	*n*	two-way directional-control valve (TCS)	*n*
distributeur d'allumage	*m*	Zündverteiler	*m*	ignition distributor	*n*
distributeur haute tension	*m*	Hochspannungsverteiler	*m*	high-voltage distributor	*n*
distributeur pilote	*m*	Vorsteuerventil (Bremskraftregler)	*n*	pilot valve (load-sensing valve)	*n*
distribution (commande des soupapes)	*f*	Ventiltrieb	*m*	valve gear	*n*
distribution (moteur à combustion)	*f*	Ventilsteuerzeit (Verbrennungsmotor)	*f*	valve timing (IC engine)	*n*
distribution de tension	*f*	Spannungsverteilung	*f*	voltage distribution	*n*
divergent d'air (KE-Jetronic)	*m*	Lufttrichter (KE-Jetronic)	*m*	air funnel (KE-Jetronic)	*n*
diviseur d'impulsions	*m*	Impulsteiler	*m*	pulse divider	*n*
diviseur de fréquence	*m*	Frequenzteiler	*m*	frequency divider	*n*
diviseur de tension	*m*	Spannungsteiler	*m*	voltage divider	*n*
division (entreprise)	*f*	Geschäftsbereich	*m*	division (business)	*n*
document technique client	*m*	Technische Kundenunterlage, TKU	*f*	technical customer information	*n*
doigt de distributeur (allumage)	*m*	Zündverteilerläufer	*m*	distributor rotor (ignition)	*n*
domaine de spécialisation	*m*	Geschäftsfeld	*n*	business area	*n*
dommages par cavitation	*mpl*	Kavitationsschaden	*m*	cavitation damage	*n*
dosage	*m*	Dosierung	*f*	meter	*v*
dosage à l'admission	*m*	Zulaufmessung	*f*	inlet metering	*n*
dosage air-carburant	*m*	Luft-Kraftstoff-Verhältnis	*n*	air-fuel (A/F) ratio	*n*
dosage automatique de la force de freinage en fonction de la charge	*m*	automatisch lastabhängige Bremskraftregelung, ALB	*f*	automatic load-sensitive braking-force metering	*n*
dosage du carburant	*m*	Kraftstoffzumessung	*f*	fuel metering	*n*
dosage du mélange	*m*	Gemischzumessung	*f*	air-fuel-mixture metering	*v*
dosage monotrou (injecteur)	*m*	Einlochzumessung (Einspritzventil)	*f*	single-orifice metering	*n*
dosage multitrous (injecteur)	*m*	Mehrlochzumessung (Einspritzventil)	*f*	multi-orifice metering	*n*
dosage par bague	*m*	Schieberzumessung	*f*	sleeve metering	*n*
dosage par déplacement	*m*	Shuttle-Zumessung	*f*	displacement metering	*n*
dosage par fente annulaire (injecteur)	*m*	Ringspaltzumessung (Einspritzventil)	*f*	ring-gap metering (fuel injector)	*n*
dosage par rampe et trou	*m*	Steuerkanten-Zumessung	*f*	port-and-helix metering	*n*
dosage par valve	*m*	ventilgesteuerte Zumessung	*f*	valve metering	*n*
doseur-distributeur de carburan	*m*	Kraftstoffmengenteiler	*m*	fuel distributor	*n*
double allumage	*m*	Doppelzündung	*f*	dual ignition	*n*
double battement (essuie-glace)	*m*	Zweischlag (Wischeranlage)	*m*	four-bar linkage (wiper system)	*n*
double joint	*m*	Doppeldichtung	*f*	double seal	*n*

Français		Allemand		Anglais	
double micro-arête (raclette en caoutchouc)	*f*	Mikro-Doppelkante (Wischgummi)	*f*	double microedge (wiper blade)	*n*
douille d'élément de pompage	*f*	Elementbuchse	*f*	pumping-element bushing	*n*
douille de butée	*f*	Anschlaghülse	*f*	stop sleeve	*n*
douille de guidage	*f*	Führungsbuchse	*f*	guide bushing	*n*
douille de réglage (pompe d'injection)	*f*	Regelhülse (Einspritzpumpe)	*f*	control sleeve (fuel-injection pump)	*n*
douille de serrage	*f*	Spannhülse	*f*	slotted spring pin	*n*
douille de serrage (capteur de vitesse)	*f*	Federhülse (Drehzahlsensor)	*f*	spring sleeve (wheel-speed sensor)	*n*
douille élastique (capteur de vitesse)	*f*	Federhülse (Drehzahlsensor)	*f*	spring sleeve (wheel-speed sensor)	*n*
douille en caoutchouc	*f*	Gummimanschette	*f*	rubber sleeve	*n*
drainer (filtre)	*v*	entwässern (Filter)	*v*	drain (drain)	*v*
durabilité	*f*	Dauerstandfestigkeit	*f*	service life	*n*
durabilité du filtre	*f*	Filterstandzeit	*f*	filter service life	*n*
durée d'actionnement	*f*	Betätigungsdauer	*f*	duration of application	*n*
durée d'attraction (injecteur)	*f*	Anzugszeit (Einspritzventil)	*f*	pickup time (fuel injector)	*n*
durée d'enclenchement	*f*	Einschaltdauer	*f*	operating time	*n*
durée d'incandescence	*f*	Glühdauer	*f*	glow duration	*n*
durée d'inflammation	*f*	Entflammungsdauer	*f*	flame-front propagation time	*n*
durée d'injection	*f*	Einspritzzeit	*f*	injection time	*n*
durée d'injection de base	*f*	Grundeinspritzzeit	*f*	basic injection timing	*n*
durée d'ouverture (injecteur)	*f*	Öffnungsdauer (Einspritzventil)	*f*	opening time (fuel injector)	*n*
durée de combustion (mélange air-carburant)	*f*	Brenndauer (Kraftstoff-Luft-Gemisch)	*f*	combustion time (air-fuel mixture)	*n*
durée de démarrage	*f*	Startdauer	*f*	starting time	*n*
durée de fermeture (allumage)	*f*	Schließzeit (Zündung)	*f*	dwell period (ignition)	*n*
durée de fonctionnement	*f*	Betriebsdauer	*f*	period of use	*n*
durée de l'étincelle	*f*	Funkendauer	*f*	spark duration	*n*
durée de période	*f*	Periodendauer	*f*	period duration	*n*
durée de préchauffage	*f*	Vorglühdauer	*f*	preheating time	*n*
durée de refoulement	*f*	Förderdauer	*f*	delivery period	*n*
durée de vie	*f*	Dauerstandfestigkeit	*f*	service life	*n*
dynamique des véhicules à moteur	*f*	Fahrdynamik	*f*	dynamics of vehicular operation	*n*
dynamique du freinage	*f*	Bremsdynamik	*f*	dynamic braking response	*n*
dynamique longitudinale d'un véhicule	*f*	Fahrzeuglängsdynamik	*f*	dynamics of linear motion (motor vehicle)	*n*
dynamique transversale d'un véhicule	*f*	Fahrzeugquerdynamik	*f*	dynamics of lateral motion (motor vehicle)	*n*
dynamo	*f*	Gleichstromgenerator	*m*	direct-current generator	*n*
dynamomètre (banc d'essai)	*m*	Kraftmeßeinrichtung (Rollenbremsprüfstand)	*f*	load sensor (dynamic brake analyzer)	*n*
E					
eau de refroidissement	*f*	Kühlwasser	*n*	cooling water	*n*
effet d'éblouissement (projecteur)	*m*	Blendwirkung (Scheinwerfer)	*f*	glare effect (headlamp)	*n*
effet d'étranglement	*m*	Drosselwirkung	*f*	throttling effect	*n*

Français

Français		Allemand		Anglais	
effet d'impact (filtre)	*m*	Aufpralleffekt (Filter)	*m*	impact (filter)	*n*
effet de "postcharge"	*m*	Nachladeeffekt	*m*	boost effect	*n*
effet de barrage (filtre)	*m*	Sperreffekt (Filter)	*m*	blockage (filter)	*n*
effet de diffusion (filtre)	*m*	Diffusionseffekt (Filter)	*m*	diffusion (filter)	*n*
effet de filtrage (filtre)	*m*	Siebeffekt (Filter)	*m*	straining (filter)	*n*
effet de filtration	*m*	Filterwirkung	*f*	filter effect	*n*
effet de frein moteur	*m*	Motorbremswirkung	*f*	engine braking action	*n*
effet de freinage	*m*	Bremswirkung	*f*	braking effect	*n*
effet de freinage à chaud	*m*	Heißbremswirkung	*f*	effectiveness of hot brakes	*n*
effet de freinage auxiliaire	*m*	Hilfsbremswirkung	*f*	secondary braking effect	*n*
effet de post-refoulement	*m*	Nachfördereffekt	*m*	post-delivery effect	*n*
effet de prérefoulement	*m*	Vorfördereffekt	*m*	pre-delivery effect	*n*
effet de renforcement de freinage (servofrein)	*m*	Verstärkungsfaktor (Bremskraftverstärker)	*m*	boost factor (brake booster)	*n*
effet Hall	*m*	Hall-Effekt	*m*	Hall effect	*n*
effet résiduel de freinage	*m*	Restbremswirkung	*f*	residual braking	*n*
efficacité de freinage	*f*	Abbremsung	*f*	braking factor	*n*
emballage blister	*m*	Blisterverpackung	*f*	blister pack	*n*
emballer <s'emballer> (moteur à combustion)	*v*	durchgehen (Verbrennungsmotor)	x *v*	speed up out of control (IC engine)	*v*
embase (relais)	*f*	Grundplatte (Relais)	*f*	cap (relay)	*n*
embout d'antiparasitage	*m*	Entstörstecker	*m*	suppressor	*n*
embout de bougie	*m*	Zündkerzenstecker	*m*	spark-plug connector	*n*
embrayage multidisques	*m*	Lamellenkupplung	*f*	multiplate clutch	*n*
empattement (véhicule)	*m*	Achsabstand (Fahrzeug)	*m*	wheelbase (vehicle)	*n*
EMS, commande électronique du moteur	*a*	EGAS, elektronische Motorleistungssteuerung	*a*	ETC, electronic throttle control	*a*
en barillet	*loc*	zylindrische Anordnung	*f*	cylindrical-type	*n*
en V	*loc*	V-Anordnung	*f*	vee-type	*n*
encapsulage antibruit	*m*	Geräuschkapselung	*f*	noise encapsulation	*n*
encapsulage des bagues collectrices	*m*	Schleifringkapselung	*f*	collector-ring housing	*n*
encoche d'autoretard (élément de pompage)	*f*	Startnut (Pumpenelement)	*f*	starting groove (plunger-and-barrel assembly)	*n*
engagement (pignon)	*m*	einspuren (Starterritzel)	*v*	mesh (starter pinion)	*v*
engrènement (pignon)	*m*	einspuren (Starterritzel)	*v*	mesh (starter pinion)	*v*
enregistreur infrarouge à absorption	*m*	Infrarot-Analysator	*m*	infrared analyzer	*n*
enrichir (mélange air-carburant)	*v*	anfetten (Luft-Kraftstoff-Gemisch)	*v*	enrich (air-fuel mixture)	*v*
enrichissement à l'accélération	*m*	Beschleunigungsanreicherung	*f*	acceleration enrichment	*n*
enrichissement après démarrage	*m*	Nachstartanreicherung	*f*	post-start enrichment	*n*
enrichissement au fonctionnement à froid	*m*	Kaltlaufanreicherung	*f*	cold-running enrichment	*n*
enrichissement au réchauffage	*m*	Warmlaufanreicherung	*f*	warm-up enrichment	*n*
enrichissement de départ à froid	*m*	Kaltstartanreicherung	*f*	cold-start enrichment	*n*
enrichissement de mise en action	*m*	Warmlaufanreicherung	*f*	warm-up enrichment	*n*
enrichissement de pleine charge	*m*	Vollastanreicherung	*f*	full-load enrichment	*n*

Français		Allemand		Anglais	
enrichissement de post-démarrage	*m*	Nachstartanreicherung	*f*	post-start enrichment	*n*
enrichissement du mélange	*m*	Gemischanreicherung	*f*	mixture enrichment	*n*
enrobage mou	*m*	Weichverguß	*m*	soft casting	*n*
enroulement à deux couches	*m*	Zweischichtwicklung	*f*	two-layer winding	*n*
enroulement d'appel	*m*	Einzugswicklung	*f*	pull-in winding	*n*
enroulement d'excitation	*m*	Erregerwicklung	*f*	excitation winding	*n*
enroulement d'induction	*m*	Induktionswicklung	*f*	induction coil	*n*
enroulement d'induit	*m*	Ankerwicklung	*f*	armature winding	*n*
enroulement de freinage	*m*	Bremswicklung	*f*	brake winding	*n*
enroulement de maintien	*m*	Haltewicklung	*f*	hold-in winding	*n*
enroulement en dérivation	*m*	Nebenschlußwicklung	*f*	shunt winding	*n*
enroulement en shunt	*m*	Nebenschlußwicklung	*f*	shunt winding	*n*
enroulement multiphases	*m*	Mehrphasenwicklung	*f*	polyphase winding	*n*
enroulement primaire	*m*	Primärwicklung	*f*	primary winding	*n*
enroulement rotorique	*m*	Läuferwicklung	*f*	rotor winding	*n*
enroulement secondaire	*m*	Sekundärwicklung	*f*	secondary winding	*n*
enroulement série	*m*	Reihenschlußwicklung	*f*	series winding	*n*
enroulement statorique	*m*	Ständerwicklung	*f*	stator winding	*n*
enroulement triphasé	*m*	Drehstromwicklung	*f*	three-phase winding	*n*
enroulement-tige	*m*	Stabwicklung	*f*	bar winding	*n*
enrouler (bobine)	*v*	wickeln (Spule)	*v*	wind (coil)	*v*
ensemble d'appareils de freinage	*m*	Gerätegruppe (Druckluftanlagen)	*f*	component group (air-brake systems)	*n*
ensemble de clapet de refoulement (pompe d'injection	*m*	Druckventilhalter (Einspritzpumpe)	*m*	delivery-valve holder (fuel-injection pump)	*n*
ensemble de clapet de refoulement (pompe d'injection	*m*	Druckventil (Einspritzpumpe)	*n*	delivery valve (fuel-injection pump)	*n*
ensemble de pompe d'injection	*m*	Einspritzpumpen-Kombination	*f*	injection-pump assembly	*n*
ensemble de relais	*m*	Relaiskombination	*f*	relay combination	*n*
ensemble de véhicules	*m*	Fahrzeugkombination	*f*	vehicle combination	*n*
ensemble élément-soupape	*m*	Elementverband	*m*	barrel-and-valve assembly	*n*
ensemble injecteur/porte-injecteur	*m*	Düsenhalterkombination, DHK	*f*	nozzle-and-holder assembly	*n*
ensemble intégré au réservoir +	*m*	Tankeinbaueinheit	*f*	in-tank unit	*n*
entraînement de lève-vitre	*m*	Fensterantrieb	*m*	power-window drive	*n*
entraînement du toit ouvrant	*m*	Schiebedachantrieb	*m*	power-sunroof drive unit	*n*
entraînement extérieur	*m*	Fremdantrieb	*m*	external drive	*n*
entraîneur (alternateur)	*m*	Mitnehmer (Generator)	*m*	driver (alternator)	*n*
entraîneur (piston de pompe)	*m*	Kolbenfahne (Pumpenkolben)	*f*	plunger control arm	*n*
entre-électrodes (bougie)	*m*	Elektrodenabstand (Zündkerze)	*m*	electrode gap (spark plug)	*n*
entredent	*m*	Zahnlücke	*f*	tooth space	*n*
entrée analogique	*f*	Analogeingang	*m*	anolog input	*n*
entrée climatiseur	*f*	Klimaeingang (Luftzufuhr Klimakompressor) x	*m*	air-conditioner input	*n*
entrée embrayage	*f*	Kupplungseingang	*m*	clutch input	*n*
entrefer	*m*	Luftspalt	*m*	air gap	*n*

Français

Français		Allemand		Anglais	
entrefer (électrovalve ABS)	*m*	Arbeitsluftspalt (ABS-Magnetventil)	*m*	working air gap (ABS solenoid valve)	*n*
entrefer secondaire	*m*	Sekundärluftspalt	*m*	secondary air gap	*n*
enveloppe	*f*	Hüllkurve	*f*	envelope	*n*
enveloppe à lamelles (bobine d'allumage)	*f*	Mantelblech (Zündspule)	*n*	metal jacket (ignition coil)	*n*
enveloppe d'air (injecteur)	*f*	Luftumfassung (Einspritzventil)	*f*	air-shrouding (fuel injector)	*n*
equipement automobile	*m*	Kraftfahrzeugausrüstung	*f*	automotive equipment	*n*
ergot de butée	*m*	Anschlagnase	*f*	stop lug	*n*
ergot de positionnement	*m*	Fixierstift	*m*	locating pin	*n*
erreur d'initialisation	*f*	Initialisierungsfehler	*m*	initialization error	*n*
ESP, régulation du comportement dynamique	*m*	Fahrdynamikregelung, ESP	*f*	electronic stability program, ESP	*n*
espace mort	*m*	Totraum	*m*	clearance volume	*n*
essai d'endurance	*m*	Dauerlauferprobung	*f*	endurance test	*n*
essai d'étanchéité	*m*	Dichtheitsprüfung	*f*	air-tightness test	*n*
essai d'évaporation (méthode CVS)	*m*	Verdünnungsverfahren (CVS-Methode)	*n*	dilution prodedure (CVS method)	*n*
essai de basse pression (cylindre de roue)	*m*	Niederdruckprüfung (Radzylinder)	*f*	low-pressure test (wheel-brake cylinder)	*n*
essai de dérapage	*m*	Schleuderprüfung	*f*	overspeed test	*n*
essai de fiabilité	*m*	Zuverlässigkeitsprüfung	*f*	reliability test	*n*
essai de freinage	*m*	Bremsenprüfung	*f*	brake testing	*n*
essai de haute pression	*m*	Hochdruckprüfung	*f*	high-pressure test	*n*
essai de niveau sonore	*m*	Geräuschprüfung	*f*	noise-level test	*n*
essai de pression pilote (cylindre de roue)	*m*	Vordruckprüfung (Radzylinder)	*f*	latent-pressure test (wheel-brake cylinder)	*n*
essai des freins	*m*	Bremsprüfung	*f*	brake test	*n*
essai qualitatif	*m*	Qualitätsprüfung	*f*	quality examination	*n*
essais	*mpl*	Prüfumfang	*m*	extent of inspection	*n*
essence	*f*	Ottokraftstoff	*m*	gasoline	*n*
essieu directeur	*m*	Vorlaufachse	*f*	leading axle	*n*
essieu moteur	*m*	Antriebsachse	*f*	powered axle	*n*
essieu moteur (véhicule)	*m*	Achsantrieb (Kfz)	*m*	final drive (motor vehicle)	*n*
essieu relevable	*m*	Liftachse	*f*	lifting axle	*n*
essieu suiveur	*m*	Nachlaufachse	*f*	trailing axle	*n*
essuie-glace	*m*	Scheibenwischer	*m*	windshield wiper	*n*
essuie-glace à balayage opposé	*m*	Gegenlaufsystem (Scheibenwischer)	*n*	opposed-pattern wiper system	*n*
essuie-glace à balayage parallèle	*m*	Gleichlaufsystem (Scheibenwischer)	*n*	tandem-pattern wiper system	*n*
essuie-glace arrière	*m*	Heckwischer	*m*	rear wiper	*n*
essuyage-séchage automatique	*m*	Trockenwisch-Automatik	*f*	automatic wash-and-wipe system	*n*
examen visuel	*m*	Sichtprüfung	*f*	visual examination	*n*
excentrique (valve de frein de stationnement)	*m*	Exzenter (Feststellbremsventil)	*m*	eccentric element (parking-brake valve)	*n*
excentrique compensateur	*m*	Ausgleichexzenter	*m*	compensating eccentric	*n*
excentrique d'entraînement	*m*	Antriebsexzenter	*m*	drive eccentric	*n*

Français		Allemand			Anglais	
excentrique de compensation	*m*	Ausgleichexzenter		*m*	compensating eccentric	*n*
excentrique de réglage	*m*	Verstellexzenter		*m*	adjusting eccentric	*n*
excès d'air	*m*	Luftüberschuß		*m*	excess air	*n*
excitation extérieure (machines tournantes)	*f*	Fremderregung (drehende Maschinen)		*f*	external exitation (rotating machines)	*n*
excitation par aimant permanent	*f*	Permanentmagneterregung		*f*	permanent-magnet excitation	*n*
excitation permanente	*f*	Permanentfeld		*n*	permanent-magnet field	*n*
exploitation avec remorque	*f*	Anhängerbetrieb		*m*	trailer operation	*n*
exploitation de valeur analogique	*f*	Analogwertauswertung		*f*	analog-value evaluation	*n*
extrémité polaire	*f*	Polfinger		*m*	pole finger	*n*
extrudé	*pp*	fließgepreßt		*pp*	extruded	*pp*
É						
éblouissement (projecteur)	*m*	Blendung (Scheinwerfer)		*f*	glare (headlamp)	*n*
écart angulaire de came	*m*	Nockenversatz		*m*	angular cam spacing	*n*
écart de refoulement	*m*	Förderabstand (Pumpenelement)		*m*	phasing (plunger-and-barrel assembly)	*n*
écart de réglage	*m*	Schaltspanne		*f*	operating range	*n*
écart de régulation	*m*	Regelabweichung		*f*	governor deviation	*n*
écartement des électrodes (bougie)	*m*	Elektrodenabstand (Zündkerze)		*m*	electrode gap (spark plug)	*n*
échange de chaleur	*m*	Wärmeaustausch		*m*	heat exchange	*n*
échange standard (rechanges)	*m*	Werksaustausch (Ersatzbedarf)		*m*	factory exchange (replacement requirements)	*n*
échangeur de chaleur (ralentisseur hydrodynamique)	*m*	Wärmetauscher (hydrodynamischer Verlangsamer)		*m*	heat exchanger (hydrodynamic retarder)	*n*
échangeur de pression	*m*	Druckwellenlader		*m*	pressure-wave supercharger	*n*
échappement (moteur à combustion)	*m*	Ausstoßtakt		*m*	exhaust cycle	*n*
échappement d'air (régulateur de pression)	*m*	abblasen (Druckregler)	x	*v*	blow-off (pressure regulator)	*v*
éclairage (automobile)	*m*	Beleuchtung (Kfz)		*f*	lighting (motor vehicle)	*n*
éclairage assisté par ordinateur	*m*	Computer Aided Lighting, CAI		*n*	Computer Aided Lighting, CAI	*n*
éclairage intérieur	*m*	Innenleuchte		*f*	interior light	*n*
éclairage par lampe à gaz rare	*m*	Edelgaslicht		*n*	inert-gas light	*n*
éclairage par lampe à halogène	*m*	Halogenlicht		*n*	halogen-gas light	*n*
éclairage route	*m*	Fernlicht		*n*	high beam	*n*
éclairement	*m*	Ausleuchtung		*f*	illumination	*n*
éclatement de l'étincelle (aux électrodes)	*m*	Funkenüberschlag (an den Elektroden)		*m*	flashover (at electrodes)	*n*
éclateur	*m*	Funkenbahn		*f*	creepage-discharge path	*n*
éclateur à étincelle dans l'air (bougie)	*m*	Luftfunkentechnik (Zündkerze)		*f*	air-gap design (spark plug)	*n*
éclateur dans l'air (bougie)	*m*	Luftfunkenstrecke (Zündkerze)		*f*	spark air gap (spark plug)	*n*
écrou de connexion (bougie)	*m*	Anschlußmutter (Zündkerze)		*f*	terminal nut (spark plug)	*n*
écrou de fixation d'injecteur	*m*	Düsenspannmutter		*f*	nozzle-retaining nut	*n*
écrou-raccord	*m*	Spannmutter		*f*	retaining nut	*n*

Français		Allemand		Anglais	
écrou-raccord d'injecteur	*m*	Düsenspannmutter	*f*	nozzle-retaining nut	*n*
égalisation des débits	*f*	Gleichförderung	*f*	uniformity of fuel delivery	*n*
éjecteur	*m*	Auswerfer	*m*	ejector	*n*
élasticité du moteur	*f*	Motorelastizität (Verbrennungsmotor)	*f*	engine flexibility	*n*
électro-aimant d'engrènement (démarreur)	*m*	Einrückmagnet (Starter)	*m*	starting-motor solenoid (starter)	*n*
électro-aimant d'enrichissement	*m*	Fettzugmagnet	*m*	enrichment solenoid	*n*
électro-aimant de blocage	*m*	Sperrmagnet	*m*	shut-down solenoid	*n*
électro-aimant de commande	*m*	Hubmagnet	*m*	tractive solenoid	*n*
électro-aimant de démarrage	*m*	Startmagnet	*m*	starting solenoid	*n*
électro-aimant de positionnement	*m*	Stellmagnet	*m*	actuator solenoid	*n*
électro-aimant de poussée	*m*	Druckmagnet	*m*	pushing electromagnet	*n*
électro-aimant de traction	*m*	Zugmagnet	*m*	pulling electromagnet	*n*
électrode	*f*	Elektrode	*f*	electrode	*n*
électrode centrale	*f*	Mittelelektrode	*f*	center electrode	*n*
électrode centrale composite (bougie)	*f*	Verbundmittelelektrode (Zündkerze)	*f*	compound center electrode (spark plug)	*n*
électrode centrale en platine (bougie)	*f*	Platinmittelelektrode (Zündkerze)	*f*	platinum center electrode (spark plug)	*n*
électrode composite (bougie)	*f*	Verbundelektrode (Zündkerze)	*f*	compound electrode (spark plug)	*n*
électrode de diffusion	*f*	Sprühelektrode	*f*	discharge electrode	*n*
électrode de masse	*f*	Masseelektrode	*f*	ground electrode	*n*
électrode frontale (bougie)	*f*	Dachelektrode (Zündkerze)	*f*	front electrode (spark plug)	*n*
électrode latérale (bougie)	*f*	Seitenelektrode (Zündkerze)	*f*	side electrode (spark plug)	*n*
électrode négative (batterie)	*f*	Minusplatte (Batterie)	*f*	negative plate (battery)	*n*
électrode positive (batterie)	*f*	Plusplatte (Batterie)	*f*	positive plate (battery)	*n*
électrode spéciale	*f*	Sonderelektrode	*f*	special electrode	*n*
électrolyte	*m*	Elektrolyt	*m*	electrolyte	*n*
électronique de carrosserie	*f*	Karosserie-Elektronik	*f*	body electronics	*n*
électronique de commande	*f*	Ansteuerungselektronik	*f*	drive electronics	*npl*
électronique de confort	*f*	Komfortelektronik	*f*	comfort and convenience electronics	*npl*
électronique de sécurité	*f*	Sicherheitselektronik	*f*	safety and security electronics	*npl*
électrotechnique de carrosserie	*f*	Karosserie-Elektrik	*f*	body electrics	*n*
électrovalve	*f*	Magnetventil	*n*	solenoid valve	*n*
électrovalve d'air secondaire	*f*	Sekundärluftventil	*n*	secondary-air valve	*n*
électrovalve de coupure en décélération	*f*	Schubabschaltventil	*n*	overrun fuel-cutoff valve	*n*
électrovalve de dégazage du réservoir	*f*	Regenerierventil (Abgastechnik)	*n*	canister-purge valve (emissions control technology)	*n*
électrovalve de recyclage des gaz d'échappement	*f*	Abgasrückführventil	*n*	exhaust-gas recirculation (EGR) valve	*n*
électrovalve de régénération (technique des gaz d'échappement)	*f*	Regenerierventil (Abgastechnik)	*n*	canister-purge valve (emissions control technology)	*n*
électrovalve double	*f*	Doppelmagnetventil	*n*	double solenoid-operated valve	*n*

Français		Allemand		Anglais	
électrovalve-relais	f	Magnetrelaisventil	n	solenoid relay valve	n
électrovanne	f	Magnetventil	n	solenoid valve	n
électrovanne à rapport cyclique d'ouverture	f	Taktventil	n	pulse valve	n
électrovanne de cadence	f	Taktventil	n	pulse valve	n
électrovanne de désactivation d'élément	f	Elementabschaltventil (Common Rail)	n	element switchoff valve (common rail)	n
électrovanne de variateur d'avance	f	Spritzversteller-Magnetventil	n	timing-device solenoid valve	n
électrovanne haute pression	f	Hochdruckmagnetventil	n	high-pressure solenoid valve	n
élément à deux orifices	m	Zweilochelement	n	two-port plunger-and-barrel assembly	n
élément à tiroir	m	Hubschieberelement	n	control-sleeve element	n
élément à trou borgne	m	Sacklochelement	n	blind-hole pumping element	n
élément à un orifice	m	Einlochelement	n	single-port plunger-and-barrel assembly	n
élément avec fente de préinjection	m	Split-Element	n	stepped plunger	n
élément chauffant	m	Heizelement	n	heater element	n
élément de commande	m	Stellelement	n	control element	n
élément de correction		Stellelement	n	control element	n
élément de filtre	m	Filtereinsatz	m	filter element	n
élément de mesure	m	Meßelement	n	measuring element	n
élément de pompage (groupe hydraulique ABS)	m	Pumpenelement (ABS-Hydroaggregat)	n	pump element (ABS hydraulic modulator)	n
élément de pompage (pompe d'injection)	m	Pumpenelement (Einspritzpumpe)	n	plunger-and-barrel assembly (fuel-injection pump)	n
élément de pompage à bride	m	Flanschelement	n	barrel-and-flange-element	n
élément de refoulement	m	Pumpenelement (Einspritzpumpe)	n	plunger-and-barrel assembly (fuel-injection pump)	n
élément de suspension (suspension pneumatique)	m	Federelement (Luftfederung)	n	suspension element (air suspension)	n
élément filtrant en papier (filtre à air)	m	Papiereinsatz (Luftfilter)	m	paper element (air filter)	n
élément Hall	m	Hall-Element	n	Hall element	n
élément sensible	m	Sensorelement	n	sensor element	n
élément thermostatique	m	Dehnstoffelement	n	expansion element	n
élévation de tension au démarrage	f	Startspannungsanhebung	f	starting-voltage increase	n
émetteur manuel (alarme auto)	m	Handsender (Autoalarm)	m	hand transmitter (car alarm)	n
émetteur manuel infrarouge (alarme auto)	m	Infrarot-Handsender (Autoalarm)	m	infrared hand transmitter (car alarm)	n
émetteur manuel radio (alarme auto)	m	Funk-Handsender (Autoalarm)	m	radio hand transmitter (car alarm)	n
émission de fumées	f	Rauchstoß	m	cloud of smoke	n
émission de gaz d'échappement	f	Abgasemission	f	exhaust-gas emission	n
émission de particules	f	Partikelemission	f	particulate emission	n
émission de particules de suie	f	Rußemission	f	soot emission	n
émission de polluants	f	Schadstoffausstoß	m	pollutant emission	n
émission quantifiée de polluant	f	gewichtete Schadstoffemission	f	weighted emissions	n

Français		Allemand		Anglais	
émissions d'échappement	*fpl*	Abgas	*n*	exhaust gas	*n*
énergie cinétique	*f*	Bewegungsenergie	*f*	kinetic energy	*n*
énergie d'allumage	*f*	Zündenergie	*f*	ignition energy	*n*
énergie de freinage	*f*	Bremsenergie	*f*	braking energy	*n*
énergie étrangère (commande de frein)	*f*	Fremdkraft (Bremsbetätigung)	*f*	external force (brake control)	*n*
énergie perturbatrice (CEM)	*f*	Störenergie (EMV)	*f*	interference energy (EMC)	*n*
épanouissement polaire	*m*	Polschuh	*m*	pole shoe	*n*
épaulement de centrage	*m*	Zentrierbund	*m*	locating collar	*n*
épaulement de détente	*m*	Entlastungsbund	*m*	relief collar	*n*
épurateur d'air	*m*	Luftreiniger	*m*	air cleaner	*n*
équilibrage de pression	*m*	Druckausgleich	*m*	pressure compensation	*n*
équilibrage des freins	*m*	Bremsabstimmung	*f*	brake calibration	*n*
équipement auxiliaire (remorque)	*m*	Zusatzeinrichtung (Anhängefahrzeuge)	*f*	auxiliary device (trailers)	*n*
équipement d'allumage	*m*	Zündanlage	*f*	ignition system	*n*
équipement d'essuie-glace	*m*	Wischeranlage	*f*	wiper system	*n*
équipement d'injection	*m*	Einspritzausrüstung	*f*	fuel-injection equipment	*n*
équipement de démarrage	*m*	Startanlage	*f*	starting system	*n*
équipement de freinage	*m*	Bremsausrüstung	*f*	braking equipment	*n*
équipement de freinage de la remorque	*m*	Anhängerbremsausrüstung	*f*	trailer braking equipment	*n*
érosion des contacts	*f*	Kontaktabbrand	*m*	contact erosion	*n*
érosion ionique	*f*	Funkenerosion	*f*	spark erosion	*n*
érosion par arc électrique	*f*	Funkenerosion	*f*	spark erosion	*n*
étage de puissance (calculateur)	*m*	Leistungsstufe (Steuergerät)	*f*	power stage (ECU)	*n*
étage de ralenti	*m*	Leerlaufstufe	*f*	idle-speed stage	*n*
étage de sortie (calculateur)	*m*	Leistungsendstufe (Steuergerät)	*f*	driver stage (ECU)	*n*
étage de sortie d'allumage	*m*	Zündungsendstufe	*f*	ignition driver stage	*n*
étage de sortie de débit	*f*	Mengenendstufe	*f*	fuel-quantity power stage	*n*
étage final (calculateur)	*m*	Leistungsendstufe (Steuergerät)	*f*	driver stage (ECU)	*n*
étage multiplicateur (calculateur)	*m*	Multiplizierstufe (elektronisches Steuergerät)	*f*	multiplying stage (ECU)	*n*
étage principal (pompe à accélération périphérique)	*m*	Hauptstufe (Peripheralpumpe)	*f*	main stage (peripheral pump)	*n*
étalonnage de débit	*m*	Mengenabgleich	*m*	fuel-quantity compensation	*n*
étalonnage du débit de démarrage	*m*	Startmengenabgleich	*m*	starting fuel-quantity compensation	*n*
étalonnage multiplicatif	*m*	multiplikativer Abgleich	*m*	multiplicative adjustment	*n*
étancher	*v*	abdichten	*v*	seal	*v*
état de charge de la batterie	*m*	Batterieladezustand	*m*	state of charge (battery)	*n*
état de charge du moteur	*m*	Lastzustand	*m*	load condition	*n*
état de fonctionnement	*m*	Betriebszustand	*m*	operating state	*n*
état de la chaussée	*m*	Fahrbahnbeschaffenheit	*f*	road condition	*n*
étincelle d'allumage	*f*	Zündfunke	*m*	ignition spark	*n*
étincelle dans l'air (bougie)	*f*	Luftfunken (Zündkerze)	*m*	air gap (spark plug)	*n*
étincelle de la bougie	*f*	Zündfunke	*m*	ignition spark	*n*
étincelle de rupture	*f*	Abreißfunke	*m*	contact-breaking spark	*n*

Français		Allemand		Anglais	
étincelle glissante (bougie)	*f*	Luftgleitfunken (Zündkerze)	*m*	surface air-gap (spark plug)	*n*
étranglement à l'admission	*m*	Zulaufdrossel	*f*	input throttle	*n*
étranglement constant (frein moteur)	*m*	Konstantdrossel (Motorbremse)	*f*	constant throttle (engine brake)	*n*
étranglement d'arrivée	*m*	Zulaufdrossel	*f*	input throttle	*n*
étranglement de régénération (dessiccateur)	*m*	Regenerationsdrossel (Lufttrockner)	*f*	regeneration throttle (air drier)	*n*
étranglement de sortie	*m*	Ablaufdrossel	*f*	output throttle	*n*
étranglement de trop-plein	*m*	Überströmdrossel	*f*	overflow restriction	*n*
étranglement fixe	*m*	feste Drossel	*f*	fixed throttle	*n*
étranglement fixe (actionneur de pression)	*m*	Festdrossel (Drucksteller)	*f*	fixed restriction (pressure actuator)	*n*
étranglement transversal	*m*	Querdrossel	*f*	cross throttle	*n*
étrangler	*v*	drosseln	*v*	choke	*v*
étrangleur	*m*	Durchflußdrossel	*f*	flow throttle	*n*
étrier de fixation	*m*	Spannbügel	*m*	hold-down clamp	*n*
étrier de frein à disque	*m*	Bremssattel	*m*	disc-brake caliper	*n*
étrier fixe (frein)	*m*	Festsattel (Bremse)	*m*	fixed caliper (brakes)	*n*
étrier flottant (frein)	*m*	Faustsattel (Bremse)	*m*	floating caliper (brakes)	*n*
étrier monobloc	*m*	Bremssattel	*m*	disc-brake caliper	*n*
évacuation des émulsions	*f*	Mischölabführung	*f*	emulsion drain	*n*
évaluation de la qualité	*f*	Qualitätsbewertung	*f*	quality assessment	*n*
évolution de l'angle de braquage	*f*	Lenkwinkelverlauf	*m*	steering-angle characteristic	*n*
évolution de la préinjection	*f*	Voreinspritzverlauf	*m*	pre-injection characteristic	*n*
évolution de la pression	*f*	Druckverlauf	*m*	pressure characteristic	*n*
évolution de la température	*f*	Temperaturverlauf	*m*	temperature profile	*n*
évolution du débit d'injection	*f*	Fördermengenverlauf	*m*	fuel-delivery characteristics	*npl*
évolution du freinage	*f*	Anbremsvorgang	*m*	initial braking	*n*
évolution en rampe (régulation lambda)	*f*	Rampenverlauf (Lambda-Regelung)	*m*	ramp progression (lambda closed-loop control)	*n*
F					
facteur d'enrichissement (mélange air-carburant)	*m*	Anreicherungsfaktor (Luft-Kraftstoff-Gemisch)	*m*	enrichment factor (air-fuel mixture)	*n*
facteur de bobinage	*m*	Wicklungsfaktor	*m*	winding factor	*n*
facteur de mâchoire (frein)	*m*	Backenkennwert (Bremse)	*m*	shoe factor (brakes)	*n*
facteur de proportionnalité	*m*	Proportionalgrad	*m*	speed droop	*n*
facteur de qualité	*m*	Gütefaktor	*m*	quality factor	*n*
facteur de remplissage des rainures (machines tournantes)	*m*	Nutfüllfaktor (drehende Maschinen)	*m*	slot fill factor (rotating machines)	*n*
fading (frein) x	*m*	Fading (Bremse) x	*n*	fading (brakes)	*n*
faisceau code	*m*	Abblendlicht	*n*	low beam	*n*
faisceau code asymétrique	*m*	asymmetrisches Abblendlicht	*n*	asymmetrical lower beam	*n*
faisceau d'enroulements	*m*	Wicklungsstrang	*m*	phase winding	*n*
faisceau de câblage	*m*	Kabelbaum	*m*	wiring harness	*n*
faisceau de câbles	*m*	Kabelbaum	*m*	wiring harness	*n*
faisceau route	*m*	Fernlicht	*n*	high beam	*n*
fanfare	*f*	Fanfare	*f*	fanfare horn	*n*

Français

Français		Allemand		Anglais	
faux contact	*m*	Wackelkontakt	*m*	loose contact	*n*
faux rond (disque de frein)	*m*	Seitenschlag (Bremsscheibe)	*m*	side runout (brake disc)	*n*
fenêtre de régulation (actionneur de ralenti)	*f*	Stellfenster (Leerlaufsteller)	*n*	actuator window (idle actuator)	*n*
fente annulaire	*f*	Ringspalt	*m*	annular orifice	*n*
fente d'air résiduel	*f*	Restluftspalt	*m*	residual air gap	*n*
fente d'étranglement (injecteur)	*f*	Drosselspalt	*m*	throttling gap	*n*
fente d'étranglement (piston)	*f*	Steuerschlitz	*m*	metering slot	*n*
fente de dosage (KE-Jetronic)	*f*	Zumeßschlitz (KE-Jetronic)	*m*	fuel-metering slit (KE-Jetronic)	*n*
fente du poussoir à galet	*f*	Rollenstößelspalt	*m*	roller-tappet gap	*n*
feu	*m*	Leuchte	*f*	lamp	*n*
feu (véhicule automobile)	*m*	Kraftfahrzeugleuchte	*f*	motor-vehicle lamp	*n*
feu à fonction unique	*m*	Einfunktionsleuchte	*f*	single-function lamp	*n*
feu à plusieurs compartiments	*m*	Mehrkammerleuchte	*f*	multiple-compartment lamp	*n*
feu antibrouillard	*m*	Nebelscheinwerfer, NSW	*m*	fog lamp	*n*
feu arrière	*m*	Schlußleuchte	*f*	tail lamp	*n*
feu arrière de brouillard	*m*	Nebelschlußleuchte	*f*	fog warning lamp	*n*
feu avant	*m*	Frontleuchte	*f*	front lamp	*n*
feu clignotant	*m*	Blinklicht	*n*	turn signal	*n*
feu code	*m*	Abblendlicht	*n*	low beam	*n*
feu d'éclairage de plaque d'immatriculation	*m*	Kennzeichenleuchte	*f*	license-plate lamp	*n*
feu de croisement	*m*	Abblendlicht	*n*	low beam	*n*
feu de croisement asymétrique	*m*	asymmetrisches Abblendlicht	*n*	asymmetrical lower beam	*n*
feu de marche arrière	*m*	Rückfahrscheinwerfer	*m*	backup lamp	*n*
feu de plaque d'immatriculation	*m*	Kennzeichenleuchte	*f*	license-plate lamp	*n*
feu de position	*m*	Begrenzungsleuchte	*f*	side-marker lamp	*n*
feu de recul	*m*	Rückfahrscheinwerfer	*m*	backup lamp	*n*
feu de roulage de jour	*m*	Tagfahrleuchte	*f*	daytime running lamp	*n*
feu de route	*m*	Fernlicht	*n*	high beam	*n*
feu de stationnement	*m*	Parklicht	*n*		
feu de stationnement	*m*	Parkleuchte	*f*	parking lamp	*n*
feu de stop	*m*	Bremsleuchte	*f*	stop lamp	*n*
feu indicateur de changement de direction	*m*	Fahrtrichtungsanzeiger	*m*	direction-indicator lamp	*n*
feu indicateur de direction	*m*	Fahrtrichtungsanzeiger	*m*	direction-indicator lamp	*n*
feu rouge arrière	*m*	Schlußleuchte	*f*	tail lamp	*n*
feu spécial d'avertissement	*m*	Kennleuchte	*f*	identification lamp	*n*
feu spécial de signalisation	*m*	Kennleuchte	*f*	identification lamp	*n*
feu stop	*m*	Bremsleuchte	*f*	stop lamp	*n*
feu stop supplémentaire	*m*	Zusatz-Bremsleuchte	*f*	auxiliary stop lamp	*n*
feu tournant à éclats	*m*	Rundumkennleuchte	*f*	rotating beacon	*n*
feuille conductrice (capteur d'angle de rotation)	*f*	Leiterfolie (Drehwinkelsensor)	*f*	conductive foil (angle of rotation sensor)	*n*
fiabilité d'allumage	*f*	Zündsicherheit	*f*	ignition reliability	*n*
fibre optique	*f*	Lichtwellenleiter	*m*	optical waveguide	*n*
fiche	*f*	Stecker	*m*	connector	*n*

Français

Français		Allemand		Anglais	
fiche femelle	*f*	Steckhülse	*f*	receptable	*n*
fiche femelle ronde	*f*	Rundsteckerhülse	*f*	pin receptable	*n*
fiche plate	*f*	Flachstecker	*m*	blade terminal	*n*
fiche ronde	*f*	Rundstecker	*m*	pin terminal	*n*
fiche secteur	*f*	Netzstecker	*m*	mains plug	*n*
fil chaud (débitmètre massique)	*m*	Hitzdraht (Luftmassenmesser)	*m*	hot wire (air-mass meter)	*n*
fil de bobinage	*m*	Wickeldraht	*m*	winding wire	*n*
fil de cuivre laqué	*m*	Kupferlackdraht	*m*	varnished copper wire	*n*
filament chauffant	*m*	Heizwendel	*f*	helical heating wire	*n*
filament chauffant hélicoïdal	*m*	Heizwendel	*f*	helical heating wire	*n*
filiale	*f*	Tochtergesellschaft	*f*	subsidiary	*n*
filtre (projecteur)	*m*	Lichtfilter	*n*	light filter	*n*
filtre à air	*m*	Luftfilter	*n*	air filter	*n*
filtre à air à bain d'huile	*m*	Ölbadluftfilter	*n*	oil-bath air filter	*n*
filtre à air en papier	*m*	Papierluftfilter	*n*	paper air filter	*n*
filtre à carburant	*m*	Kraftstoffilter	*n*	fuel filter	*n*
filtre à disques	*m*	Spaltfilter	*n*	edge filter	*n*
filtre à étages	*m*	Stufenfilter	*n*	multistage filter	*n*
filtre à huile	*m*	Ölfilter	*n*	lube-oil filter	*n*
filtre à particules	*m*	Rußfilter	*n*	particulate filter	*n*
filtre à rechange rapide	*m*	Wechselfilter	*n*	easy-change filter	*n*
filtre à un étage	*m*	Einfachfilter	*n*	single-stage filter	*n*
filtre antiparasite	*m*	Entstörfilter	*n*	suppression filter	*n*
filtre central	*m*	Zentralfilter	*n*	centrally located air filter	*n*
filtre d'antiparasitage	*m*	Entstörfilter	*n*	suppression filter	*n*
filtre d'aspiration	*m*	Ansaugfilter	*n*	intake filter	*n*
filtre d'entrée	*m*	Eingangsfilter	*n*	input filter	*n*
filtre d'oxidation de particules	*m*	Rußabbrennfilter	*m*	soot burn-off filter	*n*
filtre dans le passage de roue	*m*	Radkastenfilter	*n*	fender-mounted air filter	*n*
filtre de conduite	*m*	Leitungsfilter	*n*	line filter	*n*
filtre en ligne	*m*	Leitungsfilter	*n*	line filter	*n*
filtre en parallèle	*m*	Parallelfilter	*n*	parallel filter	*n*
filtre en profondeur	*m*	Tiefenfilter	*n*	deep-bed filter	*n*
filtre fin	*m*	Feinfilter	*n*	fine filter	*n*
filtre grossier	*m*	Grobfilter	*n*	course filter	*n*
filtre moléculaire (dessiccateur)	*m*	Molekularfilter (Lufttrockner)	*n*	molecular filter (air drier)	*n*
filtre passe-bande	*m*	Bandpaßfilter	*n*	bandpass filter	*n*
filtre passe-bas (calculateur)	*m*	Tiefpaßfilter (Steuergerät)	*n*	low-pass filter (ECU)	*n*
filtre pour particules de suie	*m*	Rußfilter	*n*	particulate filter	*n*
filtre secondaire	*m*	Nachfilter	*n*	secondary filter	*n*
filtre-box	*m*	Boxfilter	*n*	box-type fuel filter	*n*
filtre-box à deux étages	*m*	Stufenboxfilter	*n*	two-stage box-type filter	*n*
filtre-box interchangeable	*m*	Wechselbox (Filter)	*f*	fuel-filter exchange box	*n*
filtre-tamis (pompe d'alimentation)	*m*	Siebfilter (Kraftstofförderpumpe)	*n*	strainer (fuel-supply pump)	*n*
filtre-tige	*m*	Stabfilter	*n*	edge-type filter	*n*
fin d'injection	*f*	Spritzende	*n*	end of injection	*n*

Français

Français		Allemand			Anglais	
fin de combustion	f	Verbrennungsende		n	end of combustion	n
fin de coupure de débit	f	Abregelende		n	end of breakaway	n
fin de freinage	f	Bremsende		n	end of braking	n
fin de refoulement (injection diesel)	f	absteuern (Dieseleinspritzung)		v	fuel-delivery termination (diesel fuel injection)	n
fin de refoulement (pompe d'injection)	f	Förderende (Einspritzpumpe)		n	spill (fuel-injection pump)	n
fin de régulation (injection diesel)	f	abregeln (Dieseleinspritzung)		v	regulate (diesel fuel injection)	v
fixation par bague filetée	f	Gewindehalsbefestigung		f	threaded-neck mounting	n
fixation par base plane	f	Flachbettbefestigung		f	flatbed mounting	n
fixation par bec enfichable (essuie-glace)	f	Steckschnabelbefestigung (Wischer)		f	snap-in nib fastening (wipers)	n
fixation par berceau	f	Sattelbefestigung		f	cradle mounting	n
fixation par bride	f	Flanschbefestigung		f	flange mounting	n
fixation par contre-étrier (essuie-glace)	f	Überfallbügelbefestigung (Wischer)		m	hasp-type fastening (wipers)	n
fixation par crochet (essuie-glace)	f	Hakeneinhängung (Wischer)		f	hook-type fastening (wipers)	n
fixation par enfichage (essuie-glace)	f	Steckbefestigung (Wischer)		f	snap-in fastening (wipers)	n
fixation sur carter	f	Gehäusebefestigung		f	housing mounting	n
flasque côté bagues collectrices (alternateur)	m	Schleifringlagerschild (Generator)		m	collector-ring end shield (alternator)	n
flasque côté collecteur (alternateur)	m	Kommutatorlager (Generator)		n	commutator end shield (alternator)	n
flasque côté entraînement (alternateur)	m	Antriebslagerschild (Generator)		m	drive end shield (alternator)	n
flasque de distribution	m	Verteilerflansch		m	distributor-head flange	n
flexible blindé (bobine d'allumage spéciale)	m	Panzerschlauch (Sonderzündspule)		m	armored hose (special ignition coil)	n
flexible de frein	m	Bremsschlauch		m	brake hose	n
flexible de gonflage des pneus	m	Reifenfüllschlauch		m	tire-inflation hose	n
flexible de pression	m	Druckschlauch		m	pressure hose	n
fluide de refoulement	m	Fördermedium		n	flow medium	n
fluide hydraulique	m	Hydraulikflüssigkeit		f	hydraulic fluid	n
flux d'énergie	m	Energiefluß		m	flow of energy	n
flux de gaz régénérateur	m	Regeneriergasstrom		m	regeneration-gas flow	n
flux de signaux	m	Signalfluß		m	current flow	n
flux lumineux	m	Lichtstrom		m	luminous flux	n
flux magnétique utile	m	Nutzfluß (magnetisch)		m	magnetic flux	n
flux partiel de gaz d'échappement	m	Abgasteilstrom		m	exhaust-gas partial flow	n
fonction "incidentée"	f	Notfahrfunktion		f	limp-home function	n
fonction "mode dégradé"	f	Notfahrfunktion		f	limp-home function	n
fonction d'inclinaison (suspension pneumatique)	f	Kneeling-Funktion (Luftfederung)	x	f	kneeling-function (air suspension)	n
fonction de correction	f	Verstellfunktion		f	adjustment function	n
fonction de dosage	f	Zumeßfunktion		f	metering function	n

Français

Français		Allemand		Anglais	
fonctionnement à vide (régulateur de pression)	*m*	Leerlaufbetrieb (Druckregler)	*m*	idle (pressure regulator)	*v*
fonctionnement autonome	*m*	Selbstlauf	*m*	sustained operation	*n*
fonctionnement continu	*m*	Dauerlauf	*m*	continuous running	*n*
fonctionnement de courte durée (machines électriques)	*m*	Kurzzeitbetrieb (elektrische Maschinen)	*m*	short-time-duty type (electrical machines)	*n*
fonctionnement en mode dégradé	*m*	Notfahrbetrieb	*m*	limp-home operation	*n*
fonctionnement en mode incidenté	*m*	Notfahrbetrieb	*m*	limp-home operation	*n*
fonctionnement instable	*m*	Laufunruhe	*f*	uneven running	*v*
fonctionnement intermittent (machines électriques)	*m*	Aussetzbetrieb (elektrische Maschinen)	*m*	intermittent-periodic duty (electrical machines)	*n*
fonctionnement permanent (machines électriques)	*m*	Dauerbetrieb (elektrische Maschinen)	*m*	continuous-running-duty type (electrical machines)	*n*
fonctionnement polycarburant	*m*	Mehrstoffbetrieb	*m*	multifuel operation	*n*
fonctionnement régulier (moteur à combustion)	*m*	Laufruhe (Verbrennungsmotor)	*f*	smooth running (IC engine)	*n*
fond du cylindre	*m*	Zylinderboden	*m*	cylinder base	*n*
force circonférentielle (roue)	*f*	Umfangskraft (Rad)	*f*	circumferential force (wheel)	*n*
force d'application	*f*	Anpreßkraft	*f*	downforce	*n*
force d'assistance (servofrein)	*f*	Unterstützungskraft (Bremskraftverstärker)	*m*	assisting force (brake booster)	*n*
force d'extraction	*f*	Abzugskraft	*f*	pull-off force	*n*
force de commande	*f*	Betätigungskraft	*f*	control force	*n*
force de couplage (dispositif de freinage électronique-pneumatique)	*f*	Koppelkraft (elektronisch-pneumatisches Bremssystem)	*f*	coupling force (electronic/compressed-air braking system)	*n*
force de déclivité	*f*	Hangabtriebskraft	*f*	downgrade force	*n*
force de fermeture	*f*	Schließkraft	*f*	closing force	*n*
force de fermeture de l'aiguille	*f*	Nadelschließkraft	*f*	needle closing force	*n*
force de freinage	*f*	Bremskraft	*f*	braking force	*n*
force de freinage au roulement des pneumatiques	*f*	Reifenkraft	*f*	tire force	*n*
force de freinage du pneumatique	*f*	Reifenbremskraft	*f*	tire braking force	*n*
force de freinage totale	*f*	gesamte Bremskraft	*f*	total braking force	*n*
force de friction	*f*	Reibkraft	*f*	frictional force	*n*
force de frottement	*f*	Reibungskraft	*f*	friction force	*n*
force de guidage latéral	*f*	Seitenführungskraft	*f*	lateral force	*n*
force de l'air	*f*	Luftkraft	*f*	air force (pneumatics)	*n*
force de piston	*f*	Kolbenkraft	*f*	piston force	*n*
force de propulsion	*f*	Vortriebskraft	*f*	drive force	*n*
force de rappel	*f*	Rückstellkraft	*f*	return force	*n*
force de réaction (systèmes de freinage)	*f*	Reaktionskraft (Bremse)	*f*	reaction force (brakes)	*n*
force de réglage (électrovalve ABS)	*f*	Verstellkraft (ABS-Magnetventil)	*f*	actuating force (ABS solenoid valve)	*n*
force de serrage (garnitures de frein)	*f*	Spannkraft (Bremsbeläge)	*f*	application force (brake linings	*n*

Français			Allemand		Anglais	
force du ressort		f	Federkraft	f	spring force	n
force du vent latéral		f	Seitenwindkraft	f	crosswind force	n
force excédentaire		f	Überschußkraft	f	surplus force	n
force latérale		f	Seitenkraft	f	side force	n
force latérale du pneumatique		f	Reifenseitenkraft	f	lateral tire force	n
force motrice		f	Antriebskraft	f	motive force	n
force musculaire (commande de frein)		f	Muskelkraft (Bremsbetätigung)	f	muscular force (brake control)	n
force normale		f	Normalkraft	f	normal force	n
force verticale du pneumatique		f	Reifenaufstandskraft	f	vertical tire force	n
format de message (multiplexage)		m	Botschaftsformat (CAN)	n	message format (CAN)	n
formation de l'arc (aux électrodes)		f	Funkenüberschlag (an den Elektroden)	m	flashover (at electrodes)	n
formation de suie		f	Rußbildung	f	soot production	n
formation du mélange		f	Gemischaufbereitung	f	mixture formation	n
formation du moment de lacet		f	Giermomentaufbau	m	yaw-moment build-up	n
forme de came		f	Nockenform	f	cam shape	n
forme de la chambre de combustion		f	Brennraumgestaltung	f	combustion-chamber design	n
forme des électrodes		f	Elektrodenform (Zündkerze)	f	electrode shape (spark plug)	n
forme des trous d'injection		f	Lochform (Einspritzdüse)	f	spray-hole shape (injector)	n
forme du collecteur d'admissior		f	Saugrohrgestaltung	f	intake-passage design	n
forme du jet (injection)		f	Strahlform (Einspritzung)	f	spray shape (injection)	n
formule de type		f	Typformel	f	type designation	n
fourchette d'articulation		f	Gelenkgabel	f	link fork	n
fourchette d'engrènement (démarreur)		f	Einrückhebel (Starter)	m	engagement lever (starter)	n
fourreau d'étanchéité (cylindre de roue)		m	Abdichtstulpe (Radzylinder)	f	sealing cap (wheel-brake cylinder)	n
foyer (projecteur)		m	Brennpunkt (Scheinwerfer)	m	focal point (headlamp)	n
frein		m	Bremse	f	brake	n
frein à air comprimé		m	Druckluftbremse	f	compressed-air brake	n
frein à cames		m	Nockenbremse	f	cam brake	n
frein à coin		m	Keilbremse	f	wedge-actuated brake	n
frein à coin d'écartement		m	Keilbremse	f	wedge-actuated brake	n
frein à commande hydraulique		m	hydraulische Bremse	f	hydraulic-actuated brake	n
frein à courants de Foucault		m	elektrodynamischer Verlangsamer	m	electrodynamic retarder	n
frein à disque		m	Scheibenbremse	f	disc brake	n
frein à disque ventilé		m	innenbelüftete Scheibenbremse	f	ventilated disc brake	n
frein à friction		m	Reibungsbremse	f	friction brake	n
frein à mâchoires		m	Backenbremse	f	shoe brake	n
frein à main	x	m	Handbremse	f	hand brake	n
frein à pied	x	m	Betriebs-Bremsanlage	f	service-brake system	n
frein à segments		m	Trommelbremse	f	drum brake	n
frein à segments à expansion interne		m	Innenbackenbremse	f	internal-shoe brake	n

Français

Français		Allemand		Anglais	
frein à tambour	*m*	Trommelbremse	*f*	drum brake	*n*
frein additionnel	*m*	Zusatzbremse	*f*	auxiliary brake	*n*
frein automatique	*m*	automatische Bremse	*f*	automatic brake	*n*
frein d'aiguille (afficheur de banc d'essai)	*m*	Zeigerbremse (Rollenbremsprüfstand)	*f*	indicator lock (dynamic brake analyzer)	*n*
frein de ceinture de sécurité	*m*	Gurtbremse (Sicherheitsgurt)	*f*	seat-belt brake	*n*
frein de différentiel	*m*	Getriebedifferentialbremse	*f*	differential brake	*n*
frein de réaspiration	*m*	Rückströmdrossel, RSD	*f*	return-flow restriction	*n*
frein de remorque	*m*	Anhängerbremse	*f*	trailer brake	*n*
frein de roue	*m*	Radbremse	*f*	wheel brake	*n*
frein de stationnement	*m*	Feststell-Bremsanlage	*f*	parking-brake system	*n*
frein duo-duplex	*m*	Duo-Duplexbremse	*f*	duo-duplex brake	*n*
frein duplex	*m*	Duplexbremse	*f*	duplex brake	*n*
frein électrique (démarreur)	*m*	Strombremse (Starter)	*f*	electric brake (starter)	*n*
frein électrohydraulique, EHB	*m*	elektrohydraulische Bremse, EHB	*f*	electrohydraulic braking system, EHB	*n*
frein moteur	*m*	Auspuffverlangsamer	*m*	exhaust brake	*n*
frein pneumatique	*m*	Druckluftbremse	*f*	compressed-air brake	*n*
frein simplex	*m*	Simplexbremse	*f*	simplex brake	*n*
freinage	*m*	Bremsung	*f*	braking	*n*
freinage automatique	*m*	selbsttätige Bremsung	*f*	automatic braking	*n*
freinage d'arrêt	*m*	Stoppbremsung	*f*	braking to a standstill	*n*
freinage d'urgence	*m*	Vollbremsung	*f*	full braking	*n*
freinage de l'induit	*m*	Ankerabbremsung	*f*	armature braking	*n*
freinage de service	*m*	Betriebsbremsung	*f*	service-brake application	*n*
freinage en situation de panique	*m*	Panikbremsung	*f*	panic braking	*n*
freinage en virage	*m*	Kurvenbremsung	*f*	braking during cornering	*n*
freinage mal réparti	*m*	schiefziehen (Bremse)	x *v*	brake "pull"	*n*
freinage minimal	*m*	Mindestbremswirkung	*f*	minimum braking effect	*n*
freinage partiel	*m*	Teilbremsung	*f*	partial braking	*n*
freinage prolongé	*m*	Dauerbremsung	*f*	continuous braking	*n*
freinage rapide	*m*	Schnellbremsung	*f*	emergency braking	*n*
freiner	*v*	bremsen	*v*	brake	*v*
freins d'un véhicule à moteur	*mpl*	Kraftfahrzeugbremsen	*fpl*	motor-vehicle brakes	*npl*
fréquence d'excitation	*f*	Anregungsfrequenz	*f*	stimulation frequency	*n*
fréquence d'impulsions (allumage)	*f*	Zündfolge	*f*	firing sequence	*n*
fréquence d'oscillation (multivibrateur)	*f*	Kippfrequenz (Multivibrator)	*f*	switching frequency (multivibrator)	*n*
fréquence d'utilisation	*f*	Betriebsfrequenz	*f*	operating frequency	*n*
fréquence de clignotement	*f*	Blinkfrequenz	*f*	flash frequency	*n*
fréquence de résonance	*f*	Resonanzfrequenz	*f*	resonant frequency	*n*
fréquence des impulsions	*f*	Taktfrequenz	*f*	timing frequency	*n*
fréquence limite (régulateur)	*f*	Grenzfrequenz (Regler)	*f*	cutoff frequency (governor)	*n*
fréquence perturbatrice du vilebrequin	*f*	Kurbelwellenstörfrequenz	*f*	crankshaft disturbance frequency	*n*
fréquence propre	*f*	Eigenfrequenz	*f*	natural frequency	*n*
front de flamme	*m*	Flammenfront	*f*	flame front	*n*

Français			Allemand			Anglais	
frottement (piston)		*m*	Reibungsverlust		*m*	friction loss	*n*
frottement au roulement		*m*	Rollreibung		*f*	rolling friction	*n*
frottement de glissement		*m*	Gleitreibung		*f*	sliding friction	*n*
frottement statique (adhérence)		*m*	Haftreibung		*f*	static friction	*n*
fuite		*f*	Leckage	x	*f*	leakage	*n*
fumées blanches		*fpl*	Weißrauch	x	*m*	white smoke	*n*
fumées bleues		*fpl*	Blaurauch	x	*m*	blue smoke	*n*
fumées diesel		*fpl*	Dieselrauch	x	*m*	diesel smoke	*n*
fumées noires		*fpl*	Schwarzrauch		*m*	black smoke	*n*
fumimètre		*m*	Rauchgastester		*m*	smokemeter	*n*
fût d'injecteur		*m*	Düsenschaft		*m*	nozzle stem	*n*
G							
gaine isolante		*f*	Isolierschlauch		*m*	insulating tubing	*n*
galerie d'alimentation (pompe d'injection)		*f*	Saugraum (Einspritzpumpe)		*m*	fuel gallery (fuel-injection pump)	*n*
galet de palpage de la came		*m*	Nockenlaufrolle		*f*	camshaft roller	*n*
galet de poussoir		*m*	Stößelrolle		*f*	tappet roller	*n*
galet de pression (frein à coin)		*m*	Druckrolle (Keilbremse)		*f*	pressure roller (wedge brake)	*n*
gamme de vitesses de rotation		*f*	Drehzahlbereich		*m*	speed range	*n*
garde au sol (véhicule)		*f*	Bodenfreiheit (Kfz)		*f*	ground clearance (motor vehicle)	*n*
garniture		*f*	Dichtmanschette		*f*	cup seal	*n*
garniture anti-poussière		*f*	Staubmanschette		*f*	dust sleeve	*n*
garniture de frein		*f*	Bremsbelag		*m*	brake lining	*n*
garniture de frein à disque		*f*	Scheibenbremsbelag		*m*	disc-brake pad	*n*
garniture de friction		*f*	Reibbelag		*m*	friction lining	*n*
gas-oil		*m*	Dieselkraftstoff		*m*	diesel fuel	*n*
gâteau de filtre	x	*m*	Filterkuchen		*m*	filter cake	*n*
gaz d'échappement		*mpl*	Abgas		*n*	exhaust gas	*n*
gaz de calibrage		*m*	Kalibriergas		*n*	calibrating gas	*n*
gaz de combustion		*mpl*	Verbrennungsgas		*n*	combustion gas	*n*
gaz de fuite		*mpl*	Leckgas		*n*	blowby gas	*n*
gaz de mesure (émissions)		*m*	Meßgas (Abgasprüfung)		*n*	test gas (exhaust-gas test)	*n*
gaz de référence (régulation lambda)		*m*	Referenzgas (Lambda-Regelung)		*n*	reference gas (lambda closed-loop control)	*n*
gaz étalon		*m*	Kalibriergas		*n*	calibrating gas	*n*
gaz frais (moteur à combustion)		*mpl*	Frischgas (Verbrennungsmotor)		*n*	fresh A/F mixture (IC engine)	*n*
gaz neutre (émissions)		*m*	Nullgas (Abgasprüftechnik)		*n*	zero gas (exhaust-gas test)	*n*
gaz résiduels		*mpl*	Restgas		*n*	residual exhaust gas	*n*
gaz zéro (émissions)		*m*	Nullgas (Abgasprüftechnik)		*n*	zero gas (exhaust-gas test)	*n*
gazole		*m*	Dieselkraftstoff		*m*	diesel fuel	*n*
générateur à induction (allumage)		*m*	Induktionsgeber (Zündung)		*m*	induction-type pulse-generator (ignition)	*n*
générateur acoustique (alarme auto)		*m*	Schallgeber (Autoalarm)		*m*	sonic generator (car alarm)	*n*
générateur d'impulsions		*m*	Impulsgeber		*m*	pulse generator	*n*
générateur de gaz (coussin gonflable)		*m*	Gasgenerator (Airbag)		*m*	gas inflator (airbag)	*n*

Français		Allemand		Anglais	
générateur de Hall	m	Hall-Sensor	m	Hall generator	n
générateur de pression (ASR)	m	Druckversorgung (ASR)	f	pressure generator (TCS)	n
génération d'énergie	f	Energieversorgung	f	energy supply	n
génératrice	f	Generator	m	generator	n
génératrice de courant continu	f	Gleichstromgenerator	m	direct-current generator	n
géométrie de came	f	Nockenform	f	cam shape	n
géométrie variable de turbine	f	variable Turbinengeometrie	f	variable turbine geometry	n
gestion de projet	f	Projektmanagement	n	project management	n
gestion des fonctions du moteur	f	Motormanagement	f	engine management	n
gestion du moteur	f	Motormanagement	f	engine management	n
gicleur (lavophare)	m	Spritzdüse (Scheibenwaschanlage)	f	nozzle (windshield washer)	n
gicleur d'aspiration	m	Saugdrossel	f	suction throttle	n
gicleur de départ à froid	m	Kaltstartdüse	f	starting nozzle	n
glace de diffusion (feu)	f	Lichtscheibe (Leuchte)	f	lens (lamp)	n
glace de porte-injecteur	f	Düsenhalter-Zwischenscheibe	f	adapter plate (nozzle holder)	n
glissant	adj	rutschig	adj	slippery	adj
glissement	m	Gleitvorgang	m	slip	n
glissement (pneu)	m	Reifenschlupf	m	tire slip	n
glissement (roue)	m	Schlupf (Rad)	m	wheel slip	n
glissement au freinage	m	Bremsschlupf	m	brake slip	n
glissière (tête d'accouplement)	f	Klauenführung (Kupplungskopf)	f	claw guide (coupling head)	n
gommer (pneu) x	v	radieren (Reifen) x	v	drag (tire) x	v
gonflement des élastomères (liquide de frein)	m	Elastomerquellung (Bremsflüssigkeit)	f	elastomer swelling (brake fluid)	n
gorge annulaire	f	Ringnut	f	ring groove	n
gouttelette de carburant	f	Kraftstofftröpfchen	n	fuel droplet	n
grandeur convergente	f	Hilfssteuergröße	f	auxiliary actuating variable	n
grandeur d'entrée	f	Eingangsgröße	f	input variable	n
grandeur de correction	f	Stellgröße	f	manipulated variable	n
grandeur perturbatrice (régulation)	f	Störgröße (Regelung und Steuerung)	f	disturbance value (regulation and control)	n
grandeur réglante	f	Stellgröße	f	manipulated variable	n
grandeur réglée	f	Regelgröße	f	controlled variable (closed-loop control)	n
granulat (dessiccateur)	m	Trockenmittel (Lufttrockner)	n	desiccant (air drier)	n
griffe (tête d'accouplement)	f	Klaue (Kupplungskopf)	f	claw (coupling head)	n
griffe de palonnier (essuie-glace)	f	Bügelkralle (Wischer)	f	bracket clamp (wipers)	n
grille de plomb (batterie)	f	Bleigitter (Batterie)	n	lead grid (battery)	n
grille métallique (catalyseur)	f	Metallgeflecht (Katalysator)	n	metal mesh (catalytic converter)	n
grincement (frein)	m	quietschen (Bremse)	v	squeal (brakes)	v
grippage de piston	m	Kolbenfresser	m	piston seizure	n
groupe auxiliaire	m	Nebenaggregat	n	auxiliary system	n
groupe d'adaptation	m	Anpaßeinrichtung	f	add-on module	n
groupe d'injecteurs	m	Einspritzventilgruppe	f	injection-valve group	n
groupe de freinage	m	Bremsgerätegruppe	f	brake-component group	n

Français

Français		Allemand		Anglais	
groupe de freinage à double circuit	*m*	Zweikreis-Bremsgerät	*n*	dual-circuit brake assembly	*n*
groupe de leviers	*m*	Hebelverband	*m*	lever assembly	*n*
groupe de ronflement	*m*	Schnarrgruppe	*f*	chatter group	*n*
groupe doseur-distributeur	*m*	Mengenteilerblock	*m*	fuel-distributor block	*n*
groupe électropompe	*m*	elektro-hydraulische Pumpe	*f*	electro-hydraulic pump	*n*
groupe hydraulique (ABS)	*m*	Hydroaggregat (ABS)	*n*	hydraulic modulator (ABS)	*n*
guidage du véhicule	*m*	Fahrzeugführung	*f*	vehicle handling	*n*
guide de parcage	*m*	Park-Pilot	*m*	Park Pilot	*n*
guide-aiguille	*m*	Nadelführung	*f*	needle guide	*n*
guide-coulisse (injection diesel)	*m*	Kulissenführung (Diesel-Regler)	*f*	sliding-block guide (governor)	*n*
guipé (courroie trapézoïdale)	*pp*	ummantelt (Keilriemen)	*pp*	sheathed (V-belt)	*pp*
gyrophare	*m*	Rundumkennleuchte	*f*	rotating beacon	*n*
H					
homologation	*f*	Homologation	*f*	homologation	*n*
homologation générale	*f*	Allgemeine Betriebserlaubnis, ABE	*f*	General Certification	*n*
horamètre électronique	*m*	Laufzeitelektronik	*f*	elapsed-time electronics	*n*
huile d'essai	*f*	Prüföl	*n*	calibrating oil	*n*
humidification des parois (collecteur d'admission)	*f*	Wandfilmbildung (Saugrohr)	*f*	manifold-wall fuel condensation	*n*
hystérésis du freinage	*f*	Bremshysterese	*f*	braking hysteresis	*n*
I					
identificateur de capteur	*m*	Geberkennwort	*n*	sensor ID	*n*
identification des bornes	*f*	Klemmenbezeichnung	*f*	terminal designation	*n*
impédance de champ	*f*	Feldwiderstand	*m*	field resistor	*n*
impulsion d'allumage	*f*	Zündimpuls	*m*	ignition pulse	*n*
impulsion d'injection	*f*	Einspritzimpuls	*m*	injection pulse	*n*
impulsion de commande (calculateur)	*f*	Steuerimpuls (Steuergerät)	*m*	control pulse (ECU)	*n*
impulsion de contrôle	*f*	Prüfimpuls	*m*	test pulse	*n*
impulsion de test	*f*	Prüfimpuls	*m*	test pulse	*n*
impulsion rectangulaire (calculateur)	*f*	Rechteckimpuls (Steuergerät)	*m*	square-wave pulse (ECU)	*n*
incandescence permanente	*f*	dauerglühen	*v*	continuous glowing	*v*
incompatibilité avec l'environnement	*f*	Umweltbelastung	*f*	environmental impact	*n*
incontrôlable (véhicule)	*adj*	lenkunfähig (Kfz)	*adj*	unsteerable (motor vehicle)	*adj*
incrément de débit	*m*	Mengeninkrement	*n*	fuel-quantity increment	*n*
incrément de débit en fonction de la température	*m*	temperaturabhängiges Mengeninkrement	*n*	temperature-dependent quantity increment	*n*
indétonance	*f*	Klopffestigkeit	*f*	antiknock quality	*n*
indicateur de charge	*m*	Ladezustandsanzeige	*f*	charge indicator	*n*
indicateur de consommation	*m*	Verbrauchsmodul	*m*	consumption meter	*n*
indicateur de course de régulation	*m*	Regelweganzeige	*f*	rack-travel indication	*n*
indicateur de défauts	*m*	Fehleranzeige	*f*	fault display	*n*

Français

Français		Allemand		Anglais	
indicateur de disponibilité de démarrage (moteur diesel)	*m*	Startbereitschaftsanzeige (Dieselmotor)	*f*	ready-to-start indicator (diesel engine)	*n*
indicateur-avertisseur de pression	*m*	Warndruckanzeiger	*m*	low-pressure indicator	*n*
indication de changement de direction	*f*	Fahrtrichtungsblinken	*n*	direction-indicator signal	*n*
indice caractéristique du degré thermique (bougie)	*m*	Wärmewertkennzahl (Zündkerze)	*f*	heat-range code number (spark plug)	*n*
indice d'octane	*m*	Oktanzahl, OZ	*f*	octane number	*n*
indice d'octane moteur, MON	*m*	Motor-Oktanzahl, MOZ	*f*	motor octane number, MON	*n*
indice d'octane recherche, RON	*m*	Research-Oktanzahl, ROZ	*f*	research octane number, RON	*n*
indice de cétane	*m*	Cetanzahl, CZ	*f*	cetane number, CN	*n*
indice de montage	*m*	Montagezahl	*f*	assembly number	*n*
indice de noircissement	*m*	Schwärzungszahl	*f*	smoke number	*n*
indice de noircissement Bosch	*m*	Bosch-Schwärzungszahl, BSZ	*f*	Bosch black-smoke number	*n*
indices des acides (batterie)	*mpl*	Säurewerte (Batterie)	*fpl*	electrolyte values (battery)	*npl*
induit (machines tournantes)	*m*	Anker (umlaufende Maschinen)	*m*	armature (rotating machines)	*n*
induit du moteur (pompe électrique à carburant)	*m*	Motoranker (Elektrokraftstoffpumpe)	*m*	motor armature (electric fuel pump)	*n*
induit rotatif	*m*	Drehanker	*m*	rotating armature	*n*
inertie du moteur	*f*	Motorträgheit	*f*	engine inertia	*n*
inflammabilité	*f*	Zündwilligkeit	*f*	ignition quality	*n*
inflammable	*adj*	zündwillig	*adj*	ignitable	*adj*
inflammation (allumage)	*f*	Zündung	*f*	ignition	*n*
information de production	*f*	Fertigungshinweis	*m*	manufacturing information	*n*
initialisation de la centrale de commande	*f*	Steuergeräteinitialisierung	*f*	control-unit initialization	*n*
initiateur de refoulement	*m*	lastabhängiger Förderbeginn, LFB	*m*	load-dependent start of delivery	*n*
injecteur	*m*	Einspritzventil	*n*	fuel injector	*n*
injecteur "Common Rail"	*m*	Common Rail Injektor	*m*	common-rail injector	*n*
injecteur (injection diesel)	*m*	Einspritzdüse	*f*	nozzle (diesel fuel injection)	*n*
injecteur (système "Common Rail")	*m*	Injektor (Common Rail)	*m*	injector (common rail)	*n*
injecteur à aiguille	*m*	Nadelventil	*n*	needle valve	*n*
injecteur à deux aiguilles	*m*	Doppelnadeldüse	*f*	twin-needle nozzle	*n*
injecteur à fente	*m*	Spaltlochdüse	*f*	hole-type nozzle gap	*n*
injecteur à flux axial	*m*	Einspritzventil mit axialer Zuführung ("Top-Feed")	*n*	top-feed injector	*n*
injecteur à flux radial	*m*	Einspritzventil mit radialer Zuführung ("Bottom-Feed")	*n*	bottom-feed injector	*n*
injecteur à portée oblique	*m*	Schrägschulter-Düse	*f*	chamfered-shoulder nozzle	*n*
injecteur à siège perforé	*m*	Sitzlochdüse	*f*	sac-less (vco) nozzle	*n*
injecteur à téton	*m*	Zapfendüse	*f*	pintle nozzle	*n*
injecteur à téton et étranglemen	*m*	Drosselzapfendüse	*f*	throttling pintle nozzle	*n*
injecteur à téton perforé	*m*	Lochzapfendüse	*f*	hole pintle nozzle	*n*
injecteur à téton plan	*m*	Flächenzapfendüse	*f*	flatted pintle nozzle	*n*
injecteur à trou borgne	*m*	Sacklochdüse	*f*	blind-hole nozzle	*n*
injecteur à trou(s)	*m*	Lochdüse	*f*	hole-type nozzle	*n*

Français

Français		Allemand		Anglais	
injecteur bi-jet	*m*	Zweistrahlventil	*n*	dual-stream injector	*n*
injecteur d'essai	*m*	Prüfdüse	*f*	calibrating nozzle	*n*
injecteur de départ à froid	*m*	Kaltstartventil	*n*	cold-start valve	*n*
injecteur de série	*m*	Seriendüse	*f*	standard nozzle	*n*
injecteur monojet à téton et étranglement	*m*	Einstrahl-Drosselzapfendüse	*f*	single-jet throttling-pintle nozzle	*n*
injecteur monotrou	*m*	Einstrahldüse	*f*	single-hole nozzle	*n*
injecteur multitrous	*m*	Mehrlochdüse	*f*	multihole nozzle	*n*
injecteur Pintaux	*m*	Pintaux-Düse	*f*	Pintaux-type nozzle	*n*
injecteur sans retour de fuite	*m*	lecköllose Düse	*f*	non-leak-off nozzle	*n*
injecteur-conduite-pompe	*m*	Pumpe-Leitung-Düse, UPS	*f*	unit pump system, UPS	*n*
injecteur-étalon	*m*	Prüfdüse	*f*	calibrating nozzle	*n*
injecteur-pompe	*m*	Pumpe-Düse-Einheit, UIS	*f*	unit injector system, UIS	*n*
injection (opération)	*f*	Einspritzvorgang	*m*	injection process	*n*
injection (procédé)	*f*	Kraftstoffeinspritzung	*f*	fuel injection	*n*
injection centralisée	*f*	Zentraleinspritzung	*f*	single-point fuel injection	*n*
injection d'essence	*f*	Benzineinspritzung	*f*	gasoline injection	*n*
injection de carburant	*f*	Kraftstoffeinspritzung	*f*	fuel injection	*n*
injection diesel	*f*	Dieseleinspritzung	*f*	diesel fuel injection, DFI	*n*
injection directe	*f*	Direkteinspritzung (Dieselmotor)	*f*	direct injection, DI	*n*
injection directe diesel	*f*	Dieseldirekteinspritzung	*f*	diesel direct injection	*n*
injection directe essence	*f*	Benzindirekteinspritzung, BDE	*f*	gasoline direct injection	*n*
injection électronique d'essence, Jetronic	*f*	Jetronic (elektronische Benzineinspritzung)	*f*	Jetronic (electronic fuel injection)	*n*
injection groupée	*f*	Gruppeneinspritzung	*f*	group injection	*n*
injection haute pression	*f*	Hochdruckeinspritzung	*f*	high-pressure fuel injection	*n*
injection indirecte	*f*	indirekte Einspritzung, IDI	*f*	indirect injection, IDI	*n*
injection intermittente de carburant	*f*	intermittierende Kraftstoffeinspritzung	*f*	intermittent fuel injection	*n*
injection monopoint	*f*	Zentraleinspritzung	*f*	single-point fuel injection	*n*
injection multipoint	*f*	Einzeleinspritzung	*f*	multipoint fuel injection, MPI	*n*
injection pilote	*f*	Voreinspritzung	*f*	pilot injection	*n*
injection principale	*f*	Haupteinspritzung	*f*	main injection	*n*
injection retardée	*f*	Nachspritzer (Dieseleinspritzung)	*m*	dribble (diesel fuel injection)	*n*
injection secondaire	*f*	Nacheinspritzung	*f*	secondary injection	*n*
insensible à l'inversion de polarité	*loc*	verpolungssicher	*adj*	insensitive to reverse polarity	*adj*
insensible au court-circuit	*loc*	kurzschlußsicher	*adj*	insensitive to short-circuit	*adj*
insensible aux secousses (batterie)	*loc*	rüttelfest (Batterie)	*adj*	vibration-proof (battery)	*adj*
insert de jambe de suspension	*m*	Federbeineinsatz	*m*	spring strut insert	*n*
inspection générale	*f*	Hauptuntersuchung, HU	*f*	general inspection	*n*
inspection intermédiaire (frein)	*f*	Zwischenuntersuchung, ZU (Bremse)	*f*	intermediate inspection (brakes	*n*
instabilité de fonctionnement	*f*	Laufunruhe	*f*	uneven running	*v*
installation de contrôle (émissions)	*f*	Abgasprüfzelle	*f*	emissions test cell	*n*

Français		Allemand		Anglais	
instruction de commande (calculateur)	*f*	Steuerbefehl (Steuergerät)	*m*	control command (ECU)	*n*
instruction de montage	*f*	Montagehinweis	*m*	assembly instructions	*n*
instruction de pilotage (calculateur)	*f*	Steuerbefehl (Steuergerät)	*m*	control command (ECU)	*n*
instructions d'essai	*fpl*	Prüfvorschrift	*f*	test regulations	*npl*
instructions d'utilisation	*fpl*	Bedienungsanleitung	*f*	operating instructions	*npl*
instrument du poste de pilotage	*m*	Cockpit-Instrument	*n*	cockpit instrument	*n*
insufflation d'air secondaire	*f*	Sekundärlufteinblasung	*f*	secondary-air injection	*n*
intégrateur de ralenti	*m*	Leerlaufintegrator	*m*	low-idle integrator	*n*
intégrateur de régulation poste à poste	*m*	Laufruheintegrator	*m*	cylinder-balancing integrator	*n*
intensité lumineuse	*f*	Lichtstärke	*f*	luminous intensity	*n*
intensité nominale	*f*	Sollstrom	*m*	nominal current	*n*
interface	*f*	Schnittstelle	*f*	interface	*n*
interface de diagnostic (systèmes électroniques)	*f*	Diagnoseschnittstelle (elektronische Systeme)	*f*	diagnosis interface (electronic systems)	*n*
intérieur de la pompe	*m*	Pumpenraum	*m*	pump interior	*n*
interrupteur à bouton poussoir	*m*	Wischintervallschalter	*m*	intermittent-wiper switch	*n*
interrupteur à clé (alarme auto)	*m*	Schlüsselschalter (Autoalarm)	*m*	key-operated switch (car alarm)	*n*
interrupteur à retour automatique	*m*	Tastschalter	*m*	non-locking switch	*n*
interrupteur à retour non automatique	*m*	Stellschalter	*m*	detent switch	*n*
interrupteur à tirette (alarme auto)		Zugschalter	*m*	pull switch	*n*
interrupteur à touche	*m*	Tastschalter	*m*	non-locking switch	*n*
interrupteur de circuit	*m*	Leistungsschalter	*m*	circuit breaker	*n*
interrupteur principal pour batterie	*m*	Batterieschalter	*m*	battery master switch	*n*
interrupteur-témoin de rapport de vitesse	*m*	Ganganzeigeschalter	*m*	gear-indicator switch	*n*
intervention par positionnement	*f*	Stelleingriff	*m*	actuator adjustment	*n*
intervention sur l'allumage	*f*	Zündungseingriff	*m*	ignition adjustment	*n*
intervention sur le moteur (ASR)	*f*	Motoreingriff (ASR)	*m*	engine intervention (TCS)	*n*
intervention sur le papillon (ASR)	*f*	Drosselklappeneingriff (ASR)	*m*	throttle-valve intervention (TCS)	*n*
intervention sur les freins (ASR)	*f*	Bremseneingriff (ASR)	*m*	brake application (TCS)	*n*
inverseur des clignotants	*m*	Blinkerschalter	*m*	turn-signal switch	*n*
inverseur des feux clignotants	*m*	Blinkerschalter	*m*	turn-signal switch	*n*
inversion du courant	*f*	Kommutierung	*f*	commutation	*n*
isolant (bougie)	*m*	Isolator (Zündkerze)	*m*	insulator (spark plug)	*n*
isolateur (bobine d'allumage)	*m*	Isolierkörper (Zündspule)	*m*	insulator (ignition coil)	*n*
isolateur de vibrations	*m*	Schwingungsdämpfer	*m*	vibration damper	*n*
isolation	*f*	Isolierung	*f*	insulation	*n*
isolation acoustique	*f*	Schallisolierung	*f*	soundproofing	*n*
isolation thermique (injecteur)	*f*	Wärmeschutz (Einspritzdüse)	*m*	heat shield (nozzle)	*n*

Français		Allemand			Anglais	
isolement (redressement)	*m*	Rückstromsperre (Gleichrichtung)		*f*	reverse-current block (rectification)	*n*
J						
jambe de suspension	*f*	Federbein		*n*	spring strut	*n*
jauge "bon/mauvais"	*f*	Gut-Schlechtlehre		*f*	go/no-go gauge	*n*
jauge (bougie)	*f*	Zündkerzenlehre		*f*	spark-plug-gap gauge	*n*
jauge à carburant	*f*	Kraftstoffanzeiger		*m*	fuel gauge	*n*
jauge de contrainte	*f*	Dehnmeßstreifen		*m*	strain gage	*n*
jauge de niveau	*f*	Füllstandsanzeige		*f*	fuel-level indicator	*n*
jet	*m*	Düsenstrahl (vor der Auflösung)		*m*	nozzle jet	*n*
jet conique	*m*	Kegelstrahl		*m*	tapered spray	*n*
jet d'injection	*m*	Einspritzstrahl		*m*	injection jet	*n*
jet de décharge	*m*	Absteuerstrahl		*m*	cutoff jet	*n*
jet pulvérisé	*m*	Düsenstrahl (aufgelöst)		*m*	spray	*n*
Jetronic (injection électronique d'essence)	*m*	Jetronic (elektronische Benzineinspritzung)		*f*	Jetronic (electronic fuel injection)	*n*
jeu (segments de frein)	*m*	Lüftspiel (Bremsbacken)		*n*	clearance (brake shoes)	*n*
jeu d'équipement ultérieur	*m*	Nachrüstsatz		*m*	supplementary-equipment set	*n*
jeu d'extrémité supérieure (piston)	*m*	Sicherheitsabstand (Kolbenkopf)		*m*	head clearance (piston)	*n*
jeu de balais	*m*	Kohlebürstensatz		*m*	carbon-brush set	*n*
jeu de câbles d'allumage	*m*	Zündleitungssatz		*m*	ignition-cable set	*n*
jeu de ceinture de sécurité	*m*	Gurtlose (Sicherheitsgurt)	x	*f*	seat-belt slack	*n*
jeu de contacts (allumage)	*m*	Kontaktsatz (Zündung)		*m*	contact set (ignition)	*n*
jeu de contacts d'allumage	*m*	Zündkontaktsatz		*m*	contact set	*n*
jeu de mâchoires de frein	*m*	Bremsbackensatz		*m*	brake-shoe set	*n*
jeu de ressorts	*m*	Federpaket		*n*	spring assembly	*n*
jeu de rouleaux (banc d'essai)	*m*	Rollensatz (Rollenbremsprüfstand)		*m*	roller set (dynamic brake analyzer)	*n*
jeu en tête (élément de pompage)	*m*	Kopfspiel (Pumpenelement)		*n*	head clearance (plunger-and-barrel assembly)	*n*
jeu entre dents (engrenage)	*m*	Flankenspiel (Zahnrad)		*n*	backlash (gear)	*n*
joint embouti (cylindre de roue)	*m*	Topfmanschette (Radzylinder)		*f*	cup seal (wheel-brake cylinder)	*n*
joint prisonnier (bougie)	*m*	unverlierbarer Dichtring (Zündkerze)		*m*	captive gasket (spark plug)	*n*
K						
kit batterie	*m*	Batterie-Set		*n*	battery set	*n*
kit d'accessoires	*m*	Zubehörsatz		*m*	accessory set	*n*
kit d'équipement ultérieur	*m*	Nachrüstsatz		*m*	supplementary-equipment set	*n*
kit d'étrier de frein	*m*	Bremssattel-Set		*n*	brake caliper set	*n*
kit de démarrage rapide (véhicules diesel)	*m*	Schnellstart-Satz (Dieselfahrzeuge)		*m*	rapid starting kit (diesel vehicles)	*n*
kit de pièces	*m*	Teilesatz		*m*	parts set	*n*
kit de remise en état	*m*	Reparatursatz		*m*	repair kit	*n*
L						
lacet (véhicule)	*m*	gieren (Kfz)	x	*v*	yaw (motor vehicle)	*v*
lame d'air	*f*	Luftspalt		*m*	air gap	*n*

Français		Allemand		Anglais	
lame flexible	*f*	Federschiene	*f*	spring strip	*n*
lame piézocéramique	*f*	Piezokeramikstreifen	*m*	piezo-ceramic strip	*n*
lame racleuse	*f*	Wischgummi	*n*	wiper-blade element	*n*
lame-ressort	*f*	Federschiene	*f*	spring strip	*n*
lamelle centrale (alternateur)	*f*	Mittellamelle (Generator)	*f*	center lamination (alternator)	*n*
lampe	*f*	Leuchtkörper	*m*	light source	*n*
lampe à décharge dans un gaz	*f*	Gasentladungslampe	*f*	gaseous-discharge lamp, GDL	*n*
lampe à halogène	*f*	Halogenlampe	*f*	halogen lamp	*n*
lampe à iode	+ *f*	Halogenlampe	*f*	halogen lamp	*n*
lampe de diagnostic	*f*	Diagnoselampe	*f*	diagnosis lamp	*n*
lampe de lecture	*f*	Leseleuchte	*f*	reading lamp	*n*
lampe de marchepied	*f*	Trittstufenleuchte	*f*	step light	*n*
lampe de signalisation	*f*	Informationslampe	*f*	indicator lamp	*n*
lampe de tableau de bord	*f*	Instrumentenleuchte	*f*	instrument-panel lamp	*n*
lampe de travail	*f*	Arbeitsleuchte	*f*	working lamp	*n*
lampe témoin	*f*	Funktionskontrolleuchte	*f*	function lamp	*n*
lampe témoin d'alternateur	*f*	Generatorkontrolleuchte	*f*	charge-indicator lamp	*n*
lampe témoin de charge	*f*	Generatorkontrolleuchte	*f*	charge-indicator lamp	*n*
lampe témoin de fonctionnement (ABS)	*f*	ABS-Funktionskontrolleuchte	*f*	ABS indicator lamp	*n*
lancement (moteur à combustion)	*m*	durchdrehen (Verbrennungsmotor)	x *v*	cranking (IC engine)	*n*
lanceur	*m*	Einspurgetriebe	*n*	pinion-engaging drive	*n*
lanceur (à roue libre)	*m*	Freilaufgetriebe (Starter)	*n*	overrunning clutch (starter)	*n*
lanterne (vehicule automobile)	*f*	Kraftfahrzeugleuchte	*f*	motor-vehicle lamp	*n*
lanterne à deux compartiments	*f*	Zweikammerleuchte	*f*	two-chamber lamp	*n*
lanterne à trois compartiments	*f*	Dreikammerleuchte	*f*	three-chamber lamp	*n*
laque à base de poudre	*f*	Pulverlack	*m*	powder-based paint	*n*
lave-glace	*m*	Scheibenspüler	*m*	windshield washer	*n*
lave/essuie-projecteur	*m*	Wisch-Wasch-Anlage (Scheinwerfer)	*f*	wipe/wash system (headlamp)	*n*
lavophare	*m*	Lichtwischer	*m*	headlamp wiper	*n*
lavophare	*m*	Lichtwischeranlage	*f*	beamwash	*n*
lavophare complet	*m*	Scheinwerfer-Waschanlage	*f*	headlamp washer system	*n*
législation	*f*	gesetzliche Vorschriften	*fpl*	legal requirements	*npl*
législation antipollution	*f*	Abgasgesetzgebung	*f*	emission-control legislation	*n*
lève-vitre	*m*	Fensterheber	*m*	power-window unit	*n*
levée d'excentrique	*f*	Exzenterhub	*m*	eccentric lift	*n*
levée de came	*f*	Nockenhub	*m*	cam pitch	*n*
levée de l'aiguille	*f*	Nadelhub	*m*	needle lift	*n*
lévée de soupape	*f*	Ventilhub	*m*	valve lift	*n*
levier à coulisse (régulateur diesel)	*m*	Regelhebel (Diesel-Regler)	*m*	variable-fulcrum lever (governor)	*n*
levier à fourche (démarreur)	*m*	Gabelhebel (Starter)	*m*	fork lever (starter)	*n*
levier à fourchette de commande	*m*	Einrückhebel (Starter)	*m*	engagement lever (starter)	*n*
levier à rotule	*m*	Kniehebel	*m*	toggle lever	*n*
levier articulé	*m*	Lenkhebel	*m*	linkage lever	*n*

Français		Allemand		Anglais	
levier coudé	*m*	Winkelhebel	*m*	bell crank	*n*
levier culbuteur (commande de soupapes)	*m*	Standard-Kipphebel (Ventiltrieb)	*m*	standard rocker arm (valve gear)	*n*
levier d'arrêt	*m*	Abstellhebel	*m*	stop (shutoff) lever	*n*
levier d'engrènement	*m*	Einrückhebel (Starter)	*m*	engagement lever (starter)	*n*
levier de balayage (nettoyeur de projecteurs)	*m*	Wischhebel (Scheinwerfer-Reinigungsanlage)	*m*	wiper arm (headlamp cleaning system)	*n*
levier de butée (pompe d'injection en ligne)	*m*	Anschlaghebel (Reiheneinspritzpumpe)	*m*	stop lever (in-line pump)	*n*
levier de commande (pompe d'injection en ligne)	*m*	Verstellhebel (Reiheneinspritzpumpe)	*m*	control lever (in-line pump)	*n*
levier de correction de débit	*m*	Angleichhebel	*m*	torque-control lever	*n*
levier de démarrage	*m*	Starthebel	*m*	starting lever	*n*
levier de frein	*m*	Bremshebel	*m*	brake lever	*n*
levier de guidage	*m*	Führungshebel	*m*	guide lever	*n*
levier de lavophare	*m*	Lichtwischerhebel	*m*	beamwash wiper-lever	*n*
levier de manoeuvre	*m*	Betätigungshebel	*m*	actuating lever	*n*
levier de positionnement (pompe d'injection en ligne à tiroirs)	*m*	Anlenkhebel (Hubschieberpumpe)	*m*	control-sleeve lever (control-sleeve fuel-injection pump)	*n*
levier de réglage (pompe distributrice)	*m*	Einstellhebel (Verteilereinspritzpumpe)	*m*	control lever (distributor pump)	*n*
levier de renvoi	*m*	Umlenkhebel	*m*	reverse-transfer lever	*n*
levier de stop (pompe distributrice)	*m*	Stopphebel (Verteilereinspritzpumpe)	*m*	stop lever (distributor pump)	*n*
levier de tension	*m*	Spannhebel	*m*	tensioning lever	*n*
levier de transmission (capteur de niveau)	*m*	Antriebshebel (Niveaugeber)	*m*	transfer rod (level sensor)	*n*
levier du curseur (potentiomètre)	*m*	Schleiferhebel (Potentiometer)	*m*	wiper lever (potentiometer)	*n*
levier du frein à main	*m*	Handbremshebel	*m*	hand-brake lever	*n*
levier dynamométrique (banc d'essai)	*m*	Drehmomenthebel (Rollenbremsprüfstand)	*m*	torque lever (dynamic brake analyzer)	*n*
levier en équerre	*m*	Winkelhebel	*m*	bell crank	*n*
levier oscillant (commande des soupapes)	*m*	Schlepphebel (Ventilsteuerung)	*m*	rocker arm (valve timing)	*n*
levier pivotant	*m*	Schwenkhebel	*m*	swivelling lever	*n*
lèvre d'essuyage	*f*	Wischlippe	*f*	wiper-element lip	*n*
liaison à déclic	*f*	Schnappverbindung	*f*	snap-on connection	*n*
liaison mécanique	*f*	Wirkverbindung	*f*	mechanical linkage	*n*
lieu de production	*m*	Fertigungsstandort	*m*	production location	*n*
ligne à tiroirs	*f*	Hubschieber	*m*	control sleeve	*n*
ligne de fuite	*f*	Kriechweg	*m*	leakage path	*n*
limitation de couple	*f*	Drehmomentbegrenzung	*f*	torque limitation	*n*
limitation de l'émission de fumées	*f*	Rauchbegrenzung	*f*	smoke limitation	*n*
limitation de la vitesse de rotation	*f*	Drehzahlbegrenzung	*f*	engine-speed limitation	*n*
limitation de suralimentation en décélération	*f*	Turboschubbegrenzung	*f*	turbo overrun limiting	*n*

Français

Français		Allemand		Anglais	
limitation de tension	*f*	Spannungsbegrenzung	*f*	voltage limitation	*n*
limitation de vitesse	*f*	Geschwindigkeitsbegrenzung	*f*	speed limiting	*n*
limitation de vitesse de roulage	*f*	Fahrgeschwindigkeits-begrenzung	*f*	road-speed limitation	*n*
limitation des grandeurs de correction	*f*	Stellgrößenbegrenzung	*f*	correcting-variable limit	*n*
limitation du débit de surcharge au démarrage	*f*	Startmengenbegrenzung	*f*	start-quantity limitation	*n*
limitation du débit maximal	*f*	Vollastbegrenzung	*f*	full-load limitation	*n*
limitation du moment de lacet	*f*	Giermomentbegrenzung	*f*	yaw-moment limitation	*n*
limitation du régime	*f*	Drehzahlbegrenzung	*f*	engine-speed limitation	*n*
limite clair/obscur (projecteur)	*f*	Hell-Dunkel-Grenze, HDG (Scheinwerfer)	*f*	light-dark cutoff (headlamp)	*n*
limite d'allumage	*f*	Zündgrenze	*f*	ignition limit	*n*
limite d'émission de fumées	*f*	Rauchgrenze	*f*	smoke limit	*n*
limite de blocage (roues)	*f*	Blockiergrenze (Rad)	*f*	wheel-lock limit	*n*
limite de cliquetis	*f*	Klopfgrenze	*f*	knock limit	*n*
limite de démarrage à froid	*f*	Kaltstartgrenze	*f*	cold-start limit	*n*
limite de stabilité du moteur	*f*	Laufgrenze	*f*	lean misfire limit, LML	*n*
limite de température de démarrage	*f*	Starttemperaturgrenze	*f*	start-temperature limit	*n*
limite entre la clarté et l'obcurité (projecteur)	*f*	Hell-Dunkel-Grenze, HDG (Scheinwerfer)	*f*	light-dark cutoff (headlamp)	*n*
limiteur d'écoulement	*m*	Durchflußbegrenzer	*m*	flow limiter	*n*
limiteur d'intensité	*m*	Strombegrenzer	*m*	current limiter	*n*
limiteur de course	*m*	Hubkontrolle	*f*	stroke limiter	*n*
limiteur de débit	*m*	Strombegrenzungsventil	*n*	flow-limiting valve	*n*
limiteur de dépression (Jetronic)	*m*	Unterdruckbegrenzer (Jetronic)	*m*	vacuum limiter (Jetronic)	*n*
limiteur de pression	*m*	Druckbegrenzer	*m*	pressure limiter	*n*
limiteur de pression de freinage	*m*	Bremskraftbegrenzer	*m*	braking-force limiter	*n*
limiteur de richesse	*m*	ladedruckabhängiger Vollastanschlag, LDA	*m*	manifold-pressure compensator	*n*
limiteur de vitesse de roulage	*m*	Fahrgeschwindigkeits-begrenzer, FGB	*m*	vehicle-speed limiter	*n*
linguet (rupteur)	*m*	Unterbrecherhebel (Zündung)	*m*	breaker lever (ignition)	*n*
liquide de frein	*m*	Bremsflüssigkeit	*f*	brake fluid	*n*
liquide de frein à base d'huile minérale	*m*	Mineralöl-Bremsflüssigkeit	*f*	mineral-oil-based brake fluid	*n*
liquide de frein à base de glycol	*m*	Glykol-Bremsflüssigkeit	*f*	glycol-based brake fluid	*n*
liquide de freinage	*m*	Bremsflüssigkeit	*f*	brake fluid	*n*
liquide de refroidissement	*m*	Kühlmittel	*n*	coolant	*n*
liste des reprises (échange standard)	*f*	Rücknahmeliste (Werksaustausch)	*f*	catalog of exchange parts (factory exchange)	*n*
Litronic (projecteur avec lampe à décharge)	*m*	Litronic (Scheinwerfer mit Gasentladungslampe)	*f*	Litronic (headlamp system with gaseous-discharge lamp)	*n*
logement de la bougie	*m*	Zündkerzenmulde	*f*	spark-plug recess	*n*
logiciel de surveillance	*m*	Überwachungssoftware	*f*	monitoring software	*n*
logique d'allumeur	*f*	Verteilerlogik	*f*	distributor logic	*n*

Français		Allemand		Anglais	
logique de pilotage	*f*	Vorsteuerlogik	*f*	precontrol logic	*n*
logique de régulation (calculateur)	*f*	Reglerlogik (Steuergerät)	*f*	controller logic (ECU)	*n*
loi d'injection	*f*	Einspritzverlauf	*m*	rate-of-discharge curve	*n*
longévité	*f*	Dauerstandfestigkeit	*f*	service life	*n*
longueur d'étincelle	*f*	Funkenlänge	*f*	spark length	*n*
longueur des trous d'injection	*f*	Lochlänge	*f*	spray-hole length	*n*
louvoiement (freinage)	*m*	ungleiches Bremsen	*n*	uneven braking	*v*
lumière d'admission	*f*	Zulaufbohrung (Einspritzdüse)	*f*	inlet passage (injection nozzle)	*n*
lumière de distribution	*f*	Steuerbohrung	*f*	spill port	*n*
luminance (éclairage)	*f*	Leuchtdichte (Lichttechnik)	*f*	luminance (lighting)	*n*
lunette arrière	*f*	Heckscheibe	*f*	rear window	*n*
luxmètre	*m*	Luxmeter	*n*	luxmeter	*n*
M					
mâchoire de frein à main	*f*	Handbremsbacke	*f*	hand-brake shoe	*n*
mâchoire pivotante (frein à tambour)	*f*	Drehbacke (Trommelbremse)	*f*	rotating shoe (drum brake)	*n*
mâchoire primaire	*f*	auflaufende Bremsbacke	*f*	leading shoe	*n*
mâchoire secondaire	*f*	ablaufende Bremsbacke	*f*	trailing shoe	*n*
magnétisme restant	*m*	Restmagnetismus	*m*	residual magnetism	*n*
maître-cylindre de frein	*m*	Hauptzylinder	*m*	brake master cylinder	*n*
maître-cylindre tandem	*m*	Tandemhauptzylinder	*m*	tandem master cylinder	*n*
manchette de séparation	*f*	Trennmanschette	*f*	separating cup seal	*n*
manchette primaire	*f*	Primärmanschette	*f*	primary cup seal	*n*
manchette secondaire	*f*	Sekundärmanschette	*f*	secondary cup seal	*n*
manchon à bride	*m*	Flanschbuchse	*f*	flange bushing	*n*
manchon calorifuge (injecteur)	*m*	Wärmeschutzhülse (Einspritzdüse)	*f*	thermal-protection sleeve (injection nozzle)	*n*
manchon central (régulateur diesel)	*m*	Reglermuffe (Diesel-Regler)	*f*	sliding sleeve (governor)	*n*
manchon d'étanchéité (cylindre de roue)	*m*	Abdichtstulpe (Radzylinder)	*f*	sealing cap (wheel-brake cylinder)	*n*
manchon de blindage	*m*	Abschirmhülse	*f*	shielding sleeve	*n*
manchon de réglage	*m*	Einstellhülse	*f*	setting sleeve	*n*
manchon fileté	*m*	Einschraubstutzen	*m*	screwed socket	*n*
manocontact	*m*	Druckschalter	*m*	pressure switch	*n*
manoeuvrabilité	*f*	Lenkbarkeit	*f*	steerability	*n*
manomètre	*m*	Druckmesser	*m*	pressure gauge	*n*
manque de visibilité	*m*	Sichttrübung	*f*	impairment of vision	*n*
manteau d'air (injecteur)	*m*	Luftumfassung (Einspritzventil)	*f*	air-shrouding (fuel injector)	*n*
manuel	*m*	Handbuch	*n*	manual	*n*
manuel d'atelier	*m*	Werkstatthandbuch	*n*	workshop manual	*n*
manuel de réparation	*m*	Reparaturhandbuch	*n*	repair manual	*n*
marge de tolérance	*f*	Toleranzbereich	*m*	range of tolerance	*n*
marque d'homologation	*f*	Prüfzeichen	*n*	mark of approval	*n*
marque de contrôle	*f*	Prüfzeichen	*n*	mark of approval	*n*
masse (du boîtier)	*f*	Masse (Gehäusemasse)	*f*	equipment ground	*n*
masse (du véhicule)	*f*	Masse (Fahrzeugmasse)	*f*	vehicle ground	*n*

Français		Allemand		Anglais	
masse d'air	*f*	Luftmasse	*f*	air mass	*n*
masse d'enrobage (batterie)	*f*	Vergußmasse (Batterie)	*f*	sealing compound (battery)	*n*
masse de référence (circuit de bord)	*f*	Bezugsmasse (Bordnetz)	*f*	reference ground (vehicle electrical system)	*n*
masse injectée	*f*	Einspritzmasse	*f*	injection mass	*n*
masse polaire	*f*	Polschuh	*m*	pole shoe	*n*
masse suspendue	*f*	gefederte Masse	*f*	sprung weight	*n*
masse volumique de l'électrolyte (batterie)	*f*	Säuredichte	*f*	specific gravity of electrolyte	*n*
masselotte	*f*	Fliehgewicht	*n*	flyweight	*n*
matériaux des électrodes	*mpl*	Elektrodenwerkstoffe	*mpl*	electrode materials	*npl*
matériel d'injection	*m*	Einspritzausrüstung	*f*	fuel-injection equipment	*n*
matériel de connexion (électrique)	*m*	Verbindungsmittel (elektrisch)	*n*	connecting devices (electrical)	*n*
matière active (batterie)	*f*	aktive Masse (Batterie)	*f*	active materials (battery)	*n*
mécanique du freinage	*f*	Bremsvorgang	*m*	braking action	*n*
mécanisme d'embiellage	*m*	Kurbeltrieb	*m*	crankshaft drive	*n*
mécanisme d'engrènement	*m*	Einspurgetriebe	*n*	pinion-engaging drive	*n*
mécanisme de détection	*m*	Fliehgewichtsmeßwerk	*n*	flyweight speed-sensing elemer	*n*
mécanisme de détection à masselottes	*m*	Fliehgewichtsmeßwerk	*n*	flyweight speed-sensing elemer	*n*
mécanisme de la défaillance (de l'incident)	*m*	Ausfallmechanismus	*m*	failure mechanism	*n*
mélange air-carburant	*m*	Luft-Kraftstoff-Gemisch	*n*	air-fuel mixture	*n*
mélange gazeux	*m*	Luft-Kraftstoff-Gemisch	*n*	air-fuel mixture	*n*
mélange trop riche	*m*	Überfettung x	*f*	over-enrichment	*n*
membrane à couches épaisses	*f*	Dickschicht-Membran	*f*	thick-film diaphragm	*n*
membrane active	*f*	Wirkmembran	*f*	transfer diaphragm	*n*
membrane de régulation	*f*	Regelmembran	*f*	control diaphragm	*n*
Mémento de technologie automobile (publication Bosch)	*m*	Kraftfahrtechnisches Taschenbuch (Bosch-Schriftenreihe)	*n*	Automotive Handbook (Bosch publication)	*n*
mémoire de défauts	*f*	Fehlerspeicher	*m*	fault store	*n*
mémoire de valeurs fixes, ROM	*f*	Festwertspeicher, ROM	*f*	read-only memory, ROM	*n*
mémoire vive à lecture/écriture, RAM	*f*	Schreib-Lese-Speicher, RAM	*m*	random-access memory, RAM	*n*
mémorisation des défauts	*f*	Fehlerabspeicherung	*f*	error storage	*n*
méplat de tige de piston (piston de pompe)	*m*	Kolbenfahne (Pumpenkolben)	*f*	plunger control arm	*n*
mesure de la vitesse de roulage	*f*	Fahrgeschwindigkeitsmessung	*f*	vehicle-speed measurement	*n*
méthode CVS (essai d'évaporation)	*m*	Verdünnungsverfahren (CVS-Methode)	*n*	dilution prodedure (CVS method)	*n*
méthode de balayage	*f*	Durchspülungsverfahren	*n*	flushing method	*n*
mi-charge (moteur à combustion)	*f*	Teillast (Verbrennungsmotor)	*f*	part load (IC engine)	*n*
microcontrôleur (calculateur)	*m*	Mikrocontroller, MC (Steuergerät)	*m*	microcontroller, MC (ECU)	*n*
micromécanique	*f*	Mikromechanik	*f*	micromechanics	*npl*
microrelais	*m*	Mikrorelais	*n*	microrelay	*n*

Français		Allemand		Anglais	
miroir d'orientation (éclairage)	*m*	Ausrichtspiegel (Lichttechnik)	*m*	alignment mirror (lighting)	*n*
mise à la terre	*f*	Masseverbindung	*f*	ground connection	*n*
mise en action	*f*	Warmlauf	*m*	warm-up	*v*
mise en prise (pignon)	*f*	einspuren (Starterritzel)	*v*	mesh (starter pinion)	*v*
mise en veille (alarme auto)	*f*	schärfen (Autoalarm)	*v*	prime (car alarm)	*v*
mise hors veille (alarme auto)	*f*	entschärfen (Autoalarm)	*v*	deprime (car alarm)	*v*
mode "charge" (charge de batterie)	*m*	Ladebetrieb (Batterieladung)	*m*	charging mode (battery charge)	*n*
mode "sécurité"	*m*	Sicherheitsmodus	*m*	safety mode	*n*
mode "soutien" (charge de batterie)	*m*	Stützbetrieb (Batterieladung)	*m*	backup mode (battery charge)	*n*
mode "tampon" (charge de batterie)	*m*	Pufferbetrieb (Batterieladung)	*m*	floating-mode operation (battery charge)	*n*
mode de pilotage des vannes	*m*	Ventilansteuermodus	*m*	valve-triggering mode	*n*
mode dégradé	*m*	Notlauf	*m*	limp-home x	*n*
modérable	*adj*	abstufbar	*adj*	graduable	*adj*
modulateur de pression	*m*	Druckregelmodul, DRM	*m*	pressure-control module	*n*
modulateur de commande de pression (ABS)	*m*	Drucksteuerventil (ABS)	*n*	pressure-control valve (ABS)	*n*
modulateur de freinage	*m*	Bremskraftregler	*m*	load-sensing valve	*n*
modulateur de pression (ABS)	*m*	Druckmodulator (ABS)	*m*	pressure modulator (ABS)	*n*
modulation de fréquence	*f*	Frequenzmodulation	*f*	frequency modulation, FM	*n*
modulation de la force de freinage	*f*	Bremskraftregelung	*f*	braking-force metering	*n*
modulation de la force de freinage	*f*	Bremsdruckmodulation	*f*	brake-pressure modulation	*n*
module d'accélérateur	*m*	Fahrpedalmodul	*m*	accelerator-pedal module	*n*
module d'adaptation	*m*	Anpaßeinrichtung	*f*	add-on module	*n*
module d'allumage (mélange air-carburant)	*m*	Zündmodul (Luft-Kraftstoff-Gemisch)	*m*	ignition module (air-fuel mixture)	*n*
module d'essieu double (remorque)	*m*	Doppelachsmodul (Anhänger)	*m*	twin-axle module (trailer)	*n*
module de circuit	*m*	Schaltungsgruppe	*f*	circuit group	*n*
module de commande (dessiccateur)	*m*	Steuerteil (Lufttrockner)	*n*	control section (air drier)	*n*
module de commande (lampe à décharge dans un gaz)	*m*	Vorschaltgerät (Gasentladungslampe)	*n*	ballast unit (gaseous-discharge lamp)	*n*
module de commande de l'allumage	*m*	Zündschaltgerät	*n*	ignition trigger box	*a*
module de commande du temps de préchauffage	*m*	Glühzeitsteuergerät, GZS	*n*	glow control unit	*n*
module de commande remorqu‹	*m*	Anhängersteuermodul, ASM	*m*	trailer control module, TCM	*n*
module de diagnostic	*m*	Diagnosemodul	*m*	diagnosis module	*n*
module de diodes	*m*	Diodenmodul	*m*	diode module	*n*
module de données	*m*	Datenmodul	*m*	operating-data module	*n*
module de feu clignotant	*m*	Blinklichteinsatz	*m*	turn-signal unit	*n*
module de mise à feu (coussin gonflable)	*m*	Zündmodul (Airbag)	*m*	firing module (airbag)	*n*
module de programme	*m*	Programmodul	*m*	program module	*n*

Français		Allemand		Anglais	
module de protection (alarme auto)	*m*	Vorschaltmodul (Autoalarm)	*m*	ballast module (car alarm)	*n*
module de protection (calculateur)	*m*	Schutzeinheit (Steuergerät)	*f*	protective unit (ECU)	*n*
module de puissance	*m*	Leistungsmodul	*m*	power module	*n*
module de réglage (correcteur de site)	*m*	Verstelleinheit (Leuchtweiteregelung)	*f*	adjuster (headlight vertical-aim control)	*n*
module de sécurité	*m*	Sicherheitsmodul	*m*	safety module	*n*
module de surveillance	*m*	Überwachungsmodul	*m*	monitoring module	*n*
module électronique d'exploitation	*m*	Auswertschaltgerät	*n*	signal-evaluation module	*n*
modulé en largeur d'impulsion	*pp*	pulsweitenmoduliert	*adj*	pulse width modulated, PWM	*pp*
module pilote (allumage)	*m*	Vorschaltgerät (Zündung)	*n*	ballast unit (ignition)	*n*
module relais	*m*	Relaiskombination	*f*	relay combination	*n*
moduler (force de freinage)	*v*	einsteuern (Bremskraft)	*v*	apply (braking force)	*v*
molette de correcteur de site	*f*	Regulierschalter (Leuchtweitenregelung)	*m*	regulator switch (headlight leveling control)	*n*
moment d'inertie	*m*	Massenträgheitsmoment	*n*	mass moment of inertia	*n*
moment d'inertie efficace de la roue	*m*	Radträgheitsmoment	*n*	wheel moment of inertia	*n*
moment de lacet	*m*	Giermoment	*n*	yaw moment	*n*
moment de lacet de consigne du véhicule	*m*	Fahrzeuggiersollmoment	*n*	vehicle yaw-moment setpoint	*n*
monoflux (ventilateur)	*adj*	einflutig (Lüfter)	*adj*	single-flow (fan)	*n*
montage en étoile	*m*	Sternschaltung	*f*	star connection	*n*
montage en parallèle	*m*	Parallelschaltung	*f*	parallel connection	*n*
montage en pont	*m*	Brückenschaltung	*f*	bridge circuit	*n*
montage en série	*m*	Reihenschaltung	*f*	series connection	*n*
montage en triangle	*m*	Dreieckschaltung	*f*	delta connection	*n*
montée de rampe	*f*	Rampensteigung	*f*	ramp climb	*n*
montée en pression	*f*	Druckaufbau	*m*	pressure rise	*n*
montée en régime (moteur à combustion)	*f*	hochlaufen (Verbrennungsmotor) x	*v*	run-up to speed (IC engine)	*v*
moteur à allumage par compression	*m*	Selbstzündungsmotor	*m*	compression-ignition (CI) engine	*n*
moteur à allumage par étincelle	*m*	Ottomotor	*m*	spark-ignition engine	*n*
moteur à aspiration naturelle	*m*	Saugmotor	*m*	naturally aspirated engine	*n*
moteur à auto-allumage	*m*	Selbstzündungsmotor	*m*	compression-ignition (CI) engine	*n*
moteur à chambre de tourbillonnement	*m*	Wirbelkammermotor	*m*	whirl-chamber diesel engine	*n*
moteur à chambre de turbulence	*m*	Nebenkammermotor	*m*	turbulence-chamber engine	*n*
moteur à chambre divisée	*m*	Kammermotor	*m*	indirect-injection (IDI) engine	*n*
moteur à charge stratifiée	*m*	Schichtlademotor	*m*	stratified-charge engine	*n*
moteur à combustion à volume constant	*m*	Ottomotor	*m*	spark-ignition engine	*n*
moteur à combustion interne	*m*	Verbrennungsmotor	*m*	internal-combustion (IC) engine	*n*
moteur à courant continu	*m*	Gleichstrommotor	*m*	DC motor	*n*

Français

Français		Allemand		Anglais	
moteur à engrenage	*m*	Zahnradmotor	*m*	hydraulic gear motor	*n*
moteur à essence	*m*	Ottomotor	*m*	spark-ignition engine	*n*
moteur à excitation composée	*m*	Doppelschlußmotor	*m*	compound motor	*n*
moteur à excitation compound	*m*	Doppelschlußmotor	*m*	compound motor	*n*
moteur à excitation shunt	*m*	Nebenschlußmotor	*m*	shunt-wound motor	*n*
moteur à injection	*m*	Einspritzmotor	*m*	fuel-injection engine	*n*
moteur à injection directe	*m*	Direkteinspritzmotor	*m*	direct-injection (DI) engine	*n*
moteur à injection indirecte	*m*	Kammermotor	*m*	indirect-injection (IDI) engine	*n*
moteur à pistons alternatifs	*m*	Hubkolbenmotor	*m*	reciprocating-piston engine	*n*
moteur à pistons axiaux	*m*	Axialkolbenmotor	*m*	axial-piston motor	*n*
moteur à préchambre	*m*	Vorkammermotor	*m*	prechamber engine	*n*
moteur à tension composée	*m*	Mischspannungsmotor	*m*	pulsating-voltage motor	*n*
moteur à turbocompresseur	*m*	Turbomotor	*m*	turbocharged engine	*n*
moteur compound	*m*	Doppelschlußmotor	*m*	compound motor	*n*
moteur d'essai	*m*	Prüfmotor	*m*	test engine	*n*
moteur d'essuie-glace	*m*	Wischermotor	*m*	wiper motor	*n*
moteur de lavophare	*m*	Lichtwischermotor	*m*	beamwash motor	*n*
moteur de lève-vitre	*m*	Fensterhebermotor	*m*	power-window motor	*n*
moteur de pompe (groupe hydraulique ABS)		Pumpenmotor (ABS-Hydroaggregat)	*m*	pump motor (ABS hydraulic modulator)	*n*
moteur de soufflante	*m*	Lüftermotor	*m*	fan motor	*n*
moteur électrique	*m*	Elektromotor	*m*	electric motor	*n*
moteur multicarburant	*m*	Mehrstoffmotor	*m*	multifuel engine	*n*
moteur pas à pas	*m*	Schrittmotor	*m*	stepping motor	*n*
moteur plat	*m*	Flachmotor	*m*	flat motor	*n*
moteur polycarburant	*m*	Mehrstoffmotor	*m*	multifuel engine	*n*
moteur pour mélange pauvre	*m*	Magermotor	*m*	lean-burn engine	*n*
moteur série	*m*	Reihenschlußmotor	*m*	series motor	*n*
moteur turbocompressé	*m*	Turbomotor	*m*	turbocharged engine	*n*
motoréducteur	*m*	Getriebemotor	*m*	motor-and-gear assembly	*n*
Motronic (système électronique de gestion du moteur)	*m*	Motronic (elektronische Motorsteuerung)	*f*	Motronic (electronic engine management)	*n*
mouler sous pression	*v*	druckgießen	*v*	pressure diecasting	*v*
mouvement alternatif et rotatif	*m*	Dreh-Hub-Bewegung	*f*	rotating-reciprocating movement	*n*
mouvement de lacet	*m*	Gierbewegung	*f*	yaw motion	*n*
mouvement de rotation	*m*	Abrollbewegung	*f*	rolling movement	*n*
mouvement de rotation et de translation (démarreur)	*m*	Schraubweg (Starter)	*m*	helical travel (starter)	*n*
mouvement de translation	*m*	Einspurhub	*m*	pinion travel	*n*
moyen de transmission (dispositif de freinage)	*m*	Übertragungsmedium (Bremsanlage)	*n*	transmission agent (braking system)	*n*
moyeu de régulateur	*m*	Reglernabe	*f*	governor hub	*n*
moyeu de roue	*m*	Radnabe	*f*	wheel hub	*n*
multivibrateur	*m*	Multivibrator	*m*	multivibrator	*n*
multivibrateur-diviseur de commande	*m*	Divisions-Steuer-Multivibrator	*m*	division control multivibrator	*n*

Français

Français		Allemand		Anglais	
N					
navigation automobile	*f*	Fahrzeugnavigation	*f*	vehicle navigation	*n*
nervurage en échiquier	*m*	Schachbrettverippung	*f*	chequerboard ribbing	*n*
nervure d'appui	*f*	Stützrippe	*f*	support rib	*n*
nettoyage des vitres	*m*	Scheibenreinigung	*f*	windshield and rear-window cleaning	*n*
nettoyeur de projecteurs	*m*	Scheinwerfer-Wischeranlage	*f*	headlamp wiper system	*n*
neutre (conduite de véhicule en virage)	*adj*	neutralsteuern (Kfz)	*v*	neutral steer (motor vehicle)	*v*
niveau bas (suspension pneumatique)	*m*	Tiefniveau (Luftfederung)	*n*	low level (air suspension)	*n*
niveau d'inclinaison (suspension pneumatique)	*m*	Kneeling-Niveau (Luftfederung) x	*n*	kneeling level (air suspension)	*n*
niveau de bruit	*m*	Geräuschpegel	*m*	noise level	*n*
niveau de perturbations (CEM)	*m*	Funkstörspannungspegel (EMV)	*m*	interference level (EMC)	*n*
niveau de pression acoustique	*m*	Schalldruckpegel	*m*	sound pressure level	*n*
niveau de qualité	*m*	Qualitätsstand	*m*	quality level	*n*
niveau de référence	*m*	Referenzpegel	*m*	reference level	*n*
niveau de valeur de pointe	*m*	Spitzenwertpegel	*m*	peak-value level	*n*
niveau du liquide de frein	*m*	Bremsflüssigkeitsstand	*m*	brake-fluid level	*n*
niveau haut (suspension pneumatique)	*f*	Hochniveau (Luftfederung)	*n*	high level (air suspension)	*n*
niveau normal (suspension pneumatique)	*f*	Normalniveau (Luftfederung)	*n*	normal level (air suspension)	*n*
noircissement	*m*	Schwärzung	*f*	blackening	*n*
nombre d'étincelles	*m*	Funkenzahl	*f*	sparking rate	*n*
nombre de cycles de commutation	*m*	Schaltzahl	*f*	number of switching operations	*n*
nombre de pôles	*m*	Polzahl	*f*	number of poles	*n*
nombre de spires	*m*	Windungszahl	*f*	number of coils	*n*
nombre de tours des spires de l'enroulement	*m*	Windungszahl	*f*	number of coils	*n*
nomenclature	*f*	Stückliste	*f*	parts list	*n*
notice d'application	*f*	Applikationshinweis	*m*	application instructions	*npl*
notice d'entretien	*f*	Wartungsvorschrift	*f*	maintainance instructions	*npl*
notice d'essai	*f*	Prüfanleitung	*f*	test instructions	*npl*
notice d'utilisation	*f*	Bedienungsanleitung	*f*	operating instructions	*npl*
notice de montage	*f*	Montageanleitung	*f*	installation instructions	*npl*
notice de remise en état	*f*	Reparaturanleitung	*f*	repair instructions	*npl*
noyau (groupe hydraulique ABS)	*m*	Anker (ABS-Hydroaggregat)	*m*	armature (ABS hydraulic modulator)	*n*
noyau d'actionneur	*m*	Stellwerkjoch	*m*	actuator fastening flange	*m*
noyau de cuivre (bougie)	*m*	Kupferkern (Zündkerze)	*m*	copper core (spark plug)	*n*
noyau de fer	*m*	Eisenkern	*m*	iron core	*n*
noyau de stator (alternateur)	*m*	Lamellenpaket (Generator)	*n*	stator lamination (alternator)	*n*
noyau feuilleté d'induit	*m*	Ankerpaket	*n*	armature stack	*n*
noyau plongeur	*m*	Magnetanker	*m*	solenoid armature	*n*
noyau polaire	*m*	Polkern	*m*	pole body	*n*

Français		Allemand			Anglais	
noyau synchroniseur (allumage)	*m*	Impulsgeberrad (Zündung)		*n*	trigger wheel (ignition)	*n*
numéro de châssis	*m*	Fahrgestellnummer		*f*	chassis number	*n*
numéro de montage	*m*	Montagezahl		*f*	assembly number	*n*
O						
objectif qualité	*m*	Qualitätsziel		*n*	quality objective	*n*
obturateur (tête d'accouplement)	*m*	Absperrglied (Kupplungskopf)		*n*	shutoff element (coupling head)	*n*
obturateur d'échappement	*m*	Auspuffverlangsamer		*m*	exhaust brake	*n*
onde de pression	*f*	Druckwelle		*f*	pressure wave	*n*
onde perturbatrice (CEM)	*f*	Störwelle (EMV)		*f*	interference wave (EMC)	*n*
opacimètre	*m*	Lichtabsorptionsmeßgerät		*n*	opacimeter	*n*
opacité	*f*	Trübung		*f*	opacity	*n*
opérateur à valeur minimale	*m*	Minimalwertoperator		*m*	minimum-value operator	*n*
optique de Fresnel	*f*	Fresneloptik		*f*	fresnel optics	*npl*
optique de projection (projecteur)	*f*	Projektionsoptik (Scheinwerfer)		*f*	projection optics (headlamp)	*npl*
optique de réflexion	*f*	Reflektoroptik		*f*	reflector optics	*npl*
ordinateur de bord	*m*	Bordcomputer		*m*	on-board computer	*n*
ordre d'allumage	*m*	Zündfolge		*f*	firing sequence	*n*
ordre d'injection	*m*	Einspritzfolge		*f*	injection sequence	*n*
ordre des cames	*m*	Nockenfolge		*f*	cam sequence	*n*
orifice calibré	*m*	Dämpfungsdrossel		*f*	damping throttle	*n*
orifice d'admission (injecteur)	*m*	Zulaufbohrung (Einspritzdüse)		*f*	inlet passage (injection nozzle)	*n*
orifice d'admission (pompe d'injection en ligne)	*m*	Saugloch (Reiheneinspritzpumpe)		*n*	inlet port (in-line pump)	*n*
orifice d'admission de carburant de barrage	*m*	Sperrölzulaufbohrung	+	*f*	blocking-oil inlet passage	*n*
orifice d'air	*m*	Luftanschluß		*m*	air connection	*n*
orifice d'alimentation	*m*	Saugloch (Reiheneinspritzpumpe)		*n*	inlet port (in-line pump)	*n*
orifice d'entrée	*m*	Zulaufbohrung (Einspritzdüse)		*f*	inlet passage (injection nozzle)	*n*
orifice d'étranglement	*m*	Drosselbohrung		*f*	throttle bore	*n*
orifice de balayage	*m*	Überströmbohrung		*f*	overflow orifice	*n*
orifice de décharge	*m*	Absteuerquerschnitt		*m*	cutoff bore	*n*
orifice de dégazage (batterie)	*m*	Entgasungsöffnung (Batterie)		*f*	ventilation opening (battery)	*n*
orifice de distribution	*m*	Steuerbohrung		*f*	spill port	*n*
orifice de purge d'air	*m*	Entlüftungsbohrung		*f*	vent bore	*n*
orifice de retour	*m*	Rücklaufbohrung		*f*	return passage	*n*
orifice taraudé	*m*	Gewindeanschluß		*m*	threaded port	*n*
origine étrangère	*f*	Fremdbezug		*m*	out-sourcing	*n*
oscillateur à quartz	*m*	Quarzoszillator		*m*	quartz oscillator	*n*
oscillation croissante (véhicule)	*f*	aufschaukeln (Kfz)		*v*	pitch (motor vehicle)	*v*
oscillations harmoniques	*fpl*	Oberschwingungen		*fpl*	harmonics	*npl*
outil de diagnostic	*m*	Diagnosewerkzeug		*n*	diagnosis tool	*n*
outil spécial	*m*	Sonderwerkzeug		*n*	special tool	*n*
oxygène résiduel (gaz d'échappement)	*m*	Restsauerstoff (Abgas)		*m*	exhaust-gas oxygen	*n*

Français		Allemand		Anglais	
P					
palette Europe	*f*	Europalette	*f*	euro-pallet	*n*
palier côté bagues collectrices (alternateur)	*m*	Schleifringlagerschild (Generator)	*m*	collector-ring end shield (alternator)	*n*
palier côté entraînement (alternateur)	*m*	Antriebslagerschild (Generator)	*m*	drive end shield (alternator)	*n*
palier d'appui (frein à tambour)	*m*	Stützlager (Trommelbremse)	*n*	support bearing (drum brake)	*n*
palier de baisse de pression (ABS)	*m*	Druckabbaustufe (ABS)	*f*	pressure-reduction step (ABS)	*n*
palonniers (essuie-glace)	*mpl*	Bügelsystem (Wischeranlage)	*n*	bracket system (wiper system)	*n*
papier diélectrique	*m*	Isolierpapier	*n*	insulating paper	*n*
papier isolant	*m*	Isolierpapier	*n*	insulating paper	*n*
papillon (moteur à combustion)	*m*	Drosselklappe	*f*	throttle valve (IC engine)	*n*
papillon des gaz (moteur à combustion)	*m*	Drosselklappe	*f*	throttle valve (IC engine)	*n*
paquet de lamelles de tôle (alternateur)	*m*	Lamellenpaket (Generator)	*n*	stator lamination (alternator)	*n*
par impulsion (pilotage de pression)	*loc*	pulsen (Drucksteuerung)	*v*	pulsing (pressure control)	*v*
par impulsions (modulation de pression)	*loc*	pulsierend (Drucksteuerung)	*ppr*	pulse-controlled (pressure)	*pp*
paramètre d'influence	*m*	Einflußgröße	*f*	actuating variable	*n*
paramètre de commande	*m*	Steuergröße	*f*	controlled variable (open-loop control)	*n*
paramètre de fonctionnement	*m*	Betriebsparameter	*m*	operating parameter	*n*
pare-brise	*m*	Frontscheibe	*f*	windshield	*n*
pare-gouttes (projections d'eau)	*m*	Tropfkante (Spritzwasserschutz)	*f*	drip rim (splash resistance)	*n*
paroi de la cavité du piston	*f*	Muldenwand	*f*	piston-recess wall	*n*
particules de suie	*fpl*	Rußpartikel	*n*	soot particle	*n*
partie basse pression	*f*	Niederdruckteil	*n*	low-pressure stage	*n*
partie commutateur (balai)	*f*	Kommutierungsszone (Kohlebürste)	*f*	commutating zone (carbon brush)	*n*
partie haute pression	*f*	Hochdruckteil	*n*	high-pressure stage	*n*
partie puissance (balai)	*f*	Leistungszone (Kohlebürste)	*f*	power zone (carbon brush)	*n*
pas polaire	*m*	Polteilung	*f*	pole pitch	*n*
passage de câble	*m*	Kabeldurchführung	*f*	cable lead-through	*n*
passage de pôle	*m*	Poldurchgang	*m*	pole pass	*n*
passe-fil caoutchouc	*m*	Gummitülle	*f*	rubber grommet	*n*
pastille de réglage	*f*	Ausgleichsplatte	*f*	shim plate	*n*
pastille explosive (coussin gonflable)	*f*	Zündpille (Airbag)	*f*	firing pellet (airbag)	*n*
pastille perforée	*f*	Lochplatte	*f*	orifice plate	*n*
pâte antigrippage	*f*	Gleitpaste	*f*	slip paste	*n*
pâte de cuivre	*f*	Kupferpaste	*f*	copper paste	*n*
pâte thermoconductrice	*f*	Wärmeleitpaste	*f*	thermal-conduction paste	*n*
patiner (roue motrice)	*v*	durchdrehen (Antriebsrad) x	*v*	wheel spin	*n*
patte de butée	*f*	Anschlaglasche	*f*	stop strap	*n*
patte de correction	*f*	Angleichlasche	*f*	torque-control bar	*n*

Français		Allemand		Anglais	
patte de fixation	*f*	Befestigungslasche	*f*	mounting bracket	*n*
pauvre (mélange air-carburant)	*adj*	mager (Luft-Kraftstoff-Gemisch)	*adj*	lean (air-fuel-mixture)	*adj*
pédale de frein	*f*	Bremspedal	*n*	brake pedal	*n*
pente de rampe	*f*	Rampensteigung	*f*	ramp climb	*n*
percolation	*f*	Dampfblasenbildung	*f*	vapor-bubble formation	*n*
période de l'allumage	*f*	Zündabstand	*m*	angular ignition spacing	*n*
période de mise en action (moteur à combustion)	*f*	Warmlaufphase (Verbrennungsmotor)	*f*	warm-up period (IC engine)	*n*
période de préchauffage	*f*	Glühzeitablauf	*m*	preheating sequence	*n*
période de réchauffage (moteur à combustion)	*f*	Warmlaufphase (Verbrennungsmotor)	*f*	warm-up period (IC engine)	*n*
périphériques du système	*mpl*	Systemperipherie	*f*	system peripheral equipment	*n*
perte de chaleur	*f*	Verlustwärme	*f*	heat losses	*npl*
perte de charge	*f*	Druckverlust	*m*	pressure loss	*n*
perte de charge (carburant)	*f*	Druckgefälle (Kraftstoff)	*n*	pressure drop (fuel)	*n*
perte de pression	*f*	Druckverlust	*m*	pressure loss	*n*
perte de puissance	*f*	Leistungsverlust	*m*	performance drop	*n*
perte par friction (piston)	*f*	Reibungsverlust	*m*	friction loss	*n*
perte par frottement	*f*	Reibungsverlust	*m*	friction loss	*n*
pertes au renouvellement des gaz	*fpl*	Gaswechselverlust	*m*	charge-cycle losses	*npl*
pertes cuivre (alternateur)	x *fpl*	Kupferverluste (Generator)	x *mpl*	copper losses (alternator)	x *npl*
pertes d'aimantation	*fpl*	Magnetisierungsverlust	*m*	magnetization loss	*n*
pertes d'excitation	*fpl*	Erregerverluste	*mpl*	excitation losses	*npl*
pertes de commutation	*fpl*	Umschaltverlust	*m*	switching loss	*n*
pertes de flux magnétique	*fpl*	Streuflußverluste (magnetische)	*mpl*	magnetic leakage	*n*
pertes de puissance	*fpl*	elektrische Verlustleistung	*f*	electrical power loss	*n*
pertes fer (alternateur)	x *fpl*	Eisenverluste (Generator)	x *mpl*	iron losses (alternator)	x *npl*
pertes par évaporation (alimentation en carburant)	*fpl*	Verdampfungsverluste (Kraftstoffsystem)	*mpl*	evaporative losses (fuel system)	*npl*
pertes par fuites	*fpl*	Leckverlust	*m*	leakage losses	*npl*
pertes redresseurs	*fpl*	Gleichrichterverluste	*mpl*	rectifier losses	*npl*
perturbation à bande étroite	*f*	Schmalbandstörung	*f*	narrow-band interference	*n*
perturbation à large bande	*f*	Breitbandstörung	*f*	broad-band interference	*n*
perturbation aléatoire	*f*	rauschen (Funkstörung)	x *v*	background noise (radio disturbance)	*n*
perturbation par champ continu	*f*	Gleichfeldeinstreuung	*f*	constant field pick-up	*n*
perturbation radioélectrique	*f*	Funkstörung (Ursache)	*f*	radio disturbance	*n*
PES, projecteur polyellipsoïde	*a*	Poly-Ellipsoid-Scheinwerfer, PES	*m*	PES headlamp	*n*
pèse-acide (charge de batterie)	*m*	Säureprüfer (Batterie)	*m*	hydrometer (battery charge)	*n*
petit relais	*m*	Kleinrelais	*n*	minirelay	*n*
peu extensible (courroie trapézoïdale)	*loc*	dehnungsarm (Keilriemen)	*adj*	low stretch (V-belt)	*n*
phare	+ *m*	Scheinwerfer	*m*	headlamp	*n*
phasage	*m*	Versatz	*m*	phasing	*n*
phasage (élément de pompage)	*m*	Förderabstand (Pumpenelement)	*m*	phasing (plunger-and-barrel assembly)	*n*

Français			Allemand		Anglais		
phase d'une grandeur sinusoïdale		*f*	Phasenwinkel	*m*	phase angle		*n*
phase de démarrage		*f*	Startphase	*f*	starting phase		*n*
phase de détente (moteur à combustion interne)		*f*	Expansionsphase (Verbrennungsmotor)	*f*	expansion phase (IC engine)		*n*
phase de post-chauffage		*f*	Nachheizphase	*f*	hot-soak phase		*n*
phase de post-démarrage		*f*	Nachstartphase	*f*	post-start phase		*n*
phase de refoulement		*f*	Förderphase	*f*	delivery phase		*n*
phase de remplissage		*f*	Füllphase	*f*	filling phase		*n*
phase transitoire (émissions)		*f*	Übergangsphase (Abgasprüfung)	*f*	transition phase (exhaust-gas test)		*n*
phénomène de démixtion		*m*	Entmischungsvorgang	*m*	segregation process		*n*
phénomène de mise en "portefeuille" (semi-remorque)	x	*m*	einknicken (Sattelzug)	*v*	jacknife (semitrailer unit)		*v*
pièce conductrice		*f*	Leitstück	*n*	conductive element		*n*
pièce d'étanchement		*f*	Dichtstück	*n*	seal piece		*n*
pièce d'usure		*f*	Verschleißteil	*n*	wearing part		*n*
pièce de pression (tête d'accouplement)		*f*	Druckstück (Kupplungskopf)	*n*	thrust member (coupling head)		*n*
pièce de remplissage		*f*	Füllstück	*n*	filler piece		*n*
pigeage		*m*	Vorhub (Pumpenkolben)	*m*	plunger lift to port closing		*n*
pignon d'entraînement		*m*	Starterritzel	*n*	starter pinion		*n*
pignon du démarreur		*m*	Starterritzel	*n*	starter pinion		*n*
pilotage (ABS pour véhicules utilitaires)		*m*	Vorsteuerung (Nfz-ABS)	*f*	pilot control (commercial-vehicle ABS)		*n*
pilotage (régulation ABS)		*m*	Ansteuerung (ABS-Regelung)	*f*	triggering (ABS control)		*n*
pilotage cyclique (pression de freinage)		*m*	takten (Radbremsdruck)	*v*	cyclical actuation (wheel brake-pressure)		*n*
pilotage de démarrage à froid		*m*	Kaltstartsteuerung	*f*	cold-start control		*n*
pilotage de la remorque		*m*	Anhängeransteuerung	*f*	trailer pilot control		*n*
pilotage du débit de surcharge		*m*	Startmengenvorsteuerung	*f*	excess-fuel preset		*n*
pilotage dynamique		*m*	dynamische Vorsteuerung	*f*	dynamic pilot control		*n*
piloté par cartographie (allumage)		*pp*	kennfeldgesteuert (Zündung)	*pp*	map-controlled (ignition)		*pp*
piloter		*v*	ansteuern	*v*	trigger		*v*
piloter (force de freinage)		*v*	aussteuern (Bremskraft)	*v*	output (braking force)		*v*
pince capacitive (CEM)		*f*	kapazitive Zange (EMV)	*f*	capacitive clamp (EMC)	x	*n*
pince d'intensité		*f*	Stromzange	*f*	current clamp	x	*n*
pince de batterie		*f*	Batteriezange	*f*	crocodile clip		*n*
pipe d'admission		*f*	Schwingrohr	*n*	intake runner		*n*
piste à résistance		*f*	Kollektorbahn	*f*	collector-track		*n*
piste de came		*f*	Nockenlaufbahn	*f*	cam track		*n*
piste de contact		*f*	Leiterbahn	*f*	conductor		*n*
piste de potentiomètre		*f*	Potentiometerbahn	*f*	potentiometer track		*n*
piste de régime		*f*	Drehzahlpfad	*m*	speed path		*n*
piste de roulement		*f*	Rollengleitkurve	*f*	roller race		*n*
piston (frein à disque)		*m*	Druckkolben (Scheibenbremse)	*m*	piston (disc brake)		*n*
piston (valve de nivellement)		*m*	Federkolben (Luftfederventil)	*m*	spring piston (height-control valve)		*n*

Français		Allemand		Anglais	
piston à fléau	*f*	Wiegekolben	*m*	rocking piston	*n*
piston à joint embouti	*m*	Membrankolben	*m*	diaphragm piston	*n*
piston à palettes (correcteur de freinage)	*m*	Fächerkolben (Bremskraftregler)	*m*	fan-type piston (braking-force regulator)	*n*
piston à tige-poussoir	*m*	Druckstangenkolben	*m*	push-rod piston	*n*
piston amplificateur	*m*	Verstärkerkolben	*m*	servo-unit piston	*n*
piston d'élément de pompage	*m*	Elementkolben	*m*	pumping-element plunger	*n*
piston de commande	*m*	Steuerkolben	*m*	control plunger	*n*
piston de détente	*m*	Entlastungskolben	*m*	retraction piston	*n*
piston de dosage (KE-Jetronic)	*m*	Zumeßkolben (KE-Jetronic)	*m*	fuel-metering plunger (KE-Jetronic)	*n*
piston de marche à vide (dessiccateur)	*m*	Leerlaufkolben (Lufttrockner)	*m*	idle piston (air drier)	*n*
piston de pompe (pompe d'injection)	*m*	Pumpenkolben (Einspritzpumpe)	*m*	pump plunger (fuel-injection pump)	*n*
piston de rappel	*m*	Reaktionskolben	*m*	reaction piston	*n*
piston de réaction	*m*	Schleppkolben	*m*	drag piston	*n*
piston de refoulement	*m*	Förderkolben	*m*	delivery plunger	*n*
piston de soupape	*m*	Ventilkolben	*m*	valve plunger	*n*
piston de soupape de refoulement	*m*	Druckventilkolben	*m*	delivery-valve plunger	*n*
piston de travail	*m*	Arbeitskolben	*m*	working piston	*n*
piston différentiel	*m*	Stufenkolben	*m*	stepped piston	*n*
piston distributeur	*m*	Verteilerkolben	*m*	distributor plunger	*n*
piston flotteur	*m*	Schwimmkolben	*m*	float piston	*n*
piston intermédiaire	*m*	Zwischenkolben	*m*	intermediate piston	*n*
piston-poussoir	*m*	Stößelkolben	*m*	tappet plunger	*n*
piston-relais	*m*	Relaiskolben	*m*	relay piston	*n*
pivot central	*m*	Königszapfen	*m*	fifth wheel	*n*
pivotement des portes (autobus)	*m*	Türbetätigung (Omnibus)	*f*	door control (bus)	*n*
plage d'application thermique	*f*	thermischer Anwendungsbereich	*m*	temperature limits of application	*n*
plage d'enclenchement	*f*	Einschaltbereich	*m*	cutin area	*n*
plage d'étranglement	*f*	Drosselhub	*m*	throttling stroke	*n*
plage de charge partielle	*f*	Teillastbereich	*m*	part-load range	*n*
plage de correction de débit	*f*	Angleichbereich	*m*	torque-control range	*n*
plage de coupure de débit	*f*	Abregelbereich	*m*	breakaway range	*n*
plage de fonctionnement dynamique	*f*	dynamischer Funktionsbereich	*m*	dynamic functional range, DFR	*n*
plage de pression	*f*	Druckbereich	*m*	pressure area	*n*
plage de régimes	*f*	Drehzahlbereich	*m*	speed range	*n*
plage de régulation	*f*	Regelbereich	*m*	control range	*n*
plage de vitesses de rotation	*f*	Drehzahlbereich	*m*	speed range	*n*
plage neutre	*f*	Gleichfeld	*n*	constant field	*n*
plage non régulée	*f*	ungeregelter Bereich	*m*	uncontrolled range	*n*
plan d'assemblage	*m*	Zusammenbauzeichnung	*f*	assembly drawing	*n*
plan d'offre	*m*	Angebotszeichnung	*f*	project drawing	*n*
plan de développement	*m*	Entwicklungszeichnung	*f*	draft drawing	*n*

Français		Allemand		Anglais	
planche de bord	*f*	Armaturenbrett	*n*	dashboard	*n*
plaque à came	*f*	Kurvenplatte	*f*	plate cam	*n*
plaque à circuit imprimé	*f*	Leiterplatte	*f*	printed-circuit board	*n*
plaque à diodes d'excitation	*f*	Erregerdiodenplatte	*f*	excitation-diode plate	*n*
plaque d'appui (filtre)	*f*	Stützplatte (Filter)	*f*	support plate (filter)	*n*
plaque d'identification	*f*	Typenschild	*n*	nameplate	*n*
plaque de constructeur	*f*	Typenschild	*n*	nameplate	*n*
plaque de guidage	*f*	Kurvenplatte	*f*	plate cam	*n*
plaque de réglage	*f*	Ausgleichsplatte	*f*	shim plate	*n*
plaque intermédiaire	*f*	Zwischenplatte	*f*	intermediate plate	*n*
plaque négative (batterie)	*f*	Minusplatte (Batterie)	*f*	negative plate (battery)	*n*
plaque porte-soupape (Jetronic)	*f*	Ventilplatte (Jetronic)	*f*	valve plate (Jetronic)	*n*
plaque positive (batterie)	*f*	Plusplatte (Batterie)	*f*	positive plate (battery)	*n*
plaque signalétique	*f*	Typenschild	*n*	nameplate	*n*
plaque-membrane	*f*	Membranplatte	*f*	diaphragm plate	*n*
plaque-soupape mobile	*f*	Plattenventil	*n*	plate valve	*n*
plaque-support (filtre)	*f*	Stützplatte (Filter)	*f*	support plate (filter)	*n*
plaquette calorifuge (injecteur)	*f*	Wärmeschutzplättchen (Einspritzdüse)	*n*	thermal-protection plate (injection nozzle)	*n*
plaquette de contrôle	*f*	Prüfplakette	*f*	inspection tag	*n*
plaquette de refroidissement	*f*	Kühlkörper	*m*	heat sink	*n*
plaquette semi-conductrice	*f*	Halbleiterplättchen	*n*	semiconductor wafer	*n*
plateau à cames	*m*	Hubscheibe	*f*	cam plate	*n*
plateau à griffes	*m*	Klauenpol	*m*	claw pole	*n*
plateau d'ajustage (banc d'essai)	*m*	Justierplatte (Rollenbremsprüfstand)	*f*	adjustment plate (dynamic brake analyzer)	*n*
plateau de pression (frein)	*m*	Druckplatte (Bremse)	*f*	pressure plate (brakes)	*n*
plateau en plastique	*m*	Kühlnoppe	*f*	cooling pip	*n*
plateau porte-balais	*m*	Bürstenhalterplatte	*f*	brush-holder plate	*n*
plateau-sonde (K-Jetronic)	*m*	Stauscheibe (K-Jetronic)	*f*	sensor plate (K-Jetronic)	*n*
plateau-support (correcteur d'avance)	*m*	Achsplatte (Zündversteller)	*f*	support plate (ignition-advance mechanism)	*n*
plateau-support (système de déclenchement Hall)	*m*	Trägerplatte (Hall-Auslösesystem)	*f*	carrying plate (Hall triggering system)	*n*
platine	*f*	Halteplatte	*f*	cover plate	*n*
plausibilité dynamique	*f*	dynamische Plausibilität	*f*	dynamic plausibility	*n*
plein débit	*m*	Vollförderung	*f*	maximum delivery	*n*
pleine charge	*f*	Vollast, VL	*f*	wide-open throttle, WOT	*n*
plots de contact (allumage)	*mpl*	Zündkontakt	*m*	distributor contact points	*npl*
pneumatique automobile	*f*	Fahrzeugpneumatik	*f*	automotive pneumatics	*n*
poids	*m*	Gewichtskraft	*f*	weight (force)	*n*
poids de l'essieu	*m*	Achsgewicht	*n*	axle weight	*n*
poids de mesure	*m*	Meßgewicht	*n*	measurement weight	*n*
poids total admissible	*m*	Gesamtgewichtskraft	*f*	permissible total weight	*n*
point d'allumage	*m*	Zündzeitpunkt	*m*	moment of ignition	*n*
point d'appui (cartographie)	*m*	Stützstelle (Kennfeld)	*f*	data point (program map)	*n*
point d'appui (frein)	*m*	Abstützpunkt (Bremsbacke)	*m*	fulcrum (brake shoe)	*n*

Français		Allemand			Anglais	
point d'ébullition liquide humidifié (liquide de frein)	*m*	Naßsiedepunkt (Bremsflüssigkeit)		*m*	wet boiling point (brake fluid)	*n*
point d'ébullition liquide sec (liquide de frein)	*m*	Trockensiedepunkt (Bremsflüssigkeit)		*m*	dry boiling point (brake fluid)	*n*
point d'enclenchement	*m*	Einschaltpunkt		*m*	cutin point	*n*
point d'étranglement	*m*	Drosselstelle		*f*	throttling point	*n*
point d'inflammation	*m*	Entflammungszeitpunkt		*m*	mixture ignition point	*n*
point d'injection	*m*	Abspritzstelle		*f*	point of injection	*n*
point de changement de vitesse	*m*	Schaltpunkt (Getriebesteuerung)		*m*	shifting point (transmission control)	*n*
point de contact de la roue avec la chaussée	*m*	Radaufstandspunkt		*m*	wheel contact point	*n*
point de début d'injection	*m*	Einspritzbeginn		*m*	start of injection	*n*
point de dosage	*m*	Zumeßstelle		*f*	metering point	*n*
point de pression (valve de frein de stationnement)	*m*	Druckpunkt (Feststellbremsventil)		*m*	pressure point (parking-brake valve)	*n*
point de réglage	*m*	Einstellpunkt		*m*	adjustment point	*n*
point de réglage de ralenti	*m*	Leerlaufeinstellpunkt		*m*	idle-speed adjustment point	*n*
point de régulation finale (servofrein)	*m*	Aussteuerpunkt (Bremskraftverstärker)		*m*	saturation point (brake booster)	*n*
point de rosée sous pression (dessiccation de l'air)	*m*	Drucktaupunkt (Lufttrocknung)		*m*	dew point (air drying)	*n*
point de travail du pneumatique	*m*	Reifenarbeitspunkt		*m*	tire working point	*n*
point de trouble (huile minérale)	*m*	Cloudpoint (Mineralöl)	x	*m*	cloud point (mineral oil)	*n*
point faible	*m*	Schwachstelle		*f*	problem area	*n*
point mort bas, PMB	*m*	Unterer Totpunkt, UT		*m*	bottom dead center, BDC	*n*
point mort haut, PMH	*m*	Oberer Totpunkt, OT		*m*	top dead center, TDC	*n*
point neutre	*m*	Sternpunkt		*m*	neutral point	*n*
pointe de tension	*f*	Spannungsspitze		*f*	voltage peak	*n*
pôle (batterie)	*m*	Endpol (Batterie)		*m*	terminal post (battery)	*n*
polluant	*m*	Schadstoffkomponente		*f*	pollutant component	*n*
polluants (gaz d'échappement)	*mpl*	Schadstoffe (Motorabgas)		*mpl*	pollutants (exhaust gas)	*npl*
pompe "Common Rail"	*f*	Common Rail Pumpe		*f*	common-rail pump	*n*
pompe à accélération périphérique	*f*	Peripheralpumpe		*f*	peripheral pump	*n*
pompe à air	*f*	Luftpumpe		*f*	air pump	*n*
pompe à air secondaire	*f*	Sekundärluftpumpe		*f*	secondary-air pump	*n*
pompe à canal latéral	*f*	Seitenkanalpumpe		*f*	side-channel pump	*n*
pompe à dépression	*f*	Unterdruckpumpe		*f*	vacuum pump	*n*
pompe à eau	*f*	Wasserpumpe		*f*	water pump	*n*
pompe à engrenage	*f*	Zahnradpumpe		*f*	gear pump	*n*
pompe à engrenage intérieur	*f*	Innenzahnradpumpe		*f*	internal-gear pump	*n*
pompe à fixation par berceau	*f*	Wannenpumpe	x	*f*	cradle-mounted pump	*n*
pompe à haute pression	*f*	Hochdruckpumpe		*f*	high-pressure pump	*n*
pompe à main	*f*	Handpumpe		*f*	hand primer pump	*n*
pompe à membrane	*f*	Membranpumpe		*f*	diaphragm pump	*n*
pompe à vide	*f*	Unterdruckpumpe		*f*	vacuum pump	*n*
pompe antigel	*f*	Frostschutzpumpe		*f*	antifreeze pump	*n*

Français		Allemand		Anglais	
pompe centrifuge	*f*	Strömungspumpe	*f*	flow-type pump	*n*
pompe d'alimentation (carburant)	*f*	Kraftstofförderpumpe	*f*	fuel-supply pump	*n*
pompe d'alimentation à main	*f*	Handpumpe	*f*	hand primer pump	*n*
pompe d'alimentation à palettes	*f*	Flügelzellen-Förderpumpe	*f*	vane-type supply pump	*n*
pompe d'alimentation électrique	*f*	Elektroförderpumpe	*f*	electric supply pump	*n*
pompe d'injection	*f*	Kraftstoffeinspritzpumpe	*f*	fuel-injection pump	*n*
pompe d'injection à accumulateur	*f*	Speichereinspritzpumpe	*f*	accumulator fuel-injection pump	*n*
pompe d'injection à galet	*f*	Rollenstößel-Einspritzpumpe	*f*	roller-type fuel-injection pump	*n*
pompe d'injection à piston	*f*	Hubkolbeneinspritzpumpe	*f*	piston injection pump	*n*
pompe d'injection alternative	*f*	Kolben-Einspritzpumpe	*f*	reciprocating fuel-injection pump	*n*
pompe d'injection de carburant	*f*	Kraftstoffeinspritzpumpe	*f*	fuel-injection pump	*n*
pompe d'injection diesel	*f*	Dieseleinspritzpumpe	*f*	diesel fuel-injection pump	*n*
pompe d'injection distributrice	*f*	Verteilereinspritzpumpe (VE)	*f*	distributor injection pump	*n*
pompe d'injection en ligne (PE)	*f*	Reiheneinspritzpumpe (PE)	*f*	in-line fuel-injection pump (PE	*n*
pompe d'injection en ligne à tiroirs (PE)	*f*	Hubschieber-Reiheneinspritzpumpe (PE)	*f*	control-sleeve in-line fuel-injection pump (PE)	*n*
pompe d'injection individuelle (PF)	*f*	Einzylinder-Einspritzpumpe (PF)	*f*	single-plunger fuel-injection pump (PF)	*n*
pompe d'injection monocylindrique (PF)	*f*	Einzylinder-Einspritzpumpe (PF)	*f*	single-plunger fuel-injection pump (PF)	*n*
pompe d'injection rotative	*f*	Radialkolbenpumpe (VR)	*f*	radial-piston pump	*n*
pompe d'injection rotative	*f*	umlaufende Einspritzpumpe	*f*	revolving injection pump	*n*
pompe de charge	*f*	Ladepumpe (EHB)	*f*	charging pump (EHB)	*n*
pompe de circulation d'eau	*f*	Wasserumwälzpumpe	*f*	water-circulating pump	*n*
pompe de direction assistée	*f*	Lenkhilfpumpe	*f*	power-steering pump	*n*
pompe de graissage	*f*	Schmierpumpe	*f*	lubricating pump	*n*
pompe de lave-glace	*f*	Scheibenspülerpumpe	*f*	windshield-washer pump	*n*
pompe de pré-alimentation	*f*	Vorförderpumpe	*f*	presupply pump	*n*
pompe de référence de débit	*f*	Fördermengennormal	*n*	calibration pump	*n*
pompe de référence de début de refoulement	*f*	Förderbeginn-Normal (Einspritzpumpe)	*n*	master pump	*n*
pompe de référence étalon	*f*	Fördermengenhauptnormal	*n*	audit calibration pump	*f*
pompe de refoulement (lave-glace)	*f*	Druckpumpe (Scheibenspüler)	*f*	pressure pump (windshield washer)	*n*
pompe de refoulement d'eau	*f*	Wasserdruckpumpe	*f*	water-pressure pump	*n*
pompe de retour	*f*	Rückförderpumpe	*f*	return pump	*n*
pompe de retour d'huile	*f*	Ölrückförderpumpe	*f*	oil-return pump	*n*
pompe de suralimentation haute pression (ASR)	*f*	Hochdruckladepumpe (ASR)	*f*	high-pressure charge pump (TCS)	*n*
pompe de transfert (carburant)	*f*	Kraftstofförderpumpe	*f*	fuel-supply pump	*n*
pompe distributrice	*f*	Verteilereinspritzpumpe (VE)	*f*	distributor injection pump	*n*
pompe distributrice à piston axial	*f*	Axialkolben-Verteiler-einspritzpumpe	*f*	axial-piston pump	*n*
pompe distributrice à pistons radiaux	*f*	Radialkolbenpumpe (VR)	*f*	radial-piston pump	*n*
pompe électrique à carburant	*f*	Elektrokraftstoffpumpe, EKP	*f*	electric fuel pump	*n*

Français		Allemand		Anglais	
pompe haute pression "Common Rail"	f	Common Rail Hochdruckpumpe	f	common-rail high-pressure pump	n
pompe haute pression à pistons radiaux	f	Radialkolben-Hochdruckpumpe	f	radial-piston high-pressure pump	n
pompe hydraulique	f	Hydropumpe	f	hydraulic pump	n
pompe incorporée au réservoir	f	Tankeinbaupumpe	f	in-tank pump	n
pompe multicarburant	f	Mehrstoffpumpe	f	multifuel pump	n
pompe multicellulaire à rouleaux	f	Rollenzellenpumpe	f	roller-cell pump	n
pompe multicylindrique	f	Mehrzylinder-Einspritzpumpe	f	multiple-plunger pump	n
pompe polycarburant	f	Mehrstoffpumpe	f	multifuel pump	n
pompe rotative à rouleaux	f	Rollenzellenpumpe	f	roller-cell pump	n
pompe submersible	f	Tankeinbaupumpe	f	in-tank pump	n
pompe sur conduite	f	Leitungseinbaupumpe	f	in-line pump (fuel supply)	n
pompe volumétrique	f	Verdrängerpumpe	f	positive-displacement pump	n
pont (batterie)	m	Plattenverbinder (Batterie)	m	plate strap (battery)	n
porosité (filtre)	f	Porengröße (Filter)	f	pore size (filter)	n
porte va-et-vient (autobus)	f	Schwingtür (Omnibus)	f	swinging door (bus)	n
porte-balais	m	Kohlebürstenhalter	m	brush holder	n
porte-balais tubulaire	m	Köcherbürstenhalter	m	cartridge-type brush holder	n
porte-diodes (alternateur)	m	Diodenträger (Generator)	m	diode plate (alternator)	n
porte-injecteur	m	Düsenhalter	m	nozzle-holder assembly	n
porte-injecteur à deux ressorts	m	Zweifeder-Düsenhalter	m	two-spring nozzle holder	n
porte-injecteur à un ressort	m	Einfeder-Düsenhalter	m	single-spring nozzle holder	n
porte-injecteur complet	m	Düsenhalterkombination, DHK	f	nozzle-and-holder assembly	n
porte-injecteur standard	m	Standard-Düsenhalter	m	standard nozzle holder	n
porte-masselottes	m	Fliehgewichtsträger	m	flyweight mount	n
porte-raclette (système d'essuie-glace)	m	Wischarm (Wischeranlage)	m	wiper arm (windshield wiper sytem)	n
porte-soupape	m	Ventilträger	m	valve holder	n
porte-soupape de refoulement	m	Druckventilträger	m	delivery-valve support	n
portée (projecteur)	f	Reichweite (Scheinwerfer)	f	range (headlamp)	n
portée géométrique (projecteur)	f	geometrische Reichweite (Scheinwerfer)	f	geometric range (headlamp)	n
porteur de charge (bougie)	m	Ladungsträger (Zündkerze)	m	charged carrier (spark plug)	n
position d'arrêt	f	Abschlußstellung	f	final position	n
position de contrôle (valve de frein de stationnement)	f	Prüfstellung (Feststellbremsventil)	f	test position (parking-brake valve)	n
position de démarrage	f	Startlage	f	start position	n
position de desserrage	f	Lösestellung	f	release position	n
position de fin de course	f	Endlage	f	end position	n
position de freinage	f	Bremsstellung	f	brakes-applied mode	n
position de freinage d'urgence	f	Vollbremsstellung	f	fully braked mode	n
position de freinage de stationnement	f	Feststellbremsstellung	f	parking-brake-applied position	n
position de freinage partiel	f	Teilbremsstellung	f	partially braked mode	n
position de l'éclateur	f	Funkenlage	f	spark position	n
position de l'étincelle	f	Funkenlage	f	spark position	n

Français		Allemand			Anglais	
position de la tige de réglage	f	Regelstangenstellung		f	rack position, RP	n
position de montage	f	Einbaulage		f	installation position	n
position de pleine charge	f	Vollaststellung		f	full-load position	n
position de refoulement	f	Luftförderungsstellung (Druckregler)		f	air-supply position (pressure regulator)	n
position de roulage	f	Fahrstellung		f	driving (non-braked) mode	n
position de stop	f	Stopp-Stellung		f	stop setting	n
position du papillon	f	Drosselklappenstellung		f	throttle-valve position	n
position médiane	f	Mittelstellung		f	intermediate setting	n
position stop	f	Stopp-Stellung		f	stop setting	n
positionneur de pédale de frein (contrôle des freins)	m	Pedalstütze (Bremsenprüfung)		f	pedal positioner (braking-system inspection)	n
positionneur de volant	m	Lenkradverstellung		f	steering-wheel positioner	n
post-allumage	m	Nachentflammung		f	post-ignition	n
post-combustion	f	Nachverbrennung		f	afterburning	n
post-fonctionnement	m	Nachlauf		m	after-run	n
post-incandescence	f	nachglühen		v	post-glow	n
post-injection	f	nachspritzen		v	post-injection	n
pot de giration	m	Dralltopf		m	swirl plate	n
potentiomètre	m	Potentiometer		m	potentiometer	n
potentiomètre de papillon	m	Drosselklappenpotentiometer		n	throttle-valve potentiometer	n
potentiomètre de réglage	m	Einstellpotentiometer		n	adjusting potentiometer	n
potentiomètre rotatif	m	Drehpotentiometer		n	rotary potentiometer	n
poudre isolante (bougie-crayon de préchauffage)	f	Füllpulver (Glühstiftkerze)		n	filling powder (sheathed-element glow plug)	n
poulie	f	Riemenscheibe		f	belt pulley	n
pousser (voiture, en braquage)	v	schieben (Fahrzeug, beim Lenken)	x	v	push (out to the side, vehicle)	v
poussoir (commande de soupape)	m	Stößel (Ventiltrieb)		m	tappet (valve gear)	n
poussoir (commande des portes	m	Stößel (Türbetätigung)		m	push rod (door control)	n
poussoir (porte-injecteur à deux ressorts)	m	Druckstift (Zweifeder-Düsenhalter)		m	pressure pin (two-spring nozzle holder)	n
poussoir à galet	m	Rollenstößel		m	roller tappet	n
poussoir coulissant	m	Gleitstößel		m	sliding tappet	n
pouvoir antidétonant	m	Klopffestigkeit		f	antiknock quality	n
pouvoir d'absorption calorifique	m	Wärmeaufnahmevermögen		n	heat-absorbing property	n
pouvoir de dissipation thermique	m	Wärmeleitfähigkeit		f	thermal conductivity	n
pouvoir indétonant	m	Klopffestigkeit		f	antiknock quality	n
pré-allumage	m	Vorentflammung		f	pre-ignition	n
pré-excitation (machines tournantes)	f	Vorerregung (drehende Maschinen)		f	pre-excitation (rotating machines)	n
préchambre	f	Vorkammer		f	prechamber	n
préchauffage	m	vorglühen		v	preheat	v
préchauffage du collecteur d'admission	m	Saugrohrvorwärmung		f	intake-manifold preheating	n
précision de dosage	f	Zumeßgenauigkeit		f	metering accuracy	n
précombustion	f	Vorverbrennung		f	pre-combustion	n

Français		Allemand		Anglais	
précontact (relais)	m	Vorkontakt (Relais)	m	advance contact (relay)	n
précoupure	f	Vorabregelung	f	pre-governing	n
précourse (piston de pompe)	f	Vorhub (Pumpenkolben)	m	plunger lift to port closing	n
précourse du piston (jusqu'au début de refoulement)	f	Kolbenhub bis Förderbeginn (Vorhub des Pumpenkolbens)	m	plunger lift to cutoff port closing	n
prédéshydratation (dessiccateur)	f	Vorentwässerung (Lufttrockner)	f	initial drying (air drier)	n
préfiltre (dessiccateur)	m	Vorfilter (Lufttrockner)	n	preliminary filter (air drier)	n
préfiltre (pompe d'alimentation)	m	Vorreiniger	m	preliminary filter (fuel-supply pump)	n
préfiltre à carburant	m	Kraftstoffvorreiniger	m	fuel prefilter	n
préinjection	f	Voreinspritzung	f	pilot injection	n
premier démarrage	m	Erststart	m	first start	n
premier étage (pompe à canal latéral)	m	Vorstufe (Seitenkanalpumpe)	f	first stage (side-channel pump)	n
préparation du mélange	f	Gemischaufbereitung	f	mixture formation	n
prescriptions de sécurité	fpl	Sicherheitsvorschriften	fpl	safety regulations	npl
présélecteur de vitesses	m	Gangvorwahlschalter	m	gear-preselector switch	n
préséparateur (Jetronic)	m	Vorabscheider (Jetronic)	m	preliminary filter (Jetronic)	n
préséparateur à cyclone (filtre à air en papier)	m	Zyklon-Vorabscheider (Papierluftfilter)	m	cyclone prefilter (paper filter)	n
pression à l'intérieur de la pompe	f	Pumpendruck	m	pump interior pressure	n
pression acoustique	f	Schalldruck	m	sound pressure	n
pression calculée (effet de freinage)	f	Berechnungsdruck (Bremswirkung)	m	design pressure (braking action)	n
pression d'accouplement	f	Aufsatteldruck (Sattelschlepper)	m	kingpin load	n
pression d'actionnement	f	Betätigungsdruck	m	applied pressure	n
pression d'admission	f	Saugrohrdruck	m	intake-manifold pressure	n
pression d'air	f	Luftdruck	m	air pressure	n
pression d'air corrigée	f	korrigierter Luftdruck	m	corrected air pressure	n
pression d'alimentation (ESP)	f	Vordruck (ESP)	m	admission pressure (ESP)	n
pression d'alimentation (frein)	f	Vorratsdruck (Bremse)	m	supply pressure (brakes)	n
pression d'alimentation (Jetronic)	f	Versorgungsdruck (Jetronic)	m	supply pressure (Jetronic)	n
pression d'appui (garniture de frein)	f	Belagbelastung (Bremsbelag)	f	lining load	n
pression d'aspiration	f	Saugdruck	m	suction pressure	n
pression d'enclenchement	f	Einschaltdruck	m	cutin pressure	n
pression d'injection	f	Einspritzdruck	m	injection pressure	n
pression d'intervention (garnitures de frein)	f	Spannkraft (Bremsbeläge)	f	application force (brake linings)	n
pression d'ouverture	f	Öffnungsdruck	m	opening pressure	n
pression d'ouverture de l'injecteur	f	Düsenöffnungsdruck	m	nozzle-opening pressure	n
pression dans conduite	f	Leitungsdruck	m	line pressure	n
pression dans l'élément	f	Elementdruck	m	pump-side pressure	n
pression de blocage (frein)	f	Blockierdruck	m	locking pressure (brakes)	n

Français		Allemand		Anglais	
pression de circuit (ESP)	*f*	Kreisdruck (ESP)	*m*	circuit pressure (ESP)	*n*
pression de combustion	*f*	Verbrennungsdruck	*m*	combustion pressure	*n*
pression de commande	*f*	Steuerdruck	*m*	control pressure	*n*
pression de coupure	*f*	Abschaltdruck	*m*	cutoff pressure	*n*
pression de desserrage	*f*	Lösedruck	*m*	release pressure	*n*
pression de fermeture	*f*	Schließdruck	*m*	closing pressure	*n*
pression de freinage	*f*	Bremsdruck	*m*	braking pressure	*n*
pression de freinage continue	*f*	Dauerbremsdruck	*m*	sustained braking pressure	*n*
pression de freinage partielle	*f*	Teilbremsdruck	*m*	partial braking pressure	*n*
pression de freinage sur roue	*f*	Radbremsdruck	*m*	wheel brake pressure	*n*
pression de l'accumulateur	*f*	Speicherdruck	*m*	storage pressure	*n*
pression de l'air de suralimentation	*f*	Ladedruck	*m*	charge-air pressure	*n*
pression de modulation (commande de boîte de vitesses)	*f*	Modulationsdruck (Getriebesteuerung)	*m*	modulation pressure (transmission control)	*n*
pression de pointe	*f*	Spitzendruck	*m*	peak injection pressure	*n*
pression de rappel	*f*	Rückstelldruck	*m*	retraction pressure	*n*
pression de référence	*f*	Referenzdruck	*m*	reference pressure	*n*
pression de refoulement	*f*	Förderdruck	*m*	delivery pressure	*n*
pression de réponse	*f*	Ansprechdruck	*m*	response pressure	*n*
pression de sécurité	*f*	Sicherungsdruck	*m*	safety pressure	*n*
pression de service	*f*	Betriebsdruck	*m*	operating pressure	*n*
pression de suralimentation	*f*	Ladedruck	*m*	charge-air pressure	*n*
pression de tarage	*f*	Öffnungsdruck	*m*	opening pressure	*n*
pression de tarage de l'injecteur	*f*	Düsenöffnungsdruck	*m*	nozzle-opening pressure	*n*
pression de transfert	*f*	Förderdruck	*m*	delivery pressure	*n*
pression de transfert (pompe d'alimentation)	*f*	Förderpumpendruck	*m*	supply-pump pressure	*n*
pression de vapeur (essence)	*f*	Dampfdruck (Benzin)	*m*	vapor pressure (gasoline)	*n*
pression différentielle	*f*	Differenzdruck	*m*	differential pressure	*n*
pression du pneu	*f*	Reifendruck	*m*	tire pressure	*n*
pression du système (Jetronic)	*f*	Systemdruck (Jetronic)	*m*	primary pressure (Jetronic)	*n*
pression maximale	*f*	Spitzendruck	*m*	peak injection pressure	*n*
pression maximale (servofrein)	*f*	Aussteuerdruck (Bremskraftverstärker)	*m*	output pressure (brake booster)	*n*
pression nominale	*f*	Nenndruck	*m*	nominal pressure	*n*
pression primaire (frein)	*f*	Vorratsdruck (Bremse)	*m*	supply pressure (brakes)	*n*
pression résiduelle	*f*	Restdruck	*m*	residual pressure	*n*
pression secondaire (frein)	*f*	Sekundärdruck (Bremse)	*m*	secondary pressure (brakes)	*n*
pression soufflet	*f*	Balgdruck (Luftfeder)	*m*	bellows pressure	*n*
pression statique	*f*	Standdruck	*m*	static pressure	*n*
prétension de courroie	*f*	Riemenvorspannung	*f*	belt pre-tension	*n*
prétensionneur de ceinture	*m*	Gurtstraffer (Sicherheitsgurt)	*m*	seat-belt tightener	*n*
principe bicalculateur (régulation ABS)	*m*	Zweirechner-Prinzip (ABS-Regelung)	*n*	dual-processor principle (ABS control)	*n*
principe de décharge	*m*	Überströmprinzip	*n*	overflow principle	*n*
principe de reflux (ABS)	*m*	Rückförderprinzip (ABS)	*n*	return principle (ABS)	*n*

Français		Allemand		Anglais	
principe de transfert	*m*	Durchströmprinzip	*n*	throughflow principle	*n*
prise	*f*	Steckdose	*f*	socket	*n*
prise de diagnostic	*f*	Diagnosesteckdose	*f*	diagnosis socket	*n*
prise de stationnement (ABS pour remorque)	*f*	Parkdose (Anhänger-ABS) x	*f*	parking socket (trailer ABS)	*n*
prise de tension (capteur de niveau)	*f*	Spannungsabgriff (Niveaugeber)	*m*	contact wiper (level sensor)	*n*
prise de test (frein à air comprimé)	*f*	Prüfanschluß (Druckluftbremse)	*m*	pressure test connection (compressed-air brake)	*n*
procédé d'injection directe	*m*	Direkteinspritzverfahren	*n*	direct-injection (DI) process	*n*
procédé de combustion	*m*	Verbrennungsverfahren	*n*	combustion system	*n*
procédé de suralimentation	*m*	Aufladeverfahren	*n*	supercharging process	*n*
procès-verbal d'essai	*m*	Prüfprotokoll	*n*	test record	*n*
processus de combustion	*m*	Verbrennungsablauf	*m*	combustion characteristics	*npl*
production propre	*f*	Eigenfertigung	*f*	in-house production	*n*
produit d'autre marque	*m*	Fremderzeugnis	*n*	non-Bosch product	*n*
produit d'échange standard	*m*	Austausch-Erzeugnis	*n*	exchange product	*n*
profil de came	*m*	Nockenablauf	*m*	cam profile	*n*
profil de courbe	*m*	Kurvenprofil	*n*	curve profile	*n*
programme Commerce	*m*	Handelsprogramm	*n*	aftermarket program	*n*
programme d'échange standard	*m*	Austauschprogramm (Werksaustausch)	*n*	exchange program (factory exchange)	*n*
programme d'essai (émissions)	*m*	Prüfprogramm (Abgasprüfung)	*n*	test program (exhaust-gas test)	*n*
projecteur	*m*	Scheinwerfer	*m*	headlamp	*n*
projecteur antibrouillard	*m*	Nebelscheinwerfer, NSW	*m*	fog lamp	*n*
projecteur code	*m*	Abblendscheinwerfer	*m*	low-beam headlamp	*n*
projecteur complémentaire	*m*	Zusatzscheinwerfer, ZSW	*m*	auxiliary lamp	*n*
projecteur d'ambiance	*m*	Flutlichtstrahler	*m*	floodlight	*n*
projecteur de croisement	*m*	Abblendscheinwerfer	*m*	low-beam headlamp	*n*
projecteur de recherche	*m*	Suchscheinwerfer	*m*	spot lamp	*n*
projecteur de travail	*m*	Arbeitsscheinwerfer	*m*	floodlamp	*n*
projecteur encastrable	*m*	Einbauscheinwerfer	*m*	flush-fitting headlamp	*n*
projecteur escamotable	*m*	Klappscheinwerfer	*m*	retractable headlight	*n*
projecteur extérieur	*m*	Anbauscheinwerfer	*m*	external-fitting headlamp	*n*
projecteur longue portée	*m*	Weitstrahlscheinwerfer	*m*	long-range driving lamp	*n*
projecteur orientable	*m*	Suchscheinwerfer	*m*	spot lamp	*n*
projecteur polyellipsoïde	*m*	Poly-Ellipsoid-Scheinwerfer, PES	*m*	PES headlamp	*n*
projecteur portable	*m*	Handscheinwerfer	*m*	hand-portable searchlight	*n*
projecteur route	*m*	Fernscheinwerfer	*m*	driving lamp	*n*
projecteur route supplémentaire	*m*	Zusatz-Fernlichtscheinwerfer	*m*	auxiliary driving lamp	*n*
propriété de friction (garniture de frein)	*f*	Reibeigenschaft (Bremsbelag)	*f*	friction properties (brake lining	*n*
propulsion (véhicule)	*f*	Vortrieb (Kfz)	*m*	accelerative force (motor vehicle)	*n*
protection à maximum de tension	*f*	Überspannungsschutz	*m*	overvoltage protection	*n*
protection anticapotage	*f*	Überschlagschutz	*m*	rollover protection	*n*

Français

Français		Allemand		Anglais	
protection anticorrosion	*f*	Korrosionsschutz	*m*	corrosion protection	*n*
protection contre l'inversion de polarité (charge de batterie)	*f*	Verpolungsschutz (Batterieladung)	*m*	reverse-polarity protection (battery charge)	*n*
protection contre la corrosion	*f*	Korrosionsschutz	*m*	corrosion protection	*n*
protection contre le remorquage (alarme auto)	*f*	Abschleppschutz (Autoalarm)	*m*	tow-away protection (car alarm)	*n*
protection contre le vieillissement (essence)	*f*	Alterungsschutz (Kraftstoff)	*m*	anti-aging additive (gasoline)	*n*
protection contre le vol des roues (alarme auto)	*f*	Radschutz (Autoalarm)	*m*	wheel-theft protection (car alarm)	*n*
protection contre le vol des roues et le remorquage (alarme auto)	*f*	Rad- und Abschleppschutz (Autoalarm)	*m*	wheel theft and tow-away protection (car alarm)	*n*
protection contre les éclaboussures	*f*	Spritzschutz (Wasser)	*m*	splash guard (water)	*n*
protection contre les incidences (surtension)	*f*	Folgeschadenschutz (Überspannung)	*m*	consequential-damage protection (overvoltage)	*n*
protection contre les projections d'eau	*f*	Spritzschutz (Wasser)	*m*	splash guard (water)	*n*
protection contre les radiations	*f*	Strahlungsschutz	*m*	radiation shield	*n*
protection contre les surtension:	*f*	Überspannungsschutz	*m*	overvoltage protection	*n*
protection contre manipulation	*f*	Manipulationsschutz	*m*	protection against manipulation	*n*
protection de l'habitacle par ultrasons (alarme auto)	*f*	Ultraschall-Innenraumschutz (Autoalarm)	*m*	ultrasonic passenger-compartment protection (car alarm)	*n*
protection de surchauffage	*f*	Überhitzungsschutz	*m*	overheat protection	*n*
protection de surrégime	*f*	Überdrehzahlschutz	*m*	overspeed protection	*n*
protection des circuits d'alimentation (système de freinage)	*f*	Kreisabsicherung (Bremssystem)	*f*	circuit safeguard (braking system)	*n*
protection du coffre (alarme auto)	*f*	Kofferraumsicherung (Autoalarm)	*f*	trunk protection (car alarm)	*n*
protégé contre l'inversion de polarité	*loc*	verpolungssicher	*adj*	insensitive to reverse polarity	*adj*
protégé contre la poussière	*pp*	staubgeschützt	*adj*	dust-protected	*pp*
puissance absorbée	*f*	Leistungsaufnahme	*f*	power input	*n*
puissance d'entraînement	*f*	Antriebsleistung	*f*	drive power	*n*
puissance de démarrage	*f*	Startleistung	*f*	starting power	*n*
puissance de l'alternateur	*f*	Generatorleistung	*f*	alternator output power	*n*
puissance débitée (machines électriques)	*f*	Leistungsabgabe (elektrische Maschinen)	*f*	power output (electrical machines)	*n*
puissance des récepteurs	*f*	Verbraucherleistung	*f*	electrical load requirements	*n*
puissance du moteur	*f*	Motorleistung	*f*	engine performance	*n*
puissance électrique dissipée	*f*	elektrische Verlustleistung	*f*	electrical power loss	*n*
puissance instantanée de freinage	*f*	Bremsleistung	*f*	instantaneous braking power	*n*
puissance motrice	*f*	Antriebsleistung	*f*	drive power	*n*
puissance requise (récepteurs électriques)	*f*	Verbraucherleistung	*f*	electrical load requirements	*n*
pulsation de pression	*f*	Druckschwingung	*f*	pressure pulsation	*n*

Français		Allemand		Anglais	
pulvérisation du carburant	*f*	Kraftstoffzerstäubung	*f*	fuel atomization	*n*
purge d'air	*f*	entlüften	*v*	bleed	*v*
purgeur d'eau	*m*	Entwässerungsventil	*n*	drain valve	*n*
purgeur rapide (frein)	*m*	Schnellentlüftungsventil (Bremse)	*n*	rapid-bleeder valve (brakes)	*n*
Q					
qualité de séparation (filtre)	*f*	Abscheidegüte (Filter)	*f*	filtration efficiency	*n*
quantité d'oxygène résiduelle (gaz d'échappement)	*f*	Restsauerstoff (Abgas)	*m*	exhaust-gas oxygen	*n*
quantité de base injectée	*f*	Grundeinspritzmenge	*f*	basic injection quantity	*n*
quantité de carburant injectée	*f*	Einspritzmenge	*f*	injected fuel quantity	*n*
quantité de saturation (humidité de l'air)	*f*	Sättigungsmenge (Luftfeuchtigkeit)	*f*	saturation point (water content)	*n*
queue de l'étincelle	*f*	Funkenschwanz	*m*	spark tail	*n*
queue de pignon	*f*	Ritzelschaft	*m*	pinion shaft	*n*
queue de piston	*f*	Kolbenschaft (Druckventil)	*m*	pressure-valve stem	*n*
R					
raccord	*m*	Anschlußstutzen	*m*	fitting	*n*
raccord d'accouplement	*m*	Kupplungsanschluß	*m*	coupling port	*n*
raccord d'aspiration	*m*	Sauganschluß	*m*	suction connection	*n*
raccord d'eau de refroidissemen	*m*	Kühlwasseranschluß	*m*	water port	*n*
raccord d'essai (frein à air comprimé)	*m*	Prüfanschluß (Druckluftbremse)	*m*	pressure test connection (compressed-air brake)	*n*
raccord d'huile de fuite	*m*	Leckölanschluß	*m*	leakage-fuel connection	*n*
raccord de commande	*m*	Steueranschluß	*m*	control connection	*n*
raccord de gonflage des pneus	*m*	Reifenfüllanschluß	*m*	tire-inflation fitting	*n*
raccord de pression	*m*	Druckanschluß	*m*	pressure connection	*n*
raccord de refoulement (pompe d'injection)	*m*	Druckanschluß (Einspritzpumpe)	*m*	pressure connection (fuel-injection pump)	*n*
raccord de sortie (pompe d'injection)	*m*	Druckventilhalter (Einspritzpumpe)	*m*	delivery-valve holder (fuel-injection pump)	*n*
raccord de surpression	*m*	Überdrucknippel	*m*	overpressure nipple	*n*
raccord fileté	*m*	Anschlußnippel	*m*	connection fitting	*n*
raccord rapide	*m*	Schnellkupplung	*f*	rapid coupling	*n*
raccordement de frein	*m*	Bremsanschluß	*m*	brake connection	*n*
raclette d'essuie-glace	*f*	Wischblatt	*n*	wiper blade	*n*
raclette de lavophare	*f*	Lichtwischerblatt	*n*	beamwash wiper-blade	*n*
raclette de lunette arrière	*f*	Heck-Wischblatt	*n*	rear-window wiper blade	*n*
raclette de pare-brise	*f*	Front-Wischblatt	*n*	front wiper blade	*n*
raclette en caoutchouc	*f*	Wischgummi	*n*	wiper-blade element	*n*
radiateur	*m*	Kühlkörper	*m*	heat sink	*n*
radiocommande	*f*	Funk-Fernbedienung	*f*	radio remote control	*n*
raideur de ressort	*f*	Federrate	*f*	spring rate	*n*
raidisseur nervuré	*m*	Versteifungsrippe	*f*	strengthening rib	*n*
rail (Common Rail)	*m*	Hochdruckspeicher (Common Rail)	*m*	high-pressure accumulator (common rail)	*n*
rail de contact (rampe distributrice)	*m*	Kontaktschiene (Kraftstoffverteiler)	*f*	contact rail (fuel rail)	*n*

Français

Français		Allemand		Anglais	
rainure annulaire	*f*	Ringnut	*f*	ring groove	*n*
rainure annulaire de piston	*f*	Kolbenringnut	*f*	piston-ring groove	*n*
rainure de barrage	*f*	Sperrnut	*f*	oil-block groove	*n*
rainure de distribution	*f*	Verteilernut	*f*	distributor slot	*n*
rainure de guidage	*f*	Führungsschlitz	*m*	guide slot	*n*
rainure de retour des fuites	*f*	Leckrückführnut	*f*	leakage-return slot	*n*
rainure de stop	*f*	Stoppnut	*f*	stop slot	*n*
rainure longitudinale (piston de pompe)	*f*	Längsnut (Pumpenkolben)	*f*	vertical groove (pump plunger)	*n*
rainure verticale (piston de pompe)	*f*	Längsnut (Pumpenkolben)	*f*	vertical groove (pump plunger)	*n*
ralenti	*m*	Leerlauf	*m*	idle	*n*
ralenti accéléré	*m*	Leerlaufanhebung	*f*	idle-speed increase	*n*
ralentir	*v*	verlangsamen	*v*	slow down	*v*
ralentisseur	*m*	Verlangsamer	*m*	retarder	*n*
ralentisseur électrique	*m*	Strombremse (Starter)	*f*	electric brake (starter)	*n*
ralentisseur électromagnétique	*m*	elektrodynamischer Verlangsamer	*m*	electrodynamic retarder	*n*
ralentisseur hydrodynamique	*m*	hydrodynamischer Verlangsamer	*m*	hydrodynamic retarder	*n*
ralentisseur sur échappement	*m*	Auspuffverlangsamer	*m*	exhaust brake	*n*
rampe à billes (commande des portes, direction)	*f*	Kugelumlauf (Türbetätigung, Lenkung)	*m*	recirculating-ball device (door control, steering system)	*n*
rampe à profil (correcteur d'avance)	*f*	Wälzbahn (Zündversteller)	*f*	contact path (advance mechanism)	*n*
rampe d'injection (injection multipoint)	*f*	Kraftstoffverteilerstück (Einzeleinspritzung)	*n*	fuel-distribution pipe (multipoint fuel injection)	*n*
rampe de contact (potentiomètre)	*f*	Potentiometerbahn	*f*	potentiometer track	*n*
rampe de distribution (élément de pompage)	*f*	Steuerkante (Pumpenelement)	*f*	helix (plunger-and-barrel assembly)	*n*
rampe de travail	*f*	Rollengleitkurve	*f*	roller race	*n*
rampe de vitesse	*f*	Geschwindigkeitsrampe x	*f*	vehicle-speed ramp	*n*
rampe distributrice	*f*	Kraftstoffverteiler	*m*	fuel rail	*n*
rampe distributrice (injection multipoint)	*f*	Kraftstoffverteilerstück (Einzeleinspritzung)	*n*	fuel-distribution pipe (multipoint fuel injection)	*n*
rampe distributrice de carburant	*f*	Kraftstoffverteiler	*m*	fuel rail	*n*
rampe distributrice haute pression "Common Rail"	*f*	Common Rail Hochdruckverteilerleiste	*f*	common-rail high-pressure fuel rail	*n*
rampe hélicoïdale (élément de pompage)	*f*	Steuerkante (Pumpenelement)	*f*	helix (plunger-and-barrel assembly)	*n*
rapport air-carburant	*m*	Luft-Kraftstoff-Verhältnis	*n*	air-fuel (A/F) ratio	*n*
rapport cyclique d'impulsions	*m*	Tastverhältnis	*n*	on/off ratio	*n*
rapport d'amplification	*m*	Verstärkungsverhältnis	*n*	amplification ratio	*n*
rapport d'impulsions	*m*	Tastverhältnis	*n*	on/off ratio	*n*
rapport de régulation (valve de frein)	*m*	Regelverhältnis (Bremsventil)	*n*	control ratio (brake valve)	*n*
rapport de roulage	*m*	Fahrstufe	*f*	gear selection	*n*
rapport de transformation (nombre de spires)	*m*	Windungsverhältnis	*n*	turn ratio	*n*

Français		Allemand		Anglais	
rapport de transmission de la boîte de vitesses	*m*	Getriebeübersetzung	*f*	gearbox step-up ratio	*n*
rapport de vitesse	*m*	Getriebefahrstufe	*f*	gearbox stage	*n*
rapport volumétrique	*m*	Verdichtungsverhältnis	*n*	compression ratio	*n*
ratés d'allumage	*mpl*	Zündaussetzer	*m*	misfiring	*n*
ratés d'inflammation	*mpl*	Entflammungsaussetzer	*m*	ignition miss	*n*
ratés de combustion	*mpl*	Verbrennungsaussetzer	*m*	combustion miss	*n*
rattrapage de jeu (frein)	*m*	Bremsennachstellung	*f*	brake adjustment	*n*
rayon actif	*m*	Wirkradius	*m*	effective radius	*n*
rayon de courbure (virage)	*m*	Kurvenradius (Fahrbahn)	*m*	radius of bend (road)	*n*
rayon du cercle de braquage	*m*	Spurkreisradius	*m*	turning radius	*n*
rayonnement (CEM)	*m*	Abstrahlung (EMV)	*f*	radiation (EMC)	*n*
rayonnement de signaux perturbateurs (CEM)	*m*	Störstrahlung (EMV)	*f*	interference radiation (EMC)	*n*
rayonnement incident (CEM)	*m*	Einstrahlung (EMV)	*f*	incident radiation (EMC)	*n*
rayonnement parasite (CEM)	*m*	Störstrahlung (EMV)	*f*	interference radiation (EMC)	*n*
rayonnement thermique	*m*	Wärmestrahlung	*f*	heat radiation	*n*
réaction (régulation)	*f*	Rückkoppelung (Regelung)	*f*	feedback (control)	*n*
réaction d'induit	*f*	Ankerrückwirkung	*f*	armature reaction	*n*
réaction de contre-pression	*f*	Gegendruck	*m*	back-pressure reaction	*n*
réaction transitoire	*f*	Übergangsverhalten	*n*	transition response	*n*
réaction transitoire de lacet (dynamique d'un véhicule)	*f*	Lenkwinkelsprung (Kfz-Dynamik)	*m*	sudden steering input (vehicle dynamics)	*n*
réalisation d'échantillons	*f*	Musterbau	*m*	prototype manufacture	*n*
rebondissement des contacts	*m*	Kontaktprellung	*f*	contact chatter	*n*
rebord de fixation (batterie)	*m*	Bodenleiste (Batterie)	*f*	bottom rail (battery)	*n*
récepteur à fonctionnement de courte durée	*m*	Kurzzeitverbraucher	*m*	short-term load	*n*
récepteur à ultrasons	*m*	Ultraschallsensor	*m*	ultrasonic receiver	*n*
récepteur d'air comprimé	*m*	Druckluftverbraucher	*m*	compressed-air load	*n*
récepteur permanent	*m*	Dauerverbraucher	*m*	permanent load	*n*
récepteurs auxiliaires (dispositif de freinage à air comprimé)	*mpl*	Nebenverbraucher (Druckluftanlage)	*mpl*	secondary loads (compressed-air system)	*npl*
réchauffage	*m*	Warmlauf	*m*	warm-up	*v*
réchauffage du filtre	*m*	Filteraufheizung	*f*	filter heating	*n*
réchauffeur de voiture	*m*	Wagenheizung	*f*	vehicle heater	*n*
recirculation des gaz d'échappement	*f*	Abgasrückführung, AGR	*f*	exhaust-gas recirculation, EGR	*n*
recyclage des gaz d'échappement	*m*	Abgasrückführung, AGR	*f*	exhaust-gas recirculation, EGR	*n*
RED, régulation électronique diesel	*a*	elektronische Dieselregelung, EDC	*f*	electronic diesel control, EDC	*n*
redémarrage	*m*	Wiederstart x	*m*	repeat start	*n*
redressement (courant alternatif)	*m*	Gleichrichtung (Wechselstrom)	*f*	rectification (alternating current)	*n*
redressement à deux alternance:	*m*	Zweiweggleichrichtung	*f*	full-wave rectification	*n*
redressement biplaque	*m*	Zweiweggleichrichtung	*f*	full-wave rectification	*n*
redressement pleine-onde	*m*	Zweiweggleichrichtung	*f*	full-wave rectification	*n*

Français		Allemand		Anglais	
redresseur (alternateur)	*m*	Gleichrichter (Generator)	*m*	rectifier (alternator)	*n*
redresseur à deux alternances	*m*	Zweiweggleichrichter	*m*	full-wave rectifier	*n*
redresseur demi-onde	*m*	Einweggleichrichter	*m*	half-wave rectifier	*n*
redresseur pleine-onde	*m*	Zweiweggleichrichter	*m*	full-wave rectifier	*n*
réducteur	*m*	Vorgelege	*n*	reduction gear	*n*
réducteur à course de levée	*m*	Hubgetriebe	*n*	lifting gear assembly	*n*
réducteur de débit	*m*	Mindermengeneinsteller	*m*	fuel-flow reducing device	*n*
réducteur de freinage	*m*	Bremskraftminderer	*m*	braking-force reducer	*n*
réducteur de pression	*m*	Reduzierventil	*n*	reducing valve	*n*
réducteur de pression de freinage	*m*	Bremsdruckminderer	*m*	proportioning valve (brakes)	*n*
réduction de débit	*f*	Mindermenge	*f*	reduced delivery	*n*
référence	*f*	Bestellnummer	*f*	part number	*n*
réflecteur	*m*	Reflektor	*m*	reflector	*n*
réflecteur bifocal	*m*	Bifokalreflektor	*m*	bifocal reflector	*n*
réflecteur de base	*m*	Grundreflektor	*m*	basic reflector	*n*
réflecteur étagé	*m*	Stufenreflektor	*m*	stepped reflector	*n*
réflecteur homofocal	*m*	Homofokal-Reflektor	*m*	homofocal reflector	*n*
réflecteur multifocal	*m*	Multi-Focus-Reflektor, MFR	*m*	Multi-Focus-Reflector, MFR	*n*
réflecteur supplémentaire	*m*	Zusatzreflektor	*m*	supplementary reflector	*n*
reflux des gaz	*m*	rückblasen	*v*	blowback	*n*
refoulement (air comprimé)	*m*	Druckförderung (Druckluft)	*f*	pressure delivery (compressed air)	*n*
refoulement à chaud	*m*	Heißförderung	*f*	hot-fuel delivery	*n*
refoulement basse pression	*m*	Niederdruckförderung	*f*	low-pressure delivery	*n*
refoulement du carburant	*m*	Kraftstofförderung	*f*	fuel supply and delivery	*n*
refoulement haute pression	*m*	Hochdruckförderung	*f*	high-pressure delivery	*n*
refroidi par air	*pp*	luftgekühlt	*pp*	air-cooled	*pp*
refroidissement	*m*	Kühlung	*f*	cooling	*n*
refroidissement de l'air de suralimentation	*m*	Ladeluftkühlung, LLK	*f*	charge-air cooling	*n*
refroidissement de la charge d'air	*m*	Ladeluftkühlung, LLK	*f*	charge-air cooling	*n*
refroidissement par air	*m*	Luftkühlung	*f*	air cooling	*n*
refroidisseur	*m*	Kühlkörper	*m*	heat sink	*n*
refroidisseur d'air de suralimentation	*m*	Ladeluftkühler	*m*	charge-air cooler	*n*
refroidisseur nervuré	*m*	Rippenkühlkörper	*m*	heat sink with ribs	*n*
régénération (dessiccateur)	*f*	Regeneration (Lufttrockner)	*f*	regeneration (air drier)	*n*
régénération forcée	*f*	Zwangsregeneration	*f*	forced regeneration	*n*
régime à charge partielle	*m*	Teillastdrehzahl	*f*	part-load speed	*n*
régime accéléré de démarrage	*m*	Startdrehzahlanhebung	*f*	cranking-speed increase	*n*
régime autorisé en pleine charge	*m*	obere Vollastdrehzahl	*f*	maximum full-load speed	*n*
régime consigne de ralenti	*m*	Leerlauf-Solldrehzahl	*f*	low-idle setpoint speed	*n*
régime d'enclenchement	*m*	Einschaltdrehzahl (Generator)	*f*	cutting-in speed (alternator)	*n*
régime de charge (batterie)	*m*	Batterieladestrom	*m*	battery charge current	*n*
régime de coupure	*m*	Abschaltdrehzahl	*f*	cutoff speed	*n*

Français		Allemand		Anglais	
régime de décélération	*m*	Schiebebetrieb	*m*	overrun	*n*
régime de décrochage	*m*	Abspringdrehzahl	*f*	no-follow speed	*n*
régime de démarrage	*m*	Startdrehzahl	*f*	cranking speed	*n*
régime de fonctionnement	*m*	Betriebsdrehzahl	*f*	operating speed	*n*
régime de frein-moteur	*m*	Schiebebetrieb	*m*	overrun	*n*
régime de pleine charge	*m*	Vollastdrehzahl	*f*	full-load speed	*n*
régime de ralenti	*m*	Leerlaufdrehzahl	*f*	idle speed	*n*
régime de seuil	*m*	Schwellendrehzahl	*f*	threshold speed	*n*
régime en fin de démarrage	*m*	Startabwurfdrehzahl	*f*	starting cutout speed	*n*
régime inférieur de pleine charge	*m*	untere Vollastdrehzahl	*f*	minimum full-load speed	*n*
régime intermédiaire	*m*	Zwischendrehzahl	*m*	intermediate speed	*n*
régime limite	*m*	Grenzdrehzahl	*f*	limit speed	*n*
régime limite supérieur	*m*	obere Vollastdrehzahl	*f*	maximum full-load speed	*n*
régime maximum à vide	*m*	obere Leerlaufdrehzahl	*f*	high idle speed	*n*
régime minimum à vide	*m*	untere Leerlaufdrehzahl	*f*	low-idle speed	*n*
régime minimum de démarrage	*m*	Startmindestdrehzahl	*f*	minimum starting speed	*n*
régime moteur	*m*	Motordrehzahl	*f*	engine speed	*n*
régime nominal	*m*	Nenndrehzahl	*f*	rated speed	*n*
réglage de la précourse	*m*	Vorhubeinstellung	*f*	prestroke adjustment	*n*
réglage de rétroviseur	*m*	Spiegelverstellung	*f*	mirror adjuster	*n*
réglage des sièges	*m*	Sitzverstellung	*f*	seat adjustment	*n*
réglage du dossier de siège	*m*	Lehnenverstellung	*f*	backrest adjuster	*n*
réglementation antipollution	*f*	Abgasgesetzgebung	*f*	emission-control legislation	*n*
réglophare	*m*	Scheinwerfer-Einstellprüfgerät	*n*	headlight aiming device	*n*
régulateur (injection diesel)	*m*	Drehzahlregler (Dieseleinspritzung)	*m*	governor (diesel fuel injection)	*n*
régulateur à caractéristique coudée (frein)	*m*	Knickregler (Bremse) x	*m*	dynamic load-sensing valve (brakes)	*n*
régulateur à deux positions (régulation lambda)	*m*	Zweipunktregler (Lambda-Regelung)	*m*	two-position controller (lambda closed-loop control)	*n*
régulateur à échelons	*m*	Stufendrehzahlregler	*m*	combination governor	*n*
régulateur à vibreur	*m*	Kontaktregler	*m*	contact regulator	*n*
régulateur à vitesse continue	*m*	Enddrehzahlregler	*m*	maximum-speed governor	*n*
régulateur bicontact	*m*	Zweikontaktregler	*m*	double-contact regulator	*n*
régulateur centrifuge	*m*	Fliehkraftregler	*m*	mechanical governor	*n*
régulateur d'air additionnel	*m*	Zusatzluftschieber	*m*	auxiliary-air device	*n*
régulateur d'alternateur	*m*	Spannungsregler (Generator)	*m*	voltage regulator (alternator)	*n*
régulateur d'état (ESP)	*m*	Zustandsregler (ESP)	*m*	state controller (ESP)	*n*
régulateur d'intensité	*m*	Stromregler	*m*	current regulator	*n*
régulateur de climatisseur	*m*	Klimaregelung	*f*	air-conditioning	*n*
régulateur de courant	*m*	Stromregler	*m*	current regulator	*n*
régulateur de débit	*m*	Stromregelventil	*n*	flow-control valve	*n*
régulateur de dynamique de roulage	*m*	Fahrdynamikregler	*m*	vehicle dynamics controller	*n*
régulateur de freinage (ASR)	*m*	Bremsregler (ASR)	*m*	brake controller (TCS)	*n*
régulateur de glissement (ESP)	*m*	Schlupfregler (ESP)	*m*	slip controller (ESP)	*n*

Français		Allemand		Anglais	
régulateur de la stabilité de fonctionnement	*m*	Laufruheregler	*m*	smooth-running regulator	*n*
régulateur de luminosité (projecteur)	*m*	Helligkeitsregler (Scheinwerfer	*m*	luminosity controller (headlamp)	*n*
régulateur de mélange (Jetronic)	*m*	Gemischregler (Jetronic)	*m*	mixture-control unit (Jetronic)	*n*
régulateur de mise en action	*m*	Warmlaufregler	*m*	warm-up regulator	*n*
régulateur de pression	*m*	Druckregler	*m*	pressure regulator	*n*
régulateur de pression à membrane	*m*	Membrandruckregler	*m*	diaphragm governor	*n*
régulateur de pression à piston	*m*	Kolbendruckregler	*m*	plunger-type pressure regulator	*n*
régulateur de pression à trop-plein	*m*	Überströmdruckregler	*m*	overflow pressure regulator	*n*
régulateur de pression d'alimentation	*m*	Systemdruckregler	*m*	primary-pressure regulator	*n*
régulateur de pression de carburant	*m*	Kraftstoffdruckregler	*m*	fuel-pressure regulator	*n*
régulateur de pression de suralimentation	*m*	Ladedruckregler	*m*	pressure-charging regulator	*n*
régulateur de pression différentielle	*m*	Differenzdruckventil	*n*	differential-pressure valve	*n*
régulateur de pression du système	*m*	Systemdruckregler	*m*	primary-pressure regulator	*n*
régulateur de ralenti	*m*	Leerlaufregler	*m*	idle controller	*n*
régulateur de roulage en mode incidenté	*m*	Notfahrstellregler	*m*	limp-home position governor	*n*
régulateur de tension (alternateur)	*m*	Spannungsregler (Generator)	*m*	voltage regulator (alternator)	*n*
régulateur de ventilateur	*m*	Gebläseregler	*m*	blower control unit	*n*
régulateur de vitesse	*m*	Drehzahlregler (Dieseleinspritzung)	*m*	governor (diesel fuel injection)	*n*
régulateur de vitesse de roulage	*m*	Fahrgeschwindigkeitsregler, FGR	*m*	vehicle-speed controller	*n*
régulateur de vitesse maximale	*m*	Enddrehzahlregler	*m*	maximum-speed governor	*n*
régulateur du moteur (ASR)	*m*	Motorregler (ASR)	*m*	engine controller (TCS)	*n*
régulateur hybride	*m*	Hybridregler	*m*	hybrid regulator	*n*
régulateur isodromique	*m*	Isodromregler	*m*	isodromous governor	*n*
régulateur mécanique	*m*	Fliehkraftregler	*m*	mechanical governor	*n*
régulateur mécanique mini-maxi	*m*	Leerlauf- und Enddrehzahlregler	*m*	minimum-maximum-speed governor	*n*
régulateur mini-maxi	*m*	Leerlauf- und Enddrehzahlregler	*m*	minimum-maximum-speed governor	*n*
régulateur monocontact	*m*	Einkontaktregler	*m*	single-contact regulator	*n*
régulateur monolithe	*m*	Monolithregler	*m*	monolithic regulator	*n*
régulateur proportionnel de pression	*m*	Druckverhältnisventil	*n*	adapter valve	*n*
régulateur tous régimes	*m*	Alldrehzahlregler	*m*	variable-speed governor	*n*
régulateur toutes vitesses	*m*	Alldrehzahlregler	*m*	variable-speed governor	*n*
régulation anti-à-coups	*f*	aktive Ruckeldämpfung, ARD	*f*	surge damping control	*n*
régulation auto-adaptative de la distance	*f*	adaptive Fahrgeschwindigkeitsregelung, ACC	*f*	adaptive cruise control, ACC	*n*

Français		Allemand		Anglais	
régulation auto-adaptative de vitesse de roulage	*f*	adaptive Fahrgeschwindigkeitsregelung, ACC	*f*	adaptive cruise control, ACC	*n*
régulation cartographique	*f*	Kennfeldregelung	*f*	map-based control	*n*
régulation d'antipatinage à la traction, ASR	*f*	Antriebsschlupfregelung, ASR	*f*	traction control system, TCS	*n*
régulation d'antipatinage, ASR	*f*	Antriebsschlupfregelung, ASR	*f*	traction control system, TCS	*n*
régulation de débit	*f*	Fördermengenregelung	*f*	fuel-delivery control	*n*
régulation de freinage	*f*	Bremsregelung	*f*	brake control system	*n*
régulation de la fin de refoulement	*f*	Förderenderegelung	*f*	end-of-delivery control	*n*
régulation de la force de freinage	*f*	Bremskraftregelung	*f*	braking-force metering	*n*
régulation de la pression de suralimentation	*f*	Ladedruckregelung	*f*	boost-pressure control	*n*
régulation de la stabilité de fonctionnement	*f*	Laufruheregelung	*f*	smooth-running control	*n*
régulation de la vitesse de ralenti	*f*	Leerlaufregelung, LLR	*f*	idle-speed control	*n*
régulation de la vitesse de rotation	*f*	Drehzahlregelung	*f*	rotational-speed control	*n*
régulation de la vitesse de roulage	*f*	Fahrgeschwindigkeitsregelung	*f*	cruise control (system)	*n*
régulation de position	*f*	Lageregelung	*f*	closed-loop position control	*n*
régulation de pression	*f*	Druckregelung	*f*	pressure control	*n*
régulation de pression de freinage	*f*	Bremsdruckregelung	*f*	braking-pressure control	*n*
régulation de régime	*f*	Drehzahlregelung	*f*	rotational-speed control	*n*
régulation de richesse	*f*	Lambda-Regelung	*f*	lambda closed-loop control	*n*
régulation de tension	*f*	Spannungsregelung	*f*	voltage regulation	*n*
régulation de vitesse maximale (pompe d'injection)	*f*	Endabregelung (Einspritzpumpe)	*f*	full-load speed regulation (fuel-injection pump)	*n*
régulation de vitesses intermédiaires	*f*	Zwischendrehzahlregelung	*f*	intermediate-speed regulation	*n*
régulation des débits d'injection	*f*	Fördermengenregelung	*f*	fuel-delivery control	*n*
régulation diesel	*f*	Dieselregelung	*f*	governing (diesel engine)	*n*
régulation du chauffage	*f*	Heizungsregelung	*f*	heating regulator	*n*
régulation du cliquetis	*f*	Klopfregelung	*f*	knock control	*n*
régulation du comportement dynamique, ESP	*f*	Fahrdynamikregelung, ESP	*f*	electronic stability program, ESP	*n*
régulation du couple d'inertie du moteur	*f*	Motorschleppmoment-regelung, MSR	*f*	engine drag-torque control	*n*
régulation du début de refoulement	*f*	Förderbeginnregelung	*f*	start-of-delivery control	*n*
régulation du recyclage des gaz d'échappement	*f*	Abgasrückführregelung	*f*	exhaust-gas recirculation (EGR) control	*n*
régulation du régime de ralenti	*f*	Leerlaufregelung, LLR	*f*	idle-speed control	*n*
régulation du remplissage des cylindres	*f*	Füllungsregelung (Luftversorgung)	*f*	charge adjustment (air supply)	*n*
régulation électronique de pression de freinage, EPC	*f*	elektronische Bremsdruckregelung, EPC	*f*	electronic braking-pressure control, EPC	*n*

Français		Allemand		Anglais	
régulation électronique diesel, RED	f	elektronische Dieselregelung, EDC	f	electronic diesel control, EDC	n
régulation électronique du niveau	f	Niveauregelung	f	level control	n
régulation électronique du ralenti	f	elektronische Leerlaufregelung, ELR	f	electronic idle-speed control	n
régulation individuelle (ABS)	f	Einzelradregelung (ABS)	f	individual control, IR (ABS)	n
régulation individuelle modifiée (ABS)	f	modifizierte Individual-regelung, IRM (ABS)	f	modified individual control, IRM (ABS)	n
régulation lambda	f	Lambda-Regelung	f	lambda closed-loop control	n
relais	m	Relais	n	relay	n
relais à armature battante	m	Klappankerrelais	n	hinged-armature relay	n
relais à armature pivotante	m	Drehankerrelais	n	rotating armature relay	n
relais à courant continu	m	Gleichstromrelais	n	DC relay	n
relais à noyau plongeur	m	Tauchankerrelais	n	solenoid plunger relay	n
relais cadenceur d'essuie-glace	m	Wischintervallrelais	n	intermittent-wiper relay	n
relais commutateur de tonalités	m	Tonfolgeschalter	m	tone-sequence control device	n
relais de blocage du démarreur	m	Startsperrelais	n	start-locking relay	n
relais de commande	m	Steuerrelais	n	control relay	n
relais de commande de moteur (ABS)	m	Motorrelais (ABS)	n	motor relay (ABS)	n
relais de coupure de batterie	m	Batterietrennrelais	n	battery-cutoff relay	n
relais de découplage de batterie	m	Batterietrennrelais	n	battery-cutoff relay	n
relais de démarreur	m	Starterrelais	m	starting-motor relay	n
relais de protection	m	Schutzrelais	n	protective relay	n
relais de puissance	m	Leistungsrelais	n	power relay	n
relais de sécurité (calculateur)	m	Sicherheitsrelais (Steuergerät)	n	safety relay (ECU)	n
relais des électrovalves (ABS)	m	Ventilrelais (ABS)	n	valve relay (ABS)	n
relais du moteur (ABS)	m	Motorrelais (ABS)	n	motor relay (ABS)	n
relais du ralentisseur	m	Dauerbremsrelais, DBR	n	retarder relay	n
relais du signal de détresse	m	Warnblinkrelais	n	hazard-warning and turn-signal relay	n
relais intermittent d'essuie-glac(	m	Wischintervallrelais	n	intermittent-wiper relay	n
relais pour cartes imprimées	m	Leiterplattenrelais	n	PC-board relay	n
relais principal	m	Hauptrelais	n	main relay	n
rémanence	f	Restmagnetismus	m	residual magnetism	n
remise en état	f	Instandsetzung	f	repairing	n
remise en veille (alarme auto)	f	rückschärfen (Autoalarm)	v	reprime (car alarm)	v
remorque	f	Anhängefahrzeug	n	trailer	n
remorque à essieu central	f	Zentralachsanhänger	m	centre-axle trailer	n
remorque à timon articulé	f	Gelenk-Deichselanhänger	m	draw bar trailer	n
remplissage d'air	m	Luftfüllung	f	air charge	n
remplissage du cylindre	m	Zylinderladung	f	cylinder charge	n
rendement (technique d'enroulement)	m	Ausnutzungsgrad (Wickeltechnik)	m	power/space ratio (winding technique)	n
rendement volumétrique (moteur à combustion)	m	Liefergrad (Verbrennungsmotor)	m	volumetric efficiency (IC engine)	n
reniflard (valve de frein)	m	Schnorchel (Bremsventil)	m	snorkel (brake valve)	n

Français		Allemand		Anglais	
renouvellement des gaz	m	Gaswechsel	m	gas exchange	n
réparation	f	Instandsetzung	f	repairing	n
répartiteur de carburant	m	Kraftstoffmengenteiler	m	fuel distributor	n
répartiteur de force de freinage	m	Bremskraftverteiler	m	braking-force metering device	n
répartiteur de freinage (frein hydraulique)	m	Bremskraftverteiler	m	braking-force metering device	n
répartition de la charge par essieu	f	Achslastverteilung	f	axle-load distribution	n
répartition de la force de freinage	f	Bremskraftverteilung	f	braking-force distribution	n
répartition de la lumière (éclairage)	f	Lichtverteilung (Lichttechnik)	f	light pattern (lighting)	n
répartition des circuits de freinage	f	Bremskreisaufteilung	f	brake-circuit configuration	n
répartition du carburant	f	Kraftstoffverteilung	f	fuel distribution	n
répartition du mélange	f	Gemischverteilung	f	mixture distribution	n
répartition du poids (frein)	f	Gewichtsverteilung (Bremse)	f	weight distribution (brakes)	n
répartition uniforme (mélange air-carburant)	f	Gleichverteilung (Luft-Kraftstoff-Gemisch)	f	even mixture distribution (air-fuel mixture)	n
repère d'allumage	m	Zündmarke	f	ignition mark	n
repère de consigne	m	Bezugsmarke	f	reference mark	n
repère de référence	m	Bezugsmarke	f	reference mark	n
réponse (véhicule)	f	Übertragungsverhalten (Kfz)	n	response (motor vehicle)	n
report de charge	m	Achslastverlagerung	f	axle-load transfer	n
report de charge (frein)	m	Gewichtsverlagerung (Bremse)	f	weight transfer (brakes)	n
report de charge dynamique	m	dynamische Gewichtsverlagerung	f	dynamic weight transfer	n
report de charge dynamique de l'essieu	m	Achslastverlagerung	f	axle-load transfer	n
réserve d'air comprimé	f	Druckluftvorrat	m	compressed-air reserve	n
réserve d'énergie (coussin d'air)	f	Energiereserve (Airbag)	f	energy reserve (airbag triggering system)	n
réserve de tension d'allumage	f	Zündspannungsreserve	f	voltage reserve	n
réservoir d'air comprimé (pneumatique)	m	Druckluftbehälter (Pneumatik)	m	compressed-air reservoir (pneumatics)	n
réservoir d'air de régénération	m	Regenerationsluftbehälter	m	regeneration-air tank	n
réservoir de carburant	m	Kraftstoffbehälter	m	fuel tank	n
réservoir de compensation (frein)	m	Ausgleichsbehälter (Bremse)	m	compensating reservoir (brakes	n
réservoir de fluide hydraulique	m	Hydraulikbehälter +	m	hydraulic fluid reservoir	n
réservoir de liquide de frein	m	Bremsflüssigkeitsbehälter	m	brake-fluid reservoir	n
réservoir en charge	m	Falltankbetrieb	m	gravity-feed fuel-tank operation	n
résidus de la combustion	mpl	Verbrennungsrückstände	mpl	combustion residues	npl
résistance à l'abrasion	f	Abriebfestigkeit	f	abrasion resistance	n
résistance à l'engrènement (démarreur)	f	Einrückwiderstand (Starter)	m	meshing resistance (starter)	n
résistance à l'environnement	f	Umweltbeständigkeit	f	environmental resistance	n
résistance à la corrosion	f	Korrosionsfestigkeit	f	corrosion resistance	n
résistance à la déformation	f	Verformungsfestigkeit	f	dimensional stability	n

Français

Français		Allemand		Anglais	
résistance à la pression	*f*	Druckfestigkeit	*f*	resistance to pressure	*n*
résistance à la tension	*f*	Spannungsfestigkeit	*f*	electric strength	*n*
résistance active	*f*	Wirkwiderstand	*m*	active resistance	*n*
résistance additionnelle	*f*	Vorwiderstand	*m*	series resistor	*n*
résistance antiparasite	*f*	Entstörwiderstand	*m*	interference-suppression resisto	*n*
résistance au courant	*f*	Strömungswiderstand	*m*	resistance to flow	*n*
résistance au roulement	*f*	Rollwiderstand	*m*	rolling resistance	*n*
résistance aux chocs thermique:	*f*	Temperaturwechselfestigkeit	*f*	resistance to thermal cycling	*n*
résistance aux secousses	*f*	Schüttelfestigkeit	*f*	vibration strength	*n*
résistance aux vibrations	*f*	Schwingfestigkeit	*f*	vibrational strength	*n*
résistance CTN	*f*	NTC-Widerstand	*m*	NTC resistor	*n*
résistance d'antiparasitage	*f*	Entstörwiderstand	*m*	interference-suppression resisto	*n*
résistance d'enroulement	*f*	Wicklungswiderstand	*m*	winding resistance	*n*
résistance de contact	*f*	Übergangswiderstand	*m*	contact resistance	*n*
résistance de glissement (banc d'essai)	*f*	Gleitwiderstand (Rollenbremsprüfstand)	*m*	slip resistance (dynamic brake analyzer)	*n*
résistance de l'air	*f*	Luftwiderstand	*m*	aerodynamic drag	*n*
résistance de l'enroulement primaire	*f*	Primärwiderstand	*m*	primary resistance	*n*
résistance de lancement du moteur	*f*	Durchdrehwiderstand (Verbrennungsmotor)	*m*	resistance to rotation (IC engine)	*n*
résistance de régulation	*f*	Regelwiderstand	*m*	regulating resistor	*n*
résistance électrique fixe	*f*	Festwiderstand	*m*	fixed resistor	*n*
résistance en côte	*f*	Steigungswiderstand	*m*	climbing resistance	*n*
résistance série	*f*	Vorwiderstand	*m*	series resistor	*n*
résistance thermique	*f*	Temperaturbeständigkeit	*f*	temperature resistance	*n*
résistance totale à l'avancement	*f*	Gesamtfahrwiderstand	*m*	total running resistance	*n*
résistant à l'usure	*ppr*	verschleißfest	*adj*	wear-resistant	*adj*
résistant au gazole	*ppr*	dieselbeständig	*adj*	diesel-fuel resistant	*ppr*
résistant aux chutes	*ppr*	fallbeständig	*adj*	drop-proof	*adj*
résistant aux courts-circuits	*ppr*	kurzschlußfest	*adj*	short-circuit resistant	*adj*
résistant aux cycles alternés (batterie)	*ppr*	zyklenfest (Batterie)	*adj*	deep-cycle resistant (battery)	*ppr*
résonance des essieux	*f*	Achsresonanz	*f*	axis resonance	*n*
résonateur d'admission	*m*	Saugresonator	*m*	suction resonator	*n*
responsabilité du fabricant	*f*	Produzentenhaftung	*f*	manufacturers responsibility	*n*
responsabilité produit	*f*	Produkthaftung	*f*	product liability	*n*
ressort à cran d'arrêt	*m*	Rastfeder	*f*	stop-spring	*n*
ressort à déclic	*m*	Verschlußfeder	*f*	sealing spring	*n*
ressort à lames	*m*	Blattfeder	*f*	leaf spring	*n*
ressort additionnel de ralenti	*m*	Leerlauf-Zusatzfeder	*f*	auxiliary idle-speed spring	*n*
ressort compensateur	*m*	Schleppfeder	*f*	drag spring	*n*
ressort correcteur de débit	*m*	Angleichfeder	*f*	torque-control spring	*n*
ressort d'engrènement	*m*	Einspurfeder	*f*	meshing spring	*n*
ressort d'injecteur	*m*	Düsenfeder	*f*	nozzle spring	*n*
ressort de contact	*m*	Federkontakt	*m*	spring contact	*n*
ressort de correction de débit	*m*	Angleichfeder	*f*	torque-control spring	*n*

Français		Allemand			Anglais	
ressort de couplage	*m*	Koppelfeder		*f*	coupling spring	*n*
ressort de démarrage	*m*	Startfeder		*f*	starting spring	*n*
ressort de piston	*m*	Kolbenfeder (Pumpenkolben)		*f*	plunger return spring	*n*
ressort de pression	*m*	Druckfeder		*f*	compression spring	*f*
ressort de ralenti	*m*	Leerlauffeder		*f*	idle-speed spring	*n*
ressort de ralenti solidaire du corps de pompe	*m*	gehäusefeste Leerlauffeder, LFG	x	*f*	idle-speed spring attached to governor housing	*n*
ressort de rappel	*m*	Rückholfeder		*f*	return spring	*n*
ressort de rappel (valve de frein de stationnement)	*m*	Reaktionsfeder (Feststellbremsventil)		*f*	reaction spring (parking-brake valve)	*n*
ressort de rappel du piston (piston de pompe)	*m*	Kolbenfeder (Pumpenkolben)		*f*	plunger return spring	*n*
ressort de régulateur (injection diesel)	*m*	Regelfeder		*f*	governor spring	*n*
ressort de régulation	*m*	Regelfeder		*f*	governor spring	*n*
ressort de régulation de vitesse maximale	*m*	Endregelfeder		*f*	maximum-speed spring	*n*
ressort de valve	*m*	Ventilfeder		*f*	valve spring	*n*
ressort hélicöidal	*m*	Spiralfeder		*f*	spiral spring	*n*
ressort hélicoïdal de compression	*m*	Schraubendruckfeder		*f*	helical compression spring	*n*
ressort limiteur de course	*m*	Wegfeder		*f*	travel-limiting spring	*n*
ressort toroïde (suspension)	*m*	Torusbalgfeder (Luftfeder)		*f*	toroid bellows (air spring)	*n*
résultat du test de particules (fumées diesel)	*m*	Feststoff-Testergebnis (Dieselrauch)		*n*	particulates test result (diesel smoke)	*n*
retard de phase (frein de remorque)	*m*	Nacheilung (Anhängerbremse)		*f*	negative offset (trailer brake)	*n*
retard (angle d'allumage)	*m*	Spätverstellung (Zündwinkel)		*f*	ignition retard	*n*
retour (électrovalve ABS)	*m*	Rücklauf (ABS-Magnetventil)		*m*	return line (ABS solenoid valve)	*n*
retour d'allumage	*m*	Saugrohrrückzündung		*f*	backfiring	*n*
retour de l'huile de graissage	*m*	Schmierölrücklauf		*m*	lube-oil return	*n*
retour par la masse	*m*	Masserückführung		*f*	ground return	*n*
revêtement de poudre	*m*	pulverbeschichtet		*pp*	powder coated	*pp*
riche (mélange air-carburant)	*adj*	fett (Luft-Kraftstoff-Gemisch)		*adj*	rich (air-fuel mixture)	*adj*
rigidité diélectrique	*f*	spannungsfest		*adj*	surge-proof	*adj*
rigidité du pneumatique	*f*	Reifensteifigkeit		*f*	tire rigidity	*n*
robinet à quatre voies	*m*	Vierwegehahn		*m*	four-way cock	*n*
robinet d'arrêt	*m*	Absperrhahn		*m*	stopcock	*n*
robinet de batterie	*m*	Batterieschalter		*m*	battery master switch	*n*
robinet de secours (commande des portes)	*m*	Nothahn (Türbetätigung)		*m*	emergency valve (door control	*n*
rondelle Belleville	+ *f*	Tellerfeder		*f*	disc spring	*n*
rondelle calorifuge (injecteur)	*f*	Wärmeschutzscheibe (Einspritzdüse)		*f*	thermal-protection disc (injection nozzle)	*n*
rondelle court-circuit	*f*	Kurzschlußscheibe		*f*	short-circuit shim	*n*
rondelle d'obturation	*f*	Verschlußscheibe		*f*	sealing washer	*n*
rondelle de compensation	*f*	Ausgleichscheibe		*f*	shim (delivery-valve holder)	*n*
rondelle de friction (démarreur)	*f*	Anlaufscheibe (Starter)		*f*	friction washer (starter)	*n*

Français		Allemand			Anglais	
rondelle de réglage	*f*	Einstellscheibe		*f*	shim (nozzle-holder assembly)	*n*
rondelle isolante	*f*	Isolierscheibe		*m*	insulating washer	*n*
rondelle-ressort	*f*	Tellerfeder		*f*	disc spring	*n*
ronflement	*m*	Schnarrverhalten		*n*	chatter <noun>	*n*
ronflement (perturbation)	*m*	brummen (Funkstörung)		*v*	hum (radio disturbance)	*v*
ronfler	*v*	schnarren		*v*	chatter <to chatter>	*v*
rotation à droite	*f*	Rechtslauf		*m*	clockwise rotation	*n*
rotation à gauche	*f*	Linkslauf		*m*	counterclockwise rotation	*n*
rotation antihoraire	*f*	Linkslauf		*m*	counterclockwise rotation	*n*
rotation du pignon	*f*	Ritzelverdrehung		*f*	pinion rotation	*n*
rotation horaire	*f*	Rechtslauf		*m*	clockwise rotation	*n*
rotor (échangeur de pression)	*m*	Rotor (Druckwellenlader)		*m*	rotor (pressure-wave supercharger)	*n*
rotor (pompe à accélération périphérique)	*m*	Laufrad (Peripheralpumpe)		*n*	impeller ring (peripheral pump)	*n*
rotor à cages (pompe multicellulaire à rouleaux)	*m*	Läuferscheibe (Rollenzellenpumpe)		*f*	rotor plate (roller-cell pump)	*n*
rotor à disque	*m*	Scheibenläufer		*m*	disc rotor	*n*
rotor à griffes	*m*	Klauenpolläufer		*m*	claw-pole rotor	*n*
rotor à pièce conductrice (alternateur)	*m*	Leitstückläufer (Generator)		*m*	windingless rotor (alternator)	*n*
rotor à pôles saillants	*m*	Einzelpolläufer		*m*	salient-pole rotor	*n*
rotor d'actionneur	*m*	Stellwerkrotor		*m*	actuator rotor	*n*
rotor de freinage	*m*	Bremsrotor		*m*	braking rotor	*n*
rotor distributeur (allumage)	*m*	Zündverteilerläufer		*m*	distributor rotor (ignition)	*n*
rotor excentré (suralimentation)	*m*	Verdränger (Aufladung)		*m*	displacer element (supercharging)	*n*
rotor sans enroulement (alternateur)	*m*	Leitstückläufer (Generator)		*m*	windingless rotor (alternator)	*n*
rotule	*f*	Kugelbolzen		*m*	ball pin	*n*
roue à denture intérieure	*f*	Hohlrad		*n*	internal gear (ring gear)	*n*
roue à palettes (ralentisseur hydrodynamique)	*f*	Schaufelrad (hydrodynamischer Verlangsamer)		*n*	blade wheel (hydrodynamic retarder)	*n*
roue à sélection "basse" (ABS)	*f*	Low-Rad (ABS)	x	*n*	low wheel (ABS)	*n*
roue à sélection "haute" (ABS)	*f*	High-Rad (ABS)	x	*n*	high wheel (ABS)	*n*
roue de compresseur centrifuge	*f*	Verdichterrad		*n*	compressor wheel	*n*
roue libre (démarreur)	*f*	Rollenfreilauf (Starter)		*m*	roller-type overrunning clutch (starter)	*n*
roue menante	*f*	Antriebsrad (Elektrokraftstoffpumpe)		*n*	driving wheel	*n*
roue motrice (véhicule)	*f*	Antriebsrad (Kfz)		*n*	driven wheel (motor vehicle)	*n*
roue planétaire	*f*	Planetenrad		*n*	planet gear	*n*
roue polaire	*f*	Polrad		*n*	pole wheel	*n*
roue solaire	*f*	Sonnenrad		*n*	sun gear	*n*
rouleau d'entraînement (banc d'essai)	*m*	Antriebsrolle (Rollenbremsprüfstand)		*f*	drive roller (dynamic brake analyzer)	*n*
rouleau de contact (banc d'essai)	*m*	Tastrolle (Rollenbremsprüfstand)		*f*	sensor roller (dynamic brake analyzer)	*n*

Français		Allemand		Anglais	
rouleau de papier (filtre à carburant)	*m*	Papierwickel (Kraftstoffilter)	*m*	paper element (fuel filter)	*n*
rouleau palpeur (banc d'essai)	*m*	Tastrolle (Rollenbremsprüfstand)	*f*	sensor roller (dynamic brake analyzer)	*n*
rouleau suiveur (banc d'essai)	*m*	Auflaufrolle (Rollenbremsprüfstand)	*f*	secondary roller (dynamic brake analyzer)	*n*
roulement de roue	*m*	Radlager	*n*	wheel bearing	*n*
rupteur (allumage)	*m*	Zündunterbrecher	*m*	ignition contact breaker	*n*
rupture de câble	*f*	Kabelbruch	*m*	cable break	*n*
rupture de conduite (système de freinage)	*f*	Leitungsbruch (Bremssystem)	*m*	line break (braking system)	*n*
rythme de commutation	*m*	Schaltrhythmus (Relais)	*m*	switching frequency	*n*
S					
sac d'injecteur	*m*	Sackloch (Einspritzventil)	*n*	blind hole (injector)	*n*
saisie de valeur analogique	*f*	Analogwerterfassung	*f*	analog-value sampling	*n*
saisie des mesures	*f*	Meßdatenerfassung	*f*	measuring-data acquisition	*n*
saisie des paramètres opérationnels	*f*	Betriebsdatenerfassung	*f*	data acquisition	*n*
sans bagues collectrices (alternateur)	*loc*	schleifringlos (Generator)	*adj*	brushless (alternator)	*adj*
sans entretien	*loc*	wartungsfrei	*adj*	maintenance-free	*adj*
sans plomb (essence)	*loc*	bleifrei (Benzin)	*adj*	unleaded (gasoline)	*pp*
sans rupteur mécanique	*loc*	kontaktlos	*adj*	breakerless	*adj*
saut de tension	*m*	Spannungssprung	*m*	voltage jump	*n*
schéma de bobinage	*m*	Wickelschema	*n*	winding diagram	*n*
schéma de connexion	*m*	Anschlußplan	*m*	terminal diagram	*n*
schéma de principe	*m*	Übersichtsschaltplan	*m*	block diagram	*n*
schéma des bornes	*m*	Anschlußplan	*m*	terminal diagram	*n*
schéma des circuits	*m*	Stromlaufplan	*m*	schematic diagram	*n*
schéma électrique	*m*	Schaltplan	*m*	diagram	*n*
schéma fonctionnel	*m*	Übersichtsschaltplan	*m*	block diagram	*n*
secteur (entreprise)	*m*	Unternehmensbereich	*m*	business sector	*n*
secteur denté	*m*	Zahnsegment	*n*	control-sleeve gear	*n*
section d'écoulement	*f*	Ausflußquerschnitt	*m*	outlet cross-section	*n*
section de câble	*f*	Kabelquerschnitt	*m*	cable cross-section	*n*
section de passage de flux	*f*	Strömungsquerschnitt	*m*	flow cross-section	*n*
section du conducteur	*f*	Leiterquerschnitt	*m*	conductor cross section	*n*
sécurité antirotation (commande des portes)	*f*	Verdrehsicherung (Türbetätigung)	*f*	anti-rotation element (door control)	*n*
sécurité de fonctionnement	*f*	Betriebssicherheit	*f*	functional security	*n*
sécurité de mise en veille (alarme auto)	*f*	Aktivierungssperre (Autoalarm)	*f*	activation blocking (car alarm)	*n*
sécurité en cas de panne (alarme auto)	*f*	Ausfallsperre (Autoalarm)	*f*	failure protection (car alarm)	*n*
segment de frein	*m*	Bremsbacke	*f*	brake shoe	*n*
segment denté	*m*	Zahnsegment	*n*	control-sleeve gear	*n*
sélecteur de circuit	*m*	Wechselventil	*n*	shuttle valve	*n*
sélecteur de rapport de vitesse	*m*	Getriebewählhebel	*m*	selector lever	*n*

Français		Allemand			Anglais	
sélection basse (ABS/ASR)	*f*	Select-low-Regelung, SL (ABS/ASR)	x	*f*	select-low control, SL (ABS/TCS)	*n*
sélection haute (ABS/ASR)	*f*	Select-high-Regelung, SH (ABS/ASR)	x	*f*	select-high control, SH (ABS/TCS)	*n*
sélection idéale (ABS/ASR)	*f*	Select-smart-Regelung, SSM (ABS/ASR)	x	*f*	select-smart control, SSM (ABS/TCS)	*n*
self antiparasite	*f*	Entstördrossel		*f*	interference-suppression choke	*n*
self d'antiparasitage	*f*	Entstördrossel		*f*	interference-suppression choke	*n*
self-induction	*f*	Selbstinduktion		*f*	self-induction	*n*
sellette de semi-remorque	*f*	Aufsattelkupplung		*f*	fifthwheel coupling	*n*
sens d'écoulement	*m*	Strömungsrichtung		*f*	flow direction	*n*
sens d'action	*m*	Wirkrichtung		*f*	force-transfer direction	*n*
sens d'écoulement inverse	*m*	Rückströmrichtung		*f*	return-flow direction	*n*
sens d'injection	*m*	Einspritzrichtung		*f*	injection direction	*n*
sens de refoulement	*m*	Förderrichtung		*f*	delivery direction	*n*
sens de rotation	*m*	Drehrichtung		*f*	direction of rotation	*n*
sensibilité transversale (capteur)	*f*	Querempfindlichkeit (Sensor)		*f*	cross sensitivity (sensor)	*n*
séparateur (batterie)	*m*	Separator (Batterie)		*m*	separator (battery)	*n*
séparateur (filtre)	*m*	Abscheider (Filter)		*m*	separator (filter)	*n*
séparateur à filtration	*m*	Filtrationsabscheider		*m*	filtration separator	*n*
séparateur centrifuge	*m*	Fliehkraftabscheider		*m*	centrifugal separator	*n*
séparateur d'air du carburant	*m*	Kraftstoffluftabscheider		*m*	fuel-air separator	*n*
séparateur d'eau	*m*	Wasserabscheider		*m*	water separator	*n*
séparateur d'eau du carburant	*m*	Kraftstoffwasserabscheider		*m*	fuel-water separator	*n*
séparateur d'huile	*m*	Ölabscheider		*m*	oil separator	*n*
séparateur de particules de suie	*m*	Rußabscheider		*m*	soot separator	*n*
séparateur électrique	*m*	Elektroabscheider		*m*	electrical separator	*n*
séquentiel	*adj*	sequentiell		*adj*	sequential	*adj*
série	*f*	Baureihe		*f*	series	*n*
série de courses	*f*	Hubphase		*f*	stroke phase	*n*
série pilote	*f*	Nullserie		*f*	pilot run	*n*
sériel	*adj*	seriell		*adj*	serial	*adj*
serpentin	*m*	Rohrschlange		*f*	coiled pipe	*n*
serrure à barillet (bobine d'allumage spéciale)	*f*	Schloßzylinder (Sonderzündspule)		*m*	lock barrel (special ignition coil)	*n*
sertir	*v*	crimpen		*v*	crimp	*v*
serveur de ceinture	*m*	Gurtbringer		*m*	seat-belt extender	*n*
service après-vente	*m*	Kundendienst		*m*	service	*n*
service continu (machines électriques)	*m*	Dauerbetrieb (elektrische Maschinen)		*m*	continuous-running-duty type (electrical machines)	*n*
service freins	*m*	Bremsendienst		*m*	brake repair service	*n*
service intermittent (machines électriques)	*m*	Aussetzbetrieb (elektrische Maschinen)		*m*	intermittent-periodic duty (electrical machines)	*n*
servofrein (frein à tambour)	*m*	Servobremse (Trommelbremse)		*f*	servo brake (drum brake)	*n*
servofrein (voiture)	*m*	Bremskraftverstärker (Pkw)		*m*	brake booster (passenger car)	*n*
servofrein à air comprimé	*m*	pneumatische Hilfskraft-Bremsanlage		*f*	air-assisted braking system	*n*

Français		Allemand		Anglais	
servofrein à dépression	*m*	Unterdruck-Bremskraftverstärker	*m*	vacuum brake booster	*n*
servofrein duo	*m*	Duo-Servobremse	*f*	duo-servo brake	*n*
servofrein hydraulique	*m*	Hydraulik-Bremskraftverstärker	*m*	hydraulic brake booster	*n*
servomoteur	*m*	Stellmotor	*m*	servomotor	*n*
servopompe d'injection	*f*	Servoeinspritzpumpe	*f*	servo fuel-injection pump	*n*
seuil croissant (capteur d'accélérateur)	*m*	Anstiegsschwellwert (Fahrpedalsensor)	*m*	increase threshold value (accelerator-pedal sensor)	*n*
seuil d'autonettoyage	*m*	Freibrenntemperatur	*f*	self-cleaning temperature	*n*
seuil d'enclenchement	*m*	Einschaltschwelle	*f*	switch-on threshold	*n*
seuil de consigne	*m*	Referenzpegel	*m*	reference level	*n*
seuil de coupure	*m*	Ausschaltschwelle	*f*	shut-off threshold	*n*
seuil de déclenchement	*m*	Auslöseschwelle	*f*	trigger threshold	*n*
seuil de glissement (ABS)	*m*	Schlupfschaltschwelle (ABS)	*f*	slip switching threshold (ABS)	*n*
seuil de régime	*m*	Drehzahlschwelle	*f*	engine-speed threshold	*n*
seuil de régulation	*m*	Regelschwelle	*f*	control threshold	*n*
seuil de réponse	*m*	Ansprechschwelle	*f*	response threshold	*n*
seuil de température	*m*	Temperaturschwelle	*f*	temperature threshold	*n*
seuil décroissant (capteur d'accélérateur)	*m*	Abfallschwellwert (Fahrpedalsensor)	*m*	decrease threshold value (accelerator-pedal sensor)	*n*
shunt	*m*	Nebenschluß	*m*	shunt	*n*
siège conique	*m*	Kegeldichtsitz	*m*	conical seat	*n*
siège d'admission (moteur à combustion)	*m*	Einlaßventilsitz (Verbrennungsmotor)	*m*	intake-valve seat (IC engine)	*n*
siège d'échappement	*m*	Auslaßventilsitz	*m*	discharge-valve seat	*n*
siège d'étanchéité	*m*	Dichtsitz	*m*	seal seat	*n*
siège d'injecteur	*m*	Düsensitz	*m*	nozzle seat	*n*
siège de l'aiguille d'injecteur	*m*	Düsennadelsitz	*m*	nozzle-needle seat	*n*
siège de soupape	*m*	Ventilsitz	*m*	valve seat	*n*
siège de soupape de refoulement	*m*	Druckventilsitz	*m*	delivery-valve seat	*n*
siège plat	*m*	Flachdichtsitz	*m*	flat seat	*n*
signal clignotant	*m*	Blinksignal	*n*	flashing signal	*n*
signal d'enrichissement au démarrage	*m*	Startanhebung	*f*	starting enrichment	*n*
signal de charge	*m*	Lastsignal	*n*	load signal	*n*
signal de charge sur essieu	*m*	Achslastsignal	*n*	axle-load signal	*n*
signal de commande	*m*	Steuersignal	*n*	control signal (open loop)	*n*
signal de défaut	*m*	Fehlersignal	*n*	error signal	*n*
signal de détresse	*m*	Warnsignal	*n*	warning signal	*n*
signal de pilotage	*m*	Ansteuersignal	*n*	triggering signal	*n*
signal de rampe	*m*	Rampensignal	*n*	ramp signal	*n*
signal de réduction (ASR)	*m*	Reduziersignal (ASR)	*n*	reduction signal (TCS)	*n*
signal de réglage	*m*	Stellsignal	*n*	command signal	*n*
signal de régulation	*m*	Regelsignal	*n*	control signal (closed loop)	*n*
signal lumineux	*m*	Lichtsignal	*n*	visual signal	*n*
signal optique	*m*	Lichthupe	*f*	headlamp flasher	*n*

Français

Français		Allemand		Anglais	
signal pilote	*m*	Ansteuersignal	*n*	triggering signal	*n*
signal rectangulaire (calculateur)	*m*	Rechtecksignal (Steuergerät)	*n*	square-wave signal (ECU)	*n*
signal utile (antiparasitage)	*m*	Nutzsignal (Entstörung)	*n*	wanted signal (interference suppression)	*n*
signalisation "détresse"	*f*	warnblinken	*v*	hazard flashing	*v*
silencieux (régulateur de pression)	*m*	Schalldämpfer (Druckregler)	*m*	silencer (pressure regulator)	*n*
silencieux à réflexion	*m*	Reflexionsschalldämpfer	*m*	reflection muffler	*n*
silencieux arrière	*m*	Nachschalldämpfer	*m*	rear muffler	*n*
silencieux avant	*m*	Vorschalldämpfer	*m*	front muffler	*n*
silencieux médian	*m*	Mittelschalldämpfer	*m*	exhaust-gas center silencer	*n*
simulation des défauts	*f*	Fehlersimulation	*f*	error simulation	*n*
simultané	*adj*	simultan	*adj*	simultaneous	*adj*
situation de freinage	*f*	Bremszustand	*m*	braking condition	*n*
société régionale	*f*	Regionalgesellschaft	*f*	regional subsidiary	*n*
sonde altimétrique	*f*	Höhensensor	*m*	altitude sensor	*n*
sonde d'oxygène lambda	*f*	Lambda-Sonde	*f*	lambda sensor	*n*
sonde de champ magnétique terrestre (système de navigation)	*f*	Erdmagnetfeldsonde (Navigationssystem)	*f*	geomagnetic sensor (navigation system)	*n*
sonde de débit d'air	*f*	Luftmengenmesser	*m*	air-flow sensor	*n*
sonde de prélèvement	*f*	Entnahmesonde	*f*	exhaust-sample probe	*n*
sonde de pression	*f*	Drucksensor	*m*	pressure sensor	*n*
sonde de richesse	*f*	Lambda-Sonde	*f*	lambda sensor	*n*
sonde de richesse chauffée	*f*	beheizte Lambda-Sonde, LSH	*f*	heated lambda sensor, LSH	*n*
sonde de température	*f*	Temperatursensor	*m*	temperature sensor	*n*
sonde lambda	*f*	Lambda-Sonde	*f*	lambda sensor	*n*
sonde lambda planaire	*f*	planare Lambda Sonde	*f*	planar Lambda sensor	*n*
sortie	*f*	Auslaß	*m*	outlet	*n*
sortie centrale (bobine d'allumage)	*f*	Mitteldom (Zündspule)	*m*	center tower (ignition coil)	*n*
sortie de diagnostic	*f*	Diagnoseausgabe	*f*	diagnosis output	*n*
soufflante à piston rotatif	*f*	Drehkolben-Gebläse	*n*	rotary-piston blower	*n*
soufflante Roots	*f*	Drehkolben-Gebläse	*n*	rotary-piston blower	*n*
soufflerie	*f*	Windkanal	*m*	wind tunnel	*n*
soufflet	*m*	Faltenbalg	*m*	gaiter seal	*n*
soufflet à air	*m*	Luftfederbalg	*m*	air-spring bellows	*n*
soufflet de protection	*m*	Schutzbalg	*m*	protective bellows	*n*
soufflet de suspension	*m*	Luftfeder	*f*	air spring	*n*
soufflet en caoutchouc	*m*	Gummirollbalg	*m*	rubber bellows	*n*
soufflet en U (suspension)	*m*	Rollbalgfeder (Luftfeder)	*f*	roll bellows (air spring)	*n*
soupape à piston (piston de pompe)	*f*	Kolbenventil (Pumpenkolben)	*n*	plunger-type valve	*n*
soupape à plaque	*f*	Plattenventil	*n*	plate valve	*n*
soupape à pression différentiell	*f*	Differenzdruckventil	*n*	differential-pressure valve	*n*
soupape à siège plan	*f*	Flachsitzventil	*n*	flat-seat valve	*n*
soupape à trois ailettes	*f*	Dreiflügelventil	*n*	triple-fluted valve	*n*

Français		Allemand		Anglais	
soupape auxiliaire de démarrage	*f*	Kaltstartventil	*n*	cold-start valve	*n*
soupape centrale	*f*	Zentralventil	*n*	central valve	*n*
soupape d'admission (moteur à combustion)	*f*	Einlaßventil	*n*	intake valve	*n*
soupape d'arrivée	*f*	Zulaufventil	*n*	inlet valve	*n*
soupape d'aspiration (pompe d'alimentation)	*f*	Saugventil (Kraftstofförderpumpe)	*n*	suction valve (fuel-supply pump)	*n*
soupape d'échappement (moteur à combustion)	*f*	Auslaßventil (Verbrennungsmotor)	*n*	exhaust valve (IC engine)	*n*
soupape de balayage	*f*	Überströmventil	*n*	overflow valve	*n*
soupape de compensation	*f*	Speicherventil	*n*	compensation valve	*n*
soupape de correction de débit	*f*	Angleichventil	*n*	torque-control valve	*n*
soupape de coupure	*f*	Absperrventil	*n*	shutoff valve	*n*
soupape de coupure d'élément	*f*	Element-Abschaltventil	*n*	element cutoff valve	*n*
soupape de décharge	*f*	Druckablaßventil	*n*	pressure relief valve	*n*
soupape de décharge à calibrage	*f*	Überströmdrosselventil	*n*	overflow throttle valve	*n*
soupape de décharge de l'accumulateur	*f*	Speicherüberströmventil	*n*	accumulator overflow valve	*n*
soupape de décharge du coulisseau	*f*	Schieber-Überströmventil	*n*	spool overflow valve	*n*
soupape de dosage (pompe d'injection)	*f*	Auslaßventil (Einspritzpumpe)	*n*	metering spill (fuel-injection pump)	*n*
soupape de dosage de débit de retour	*f*	Überströmdosierventil	*n*	overflow metering valve	*n*
soupape de frein de réaspiratior	*f*	Rückströmdrosselventil	*n*	orifice check valve	*n*
soupape de maintien de la pression (injection diesel)	*f*	Druckhalteventil (Dieseleinspritzung)	*n*	pressure-holding valve (diesel fuel injection)	*n*
soupape de marche à vide	*f*	Leerlaufventil	*n*	idle valve	*n*
soupape de pression à méplat	*f*	Flächendruckventil	*n*	delivery-valve with flat	*n*
soupape de ralenti	*f*	Leerlaufventil	*n*	idle valve	*n*
soupape de trop-plein	*f*	Überströmventil	*n*	overflow valve	*n*
soupape modulatrice de pression	*f*	Druckregelventil	*n*	pressure-control valve	*n*
souplesse de fonctionnement (moteur à combustion)	*f*	Laufruhe (Verbrennungsmotor)	*f*	smooth running (IC engine)	*n*
source acoustique	*f*	Schallquelle	*f*	acoustic source	*n*
source d'énergie	*f*	Energiequelle	*f*	source of energy	*n*
source de perturbations (CEM)	*f*	Störquelle	*f*	radio-interference source	*n*
sous écran	*loc*	geschirmt	*pp*	shielded	*pp*
sous-ensemble	*m*	Baugruppe	*f*	assembly	*n*
sous-tension	*f*	Unterspannung	*f*	under-voltage	*n*
sous-virage (véhicule)	*m*	untersteuern (Kfz)	*v*	understeer (motor vehicle)	*v*
spécification client	*f*	Kundenspezifikation	*f*	customer specification	*n*
spécification du produit	*f*	Produktspezifikation	*f*	product specification	*n*
spirale de régulation	*f*	Regelwendel	*f*	control filament	*n*
spot de lecture	*m*	Leseleuchte	*f*	reading lamp	*n*
spray au cuivre	*m*	Kupferspray	*m*	copper spray	*n*

Français		Allemand		Anglais	
stabilisateur	*m*	Stabilisator	*m*	stabilizer	*n*
stabilisateur de tension	*m*	Spannungsstabilisator	*m*	voltage stabilizer	*n*
stabilisation de la tension	*f*	Spannungsstabilisierung	*f*	voltage stabilisation	*n*
stabilisation du ralenti	*f*	Leerlaufstabilisierung	*f*	idle stabilization	*n*
stabilité de trajectoire (comportement de roulage)	*f*	Fahrtrichtungsstabilität (Kfz)	*f*	directional stability (driveability)	*n*
stabilité directionnelle (comportement de roulage)	*f*	Fahrtrichtungsstabilität (Kfz)	*f*	directional stability (driveability)	*n*
stabilité du fonctionnement (moteur à combustion)	*f*	Laufruhe (Verbrennungsmotor)	*f*	smooth running (IC engine)	*n*
stabilité du véhicule (au freinage)	*f*	Fahrzeugstabilität (beim Bremsen)	*f*	vehicle stability (during braking)	*n*
stade de maintien de la pressior (ABS)	*m*	Druckhaltephase (ABS)	*f*	pressure-holding phase (ABS)	*n*
standardisation	*f*	Standardisierung	*f*	standardization	*n*
statisme	*m*	Proportionalgrad	*m*	speed droop	*n*
stator (alternateur)	*m*	Stator (Generator)	*m*	stator (alternator)	*n*
stator de freinage	*m*	Bremsstator	*m*	braking stator	*n*
stœchiométrique	*adj*	stöchiometrisch	*adj*	stoichiometric	*adj*
stop (régulateur)	*m*	Abschaltung (Regler)	*f*	shutoff (governor)	*n*
stratification de la charge	*f*	Ladungsschichtung	*f*	charge stratification	*n*
structure du bus	*f*	Busstruktur (CAN)	*f*	bus configuration (CAN)	*n*
substances toxiques (gaz d'échappement)	*fpl*	Schadstoffe (Motorabgas)	*mpl*	pollutants (exhaust gas)	*npl*
support (catalyseur)	*m*	Trägersystem (Katalysator)	*n*	substrate system (catalytic converter)	*n*
support à billes (catalyseur)	*m*	Schüttgutträger (Katalysator)	*m*	pelleted substrate (catalytic converter)	*n*
support d'engrenage planétaire	*m*	Planetenträger	*m*	planetary-gear carrier	*n*
support de frein	*m*	Bremsträger (Bremse)	*m*	brake anchor plate (brakes)	*n*
support en céramique	*m*	Keramikträger	*m*	ceramic substrate	*n*
support en forme d'étoile (frein à courants de Foucault)	*m*	Haltestern (Wirbelstrombremse)	*m*	star-shaped bracket (electromagnetic retarder)	*n*
support monolythique (catalyseur)	*m*	Monolith (Katalysator)	*m*	monolith (catalytic converter)	*n*
suralimentation (moteur à combustion)	*f*	Aufladung (Verbrennungsmotor)	*f*	pressure-charging (IC engine)	*n*
suralimentation dynamique	*f*	dynamische Aufladung	*f*	dynamic supercharging	*v*
suralimentation par collecteur de résonance	*f*	Registerresonanzaufladung	*f*	register resonance pressure-charging	*n*
suralimentation par ondes de pression	*f*	Druckwellenaufladung	*f*	pressure-wave supercharging	*n*
suralimentation par oscillation d'admission	*f*	Schwingsaugrohr-Aufladung	*f*	ram-effect supercharging	*v*
suralimentation par résonance	*f*	Resonanzaufladung	*f*	tuned-intake pressure-charging	*n*
suralimentation par turbocompresseur	*f*	Abgasturboaufladung	*f*	exhaust-gas turbocharging	*n*
suralimentation par turbosoufflante	*f*	Abgasturboaufladung	*f*	exhaust-gas turbocharging	*n*
suralimentation pulsatoire	*f*	Stoßaufladung	*f*	pulse turbocharging	*v*

Français		Allemand		Anglais	
suralimenter (moteur à combustion)	*v*	aufladen (Verbrennungsmotor)	*v*	supercharge (IC engine)	*v*
surcharge (batterie)	*f*	Überladung (Batterie)	*f*	overcharge (battery) <noun>	*n*
surcharge à déverrouillage mécanique	*f*	mechanisch entriegelte Startmenge	*f*	mechanically controlled starting quantity	*n*
surcharge automatique au démarrage	*f*	automatische Startmenge	*f*	automatic starting quantity	*n*
surcharge étagée	*f*	gestufte Startmenge, GST	*f*	graded start quantity	*n*
surcharge variable en fonction de la température	*f*	temperaturabhängige Startmenge	*f*	temperature-dependent excess-fuel quantity	*n*
surcharger (batterie)	*v*	überladen (Batterie)	*v*	overcharge (battery) <to overcharge>	*v*
surchauffer (frein)	*v*	heißfahren (Bremse)	*v*	overheat (brakes)	*v*
surcroît de débit	*m*	Mengenüberhöhung	*f*	excess fuel quantity	*n*
surdébit de carburant	*m*	Kraftstoff-Mehrmenge	*f*	excess fuel	*n*
surdébit de démarrage	*m*	Startmehrmenge	*f*	excess fuel for starting	*n*
surenrichir (mélange air-carburant)	*v*	überfetten (Luft-Kraftstoff-Gemisch)	*v*	over-enrich (air-fuel mixture)	*v*
surface annulaire	*f*	Ringfläche	*f*	ring-shaped area	*n*
surface d'appui (pneu)	*f*	Reifenaufstandsfläche	*f*	tire contact patch	*n*
surface d'arrêt	*f*	Anschlagfläche	*f*	stop surface	*n*
surface d'impact (injection diesel)	*f*	Prallfläche (Dieseleinspritzung)	*f*	baffle surface (diesel fuel injection)	*n*
surface de contact du pneu	*f*	Reifenaufstandsfläche	*f*	tire contact patch	*n*
surface de friction (tambour, disque de frein)	*f*	Lauffläche (Bremstrommel, Bremsscheibe)	*f*	contact surface (brake drum, brake disc)	*n*
surface de guidage des rouleaux	*f*	Rollenlaufbahn	*f*	roller path	*n*
surface de sortie de la lumière (éclairage)	*f*	Lichtaustrittsfläche (Lichttechnik)	*f*	lens aperture area (lighting)	*n*
surface efficace	*f*	Wirkfläche	*f*	effective area	*n*
surface utile	*f*	Wirkfläche	*f*	effective area	*n*
surfreiner	*v*	überbremsen	*v*	overbrake	*v*
surpresseur	*m*	Lader	*m*	supercharger	*n*
surrégime	*m*	Überdrehzahl	*f*	overspeed	*n*
surveillance de l'habitacle (véhicule)	*f*	Innenraumüberwachung (Kfz)		intrusion detection (motor vehicle)	*n*
surveillance de la qualité	*f*	Qualitätsüberwachung	*f*	quality surveillance	*n*
survirage (véhicule)	*m*	übersteuern (Kfz)	*v*	oversteer (motor vehicle)	*v*
suspension de débit	*f*	Mengenabstellung	*f*	fuel shutoff	*n*
suspension pneumatique	*f*	Luftfederung	*f*	pneumatic suspension	*n*
suspension pneumatique à régulation électronique, ELF	*f*	elektronisch geregelte Luftfederung, ELF	*f*	electronically controlled pneumatic suspension, ELF	*n*
symbole graphique	*m*	Schaltzeichen	*n*	symbol	*n*
système "Common Rail"	*m*	Common Rail System, CR	*n*	common-rail system, CR	*n*
système à deux chambres (dispositif de freinage à dépression)	*m*	Zweikammerbetrieb (Vakuum-Bremsanlage)	*m*	dual-chamber operation (vacuum-brake system)	*n*
système à deux projecteurs	*m*	Zweischeinwerfer-System	*n*	two-headlamp system	*n*
système à double pot d'échappement	*m*	Doppel-Auspuffanlage	*f*	dual exhaust system	*n*

Français		Allemand		Anglais	
système à quatre projecteurs	*m*	Vier-Scheinwerfer-System	*n*	four-headlamp system	*n*
système à quatre soupapes par cylindre	*m*	Vierventil-Technik	*f*	four-valve design	*n*
système antagoniste (essuie-glace)	*m*	Gegenlaufsystem (Scheibenwischer)	*n*	opposed-pattern wiper system	*n*
système antiblocage, ABS	*m*	Antiblockiersystem, ABS	*n*	antilock braking system, ABS	*n*
système asservi	*m*	Regelstrecke	*f*	controlled system	*n*
système d'admission (moteur à combustion)	*m*	Ansaugsystem (Verbrennungsmotor)	*n*	air-intake system (IC engine)	*n*
système d'admission à géométrie variable	*m*	Schalt-Ansaugsystem	*n*	variable-configuration intake manifold	*n*
système d'aide au démarrage	*m*	Starthilfsanlage	*f*	start-assist system	*n*
système d'aide au parcage	*m*	Park-Pilot	*m*	Park Pilot	*n*
système d'alimentation en carburant	*m*	Kraftstoffsystem	*n*	fuel system	*n*
système d'allumage	*m*	Zündanlage	*f*	ignition system	*n*
système d'allumage double	*m*	Doppelzündung	*f*	dual ignition	*n*
système d'antiblocage des roues, ABS	*m*	Antiblockiersystem, ABS	*n*	antilock braking system, ABS	*n*
système d'échappement	*m*	Abgasanlage	*f*	exhaust-gas system	*n*
système d'engrènement	*m*	Einspursystem	*n*	engaging system	*n*
système d'excitation	*m*	Erregersystem	*n*	excitation system	*n*
système d'information de l'automobiliste	*m*	Fahrerinformationssystem	*n*	driver-information system	*n*
système d'injection	*m*	Einspritzanlage	*f*	fuel-injection installation	*n*
système d'injection à accumulateur	*m*	Common Rail System, CR	*n*	common-rail system, CR	*n*
système d'injection à pression modulée (Common Rail)	*m*	Common Rail System, CR	*n*	common-rail system, CR	*n*
système d'injection d'essence à commande électronique, Jetronic	*m*	Jetronic (elektronische Benzineinspritzung)	*f*	Jetronic (electronic fuel injection)	*n*
système de contrôle des pneumatiques	*m*	Reifenkontrollsystem	*n*	tire-pressure monitoring system	*n*
système de correction "avance"	*m*	Früh-Verstellsystem	*n*	early (advance) adjustment system	*n*
système de correction "retard"	*m*	Spät-Verstellsystem	*n*	late (retard) adjustment system	*n*
système de déclenchement	*m*	Auslösessystem	*m*	triggering system	*n*
système de déclenchement Hall	*m*	Hall-Auslösesystem	*n*	Hall triggering system	*n*
système de diagnostic	*m*	Diagnosesystem	*n*	diagnostics system	*n*
système de freinage	*m*	Bremsanlage	*f*	braking system	*n*
système de freinage à circuit unique	*m*	Einkreis-Bremsanlage	*f*	single-circuit braking system	*n*
système de freinage à double circuit	*m*	Zweikreis-Bremsanlage	*f*	dual-circuit braking system	*n*
système de localisation à l'estime (système de navigation	*m*	Koppelortungssystem (Navigationssystem)	*n*	compound navigation (navigation system)	*n*
système de localisation par satellite (système de navigation	*m*	Satellitenortungssystem (Navigationssystem)	*n*	satellite positioning system (navigation system)	*n*
système de navigation	*m*	Navigationssystem	*n*	navigation system	*n*

Français		Allemand		Anglais	
système de navigation (automobile)	m	Navigationssystem (Kfz)	n	navigation system (motor vehicle)	n
système de projecteurs	m	Scheinwerfersystem	n	headlamp system	n
système de protection des passagers	m	Insassenschutzsystem	n	occupant-protection system	n
système de protection des véhicules	m	Fahrzeug-Sicherungssystem	n	vehicle security system	n
système de réglage des rétroviseurs	m	Spiegelverstellsystem	n	mirror adjusting system	n
système de retenue des vapeurs de carburant	m	Kraftstoffverdunstungs-Rückhaltesystem	n	evaporative-emissions control system	n
système de roues planétaires	m	Planetenradsystem	n	planetary-gear system	n
système de sécurité	m	Sicherheitssystem	n	safety and security system	n
système de stabilisation (véhicules)	+ m	Fahrdynamikregelung, ESP	f	electronic stability program, ESP	n
système de suspension	m	Fahrwerksystem	n	chassis system	n
système de transmission intégrale	m	Allradsystem	n	all-wheel-drive system	n
système électronique de gestion du moteur, Motronic	m	elektronische Motorsteuerung, Motronic	f	electronic engine-management system, Motronic	n
système incrémentiel angle-temps	m	Inkremental-Winkel-Zeit-System	n	increment-angle-time system	n
système monobras (essuie-glace)	m	Einhebelsystem (Scheibenwischer)	n	single-arm wiper system	n
système pompe-conduite-injecteur	m	Pumpe-Leitung-Düse, UPS	f	unit pump system, UPS	n
système régulé	m	Regelstrecke	f	controlled system	n
système tandem (essuie-glace)	m	Gleichlaufsystem (Scheibenwischer)	n	tandem-pattern wiper system	n
systèmes de confort	mpl	Komfortsysteme	npl	comfort and convenience systems	npl
T					
table de correspondance	f	Gegenüberstellung	f	cross-reference	n
tableau de bord	m	Armaturenbrett	n	dashboard	n
tachographe	m	Fahrtschreiber	m	trip recorder	n
tachymètre (terme général)	m	Drehzahlmesser (allgemein)	m	tachometer (general term)	n
taille de particule (filtre)	f	Teilchengröße (Filter)	f	particle size (filter)	n
taille de pompe	f	Pumpengröße	f	pump size	n
taille des pores (filtre)	f	Porengröße (Filter)	f	pore size (filter)	n
talon de galet	m	Rollenschuh	m	roller support	n
tambour de frein	m	Bremstrommel	f	brake drum	n
tamis de filtre	m	Filtersieb	n	filter strainer	n
tarage du ressort	m	Federvorspannung	f	initial spring tension	n
taré (ressort)	pp	vorgespannt (Feder)	pp	pre-loaded (spring)	pp
taré par ressort	pp	federbelastet	pp	spring-loaded	pp
taux d'admission de charge	m	Liefergrad (Verbrennungsmotor)	m	volumetric efficiency (IC engine)	n
taux d'enrichissement	m	Anreicherungsrate	f	enrichment quantity	n
taux d'injection	m	Spritzrate	f	injection rate	n
taux de compression	m	Verdichtungsverhältnis	n	compression ratio	n

Français		Allemand		Anglais	
taux de correction de débit	*m*	Angleichrate	*f*	torque-control rate	*n*
taux de freinage	*m*	Abbremsung	*f*	braking factor	*n*
taux de freinage minimum	*m*	Mindestabbremsung	*f*	minimum retardation	*n*
taux de polluants	*m*	Schadstoffanteil	*m*	noxious constituents	*npl*
taux de recyclage des gaz d'échappement	*m*	Abgasrückführrate	*f*	exhaust-gas recirculation (EGR) rate	*n*
taux de refoulement	*m*	Förderrate	*f*	fuel-delivery rate	*n*
taux de remplissage (batterie)	*m*	Füllungsgrad (Batterie)	*m*	electrolyte level (battery)	*n*
taux de transmission (multiplexage)	*m*	Übertragungsrate (CAN)	*f*	transfer rate (CAN)	*n*
technique à couches épaisses	*f*	Dickschichttechnik	*f*	thick-film techniques	*npl*
technique à couches minces	*f*	Dünnschichttechnik	*f*	thin-film techniques	*npl*
technique bipolaire	*f*	Bipolartechnik	*f*	bipolar technology	*n*
technique d'analyse des gaz d'échappement	*f*	Abgasprüftechnik	*f*	exhaust-gas analysis techniques	*npl*
technique d'éclairage	*f*	Lichttechnik	*f*	lighting techniques	*n*
technique d'injection	*f*	Kraftstoffeinspritzung	*f*	fuel injection	*n*
technique de contrôle et d'essai	*f*	Prüftechnik	*f*	test technology	*n*
technique de mesure des gaz d'échappement	*f*	Abgasmeßtechnik	*f*	exhaust-gas measuring techniques	*npl*
technique de radioguidage de la circulation	*f*	Verkehrsleittechnik	*f*	traffic-control engeneering	*n*
technique des gaz d'échappement	*f*	Abgastechnik	*f*	emissions-control technology	*n*
technique hybride	*f*	Hybridtechnik	*f*	hybrid technology	*n*
technique modulaire	*f*	Modultechnik	*f*	modular system	*n*
technique monolithe	*f*	Monolithtechnik	*f*	monolithic techniques	*npl*
télécommande radio	*f*	Funkfernbedienung	*f*	radio remote control	*n*
témoin d'alerte	*m*	Warnlampe	*f*	warning lamp	*n*
témoin de diagnostic	*m*	Diagnoselampe	*f*	diagnosis lamp	*n*
témoin de fonctionnement	*m*	Funktionskontrolleuchte	*f*	function lamp	*n*
témoin de préchauffage	*m*	Vorglühanzeige	*f*	pre-glow indicator	*n*
température d'autoallumage	*f*	Selbstzündtemperatur	*f*	auto-ignition temperature	*n*
température d'autonettoyage	*f*	Freibrenntemperatur	*f*	self-cleaning temperature	*n*
température d'inflammation	*f*	Zündtemperatur	*f*	ignition temperature	*n*
température de couleur (éclairage)	*f*	Farbtemperatur (Lichttechnik)	*f*	color temperature (lighting)	*n*
température de démarrage	*f*	Starttemperatur	*f*	starting temperature	*n*
température finale de fonctionnement	*f*	Enderwärmung	*f*	final operating temperature	*n*
température limite	*f*	Grenztemperatur	*f*	limit temperature	*n*
température limite de démarrage	*f*	Startgrenztemperatur	*f*	minimum starting temperature	*n*
température normale de fonctionnement	*f*	Betriebstemperatur	*f*	operating temperature	*n*
temporisateur (électrovanne de démarrage)	*m*	Verzögerungsschaltung (Startventil)	*f*	delay switch (start valve)	*n*
temporisation de la formation du couple de lacet	*f*	Giermomentaufbau-verzögerung, GMA	*f*	yaw moment buildup delay	*n*

Français		Allemand		Anglais	
temps d'accroissement (freinage)	*m*	Schwelldauer (Bremsvorgang)	*f*	pressure build-up time (braking)	*n*
temps d'admission	*m*	Ansaugtakt	*m*	induction stroke	*n*
temps d'arrêt (freinage)	*m*	Anhaltezeit (Bremsvorgang)	*f*	stopping time (braking)	*n*
temps d'attente en fonction de la température	*m*	temperaturabhängige Wartezeit	*f*	temperature-dependent waiting period	*n*
temps d'injection	*m*	Einspritzzeit	*f*	injection time	*n*
temps d'interruption de l'injection (Jetronic)	*m*	Einspritzausblendungszeit (Jetronic)	*f*	injection blank-out period (Jetronic)	*n*
temps de charge (batterie)	*m*	Ladezeit (Batterie)	*m*	charging time (battery)	*n*
temps de combustion	*m*	Arbeitshub	*m*	working stroke	*n*
temps de commande	*m*	Steuerzeit	*f*	control time	*n*
temps de compression (moteur à combustion)	*m*	Verdichtungstakt (Verbrennungsmotor)	*m*	compression cycle (IC engine)	*n*
temps de desserrage (frein)	*m*	Lösedauer (Bremse)	*f*	release time (brakes)	*n*
temps de fermeture (allumage)	*m*	Schließzeit (Zündung)	*f*	dwell period (ignition)	*n*
temps de fermeture (injecteur)	*m*	Abfallzeit (Einspritzventil)	*f*	release time (fuel injector)	*n*
temps de freinage	*m*	Bremsdauer	*f*	braking time	*n*
temps de freinage actif	*m*	Bremswirkungsdauer	*f*	effective braking time	*n*
temps de montée en pression (freinage)	*m*	Schwellzeit (Bremsvorgang)	*f*	pressure build-up time (braking)	*n*
temps de montée en régime	*m*	Hochlaufdauer	*f*	running-up time	*n*
temps de post-incandescence	*m*	Nachglühzeit	*f*	post-glow time	*n*
temps de préchauffage	*m*	Vorglühdauer	*f*	preheating time	*n*
temps de réaction (freinage)	*m*	Reaktionsdauer (Bremsbetätigung)	*f*	reaction time (brake actuation)	*n*
temps de rebondissement (relais)	*m*	Prellzeit (Relais)	*f*	bounce time (relay)	*n*
temps de régulation du courant	*m*	Stromregelzeit	*f*	current control time	*n*
temps de relâchement (relais)	*m*	Rückfallzeit (Relais)	*f*	release time (relay)	*n*
temps de réponse	*m*	Ansprechzeit	*f*	response time	*n*
temps de réponse des freins	*m*	Bremsenansprechdauer	*f*	brake response time	*n*
temps de réponse initial	*m*	Ansprechdauer	*f*	initial response time	*n*
temps de rétablissement	*m*	Ausregelzeit	*f*	settling time	*n*
temps de transit des gaz (régulation lambda)	*m*	Gaslaufzeit (Lambda-Regelung)	*f*	gas travel time (lambda closed-loop control)	*n*
temps maximum de détection (régulateur)	*m*	Abtastzeitmaxima	*npl*	maximum sampling time	*n*
temps mort (effet de freinage)	*m*	Verlustzeit (Bremsvorgang)	*f*	reaction time (braking action)	*n*
temps moteur	*m*	Arbeitstakt	*m*	power cycle	*n*
temps opérationnel du programme principal	*m*	Hauptprogrammlaufzeit	*f*	main-program running time	*n*
temps total de freinage	*m*	Gesamtbremsdauer	*f*	total braking time	*n*
tendance au blocage (roue)	*f*	Blockierneigung (Rad)	*f*	incipient lock (wheel)	*n*
tendance au cliquetis	*f*	Klopfneigung	*f*	tendency to knock	*n*
tendance au rampement (véhicules à boîte automatique)	*f*	Kriechneigung (Fahrzeuge mit Automatikgetriebe)	*f*	creep tendency (vehicles with automatic gearbox)	*n*
tendeur de courroie	*m*	Riemenspanner	*m*	belt tensioner	*n*

Français		Allemand		Anglais	
tension à l'état bloqué (semi-conducteur)	*f*	Sperrspannung (Halbleiter)	*f*	off-state voltage (semiconductor)	*n*
tension à l'état passant (diode redresseuse)	*f*	Durchlaßspannung (Gleichrichterdiode)	*f*	forward voltage (rectifier diode	*n*
tension alternative	*f*	Wechselspannung	*f*	alternating voltage	*n*
tension au repos (batterie)	*f*	Ruhespannung (Batterie)	*f*	steady-state voltage (battery)	*n*
tension aux bornes	*f*	Klemmenspannung	*f*	terminal voltage	*n*
tension d'alimentation	*f*	Versorgungsspannung	*f*	supply voltage	*n*
tension d'allumage	*f*	Zündspannung	*f*	ignition voltage	*n*
tension d'arc (bougie)	*f*	Brennspannung (Zündkerze)	*f*	spark voltage (spark plug)	*n*
tension d'essai	*f*	Prüfspannung	*f*	test voltage	*n*
tension d'excitation	*f*	Erregerspannung	*f*	excitation voltage	*n*
tension d'induction	*f*	Induktionsspannung	*f*	induction voltage	*n*
tension de charge	*f*	Ladespannung (Batterie)	*f*	charge voltage	*n*
tension de claquage	*f*	Durchbruchspannung	*f*	breakdown voltage	*n*
tension de combustion	*f*	Brennspannung (Zündkerze)	*f*	spark voltage (spark plug)	*n*
tension de crête	*f*	Scheitelspannung	*f*	peak voltage	*n*
tension de dégagement gazeux	*f*	Gasungsspannung	*f*	gassing voltage	*n*
tension de maintien	*f*	Haltespannung	*f*	holding voltage	*n*
tension de rampe	*f*	Rampenspannung	*f*	ramp voltage	*n*
tension de régulation	*f*	Regelspannung	*f*	regulator response voltage	*n*
tension de relâchement	*f*	Rückfallspannung	*f*	dropout voltage	*n*
tension de réponse	*f*	Ansprechspannung	*f*	response voltage	*n*
tension de rupture	*f*	Schaltspannung	*f*	switched voltage	*n*
tension de service	*f*	Betriebsspannung	*f*	operating voltage	*n*
tension de seuil	*f*	Schwellenspannung	*f*	threshold voltage	*n*
tension de sortie	*f*	Ausgangsspannung	*f*	output voltage	*n*
tension du circuit de bord	*f*	Bordnetzspannung	*f*	vehicle system voltage	*n*
tension du générateur d'impulsions	*f*	Geberspannung	*f*	pulse-generator voltage	*n*
tension Hall	*f*	Hall-Spannung	*f*	Hall voltage	*n*
tension initiale du ressort	*f*	Federvorspannung	*f*	initial spring tension	*n*
tension inverse (diode)	*f*	Sperrspannung (Diode)	*f*	reverse voltage (diode)	*n*
tension moyenne	*f*	Mittelspannung	*f*	medium voltage, MV	*n*
tension nominale	*f*	Nennspannung	*f*	nominal voltage	*n*
tension partielle	*f*	Teilspannung	*f*	partial voltage	*n*
tension perturbatrice (CEM)	*f*	Funkstörspannung (EMV)	*f*	radio interference voltage (EMC)	*n*
tension secondaire	*f*	Sekundärspannung	*f*	secondary voltage	*n*
tension Zener	*f*	Zenerspannung	*f*	Zener voltage	*n*
tenue au rayonnement incident (CEM)	*f*	Einstrahlfestigkeit (EMV)	*f*	resistance to incident radiation (EMC)	*n*
tenue aux ondes de pression	*f*	Druckschwellfestigkeit	*f*	compression pulsating fatigue strength	*n*
tenue aux vibrations	*f*	Schwingungsfestigkeit	*f*	resistance to vibrations	*n*
test au brouillard salin	*m*	Salzsprühtest	*m*	salt spray test	*n*
test automatique	*m*	Selbsttest	*m*	self test	*n*
test d'émission de fumées	*m*	Rauchprüfung	*f*	smoke emission test	*n*

Français		Allemand		Anglais	
test d'évaporation	*m*	Verdunstungsprüfung	*f*	evaporative-emissions test	*n*
test des gaz d'échappement	*m*	Abgastest	*m*	exhaust-gas test	*n*
test du relais principal	*m*	Hauptrelaistest	*m*	main-relay test	*n*
test final	*m*	Endkontrolle	*f*	final inspection	*n*
testeur de batteries	*m*	Batterie-Tester	*m*	battery tester	*n*
testeur de diagnostic	*m*	Diagnosetestgerät	*n*	diagnosis tester	*n*
testeur pour moteur	*m*	Motortestgerät	*n*	engine analyzer	*n*
tête coulissante	*f*	Gleitstein	*m*	sliding block	*n*
tête d'accouplement	*f*	Kupplungskopf	*m*	coupling head	*n*
tête d'accouplement "alimentation"	*f*	Kupplungskopf "Vorrat"	*m*	coupling head "supply"	*n*
tête d'accouplement "frein"	*f*	Kupplungskopf "Bremse"	*m*	coupling head "brakes"	*n*
tête d'allumeur	*f*	Zündverteilerkappe	*f*	distributor cap	*n*
tête de bobine (stator)	*f*	Wickelkopf (Ständer)	*m*	winding head (stator)	*n*
tête de cylindre (compresseur d'air)	*f*	Zylinderdeckel (Luftkompressor)	*m*	cylinder head (air compressor)	*n*
tête de distributeur	*f*	Zündverteilerkappe	*f*	distributor cap	*n*
tête de distribution (pompe distributrice)	*f*	Verteilerkörper (Verteilereinspritzpumpe)	*m*	distributor head (distributor pump)	*n*
tête de l'élément de pompage	*f*	Elementkopf (Pumpenelement)	*m*	plunger-and-barrel head	*n*
tête de l'étincelle	*f*	Funkenkopf	*m*	spark head	*n*
tête hydraulique (pompe distributrice)	*f*	Verteilerkörper (Verteilereinspritzpumpe)	*m*	distributor head (distributor pump)	*n*
téton d'étranglement	*m*	Drosselzapfen	*m*	throttling pintle	*n*
téton d'injection	*m*	Spritzzapfen	*m*	pintle	*n*
téton de pression (injecteur à téton et étranglement)	*m*	Druckzapfen (Drosselzapfendüse)	*m*	pressure pin (throttling-pintle nozzle)	*n*
thermistance CTN	*f*	NTC-Widerstand	*m*	NTC resistor	*n*
thermocontact	*m*	Thermoschalter	*m*	thermostatic switch	*n*
thermocontact temporisé	*m*	Thermozeitschalter	*m*	thermo-time switch	*n*
thermocontacteur	*m*	Thermoschalter	*m*	thermostatic switch	*n*
thermostat	*m*	Thermostat	*m*	thermostat	*n*
tige centrale	*f*	Anschlußbolzen	*m*	terminal stud	*n*
tige chauffante (dessiccateur)	*f*	Heizstab (Lufttrockner)	*m*	heating element (air drier)	*n*
tige d'engrènement (démarreur)	*f*	Einrückstange (Starter)	*f*	engagement rod (starter)	*n*
tige de commande d'injecteur	*f*	Ventilsteuerkolben	*m*	valve control plunger	*n*
tige de connexion	*f*	Anschlußbolzen	*m*	terminal stud	*n*
tige de guidage	*f*	Führungsstift	*m*	guide pin	*n*
tige de piston	*f*	Kolbenstange	*f*	piston rod	*n*
tige de piston (clapet de refoulement)	*f*	Kolbenschaft (Druckventil)	*m*	pressure-valve stem	*n*
tige de poussoir (servofrein)	*f*	Druckstange (Bremskraftverstärker)	*f*	push rod (brake booster)	*n*
tige de pression	*f*	Druckstift (Zweifeder-Düsenhalter)	*m*	pressure pin (two-spring nozzle holder)	*n*
tige de réglage (pompe d'injection en ligne)	*f*	Regelstange (Reiheneinspritzpumpe)	*f*	control rack (in-line pump)	*n*
tige de soupape	*f*	Ventilstift	*m*	valve pin	*n*
tige de soupape de refoulement	*f*	Druckventilschaft	*m*	delivery-valve stem	*n*

Français

Français		Allemand		Anglais	
tige de traction (correcteur d'avance)	*f*	Zugstange (Zündversteller)	*f*	vacuum advance arm (advance mechanism)	*n*
tige-poussoir	*f*	Druckbolzen	*m*	pressure pin	*n*
timon (remorque)	*m*	Deichsel	*f*	drawbar	*n*
timonerie d'accélérateur	*f*	Gasgestänge	*n*	accelerator-lever linkage	*n*
timonerie de frein	*f*	Bremsgestänge	*n*	brake linkage	*n*
tiroir d'air additionnel	*m*	Zusatzluftschieber	*m*	auxiliary-air device	*n*
tiroir de régulation (pompe distributrice)	*m*	Regelschieber (Verteilereinspritzpumpe)	*m*	control collar (distributor pump)	*n*
tiroir rotatif	*m*	Drehschieber	*m*	rotating slide	*n*
toît ouvrant	*m*	Schiebedach	*n*	sliding sunroof	*n*
tôle magnétique	*f*	Elektroblech	*n*	electrical sheet steel	*n*
tolérance de régulation	*f*	Regeltoleranz	*f*	control tolerance	*n*
tonalité continue (alarme auto)	*f*	Dauerton (Autoalarm)	*m*	continuous tone (car alarm)	*n*
tonalité d'alerte (alarme auto)	*f*	Alarmton (Autoalarm)	*m*	alarm tone (car alarm)	*n*
touche	*f*	Tastschalter	*m*	non-locking switch	*n*
toucheau (rupteur)	*m*	Gleitstück (Unterbrecherhebel)	*n*	cam follower (breaker lever)	*n*
tourbillon	*m*	Drall	*m*	swirl	*v*
tourbillon à l'admission	*m*	Einlaßdrall (Saugrohr)	*m*	intake swirl (intake manifold)	*n*
tourbillonnement	*m*	Verwirbelung	*f*	swirl effect	*n*
tourbillonnement de l'air	*m*	Luftverwirbelung	*f*	air turbulence	*n*
tourillon sphérique	*m*	Kugelzapfen	*m*	ball pivot	*n*
trace d'usure (tambour, frein à disque)	*f*	Einlaufstelle (Bremstrommel, Bremsscheibe)	*f*	scoring (brake drum, brake disc)	*n*
tracer	*v*	plotten	*v*	plot	*v*
traces d'abrasion dues au freinage	*fpl*	Bremsabrieb	*m*	brake dust	*n*
traceur	*m*	Plotter	*m*	plotter	*n*
tracteur	*m*	Zugfahrzeug	*n*	tractor vehicle	*n*
traction avant	*f*	Frontantrieb	*m*	front-wheel drive	*n*
train épicycloïdal	*m*	Planetengetriebe	*n*	planetary gear	*n*
train longitudinal (système de transmission intégrale)	*m*	Längsstrang (Allradantrieb)	*m*	longitudinal train (all-wheel drive)	*n*
train planétaire	*m*	Planetengetriebe	*n*	planetary gear	*n*
trains d'étincelles	*mpl*	Folgefunken	*m*	follow-up spark	*n*
traitement à l'étage de sortie (calculateur)	*m*	Endstufenbearbeitung (Steuergerät)	*f*	driver-stage processing (ECU)	*n*
traitement des paramètres de fonctionnement	*m*	Betriebsdatenverarbeitung	*f*	operating-data processing	*n*
traitement secondaire des gaz d'échappement	*m*	Abgasnachbehandlung	*f*	exhaust-gas treatment	*n*
trajectoire	*f*	Fahrspur	*f*	lane	*n*
trajectoire (véhicule)	*f*	Spurtreue (Kfz)	*f*	vehicle stability (staying in lane)	*n*
trajectoire rectiligne (véhicule)	*f*	Geradeauslauf (Kfz)	*m*	straight-ahead running stability (motor vehicle)	*n*
tranche (semi-conducteur)	*f*	Wafer (Halbleiter) x	*m*	wafer (semiconductor)	*n*
transducteur d'accélérateur x	*m*	Fahrpedalsensor	*m*	pedal-travel sensor	*n*

Français		Allemand			Anglais		
transducteur-récepteur (alarme auto)	*m*	Empfänger-Wandler (Autoalarm)		*m*	receiver transducer (car alarm)		*n*
transformateur d'allumage	*m*	Zündtrafo		*m*	ignition tranformer		*n*
transistor d'allumage	*m*	Zündtransistor		*m*	ignition transistor		*n*
transistor d'attaque	*m*	Treibertransistor		*m*	driving transistor		*n*
transistor de puissance	*m*	Leistungstransistor		*m*	power transistor		*n*
transmetteur tachymétrique	*m*	Tachogenerator		*m*	speedometer generator		*n*
transmission	*f*	Antriebsvorrichtung		*f*	drive assembly		*n*
transmission (correcteur de freinage)	*f*	Antrieb (Bremskraftregler)		*m*	drive element (braking force regulator)		*n*
transmission (dispositif de freinage)	*f*	Übertragungseinrichtung (Bremsanlage)		*f*	transmission (braking system)		*n*
transmission à courroie	*f*	Riementrieb		*m*	belt drive		*n*
transmission combinée (dispositif de freinage)	*f*	gemischte Übertragungs-einrichtung (Bremsanlage)		*f*	combined transmission (braking system)		*n*
transmission de données	*f*	Datenübertragung		*f*	data transmission		*n*
transmission intégrale	*f*	Allradantrieb		*m*	all-wheel drive, AWD		*n*
transmission intermédiaire	*f*	Vorgelege		*n*	reduction gear		*n*
transmission quatre roues	*f*	Vierradantrieb		*m*	four-wheel drive, FWD		*n*
travail de déformation (pneu)	*m*	Formänderungsarbeit (Reifen)		*f*	deformation process (tire)		*n*
travail de freinage	*m*	Bremsarbeit		*f*	braking work		*n*
tréfilage (enroulement)	*m*	Einziehtechnik (Wicklung)		*f*	pull-in technique (winding)		*n*
tringlerie du régulateur	*f*	Reglergestänge		*n*	governor linkage		*n*
trou à l'accélération	*m*	Beschleunigungsloch	x	*n*	flat spot		*n*
trou borgne (injecteur)	*m*	Sackloch (Einspritzventil)		*n*	blind hole (injector)		*n*
trou d'injecteur	*m*	Spritzloch		*n*	injection orifice		*n*
trou d'injection	*m*	Spritzloch		*n*	injection orifice		*n*
trou de fin d'injection étagé	*m*	gestufter Absteuerquerschnitt		*m*	stepped spill port		*n*
trou de fixation	*m*	Befestigungsloch		*n*	fixing hole		*n*
trou de suralimentation	*m*	Turboloch	x	*n*	turbo lag	x	*n*
trou pilote (injecteur)	*m*	Sackloch (Einspritzventil)		*n*	blind hole (injector)		*n*
tube "Common Rail"	*m*	Common Rail Leitung		*f*	common-rail pipe		*n*
tube à résonance	*m*	Resonanzrohr		*n*	resonance tube		*n*
tube chauffant	*m*	Heizrohr		*n*	heating tube		*n*
tube de refoulement	*m*	Druckleitung		*f*	fuel-injection tubing		*n*
tube de vaporisation	*m*	Verdampferrohr		*n*	evaporator tube		*n*
tube incandescent	*m*	Glührohr		*n*	glow tube		*n*
tubulure d'admission	*f*	Einzelschwingrohr		*n*	individual runner		*n*
tubulure d'aspiration d'air	*f*	Luftansaugstutzen		*m*	air-intake fitting		*n*
tubulure d'échappement (régulateur de pression)	*f*	Ablaßstutzen (Druckregler)		*m*	blow-off fitting (pressure regulator)		*n*
tubulure de mise à l'atmosphère	*f*	Entlüftungsstutzen		*m*	vent connection		*n*
tunnel de dilution (méthode CVS)	*m*	Verdünnungstunnel (CVS-Methode)		*m*	dilution tunnel (CVS method)		*n*
turbine à gaz d'échappement	*f*	Abgasturbine		*f*	exhaust-gas turbine		*n*
turbocompresseur	*m*	Abgasturbolader		*m*	exhaust-gas turbocharger		*n*
turbomachine	*f*	Strömungsmaschine		*f*	turbo element		*n*
turbosoufflante	*f*	Abgasturbolader		*m*	exhaust-gas turbocharger		*n*

Français		Allemand		Anglais	
turbulence	*f*	Verwirbelung	*f*	swirl effect	*n*
turbulence de l'air	*f*	Luftverwirbelung	*f*	air turbulence	*n*
turbulence du mélange	*f*	Gemischturbulenz	*f*	mixture turbulence	*n*
tuyau d'échappement	*m*	Abgasrohr	*n*	exhaust pipe	*n*
tuyau de refoulement	*m*	Druckleitung	*f*	fuel-injection tubing	*n*
tuyau flexible	*m*	flexible Leitung	*f*	flexible line	*n*
tuyau flexible de frein	*m*	Bremsschlauch	*m*	brake hose	*n*
tuyauterie d'admission	*f*	Saugrohr	*n*	intake manifold	*n*
tuyauterie de carburant	*f*	Kraftstoffleitung	*f*	fuel line	*n*
tuyauterie de référence	*f*	Referenzleitung	*f*	reference line	*n*
tuyauterie de refoulement	*f*	Druckleitung	*f*	fuel-injection tubing	*n*
tuyauterie haute pression	*f*	Hochdruckleitung	*f*	high-pressure delivery line	*n*
type à bloc redresseur compact (alternateur)	*m*	Topfbauart (Generator)	*f*	compact-diode-assembly model (alternator)	*n*
type de défaut	*m*	Fehlerart	*f*	failure mode	*n*
type de véhicule	*m*	Fahrzeugtyp	*m*	vehicle type	*n*
U					
uniformité des débits	*f*	Gleichförderung	*f*	uniformity of fuel delivery	*n*
unité d'affichage (ordinateur de bord)	*f*	Anzeigeeinheit (Fahrdatenrechner)	*f*	display unit (trip computer)	*n*
unité d'entraînement (banc d'essai)	*f*	Antriebseinheit (Rollenbremsprüfstand)	*f*	drive unit (dynamic brake analyzer)	*n*
unité d'injection (Mono-Jetronic)	*f*	Einspritzaggregat (Mono-Jetronic)	*n*	central injection unit (Mono-Jetronic)	*n*
unité de calcul (calculateur)	*f*	Rechenwerk (Steuergerät)	*n*	arithmetic-logic processor (ECU)	*n*
unité de gicleur d'aspiration	*f*	Saugdrosseleinheit	*f*	inlet metering unit	*n*
unité de piston de charge (ESP)	*f*	Ladekolbeneinheit (ESP)	*f*	charging-piston unit (ESP)	*n*
unité de puisage	*f*	Tankeinbaueinheit	*f*	in-tank unit	*n*
unité de sélection (ordinateur de bord)	*f*	Bedieneinheit (Fahrdatenrechner)	*f*	control unit (trip computer)	*n*
unité de traitement (ordinateur de bord)	*f*	Zentraleinheit (Fahrdatenrechner)	*f*	central processing unit (on-board computer), CPU	*n*
usure de garniture de frein	*f*	Belagverschleiß	*m*	lining wear	*n*
usure des balais	*f*	Bürstenverschleiß	*m*	brush wear	*n*
usure des électrodes	*f*	Elektrodenverschleiß	*m*	electrode wear	*n*
usure du pneu	*f*	Reifenverschleiß	*m*	tire wear	*n*
V					
valeur brute (capteur d'accélérateur)	*f*	Rohwert (Fahrpedalsensor)	*m*	raw value (accelerator-pedal sensor)	*n*
valeur consigne de l'actionneur de débit	*f*	Mengenstellersollwert	*m*	fuel-quantity positioner setpoint value	*n*
valeur d'émission de fumées	*f*	Rauchwert	*m*	smoke-emission value	*n*
valeur d'excitation	*f*	Anregungskennwert	*m*	stimulation characteristic value	*n*
valeur de seuil de débit	*f*	Mengenschwellwert	*m*	fuel-quantity threshold value	*n*
valeur initiale de débit demandé	*f*	Wunschmengenanfangswert	*m*	demand-value starting point	*n*
valeur limite d'émission	*f*	Abgasgrenzwert	*m*	emission limits	*n*
valeur thermique (bougie)	*f*	Wärmewert (Zündkerze)	*m*	heat range (spark plug)	*n*

Français		Allemand		Anglais	
valeurs d'émission	*fpl*	Emissionswerte	*mpl*	emission values	*npl*
valeurs d'essai	*fpl*	Prüfwerte	*mpl*	test specifications	*npl*
valeurs limites de fonctionnement	*fpl*	Betriebsgrenzwert	*m*	operating limits	*n*
validation	*f*	Freigabe (Fertigung)	*f*	release (manufacturing)	*n*
valve à bouton poussoir	*f*	Druckknopfventil	*n*	push-button valve	*n*
valve à bouton rotatif	*f*	Drehknopfventil	*n*	rotary-knob valve	*n*
valve à deux positions	*f*	Zweistellungsventil	*n*	two-position valve	*n*
valve à double siège	*f*	Doppelsitzventil	*n*	double-seat valve	*n*
valve à impulsions progressives (ELB)	*f*	Hochtaktventil (ELB)	*n*	pressure-buildup valve (ELB)	*n*
valve à membrane	*f*	Membranventil	*n*	diaphragm valve	*n*
valve à trois positions	*f*	Dreistellungsventil	*n*	three-position valve	*n*
valve asservie à la charge (ASR)	*f*	Lastventil (ASR)	*n*	load valve (TCS)	*n*
valve by-pass	*f*	Bypassventil	*n*	wastegate	*n*
valve d'admission	*f*	Einlaßventil	*n*	intake valve	*n*
valve d'air additionnel	*f*	Zusatzluftventil	*n*	auxiliary-air valve	*n*
valve d'amortissement (pivotement des portes)	*f*	Drosselventil (Türbetätigung)	*n*	throttle valve (door control)	*n*
valve d'arrêt	*f*	Sperrventil	*n*	check valve	*n*
valve d'étranglement (pivotement des portes)	*f*	Drosselventil (Türbetätigung)	*n*	throttle valve (door control)	*n*
valve de barrage	*f*	Absperrventil	*n*	shutoff valve	*n*
valve de barrage (tête d'accouplement)	*f*	Absperrglied (Kupplungskopf)	*n*	shutoff element (coupling head)	*n*
valve de barrage ASR	*f*	ASR-Sperrventil	*n*	TCS lock valve	*n*
valve de commande	*f*	Steuerventil	*n*	control valve (open loop)	*n*
valve de commande de remorque	*f*	Anhängersteuerventil	*n*	trailer-control valve	*n*
valve de commande de remorque à deux conduites	*f*	Zweileitungs-Anhängersteuerventil	*n*	dual-line trailer-control valve	*n*
valve de contrôle	*f*	Prüfventil	*n*	test valve	*n*
valve de décharge	*f*	Überströmventil	*n*	overflow valve	*n*
valve de dégazage	*f*	Entlüftungsventil	*n*	bleeder valve	*n*
valve de dérivation	*f*	Bypassventil	*n*	wastegate	*n*
valve de desserrage	*f*	Löseventil	*n*	release valve	*n*
valve de desserrage rapide (frein)	*f*	Schnellöseventil (Bremse)	*n*	quick-release valve (brakes)	*n*
valve de drainage	*f*	Entwässerungsventil	*n*	drain valve	*n*
valve de frein	*f*	Bremsventil	*n*	brake valve	*n*
valve de frein à main	*f*	Handbremsventil	*n*	hand-brake valve	*n*
valve de frein de remorque	*f*	Anhängerbremsventil	*n*	trailer-brake valve	*n*
valve de frein de secours	*f*	Hilfsbremsventil	*n*	secondary-brake valve	*n*
valve de frein de service	*f*	Betriebsbremsventil	*n*	service-brake valve	*n*
valve de frein de service à double circuit	*f*	Zweikreis-Betriebsbremsventil	*n*	dual-circuit service-brake valve	*n*
valve de frein de stationnement	*f*	Feststellbremsventil	*n*	parking-brake valve	*n*
valve de maintien (ABS)	*f*	Halteventil (ABS)	*n*	pressure-holding valve (ABS)	*n*

Français		Allemand		Anglais	
valve de nivellement	*f*	Luftfederventil	*n*	height-control valve	*n*
valve de pression d'admission	*f*	Vordruckventil	*n*	admission-pressure valve	*n*
valve de purge air	*f*	Entlüftungsventil	*n*	bleeder valve	*n*
valve de régulation	*f*	Regelventil	*n*	control valve (closed loop)	*n*
valve de secours	*f*	Rückhalteventil	*n*	backup valve	*n*
valve de sécurité (dessiccateur)	*f*	Sicherheitsventil (Lufttrockner)	*n*	safety valve (air drier)	*n*
valve de sécurité (frein)	*f*	Schutzventil (Bremse)	*n*	protection valve (brakes)	*n*
valve de sécurité à deux circuits	*f*	Zweikreis-Schutzventil	*f*	dual-circuit protection valve (brakes)	*n*
valve de sécurité à quatre circuits	*f*	Vierkreis-Schutzventil	*n*	four-circuit protection valve	*n*
valve de sécurité à trois circuits	*f*	Dreikreis-Schutzventil	*n*	triple-circuit protection valve	*n*
valve de sécurité multicircuits	*f*	Mehrkreisschutzventil	*n*	multiple-circuit protection valve	*n*
valve de verrouillage	*f*	Verriegelungsventil	*n*	locking valve	*n*
valve électromagnétique	*f*	Magnetventil	*n*	solenoid valve	*n*
valve modulatrice de pression	*f*	Wastegate-Regelventil	*n*	waste-gate control valve	*n*
valve modulatrice de pression (ABS)	*f*	Drucksteuerventil (ABS)	*n*	pressure-control valve (ABS)	*n*
valve pilote (modulateur de freinage)	*f*	Vorsteuerventil (Bremskraftregler)	*n*	pilot valve (load-sensing valve)	*n*
valve proportionnelle (ASR)	*f*	Proportionalventil (ASR)	*n*	proportioning valve (TCS)	*n*
valve thermostatique	*f*	Thermostatventil	*n*	thermostatic valve	*n*
valve vide-charge	*f*	Last-Leer-Ventil	*n*	load-proportioning valve	*n*
valve-relais	*f*	Relaisventil	*n*	relay valve	*n*
valve-relais de remorque	*f*	Anhängerrelaisventil	*n*	trailer relay valve	*n*
vanne commandée par servomoteur	*f*	Servoventil	*n*	servo valve	*n*
vanne d'aspiration (ABS/ABD)	*f*	Ansaugventil, ASV (ABS/ABD)	*n*	suction valve (ABS/ABD)	*n*
vanne d'eau chaude	*f*	Heizwasserventil	*n*	hot-water valve	*n*
vanne d'inversion (ABS/ASR)	*f*	Umschaltventil (ABS/ASR)	*n*	pilot valve (ABS, TCS)	*n*
vanne d'isolement (banc d'essai de pompes)	*f*	Trennschieber (Pumpenprüfstand)	*m*	shut-off slide (injection-pump test bench)	*n*
vanne de commutation (ABS/ASR)	*f*	Umschaltventil (ABS/ASR)	*n*	pilot valve (ABS, TCS)	*n*
vanne de recyclage de carburan	*f*	Kraftstoffrückführventil	*n*	fuel-recirculation valve	*n*
vaporisation du carburant	*f*	Kraftstoffverdampfung	*f*	fuel vaporization	*n*
variateur d'avance	*m*	Spritzversteller	*m*	timing device	*n*
variation de la charge	*f*	Lastwechsel	*m*	load changes	*npl*
variation de pression	*f*	Druckschwankung	*f*	pressure variation	*n*
variation de qualité	*f*	Qualitätsabweichung	*f*	quality deviation	*n*
variation du calage de l'arbre à cames	*f*	Nockenwellenumschaltung	*f*	camshaft lobe control	*n*
véhicule articulé	*m*	Gelenkfahrzeug	*n*	articulated vehicle	*n*
véhicule électrique	*m*	Elektrofahrzeug (Straßenfahrzeug)	*n*	electric vehicle, EV	*n*
véhicule tracté	*m*	Anhängefahrzeug	*n*	trailer	*n*
véhicule tracteur	*m*	Zugfahrzeug	*n*	tractor vehicle	*n*
véhicule utilitaire	*m*	Nutzfahrzeug, Nfz	*n*	commercial vehicle	*n*

Français		Allemand		Anglais	
ventilateur	*m*	Lüfter	*m*	fan	*n*
ventilateur aspirant	*m*	Ansauggebläse	*n*	intake fan	*n*
ventilateur auxiliaire	*m*	Hilfsgebläse	*n*	auxiliary ventilator	*n*
ventilateur axial	*m*	Axiallüfter	*m*	axial fan	*n*
ventilateur d'aspiration	*m*	Ansauggebläse	*n*	intake fan	*n*
ventilateur de chaufferette	*m*	Heizergebläse	*n*	heater blower	*n*
ventilateur de radiateur	*m*	Kühlergebläse	*n*	radiator blower	*n*
ventilateur radial	*m*	Radiallüfter	*m*	radial fan	*n*
ventilation	*f*	Lüftung	*f*	ventilation	*n*
ventilation externe	*f*	Fremdbelüftung	*f*	auxiliary ventilation	*n*
ventilation interne (disque de frein)	*f*	innenbelüftet (Bremsscheibe)	*pp*	internally ventilated (brake disc)	*pp*
vérin	*m*	Arbeitszylinder	*m*	working cylinder	*n*
vérin à bride	*m*	Flanschzylinder	*m*	flange cylinder	*n*
verrouillage centralisé	*m*	Zentralverriegelung	*f*	central locking system	*n*
verrouillage de ceinture de sécurité	*m*	Gurtverriegelung (Sicherheitsgurt)	*f*	seat-belt locking	*n*
verrouillage du débit de surcharge	*m*	Startverriegelung	*f*	starting-quantity deactivator	*n*
verrouillage du débit de surcharge au démarrage	*m*	Startmengenverriegelung	*f*	start-quantity locking device	*n*
verrouillage en fin de démarrage	*m*	Startabwurfsperrzeit	*f*	starting-cutout	*n*
version de série	*f*	Serienausführung	*f*	series fabrication type	*n*
version fermée	*f*	geschlossene Bauweise	*f*	closed-type design	*n*
version ouverte	*f*	offene Bauweise	*f*	open-type design	*n*
vibration due à la torsion	*f*	Drehschwingung	*f*	rotary oscillation	*n*
vibrations	*fpl*	Schüttelbeanspruchung	*f*	vibration	*n*
vibrations dues aux à-coups	*fpl*	Ruckelschwingung	*f*	bucking oscillations	*npl*
vibrations harmoniques	*fpl*	Oberschwingungen	*fpl*	harmonics	*npl*
vibreur	*m*	Warnsummer	*m*	buzzer	*n*
vis anti-érosion (injection diesel)	*f*	Prallschraube (Dieseleinspritzung)	*f*	anti-erosion screw (diesel fuel injection)	*n*
vis creuse	*f*	Hohlschraube	*f*	hollow screw	*n*
vis d'étranglement	*f*	Drosselschraube	*f*	throttle screw	*n*
vis de butée	*f*	Anschlagschraube	*f*	stop screw	*n*
vis de butée de ralenti	*f*	Leerlaufanschlagschraube	*f*	idle-speed stop screw	*n*
vis de purge	*f*	Entlüftungsschraube	*f*	vent screw	*n*
vis de purge d'air	*f*	Entlüftungsschraube	*f*	vent screw	*n*
vis de purge d'eau (filtre à carburant)	*f*	Wasserablaßschraube (Kraftstoffilter)	*f*	drain screw (fuel filter)	*n*
vis de réglage	*f*	Einstellschraube	*f*	adjusting screw	*n*
vis de réglage de pleine charge	*f*	Vollasteinstellschraube	*f*	full-load screw	*n*
vis-pointeau	*f*	Drosselschraube	*f*	throttle screw	*n*
visco-coupleur (transmission intégrale)	*m*	Viscokupplung (Allradantrieb)	*f*	viscous coupling (all-wheel drive)	*n*
viscosité à basse température	*f*	Tieftemperaturviskosität	*f*	cold viscosity	*n*
viscosité à froid	*f*	Tieftemperaturviskosität	*f*	cold viscosity	*n*

Français		Allemand			Anglais	
visibilité	*f*	Sichtweite		*f*	visual range	*n*
visualiser (code de défaut)	*v*	auslesen (Fehlercode)	x	*v*	read out (error code)	*v*
visuel d'information (ABS)	*m*	Informationsanzeige, INA (ABS)	+	*f*	info display (ABS)	*n*
vitesse à charge partielle	*f*	Teillastdrehzahl		*f*	part-load speed	*n*
vitesse d'amorçage (alternateur)	*f*	Einschaltdrehzahl (Generator)		*f*	cutting-in speed (alternator)	*n*
vitesse d'auto-excitation (machines tournantes)	*f*	Angehdrehzahl (drehende Maschinen)	x	*f*	self-excitation speed (rotating machines)	*n*
vitesse d'écoulement	*f*	Strömungsgeschwindigkeit		*f*	flow velocity	*n*
vitesse d'entretien (moteur à combustion)	*f*	Selbstdrehzahl (Verbrennungsmotor)		*f*	self-sustaining speed (IC engine)	*n*
vitesse d'équilibre	*f*	Beharrungsdrehzahl		*f*	steady-state speed	*n*
vitesse d'essai	*f*	Prüfgeschwindigkeit		*f*	test speed	*n*
vitesse de braquage (dynamique d'un véhicule)	*f*	Giergeschwindigkeit (Kfz-Dynamik)		*f*	yaw velocity (vehicle dynamics)	*n*
vitesse de chauffe	*f*	Aufheizgeschwindigkeit		*m*	pre-heating rate	*n*
vitesse de coupure	*f*	Abregeldrehzahl		*f*	breakaway speed	*n*
vitesse de démarrage	*f*	Startdrehzahl		*f*	cranking speed	*n*
vitesse de fonctionnement	*f*	Betriebsdrehzahl		*f*	operating speed	*n*
vitesse de pleine charge	*f*	Vollastdrehzahl		*f*	full-load speed	*n*
vitesse de ralenti	*f*	Leerlaufdrehzahl		*f*	idle speed	*n*
vitesse de référence	*f*	Referenzgeschwindigkeit		*f*	reference speed	*n*
vitesse de régulation	*f*	Stellgeschwindigkeit		*f*	positioning rate	*n*
vitesse de rotation de la roue	*f*	Radgeschwindigkeit		*f*	wheel speed	*n*
vitesse de rotation du moteur	*f*	Motordrehzahl		*f*	engine speed	*n*
vitesse de rotation minimale	*f*	Mindestdrehzahl		*f*	minimum speed	*n*
vitesse de rotation nominale	*f*	Nenndrehzahl		*f*	rated speed	*n*
vitesse de rotation prescrite	*f*	Solldrehzahl		*f*	set speed	*n*
vitesse de rotation réelle	*f*	Istdrehzahl		*f*	actual speed	*n*
vitesse de roulage	*f*	Fahrgeschwindigkeit		*f*	driving speed	*n*
vitesse de transmission (multiplexage)	*f*	Übertragungsrate (CAN)		*f*	transfer rate (CAN)	*n*
vitesse différentielle des roues	*f*	Raddifferenzgeschwindigkeit		*f*	wheel-speed differential	*n*
vitesse du véhicule	*f*	Fahrzeuggeschwindigkeit		*f*	vehicle speed	*n*
vitesse intermédiaire	*f*	Zwischendrehzahl		*m*	intermediate speed	*n*
vitesse limite en virage	*f*	Kurvengrenzgeschwindigkeit		*f*	cornering limit speed	*n*
vitesse longitudinale (dynamique d'un véhicule)	*f*	Längsgeschwindigkeit (Kfz-Dynamik)		*f*	longitudinal velocity (vehicle dynamics)	*n*
vitesse maximale	*f*	obere Leerlaufdrehzahl		*f*	high idle speed	*n*
vitesse maximale à pleine charge	*f*	obere Vollastdrehzahl		*f*	maximum full-load speed	*n*
vitesse maximale à vide	*f*	obere Leerlaufdrehzahl		*f*	high idle speed	*n*
vitesse périphérique	*f*	Umfangsgeschwindigkeit		*f*	circumferential speed	*n*
vitesse relative	*f*	Relativgeschwindigkeit		*f*	relative speed	*n*
vitesse transversale (dynamique d'un véhicule)	*f*	Quergeschwindigkeit (Kfz-Dynamik)		*f*	lateral velocity (vehicle dynamics)	*n*
vitre arrière	*f*	Heckscheibe		*f*	rear window	*n*
voilage (disque de frein)	*m*	Seitenschlag (Bremsscheibe)		*m*	side runout (brake disc)	*n*

Français		Allemand		Anglais	
volant	*m*	Schwungrad	*n*	flywheel	*n*
volant d'inertie	*m*	Schwungrad	*n*	flywheel	*n*
volant d'inertie à deux masses	*m*	Zweimassenschwungrad	*n*	dual-mass flywheel	*n*
volant moteur	*m*	Schwungrad	*n*	flywheel	*n*
volatibilité (essence)	*f*	Flüchtigkeit (Benzin)	*f*	volatility (gasoline)	*n*
volet d'échappement (frein moteur)	*m*	Auspuffklappe (Motorbremse)	*f*	butterfly valve (engine brake)	*n*
volet de compensation	*m*	Kompensationsklappe	*f*	compensation flap	*n*
volet-sonde (L-Jetronic)	*m*	Stauklappe (L-Jetronic)	*f*	sensor plate (L-Jetronic)	*n*
volume d'air additionnel	*m*	Zusatzluftmenge	*f*	auxiliary air	*n*
volume d'amortissement	*m*	Dämpfungsvolumen	*n*	damping volume	*n*
volume de carburant injecté	*m*	Einspritzvolumen	*n*	injected fuel volume	*n*
volume de compensation	*m*	Ausgleichsvolumen	*n*	compensation volume	*n*
volume de compression	*m*	Kompressionsvolumen	*n*	compression volume	*n*
volume de correction	*m*	Korrekturmenge	*f*	correction quantity	*n*
volume de détente	*m*	Entlastungsvolumen	*n*	retraction volume (in-line pump)	*n*
volume de détente (électrovalve ABS)	*m*	Tauchstufe (ABS-Magnetventil)	*f*	recess step (ABS solenoid valve)	*n*
volume de fuite	x *m*	Leckmenge	*f*	leak-fuel quantity	*n*
volume de protection anti-ébullition	*m*	Kochschutzmenge	*f*	overheat-protection quantity	*n*
volume de réaspiration	*m*	Entlastungsvolumen	*n*	retraction volume (in-line pump)	*n*
volume des gaz d'échappement	*m*	Abgasvolumen	*n*	exhaust-gas volume	*n*
volume engendré (moteur à combustion)	*m*	Hubvolumen (Verbrennungsmotor)	*n*	piston displacement (IC engine)	*n*
volume entre les palettes du rotor (ralentisseur hydrodynamique)	*m*	Schaufelraum (hydrodynamischer Verlangsamer)	*m*	rotor chamber (hydrodynamic retarder)	*n*
volume mort	*m*	Totvolumen	*n*	dead volume	*n*
voyant lumineux	*m*	Funktionskontrolleuchte	*f*	function lamp	*n*
Z					
zone de coincement (mélange air-carburant)	*f*	Quench-Zone (Luft-Kraftstoff-Gemisch)	*f*	quench zone (air-fuel mixture)	*n*
zone de contraction et de rétraction à chaud (bougie)	*f*	Warmschrumpfzone (Zündkerze)	*f*	heat-shrinkage zone (spark plug)	*n*